Endorsements for Poythress and Grudem, *The Gender-Neutral Bible Controversy* (Broadman & Holman, 2000)

"Vern Poythress and Wayne Grudem have brought up some very heavy artillery so one might suppose that they are dealing with a very serious danger. Indeed, that is so. The gender-inclusivization of the Word of God is the first time anyone, apart from certain cults (such as the Jehovah's Witnesses), has ventured to strain the Bible through an ideological sieve, and such translations deserve to be subjected to heavy fire."

Harold O. J. Brown, Professor of Theology
Reformed Theological Seminary, Charlotte

"In an earnest plea for reduction of ideological interests, the authors probe the need for setting higher standards of accuracy in translation of gender-related terms."

Frederick W. Danker
Editor, Bauer-Danker-Arndt-Gingrich
Greek-English Lexicon of the New Testament
Emeritus Professor of New Testament
Lutheran School of Theology at Chicago

"In this thorough and multifaceted study, authors Poythress and Grudem have made a thoughtful and far-reaching contribution to our understanding of the inclusive-language controversy in its historical, linguistic, social, and theological dimensions. No one concerned for biblical literacy or troubled by the proliferation of customer-accommodated designer translations of the Bible can afford to ignore their concerns."

David Lyle Jeffrey
Distinguished Professor of Literature and Humanities
Baylor University

"This is an important book. Grudem and Poythress are patient to explain their position, clearing up a great deal of misunderstanding. Any responsible engagement in the debate over gender-inclusive translations cannot ignore the evidence, arguments, or conclusions of *The Gender-Neutral Bible Controversy*."

Daniel B. Wallace
Professor of New Testament Studies
Dallas Theological Seminary

"Anyone who wants to carefully analyze and understand the translation issues involved in the gender-neutral controversy must read this volume. A serious, scholarly contribution to the ongoing discussion."

Luder G. Whitlock Jr., President
Reformed Theological Seminary

"Vern Poythress and Wayne Grudem have succeeded in producing a book that not only provides remarkable scholarly insight to a present debate, but also in the process of doing so takes another step in the direction of the defense of the Biblical worldview of family and church relationships."

Paige Patterson, President
Southeastern Baptist Theological Seminary, Wake Forest, N.C.
Past President, Southern Baptist Convention

"The authors are commended for continuing the discussion of gender-related issues in biblical translation. It is a complex issue in view of their commitment to Scripture and of their interest in being culturally relevant. It is my hope that the discussion among the parties will continue so as to clarify the issues of interpretation and to assist all people in hearing God's Word afresh in our time."

Willem A. VanGemeren
Professor of Old Testament and Director of Academic Doctoral Program
Trinity Evangelical Divinity School
Editor, *New International Dictionary of Old Testament Theology and Exegesis*

"The goal in Bible translation is to convey accurately the meaning of the original text. Poythress and Grudem show that gender-neutral versions fail this test. The book is irenic but forceful, long but remarkably clear. It deserves a wide reading."

Thomas Schreiner
Professor of New Testament
The Southern Baptist Theological Seminary

"I am glad for this book for at least three reasons. It is unmodern in its allegiance to the objective, original meanings of inspired Biblical writers who have reasons for their specific words that often go deeper than we think. It is unique in that there is simply no other book on this issue so thorough and so careful. It is useful to scholar and layman alike because, for example, the table of contents is so detailed you can find the very issue you want to read about without having to wade through the whole book. I highly recommend this unmodern, unique, useful book."

John Piper, Pastor
Bethlehem Baptist Church, Minneapolis

"The authors' insistence that a translation should express what the writer intended to convey to *his* readers is much to be welcomed."

Peter G. W. Glare
Editor, *Liddell-Scott Greek-English Lexicon: Supplement* and
Oxford Latin Dictionary

The Gender-Neutral
Bible Controversy

The Gender-Neutral
Bible Controversy

Vern S. Poythress

· · · · ·

Wayne A. Grudem

BROADMAN
&HOLMAN
PUBLISHERS

Nashville, Tennessee

Ten-Digit ISBN: 0–8054–3193–4
Thirteen-Digit ISBN: 978–0–8054–3193–3

Published by Broadman & Holman Publishers, Nashville, Tennessee

Dewey Decimal Classification: 220.52
Subject Heading: BIBLE—VERSIONS \
NONSEXIST LANGUAGE—RELIGIOUS ASPECTS

2 3 4 5 6 7 8 9 10 08 07 06 05

Where this book refers to the TNIV, we have used the 2002 text of the New Testament in Today's New International Version. We understand that a full-Bible TNIV is scheduled to be published in early 2005, and we do not know if any of the verses we take issue with in this book will be changed in that edition. If any specific verses are changed to reflect more accurately in English the male-oriented details of meaning that are found in the original Greek text, we are thankful for such changes.

At press time, though, we have no information that there has been any change in the overall pattern in the TNIV, namely that it often eliminates male-oriented details of meaning that are in the original text in order to produce a more gender-neutral translation.

Vern Poythress and Wayne Grudem

Contents

Chapter 9: The Bible: The Word of God   149

Chapter 17: Ordinary People Can Understand Generic "He"   **335**

Chapter 18: More Issues in Translating Gender: Man, Son of Man, Fathers, Brother, Son, and the Extent of the Changes   **345**

Foreword

by Valerie Becker Makkai
Associate Professor of Linguistics, University of Illinois-Chicago
Past President, Linguistic Association of Canada and the United States

As a professor of linguistics with a keen interest in the theory and practice of translation, and as a committed Christian, my reading of various translations of the Bible has always been accompanied by a desire to know the original Hebrew and Greek wording on which the varying translations were based. Some knowledge of ancient Greek and of the Semitic languages, as well as study of commentaries, has only piqued my curiosity. As I read and study the Bible I find myself constantly wondering how closely and accurately each translation reflects the original. Thus I have followed with great interest the debate that has arisen over gender-neutral Bible translations in general, and the NIVI *(New International Version: Inclusive Language Edition)* in particular, and I was pleased to be asked to write the foreword to the present contribution to this debate.

In the present volume Vern Poythress and Wayne Grudem have presented a well-reasoned and level-headed argument for their case. Indeed, they are a voice of reason in a dispute that is fraught with emotion and misinformation. They clearly understand the fluid and changing nature of language and their arguments are based on sound linguistic principles, some of which bear emphasizing here.

First, one of the basic facts about language is that all languages are constantly undergoing change. At any point in time, changes in pronunciation, grammar, and vocabulary are in progress. Most of the time the speakers of the language are not aware of the changes. But if we look back in time we can see that at earlier stages the language was different. We sometimes have trouble understanding the King James Version of the Bible or the plays of Shakespeare because they were written some four centuries ago and English has undergone many changes in that time. If we go back two hundred years farther in time, say to Chaucer's *Canterbury Tales,* we have an even harder time understanding. And if we go back five hundred more years to something that was written in Old English, such as *Beowulf*, we can't understand it at all—we have to read it in Modern English translation. Or look at Latin. In the course of less than two thousand years Latin has changed so much that it isn't Latin at all any more—it has become French and Spanish and Italian and several other languages. And so it is with all languages.

A second basic fact of language is that we cannot consciously control the changes that languages undergo. We cannot prevent the changes, we cannot stop a change once it is underway, we cannot predict what will change and what will not, and very seldom if ever can we consciously cause a grammatical change to occur. The reason for this lies in the fact that historically changes have originated as "mistakes" in pronunciation or grammar or word usage that children or others make. These "mistakes" often originate because the language contains some sort of irregularity in structure that people are unconsciously trying to regularize. If enough people make the same "mistake" over a long enough period of time, the new creation begins to be seen as less of a mistake—it becomes more acceptable, and eventually, if the more educated speakers of the language begin to use it, the new form becomes an accepted part of the language. Not all such "mistakes" are ultimately incorporated into the language, however, so we can never tell the end result until many years (often a century or more) have gone by.

As an example of this process, take the pronoun *you* in English. It can refer to one person or more than one. But in English we are accustomed to being able to distinguish between singular and plural, so our inability to make that distinction with *you* bothers us on some unconscious level. Thus, in various parts of the country a new "plural" *you* has been created (albeit without conscious intent): *you-all* or *y'all* (primarily in the South), *you guys, yous,* and even *yous guys*. These are all relatively recent creations, and they have experienced varying degrees of acceptance. In the south even educated speakers now use *you-all* or *y'all*, so this has become acceptable usage there. In other parts of the country *you guys* is commonly used, but is generally regarded as slang or quite informal—it has not been totally accepted even though some educated speakers may use it in very informal situations. *Yous* and *yous guys*, while often heard, are generally used only by less educated speakers, those who are less particular about grammatical correctness. It is important to realize that there is nothing *inherently* good or bad about *any* of these forms. They are all ones that various speakers, for various reasons, have created to fill in a perceived gap in English structure. Which one of them, if any, will eventually take over as "the plural" of *you* is still anybody's guess. But ultimately the decision is not made by grammarians or scholars or anyone else who might have an ax to grind. It is made by all the millions of average speakers of the language who, by consistently using a given form over and over, turn it into an acceptable part of the grammar.

Attempts have often been made to stop such language changes in progress, but to no avail. One of the most interesting cases comes to us from Classical Latin times. A language purist (whose name has not come down to us) wrote a document which is called the *Appendix Probii*. It consists of a list of some three hundred Classical Latin words which, the author complained, everyone was mispronouncing. He carefully indicated the proper classical pronunciations (what "you should say") alongside the mispronunciations (what "you should not say"). No doubt he was not the only scholar of the times who was appalled at the common people's lack of knowledge of their language. Yet as we look at later Latin and at the languages that have descended from Latin, we find that every one of the "mistakes" that the author complained about took hold and is reflected in the daughter languages. No one, apparently, paid any attention to the instructions of the grammar teachers and scholars. They just went on saying "what came naturally," which was what they heard other people saying.

This is essentially what we all do, even though we may "know better." How many of us have said *it's me* in answer to the question *Who's there?* Do we know that *It's me* is bad grammar and that we're supposed to say *It is I?* Probably. Then why do we say it? Most people would reply, "because that's what everyone else says," or "it would sound stilted or silly to say *It is I*," and so on. The point is that the language is changing, and we say what we hear others saying. The purpose of language is to communicate, and if we don't communicate in the way others do we are in danger of being misunderstood or being thought of as weird or pedantic or a jokester.

With all this in mind, when we consider the question of "politically correct" language, we can see that there is a totally different process at work in this case. Instead of letting the language change naturally, as the speakers feel the need for new forms, those who are pushing political correctness are trying to impose change on language from the outside. The politically correct language movement attempts to speed up and control the direction of language change. It is a conscious attempt to mold the language into the form that certain people think it should take rather than let it take its normal course. From a theoretical linguistic point of view such an attempt would be doomed to failure, as we have seen, if it weren't for the fact that those who are controlling the movement have managed to give us a guilty conscience on the subject. We have been made to feel that somehow we are being insensitive to the feelings of various groups if we say the wrong thing, and so we try to follow the dictates of the "language police," as Poythress and Grudem have termed them. This has resulted in a number of words being replaced by other, "more acceptable" words, not through a natural process of change, but because of outside pressure to do so.[1] And for the

---

[1]For a detailed discussion of this subject, the reader may wish to look at my "Correctness in Language: Political and Otherwise," 1996 Presidential Address, *The Twenty-third LACUS*

most part these changes have occurred first among educated, scholarly speakers, those who are doing the writing and who do not want their writings to be stigmatized as insensitive or prejudiced. That is, the changes have occurred first in the written word, and have only later trickled down to the spoken language of some people, though by no means all. This is the exact reverse of the usual process of language change, and it remains to be seen whether changes introduced in this fashion will stick. There is a considerable amount of backlash against politically correct language, taking the form of humor, or derision, or simple refusal to use the new forms.

With regard to the issue at hand in the present volume, namely gender-neutral forms, and in particular the issue of generic *he*, there is even more resistance to the changes that the "language police" would have us make. There are several reasons for this. One is that it is relatively easier to replace one vocabulary item with another (to replace *blind* with *visually impaired*, for example) than to change a person's understanding of the meaning of a word (e.g., to claim that *man* can no longer be used to mean "humanity" in general). Secondly, in the case of *he* in particular, if we say that this word can no longer be used in a generic sense (to mean one person, unspecified as to gender) there is no good way to express the concept. We have no good replacement term, although a number of (rather silly) possibilities have been suggested. Thirdly, and most importantly, the speakers of English do not perceive a need within the language for such a change (as they do, for example, in the case of *you* discussed above). As long as the average speaker (and writer, as Poythress and Grudem illustrate in Chapter 16 and elsewhere) does not feel the need for such a change, and has no ready form to use as a replacement, it will not happen.

Poythress and Grudem show a clear understanding of the basic principles of language change, as outlined above, and have applied them to the subject of Bible translation with great sensitivity to the holiness of the task at hand. They clearly recognize that language does change, and that Bible translations must be revised from time to time to keep up with these changes. On the other hand, they also recognize that there are reasons not to jump the gun. They present statistics (Chapter 8) that show that in both 1996 and 1999 23.5% of Bibles purchased in the United States were the King James Version—written in four-hundred-year-old language! Not everyone is clamoring for a Bible in the most up-to-date language. Some people like the archaic flavor of the language of the King James Version; they find it beautiful; they trust it. On the other hand, modern language translations are also clearly needed—people want to be sure they understand what the Bible says and they don't want to have to struggle to follow the language. Where the adherents of politically correct Bible translations go wrong, however, is that

---

Forum 1996, ed. Alan K. Melby (Chapel Hill, N.C.: The Linguistic Association of Canada and the United States, 1997), 5–25.

they are rushing to judgment. They are hastening to make changes that the average speaker of English has not yet made and may never make. We do not yet know, for instance, what the ultimate fate of generic *he* will be, and we probably will not know for years. It is not the job of the Bible translator (it is not even the job of the grammar book writer or the dictionary writer) to lead the charge in such a case. It is, rather, their job, as Poythress and Grudem recognize, to follow the patterns of grammar and vocabulary that have already been firmly established through common usage.

As the authors point out again and again, a translator, and most particularly a Bible translator, does not have the option of injecting personal ideas and interpretations into the translation. If we are going to call the result a "translation," then we must *translate*—not rephrase or paraphrase. Many participants in the translation dispute seem to have an agenda of political correctness which is fueled by the feminist revolution. They want to change gender references and other terms to reflect current views and attitudes toward women. But as Poythress and Grudem state, our only agenda should be to represent God's Word as it was written, not what we wish His Word had said, nor what we think His Word would have said if it had been written today. Working with a translation that reflects as closely as possible the meaning of the original, Biblical scholars and others who want to interpret the Bible and to understand its meaning in today's setting are free to do so. But if the translation is done in such a way that the original meaning is obscured or changed, all Christians are deprived of the opportunity to read God's Word as it was given and then to interpret it according to our own beliefs. In essence we are being *told* what to believe.

This point strikes at the heart of my own personal faith. For most of my life I have belonged to the Christian Church (Disciples of Christ), a denomination which grew out of the Presbyterian and Methodist movements in the early 1800s. It arose from a commitment to the unity of all Christians and thus it rejected the various doctrinal requirements of different churches of that time. We take the Bible as our only creed, and the statement is often made that "where the Scriptures speak, we speak; where the Scriptures are silent, we are silent." This does not necessarily mean that we subscribe to a strictly literal interpretation of Scripture. In fact, most Disciples, for instance, believe that it is acceptable in modern times to have women as pastors and in roles of leadership in the church. I personally have been an elder in my local congregation for over ten years and I also currently hold the office of President of the Congregation and Chair of the General Board. I understand that the teachings of the Bible were intended for people of a different era, and I am perfectly capable of interpreting those teachings and applying them to modern times. It is not necessary for translators to do that for me, nor do I want them to. On the contrary, it is of utmost importance to me, as a Christian, to know exactly what the Scriptures say, in a translation that reflects as closely as possible the exact meaning of the original. Only then can I decide how the Biblical teachings apply to my life today. As Poythress and Grudem imply, it is insulting to me as a woman and as a thoughtful reader of the Bible to insinuate that I cannot appreciate the differences between ancient and modern cultures, that I am incapable of understanding accurately the meaning of something like generic *he,* and that I have to be catered to lest I be offended by such a "sexist" usage.

This attitude is evident in the fact that some participants in the translation debate take the position that for modern times the Bible ought to be modernized. Poythress and Grudem include the following quote from the Preface to the *Inclusive Language Edition* of the NIV: ". . . it was recognized that it was often appropriate to mute the patriarchalism of the culture of the biblical writers . . . ."[2] And (from a set of internal guidelines used by the Committee on Bible Translation for the NIVI): "The patriarchalism . . . of the ancient cultures in which the Biblical books were composed is pervasively reflected in forms of expression that . . . deny the common human dignity of all hearers and readers." As Poythress and Grudem forcefully maintain, how does anyone dare condemn God's own Word as denying the "common human dignity" of His creation! It is rather *we,* in the supreme egotism of assuming that our culture is better than that of the patriarchs, who deny *their* human dignity. How much better to simply say that we will translate God's Word as it was written, without changing meanings and nuances any more than we absolutely have to, and then allow modern Christians to interpret the message of God's Word for modern times in whatever way seems best to them.

One of the major problems in translating, which the authors discuss at length, is that one cannot always easily translate all of the meanings contained in a passage. Connotations of words (the extra meanings or associations that a word brings to mind which are not part of the dictionary definition of the word) are an important part of the process of communication, and the connotations of a word in one language are rarely the same as the connotations of the corresponding word in a another language. The choice of one or another translation of a word or phrase may significantly affect the reader's understanding of a passage. Thus, as the authors point out, it is of great importance that the translation reflect as many as possible of the connotations and nuances of meaning of the original.

Some adherents of gender-neutral language seem not to understand a basic principle which Poythress and Grudem clearly recognize—that nuances of meaning are of tremendous importance in translation (as indeed they are in any act of communication). Linguists are in agreement that *any* change in grammar or wording, no matter how slight, *always changes meaning.* Take as an example the following situation: eight-year-old twins, Susie and Billy, are in the kitchen. Their mother comes in and finds milk spilled

---

[2]See Chapter 14 for the full text of this and the following quote.

all over the table. She asks "Who spilled the milk?" and Susie replies "Billy did." The mother then says one of the following:

(to Billy)	You need to wipe it up right now!
(to Susie)	He needs to wipe it up right now!
	Whoever spilled it needs to wipe it up right now!
	We need to wipe it up right now!
	It needs to be wiped up right now!
	Wiping it up right now would be a good thing!

Which of the above will Billy take more seriously? Which sentence will be most likely to cause him to jump into action? The same basic message (wiping up the milk) is present in all the sentences. Yet there is a clear difference in tone (in nuance) conveyed by the shift from second person ("you"), to third person ("he," "whoever"), to first person ("we"), to passive—focusing on the milk ("it needs . . ."), to focusing on the action ("wiping it up . . ."). Does it make a difference which sentence the mother chooses to say? It most definitely does, as anyone familiar with children will immediately recognize.

While the above example does not involve generic *he*, the same principle applies to this and to all differences in word choice. The nuances of difference in meaning may at times seem trivial, but this is never the case —especially when we are dealing with Biblical texts which (in sermons, commentaries, and so on) are routinely subjected to intense scrutiny, with each word and its exact implications being carefully analyzed. Throughout their discussion Poythress and Grudem quite rightly emphasize that loss of nuance, with the resulting loss of details of meaning of the original, is something that should be avoided if at all possible. And their claim that substituting gender-neutral language does indeed change nuance and meaning is entirely linguistically sound.

While "translation is not treason," as the authors point out (Chapter 10), bitter disputes over the translation of God's Holy Word might be so regarded. It cannot please God to see the dissension that has arisen over what should be a joyous and loving part of fulfilling the Great Commission. Poythress and Grudem have attempted to set the record straight on a number of misunderstood issues in the inclusive language debate. It is to be hoped that all involved in the discussion will read this book carefully.

Preface

This is new book consists of two parts.

Chapters 1–6 include material that we and others wrote in 2002 in response to the publication of the New Testament in *Today's New International Version* (the TNIV),[1] and they analyze the TNIV as the most recent and most prominent of the gender-neutral Bible translations. These chapters were written in the midst of an intense controversy that began when Zondervan and the International Bible Society surprised the evangelical world with their announcement of the publication of the TNIV New Testament on January 28, 2002.

In chapters 1–6 we disagree explicitly with other scholars and friends in the evangelical world who wrote in defense of the TNIV, and the chapters show evidence of that clear disagreement. Yet we believe the chapters also reflect the respect we have for those on the other side of this controversy. Furthermore, we count it evidence of God's grace that numerous private conversations and even the public debates on these matters in 2002 and 2003 were able to be conducted in a cordial and open atmosphere that was evidence of our common commitment to Jesus Christ.

Some people might wonder, "Why do you spend so much time arguing about *the Bible*, for goodness' sake? Haven't we had enough of such controversies?" Our reply is that when accurate translation of the Bible is at stake, it is hard to think of anything in the world that is more important to argue about, because it is hard to think of anything in the world that is more important than the words of the Bible for our daily lives and our relationship with God himself. Not all arguments are harmful, and in this book we hope that readers will find our arguments to be fair, reasonable, truthful, and kind to those with whom we disagree. We also hope that out of this

---

[1]All of the material in chapters 1–6 appeared in *Journal for Biblical Manhood and Womanhood* 7/2 (fall, 2002). Footnote references to pages in our earlier book, *The Gender-Neutral Bible Controversy* (2000), have been updated so that they now refer to pages in this new book, and a few changes have been made in formatting. Otherwise these chapters are printed as they appeared in 2002.

ongoing controversy the church will reach a better understanding and eventually a clearer consensus on what kind of accuracy it will seek in the translation of God's Word.

The second part of the book contains chapters 7–21 and appendices 1–6. These chapters (and the Foreword and the Preface to the 2000 book, which refer specifically to these chapters) were earlier published as *The Gender-Neutral Bible Controversy: Muting the Masculinity of God's Words*, by Vern S. Poythress and Wayne A. Grudem (Nashville: Broadman and Holman: 2000). We have reprinted these chapters here in this current book because they provide the theoretical and linguistic arguments that support in more detail our concerns about the gender-neutral translation policy followed by the TNIV, and they contain numerous examples from other gender-neutral Bible translations as well.

We expect that in early 2005 Zondervan and the International Bible Society will publish a whole-Bible edition of the TNIV, including the Old Testament. If the pattern the translators followed in the New Testament is any guide, the TNIV Old Testament will parallel in many respects an earlier gender-neutral edition of the NIV, called the *NIV-Inclusive Language Edition* (NIVI). The NIVI was published in England in 1996, and the expectation that the NIVI would soon be published in the United States was what led to a huge controversy in the U.S. in 1997. After the TNIV Old Testament is published, readers can examine the concerns we expressed about the NIVI Old Testament in chapters 12, 13, 18, and 19, to see if the TNIV Old Testament has retained or changed most of the same problems that first led to such a public outcry in 1997.

The Council on Biblical Manhood and Womanhood (CBMW) Web site (www.cbmw.org or direct access to TNIV material at www.no-tniv.com) contains much more information about the TNIV, and CBMW will continue to add updated information about the TNIV to its Web site from time to time. On the other side of the question, arguments in support of the TNIV may be found at the TNIV Web site, www.tniv.info. We welcome free and open discussion of these issues, we offer this book as a contribution to such discussion, and we encourage readers to consider the arguments on both sides and to come to their own conclusions about these important questions regarding the translation of the Word of God.

We appreciate the help of Travis Buchanan of Phoenix Seminary in helping to research and typing much of this material, and in preparing the author and Scripture indices. We also wish to thank Steve Eriksson of Phoenix Seminary, who prepared the subject index, and Randy Stinson, Chris Cowan, Rob Lister, Sarah Affleck, Heidi Frye, Jason Meyer, Todd Miles, Matt Perman, Gary and Amy Steward, and Dan Stone of the CBMW office in Louisville, Kentucky, who helped at several points with chapter 3.

Vern Poythress and Wayne Grudem
June, 2004

Preface to *The Gender-Neutral Bible Controversy**

Both of us authors think that the issue of Bible translation deserves careful reflection, and that Christians need to be aware of the problems with gender-neutral translations. So we have undertaken to co-author this book. Though some of the material derives originally from one or the other author, we have both gone through the whole book and we speak with a unified voice.

Because we are writing with all interested Christians in mind, we have tried to explain the issues in ordinary English and to stay free of technicalities as much as possible. Where references to Hebrew and Greek are necessary, we have used transliteration into English letters and tried to keep the argument understandable to ordinary readers. Scholarly readers must understand that in a number of cases, to keep the argument from becoming excessively complex, we have simplified the discussion. In language analysis, almost any generalization has exceptions, and we have refrained from tediously cataloguing them. But we believe that careful investigation will show that the points we are making can be expressed if necessary in more elaborate, precise terms.[1]

Many people have contributed to our understanding. We appreciate our Christian fellowship with all those who participated in the Colorado Springs meeting in May 1997; but special thanks go to James Dobson and Charles Jarvis for organizing the meeting. We are grateful to Kenneth Barker, Ronald Youngblood, Lars Dunberg, and Bruce Ryskamp, because they were willing to engage in kind, patient, and fruitful dialog at that meeting, and subsequently, in spite of earlier differences of opinion.

---

*The text of *The Gender-Neutral Bible Controversy* (Nashville: Broadman & Holman, 2000) is now reprinted as Chapters 7–21 and appendices 1–6 of this book.

[1] See especially our discussion of "levels" of analysis of linguistic complexity in the excursus at the end of Chapter 10.

We have also profited from interaction with D. A. Carson, Grant Osborne, and Mark L. Strauss, and we are grateful to them for supplying us with earlier drafts of their work. We now have their published books and articles as well. We appreciate their stimulus and their friendship, even though we do not agree with many of their conclusions.

We appreciate the careful work of Roy and Joi Christians, students at Trinity Evangelical Divinity School who took a collection of various articles and unpublished manuscripts that both of us authors had written and helped us combine our work by weaving the bits and pieces into a first draft manuscript from which we could then work. We are also grateful to Aaron Thurber for quickly and accurately compiling the index of persons and the index of Scripture references and to Susanne Henry for her cheerful and faithful secretarial help in the process of writing this book.

We also wish to thank the members of Fellowship Bible Church of Little Rock, Arkansas, who generously provided a grant that enabled us to finish much of the work in the final months of this project.

We are thankful to journal editors and publishers for their permissions to republish some material here. We have incorporated in revised form pieces from Vern S. Poythress, "Gender in Bible Translation: Exploring a Connection with Male Representatives," *Westminster Theological Journal* 60/2 (1998): 225–253; Vern S. Poythress, "Explanation of the Colorado Springs Guidelines," at the Web site of the Council on Biblical Manhood and Womanhood, www.cbmw.org; Wayne Grudem, *Bible Doctrine: Essential Teachings of the Christian Faith* (Grand Rapids: Zondervan, and Leicester: InterVarsity, 1999), 33–48; and Wayne A. Grudem, "NIV Controversy: Participants Sign Landmark Agreement," *CBMW News* 2/3 (June 1997): 1, 3–6.

Abbreviations

Gender-specific Bible versions

KJV King James Version (1611)
ASV American Standard Version (1901)
RSV Revised Standard Version (1946, 1952, 1971)
NASB New American Standard Version (New American Standard Bible) (1963, 1995)
NEB New English Bible (1970)
GNB (1976) Good News Bible: The Bible in Today's English Version (1976)
NKJV New King James Version (1982)
NIV New International Version (1984)
REB Revised English Bible (1989)
NIrV (1998) New International Reader's Version (1998 revision)

Gender-neutral Bible versions

NRSV New Revised Standard Version (1989)
NCV New Century Version (1987, 1991)
GNB Good News Bible: Today's English Version Second Edition (1992)
CEV Contemporary English Version (1995)
GW God's Word (1995)
NIrV(1995) New International Reader's Version (1995)
NIVI New International Version Inclusive Language Edition (1995, 1996)
NLT New Living Translation (1996)
NLT revised edition New Living Translation (1996) (see Chapter 14 for a discussion of the revision)

Culturally adapted imaginative renderings of the Bible

Kenneth N. Taylor, *The Living Bible—Paraphrased* (1971)
Eugene Peterson, *The Message* (1995)

Other Abbreviations

BAGD Walter Bauer, *A Greek-English Lexicon of the New Testament and Other Early Christian Literature*, 2d ed., ed. William F. Arndt, F. Wilbur Gingrich, and Frederick W. Danker (Chicago: University of Chicago Press, 1979).

BDB Francis Brown, S. R. Driver, and Charles A. Briggs, *A Hebrew and English Lexicon of the Old Testament* ... (Oxford: Oxford University Press, 1907).

CBT The Committee on Bible Translation, the central committee of scholars charged with translating the New International Version, and later revising it.

CSG The Colorado Springs Guidelines, a statement drawn up in Colorado Springs on May 27, 1997, and later refined. The complete text is found in appendix 1.

Debate D. A. Carson, *The Inclusive-Language Debate: A Plea for Realism* (Grand Rapids: Baker, 1998).

Distorting Mark. L. Strauss, *Distorting Scripture? The Challenge of Bible Translation & Gender Accuracy* (Downers Grove, IL: InterVarsity, 1998).

Explanation

We classify versions as "gender-neutral" primarily on the basis of their avoidance of generic "he" (not that this is the only important issue, but it results in the most changes, and it usually signals other changes as well). For an explanation of the term "gender-neutral," see Chapter 7. For a discussion of generic "he," see Chapters 13–17.

We need some special explanation of the REB, the *Living Bible*, and *The Message*. The *Revised English Bible* (REB), a revision of the *New English Bible* (NEB) published in 1989, showed some tendencies toward gender-neutral language, and made some changes of which we are critical later in this book. But on the most decisive issue, the use of generic "he," it refused to engage in large-scale rewording; it did not eliminate generic "he." On this basis, we have not classified it as gender-neutral.

The Message (1995), by Eugene H. Peterson, consists of the New Testament, Psalms, and Proverbs, rendered in a loose paraphrase and in culturally updated language.[1] Kenneth N. Taylor's *The Living Bible—Paraphrased* (1971) uses similar procedures.[2] Unlike ordinary translators, Peterson and Taylor do not intend merely to represent an original meaning in another language, but to represent the message in another culture. Nuances are thus freely altered.

For example, corresponding to "Greet one another with a holy kiss" (1 Cor. 16:20), Taylor says, "Give each other a loving handshake when you meet," while Peterson says, "Pass the greetings around with holy

---

[1]Eugene H. Peterson, *The Message* (Colorado Springs, CO: Navpress, 1995).
[2]Kenneth N. Taylor, *The Living Bible—Paraphrased* (Wheaton, IL: Tyndale House, 1971).

embraces!" Taylor updates 1 Corinthians to picture American churches where a handshake is customary, while Peterson thinks of American churches where hugs are common.

Peterson has given us—what? Not exactly the New Testament, but a creative modern evangelistic book illustrating what the biblical message might sound like when transformed part way into a modern setting. The book exhibits the problems that we discuss later in the area of cultural updating (see Chapter 15). But because it is entitled *The Message,* and the name of the author Eugene H. Peterson is found on the cover, the spine, and the title page (at least in the edition that we have), there is not so much danger that people will confuse it with an actual translation. In addition, the chapters have no verse numbers, a subtle hint that the book is not supposed to be used for detailed study, but only for general effect.

Peterson drops male meaning components on occasion. But this result is not widespread. It appears to be the unintended effect of loose paraphrasing, rather than a deliberate and systematic attempt to eliminate male-oriented language. Generic "he" remains in place. Hence, *The Message* should *not* be classified as gender-neutral. Similarly, *The Living Bible* is *not* gender-neutral.

Since these two works engage in imaginative updating, they make stimulating reading, but neither is reliable as a basis for detailed study.

CHAPTER 1

A Brief Summary
of Concerns about the TNIV

by Wayne Grudem

Of course I agree with removing male-oriented words when there is no male-oriented meaning in the original Greek or Hebrew text. But when there is a male meaning, we dare not under-translate and conceal that meaning just because that emphasis is unpopular today.

The heart of the controversy is this: In hundreds of verses the TNIV *translates only the general idea* of a passage and *omits male-oriented details.* Such changes may sound more acceptable to modern culture, but details of meaning in the underlying Greek text are lost. Here are some examples:

A. Changes affecting singular "father" (Greek *patēr*)
and singular "son" (Greek *huios*)

NIV Hebrews 12:7 Endure hardship as discipline; God is treating you as sons. For what **son** is not disciplined by his **father**?

TNIV . . . what **children** are not disciplined by their **parents**?

The TNIV mistranslates the Greek terms *huios* ("son") and *patēr* ("father"), which in their singular forms do not mean "child" or "parent," and surely not "children" or "parents." It also obscures the parallel with God as Father in this passage.

Is it true that children are disciplined by their parents? Yes. Is that what this verse says? No. The author is using a specific male example, yet the TNIV has changed it to a generalization.

In defending this rendering for Hebrews 12:7, the TNIV web site incorrectly claims that *patēr* in the singular means "parent." Though the TNIV does not yet call God our "Parent," this claim opens a wide door for calling

God "Parent" in Hebrews 12:7 and elsewhere in future editions. In fact, in line with "political correctness" in language, the new BDAG *Lexicon* has already added "Parent" as a definition of *patēr* when used of God the Father (with no new evidence to support this new definition, p. 787). If we accept the TNIV in 2002, we should get ready for "Our Parent in heaven..." in 2010.

B. Changes affecting singular "brother" (Greek *adelphos*)

> NIV Luke 17:3 If your **brother** sins, rebuke **him**, and if he repents, forgive **him**.
>
> TNIV If any **brother or sister** sins against you, rebuke **the offender**; and if **they** repent, forgive **them**.

The TNIV inserts "or sister," which Jesus did not say. Jesus is using a single male individual ("your brother") as an example of a general truth, but the TNIV will not let him do this. I agree that the verse *applies* to sisters who sin, but that is *application*; it is not *translation*.

The Bible often points to a single individual to teach a general truth, as in the parable of the prodigal son—which *applies* to prodigal daughters, but it should not be *translated* prodigal "son or daughter" (as even the TNIV recognizes). Similarly, in the Ten Commandments, "You shall not covet your neighbor's wife" also *applies* to not coveting your neighbor's husband, but we should not change the words of God to *translate* Exodus 20:17 as "You shall not covet your neighbor's wife *or husband*." God's words are not ours to tamper with as we please.

C. Changes affecting "he/him/his" (Greek *autos*)

> NIV (1984) 1 Corinthians 14:28 If there is no interpreter, the speaker should keep quiet in the church and speak **to himself** and God.
>
> TNIV 1 Corinthians 14:28 If there is no interpreter, the speaker should keep quiet in the church and speak to God **when alone**.

The TNIV translators thought (mistakenly) that modern readers might read the word "himself" and decide that this verse did not apply to women, so they changed it to "when alone." But there is nothing that means "when alone" in the Greek text (the dative pronoun *heautō* here means "to himself"). The suggestion that this means "when the speaker is alone" may be some commentator's further *explanation* of the passage, but it is probably an overly restrictive explanation, and it is surely not an accurate *translation* of the passage. Prior to the TNIV, people could differ over whether Paul allowed uninterpreted prayer in tongues in small private groups outside the church meeting, but here the TNIV invents a new rule that Paul (and God) never said: someone praying in tongues must be "alone."

NIV Revelation 22:18: If **anyone** adds anything to them, God will add to **him** the plagues …
TNIV If **anyone of you** adds anything to them, God will add to **you** the plagues …

The TNIV implies that if any one person in your group adds to Scripture, "you" *all*, the whole group, will receive the plagues. The TNIV changes the meaning of the very verse that tells us never to change the words of Scripture!

D. Other changes

NIV (1984) Hebrews 2:6 What is **man** that you are mindful of him, **the son of man** that you care for **him**?
TNIV (2002) What are **mere mortals** that you are mindful of them, **human beings** that you care for **them**?

The TNIV needlessly obscures the possible connection of this verse with Jesus, who often called himself "the Son of Man." It mistranslates the singular Greek words *huios* ("son") and *anthropōs* ("man"). It no longer refers to the human race as a unity named "man" (the best translation of the name given by God in Gen. 5:2), but "mere mortals."

NIV Hebrews 2:17: For this reason he had to be made like his **brothers** in every way, in order that he might become a merciful and faithful high priest …
TNIV For this reason he had to be made like his **brothers and sisters** in every way, in order that he might become a merciful and faithful high priest …

Did Jesus have to become like his sisters "in every way" in order to become a "high priest in service to God"? All the Old Testament priests were men, and surely the high priest was a man. This text does not quite proclaim an androgynous Jesus (who was both male and female), but it surely leaves open a wide door for misunderstanding, and almost invites misunderstanding. Meditate on that phrase "in every way" and see if you can trust the TNIV.

Some TNIV defenders claim precedent for such changes in the New Testament authors' quotations of the Old Testament in verses like 2 Cor. 6:18, where Paul adds "and daughters" to 2 Samuel 7:14 and says, "you will be *sons and daughters* to me, says the Lord Almighty."

The problem with this argument is that the New Testament authors *freely adapt* Old Testament verses to apply to the situation at hand. Paul is not purporting to give an exact translation of 2 Samuel 7:14. We can see this from the fact that no Bible translation has ever taken Paul's adapted rendering and put it back into 2 Samuel 7:14 as the proper translation! That would give an impossible translation in which God says to David, "I will raise up your offspring after you .... He shall build a house for my name, and I will establish the throne of his kingdom forever. I will be a father to *you*, and *you* shall be *sons and daughters* to me. When he commits iniquity, I will discipline him with the rod of men ..." This makes no sense, and it is an impossible translation of the Hebrew. Paul is not translating; he is adapting and applying.

There are many other problems, such as changing "Jews" to "Jewish leaders" in Acts 13:50 and 21:11 (and several times in John) with no justification in the Greek text, thus obscuring larger corporate responsibility. With respect to gender language, "he" is changed to plural "they" 271 times (and to so-called "singular they" 112 times), "he" is changed to "you" 90 times, to "we" 9 times, and simply omitted 48 times. "Father/fathers/forefathers" are removed 39 times. Singular "brother" is changed to "brother or sister" or something like "believer" 43 times. "Man" (when translating the male-specific term *anēr*) is changed to things like "people" or "friends" 26 times. In each case these changes remove details of meaning that are there in the Greek text.

The TNIV distorts the meaning of Scripture in hundreds of such changes, *not* because the original Greek words have changed, and *not* because the meanings of ancient Greek words have changed (they haven't!), but merely to avoid five simple words that many in our culture find offensive: "man," "father," "son," "brother," and "he/him/his."

E. Widespread concern about the TNIV

Soon after the TNIV was released, over thirty-five evangelical scholars (the majority with Ph.D.s in New Testament) signed a "Statement of Concern" saying: "In light of troubling translation inaccuracies—primarily (but not exclusively) in relation to gender language—that introduce distortions of the meanings that were conveyed better by the original NIV, we cannot endorse the TNIV translation as sufficiently accurate to commend to the church" (see statement and names at on pages 111–12, below).

Then in June, 2002, over 100 respected evangelical leaders signed a public "Statement of Concern" opposing the TNIV (see more details and verses on pages 101–109, below). And the Southern Baptist Convention and the Presbyterian Church in America in 2002 overwhelmingly passed denominational resolutions opposing the TNIV. But the International Bible Society, which owns the copyright and makes the final decision, continues to promote the TNIV.

If the TNIV should gain wide acceptance, the precedent will be established for other Bible translations to mute unpopular nuances and details of meaning for the sake of "political correctness." The loss of many other doctrines unpopular in the culture will soon follow. And at every case Bible readers will never know if what they are reading is really the Word of God or the translators' ideas of something that would be a little less offensive than what God actually said.

"You shall not add to the word that I command you, nor take from it" (Deut. 4:2).

CHAPTER 2

Are the Criticisms of the TNIV Bible Really Justified?

An Interaction with Craig Blomberg, Darrell Bock, Peter Bradley, D. A. Carson, and Bruce Waltke

by Wayne Grudem, Research Professor of Bible and Theology, Phoenix Seminary, Scottsdale, AZ

Introduction

On September 4, 2002, Zondervan Publishing House sent to all members of the Evangelical Theological Society and all members of the Institute for Biblical Research a packet of information about *Today's New International Version* (TNIV). That packet contained articles written by Craig Blomberg,[1] Don Carson,[2] and Bruce Waltke,[3] all defending the TNIV in one way or another. In addition, the packet contained an interview with Peter Bradley,[4] the president of the International Bible Society, published in an edition of the IBS publication *Light Magazine* (July 2002). In addition to these four articles, Craig Blomberg's article mentions a widely circulated article by Darrell Bock, in which he supports the legitimacy of several of the passages that have been criticized in the TNIV.[5]

---

[1]Craig L. Blomberg, "*Today's New International Version*: The Untold Story of a Good Translation." Blomberg includes a very helpful section on translational improvements in the TNIV (pp. 4–14).

[2]D. A. Carson, "The Limits of Functional Equivalence in Bible Translation—and Other Limits, Too" (forthcoming in *The Challenge of Bible Translation: Essays in Honor of Ronald F. Youngblood*, ed. by Glen Scorgie, Mark Strauss and Steven Voth (Zondervan, 2003).

[3]Bruce Waltke, "Personal Reflections on the *TNIV*."

[4]"Peter Bradley and the Truth About the TNIV," *Light Magazine* (July, 2002), 6–11.

[5]Darrell L. Bock, "Do Gender Sensitive Translations Distort Scripture? Not Necessarily," available at www.tniv.info.

I count it a privilege to be able to interact with these five men, each of whom is highly respected in the evangelical world. Craig Blomberg, Darrell Bock, and Don Carson have contributed enormously to the work of evangelical scholarship in New Testament in our generation, and Bruce Waltke has likewise made enormous contributions to the academic study of the Old Testament. I have profited many times both from the academic writings of these men and from personal interaction with each of them.

Peter Bradley is president of a remarkable organization, the International Bible Society, that distributes Bibles in over 100 countries today, and that has been responsible for distributing many millions of Bibles since its founding in 1809. Peter Bradley himself, in several personal conversations with me during the past year, has consistently exhibited personal graciousness and an eagerness to honor Christ in the way we deal with this controversy, as have others involved with Zondervan Publishing House and with the NIV's Committee on Bible Translation (the CBT).

I am sure that people on both sides of this controversy wish that somehow it would go away. Yet people on both sides are convinced that important principles are at stake, and neither side has felt that it could, in good conscience before God, remain silent.[6]

Someone might ask, how could you think to disagree with men of such integrity, such commitment to the Word of God, and such academic expertise? For reasons I will explain in detail below, in spite of the high respect in which I hold the writings of these men on other subjects, I think they have reached an incorrect conclusion regarding a specific matter, namely, the translation into English of certain kinds of male-oriented details of meaning that are present in the original Hebrew and Greek texts of the Bible. This may at first sound like a small question, but, as those familiar with the controversy already know, it affects something like 4000 verses in the entire Bible.

Is it possible that such esteemed scholars could have come to an incorrect conclusion on this matter? It is certainly possible, for no human teacher is perfect in this age. James says, "We all stumble in many ways, and if anyone does not stumble in what he says, he is a perfect man, able also to bridle his whole body" (James 3:2, ESV).

In fact, there are respected Christian scholars and other leaders on both sides of this question. So I simply ask that readers evaluate the reasons and evidence on both sides, including the material below, and come to their own decisions based on the evidence, not simply by following one personality or another in this dispute.

---

[6]In addition, the five men with whom I differ in this article all share with me a common commitment to the inerrancy of the Bible as the Word of God, and to the "complementarian" conviction that God created men and women equal in value yet different in our roles in the home and in the church. Therefore we approach this difference both with a considerable measure of good will and with much common ground in our convictions. Yet our differences persist.

A. What is the main point of disagreement?

The heart of the difference can be summarized in one sentence:

Is it acceptable to translate only the general idea of a passage and systematically omit male-oriented details of meaning that are present in the original Hebrew or Greek text?

Our concern from the beginning has not been with the loss of *any* kind of male-oriented meaning in English translations, but with *the loss of male details of meaning that are present in the original Greek or Hebrew text.*[7]

Therefore, it just confuses the discussion, and completely misunderstands what several of us have been saying since at least 1997, when Mark Strauss, for example, publishes an article, "The Gender-Neutral Language of the *English Standard Version* (ESV),[8] in which he compiles a long list of verses in Matthew and Romans where the words "men" and "man" are changed to "people" or "person" in the *English Standard Version* (ESV, a revision of the 1971 *Revised Standard Version*).[9] Strauss says,

Below is a very small sampling of the gender-inclusive language of the ESV.... This list could be multiplied many times over...in this way, the ESV is very much like the recently published *Today's New International Version* (TNIV), which revises the *New International Version* (NIV) in a similar manner.[10]

What Strauss fails to mention in his paper is that the ESV makes such changes *where there is no male meaning in the original text.* These are cases that use *anthrōpos* (which everyone has known for centuries can mean either "man" or "person" depending on the context), or use pronouns like *tis* (which means "someone") or *oudeis* (which means "no one"), and so forth. *These translations of words that have no male meaning in the original Greek are not under dispute, and they have never been under dispute in this entire controversy.* Therefore it is misleading for Strauss to criticize "attacks against the gender language of the TNIV" as "coming from those who produced *similar gender*

---

[7]That is why the "Colorado Springs Guidelines" (released June 3, 1997, and revised September 9, 1997) *approved* things like changing "any man" to "anyone" for Greek *tis*, and changing "men" to "people" for Greek *anthrōpoi*, and why the CSG approved the translation "children" instead of "sons" for the plural Hebrew word *banîm*, and so forth.

[8]Quoted by Carson (pp. 17, 21) and posted online at www.Biblepacesetter.org/bibletranslation/files/gender-inclusive-ESV.doc. Although I interact with Mark Strauss only at this one point in this present paper, I have appreciated his Christian graciousness in my two public debates with him on this matter, and his book *Distorting Scripture? The Challenge of Bible Translation and Gender Accuracy* (Downers Grove: InterVarsity, 1998) is one of the two main books supporting the TNIV's position regarding gender language. Vern Poythress and I interacted with Strauss's book extensively in our book, *The Gender-Neutral Bible Controversy: Muting the Masculinity of God's Words* (Nashville: Broadman & Holman, 2000) (cited henceforth in this article as GNBC).

[9]In the interests of fair disclosure I should note here that I was a member of the Translation Oversight Committee for the ESV. I was paid for this work, but I do not receive any ongoing compensation from sales of the ESV.

[10]Strauss, *ibid.*, 1.

changes in the ESV."[11] The changes are not similar at all. The issue is whether there is a male meaning in the original Greek text or not.

We are now five years into this debate. The Colorado Springs Guidelines were released June 3, 1997. The CSG distinguished several types of translation where there was *no male meaning in the original text*[12] from several other categories of translation where there *was male-oriented meaning in the original text.*[13] But Strauss's paper, five years after the CSG, still shows no awareness of this fundamental distinction that is at the heart of the controversy.

In 2000, Vern Poythress and I wrote,

> The real issue is not the *frequency* with which a translation uses masculine terms like "man" and "he" and "father" and "brother," etc. Nor is the issue whether changes in gender language are made to conform to modern English style. The issue is whether a Bible translation systematically excludes male components of meaning that are there in the original text. If it does, the translation is "gender-neutral," and we argue in this book that such a translation does not properly translate some of the details in the Word of God.[14]

Now if one wishes, one can choose, in a debate, to go on for five years responding to a position that nobody ever held, but it certainly adds no clarity to the debate. And it is misleading to charge that we approve of "similar" changes without indicating to readers that these are all changes where *everyone agrees* there is no male meaning in the original.

B. Other Bibles

1. Have 18 of 19 recent Bible translations used gender-neutral language like the TNIV?

In the special edition of *Light Magazine*, Peter Bradley says,

> Those who are critical of the TNIV often neglect to mention that since 1985, at least 19 Bible revisions and translations have been produced in English, of which 18 contain some type of inclusive language. In fact even the *King James Version* and the *New Holman Christian Standard Bible* [produced by an agency of the Southern Baptist Convention] make extensive use of inclusive language.[15]

That simply misleads ordinary readers. It is counting as "inclusive language" any kinds of change from "men" to "people" *even when there is no male meaning in the Greek text.* It is based on counting as "inclusive

---

[11]Ibid.

[12]For example, *tis, oudeis,* forms like *ho pisteuōn,* and *anthrōpoi* when referring to mixed groups.

[13]For example, singular *adelphos* ("brother"), singular *huios* ("son"), singular *patēr* ("father"), or the male-specific word *anēr* ("man," "husband").

[14]GNBC, 116.

[15]Peter Bradley, "Truth About the TNIV," p. 9.

language" verses like Matthew 5:15, which Mark Strauss quotes among dozens of examples of "inclusive language":

RSV: Nor do **men** light a lamp and put it under a bushel,
ESV: Nor do **people** light a lamp and put it under a bushel,

But there is no word for "men" at all in the Greek text. It simply has the plural verb *kaiousin* "to light, to cause to burn."

No one has objected to changes like this. All modern translations and all modern translators agree that these are correct. So why does Bradley, in an interview responding to criticisms that have only objected to changes *where there is a male meaning in Greek*, respond that everybody makes changes (referring to places *where there is no male meaning in Greek*)?

Let's say a high school student cheats on a test by opening the textbook and copying answers from it. The teacher catches the student and sends the student to the principal. The principal says, "I hear you copied answers from the textbook." Then the student answers, "I just checked with some other students and 18 out of 19 students copied answers from the textbook." Now the principal thinks this student is being singled out unfairly, and wonders if the teacher didn't give misleading instructions, since "everybody" is doing this. So the student gets away with it.

But what the student didn't reveal to the principal is that 18 out of 19 students copied answers *in last week's "open book" test*, not in today's test where they could not use any books or notes. So the student has answered the charges against him by making reference to another situation that nobody has ever said was wrong.

This is similar to what is happening in Bradley's statement about 18 out of 19 translations using "some type of inclusive language" and the KJV and HCSB making "extensive use of inclusive language." It can be summarized like this:

TNIV critics: You are removing male meaning that is there in Greek.
IBS: Everybody removes male meaning [unstated: where it is not there in Greek].

For Bradley to claim that these other translations use "inclusive language," and to imply that the TNIV is doing nothing different, may be convincing to unsuspecting readers of *Light Magazine*, but it is misleading. He is not talking about the kind of verses where the opponents have challenged the TNIV. His statement fails to show an understanding of the very heart of the controversy.

What has actually happened in recent Bible translations? In fact, since the publication of the "Colorado Springs Guidelines" in 1997, I am aware of six new Bible versions that have been published in whole or part: the *English Standard Version* (ESV), the *Holman Christian Standard Bible* (HCSB), the *International Christian Standard Bible* (ICSB), the *NET Bible* (NET), the *New International Reader's Version* (NIrV, 1998 revision), and *Today's New*

International Version (TNIV). All of these versions conform to the *Colorado Springs Guidelines*, with the exception of the TNIV. These other recent translations use male-oriented terminology in English where there is a male meaning in Greek or Hebrew, and they avoid male-oriented terminology where there is no male meaning in Greek or Hebrew. To call them all "inclusive language" versions is simply to confuse the discussion.

2. Did even the King James Version use gender-neutral language like the TNIV?

Peter Bradley's statement says, "Even the *King James Version* and the *New Holman Christian Standard Bible*...make extensive use of inclusive language (p. 9).

Does this mean that the King James Version itself provides a precedent that validates the TNIV? Did the King James Version make the kind of gender-neutral changes for which we have criticized the TNIV? The following table makes a comparison:

Did the KJV use gender-neutral language to leave out male meaning that is present in Greek?

FROM (NIV)	TO (TNIV)	TOTAL TNIV	TOTAL KJV
son (*huios*, singular)	child, children, human beings	6	3 (odd verses)
father, fathers, forefathers (*patēr*)	parents (where inaccurate), people, ancestors	39	0 (Heb. 11:23 has "parents" correctly)
brother (*adelphos*, sing.)	(fellow) believer, brother or sister, other	43	0
brothers (*adelphos*, plural)	associates, dear friends, believers [not counted here: "brothers & sisters"]	42	0
man (*aner*, in non-idiomatic uses)	people, friends, believers, someone, those, or omitted	26	0
he/him/his/himself	they, you, we, or omitted	530	0 (not all checked)
TOTAL		686	3

What this chart shows is that the King James Version accurately retained male-oriented meaning when it was there in the original Greek text.[16] Even the three translations of the singular *huios* as "child" would be what the Colorado Springs Guidelines allow as "unusual exceptions in certain contexts." By contrast, the TNIV inappropriately omits male-oriented meaning for these terms 686 times. To claim that the KJV uses "inclusive language," and to use that as a justification for the TNIV, without telling readers that the KJV is 0.4% as "gender-neutral" as the TNIV in the kinds of changes criticized by the TNIV opponents, is again misleading readers who have no way of checking the Greek for themselves. In terms of removing male meaning that is there in the Greek, the KJV is not a gender-neutral Bible. But the TNIV is.[17]

C. Endorsements and Guidelines

1. Does the Forum of Bible agencies endorse the gender language in the TNIV?

Peter Bradley says,

"The TNIV adheres to the Forum of Bible Agencies' translation principles and procedures."

And Craig Blomberg states,

"…the Forum of Bible Agencies, which represents roughly 90% of all contemporary Bible translation work, has gone on record stating that the TNIV "falls within the forum's translation principles and procedures." (p. 4).

Two things are not disclosed to readers in these statements. First, it would at least seem fair to readers to insert a disclaimer stating that the

---

[16]For further details on these verses, see www.cbmw.org/tniv/categorized_list.html. The three verses where the KJV translated the singular term *huios* ("son") as "child" are: Matthew 23:15 ("child of hell"); Acts 13:10 ("child of the devil"); and Revelation 12:5 ("a man child"), all of which are unusual and probably idiomatic cases (and the Colorado Springs Guidelines allowed for "unusual exceptions in certain contexts"). But the KJV translated singular *huios* as "son" 307 times. The KJV also translated the plural *huioi* as "children" 47 times, which probably reflects understanding of the plural as a Hebraism reflecting the Old Testament's frequent use of Hebrew *banîm* to mean "children." I have not put plural *huioi* in the chart because Vern Poythress and I see the translation of plural *huioi* as "children" or "sons" as a difficult question requiring a judgment call (GNBC, p. 262) and this has not been a central focus of our concerns about the TNIV or gender-neutral translations generally.

[17]The TNIV web site (www.tniv.info, under Luke 17:3 and elsewhere) claims precedent in the KJV translation of Philippians 2:3, "Let nothing be done through strife or vainglory; but in lowliness of mind let each esteem other better than *themselves*." But this is not an instance of changing a singular Greek word to plural, because the entire last clause is plural in Greek, and "themselves" translates the genitive plural pronoun *heautōn*.

Nor should Matthew 18:35 from the KJV be used to justify changing singulars to plurals, "If ye from your hearts forgive not everyone his brother their trespasses," because the Byzantine text tradition, which the KJV translators use, had *ta paraptōmata autōn*, a plural expression which the KJV translated literally as "their trespasses."

In each case the KJV translated singulars as singulars and plurals as plurals, and therefore it gives no precedent for translating singulars and plurals (as in the TNIV).

Forum of Bible Agencies does not endorse any specific translation and has not endorsed the TNIV. When Blomberg says the FBA "has gone on record" stating that the TNIV "falls within the forum's translation principles and procedures," it sounds very much to the unsuspecting ear like an FBA endorsement of the TNIV, and no doubt many readers of the Zondervan packet took it that way.

But in fact the FBA has not endorsed the TNIV. What neither Bradley nor Blomberg mention by way of disclaimer is the June 24, 2002, press release from the Forum of Bible Agencies that was issued for the very purpose of clearing up such misunderstanding:

FORUM OF BIBLE AGENCIES DOES NOT ENDORSE TNIV
NEW YORK—June 24 Contrary to June 11th news release issued by the International Bible Society (IBS) and Zondervan, the Forum of Bible Agencies (FBA) today announced it has neither approved nor disapproved *Today's New International Version* (TNIV) of the Bible.

In addition, the FBA emphasized it has never endorsed the TNIV, as strongly implied in the release issued by forum member IBS in conjunction with Zondervan. Other forum members are aggrieved by the release because of the confusion it has generated among their constituents, as it is not the policy of the FBA to approve, endorse, or support members' translations.

The forum has adopted basic "principles and procedures for Bible translation." This set of guidelines for best practiced translation is mutually agreed upon and accepted by all members....[18]

Why was not this June 24 press release mentioned in the September 2 mailing from Zondervan?

The second thing that is not disclosed to the readers is what the FBA principles actually say about the translation of gender language. In the context of this major public statement by the president of the IBS responding to a controversy over gender language, when he says that "the TNIV adheres to the Forum of Bible Agencies' translation principles and procedures," we naturally assume that those FBA principles make statements about the issue he is talking about, the issue of gender language. In fact, Bradley must understand that readers will *think* the FBA principles endorse the TNIV's use of gender language, or why would he highlight the FBA principles as his *response to criticisms about gender language*?

---

[18]On July 25 the FBA followed this statement with a caution that the ongoing debate about the TNIV "is obscuring more critical Scripture translation and distribution needs worldwide, of which most Christians in the United States are unresponsive or unaware." It also reaffirmed, "contrary to recent news reports, by charter the FBA neither approves nor disapproves of specific English translations of the Bible—including *Today's New International Version* (TNIV)." The June 24 press release can be seen at www.no-tniv.com or www.cbmw.org , under the TNIV section.

But when we read further in the July 25 press release from the Forum of Bible Agencies, we find this:

Recognizing that translation is a complex process for which there are widely differing opinions on appropriate methodology, the FBA adopted basic "principles and procedures for Bible translation" that were mutually agreed upon and accepted for all members. *These standards represent a broad tent,* in that they are not language specific and do not address issues of culture *or gender* (emphasis added).

What do these FBA principles say about the translation of gender language? Zero. They do not address it.[19] It is hard for me to understand why neither Bradley nor Blomberg mention this in their claims about the FBA principles, when gender language is the whole point in dispute.

To take an example, let's say that you are planning to buy a used car from me without seeing it, because you trust me as your friend. When you call to ask me about the condition of the car, I assure you that it recently passed a safety inspection at the local Firestone dealer, including brakes, headlights, transmission, tires, and so forth. So you send me a check for the car and an additional $500 for shipping, and I ship the car to you across the country. When you get the car you see that the body has massive rust spots all over it, and has actually rusted through in several places. You call me in protest, saying that you thought that it had passed an inspection at the local Firestone dealer. And then I say, "Yes, but that was a safety inspection and it really didn't include anything about rust." You would rightly be upset with me and think that I had misled you. (And in fact I would never sell a car in that way!)

But in a similar way, when the International Bible Society and Zondervan put out materials saying that the TNIV "adheres to the Forum of Bible Agencies' translation principles and procedures," without mentioning that these principles are a "broad tent" that say *nothing* about gender language, and when they do that *in a packet of information that is focused specifically on the translation of gender language in the TNIV,* then I think readers are right to feel that they have been misled. The IBS and Zondervan make it look as though the FBA supports the translation of gender language in the TNIV, but in fact that is not true.

2. Do the translation principles of the Forum of Bible Agencies conflict with the Colorado Springs Guidelines?

After mentioning the Forum of Bible Agencies, Peter Bradley goes on to say that the IBS had to withdraw from the Colorado Springs Guidelines (CSG) because they were in conflict with the FBA guidelines and they could not endorse both. Here is his statement:

---

[19]I have reprinted these FBA principles in full in the following section.

...the TNIV adheres to the Forum of Bible Agencies' translation principles and procedures. And yet, we know, as do those opposed to the TNIV, that the TNIV does not adhere to the CSG. *The bottom line is that the Forum's translation guidelines conflict with the CSG,* and we firmly believe we have to abide by the Forum's. After all, the Forum is responsible for nearly 90 percent of translation work done worldwide—they know what they're doing (p. 8).

But is it true that these lists of principles are in "conflict" with one another? It is easy for readers to check this for themselves. I have listed below the FBA's principles and the Colorado Springs Guidelines. The FBA principles contain fifteen statements, *not one of which says anything about the translation of gender language.* The Colorado Springs Guidelines contain thirteen statements, *all of which relate to the translation of gender language.* There is no conflict, because they are talking about different subjects.

Forum of Bible Agencies
Basic Principles and Procedures for Bible Translation

After discussion over a period of two years and wide review within each member organization, the following joint statement on basic principles and procedures for Bible translation was unanimously agreed by all member organizations of the Forum of Bible Agencies, Translation section, at their meeting on April 21, 1999.

As member organizations of the Forum of Bible Agencies, we affirm the inspiration and authority of the Holy Scriptures and commit ourselves to the following goals.

Concerning translation principles:
1. To translate the Scriptures accurately, without loss, change, distortion or embellishment of the meaning of the original text. Accuracy in Bible translation is the faithful communication, as exactly as possible, of that meaning, determined according to sound principles of exegesis.
2. To communicate not only the informational content, but also the feelings and attitudes of the original text. The flavor and impact of the original should be re-expressed in forms that are consistent with normal usage in the receptor language.
3. To preserve the variety of the original. The literary forms employed in the original text, such as poetry, prophecy, narrative and exhortation, should be represented by corresponding forms with the same communicative functions in the receptor language. The impact, interest, and mnemonic value of the original should be retained to the greatest extent possible.
4. To represent faithfully the original historical and cultural context. Historical facts and events should be expressed without distortion. At the same time the translation should be done in such a way that

the receptor audience, despite differences of situation and culture, may understand the message that the original author was seeking to communicate to the original audience.

5. To make every effort to ensure that no contemporary political, ideological, social, cultural, or theological agenda is allowed to distort the translation.

6. To recognize that it is sometimes necessary to restructure the form of a text in order to achieve accuracy and maximal comprehension. Since grammatical categories and syntactic structures often do not correspond between different languages, it is often impossible or misleading to maintain the same form as the source text. Changes of form will also often be necessary when translating figurative language. A translation will employ as many or as few terms as are required to communicate the original meaning as accurately as possible.

7. To use the most reliable original language Scripture texts as the basis for translation, recognizing that these are always the primary authority. However, reliable Bible translations in other languages may be used as intermediary source texts.

Concerning translation procedures:

8. To determine, after careful linguistic and sociolinguistic research, the specific target audience for the translation and the kind of translation appropriate to that audience. It is recognized that different kinds of translation into a given language may be valid, depending on the local situation, including, for example, both more formal translations and common language translations.

9. To recognize that the transfer into the receptor language should be done by trained and competent translators who are translating into their mother tongue. Where this is not possible, mother-tongue speakers should be involved to the greatest extent possible in the translation process.

10. To give high priority to training mother-tongue speakers of the receptor language in translation principles and practice and to providing appropriate professional support.

11. To test the translation as extensively as possible in the receptor community to ensure that it communicates accurately, clearly and naturally, keeping in mind the sensitivities and experience of the receptor audience.

12. To choose the media for the translation that are most appropriate for the specific target audience, whether audio, visual, electronic, print, or a combination of these. This may involve making adjustments of form that are appropriate to the medium and to the cultural setting, while ensuring that the translated message remains faithful to the original message.

13. To encourage the periodic review of translations to ascertain when revision or a new translation is needed.

Concerning partnership and cooperation:

14. To organize translation projects in a way that promotes and facilitates the active participation of the Christian and wider community, commensurate with local circumstances. Where there are existing churches, we will encourage these churches to be involved in the translation and to carry as much responsibility for the translation project as is feasible.

15. To partner and cooperate with others who are committed to the same goals.

*****

Colorado Springs Guidelines for Translation of Gender-Related Language in Scripture

A. Gender-related renderings of Biblical language which we affirm:

1. The generic use of "he, him, his, himself" should be employed to translate generic 3rd person masculine singular pronouns in Hebrew, Aramaic and Greek. However, substantival participles such as *ho pisteuōn* can often be rendered in inclusive ways, such as "the one who believes" rather than "he who believes."

2. Person and number should be retained in translation so that singulars are not changed to plurals and third person statements are not changed to second or first person statements, with only rare exceptions required in unusual cases.

3. "Man" should ordinarily be used to designate the human race, for example in Genesis 1:26–27; 5:2; Ezekiel 29:11; and John 2:25.

4. Hebrew *îsh* should ordinarily be translated "man" and "men," and Greek *anēr* should almost always be so translated.

5. In many cases, *anthrōpoi* refers to people in general, and can be translated "people" rather than "men." The singular *anthrōpos* should ordinarily be translated "man" when it refers to a male human being.

6. Indefinite pronouns such as *tis* can be translated "anyone" rather than "any man."

7. In many cases, pronouns such as *oudeis* can be translated "no one" rather than "no man."

8. When *pas* is used as a substantive it can be translated with terms such as "all people" or "everyone."

9. The phrase "son of man" should ordinarily be preserved to retain intracanonical connections.

10. Masculine references to God should be retained.

B. Gender-related renderings which we will generally avoid, though there may be unusual exceptions in certain contexts:

1. "Brother" (*adelphos*) should not be changed to "brother or sister"; however, the plural *adelphoi* can be translated "brothers and sisters" where the context makes clear that the author is referring to both men and women.
2. "Son" (*huios, ben*) should not be changed to "child," or "sons" (*huioi*) to "children" or "sons and daughters." (However, Hebrew *banîm* often means "children.")
3. "Father" (*patēr, 'āb*) should not be changed to "parent," or "fathers" to "parents" or "ancestors."

C. *We understand these guidelines to be representative and not exhaustive, and that some details may need further refinement.*

It is difficult for me to understand, therefore, how Peter Bradley can say that "the Forum's translation guidelines conflict with the CSG," and to give that as the reason why the International Bible Society felt it had to withdraw its endorsement of the Colorado Springs Guidelines.

3. Were the Colorado Springs Guidelines forced on the International Bible Society in 1997?

Peter Bradley's article, in referring to the May 27, 1997, meeting at Focus on the Family headquarters in Colorado Springs, says,

> During that meeting, IBS representatives and other attendees were surprised by the presentation of the CSG, in first draft form, to all in attendance. By the way, the CSG were drafted under the guidance of a professor who represented a special interest group called the Council on Biblical Manhood and Womanhood. Every party was asked to endorse them. However, the members of CBT who were present believed the guidelines were flawed. As a result, they chose not to sign the CSG until they could review and edit them. This process went on for a number of months...(p. 7).

I was a part of that meeting in 1997, and I suppose I am the "professor" to whom Peter Bradley refers. Bradley's statement makes the process appear adversarial and makes it sound as though the CBT members had serious objections to the Colorado Springs Guidelines from the beginning.

In order that Bradley's view of the CSG as flawed from the beginning not be established as a balanced report of the origins of the CSG, I present here a different account of that May 27, 1997, meeting at Dr. Dobson's headquarters in Colorado Springs. *This account was written almost immediately after the meeting.* But is it accurate? Before it was published, I sent it to all the participants to check it for factual accuracy (and some suggested corrections, which I made). *Both of the NIV representatives who stayed for the whole meeting* (Bruce Ryskamp, president of Zondervan, and Ken Barker, secretary of the NIV's Committee on Bible Translation) *approved this account as accurate before I published it,* as did those of us who came to the meeting with objections about the TNIV (Tim Bayly, Joel Belz, James Dobson, Charles

Jarvis, John Piper, Vern Poythress, and R. C. Sproul).[20] This account was published in June 1997.[21]

I first described the opening discussions of the meeting, including brief statements that were presented by R. C. Sproul, John Piper, and Vern Poythress. Then the report says that "I presented a list of suggestions for guidelines involving the translation of gender-related language in Scripture" (p. 305). And then the narrative continues:

> As our discussions continued through the morning, however, we found that we shared even more common ground…. *We found that Ken Barker had a list of translation guidelines that he had prepared in recent thinking about these issues, and his list was similar to the list that our group had presented.* Several of us saw this as evidence that God had prepared the way for us to reach agreement on a wide number of these issues. From that point on in the meeting, we began to work on a joint statement that could be issued as a press release from Focus on the Family (p. 306, emphasis added).
>
> …. We reached substantial agreement on all of these points before the meeting broke up about 2:30 in the afternoon on May 27, but the document had to be circulated by fax and phone three times throughout the subsequent five days, before total agreement was reached on the final wording of all the guidelines. Then on Saturday night, May 31, complete agreement on the wording of the guidelines was finally reached by phone. By Monday morning, June 2, all twelve participants had signed the final document and faxed their signatures to the Focus on the Family headquarters. The press release was then issued on June 3 (pp. 311–312).

In fact, during that afternoon, the first draft of the "Colorado Springs Guidelines" was prepared by four of us working together: Ken Barker of the CBT, along with Vern Poythress, John Piper, and me. We did not use my first draft, but *began instead with Ken Barker's notes that he had brought to the meeting* (and of which I still have a copy in his handwriting). His draft statement was called "A Balanced, Mediating, Middle Ground Approach to Inclusive Language" and under "Practices to continue/Areas Not Open to Change" it included "generic use of he, his, him," and "don't change from singular to plural or from third person to second person to avoid man, he, his, him," along with several other points that were eventually included in the Colorado Springs Guidelines.[22]

---

[20]Due to prior conflicts, Ron Youngblood of the CBT and Lars Dunberg, then president of the IBS, had to leave the meeting early and so did not have first-hand knowledge of the development of the guidelines through that afternoon.

[21]Wayne A. Grudem, "NIV Controversy: Participants Sign Landmark Agreement," *CBMW News* 2/3 (June 1997): 1, 3–6. The account has been reprinted in Vern Poythress and Wayne Grudem, *The Gender-Neutral Bible Controversy: Muting the Masculinity of God's Words* (Nashville: Broadman and Holman, 2000), 304–315.

[22]After our June 3, 1997, press release, we received considerable comment from many other scholars, and as a result made three modifications to the Colorado Springs Guidelines on September 9, 1997, including endorsing the legitimacy of translating Greek *adelphoi* (plural) as "brothers and sisters" where the context allowed it.

I want to be very clear that I think the International Bible Society, and the NIV's Committee on Bible Translation, and all individual scholars, are completely free to endorse or not endorse the Colorado Springs Guidelines or any other set of guidelines they wish to formulate. I also believe that the Colorado Springs Guidelines are not perfect and are not set in concrete but are open to further refinement and revision, as we said in the last statement of the guidelines: "We understand these guidelines to be representative and not exhaustive, and that some details may need further refinement."

But I do not think it is correct to say that these guidelines contradict the Forum of Bible Agencies' principles, or to say that "the members of the CBT that were present believed the guidelines were flawed," when in fact Ken Barker was the only CBT member remaining in the meeting when they were formulated, and we used his handwritten first draft of principles as the foundation upon which the guidelines were built. Nor is it correct to say that the CBT members "chose not to sign the CSG until they could review and edit them" and then to say that "this process went on for a number of months," without mentioning that the president of the IBS, the president of Zondervan, and both CBT members (Ron Youngblood and Ken Barker) all agreed to the exact wording of the guidelines within four days of the meeting and all signed that wording within six days of that meeting.

4. Are most New Testament scholars in favor of the TNIV?

Craig Blomberg's paper says, "An advertisement has circulated with the signatures of 100 well-known, largely American Christian leaders condemning the new translation, though few are bona fide New Testament scholars" (p. 3). In a footnote to this statement Blomberg says, "Approximately 10% are fully credentialed New Testament scholars." The impression given is that few genuine New Testament scholars oppose the TNIV.

What Blomberg fails to mention is that prior to the publication of an advertisement with the names of 100 evangelical leaders objecting to the TNIV there was a statement signed by 37 evangelical scholars. Here is that "Statement of Concern" issued February 1, 2002, shortly after the advanced copy of the TNIV was published:

Statement of Concern by Evangelical Scholars:
Released Feb. 1, 2002 (list updated with 37 names, Feb. 7, 2002)

In light of troubling translation inaccuracies—primarily (but not exclusively) in relation to gender language—that introduce distortions of the meanings that were conveyed better by the original NIV, we cannot endorse the TNIV translation as sufficiently accurate to commend to the church.

Gregg R. Allison, Ph.D., Western Seminary, Portland, OR, **Henry S. Baldwin, Ph.D.**, Singapore Bible College, Singapore, **S. M. Baugh, Ph.D.**,

Westminster Theological Seminary in California, Escondido, CA, **Hans F. Bayer, Ph.D.**, Covenant Seminary, St. Louis, MO, **James Borland, Th.D.**, Liberty University, Lynchburg, VA, **Harold O. J. Brown, Ph.D.**, Reformed Theological Seminary, Charlotte, NC, **Ardel B. Caneday, Ph.D.**, Northwestern College, St. Paul, MN, **E. Ray Clendenen, Ph.D.**, Lifeway Christian Resources, Nashville, TN, **Clifford John Collins, Ph.D.**, Covenant Seminary, St. Louis, MO, **William Cook, Ph.D.**, Southern Baptist Theological Seminary, Louisville, KY, **Jack Cottrell, Ph.D.**, Cincinnati Bible College and Seminary, Cincinnati, OH, **Daniel Doriani, Ph.D.**, Covenant Seminary, St. Louis, MO, **J. Ligon Duncan III, Ph.D.**, First Presbyterian Church, Jackson, MS, **John M. Frame, M.Phil.**, Reformed Theological Seminary, Orlando, FL, **Paul D. Gardner, Ph.D.**, Church of England Evangelical Council, Hartford, England, **Wayne Grudem, Ph.D.**, Phoenix Seminary, Scottsdale, AZ, **C.E. Hill, Ph.D.**, Reformed Theological Seminary, Orlando, FL, **H. Wayne House, Ph.D.**, Faith Seminary, Tacoma, WA, **W. Bingham Hunter, Ph.D.**, Pastor of Adult Ministries, Harvest Bible Chapel, Former Academic Dean of Trinity Evangelical Divinity School and Talbot School of Theology, **Peter Jones, Ph.D.**, Westminster Theological Seminary, Escondido, CA, **Reggie M. Kidd, Ph.D.**, Reformed Theological Seminary, Orlando, FL, **George W. Knight, III, Ph.D.**, Greenville Presbyterian Seminary, Taylors, SC, **J. Carl Laney, Th.D.**, Western Seminary, Portland, OR, **Al Mawhinney, Ph.D.**, Reformed Theological Seminary, Orlando, FL, **R. Albert Mohler, Ph.D.**, Southern Baptist Theological Seminary, Louisville, KY, **William D. Mounce, Ph.D.**, Cornerstone Fellowship, Spokane, WA, **Raymond C. Ortlund, Jr., Ph.D.**, First Presbyterian Church, Augusta, GA, **Paige Patterson, Th.D.**, Southeastern Baptist Theological Seminary, Wake Forest, NC, **John Piper, D. theol.**, Bethlehem Baptist Church, Minneapolis, MN, **Vern S. Poythress, Ph.D., Th.D.**, Westminster Theological Seminary, Philadelphia, PA, **Mark R. Saucy, Ph.D.**, Kyiv Theological Seminary, **Thomas R. Schreiner, Ph.D.**, Southern Baptist Theological Seminary, Louisville, KY, **R. C., Sproul, DRS, Ph.D.**, Ligonier Ministries, Lake Mary, FL, **Bruce Ware, Ph.D.**, Southern Baptist Theological Seminary, Louisville, KY, **William Weinrich, Ph.D.**, Concordia Seminary, Ft. Wayne, IN, **Dean O. Wenthe, Ph.D.**, Concordia Theological Seminary, Fort Wayne, IN, **Robert Yarbrough, Ph.D.**, Trinity Evangelical Divinity School, Deerfield, IL

Of the signers on this list:
21 have Ph.D.'s in New Testament
3 have Ph.D.'s in Old Testament
11 have served as paid professional translators or translation consultants for three different English translations of the Bible.

The initial letter asking for signers to this list was sent out from the CBMW office by Bruce Ware and me, and also included as initial signers William Mounce (whose *Basics of Biblical Greek* in the largest-selling Greek textbook in the US, and perhaps in the world), John Piper (who has a doctorate in New Testament from the University of Munich and whose dissertation was published in the prestigious SNTS Monograph Series), Vern Poythress (widely-published New Testament professor from Westminster Seminary in Philadelphia), and Tom Schreiner (widely-published New Testament professor at Southern Seminary in Louisville).

In addition, J. I. Packer, who did not sign the statement, issued his own statement saying, "This is a retrograde move that the translators have made.... The gains that this translation seeks to achieve are far outweighed by the loss. I appreciate the NIV, and I think they have taken a wrong turn" (Baptist Press, Feb. 1, 2002; http://baptistpress.org/bpnews.asp?ID= 12653).

If we move outside the field of New Testament to the field of linguistics, we might ask, is there some special competence in the field of linguistics, some "inside knowledge" that perhaps gives validity to the TNIV? Is there some special theory of linguistics that is unknown to seminary graduates and even to New Testament professors, which justifies the TNIV's removal of male-oriented language that is there in the original text? Some TNIV supporters seem to have suggested that, but there is an alternative perspective by an established professional linguist, one who was in fact the president of a professional society for linguists. Here is the endorsement of Vern Poythress' and my book, *The Gender-Neutral Bible Controversy*, which was made by a woman who is both a professor of linguistics and an elder in the Christian Church (Disciples of Christ):

> In the present volume Vern Poythress and Wayne Grudem have presented a well-reasoned and level-headed argument for their case. Indeed, they are a voice of reason in a dispute that is fraught with emotion and mis-information. *They clearly understand the fluid and changing nature of language and their arguments are based on sound linguistic principles...* (from "Foreword" to *The Gender-Neutral Bible Controversy*, p. xvii).
> Valerie Becker Makkai (Ph.D., Yale; Associate Professor of Linguistics, University of Illinois-Chicago; past president, Linguistic Association of Canada and the United States).

Of course I realize that the TNIV web site also includes endorsement by a number of scholars. On both lists one can find some scholars who are less well known and some who are more well known. So where does that leave us? The bottom line is that there are competent scholars on both sides of this issue.

But is this issue really supposed to be decided by who has the "most famous" scholars? I hope that no one will decide this issue simply based on allegiance to one scholar or another like the Corinthians who were saying,

"I follow Paul," or "I follow Apollos," or "I follow Cephas," or "I follow Christ" (1 Cor. 1:12). Rather, I hope that people will look for themselves at the patterns of changes in the translation of verses, and will be like the noble Bereans who went back to the Bible for themselves, "examining the Scriptures daily to see if these things were so" (Acts 17:11).

Nor should we dismiss lightly the mature wisdom of 113 Christian leaders who signed a public statement saying the TNIV was not "sufficiently trustworthy" (www.no-tniv.com; also printed below on pages 101–109). Many of these leaders have solid seminary training and continue to work daily with their Greek and Hebrew Bibles, ministering to thousands of people through solid, expository preaching. They do understand the issues well enough to make a responsible judgment, and they know that something is deeply wrong with the TNIV.[23]

5. Can only scholars understand this dispute?

Some of the TNIV materials give the impression that only scholars can understand this issue (and in fact, the tone sometimes sounds like they think that only pro-TNIV scholars can understand this issue). This seems to me to be a smokescreen. Most of the dispute has to do with some simple English words, and the very common Greek words behind them:

father
son
brother
man
he/him/his

At times when lay persons have asked me, "How can I decide this issue when I am not a Greek and Hebrew expert?" I have pointed out that the issue is mostly over the meaning of those five words. And if a pro-TNIV scholar challenges them, "How are you qualified to make a decision on this?" I suggest that they ask the following questions:

(1) Have the *Greek words* behind these five terms changed since the 1984 NIV? (No.)

(2) Have the *meanings* of those Greek words changed since the 1984 NIV? (No.)

(3) So isn't the real question mostly one of English usage? (Yes.)

---

[23]On a personal note, I can say that in the process of circulating e-mails and faxes asking if people would sign a statement of concern about the TNIV, what surprised me was how seriously people felt about this issue. Many scholars and pastors and other Christian leaders who seldom put their names on any endorsement of anything (to say nothing of a criticism of a Bible!) felt they had no choice but to take a stand against the direction taken by the TNIV. There were also some people (both scholars and others) who declined to add their names but who said to us privately that they thought the TNIV was wrong. What surprised me was how so few people (almost no one, but a few) declined to sign our statement because they thought the TNIV was right in what it was doing.

(4) So I speak English. Are you saying that I don't know English well enough to make a good decision on this?

In fact, the TNIV's preface places the focus on changes *in English*, because it introduces the changes in gender language by saying, "While a basic core of the *English language* remains relatively stable, many diverse and complex cultural forces continue to bring about *subtle shifts in the meanings and/or connotations* of even old, well-established words and phrases" (p. vii).

The question then is whether the English language today *requires* us to change "father" (singular) to "parents," or "son" (singular) to "children," or "he" to "they" or "we" or "you" in the hundreds of verses where the TNIV has made these changes (see the categorized list of 900 examples at www.cbmw.org). Ordinary English speakers have a good sense of these changes, and they quickly recognize that these changes follow the same pattern as the "politically correct" speech codes that object to any greater use of male examples than female examples.

In fact, the implicit claim that "only scholars can understand this dispute" (or even that "only pro-TNIV scholars can understand this; anti-TNIV scholars don't understand it") sounds to me dangerously like the claim of the Roman Catholic Church during the Reformation—the claim that only experts could understand the Bible rightly.

I don't agree with this view. I think that English-speaking Christians who know their Bibles and can see the evidence and arguments on both sides are very capable of making a right decision on this matter, and they are making it overwhelmingly on the side of rejecting the TNIV Bible.

D. The English language

I. Has English changed so much that gender-neutral Bibles are needed today?

Probably the fundamental claim of the TNIV supporters is that the English language has changed so much that a translation like the TNIV is needed, particularly to communicate to a younger generation of readers. Peter Bradley says,

> The fact is, inclusive language is simply the way English usage is rapidly moving....The use of generic masculine language is rapidly fading. As a result, there is an entire generation of young people who don't use it and don't understand its usage (p. 7).

Similarly, Don Carson says, "I have been doing university missions for thirty years, and in such quarters inclusive language dominates. Not to use it is offensive" (p. 21). And Bruce Waltke says, interestingly, "Although I resent it, the English language has been impacted by secular (non-biblical) feminism and many students today are trained to hear 'man' and 'he' and their equivalents as referring only to males, excluding females" (p. 1–2).

The problem with these statements is that they are too vague. These authors do not specify what they mean by "inclusive language." Vern Poythress and I in our book, and the CSG, approve of several kinds of "inclusive language," such as saying *"No one* is justified by faith" instead of *"No man* is justified by faith." To speak of "inclusive language" in a general way is to blur the main point under dispute. Similarly, to say, "The use of generic masculine language is rapidly fading" is too vague. What kind of "generic masculine" is meant? Everyone has agreed from 1997 onward that we can remove "generic masculine language" like "he who" and "no man" and "any man" and "all men" *when there is no male meaning in the original.* So what does Bradley mean?

But if we assume for a moment that Bradley means that the use of "he/him/his" in generic statements is "rapidly fading," what does that tell us? The statement is still (a) an admission that this language is still used, and (b) an implicit prediction of the absence of such language in the future.

But the translators of the NIV ten years ago, back in 1992, were convinced that such language was "rapidly fading" and instituted policies that produced the ill-fated *NIV-Inclusive Language Edition* in 1996. Apparently ten years later such language is still rapidly fading. We begin to wonder if this "rapid fading" might continue for another twenty or fifty or one hundred years. Or if the personal perception of rapid fading is incorrect (see counter-evidence below).

A more sober evaluation is the last sentence in the 1996 *American Heritage Dictionary.* After it devotes an entire column to discussion about the use of "he" to refer to "a male who is to be taken as the representative member of the group," the last sentence says, "The entire question is unlikely to be resolved in the near future" (p. 831).

Here is the real point at issue regarding the English language:

Do readers today *understand* male specific language correctly when it represents male-specific meaning in the original text, especially in statements that have a broader application to all people?

The question is not exactly frequency of use, because when people read, they *understand* all kinds of expressions they don't use frequently themselves. And high school and college English departments can arbitrarily force students to abandon certain expressions that are still used in the Bible and elsewhere, expressions that students still understand very well when they read it in literature that was written outside their own school setting.

For example, consider the following:

NIV Luke 17:3–4: "If your **brother** sins rebuke **him,** and if **he** repents, forgive **him,** and if **he** sins against you seven times in the day, and turns to you seven times, saying, 'I repent,' you must forgive **him.**"

Jesus is using a single male individual ("your brother") as an example of a general truth. He wants the reader to envision a situation where a "brother" (a male human being who is a fellow believer) sins. He goes on to tell how to deal with such a situation. And he expects that his hearers will be able to extrapolate from that specific situation to a general principle that would of course apply to a "sister" who sins as well.

Now the question is, would a modern day reader (whether the "young people" whom Bradley mentions or the university students whom Carson mentions) first picture a "brother" who sins, and second realize that the principle has application to a "sister" who sins as well?

I think it is beyond question that readers today would understand that the principle has a *broader application* to women as well as to men. I doubt that any significant group of readers in the English-speaking world today would see that verse and reason, "That verse only applies to men, and it has no application to a situation where a woman believer has sinned."[24]

Now some people may *dislike* the fact that Jesus is using a male individual as an example. But that is different from not *understanding* that it *applies* to women as well as to men. And the fact remains that Jesus used a male-specific term (singular *adelphos*, "brother") and did not teach by using an example of a "brother or sister" or an example of a "person." He taught by using a concrete example of a "brother."

In fact, the Bible often points to a single individual as a way of teaching a general truth. Jesus uses the parable of the prodigal son (Luke 15:11–32), but surely people can understand that it also *applies* to prodigal daughters. That is the difference between *translation* and *application*. The parable of the "persistent widow" (Luke 18:1–8) also *applies* to men and teaches us all about persistence in prayer, but we should not *translate* it to be the parable of "the persistent widow or widower." And in the Ten Commandments, when we read, "You shall not covet your neighbor's *wife*," we can easily realize that the specific female example given here ("your neighbor's wife") teaches a principle that also *applies* to not coveting a neighbor's husband.

---

[24]I realize that children may misunderstand such a statement, just as children misunderstand many things in the Bible and in other things they read. Blomberg makes much of a young girl's misunderstanding of a Bible text (pp. 29–30), but the verse he quotes is the 1611 KJV's rendering of 2 Cor. 5:17, "If any **man** be in Christ, he is a new creation." The Greek has *tis* and all modern translations have "anyone" or equivalent. Why quote a place where the KJV is wrongly male-oriented, where the CSG would say to change to "anyone," *as a criticism of the CSG?*

In another article in *Light Magazine*, Phil Ginsburg tells of a third-grade girl who asked, "Daddy, why is the Bible only written to boys?" (p. 16). He gives no explanation of what passage or what translation prompted this question. It may have been the archaic KJV, in which overly male-specific language should of course be corrected. Or it may have been the warnings from a father to a son about relationships to women in Proverbs 5–7, which we cannot change. Surely it was not Proverbs 31, about the excellent wife. Surely it was not the story of Ruth, or Esther, or Sarah, or Rebecca, or Mary.

Our response to such a story should be to translate the Bible accurately. *If we begin to change our Bible translations because of stories of misunderstandings by children, the process will never stop.*

Do we have to change the parable of the prodigal son to make it the parable of the prodigal "son or daughter" in order for modern university students to understand that it has a broader application? Certainly not. Do we have to change the Ten Commandments so that they say, "You shall not covet your neighbor's *wife or husband*" in order to be sure that modern university students will realize that it also *applies* to wives not coveting husbands? Certainly not—not even in the university settings that Carson mentions, where "inclusive language dominates." Ordinary English readers can make such steps from translation to broader application quite well.

But in Luke 17:3, the TNIV imposed just this kind of change on Jesus' words. Jesus taught using a single male ("your brother") as an example of a general truth, but the TNIV will not let him do this:

> NIV: If your **brother** sins rebuke **him**, and if **he** repents, forgive **him**, and if **he** sins against you seven times in the day, and turns to you seven times, saying, 'I repent,' you must forgive **him**."
>
> TNIV: If any **brother or sister** sins against you, rebuke **the offender**; and if **they** repent forgive **them**. Even if **they** sin against you seven times in a day and seven times come back to you saying, "I repent," you must forgive **them**.

This is the kind of change to "inclusive language" that the TNIV translators say is necessary because of changes in modern English.

Readers today are perfectly capable of understanding that a male-specific example (or a female-specific example, such as the woman with the lost coin, or the persistent widow with the judge) has a broader application to people in general. No changes in English speech patterns today have taken away that ability. In fact, I doubt that any future changes in English will ever take away the ability to understand such statements readily. The ability to understand this kind of specific example used to teach a general truth is something inherent in ordinary human life.

Now someone may say that he or she does not *like* the fact that the Bible uses more male examples than female examples to teach such truths. But we cannot do anything about that, for the Bible is what it is, and while it does use both men and women as examples of general truth, it uses male examples more frequently. Should we try to conceal that fact from modern readers? The TNIV does so hundreds of times.

Another example is 1 Corinthians 14:28, about speaking in tongues in the church service:

> NIV: If there is no interpreter, the speaker should keep quiet in the church and speak **to himself** and God.

The question here is, can modern readers understand that Paul's example here also *applies* to women who speak in tongues? Do the TNIV translators actually think that there are significant numbers of women in the English-speaking world who have read that verse and decided that it *only applies to men*, so that women are free to speak in tongues in church without interpretation as often as they wish? Do we know of cases where women have been speaking in tongues without interpretation in church services, arguing that this is just fine because Paul used the word "himself" and therefore the verse only applies to men? Of course this has not happened.

Now people may not *like* the fact that Paul uses a masculine pronoun that makes it more likely that the reader will first picture a male speaker and second realize that it has broader application to all people, but the fact is that in Greek as well as English, to use a singular pronoun to refer to persons, one has to choose either a masculine or a feminine pronoun. If Paul had used a feminine pronoun, we would have to translate, "If there is no interpreter, the speaker should keep quiet in the church and speak **to herself** and God," and we would in that case first think of a female speaker and then immediately realize of course that it had broader application to a male speaker as well. But that is not what Paul wrote, and we do not have freedom to translate it as "to herself."

Nor is the issue here one of modern stylistic preferences for an author composing his or her own new writings. Many modern English style books would look at 1 Corinthians 14:28 and suggest that Paul should rewrite it with plurals, "The **speakers** should keep quiet in the church and speak **to themselves** and God." If modern writers are composing their own sentences and wish to recast a sentence in this way, or if they want to say "speak *to himself or to herself* and God," or if they want to change their sentence in some other way, then they are free to do so, *provided that they are writing their own sentences and not translating the words of the Bible.* But if we are translating what Paul wrote, then we are not free to change his male-specific example into a plural sentence or something else that fails to represent accurately what he wrote.

What does the TNIV do with this verse? It changes it as follows:

NIV 1 Cor. 14:28: If there is no interpreter, the speaker should keep quiet in the church and speak **to himself** and God.

TNIV 1 Cor. 14:28: If there is no interpreter, the speaker should keep quiet in the church and speak to God **when alone**.

The problem is that there is nothing that means "when alone" in the Greek text (the dative pronoun *heautō* here means "to himself" in parallel with the dative phrase *tō theō*, "to God"). The TNIV's interpretation that this means "when the speaker is *alone*" may be some commentator's further *explanation* of the passage, but it is probably an overly restrictive explanation, and it is surely not an accurate *translation* of the passage.

This is important because, prior to the TNIV, people could disagree over whether Paul allowed uninterpreted prayer in tongues in small private groups outside the church meeting; but here the TNIV invents a new rule that Paul (and God) never stipulated: Someone praying in tongues must be "alone."

The TNIV translators perhaps did not even realize how they were altering the meaning of this verse (or perhaps they did; I don't know). But the point is that they did so in an attempt to *avoid* the faintly male-specific example which Paul implied when he used a masculine singular pronoun meaning "to himself." That translation is accurate, it is faithful to what Paul wrote, and no changes in the English language have occurred that take away people's ability to understand Paul's meaning and the broader application of the specific example.

Another example is found in Revelation 22:18:

NIV: I warn everyone who hears the words of the prophecy of this book: If **anyone** adds anything to them, God will add to **him** the plagues described in this book.

TNIV: I warn everyone who hears the words of the prophecy of this scroll: If **any one of you** adds anything to them, God will add to **you** the plagues described in this scroll.

Once again the question is this: does anyone seriously believe that any significant group of people were reading the NIV, "If **anyone** adds anything to them, God will add to **him** the plagues," and thinking that the warning *did not apply to women*? Have there been any groups of women who have decided that they were free to add to the words of the book of Revelation, because this warning did not apply to them? Of course not.

I realize that we may find people who do not *like* the fact that the verse hints first at an example of a male human being who would add to these words, because it does use the pronoun "him." But the Greek text as the apostle John wrote it also used a masculine singular pronoun, and also suggested in the first instance a picture of a male human being adding to these words, with the realization that people would automatically understand that it also *applied to* any women who would think of adding to the words of that book. The fact that someone might not like something that is in the Bible does not give warrant for changing what it says.

And the TNIV has in fact changed the meaning of the verse. Previously the verse warned that God would add the plagues only to the specific individual who added to the words of the book ("God will add *to him* the plagues"). *But now the TNIV has God adding the plagues to the whole group!* When the sentence starts out, "If any one of you," the "you" has to include all of the readers in the group to which John is writing (for the "any one" refers to one person out of the whole group of "you"). But the TNIV does not say God will add the plagues to "that person" or "that one," but, in a way that should terrify us if we think about it, the TNIV has God adding the plagues to the whole group: "If any one *of you* adds anything to them, God will add *to you* the plagues described in this scroll." And so, under cover of the argument that "the English language has changed" the NIV has unnecessarily and inappropriately changed the meaning of the very verse that tells us not to change the words of this book of Scripture! And there are hundreds of such changes like this in the TNIV.

2. Do people think that generic "he" does not apply to women today?

Because the use of "he/him/his/himself" is so frequently changed in gender-neutral Bibles, especially in examples like the ones given above, the argument that "the English language has changed" provides an important defense for the removal of such words. Blomberg says,

> …in spoken English I almost never hear anyone any more completing a sentence of the form, "Everyone who comes to class tomorrow should bring _____ textbook with _____," with anything other than "their" and "them" respectively" (pp. 22–23).

And Carson says,

> …if for the envisaged readership of TNIV the pronouns "him" and "he" have the effect…of excluding approximately half of humanity, one could responsibly argue that the TNIV is, for such a readership, a *more accurate, more faithful* translation than the NIV or the ESV (p. 28).

But the question is not how frequently people say, "Everyone should bring their textbook with them" in spoken English today. The questions are rather: (1) What English translation most accurately represents what the biblical text actually said? and (2) Will people understand the meaning of such a translation?

As far as most accurately representing what the Biblical text actually said, I agree with Blomberg who correctly says (in this very context), "… there is no question that a change of person or number renders a translation less than fully literal" (p. 23).

Will people understand the use of "he" in a statement of a general principle like, "If anyone adds anything to them, God will add to **him** the plagues described in this book"? I think it is beyond question that people today *do understand* the generic use of "he" in sentences like that. What is the evidence that people will understand it? It is still found in ordinary English publications from a wide variety of sources. Just this month the following sentence appeared in *Christianity Today*:

> If the translator doesn't know what *he's* talking about, why should *he* be translating? (Eugene Nida, in "Meaning-full Translations," a report of an interview by David Neff, *Christianity Today*, October 7, 2002, p. 49).

Does anyone seriously think that readers thought Eugene Nida's sentence did not *apply to* women translators? Or that he was implying that women translators who do not know what they are talking about *should* be translating, men who do not know what they are talking about *should not* be translating? Of course not.

"...a passenger assisting in an emergency, for example, could put *himself* in the line of fire of an armed air marshal" (*USA Today,* September 17, 2002, p. 9E, in an article on how passengers should react in the case of an airline hijacking).

Did readers of *USA Today* misunderstand that sentence? Did the women airline travelers reading *USA Today* think, "Oh, then I am free to try to assist by attacking a terrorist because *USA Today* said that only men who did this would put themselves in the line of fire of an armed air marshal"? Of course not. Such usage is ordinary English.

"First, the person who buys the policy reports on **his** tax return only a small portion of what **he** really paid in premiums....The buyer is allowed to declare on **his** tax return the insurance company's lowest premium for that amount of insurance" (*Arizona Republic* July 28, 2002, p. A2, quoting an article by David Cay Johnston in the *New York Times* about wealthy people who buy certain types of life insurance to avoid taxes.)

There is no possibility that readers would think this article does not apply to wealthy women who buy such insurance policies.

"Mr. Baer's CIA is a place where...anyone who takes the initiative runs the risk of derailing **his** career" (*Wall Street Journal* February 7, 2002, p. A15).

Again, would any reader think that this means there are no women working at the CIA? Or that the sentence means that a woman who takes the initiative to point out a problem in intelligence gathering would not ruin her career? Of course not.

"Should you quit work to stay home with the baby? No, wait till **he's** eleven" (headline in *Wall Street Journal,* August 29, 2002, p. D1).

Do Bradley and Blomberg and Carson actually think that readers of the *Wall Street Journal* did not realize that the article applies also to baby girls (whatever we may think of the strange advice given in the article)?

"Wal-Mart is a reflection of America...if [a manager has] three shifts of people working for **him**, it's going to be a real challenge to know everyone" (*American Way Magazine* (American Airlines), June 15, 2002, p. 50, quoting Wal-Mart spokesman Jay Allen.)

Does this imply to modern readers that there are no women managers at Wal-Mart? Or that women managers have no challenge getting to know their employees but men managers do have a challenge? Of course not. People today do not really *misunderstand* such sentences. Some self-appointed guardians of "politically correct" speech may object to such sentences, of course, but they do not misunderstand them.[25]

---

[25]As a matter of fact, my nephew's wife is a manager at Wal-Mart, and there are many women managers at Wal-Mart.

"Next time your friend wants to drive drunk, do whatever it takes to stop **him**" (radio advertisement by the Ad Council, on news radio KXEM (1010 AM) in Phoenix, June 30, 2002, at 4:06 p.m.).

I wonder if Peter Bradley would say that teenagers hearing that ad thought that it did not apply to a high school girl who wanted to drive drunk? Or if Don Carson would say that this sentence has the "effect..of excluding approximately half of humanity"?

Or would they say that the Ad Council, a secular ad organization, doesn't understand how to use current English? If "the English language has changed" so much *that people cannot understand such sentences correctly,* then why do secular writers in all sorts of formats still use such statements?[26]

Now someone may answer that some of these sentences actually hint slightly at a male representative example, because it is men who are more likely to drive drunk, and men are more likely to work for the CIA, and men are more likely to attack a hijacker. I would respond that I agree completely. Those three sentences do hint slightly at a male representative example. And that is exactly the pattern of speech that we find in the New Testament, where Jesus and the New Testament authors were accustomed to teaching a general truth by speaking of or hinting at a male representative example. We should translate their sentences using "he" in this "representative generic" sense and convey exactly the meaning of what they wrote.

But what about generic "they" and generic "she"? Aren't these also used today? Of course they are (and I could provide many quotations like that as well). But it is not enough to demonstrate that the English language *also* allows for "they" and "she" in such constructions. The fact of the matter is that English today uses and allows for at least four kinds of statements: generic "he," generic "he or she," generic "she," and generic "they." As Vern Poythress and I said in our book in 2000:

> In matters of usage in modern English, we see nothing necessarily wrong with a whole spectrum of typical modern uses. Some people may continue to use generic "he" while others may avoid it, and instead use "he or she" or "you" or "they." Some people may use "man" to designate the human race, others may not....a writer today has authority over what he or she writes. A Bible translator does *not* have this authority because the meaning belongs not to him but to God.[27]

The question is, *out of these legitimate and understandable options,* which one most faithfully represents the Bible's use of masculine singular pronouns in such statements? The answer is that generic "he" represents the

---

[26]For several pages of additional examples like this, see GNBC, pp. 203–213.
[27]Poythress and Grudem, p. 7.

usage of the biblical authors most accurately in these sentences (where there is a masculine singular pronoun in the original).

The 2002 edition of the *Associate Press Stylebook and Briefing on Media Law* says,

> ...use the pronoun *his* when an indefinite antecedent may be male or female: *A reporter attempts to protect his sources.* (Not *his or her* sources...)[28]

We may ask Bradley and Blomberg and Carson and others, "If 'the English language has changed' *so much that you cannot use generic "he" in Bible translation,* then why does the Associated Press, probably the largest association of news writers in the world, not realize that the language has changed in this way? And why do *USA Today* and the *Wall Street Journal* and the *Arizona Republic* (the largest newspaper in Arizona) and *Christianity Today* and the writers for the passenger magazine for American Airlines (the largest airline in the United States) not realize that the language has changed in this way?

In addition, these writers are writing their own new sentences today, not *translating* the words of an author who wrote 2000 years ago and who used masculine singular pronouns in sentences that have generic application to men as well as women.

3. Does the common use of "singular they" in English today validate its use in the TNIV?

I recognize that in spoken English today, and somewhat in written English, people use "they" to refer to a singular antecedent. This is thought to justify the TNIV's change to "they" in sentences such as Luke 17:3:

> NIV: If your brother sins, rebuke **him**, and if **he** repents, forgive **him**.
> TNIV: If any brother or sister sins against you, rebuke **the offender**; and if **they** repent, forgive **them**.

> Or, similarly, in James 5:20:
> NIV: Whoever turns a sinner from the error of **his** way will save **him** from death and cover over a multitude of sins.
> TNIV: Whoever turns a sinner from the error of **their** way will save **their** soul from death and cover a multitude of sins.

But does good written English *require* such a use of "they" in order to be understandable, or even in order to be consistent with current English idiom? Craig Blomberg apparently thinks so, for he claims:

> And since the late 1980s, the Modern Language Association, the primary American organization that pontificates on what is or isn't

---

[28]Norm Goldstein, editor *Associated Press Stylebook and Briefing on Media Law* (Cambridge, Mass.: Perseus, 2002), p. 114. The entry goes on to recommend consideration of the option of changing the sentence to plural, but it gives no endorsement for the use of "she" or "they" in such sentences.

acceptable in written English, has approved of and even encouraged the use of plural pronouns to refer back to generic singular antecedents.[29]

But is Blomberg's claim true? The *MLA Handbook for Writers of Research Papers*, Fifth Edition, edited by Joseph Gibaldi (New York: Modern Language Association of America, 1999), says:

> ...many writers no longer use *he, him,* or *his* to express a meaning that includes women or girls: "If a young artist is not confident, he can quickly become discouraged." The use of *she, her,* and *hers* to refer to a person who may be of either sex can also be distracting and momentarily confusing.... Both usages can often be avoided through a revision that recasts the sentence into the plural, or that eliminates the pronoun .... Another technique is to make the discussion refer to a person who is identified, so that there is a reason to use a specific singular pronoun. <u>They, them, their,</u> and <u>theirs cannot logically be applied to a single person,</u> and *he or she* and *her or him* are cumbersome alternatives to be used sparingly (112, underlining added).

Far from approving and encouraging the TNIV's use of "singular they," as Blomberg claims, the MLA specifically says it is not logical to do so. So today's high school students reading the TNIV will find over a hundred times in the New Testament alone that their Bible uses grammatical constructions that their MLA style book says cannot logically be used, constructions like, "Whoever turns a sinner from the error of **their** way will save **their** soul from death..."

We should also notice that the MLA does not say the use of "he" in such generic statements is wrong, only that "many writers" no longer use this construction. And they are talking about constructing one's own sentences today, so it certainly does not imply that *English translations* from a writer in another language who uses masculine singular pronouns in this way should avoid such similar expressions in English.

My primary concern in this issue is not grammar, of course, but accuracy in Bible translation. If Zondervan and the IBS wish to publish a Bible with constructions that many today find to be grammatically incorrect, that is their decision and I will not object to it on the basis of grammar alone, nor would I take time to write an article about it, much less a book, if grammar were the only issue. But when the TNIV advocates claim that such usage is *required* because "the English language has changed," then some analysis of that claim is called for.

The TNIV web site (www.tniv.info, under Luke 17:3) also claims support for such changes from two English reference works:

> Respected dictionaries and style guides such as *Merriam-Webster's Collegiate Dictionary* and *The Chicago Manual of Style* also affirm its use.

---

[29]Blomberg, p. 23 (he gives no documentation except to refer to an online article he wrote, which contains the same claim, with no documentation or other support).

I agree that there are some dictionaries that approve this use, and *Merriam-Webster's Collegiate Dictionary* (2001 edition) does approve some types of singular they. But what the TNIV web site does not tell us is: (a) This dictionary only approves such use "to refer to indefinite pronouns (as *everyone, anyone, someone*)" (p. 1220). It does not approve the use of "they" to refer to definite nouns, as in the TNIV's "Whoever turns **a sinner** from the error of **their** way" (James 5:20) or "rebuke **the offender**; and if **they** repent, forgive **them**" (Luke 17:3). So this dictionary should not rightly be cited to support the TNIV's rendering of Luke 17:3. It gives no support for such use. (b) The entry goes on to approve generic "he" in such sentences as well: "This gives you the option of using the plural pronouns where you think they sound best, and of using the singular pronouns (as *he, she, he or she,* and their inflected forms) where you think they sound best" (p. 1221). And under "he," their second meaning is "used in a generic sense or when the sex of the person is unspecified" (p. 533).

Then what about the other work cited, the *Chicago Manual of Style*? It did recommend using singular "they,"[30] but the editors have since withdrawn that recommendation on their web site. Here are the two relevant quotations from their "Frequently Asked Questions" guide:

Chicago Manual of Style Web Site (FAQ's) (May 16, 2002)

Q. I would swear that I saw a reference in your latest manual that approved of *the use of "their" instead of a gender-biased singular pronoun.* For example, "If the user has completed installing the program, **they** should put the CD-ROM back in the package," instead of "If the user has completed installing the program, s/he should put the CD-ROM back in the package," but on your on-line FAQ, you dance around the answer to the question and suggest that you do NOT approve of the singular "their." Can you tell us what is acceptable?

A. Yes, you saw it at 2.98 (note 9), but *there is some regret at having written it and we may change our minds in the next edition. I personally would rather avoid this usage,* but occasionally it's so difficult to find a way around it that I take comfort in this note of approval and rather dread its removal. (I should add, however, that we will do almost anything to avoid using "s/he.")

Q. PLEASE tell me what you are recommending when people need a gender-neutral singular possessive pronoun. In order to avoid saying "his mind" or "her mind" (or, God forbid, "his/her mind") people are saying "their mind"—and it blows MY mind—unless, of course, those people could be sure "they" are "of one mind"! If you

---

[30]See *The Chicago Manual of Style*, Fourteenth Edition (Chicago: University of Chicago Press, 1993), 76 (section 2.98, note 9).

have a discussion on this issue, I'd be most happy to receive it or be directed to it.

A. I'm afraid your gender-neutral pronoun (at least in the sense you need) does not exist in our lexicon. *I agree that the **plural pronoun** with a singular noun seems inadequate; I would suggest that you recast the sentence altogether* or at least make "mind" plural for agreement: their minds. Other writers alternate between using "his" and "her" in such constructions in order to give equal status to each pronoun. (http://www.press.uchicago.edu/Misc/Chicago/cmos/faq.html (Search under "singular they")

So the current *Chicago Manual of Style* editors "would rather avoid" using "singular they" and say it "seems inadequate." But this "inadequate" construction is what is used so often in the TNIV, and this "inadequate" construction is what the IBS tells us has to be used for a younger generation because "the English language has changed." In fact, when we look at the reversal in the *Chicago Manual of Style*, we may wonder if our culture is now shaking off some of the influences of radical feminism and the "politically correct" language police, and if common sense and freedom to use words the way we choose is being restored, and if the "rapid decline" mentioned by Peter Bradley is actually being reversed. Predicting the future of language change is a risky business. Building a Bible translation on one's predictions of the future is even more doubtful.

Other highly respected English authorities reject "singular they" and consider it unsuitable for standard written English. For example, the 2000 edition of Strunk and White's *The Elements of Style*, perhaps the most widely acclaimed and most respected handbook for good writing in the English language, says,

Do not use *they* when the antecedent is a distributive expression such as *each, each one, everybody, every one, many a man*. Use the singular pronoun.
[incorrect:] Every one of us knows they are fallible.
[correct:] Every one of us knows he is fallible.[31]

As noted in the earlier question, the current edition of *The Associated Press Stylebook and Libel Manual* (2002) directs, "use the pronoun *his* when an indefinite antecedent may be male or female: *A reporter attempts to protect his sources*. (Not *his or her* sources...)." While it also says that a sentence may be best recast as plural, as *Reporters attempt to protect their sources*, there is no mention of any possibility of a mixture such as *A reporter attempts to protect their sources*, which is the style we find throughout the TNIV.[32]

William Zinsser, one of this country's most highly regarded English stylists, in his book *On Writing Well*, says that simply changing "he" to "they"

---

[31]William Strunk, Jr., and E. B. White, *The Elements of Style*, Fourth Edition (Boston: Allyn and Bacon, 2000), p. 60.

[32]Norm Goldstein, ed., *The Associated Press Stylebook and Briefing on Media Law* (Cambridge, Mass.: Perseus, 2002), p. 114.

is not adequate. He says, "But let's face it: the English language is stuck with the generic masculine .... I don't like plurals; they weaken writing because they are less specific than the singular, less easy to visualize" (William Zinsser, *On Writing Well*, 5th ed. (New York: HarperCollins, 1995), p. 123).

Wilson Follett, *Modern American Usage*, revised by Erik Wensberg (New York: Hill and Wang, 1998), agrees that people use plurals to refer to a singular antecedent in colloquial speech, but he then says, "But no esteemed writer of English, early or late, has been cited as using this oddity page after page, in work after work" (p. 31). (We might add, no esteemed writer of English until the TNIV translators.)[33]

The *American Heritage Dictionary* (2000 edition) notes that of its more than 200-member "Usage Panel," consisting of a wide range of well known writers, critics, and scholars, "Eighty-two percent find the sentence *The typical student in the program takes about six years to complete their course work* unacceptable" (p. 1796).[34]

We must remember, also, that these style manuals and dictionaries are talking about how they want people to write their own sentences today, *not about how people should translate sentences from an ancient author* who actually used masculine singular pronouns to speak of an example of a general truth. *None* of the English manuals quoted tells us to translate another writer's masculine *singular* pronouns as gender-neutral *plurals*! (We can only suppose that the percent of Usage Panel experts who found that procedure "unacceptable" would be higher than 82 percent.) But this is the standard usage of the TNIV.

The IBS tells us the gender language of the TNIV is necessary in order to have a Bible to reach a "younger generation." But when this younger generation begins to read the TNIV in high school, they will find the IBS has given them a Bible that repeatedly uses a construction that the *MLA*

---

[33]At least some TNIV supporters apparently hope the use of English in the TNIV will influence the way English is used in the future, for Timothy George says, "I predict the *TNIV* will have a shaping influence on the English of the future, even as it reflects today's contemporary idiom" (www.tniv.info, under "Endorsements"). Unless I misunderstand him, I think he means that he thinks some of the usages in the TNIV are not established in the English of today, but are part of informal speech ("contemporary idiom"), and he hopes they become part of "the English of the future."

[34]Under the entry for "he," the dictionary informs us that 37% of Usage Panel members preferred the word "his" in the sentence *A taxpayer who fails to disclose the source of _____ income can be prosecuted under the new law.* As far as other responses, they say, 46 percent preferred a coordinate form like *his or her*; 7 percent felt that no pronoun was needed in the sentence; 2 percent preferred an article, usually *the*; and another 2 percent overturned tradition by advocating the use of generic *her*" (p. 807). They report *no* experts who actually preferred the plural "their" in such a sentence, yet this is the standard usage of the TNIV, and the usage the IBS tells us is *necessary* for modern English readers. (As far as informal speech, as opposed to writing, this dictionary says that 64 percent accept the sentence *No one is willing to work for those wages anymore, are they?* in "informal speech." But it does not report anyone as preferring this construction in writing, and even in informal speech they give *no* support for such a usage with a definite noun as an antecedent, as in the TNIV.)

Handbook rejects, and that *Merriam-Webster's Collegiate Dictionary* does not approve, and that the *American Heritage Dictionary* tells them is "unacceptable" to 82 percent of it Usage Panel experts. When they take advanced English composition classes in high school, they will find their Bible speaks in a way that Strunk and White tell them is wrong. When they reach college, they will have difficulty quoting a Bible that the next edition of the *Chicago Manual of Style* tells them is wrong, and that William Zinsser's *On Writing Well* tells them is wrong. And if they perhaps aspire to be journalists and write for the secular press, they will be embarrassed to quote a Bible that the *Associated Press Stylebook* tells them is wrong.[35]

When the IBS and Zondervan defend a rendering such as "rebuke the offender; and if **they** repent, forgive **them**" by saying it is *necessary* because "the English language has changed," I think it can safely be said that their claim is not true. Such a construction may be *acceptable* in modern informal spoken English, but in *written* English it is not *necessary*, and many think it is not even *acceptable*. To say that the TNIV's changes in gender language are necessary because "the English language has changed" turns out to be a remarkably weak argument.

4. Is there really a loss of meaning when "they" is used as a singular pronoun?

English speakers recognize that there remains something strange, something that seems vaguely plural, when we read "they/them/their" used in a so-called "singular" sense. That is because in the vast majority of cases we use it as plural in distinction from a singular. So when we try to use it as singular, even when the context would require a singular sense, it just does not work. Think of these sentences:

---

[35]We may wonder why Zondervan and the IBS would choose to publish a Bible with a grammatical usage that is so widely labeled as incorrect even though everyone admits that it is found in informal speech? If common use in informal speech is the deciding factor, then one might suggest that the TNIV could include some other things found in informal speech, such as "Let's not have any quarreling between you and I" (a modern informal speech rendering of Abram's statement to Lot in Genesis 13:8; the NIV actually has the correct form, "between you and me"). We could even find dictionary support for such a rendering, for the *American Heritage Dictionary* says,

> When pronouns joined by a conjunction occur as the object of a preposition such as *between, according to,* or *like,* many people use the nominative form where the traditional grammatical rule would require the objective; they say *between you and I* rather than *between you and me,* and so forth .... the phrase *between you and I* occurs in Shakespeare.... But the *Between you and I* construction is nonetheless widely regarded as a marker of grammatical ignorance and is best avoided (1996 edition, p. 892).

The parallels to "singular they" are interesting: Both constructions are found in informal speech, both are found in writers going back several centuries, and both are found unacceptable by the dictionary. Why not put such commonly heard "informal speech" in the TNIV? Because no issue of male-specific meaning is at stake, so in that case what is generally acceptable in *written* English, not what is found in informal speech, becomes the standard.

They is happy.

They is singing.

Is your husband home? Yes they is.

I am not taking phone calls this morning, but if Peter calls, I will talk to them.

In every case, the context tries to force a singular meaning, but the sentence just won't work. "They" remains stubbornly plural.

So I doubt that "they" is truly an adequate substitute for singular "he/him" even in sentences like the TNIV's "rebuke **the offender;** and if **they** repent, forgive **them**." To change "him" to "them" removes the particularity of the specific male example ("your brother...him" in Luke 17:3) and creates a broadening of the statement to a thought of all the possible people who could fall in the category of "the offender." This is why we would naturally think it strange to read,

If your brother sins, rebuke *them*.

or even

If any brother sins, rebuke *them*.

The word "them" just does not function well as a true singular in English, but leaves room for some ambiguity as to whether it is referring to a singular person or more than one.

This is relevant for the TNIV's change in Revelation 3:20:

NIV I stand at the door and knock. If anyone hears my voice and opens the door, I will come in and eat with **him**, and **he** with me.

TNIV I stand at the door and knock. If anyone hears my voice and opens the door, I will come in and eat with **them**, and **they** with me.

Is "they" truly singular? Readers will wonder. The antecedent "anyone" may make them think it is singular, but then in this context Jesus is speaking to a whole church. Consider this sentence:

If anyone comes to class today, I will teach them.

Is "them" singular or plural? We can't be sure, because the situation seems to allow for several students coming to class, and we think that maybe the "anyone" potentially includes several people. Or consider this sentence:

If anyone comes to class today, I will teach them for the first half hour and put them in discussion groups after that.

Here "them" is clearly plural, and we have no problem processing the sentence because we attribute to "anyone" a plural sense, referring to all the students who might come.

Now in Revelation 3:20, the context is "To the angel of the church in Laodicea write:" (vs. 14), and the previous verse said, "Those whom I love I rebuke and discipline. So be earnest, and repent" (vs. 19). Therefore Jesus is addressing the whole church. In such a context, it is very possible to take "them" in verse 20 as referring to the whole church: "If anyone hears my voice and opens the door, I will come in and eat with **them**, and **they** with me."

Carson says of this sentence, "But with the best will in the world, it is difficult to see how this change loses 'the teaching that Jesus has fellowship with the individual believer,' precisely because the preceding 'anyone' is preserved in both instances" (p. 27). And Blomberg says, regarding plural statements generally in the Bible, "I know of no one who assumes these do not apply to individual believers" (p. 23).

But this misses the point. Of course a promise that Jesus would eat with a whole group of people (a whole church, if readers take "them" as plural) means that the readers would be in the group, and so the promise of a "church dinner" with Jesus *applies* to them. But *what* applies to them is no longer a promise of individual fellowship between Jesus and a single person ("I will eat with *him*"). What applies to them is the changed TNIV sentence, "I will eat with *them*." The assurance of individual fellowship with Jesus is no longer there. If it is a "church supper" in view, readers who have attended a church supper with an honored guest will think, "Who knows if Jesus will even notice me in such a context, much less have extended fellowship with me?" Readers will think, "Maybe it promises me personal fellowship with Jesus, but maybe the 'them' means it is fellowship with Jesus in the context of the whole church together." They cannot be sure. There is a loss of meaning for an important, well-loved verse.

People may say, "So what? That's only one verse." But the TNIV changes "he" to plural "they" 271 times in the New Testament alone, and changes "he" to "singular they" another 112 times. "He" is changed to "you" 90 times (and we often cannot tell if "you" is singular or plural), and to "we" 9 times, and simply omitted 48 times (in every case where Greek has a singular verb or a third person masculine singular pronoun).[36] Such systematic changes constitute a significant change of emphasis in the whole New Testament, a significant loss of emphasis on individual responsibility and individual relationship with God.

E. Justifications for the TNIV

1. Do the New Testament authors' quotations from the Old Testament validate the use of gender-neutral language in the TNIV?

Darrell Bock gives several examples "where Scripture is quoted within Scripture by the inspiration of the Holy Spirit" (p. 15 in my printout from Bock's Web site; see footnote 15 above) and mentions several examples.

---

[36]See the categorized list of 900 examples of problem translations in the TNIV at www.cbmw.org.

A consideration of Acts 4:11 (quoting Psalm 118:22) and Second Corinthians 6:18 (quoting 2 Sam. 7:14) will illustrate his argument.

2 Samuel 7:14 says, "I will be to **him** a father and **he** shall be to me a **son**." Bock points out (p. 16–17) that Paul changes this in 2 Corinthians 6:18 to: "I will be a father to **you**, and **you** shall be **sons and daughters** to me, says the Lord Almighty." Paul thus changes third person "he, him" to second person "you," and changes "son" to "sons and daughters." Does this not give justification for the TNIV translators today to make the same kind of changes as Paul did under the guidance of the Holy Spirit?

To take another of Bock's examples, Psalm 118:22 says,

The stone that **the builders rejected** has become the cornerstone.

But when Peter quotes it in Acts 4:11 he says,

This Jesus is the stone **that was rejected by you, the builders,** which has become the cornerstone.

Here Peter inserts the word "you" and changes the active verb to passive. Does this not give justification for changing third person statements to second person in translating the TNIV Bible?

The answer in both of these cases is no. New Testament scholars have long recognized that there is a wide variety in how freely the New Testament authors quote or change the Old Testament text. But this varied procedure does not provide us with a new theory of translation, in which we can freely alter the meaning of the original text of the Bible to suit our purposes.

People who claim this fail to take into account what the New Testament writers were doing.[37] In quoting the Old Testament, they are like preachers making an application. They are not translators producing a base translation on which everyone will rely. A preacher who functions in this way is not *claiming* to give the most accurate translation for general purposes, but is rather giving an interpretive rendering that brings out some of the implications of the original and applies it to the situation at hand. Similarly, the New Testament often gives us interpretive renderings rather than a uniform model that provides us with a pattern for how to translate the Old Testament.

This distinction between a New Testament use of an Old Testament passage and a translation has been recognized for a long time. In the nineteenth century, opponents of biblical inerrancy were using a similar argument to this objection, saying that we do not need to insist on the truthfulness of every word of Scripture, because even the New Testament authors adapt and quote freely when using the Old Testament. But defenders of inerrancy, such as A. A. Hodge and B. B. Warfield, replied in 1881 as follows:

---

[37]This paragraph and the next two are taken from Poythress and Grudem, GNBC, p. 199.

Nor is quotation to be confounded with translation. It does not, like it, profess to give as exact a representation of the original, in *all* its aspects and on *every* side, as possible; but only to give a true account of its teaching in *one* of its bearings. There is thus always an element of application in quotation; and it is, therefore, proper in quotation to so alter the form of the original as to bring out clearly its bearing on the one subject in hand, thus throwing the stress on the element for which it is cited. This would be improper in a translation. The laws which ought to govern quotations seem, indeed, to have been very inadequately investigated by those who plead the New Testament methods of quotation against inspiration.[38]

We can see very easily that New Testament citations of the Old Testament do not show us how we should translate the Old Testament. To take these two examples which Bock quotes, if these were providing us with a pattern for *translation*, then we should be able to take the New Testament "quotation" and put it back into the Old Testament text *as the best English translation of that text*. But no translator of any version would do that in cases like these, for it would make nonsense of the original Old Testament statement, and it would be an impossible translation of the Hebrew.

For example, here is what would happen to Psalm 118 if we put Peter's quotation back into the Psalm as the accurate "translation":

> I thank you that you have answered me and have become my salvation. The stone that was rejected by **you, the builders**, which has become the cornerstone (Ps. 118:21–22, if the New Testament citation is made into a translation if the Old Testament text).

This is of course impossible as a translation. By inserting "you" into verse 22, it makes the psalmist say to God that *God* has rejected a stone but that stone has become the cornerstone anyway! The Hebrew text simply doesn't mean that, and this simply is not a legitimate *translation*.

The same thing would happen if we put Paul's citation of 2 Samuel 7:14 back into God's statement to David. It would read as follows:

> When your days are fulfilled and you lie down with your fathers, I will raise up your offspring after you, who shall come from your body, and I will establish his kingdom. He shall build a house for my name, and I will establish the throne of his kingdom forever. *I will be a father to **you**, and **you** shall be **sons and daughters** to me.* When he commits iniquity, I will discipline him with the rod of men... (2 Sam. 7:12–14).

Once again this is impossible as a *translation*. It has God saying to David that after he dies, "I will be a father to you [that is, to David], and you shall

---

[38]A. A. Hodge and B. B. Warfield, "Inspiration," *The Presbyterian Review* 2/6 (April 1881), 256, emphasis in the original. I wish to thank Tim Bayly for calling my attention to this quotation.

be sons and daughters to me." It has God telling David that after his death he will be "sons and daughters" to God! It completely omits the meaning of the Hebrew text, which is a promise that God will be a father to David's son. Once again, in 2 Corinthians 6:18 Paul *adapts* and *applies* the Old Testament statement for his own purposes in writing to the Corinthian church. But he is not purporting to give an exact *translation* of the original text, nor could this ever possibly work as a translation of the original text.

Bock argues, in addition, that Paul's introductory formula in 2 Corinthians 6:16, "As God said" (Greek aorist *eipen*) means that Paul is claiming that this is what God said in the past and "not God is now saying it as a matter of current revelation" (p. 17). But this misses the point, which is that the form in which New Testament authors cite Old Testament quotations still allows for much intermingling of adaptation and application in the midst of the citation. The phrase "as God said" in verse 16 tells the reader that Paul is citing from the Old Testament, not that he is purporting to give an exact *translation* of the Old Testament statement, but that he is citing it in the way New Testament authors commonly do, mingling with it adaptation and application to the situation at hand.

Nor is Carson's argument on this point persuasive. Referring to this same verse (2 Cor. 6:18), Carson says, "The apostle himself does not think that Hebrew singulars must always be rendered by Greek singulars, or that the Hebrew 'son' should never be rendered by the Greek 'sons and daughters.' No one, I think, would quickly charge Paul with succumbing to a feminist agenda."[39] Once again, Carson misses the point that Paul is not attempting to give us an exact *translation* but is freely adapting and applying the Old Testament text to his situation. Paul's citation simply cannot be put back into 2 Samuel 7:14 as a translation.

2. Do the New Testament authors change singulars to plurals and third person to second person and thus justify such changes in the TNIV?

Craig Blomberg apparently agrees at least in part with what I have said in the previous section, for in discussing New Testament quotations from the Old Testament he says,

> Yet at the same time, Poythress and Grudem correctly observe that the New Testament many times goes beyond mere translation to interpretation and application in its "quotations" of the Old Testament. So perhaps these examples are not as conclusive as they might at first appear. (p. 25, with reference to Poythress and Grudem, *The Gender-Neutral Bible Controversy* 198–201, where we discuss this question.)

---

[39]D. A. Carson, *The Inclusive Language Debate* (Grand Rapids: Baker, 1998), 20.

But Blomberg returns with another argument. He says there are "places where within the Greek New Testament itself, an inspired author shifts between singulars and plurals or between second and third persons, in contexts that suggest no demonstrable difference in meaning. Some of these afford strikingly close parallels to the grammatical constructions the TNIV has employed." (p. 25).

As one example, Blomberg quotes James 2:15:

If a brother or sister are (pl.) naked [or "poorly clothed"] and lack (pl.) daily food, and if any of you says to *them*, 'go (pl.) in peace, be (pl.) warm and be (pl.) well fed,' and does not give *them*..." (Blomberg's literal translation, p. 25).

Blomberg correctly points out that after the first phrase "brother or sister," James shifts consistently to plural verbs and pronouns. Apparently he sees this as justification for the TNIV's translating singular pronouns as plurals and thus changing "he" to "they" hundreds of times.

But the example is not parallel for two reasons:

(1) The sentence is an unusual grammatical construction in any case, and is cited by the grammars as an exception, and not as a general pattern. The reason is that once James has started the sentence with "If a brother or sister," then to follow it with either a singular masculine adjective or a singular feminine adjective would have sounded strange to a Greek ear, so James simply translates "according to the sense" (understanding his hypothetical situation to include more than one person) and makes the rest of the sentence plural. The Blass-Debrunner-Funk *Grammar* refers to the passage as follows: "Exception: Ja 2:15 *ean adelphos ē adelphē gumnoi hyparchōsin* (*gumnos* or *gumna* would have been harsh)."[40]

Interestingly, in 1934, A. T. Robertson commented on this verse as follows: "We have a similar difficulty in English in the use of the disjunctive and other pronouns. One will loosely say: "If anyone has left their books, they can come and get them."[41] What this shows is that Robertson also recognized the unusual and rather awkward nature of this individual example. But it also shows that nearly 70 years ago people realized that "singular they" was heard in ordinary speech (it is by no means a new phenomenon!), but no Bible translation ever felt that justified using it in the accurate translation of biblical texts.

(2) There is a difference between *translating* what an author wrote and *changing* what an author wrote. If James changed from singulars to plurals, we should translate it that way. So, in translating James 2:15, translators should translate it as James wrote it, shifting in the middle of the sentence

---

[40] BDF, 75 (section 135) (4).
[41] A. T. Robertson, *A Grammar of the Greek New Testament in the Light of Historical Research* (Nashville: Broadman, 1934), 406.

from singular to plural (it makes good sense in English, as Robertson noted in 1934), thus accurately rendering James' plural pronouns as plurals:[42]

> If a brother or sister is poorly clothed and lacking in daily food, and one of you says to *them*, "go in peace, be warmed and filled," without giving *them* the things needed for the body, what good is that? (ESV).

But translating James' *plural* pronouns accurately as plurals here does not give us the justification to translate *singular* pronouns as plurals elsewhere, and thus change what the New Testament writers said!

Another example that Blomberg gives is the list of Beatitudes in the Sermon on the Mount (Matt. 5:3–11), where most of them are in the third person ("Blessed are the poor in spirit, for *theirs* is the kingdom of heaven," for example). But then in the last one Jesus shifts to the second person: "Blessed are *you* when others revile *you* and persecute *you*..." Blomberg claims this as support for changing third person statements to second person statements in the TNIV *in places where the Greek makes no such change*.

But the answer here is the same: We should translate Jesus' third person pronouns as third person pronouns, and translate his second person pronouns as second person pronouns, and if Jesus wishes for whatever reason to shift to the more direct "you" in the last Beatitude, then we should let him do that and translate the pronouns faithfully.[43] We should *translate* what is there in the Greek, but this does not give us license to *change* the meaning that is there in the Greek to something else!

None of Blomberg's examples gives us justification for *changing* the pronouns that the New Testament author used in *any* verse, far less in the hundreds of cases where this has been done in the TNIV.[44] As I mentioned earlier, the TNIV does this in a sweeping, systematic way, so that third person singular statements that were accurately translated as "he" in the NIV text have been changed in the TNIV to "they" 271 times, to "singular they" another 112 times, to "you" 90 times, to "we" 9 times, and simply omitted 48 times. This is not faithful or accurate translation. Will readers really trust a Bible where third person masculine singular pronouns ("he") have been translated as "they" or "you" hundreds of times, with no way for readers to know where these are?

---

[42] I am not of course saying that grammatical plurals always have to be translated as plurals and grammatical singulars as singulars, for I recognize that various languages have different collective nouns where a singular form expresses a plural sense, for example. But here the sense changes to plural in Greek, and it should be translated that way.

[43] Again, there is a shift from third person to second person, not just in grammatical *form* but in *meaning,* in Jesus' original statements.

[44] Vern Poythress and I recognized in our book, and the Colorado Springs Guidelines recognized in mentioning "unusual exceptions in certain contexts," that there are some cases, especially in the Old Testament, where sudden switches back and forth in pronouns present scholars with a difficult challenge even to understand the meaning, to say nothing of then translating it into understandable English. But I am speaking here of the ordinary cases, not of such difficult exceptions.

3. Should translations exercise "translational gender sensitivity" in order to make clear the "gender scope" of passages?

This question comes from the paper by Darrell Bock, "Do Gender Sensitive Translations Distort Scripture? Not Necessarily" (see footnote 5, above). Bock distinguishes between *ideological* gender sensitive renderings," which is a radical approach that removes even male metaphors for God and Jesus because it is an attempt to "degenderize" the Bible, on the one hand, and "*translational* gender sensitivity" on the other hand which "renders terms to make clear the *gender scope* of passages" (p. 2). Bock thinks that this "translational gender sensitivity" is especially appropriate when passages "use an all encompassing reference to man or mankind to address both men and women" (p. 2).

I have two difficulties with this approach as Bock explains it. First, to use the phrase "gender sensitive" to describe what the TNIV has done is unnecessarily to prejudice the discussion in favor of the TNIV. For who wants to be insensitive? I would argue that a truly "gender sensitive" translation is one that is *sensitive* to the exact meanings and nuances of the Greek terms and thus translates those precisely and faithfully into English. And if we believe that God is infinitely wise and infinitely loving and kind, then to translate his Word as accurately as possible is the most sensitive thing in the world to do, for it is giving both men and women an accurate rendering of God's words to them.

Second, to say that translations like the TNIV are justified because they "make clear the *gender scope* of passages" is to state the case in such a vague way that it fails to represent clearly the actual issue at hand. For example, take Exodus 20:17: "You shall not covet your neighbor's wife." Now what is the "gender scope" of this passage? Judging from the rest of Bock's paper, he seems to think that a passage has an inclusive "gender scope" whenever it states a general truth that applies to both men and women. But in that case the "gender scope" of this passage also includes not coveting your neighbor's husband. Should we then change the Ten Commandments and translate this, "You shall not covet your neighbor's *wife or husband*"? Surely not, and I expect that Dr. Bock should say we should not do so either. But using the vague idea of "gender scope" as a wedge with which to broaden the gender-specific statements of Scripture would seem to do exactly this.

Bock's criterion of "gender scope" is too vague, and improperly confuses *translation* with *application*.

With regard to Psalm 34:20: "He keeps all **his** bones, not one of them is broken." Bock rightly understands that "the individualizing language of the verse is an illustration that picks up on how God defends one person, a man, as an example of how he defends any who are among the class of the righteous (Jesus included, since this verse is also mentioned in John 12:46)" (*sic*, p. 10; I think this is a misprint and Bock means John 19:36).

But after rightly noticing that this verse uses an individual man as an example of a general truth, then Bock goes on to say that "either rendering 'his' or 'their' can work here conceptually" (p. 10). He says, "The advantage of the plural is that it reminds the reader that a class of people is in view theologically which serves as the base behind the individual example" (p. 10). Thus he thinks the reading of the 1997 NIVI, "He protects all **their** bones, not one of them will be broken," is also acceptable.

My objection here is that in the original Hebrew text of this verse, David, writing under the inspiration of the Holy Spirit, chose to teach this truth *by use of a specific male example.* If God decided to teach us by use of a specific male example, then we have no right to change it into a general statement about a general truth. There are other statements in the same Psalm that make clear the broader application to people generally (see vv. 15, 17, 18, 22), and the broader application will not be lost.

But why would we even think to try to change verse 20, which teaches by means of a specific male example, into a gender-neutral broader truth ("He keeps all *their* bones")? Why do we find something objectionable about verses in God's Word that use a male example to teach a general principle? Quite frankly, I think it is because in the current culture we feel a vague uneasiness about the use of such male examples. We feel they are somehow "insensitive," especially if they are not balanced with an equal number of individual female examples used to teach a general truth. But that means that our objection is really to the fact that the example is male. Yet if God used a specific male example, we should leave it, and translate it accurately. That is the truly "gender sensitive" thing to do, and only that procedure accurately and faithfully makes clear the true "gender scope" of the passage as God originally inspired it.

4. Is the TNIV acceptable because some loss of meaning is necessary in all translations?

A common theme in D. A. Carson's paper is that all translation work involves judgment and careful balancing of alternatives, and frequently some aspects of meaning have to be lost in order for others to be preserved. He argues that the TNIV should not be criticized for doing just what other translations have done, since the TNIV is just making somewhat different judgments on the details of what is preserved and what is lost in each case. Carson says:

> While the goal is certainly to preserve as much meaning as possible, translation is an inexact discipline, and something is invariably lost in any basic translation. One is constantly forced to make decisions. That is one of the fundamental reasons why there are commentaries and preachers. But somewhere along the line, Poythress and Grudem start referring to any loss of any meaning at any level as a "distortion" and an "inaccuracy".... But all translators, including Poythress and Grudem, are inevitably bound up

with making choices about "nuances" they get across....Poythress and Grudem articulate reasonably sound theory, but every time a decision goes against their favorite "nuance," they accuse their opponents of distorting Scripture and introducing inaccuracies (pp. 19–21).

I find I cannot agree with this assessment for two reasons. First, it is not true to say that "Poythress and Grudem start referring to any loss of any meaning at any level as a 'distortion' and an 'inaccuracy.'" What we actually say is this:

> Because the task is so complex, no translation can attain the ideal and communicate into the second language absolutely *everything* that is meant in any speech or writing in the first. So what do translators do in practice? They try to do the best they can. They make hard choices and settle for compromises.[45]

We go on to say,

> We must face a central fact: at a fine-grained level translators cannot avoid trade-offs.... All translations should endeavor to include as much as they can. But differences of priorities among the different translation strategies will sometimes lead to different solutions in detail.[46]

So we explicitly recognize that there is a loss of nuance at various places in translation, and sometimes difficult choices have to be made. Never do we make the foolish claim that *any* loss of *any* meaning at *any* level is a "distortion."

Second, we are not criticizing just any loss of meaning or nuance that goes against our preferences, but rather (a) a systematic program of excluding a certain kind of male-oriented meaning that is in the original text, when (b) the English language is clearly capable of representing that meaning in translation today. Thus, we are criticizing *a systematic and unnecessary removal of male aspects of meaning that are in the original text.*

We say:

> The issue is whether a Bible translation systematically excludes male components of meaning that are there in the original text. If it does, the translation is "gender-neutral," and we argue in this book that such a translation does not properly translate some of the details in the Word of God....We ought not to tolerate these losses of meaning as long as a way exists of avoiding the losses.[47]

It is hard to understand how Carson can miss this point. We give literally hundreds of examples in our book, all of which focus on the loss of male components of meaning that were represented quite well in the original NIV and can still be represented well in English today.

---

[45]Poythress and Grudem, 70.
[46]Ibid., 79–81.
[47]Poythress and Grudem, 116–17.

For example, consider Matthew 7:3:

NIV: Why do you look at the speck of sawdust in your **brother's eye** and pay no attention to the plank in your own eye?
TNIV: Why do you look at the speck of sawdust in **someone else's** eye and pay no attention to the plank in your own eye?

Here the Greek text has *tou adelphou sou*. The word *adelphos* ("brother") can mean either "(1) a male from the same womb as the reference person, *brother*" or, in an extended sense, "(2) a person viewed as a brother in terms of a close affinity, *brother, fellow member, member, associate* figurative extension of 1" (BDAG, p. 18). All the meanings and uses of the term carry the sense of someone who has a personal relationship with another, a relationship strong enough that it can be thought of in terms of the familial language of "brother." And the genitive pronoun *sou* is rightly translated by the possessive pronoun "your."

Jesus is using a specific example of "your brother" to express a general principle. This is the way he often teaches, using a specific example to teach a general truth. It will not do to say "the English language has changed" and to use that as a reason for changing the verse, for it is perfectly understandable and perfectly clear English to speak of "the speck of sawdust in your brother's eye."

Why then did the TNIV change it to "the speck of sawdust in *someone else's* eye"? Not because of any change in English, and not because the meanings of the Greek words have changed, but simply because Jesus' use of a male-specific example was objectionable. This is an example of a loss of meaning that is both systematic and unnecessary in the TNIV.

It gets worse in the next verse, Matthew 7:4:

NIV: How can you say **to your brother** "let me take the speck out of your eye," when all the time there is a plank in your own eye?
TNIV: How can you say _____ "let me take the speck out of your eye," when all the time there is a plank in your own eye? [The TNIV has no words where I have inserted a blank line to show the change.]

Here again the Greek specifies that Jesus said, "to your brother" (*tō adelphō sou*) and the NIV got it exactly right. But *the TNIV left the phrase out completely.* In Jesus' statement, he specified the indirect object: "to your brother." He emphasized once again the personal relationship of the one to whom the person is speaking, one who is considered "your brother." But the TNIV translators apparently did not think that these three words of Jesus had any importance whatsoever, for they simply omitted them. Shall we simply delete some of Jesus' words that we find objectionable?

Why do they do this? Not because "the English language has changed," for the expression, "How can you say to your brother...?" is simple, clear

English. But "to your brother" was left out because it was a male-specific example by which Jesus was teaching a general truth.

When we find several hundred examples like this in the TNIV, then we object that this is not just the kind of "loss of nuance" that is necessary in any translation, and this is not just Poythress and Grudem complaining because something goes against their personal preferences, but it is rather a thoroughgoing, systematic removal of a certain kind of male-oriented meaning, a removal that is unnecessary and that could easily be avoided with ordinary English (as the NIV itself clearly shows). It is not true to say that we are objecting to any loss of nuance at any level. We are objecting to a systematic and unnecessary removal of a male-oriented meaning that is in the original text.

5. Is this just an argument between advocates of two legitimate views of Bible translation, formal equivalence and dynamic (or functional) equivalence?

The claim that critics of the TNIV are simply trying to preserve "formal equivalence" comes up again and again. For instance, Carson says,

> That is not to say that preservation of formal equivalence is *always* a bad thing; it is to say, rather, that appeal to loyalty and faithfulness toward the Word of God as the ground for preserving formal equivalence is both ignorant and manipulative, precisely because the significance and range of use of a masculine pronoun in Hebrew are demonstrably not the same as the significance and range of use of a masculine pronoun in English (pp. 25–26).

But that is not at all what we claimed in our book. With regard to a spectrum of translations from "more preservation of form" (or "more literal") to "more changing of form" (or "paraphrastic"), we say,

> We think that there is room for a spectrum of approaches here, *provided that readers understand the limitations as well as the advantages of the different approaches* (Gender-Neutral Bible Controversy, pp. 79–80).

In fact, in that 2000 book, we responded directly to a similar charge that Carson had made earlier, that we were simply trying to preserve "formal equivalence" and that that was an incorrect approach to translation. We pointed out that the Colorado Springs Guidelines themselves in several places encourage the change of "form" (namely, masculine grammatical gender) in order to adequately represent *meaning*. If our concern were simply the preservation of grammatical "form," we of course would not approve such changes. But our concern is preservation of meaning, not preservation of form.

Here is the statement we made earlier:

What these two guidelines do claim is *not* that Hebrew, Greek, and English are "exactly" the same in pronoun use but that in the generic constructions mentioned they are *substantially* the same—so much so that (with few exceptions) generic third person singular masculine pronouns in Hebrew in Greek are best translated by generic third person singular masculine pronouns in English....What we have claimed is that a translation of a personal pronoun that uses the same gender and number often conveys the maximal amount of meaning. And this is nothing new—it has been followed for all English translations until the advent of gender-neutral Bibles beginning in 1986.

Guideline	Heb. or Greek word or phrase	Grammatical gender in Heb. or Greek	Approved English translation	Grammatical gender in Heb. or Greek
A.1	*ho pisteuōn*	*masculine*	the one who believes	unspecified
A.5	*anthrōpoi*	*masculine*	people	unspecified
A.7	*oudeis*	*masculine*	no one	unspecified
A.8	*pas*	*masculine*	all people, everyone	unspecified
B.1	*adelphoi*	*masculine*	brothers and sisters	male and female
B.3	*banîm*	*masculine*	children	unspecified

...the CSG did not insist on "formal equivalence" but on preserving meaning. It is surprising that Dr. Carson can write this [a statement that we were "blinded" to the fact that "formal equivalents are often impossible"] when the CSG themselves affirm at least six examples of translation that do not preserve formal equivalents:

Carson has simply attributed to the Guidelines a position that exists only in his own mind, and one that is explicitly contradicted by the Guidelines.[48]

Though we wrote this in our 2000 book, and though we wrote it in explicit response to a similar claim by Carson, in his 2002 paper he continues to raise the same objection.

Another way to answer the objection that this is just a controversy between "dynamic/functional equivalence" and "formal equivalence" is to note that the kind of male-specific meaning that is left out of the TNIV can

---

[48]GNBC, pp. 130–132.

easily be represented in a translation that is far over on the "dynamic/functional equivalence" end of the spectrum. For example, the *New Living Translation* (NLT) in Matthew 7:3, says:

> And why worry about a speck in *your friend's* eye when you have a log in your own?

Now there is nothing in the theory of functional equivalence that would prevent the change of one word so that the verse would read:

> And why worry about a speck in *your brother's* eye when you have a log in your own?

Or, to take another verse from the NLT, consider Luke 17:3:

> If another believer sins, rebuke *him*; then if *he* repents, forgive *him*.

Here the NLT, clearly a "dynamic/functional equivalence" translation, has used "he" and "him" in a representative generic statement, thus preserving the singular force of Jesus' example. So a "dynamic equivalence" translation *can* do this, and it preserves the singular and the male component of meaning. As far as the phrase "another believer," there is nothing in this translation theory that would prevent such a translation from rendering the verse as follows:

> If your brother sins, rebuke him; then if he repents, forgive him.

In fact, the NLT in its marginal note says "Greek *your brother*." Now the policy of the NLT toward gender language probably led to their decision not to put the literal translation "your brother" in the verse itself, but it was a policy regarding gender language which led to that decision, not anything about the difference between "dynamic/functional equivalence" and "formal equivalence" in translation theory.

Therefore, as Vern Poythress and I indicated in our book in 2002, our objection is not against a certain theory of translation. Our objection is against the systematic and unnecessary removal of male-oriented components of meaning that are there in the original text. Any kind of translation can include these.

6. Are the TNIV critics angry, incompetent, and ignorant?

I was somewhat surprised to see the choice of words that Dr. Carson used in his paper to describe those who disagreed with him or to describe their arguments. Here are some examples:

"positively cranky" (p. 7)
"betrays linguistic and…theological naiveté" (p. 9)
"hopelessly naïve" (p. 10)
"astonishing naiveté" (p. 11)
"shockingly ignorant" (p. 11)
"linguistically indefensible….even worse…inexcusable" (p. 12–13)
"deceptive and manipulative" (p. 15)

"manipulative rhetoric" (p. 15)
"theological naiveté" (p. 15)
"uninformed and misdirected" (p. 16)
"reactionary wing" (p. 16)
"demonized functional equivalence" (p. 16)
"linguistically uninformed" (p. 16)
"rarely balanced and ... sometimes shrill" (p. 16)
"thoughtful and informed" (p. 17)
"patiently explains its authors' position" (p. 17)[49]
"scathingly" (p. 21)
"a rather heated review" (p. 22)
"increasingly shrill polemic that so roundly condemns
     fellow complementarians" (p. 24)
"both ignorant and manipulative" (p. 25)
"their wrath knows few bounds" (p. 26)[50]

In addition, there are some comments that imply that those who differ with Carson do not really understand Hebrew or Greek very well. He says, "Even many teachers of Greek and Hebrew in colleges, seminaries, and universities do not enjoy much facility in the languages they are teaching. These are precisely the kinds of people who are least likely to be sensitive to the demands of functional equivalence" (p. 46). On the next page he says, "It is the student of Greek and Hebrew who has a mechanical view of language who will have most difficulty grasping these elementary points, and who in the name of fidelity will demand more "direct" translations..." (p. 47).

With regard to the motives of those who are saying we need more accuracy in translation, Carson has this comment:

> As one very sophisticated linguist wryly said, after reading his way into this debate, perhaps one of the reasons that impels some people to lay more stress on "accuracy" (by which they usually mean a greater tilting to more direct translation, though in all fairness accuracy is more complicated matter than that) is that what they really want is not so much a better translation as a "crib" on the original languages (Carson, p. 7).

Now a "crib" is "A word-for-word translation of a foreign language text, especially one used secretly by students as an aid in studying or test taking" (*American Heritage Dictionary*). The implication of this sentence is that Carson's opponents do not know Greek and Hebrew very well and really want a more literal translation so they can cover up their ignorance.

The net effect of these comments scattered throughout Carson's paper is to build up an impression of his opponents as academically incompetent to understand or discuss the complexities of these issues, incapable of making balanced judgments, driven by wrongful anger against those who differ

---

[49]I note with appreciation that these two descriptions on page 17 are used by Carson to refer to Vern Poythress' and my book *Gender-Neutral Bible Controversy*.

[50]Unfortunately, this description is also applied to Vern Poythress and me.

("scathingly," "heated," "wrath"), and secretly motivated by a desire for a literal translation that will help them hide their ignorance of Hebrew and Greek.

Such characterizations of one's opponents are known as *ad hominem* arguments, that is, arguments "against the person" rather than against the arguments that the person is making. Such *ad hominem* arguments should find no place in this discussion (and, I am glad to say, such language is not found in the papers by Blomberg, Bock, Bradley, and Waltke). It is disappointing to see it in Dr. Carson's essay, and it is also disappointing that Zondervan would include it in a packet that was mailed to all members of the Evangelical Theological Society and the Institute for Biblical Research.

Now some of the phrases I quoted above are not directly applied to persons but to positions that Carson says these persons hold. But as I read through Dr. Carson's paper, it seemed to me in a number of cases that the use of such language occurred in cases where Carson was not responding to a position that his opponent actually held, but to a position that Carson wrongly attributed to the opponent. For example, Carson discusses Tony Payne's argument that Romans 1:17 should be translated "righteousness of God" in order to preserve the ambiguity that is in the original genitive *theou*, rather than the NIV's translation "righteousness from God" (which excludes the other possible meaning of the genitive, "righteousness that belongs to God" or "God's righteousness"). Carson reports Payne as saying that in allowing only the one sense "righteousness *from* God," the NIV "places the responsibility for interpretation in the hands of the translator, rather than the reader" (p. 11). Carson's response is to say, "Surely we are not to return to the astonishing naiveté that thought that translation could be done without interpretation?....The notion that one can translate responsibly *without* interpretation is, quite frankly, shockingly ignorant of the most basic challenges facing translators" (p. 11).

But did Payne ever say that translation can be done "without interpretation"? Certainly not in the sense that translators first have to understand a text clearly ("interpret it") before they can translate it rightly, and certainly not in a sense that every translation is in some sense an "interpretation" (even the translation that leaves the ambiguous expression "righteousness of God"). What Payne was objecting to was translations that *could* translate in a way that left open for English readers both possible interpretations, so that readers today would have to do the same thing that the original readers had to do, namely, decide from the sense of the context which interpretation was appropriate. A sympathetic reading of Payne would have made that clear, but instead Carson attributes to him a foolish position that he never held (that translation can be done with no interpretation at all), and then criticizes Payne as if he in fact did hold that position.[51] So this procedure first misrepresents Payne and then maligns him.

---

[51]Carson uses a similar approach on page 15 where he responds to Payne's statement, "Better to have something simple, the NIV seems to think, even if it is not what the original

As to whether Vern Poythress and I use language that is "shrill" and speaks "scathingly" of others and whether our "wrath knows few bounds when the TNIV deploys a plural instead of a singular" (p. 26), it may be helpful to quote again what we said in 2000:

> We are not criticizing the personal motives of the translators. Only God can judge people's hearts. We do not know our own motives perfectly, let alone the motives of others (p. 7).
>
> It is inappropriate to make this issue an occasion for personal attacks. We must beware of overreacting and firing ourselves with a zeal that is "not based on knowledge" (Rom. 10:2). "For man's anger does not bring about the righteous life that God desires" (James 1:20). The law of love requires us to hope for the best concerning other people's motives (1 Cor. 13:7).... However...it is not amiss to warn others about temptations that we see impinging (pp. 293–294).

In this more recent controversy over the TNIV, we have continually sought to exclude from our web site (www.no-tniv.com or www.cbmw.org) any *ad hominem* statements or any negative comments about the persons involved on the other side of this issue. We have attempted never to write or speak out of anger. If we have failed in this attempt and have wrongfully spoken of others or said anything in anger at any point, then we certainly want others to call us to account for it. But it is troubling to be charged with acting in "wrath" when we are not aware of that attitude toward others in our own hearts.

---

text actually says." Carson says that is "deceptive and manipulative" because "the original text does not actually *say* "flesh" and "walk" and the like; it says *sarx* and *peripateō* and the like....What the original text actually says is in Aramaic and Hebrew and Greek..." (p. 15). But Payne was not denying that the original text is in Hebrew and Aramaic and Greek, nor was he unaware of that. When he used the phrase "what the original text actually says," the context of his discussion makes clear that he was simply speaking in ordinary English about what a literal translation of the Greek text would say.

In fact, Carson himself speaks this way on page 31, note 61, where he says, "Most emphatically this does *not* give us the right to change *what the Bible actually says*, as if the agendas of contemporary culture could ever have the right to domesticate Scripture" (second emphasis added). In context he is referring to translation, not of course to the original Hebrew or Greek texts. But in referring to translation he speaks of what the Bible "actually says." And frequently in his other writings he can refer to what the Greek literally says, as in his outstanding commentary on Matthew (*Expositor's Bible Commentary*, Volume 8 (Grand Rapids: Zondervan, 1984), p. 405, where he says, "The Greek is literally 'how many times will my brother sin against me and I will forgive him?'" But here Dr. Carson uses *English* words to tell us what "the Greek is literally." (And so frequently throughout his commentary.) Even Paul himself talks about what the Scripture "says" and then reports this in Greek translation, not by writing the original Hebrew words, as when he says, "It does not say, 'And to offsprings (Greek *spermasin*),' referring to many, but referring to one, 'And to your offspring (Greek *spermati*),' who is Christ" (Gal. 3:16; see also Rom. 9:17, 25; 10:11, 16; 11:2; 15:12). And so it seems to me unduly harsh for Carson to criticize Payne for using the phrase "what the original text actually says" when it is clear that what Payne is talking about is a literal rendering of the Greek text.

F. Questions about specific verses

Although I have discussed a number of specific verses up to this point, there are some important and representative verses that received extended discussion in the September 2, 2002, Zondervan packet, and it is appropriate to include a brief discussion of them here.

1. In Hebrews 2:17, is it appropriate to say that Jesus was made like his "brothers and sisters"?

Here is the TNIV change in Hebrews 2:17:

NIV For this reason he had to be made like his **brothers** in every way, in order that he might become a merciful and faithful high priest....

TNIV For this reason he had to be made like his **brothers and sisters** in every way, in order that he might become a merciful and faithful high priest....

I agree that the plural Greek word *adelphoi* can mean "brothers and sisters" when the context supports that understanding (and the Colorado Springs Guidelines allow this). But here the change to "brothers and sisters" is not appropriate. All the Old Testament priests were men, and surely the high priest was a man. So it is appropriate to keep the NIV translation, "like his *brothers* in every way."

The problem with "like his *brothers and sisters* in every way" is that it hints at an androgynous Jesus, one who was both male and female. The TNIV translation does not actually require that sense, but it surely leaves open a wide door for misunderstanding, and almost invites misunderstanding. Meditate on that phrase "in every way" and see if you can trust the TNIV. As the TNIV's readers begin to meditate on the phrase "in *every* way" and to preach on "in *every* way," it will be hard to avoid thinking that Jesus was somehow both male and female.

Carson's response is to say that even the phrase, "like his brothers in every way," which is the 1984 NIV's translation, "does not mean that Jesus must be like each 'brother' in every conceivable way: as short as all of them, as tall as all of them, as old or young as all of them..." (p. 29). Of course not, but it *does* mean that he shared "in every way" in the characteristics common to "brothers."

Second, he says, "if the focus is on being human, then for Jesus to become 'like his brothers and sisters in every way' is not contextually misleading" (p. 30). Carson's line of reasoning here is representative of what we find often in defenses of the TNIV: (1) appeal to the vague, general meaning ("being human") and (2) then say that the male-specific details ("like his brothers") do not matter. That brings us back to the exact question with which we began this paper, the question at the heart of the controversy:

Is it acceptable to translate only the general idea of a passage and omit male-oriented details of meaning that are present in the original Hebrew or Greek text?

Here the specific male meaning ("brothers") is excluded by appeal to the vague general meaning ("being human"). The original readers, however, in reading *adelphoi* in connection with Jesus' becoming a high priest, would have thought of being "like his *brothers*," not of being "like *human beings*" generally. The TNIV omits the male-specificity of the original.

Third, Carson says the phrase "brothers and sisters" is a "unified pair that must be taken together" (p. 30), somewhat like the phrase "flesh and blood" in verse 14, "Since the children have *flesh and blood*, he too shared in their humanity...." In response, I agree with Carson that "flesh and blood" will be understood by TNIV readers as a helpful parallel to the phrase "brothers and sisters" just three verses later in verse 17. But just as verse 14 clearly implies that Jesus had "blood," and just as saying he had "flesh *and blood*" has additional meaning that "flesh" alone would not have, so by this parallel we have further reason to say that "brothers and sisters" has additional meaning that "brothers" alone did not have: it affirms that Jesus was somehow like his "sisters" in every way as well, and that being like his "sisters" added something to him that he did not have in merely being "like his brothers in every way." The more readers look at this parallel, the more they will wonder if the verse teaches an androgynous Jesus.

But what is the point of this change in the TNIV? What is objectionable about saying that Jesus, in order to become a high priest, had to become "like his brothers in every way"? What is objectionable is the male-specific meaning. So the TNIV removes it. Once again, this has nothing to do with any claims that "the English language has changed," for modern English is perfectly capable of saying that Jesus was made "like his brothers in every way." The reason is not a change in English but a systematic and unnecessary removal of male-specific meaning that is there in the original text.

2. In Hebrews 2:6, is it legitimate to remove the phrase "son of man"?

The TNIV in Hebrews 2:6 changes "son of man" to "human beings":

NIV What is man that you are mindful of him, **the son of man** that you care for **him**?

TNIV What are mere mortals that you are mindful of them, **human beings** that you care for **them**?

Our objection to this change has been that the TNIV needlessly obscures the possible connection of this verse with Jesus, who often called himself "the Son of Man." (This verse is a quotation from Psalm 8:4.) And in changing "son of man" to "human beings," it incorrectly translates the singular Greek words *huios* ("son") and *anthrōpos* ("man").

Carson's response to this is to argue that the majority of commentators on Hebrews do not think that "son of man" here is a messianic title:

> Scanning my commentaries on Hebrews (I have about forty of them), over three-quarters of them do not think that "son of man" here functions as a messianic title, but simply as a gentilic, as in Psalm 8 (pp. 28–29; Carson explains that "in Hebrew gentilic nouns are often singular in form but plural in referent").

There are at least three problems with this explanation. First, all the "gentilic" nouns listed in the grammars by Gesenius and by Waltke and O'Connor are formed in a different way from what we have in Psalm 8:4: they are constructed by adding a *hîreq-yod* to the end of a noun, and they "frequently (often even as a rule) take the article" (Gesenius, section 125d; see also 127d), as in *ha'ibri* "the Hebrew" or *hakkena'anî*," "the Canaanite." Waltke-O'Connor say, "Names with the *-î* suffix are called gentilics" (5.7c; see also 7.2.2). And they say, "Both singular and plural gentilics regularly take the article in referring to the entire group" (13.5.1f). So if Carson wishes to claim *ben-'ādām* is a "gentilic" noun in Psalm 8:4 (vs. 5 in Hebrew), he at least needs to explain how he can know this, since it has no article and no *hireq-yod* ending, and thus is different from both the examples and the rules listed in these standard grammars.

Second, when Carson says that three-quarters of the commentators on Hebrews do not see "son of man" as a messianic title in Hebrews 2:6, while admitting that "there are competent interpreters" who do see it as messianic (p. 29), he actually indicates the problem with the TNIV rendering "human beings." The problem is that *this legitimate interpretive possibility is excluded by the TNIV.* The original readers of Hebrews could see that Hebrews 2:6 had the Greek phrase *huios anthrōpou* ("son of man"), and they could realize that that was the same phrase as *huios anthrōpou* ("son of man") in the Septuagint of Psalm 8. The original readers could also realize that Jesus used these same two words when he called himself "the Son of Man." Then they could ponder whether there was a connection between Psalm 8:4, and Jesus' calling himself *"the* Son of Man," and Hebrews 2:6. But none of these options is open to readers of the TNIV, for the phrase "son of man" has disappeared. Why? It is too male-oriented.

In addition, we should realize that there are other possibilities than "this is a messianic title" or "this is not a messianic title" in Psalm 8:4. Psalm 8 points to the creation plan of God to have human beings ruling over creation: "You have given him dominion over the works of your hands; you have put all things under his feet" (Ps. 8:6). Even if "son of man" is not specifically a messianic title in Psalm 8:4, it still uses a singular expression in the second line ("the son of man" or "a son of man"), and it thus invites the reader to narrow the focus from the whole race in the first line ("What is man, that you are mindful of him") to a singular example in the second ("the son of man"). The Hebrew parallelism in this case (as often) is not exactly synonymous, but it repeats the idea of the first line with increased specificity in the second line.

Thus, even if readers don't see "son of man" in Psalm 8:4 as a messianic title, surely Jesus saw himself as the fulfillment of the world-rule intention of God spoken at creation (Gen 1:28) and reaffirmed in Psalm 8 (and the author of Hebrews affirms in Heb. 2:9 that Jesus does fulfil that role). As Blomberg correctly says, "Jesus has come and proved to be the perfect human that Adam and Eve failed to be: 'But we do see Jesus' (v. 9)" (p. 20). Therefore, whether "son of man" is strictly a messianic title, or whether for some other reason it just speaks in the singular of "a son of man" whom God planned to have dominion over the earth, it is likely that Jesus saw himself as the fulfillment of Psalm 8. This means that when Jesus called himself "the Son of Man" it is likely that he had in mind not only the prophecy in Daniel 7:13 but also other "son of man" themes in the Old Testament, including that of Psalm 8:4. The TNIV should not prevent readers from seeing these possibilities.

Third, the TNIV's plural expression "human beings" in Hebrews 2:6 is simply not an appropriate translation of the singular Greek expression *huios anthrōpou*. Two components of meaning are unnecessarily left out: (a) The TNIV does not even have "human being" but "human beings," thus unnecessarily translating the singular phrase as plural. But the singular phrase is part of the inspired text.[52] (b) The sonship component of meaning in both the singular Hebrew *bēn* and the singular Greek *huios* is lost. Even if *huios anthrōpou* ("son of man") referentially indicates a human being, it does so by means of a specific phrase which includes the indication of descent from another human being, which I suspect is why even the gender-inclusive NRSV in Psalm 8:4 adds a footnote, "Heb *ben adam*, lit. *son of man.*"[53]

What is the reason for such a loss of meaning in the TNIV? The reason is not that the phrase "son of man" cannot be understood today due to changes in the English language, for the words "son" and "man" are not difficult words. The reason is that "son of man" is male-specific, and so the TNIV changed it to something "gender-neutral." Such a change is again part of a systematic and unnecessary loss of male-specific meaning that is there in the original text.

---

[52]Even if TNIV supporters believe that "son of man" in Psalm 8:4 refers to the human race as a whole, it is incorrectly confusing the meaning of the phrase with the thing it refers to to say that therefore it makes no difference to translate it "human beings." As the "Statement of Concern" by 113 Christian leaders [see appendix] said in another context, it is "like justifying translating 'sweetheart' as 'wife' because that's who it refers to." The specific meaning of the phrase "son of man" is lost, and the possible connections to that phrase in the rest of Scripture.

[53]It is interesting that in Carson's book, *The Inclusive Language Debate* (Grand Rapids: Baker, 1998), he says that "the constant use of the expression ["son of man"] in the Old Testament to refer to a human being is precisely what lends some of the ambiguity to Jesus's use of it," and he then says, "As cumbersome as it is, therefore, on the whole I favor a retention of "son of man," at least in the majority of its Old Testament occurrences..." (p. 173).

3. Can *anēr* ("man, husband") sometimes mean "person"?

We have objected to changing verses such as Acts 4:4:

NIV: But many who heard the message believed, and the number of **men** grew to about five thousand.

TNIV: But many who heard the message believed, and the number of **believers** grew to about five thousand.

Of course, this makes quite a difference, for if there were 5000 men, then the size of the church was 10,000 or more.[54] The Greek word is *anēr* (in this case plural). Whereas earlier Bible translations regularly translated *anēr* as "man" or "husband," the TNIV translates it in some gender-neutral way like "people" 26 times.

Craig Blomberg defends this translation by saying, "...one well-attested meaning of the word is as a synonym for anthrōpos" (p. 15). He then cites definitions from the standard BDAG lexicon (p. 79) as well as two theological dictionaries.[55]

But these entries have to be read carefully, and it is not clear that the citations they provide actually demonstrate that *anēr* can take the meaning "person," for several reasons:

(1) *Where is the convincing data from citations of ancient sources?* It is still not clear that there are any examples in the New Testament where the sense "person" is required instead of the sense "man." As for literature outside the Bible, what is the new data on *anēr* that anyone has produced in the last five years that shows that Bible translations have understood *anēr* wrongly up to this point? It has been well-known by Greek scholars for centuries that the term *anthrōpos* can mean either "person" or "man," depending on the context, and *anēr* always (outside of special idioms) means "man" or "husband." Nobody in the last several years of the gender-neutral Bible controversy has "discovered" any new examples that prove a new meaning for *anēr*. (And when we check the evidence for the meaning "person" given in some reference works, it turns out to give no new support for the supposed meaning "person"; see below.)

(2) *Anthrōpos* **and** *anēr*: Given the way language works, it is highly improbable linguistically that Greek would have two different words, *anthrōpos* and *anēr*, and that *both* words would mean both "man" and "person." That would leave Greek an amazing linguistic vacuum of having no common noun that could be used to speak specifically of a male human being.[56]

---

[54]The TNIV footnote "Or *men*" allows for that possibility but does not see it as most likely, since it is not in the text.

[55]*New International Dictionary of New Testament Theology*, ed. Colin Brown (Grand Rapids: Zondervan, 1976), vol. 2, pp. 562–563, and *Exegetical Dictionary of the New Testament*, ed. Horst Balz and Gerhard Schneider (Grand Rapids: Eerdmans, 1990), vol. 1, pp. 98–99.

[56]There is the word *arsēn*, but it is most frequently used as an adjective, and is far less common.

(3) **Liddell-Scott:** The standard reference work, the Liddell-Scott *Lexicon* (p. 138) for all of ancient Greek, gives no meaning "person," but only "man, husband," and some specific variations on those. This is very significant because *anēr* is not a rare word: it is *extremely* common in Greek. Thousands upon thousands of examples of it are found in Greek from the 8th century BC (Homer) onward. If any meaning "person" existed, scholars likely would have found clear examples centuries ago.

(4) **BDAG:** The Bauer-Danker-Arndt Gingrich *Greek-English Lexicon of the New Testament and Other Early Christian Literature* (Chicago: Univ. of Chicago Press, 2000), needs to be read carefully so that it is not misquoted. Although they list one meaning as "equivalent to *tis*, someone, a person" (p. 79), we should note first that that is subordinate meaning (2) under the general meaning at the beginning of the entry, "a male person."

And in this entry under "equivalent to *tis*, someone, a person," every one of the examples they cite can easily be understood to refer to a man or men (such as Luke 19:2, "a man named Zacchaeus"; Acts 10:1 "a man named Cornelius"; or Luke 5:18 "some men were bringing on a bed a man who was paralyzed"). So the entry in BDAG really shows that *anēr* can mean "someone, a person (but always male)."

Now someone could argue, "But maybe there was a woman helping to carry the paralytic." The answer is that lexical definitions cannot be built on maybes. There is no factual evidence that a woman was helping. And the clear pattern of thousands of other examples pushes us to say *anēr* (plural) here must have meant "men" to first-century readers as well, unless we find some clear counter-examples.

The situation is similar in Romans 4:8, "Blessed is the man (*anēr*) whose sin the Lord will never count against him." The context does not require the sense "person," and this is a quotation from Psalm 32:2 where David is speaking (as several times in the Wisdom Literature) of the "blessed man" who is an example for all the godly to follow, as in Psalm 1:1, "Blessed is the man who walks not in the counsel of the wicked."

Of course these verses *apply* to women as well as men, just as the parable of the prodigal son applies to women as well as men, and the parable of the woman with the lost coin applies to men as well as women, but in none of these cases should we *translate* it to be the parable of the prodigal *child* or the parable of a *person* with a lost coin.

There is one other verse that people have sometimes mentioned, but it is ambiguous at best. Acts 17:34 says, "A few men (*anēr*, plural) became followers of Paul and believed. Among them was Dionysius, a member of the Areopagus, also a woman named Damaris, and a number of others" (NIV). This verse does not mean that Damaris is included in the "some men" (*anēr* plural), as both F. F. Bruce's commentary and the BDAG *Lexicon* itself make clear (p. 79; note the word *kai*, "also"). It just means some men (on the Areopagus where Paul spoke and addressed them as "men of

Athens," vs. 22) believed, and some others like Dionysius and Damaris were added to them.

BDAG also cite several references to extra-biblical literature in this entry. I have looked up every reference and they all either clearly refer to male human beings (as 1 Maccabees 13:34, "Simon also chose *men* and sent them to Demetrius the king with a request to grant relief to the country..."), or the context is not determinative but the meaning "man" makes good sense and the meaning "person" is not required (as Psalms of Solomon 6:1, "Happy is the man (*makarios anēr*, in likely imitation of Psalm 1:1) whose heart is ready to call on the name of the Lord").

There is an idiomatic use, *kat'andra*, which BDAG also note at the end of this entry, with several references. This idiom means "man for man, individually," and clearly includes women in some instances, but that idiom does not occur in the New Testament. The LSJ Lexicon (p. 138) also notes the idiom *kat'andra*, with a similar meaning. The LSJ Lexicon does not give the meaning "person" for *anēr*, but rather, "man, opposed to women," "man, opposed to god," "man, opposed to youth," "man emphatically, man indeed," "husband," and some special usages.[57]

(5) *Louw-Nida:* The Louw-Nida Lexicon does not treat *anēr* by itself, but defines both *anēr* and *anthrōpos* in the same two entries (9.1, under the category "Human Beings" and 9.24, under the category "Males"). It is surprising that they make no distinction between these two words, about which other lexicons regularly recognize a difference, with *anēr* being a male-specific term.

In entry 9.1, with respect to *anēr*, Louw-Nida quote Romans 4:8 as meaning, "happy is the *person* to whom the Lord does not reckon sin." They then say, "The parallelism in this quotation from Psalm 32:1–2 indicates clearly that the reference of *anēr* is not a particular male but any person." They then quote Matthew 14:35 as meaning, "when the *people* of that place recognized him," and then say, "one may argue that *hoi andres* refers specifically to males, but the context would seem to indicate that the reference is to people in general" (p. 104).

What has happened here? They have given a new meaning for *anēr* with no new evidence. Translators and authors of lexicons have known about Romans 4:8 and Matthew 14:35 for centuries, and those two verses in their contexts have not been sufficiently clear to persuade them that a new meaning for *anēr* should be established. Louw-Nida have just asserted this new meaning while producing no new evidence to prove that meaning.

As we indicated above, in Rom. 4:8, the context does not require the sense "person," because "man" makes perfect sense, especially since this is a quotation from Ps. 32:2 where David is speaking, as often in the Wisdom

---

[57]For further discussion on the word *anēr*, "man," see Vern Poythress and Wayne Grudem, *The Gender Neutral Bible Controversy* (Nashville: Broadman & Holman, 2000), p. 101, note 2, and pages 321–333.

Literature, of the "blessed man" who is an example for all the godly to follow, as in Psalm 1:1, "Blessed is the man who walks not in the counsel of the wicked." As for Matt. 14:35, when Jesus landed at Gennesaret (vs. 34) it would be natural that the first people to see him and recognize him, and then send people to bring the sick to him, would be the men out working along the shore or in nearby fields. The translation "the men of that place" makes good sense.

The principle that would keep us from adopting the additional sense "person" for *anēr* is that *if a well-established meaning makes sense in the context, then we should not adopt a previously unattested meaning in its place.* Such a general principle of lexicography is well stated by Cambridge lexicographer John Chadwick, whose book *Lexicographica Graeca: Contributions to the Lexicography of Ancient Greek* is a collection of specialized studies that reflect his years of experience on the team overseeing a supplement to the Liddell-Scott *Lexicon*:

> A constant problem to guard against is the proliferation of meanings.... It is often tempting to create a new sense to accommodate a difficult example, but we must always ask first, if there is any other way of taking the word which would allow us to assign the example to an already established sense.... As I have remarked in several of my notes, there may be no reason why a proposed sense should not exist, but is there any reason why it must exist? (John Chadwick, *Lexicographica Graeca: Contributions to the Lexicography of Ancient Greek* (Oxford: Clarendon Press, 1996), pp. 23–24).

In other words, the burden of proof is on the person who postulates a new sense. If an already established sense can account for a particular use, one must not postulate a new sense.

So the Louw-Nida *Lexicon* has asserted a new meaning for *anēr*, but has not supported that claim with any new or convincing evidence.[58]

(6) *Other reference works:* Blomberg also mentions two other reference works. With regard to the NIDNTT entry, perhaps Blomberg just cited the entry without checking the supporting citations from ancient literature, because they do not support the meaning "person." The meaning "adult" which Blomberg (p. 15) mentions from NIDNTT (p. 562) is supported by just one piece of evidence, Xenophon, *Cyropaedia*. 8.7,6, in which Cyrus, king of Persia, is recounting his life, telling about "when I was a boy," then "when I became a youth," then "when I became a mature man (*anēr*)." The fact that Cyrus calls himself an *anēr* hardly proves that *anēr* can include women!

With regard to the entry in *Exegetical Dictionary of the New Testament*, the situation is the same as with the Louw-Nida *Lexicon*: no new, decisive

---

[58]For further information on some blurring of meanings generally in Louw-Nida, see Vern S. Poythress, "Comparing Bauer's and Louw-Nida's Lexicons," JETS 44 (2001), pp. 285–296.

examples are cited from extra-biblical literature, but the same New Testament verses we have always known about are claimed as evidence that *anēr* "can denote any *human being*" (p. 99). The verses given as evidence include Matthew 14:35 (the *men* of Gennesaret); Luke 5:18 ("some *men* were bringing on a bed a man who was paralyzed") and Mark 6:44 ("those who ate the loaves were five thousand *men*"). This last verse in Mark about the feeding of the five thousand is said to be a different meaning from the use of *anēr* in the parallel account of the same event in Matthew 14:21, "And those who ate were about five thousand *men*, besides women and children." But if this is right, then Matthew and Mark have vastly different reports of the number who were fed at the same event: with Mark (according to this entry in *Exegetical Dictionary of the New Testament*), there were 5000 people, total, but according to Matthew there were 5000 men, plus (we suppose) at least an equal number of women and children, giving a total of more than 10,000 people. These accounts would thus stand as significant factual discrepancies in the Gospels. And all in order to demonstrate that sometimes *anēr* can mean "person." I have to admit that I do not find such evidence convincing. I return to the question with which I began: If *anēr* really does mean "person," and not just "man," where is the convincing data from quotations of ancient sources?[59]

(7) **But could new information change my mind about anēr?** I do not wish to deny the *possibility* that the plural of *anēr* could take on a wider sense such as "people" in the fixed idiomatic expression, *andres* + plural noun, such as "men of Athens," "men of Israel," etc. If substantial evidence is forthcoming, I would be happy to change my understanding of plural *andres*, and I recognize that there may be such evidence that I have not yet seen, especially with regard to fixed idioms such as "men of Athens," etc. (In any case the CSG allow for unusual exceptions in certain cases.) But I have not yet seen clear evidence that this is the case. So I cannot at this point agree with the claim on the TNIV web site that *anēr* "was occasionally used as a generic term for human beings."

I think the perspective of Steve Baugh, an expert in the history and culture of the ancient Greek world, is helpful at this point. Baugh writes (in an e-mail to Wayne Grudem on Feb. 20, 2002, quoted with permission):

> The ANDRES EPHESIOI ("Gentlemen of Ephesus") in Acts 19 is pretty standard type of formal public address to an assembly. So, for instance, the "W ANDRES ATHHNAIOI" ("O gentlemen of Athens") with which Socrates opens his address in the Apology.
>
> That women might be present in such a crowd does not take away from the fact that ANDRES (as also "gentlemen") addresses the preponderant male constituents. I've always thought that Pliny the

---

[59]The same considerations apply to the entry in Kittel, TDNT 1, 360–361. The papyrus references, when checked, turn out to be ambiguous and in some cases (BGU 902,2) so fragmentary that one cannot even be sure that the word *anēr* is in the text.

Younger's letter (4.19) regarding his wife's practice of attending his public readings "seated discretely behind a curtain nearby" *(in proximo discreta velo sedet)* to be quite telling on ancient practice. Any respectable women in public venues were expected to be discretely out of the spotlight. Hence the traditional "gentlemen" opening to a public address.

So it seems to me that the burden of proof is still on those who say that *anēr* could lose its male meaning. Before I would agree that *anēr* can sometimes mean "person," I would hope to see some unambiguous examples from the Bible or from other ancient literature. This kind of evidence is simply what is required in all lexicography, especially concerning such a common word. Unless such examples are forthcoming, it seems unjustified to translate *anēr* as "person" or the plural form *andres* as "people."

And even if someone produces some unambiguous examples that *anēr* can mean "person" without implying a male person (as there are many unambiguous examples with *anthrōpos),* this would still be an uncommon sense, not the "default" sense that readers assume without contextual specification. And even in such cases the male-oriented connotation or overtone would probably still attach (with the sense that the people referred to are mostly or primarily male). But until substantial evidence in that regard is found, we cannot agree with the procedure of systematically changing many NT examples of *anēr* to "person" or "persons." What seems to be driving the decision at this point is not the preponderance of evidence but an attempt to eliminate male-oriented meanings.[60]

4. Other verses

There are, of course, disputes about many other verses, several of which I have treated in the earlier part of this paper. Others are treated more fully on the CBMW web site (www.cbmw.org), especially in the section "CBMW interacts with TNIV explanations of changes," and readers can consult those discussions. Many verses are discussed in detail in our book *The Gender-Neutral Bible Controversy* (reproduced as chapters 7–21 below). But perhaps what I have said to this point is sufficient to understand the kind of concerns I would have about other passages in the TNIV as well.

G. Other concerns about factual accuracy

As I read the articles in the Zondervan packet on the TNIV, I wondered about care for factual accuracy in a few other places. I mention them here by way of asking for documentation to support these claims, all of which portray TNIV critics in a negative light, and none of which is supported with any documentation.

---

[60]For further discussion of the meaning of *anēr*, see GNBC, 321–33.

1. Do we say there is nothing to be learned from feminism?

Carson writes:

"... it is important, in the face of feminist demands, not to tar the entire movement with one broad brush. One must try to assess where, in the light of Scripture, feminist agendas make telling points...and where they seem to fly in the face of Scripture.... But that is a far cry from saying that there is nothing to be learned from feminist cries, from feminist writings ...(Carson, p. 23, with reference to Poythress and Grudem).

But we say in our book, in the beginning of the chapter on feminist influence on language:

Early feminism contained some very legitimate concerns, but also some wrongheaded ideas. But God can bring good results even out of wrong human intentions (Gen. 50:20). And some good results *have* come. Not only society as a whole but also Christians in particular have received a wake-up call to pay more attention to the needs and concerns of women, and to value women as highly as they value men. As a result, we hope, Christians have become more alert to the dangers of male domineering and pride, and have gone to the Scriptures to learn and obey more thoroughly God's standards for male-female relations (p. 135).

2. Do we say the English language is not changing?

Carson writes:

I cannot help remarking, rather wryly, that in light of the ESV, the argument of Poythress and Grudem sounds a bit like this: "The language is not changing, so we do not need to respond to the demands of inclusive language. But if it is changing, the changes are driven by a feminist agenda, so they are wrong and must be opposed if we are to be faithful to Scripture. Because of the change, we will make some minor accommodations in our translations, but if others make any other changes, they are compromisers who introduce distortions and inaccuracies, and should be condemned, because changes are not necessary anyway! (p. 24).

The fact that we appreciate many of the influences from feminism was stated in the previous section. As far as the claim that we say "the language is not changing," the official statement issued with the Colorado Springs Guidelines June 3, 1997, said,

we all agree that modern language is fluid and undergoes changes in nuance that require periodic updates and revisions (GNBC, 302).

Why does Carson repeat this accusation in 2002, an accusation he also made in his 1998 book, without mentioning that we already responded to it directly in our book in 2000? Here is the relevant citation from our 2000 book:

We first quoted Carson's 1998 book, in which he said:

At the risk of caricature (in which on this issue I really do not wish to indulge), their argument runs something like this: (1) The English language is not changing, or not changing much. (2) If it is changing, we should oppose the changes because the feminists are behind the changes (pp. 183–184).

In response we said,

First, let us assure readers that Carson's description is indeed a caricature. The accompanying statement that we published with the Colorado Springs Guidelines and that was signed by all participants said, "We all agree *that modern language is fluid and undergoes changes in nuance* that require periodic updates and revisions" (*CBMW News* 2:3 [June, 1997]: 7, emphasis added). In addition, the Colorado Springs Guidelines themselves contain Guidelines that approve some changes. The following all approve changes in translations due (at least in part) to changes in English: Guidelines A.1 (approving "the one who.." rather than "he who"), A.5 (approving "people" rather than "men" for plural Greek *anthrōpoi*), A.6 (approving "anyone" rather than "any man" for Greek *tis*), A.7 (approving "no one" rather than "no man" for Greek *oudeis*), and A.8 (approving "all people" rather than "all men" for Greek *pas*).

More accurately stated, our position would be: (1) Many changes in the use of gender language in current English should be reflected in modern translations, and these changes can be made with no significant loss of meaning (see Chapter 5)....

We discussed the question of feminist influence on changes in English in Chapter 8, but it should be noted here that the CSG give approval to several changes in translation that reflect changes in English due at least in part to feminist influence. To say that we "ascribe whatever gender changes that are developing in the language to feminist influence and then heartily oppose them" (p. 183) is simply untrue. But Carson says in the very next sentence, "The latter course is being pursued by the critics of gender-inclusive translations" (p. 183). Furthermore, to say we hold that "If [the English language] is changing, we should oppose the changes because the feminists are behind the changes" (p. 184) is also simply untrue, in light of our explicit endorsement of many changes in translation due to these very changes in English.[61]

Perhaps Carson thinks it makes no difference that we denied this same caricature in 2000, and said it was simply not true. Perhaps he thinks it is valuable to repeat it anyway for rhetorical effect. Perhaps he thinks it is most

---

[61]GNBC, pp. 358–359; see also p. 92 where we approve of the loss of the plural word "men" to mean "people," a loss that we attribute to the influence of feminism on the language.

forceful if he then includes no footnote informing readers that we have already responded in print by quoting this caricature and saying that it is untrue. Perhaps he thinks it is most helpful to his case to go on making the caricature and ignoring anything that we, the targets of his caricature, might say in hopes of clarification. I really don't know why Dr. Carson has done this again. I can only say, as I have said many times when people have asked me about Carson's book, that it is impossible for readers to understand the position of the TNIV critics simply by reading about us in Carson's book.

By contrast, here is what linguistics professor Valerie Becker Makkai says about our book:

> Vern Poythress and Wayne Grudem...clearly understand the fluid and changing nature of language and their arguments are based on sound linguistic principles (GNBC, p. xvii).

We do not claim, and have never claimed, that the English language is not changing.

3. Do people repeatedly claim that Dr. Carson profits financially from the TNIV?

I find it puzzling that Carson says, "...my views have been repeatedly dismissed on the grounds (it is said) that I was a translator for the NIV and therefore benefit financially from my arguments" (p. 32; he answers with a note that he did provide free consultation regarding one book of the NIV).

I am reasonably familiar with this debate and what has been written about the issues, and I have never heard anyone claim this, much less have I heard it "repeatedly." Dr. Carson provides no documentation for this claim.

4. Have entire denominations been torn asunder in this debate?

Carson writes, "Entire denominations have been torn asunder in debate [over the issue of gender-inclusive language]" (p. 17). Again, I am reasonably familiar with the events of this debate, and I know that the Southern Baptist Convention and the Presbyterian Church in America passed resolutions against the TNIV by substantial margins (see www.cbmw.org for details). But I am not aware of any denominations that have been "torn asunder in this debate." Perhaps Dr. Carson is aware of events unknown to me, but he provides no documentation, so as it stands the claim is unnecessarily inflammatory.

H. Cultural pressures on language are not always neutral

I realize that for several decades, some English style rules imposed on students, especially in universities, have told them to avoid generic "he" (and other male-oriented expressions) and to rewrite their sentences in other ways. Of course people *can* rewrite their sentences with plurals, or change to the second person, or clutter them with "he or she," but then the sentences say something different and they sound different and their meaning is different. But if the author does not want to say the "something different," but wants to use a pronoun to hint at a *specific male example of a general truth*, then a generic third person masculine singular pronoun is needed. Since "he" is the only recognized English word that functions that way, if this use of "he" is ruled out, the result will be that the would-be rulers of the language will have told us that *there are certain things that we cannot say, even in the Bible.* We are permitted by them to say something similar, something related, something that sounds nearly the same, but we cannot say precisely this idea. It is not surprising that wise writers have resisted such a mandate, for if this kind of rule should ever prevail, our thinking would be impoverished.

This is because the pressure to conform to "politically correct" speech is primarily a pressure *not* to use certain expressions. But when our freedom to use certain expressions is taken away, then our ability to *think* in certain ways is also curtailed. For example, if all masculine generic singular statements are removed from the Bible, then the ability to *think* of such a representative male who stands for a whole group will have been removed—for we will have no acceptable words in which to formulate our thought. There will be no way to say, "If anyone loves me, **he** will keep my word, and my Father will love **him**, and we will come to **him** and make our home with **him**" (John 14:23), and thus there will be no way to think of that precise idea. Restricting certain types of expression is restricting certain types of thought.

George Orwell understood this well in his novel *1984*. One of the government functionaries who is rewriting the dictionary explains what is really happening when he revises English into the Newspeak that is required by Big Brother:

> You think, I dare say, that our chief job is inventing new words. But not a bit of it! We're destroying words — scores of them, hundreds of them, every day. We're cutting the language down to the bone.... It's a beautiful thing, the destruction of words. Of course the great wastage is in the verbs and adjectives, but there are hundreds of nouns that can be got rid of as well.... Don't you see that the whole aim of Newspeak is to narrow the range of thought? In the end we shall make thoughtcrime literally impossible, because there will be no words in which to express it.... Every year fewer and fewer words, and the range of consciousness always a little smaller...(pp. 45–46).

I. Conclusion

It is appropriate to end where we began. The heart of the difference can be summarized in one sentence:

Is it acceptable to translate only the general idea of a passage and systematically omit male-oriented details of meaning that are present in the original Hebrew or Greek text?

I have argued in this article that it is not appropriate to do this, as the TNIV has done.

I believe much is at stake. If the TNIV should gain wide acceptance, the precedent will be established for other Bible translations to mute unpopular nuances and details of meaning for the sake of "political correctness." The loss of many other doctrines unpopular in the culture will soon follow. And at every case Bible readers will never know if what they are reading is really the Word of God or the translators' ideas of something that would be a little less offensive than what God actually said. These words of the Bible are not ours to tamper with as we please. "You shall not add to the word that I command you, nor take from it" (Deut. 4:2).

CHAPTER 3

Translation Inaccuracies in the TNIV: A Categorized List of 900 Examples

Note: This list of translation inaccuracies in the TNIV now stands at 900 examples, and when we stopped collecting them we knew that more could be added. But this list seemed sufficient to indicate the scope and type of changes that have been made in *Today's New International Version* (TNIV), mostly in order to avoid using five words with masculine meaning or nuance: father, brother, son, man, and he/him/his.

It seems to us that in every case listed here the change eliminates masculine meaning or masculine nuances that are present in the underlying Greek terms, and also that these changes frequently go beyond the legitimate bounds of ordinary, well-established meanings for the common Greek words being translated (though in some cases there are differences among the lexicons, as noted in the individual categories below). These examples therefore seem to us to be "translation inaccuracies" that were included in the TNIV for the sake of producing a more "gender neutral" or "inclusive language" version.

This list was prepared under general oversight of The Council on Biblical Manhood and Womanhood, and has been compared for accuracy against the Greek New Testament. In the event that readers may find any corrections or additions that may need to be made, we would welcome your input sent to us at: office@cbmw.org.

All the changes noted are from the 1984 NIV to the 2002 TNIV.

A. Changes from singular to plural to avoid the use of he/him/his

he/him/his/himself changed to *they/them/their/themselves* (where Greek has singular verb and/or masculine singular 3rd person pronoun) (232)

Matt. 10:10, 24 (2x), 25 (2x), 38, 39 (2x); 12:35 (2x); 13:12 (3x), 19, 21 (3x), 23, 57 (2x); 16:24, 25 (2x); 18:15 (2x); 23:12 (2x); 25:29 (3x); **(31 total changes)**

Mark 2:22 (2x); 4:25 (2x); 6:4 (3x); 8:34 (2x), 35 (2x); 13:13; **(12)**

Luke 4:24; 5:37; 6:40 (2x), 45 (2x), 47, 48; 8:18 (3x); 9:23 (3x), 24 (2x); 10:7; 12:21; 14:11 (2x); 14:27; 16:16; 17:33 (2x); 18:14 (2x); 19:26; **(27)**

John 3:20 (2x), 21; 4:14 (3x), 36 (2x), 44; 7:18 (2x), 53; 11:9, 10 (2x); 12:25 (2x), 35, 45 (2x), 47, 48; 13:10 (2x), 16 (2x); 14:12; 15:15, 20; 16:2 **(33)**

Rom. 4:8; 14:4 (4x), 6, 22, 23 (2x); 15:2; **(10)**

1 Cor. 4:5; 6:18 (2x); 8:2 (2x); 11:29; 14:2 (2x), 4, 5, 13 (2x), 16, 37, 38; **(15)**

2 Cor. 9:9 (3x); 10:7 (3x), 18; 11:20; **(8)**

Gal. 4:1 (2x), 2 (2x); 6:6, 7, 8; **(7)**

Eph. 4:28 (2x); 5:29 (3x); **(5)**

Phil. 3:4

Col. 2:18 (3x), 19; 3:25; **(5)**

2 Thess. 3:14 (2x), 15 (2x); **(4)**

1 Tim. 5:18

2 Tim. 2:21

Titus 3:10 (2x), 11; **(3)**

Heb. 2:6 (2x), 7 (2x), 8 (4x); 4:10; **(9)**

Jas. 1:7, 8, 9, 10 (2x), 11 (2x), 12 (2x), 23, 24 (2x), 25 (3x), 26 (4x); 2:14, 24; 5:19; **(22)**

2 Pet. 2:19;

1 John 2:4, 5, 10 (2x), 11 (3x); 3:3 (2x), 9 (3x), 10; 4:15 (2x), 16; 5:12 (2x), 16, 18 (2x); **(21)**

Rev. 2:27, 28; 3:5 (2x), 12 (3x); 13:10 (2x); 14:10 (2x); 16:15 (2x); 21:7 (2x); **(15)**

he/him/his/himself (with singular Greek verb and/or masculine third person singular Greek pronoun) changed to *they/them/their/themselves* (with singular antecedent in English; these are examples of the so-called "singular they") (112)

Matt. 5:39, 41; 11:15; 13:9, 43; 15:4, 5, 6 (2x); 16:27; 18:6 (3x), 15 (2x), 16, 17 (3x); 24:18; **(20)**

Mark 2:21; 4:9, 23; 7:10, 11, 12 (2x); 9:42 (3x); 11:25; 13:16; **(12)**

Luke 2:3; 5:36 (2x); 8:8, 16; 14:35; 17:3 (2x), 4 (2x); **(10)**

John 3:2 (Jesus), 4 (3x), 18, 36; 6:40, 44, 65 (2x); 7:38; 10:9; 11:25; 14:21 (3x), 23 (3x); **(19)**

Acts 2:6; 4:32 (2x); 25:16 (3x); **(6)**

Rom. 2:6; 4:4 (2x), 5; 8:9, 24; 11:35 ("who"?); 14:5; **(8)**

1 Cor. 3:8 (2x); 8:10; 10:24; 14:24, 25 (2x); **(7)**

2 Cor. 5:10
1 Tim. 5:8 (2x); 6:4 (2x); **(4)**
2 Tim. 2:4; JAS. 3:13 (2x); 4:11; 5:20 (2x); **(6)**
1 John 2:5; 3:15, 17; **(3)**
2 John 1:10 (2x), 11 (2x); **(4)**
Rev. 2:7, 11, 17, 29; 3:6, 12, 13, 20 (2x), 22; 13:9; 22:12; **(12)**

he/him/his/himself (singular verb and/or masculine singular 3rd person pronoun in Greek) changed to *those (often "those who")* **(39)**
Matt. 7:8 (2x), 21; 10:22
Luke 6:47*; 11:10 (2x)
John 7:18; 15:23
Rom. 14:1, 6 (3x)
1 Cor. 1:31; 7:22 (2x); 14:4 (2x), 5, 38
2 Cor. 10:17
Eph. 4:28
2 Thess. 3:14
1 Pet. 4:1
1 John 5:12 (2x)
Rev. 2:7, 11, 17, 26; 3:5, 12, 21; 22:7, 11 (4x), 17

he/him/his/himself changed to *you/your/yourself* **(90)**
Matt. 6:24 (2x); 6:27; 7:9; 10:36; 16:26 (2x); **(7)**
Mark 7:15 (3x), 18, 19 (3x), 20; 8:36, 37, 38; 11:23 (3x); **(14)**
Luke 5:39; 9:25, 26; 11:8 (4x); 12:25; 14:28 (2x), 29 (2x), 33; 16:13 (2x); **(15)**
John 15:5 (2x), 6; 16:32; **(4)**
1 Cor. 3:18 (3x); 6:1; 7:17 (2x), 20 (2x), 24; 16:2; **(10)**
2 Cor. 9:7 (2x)
Gal. 6:3 (4x), 4 (4x), 5; **(9)**
Eph. 4:25; 6:8 (2x); **(3)**
1 Thess. 4:4
Jas. 1:5 (2x), 6 (2x), 14 (2x); 4:17; 5:13, 14 (2x), 15 (3x); **(13)**
1 Pet. 3:10 (2x)
2 Pet. 1:9 (3x);
1 John 2:15; 3:17; 5:16 (2x); **(4)**
Rev. 22:18, 19 (2x); **(3)**

he/him/his/himself changed to *we/our/ourselves* **(9)**
Rom. 14:7 (2x—ourselves); 12 (ourselves); 15:2 (ourselves)
1 John 4:20 (5x—we)

he/him/his/himself changed to *no pronoun* (sentence changed to other wording) (16)
Matt. 5:22; 18:4
Luke 6:45; 9:62; 12:8, 15, 47 (2x); 14:26
1 Thess. 4:6
1 John 2:9, 11; 3:15, 17; 4:20; 5:10

he/him/his/himself is *omitted* (29)
Matt. 5:40; 10:32, 33, 42; 12:29 (2x); 16:26; 18:15
Mark 8:34; 9:35, 41; 10:28; 13:34
Luke 9:48; 10:6; 11:8
John 3:27; 7:17
1 Cor. 2:14; 14:28
1 Thess. 4:6
2 Tim. 2:5, 21
Heb. 10:38
Jas. 4:11; 5:13, 14
1 Pet. 3:11 (2x)

he/him/his/himself changed to *other* (3)
Matt. 18:15 (omit "your" and "you")
1 Cor. 14:28 (when alone)
1 John 5:16 (any)

"whoever" (singular) changed to *those (often "those who")* (22)
Matt. 10:39 (2x); 13:12 (2x); 16:25 (2x); 23:12 (2x)
Mark 4:25 (2x); 8:35 (2x)
Luke 8:18 (2x); 9:24 (2x); 17:33 (2x)
John 3:21; 4:14
1 John 3:11
Rev. 22:17

"anyone" (singular) changed to *those (often "those who")* (9)
Matt. 10:38; 16:24 Mark 8:34
John 16:2
1 Cor. 14:2
James 1:23; 3:2
1 John 3:10
Rev. 13:18

"one" (singular) changed to *those (often "those who")* (8)
Luke 6:49
John 12:48

1 Cor. 14:5
2 Cor 10:18 (2x)
Gal. 6:8 (2x)
1 John 3:9

"everyone" (singular) changed to *those (often "those who")* **(7)**
Matt. 25:29 (2x)
Luke 14:11 (2x); 18:14
John 3:20
1 Cor. 14:3

Other changes from singular to plural for the whole sentence (20)
Matt. 10:10, 24 (2x); 13:19, 20, 57; 19:23, 24
Mark 2:22
John 11:9, 10; 12:25 (2X), 35, 44, 47; 13:10
Rom. 13:4; 14:23
Gal. 4:7
2 Tim. 2:21
1 John 2:4; 3:10
Rev. 21:7; 22:7

B. Changes to avoid the word "father" and related words

father (*patēr*, singular) changed to *parents* (2)
Acts 7:20
Heb. 12:7

fathers (*patēr*, plural) changed to *parents* or *people* (2)
(Though "parents" is sometimes acceptable as a meaning for the plural of *patēr*, in this case the context is speaking of fatherly discipline)
Acts 7:11
Heb. 12:9

fathers/forefathers (*patēr*, plural) changed to *ancestors* (34)
(The BDAG Lexicon, p. 786–87, gives "ancestors" as a possible meaning, but the LSJ Lexicon (p. 1348) only gives the meaning of "forefathers." We have included these verses in this list because they seem to us to fit the general pattern of excluding male nuances in the TNIV, and because the male nuance or connotation of the plural word *pateres* would have been evident to the original Greek readers, but "ancestors" has no evident relationship to the word "father" and no male connotation in English.)
Matt. 23:30, 32
Luke 1:55, 72; 6:23, 26; 11:47, 48
John 4:20; 6:31, 49, 58

Acts 5:30; 7:12, 15, 19, 38, 39, 44, 45, 51, 52; 13:17, 32, 36; 15:10; 22:14; 26:6;
      28:25
1 Cor. 10:1
Heb. 1:1; 3:9; 8:9
2 Pet. 3:4

C. Changes to avoid the word "brother" (or to avoid the word "sister")

brother (*adelphos*, singular) changed to *brother or sister* (19)
Matt. 5:22 (2x), 23; 18:15, 35
Luke 17:3
Rom. 14:10 (2x), 13, 15, 21
1 Cor. 8:11, 13
1 Thess. 4:6
Jas. 4:11
1 John 3:10, 17; 4:20; 5:16

brother (*adelphos*, singular) changed to *(fellow) believer* (5)
(The BDAG Lexicon, p. 18, lists "brother, fellow member, member, associate" as possible meanings for *adelphos*, but all the singular examples listed refer to male human beings. The earlier BAGD Lexicon, p. 16, did not give these meanings, and the new BDAG Lexicon (2000) gives no new examples or new arguments to justify these new meanings that it proposes. The LSJ Lexicon (p. 20) gives the meaning "brother (as a fellow Christian)," but does not give the meaning "believer.")
2 Thess. 3:6
1 John 2:9, 11; 3:15; 4:20

brother (*adelphos*, singular) changed to *(fellow) believers* (4)
1 Cor. 5:11;
2 Thess. 3:15
Jas. 1:9
1 John 2:10

brother (*adelphos*, singular) changed to *other* (15)
Matt. 5:24 (that person); 7:3 (someone else), 4 (omitted), 5 (other person);
      18:15 (them), 21 (someone)
Luke 6:41 (someone else), 42 (friend, other person)
1 Cor. 8:13 (them)
1 Thess. 4:9 ("brotherly love" to "your love for one another")
Heb. 8:11 (one another)
Jas. 4:11 (them)
2 Pet. 1:7 (mutual affection—2x)
1 John 4:21 (one another)

brothers (*adelphos*, plural) changed to *brothers and sisters* (where sisters is uncertain or doubtful) (8)
Acts 1:16; 2:29; 13:26, 38
2 Cor. 11:9
Heb. 2:17
Jas. 3:1
Rev. 19:10

brothers/brotherhood (*adelphos*, plural) changed to *fellow believers* (4)
Acts 15:22
1 Tim. 6:2
1 Pet. 2:17; 5:9

brothers (*adelphos*, plural) changed to *believers* (27)
John 21:23
Acts 9:30; 10:23; 11:1, 29; 15:1, 3, 22, 32, 33, 36, 40; 16:2, 40; 17:6, 10, 14; 18:18, 27; 21:7, 17; 28:14, 15
2 Cor. 11:26
Gal. 2:4
3 John 1:3, 10

brothers (*adelphos*, plural) changed to *other* (9)
Matt. 5:47 (own people); 22:5 (associates); 28:21 (our people)
1 Cor. 8:12 (them)
1 Thess. 4:10 (dear friends); 5:26 (God's people)
1 John 3:14 (each other), 16 (one another)
Rev. 22:9 (fellow prophets)

brothers (*adelphos*, plural) omitted (2)
Matt. 7:4
1 Cor. 15:31 (TNIV uses less likely variant reading)

D. Changes to avoid the word "man"

man or husband (*anēr*, singular) changed to *other* (7)
(The BDAG Lexicon (p. 79) gives as the general definition of *anēr* the meaning, "a male person," and under that general definition it gives as meaning 2, "equivalent to *tis*, someone, a person." All the examples they list under meaning 2 either clearly refer to a male human being (as Luke 19:2, for example, "and there was a *man* named Zacchaeus"), or the context is not determinative but the meaning "man" makes good sense and the meaning "person" is not required. BDAG at the end of this entry also notes an idiom, *kat'andra*, which clearly means "man for man, individually," and clearly

includes women in some instances, but that idiom does not occur in the New Testament. The LSJ Lexicon (p. 138) also notes the idiom *kat'andra*, with a similar meaning. The LSJ Lexicon does not give the meaning "person" for *anēr*, but rather, "man, opposed to women," "man, opposed to god," "man, opposed to youth," "man emphatically, man indeed," "husband," and some special usages. For further discussion on the word *anēr*, "man" see Vern Poythress and Wayne Grudem, *The Gender Neutral Bible Controversy* (Nashville: Broadman & Holman, 2000), p. 101, note 2, and pages 321-333; see also, "Can Greek *anēr* ("man") sometimes mean "person"? at www.cbmw.org/TNIV/aner.html.)

Rom. 4:8 (those);
1 Tim. 3:2, 12 ("husband" to "faithful" on both)
Jas. 1:12 (those), 20 (our), 23 (people); 2:2 (someone);

man (*anēr*, singular) *omitted* (2)
Jas. 1:8; 3:2

men (*anēr*, plural) changed to *people* (10)
Matt. 12:41
Luke 11:31, 32
Acts 2:22; 3:12; 13:16; 17:22, 34; 19:35; 21:28

men (*aner*, plural) changed to *other* (5)
Acts 4:4 (believers); 14:15 (friends); 17:34 (people); 19:25 (friends); 20:30 (some)

men (*anēr*, plural) *omitted* (2)
Luke 14:24
Acts 15:22 (Judas Barsabbas & Silas)

man (*anthrōpos*, singular) changed to *people* or other plural nouns (9)
Matt. 12:35 (2x); 18:7
Luke 6:45 (2x)
Rom. 1:26; 4:6
Gal. 6:7
2 Tim. 3:17

man (*anthrōpos*, singular) changed to *you/your* (10)
Matt. 10:36; 15:11, 18, 20; 16:26 (2x)
Mark 7:23; 8:36, 37
Luke 9:25

man (*anthrōpos,* singular) changed to *human being/human/mere mortal* when referring to a specific historical man (6)
Acts 10:26 (Peter)
Acts 12:22 (Herod)
1 Cor. 15:21 (Jesus)
Phil. 2:8 (Jesus)
1 Tim. 2:5 (Jesus)
Jas. 5:17 (Elijah)

men (*anthrōpos,* plural) changed to *people* when referring to male human beings (1)
Heb. 5:1 (high priests)

men (*anthrōpos,* plural) changed to *other* (8)
(Neither the meaning "man" nor the meaning "person," is represented in these verses.)
Matt. 5:9 (underfoot); 10:32 (publicly), 33 (publicly); Luke 12:8 (publicly), 9 (publicly), 36 (servants)
John 8:17 (witnesses)
1 Cor. 7:7 (you)

men (*anthrōpos,* plural) *omitted* (6)
Matt. 10:17; 19:12;
Luke 12:8
Acts 4:12 (no other name under heaven); 17:26 (all nations);
1 Tim. 5:24 (sins of some)

"man" (*anthrōpos,* singular) meaning the human race changed to *people/mortals/human* (6)
Matt. 4:4
Mark 2:27 (2x)
Luke 4:4
John 2:25
Heb. 2:6 (mere mortals); 13:6 (human beings)

E. Changes to avoid the word "son"

son (*huios,* singular) changed to *child* (3)
Matt. 23:15
Luke 14:5
Heb. 12:6

son (*huios*, singular) changed to *children* (3)
Gal. 4:7 (2x—sentence plural)
Rev. 21:7 (sentence plural)

sons (*huios*, plural) changed to *children* (16)
Matt. 5:9, 45; 17:25, 26
Luke 6:35
John 12:36
Rom. 8:14, 19; 9:26
Gal. 3:26
1 Thess. 5:5 (2x)
Heb. 12:5, 7 (2x), 8

sons (*huios*, plural) changed to *people* (2)
Matt. 13:38 (2x)

sons (*huios*, plural) changed to *sons and daughters* (1)
Heb. 2:10

F. Changes to avoid the phrase "the Jews"

the Jew(s) (*hoi ioudaioi*) changed to *Jewish leaders* (16)
The 2000 BDAG Lexicon (pages 478-479) objects to translating *hoi ioudaioi* as "the Jews" because it claims that "many readers or auditors of Bible translations do not practice the historical judgment necessary to distinguish between circumstances and events of an ancient time and contemporary ethnic-religions-social realities, with the result that anti-Judaism in the modern sense of the term is needlessly fostered through biblical texts" (p. 478). In other words, we should no longer translate *hoi ioudaioi* as "the Jews" because many Bible readers today will not realize that the Bible is talking about ancient Judaism, not modern Judaism. So it favors the translation, "Judean."

> However, we find this argument unpersuasive and believe that the term "Judean" will wrongly imply a reference to people who simply live in a certain geographical area, whether Jews or not, and will not adequately convey the religious and ethnic identification with the ancient Jewish people that the term "the Jews" implies.

> On the next page, the BDAG Lexicon discusses the phrase *hoi ioudaioi* when it is used of people who are opposed to Jesus, and says the following: "Those who are in opposition to Jesus, with special focus on hostility emanating from leaders in Jerusalem, center of Israelite belief and cult; there is no indication that John uses the term in the general ethnic sense suggested in modern use of the word *Jew*, which covers diversities

of belief and practice that were not envisaged by biblical writers ..." (p. 479). In other words, John does not use the word "Jew" to speak of modern Judaism or anything like the diversity of modern Judaism.

The implication of this BDAG comment is, again, that modern readers will not understand that John is referring to ancient Jews in the first century and that these are different from modern Jews in the twenty-first century.

While we agree that John did not use *hoi ioudaioi* to refer to modern Judaism, we believe that readers of the Bible are able to realize that they are reading about events that occurred in ancient history. To take another example, when Bible readers today read that "Jesus entered Peter's house" (Matt. 8:14), we don't avoid using the word "house" out of fear that people will think Matthew meant a modern house with electricity and air conditioning and an automatic dishwasher. Readers automatically realize that they are reading an ancient document and that "house" refers to whatever kind of house people had in first–century Palestine. Even if the BDAG Lexicon is correct in saying that *hoi ioudaioi* can be used "with special focus on hostility emanating from leaders in Jerusalem," that does not mean that *only* the leaders were involved in such opposition to Jesus, for no doubt many common people were involved as well. And there were some Jewish leaders, such as Nicodemus (see John 3) who did not join in the opposition to Jesus. So it seems to us that changing *hoi ioudaioi* from "the Jews" to "Jewish leaders" introduces an incorrect change of meaning into a translation.

The older BAGD Lexicon (1979) simply translates *hoi ioudaioi* as "the Jews" (p. 379). The LSJ Lexicon simply translates *ho ioudaios* (singular form) as "a Jew," and gives no special meaning for the plural form (p. 832). John 1:19; 5:10, 15, 16; 7:1, 11, 13; 9:22; 18:14, 36; 19:12, 31, 38; 20:19; Acts 13:50; 21:11

the Jew(s) (*hoi ioudaioi*) changed to *they or omitted* (9)
John 2:20; 5:18; 8:52, 57; 9:18, 22; 10:33; 18:31; 19:7

G. Changes that lose the nuance of holiness in "saints" (36)

"saints" (Greek *hagios*, plural) changed to "believers" (4)
Acts 9:32; 26:10 (2)
Rom. 15:31; 16:15 (2)

"saints" (Greek *hagios*, plural) changed to "people" or "God's people" (31)
Rom. 8:27; 15:25; 16:2, 15 (4)
1 Cor. 6:1, 2; 14:33; 16:15 (4)
2 Cor. 8:4; 9:1; 13:13 (3)
Eph. 1:15, 19; 3:18; 6:18 (4)
Phil. 4:22 (1)

Col. 1:4, 12, 26 (3)
1 Tim. 5:10 (1)
Philem. 1:5, 7 (2)
Jude 1:3 (1)
Rev. 5:8; 8:3; 11:18; 13:10; 16:6; 17:6; 18:24; 19:8 (8)

"saints" (Greek *hagios*, plural) changed to "those" (1)
Acts 9:13 ("those") (1)

H. Other gender-related changes

Other gender related changes (11)
John 2:4 ("woman" to "mother," also at 19:26); 21 ("woman" dropped, also
    at 20:13, 15);
Acts 12:13 ("girl" dropped); 19:24 ("craftsmen" to "workers"), 25 ("work-
    men" to "workers"), 38 ("craftsmen" to "associates");
1 Cor. 7:29 ("wives" to "husband or wife");
2 Cor. 11:13 ("workmen" to "workers")

**Other examples of unnecessary removal of masculine references to God
or Christ (5)**
John 1:33 (the one who); 6:33 (that which; margin: he who); 10:2 (the one);
Heb. 2:6 (the "son of man," apparent Messianic prophecy or theme that the
    author of Hebrews sees fulfilled in Christ, from Ps. 8:4, changed to
    "human beings")

CHAPTER 4

Avoiding Generic "He" in the TNIV

by Vern S. Poythress

Like earlier gender-neutral translations,[1] *Today's New International Version* (TNIV) consistently eliminates generic "he," and by doing so changes meanings.

The discussion of gender-neutral translations in the book *The Gender-Neutral Bible Controversy* (GNBC) continues to be relevant and applicable to this translation.[2] The TNIV, a revision of the *New International Version* of 1984, is definitely gender-neutral in its treatment of terms like "father," "brother," "son," and "man," as well as in its avoidance of generic "he."

In this article I consider only the policy of avoiding generic "he." "Generic 'he'" describes the use of the masculine singular "he," "his," "him," "himself" in the context of a general statement, typically a statement starting with "anyone," "no one," "everyone," "whoever," or "each."[3] We exclude general statements beginning with "he who," because "he who" can legitimately be re-expressed with other phrases such as "the one who," "anyone who," or "whoever."[4] But in most other occurrences, generic "he" can only be eliminated by more extended rewording, rewording that inevitably introduces meaning changes. The book GNBC devotes considerable space to the topic, because many factors and several kinds of arguments and counterarguments need discussion.[5] I do not propose to repeat or review all the arguments at this time, but rather to inspect the details of how TNIV avoids generic "he."

---

[1] On the term "gender-neutral," see Vern S. Poythress and Wayne A. Grudem, *The Gender-Neutral Bible Controversy: Muting the Masculinity of God's Words* (Nashville, TN: Broadman and Holman, 2000), 5–6 (henceforth, GNBC, and pp. 117–18 below). This book is critical of many gender-neutral policies, while D. A. Carson, *The Inclusive Language Debate: A Plea for Realism* (Grand Rapids: Baker, 1998), and Mark L. Strauss, *Distorting Scripture? The Challenge of Bible Translation & Gender Accuracy* (Downers Grove, Ill.: InterVarsity Press, 1998), are for the most part favorable.

[2] Poythress and Grudem, GNBC.

[3] See pp. 223–24.

[4] P. 223.

[5] See chapters 13–17.

We gather verses together into five categories according to the route that they use.

A. Pluralizing

First, TNIV converts many statements from third-person singular to third-person plural.[6]

Consider Revelation 2:26–28.

NIV: To *him* who overcomes and does my will to the end, I will give authority over the nations—'*He* will rule them with an iron scepter; he will dash them to pieces like pottery'—just as I have received authority from my Father. I will also give *him* the morning star.

TNIV: To *those* who are victorious and do my will to the end, I will give authority over the nations—*they* 'will rule them with an iron scepter and will dash them to pieces like pottery'—just as I have received authority from my Father. I will also give *them* the morning star.

In these verses TNIV converts all the third-person singulars ("he/him") to third-person plurals ("they/them/those"). The meanings are fairly similar; but they are not completely identical. TNIV opens up a potential ambiguity between an individualizing and a corporate interpretation. In the individualizing interpretation, each individual victor rules. In the corporate interpretation, they exercise a single joint rule, with one "iron scepter" (singular). In the corporate interpretation they also jointly receive "the morning star," a single gift to all of them together. The retention of singulars for "scepter" and "star" may push readers in the direction of a more corporate understanding.[7]

Because we are all united to Christ, who is the chief ruler, we can deduce that doubtless there is a corporate dimension to the rule of the saints. But that is the implication from other passages, not the explicit teaching of this passage.

Note also a more subtle effect. Even if we ignore the ambiguity, the use of the singular invites us to use as a starting point a sample case, "him," from which we infer a general principle applicable to every case. TNIV starts with the generality, "those," from which we infer applicability to any particular case. The directions of inferences are subtly different, and this is already a difference in meaning.[8]

---

[6] See p. 224.

[7] P. 229–35.

[8] Pp. 224–27. In fact, the ambiguities produced in this and other verses probably arise primarily from the initial difference in the starting perspective between the singular and the plural. If one starts with an individual case ("whoever, he"), the individualizing character of the application is plain. If one starts with a reference to a plurality of members of a group, it may remain unclear whether the statement applies to each member separately or to the members' interaction with one another in a more corporate fashion. Even with a corporate interpretation, there is always *some kind* of application to each individual. But what kind? Does the individual receive the morning star himself, or is he part of the group that receives it *as a group* (the corporate interpretation)?

Now consider 1 John 4:16.

NIV: ...*Whoever* lives in love lives in God, and God in *him*.

TNIV: ...*Those* who live in love live in God, and God in *them*.

The NIV again has a principle applicable to each individual. But the TNIV is ambiguous. It allows a corporate interpretation in which "living in God" and "God in them" refer to the totality of Christians together—the church lives in God and God in the church. This thought is theologically true (see 1 Cor. 3:10–15; 1 Thess. 1:1), but it is not the assertion of this verse, and the TNIV alters meaning by allowing it there.

Consider 1 John 3:3.

NIV: *Everyone* who has this hope in *him* purifies *himself*, just as he is pure.

TNIV: *All* who have this hope in *them* purify *themselves*, just as he is pure.

Again TNIV opens up a potential ambiguity between an individualizing and a corporate interpretation. In the individualizing interpretation, the purification takes place when each individual purifies himself. In the corporate interpretation, the purification takes place as each individual purifies everyone else as well as himself, or as each individual purifies the whole body through actions that help the body corporately. Corporate growth of the body of Christ is taught elsewhere (Eph. 4:11–16; 1 Cor. 12–14), so this latter interpretation is reasonable. But the singulars in Greek and in the NIV indicate unambiguously an individualizing interpretation (which, in the light of teachings elsewhere, will doubtless have some indirect corporate effects).

Consider 1 John 3:9.

NIV: *No one* who is born of God will continue to sin, because God's seed remains in *him*; *he* cannot go on sinning, because *he* has been born of God.

TNIV: *Those* who are born of God will not continue to sin, because God's seed remains in *them*; *they* cannot go on sinning, because *they* have been born of God.

Once again, TNIV converts to plurals ("those"), and thereby allows a corporate interpretation, namely that the body of people whom God has brought together through spiritual birth do not continue to sin, *as a group, when looked at as a whole*. But there may be some few exceptions that do not ruin the observation with respect to the general whole. By contrast, the singular ("no one," "him," etc.) is more explicit about disallowing exceptions. Naturally, this is not an all-or-nothing issue. We must allow that, for certain verses, the context may indicate that there are exceptions even in a case that is formulated using the singular. The point is that the singular is stronger in pushing one away from allowing exceptions.

Revelation 3:12.

NIV: *Him* who overcomes I will make a pillar in the temple of my God. Never again will *he* leave it. I will write on *him* the name of my God and the name of the city of my God, the new Jerusalem, which is coming down out of heaven from my God; and I will also write on *him* my new name.

TNIV: *Those* who are victorious I will make *pillars* in the temple of my God. Never again will *they* leave it. I will write on *them* the name of my God and the name of the city of my God, the new Jerusalem, which is coming down out of heaven from my God; and I will also write on *them* my new name.

TNIV again pluralizes and introduces the possibility of a corporate interpretation. Is the name of my God written on each person individually or once on the group as a whole? If one pictures literal pillars, one might most naturally think of the name being written on each one, but it is also possible that the name would be spelled across a group. In any case, the language of pillars is metaphorical, so it remains possible that in the reality to which the metaphor points, the name would be inscribed once on all of "them" as a group.

TNIV has converted to plurals every one of the seven promises to the "overcomers" (2:7, 11, 17, 26–28, 3: 5, 12, 21). The cumulative shift from single case to plural members of a group, over a considerable number of verses, is a fairly pronounced change.

Matthew 16:24–25.

NIV: ... If *anyone* would come after me, *he* must deny *himself* and take up *his* cross and follow me. For *whoever* wants to save *his* life will lose it, but *whoever* loses *his* life for me will find it.

TNIV: ... *Those* who want to be my disciples must deny *themselves* and take up *their* cross and follow me. For *those* who want to save their life will lose it, but *those* who lose *their* life for me will find it.

The retention of singular "cross" and singular "life" makes this saying ambiguous between a corporate and an individual interpretation.[9] (The parallel passage in Luke 9:23–24 shows a similar problem.)

John 14:12.

NIV: ... *anyone* who has faith in me will do what I have been doing. *He* will do even greater things than these, because I am going to the Father.

TNIV: ... *all* who have faith in me will do the works I have been doing, and *they* will do even greater things than these, because I am going to the Father.

John 15:20

NIV: *No servant* is greater than *his master*.

TNIV: Servants are not greater than *their* masters.

TNIV will not allow a male element even in this parable-like analogy to Christian living.

---

[9] See pp. 224–29.

1 John 5:12.

NIV: *He* who has the Son has life; *he* who does not have the Son of God does not have life.

TNIV: *Those* who have the Son have life; *those* who do not have the Son of God do not have life.

The NIV could have been changed by using "one who" or "anyone who" instead of "he who." It is unclear why the TNIV pluralized the whole. Once again, the change opens up the possibility of a corporate interpretation, where all together have a life together. This is doubtless theologically true, but not the focus on the verse.

One could produce many more examples. As a sample of the frequency of this usage, I have found the following additional examples from the Gospels: Matt 10:10, 24, 25, 38, 39; 12:35; 13:12, 19, 21, 23, 57; 23:12; 25:29; Mark 2:22; 4:25; 6:4; 8:34; 13:13; Luke 4:24; 5:37; 6:40, 45, 47–48; 8:18; 10:7; 11:10; 12:21; 14:11, 27; 16:16; 17:33; 18:14; 19:26; John 3:20, 21; 4:14, 36, 44; 7:18; 11:9–10; 12:25, 35, 45, 47, 48; 13:10, 16; 15:15.

B. Change from third person ("he") to second person ("you")

On occasion TNIV substitutes "you" for generic "he." The general principle may still be the same, or similar, but the starting point for illustration is no longer someone "out there," but "you."[10]

Luke 16:13.

NIV: *No servant* can serve two masters. Either *he* will hate the one and love the other, or *he* will be devoted to the one and despise the other. You cannot serve both God and Money.

TNIV: No one can be a slave to two masters. Either *you* will hate the one and love the other, or *you* will be devoted to the one and despise the other. You cannot be a slave to both God and Money.

The parallel in Matthew 6:24 has an analogous change.

The final sentence, "You cannot serve both God and Money," is second person in Greek and in the NIV. So far so good. But TNIV shifts into second person in the *second sentence*, one sentence *before* the Greek changes to second person. This change might not seem to be too bad, until one realizes that the first two sentences are presented as generalities about life. They picture for the listener a slave "out there." Only in the third does one hit the application, when one shifts from the generality "out there" to "you." TNIV ruins the surprise punch of the third sentence by prematurely making the second already "you."

TNIV also makes the second sentence awkward in another way. "Hate" and "love" are obviously hyperbolical when applied to a typical master-servant relation. The hyperbole can remain effective when applied to a

---

[10] See the discussion on pp. 224–26, and the response to Craig Blomberg near the end of this article.

servant "out there." But it is more likely to seem extreme when it is directly describing "you." The immediate reaction might be, "No, not me. That doesn't describe my actual experience." Again, the effectiveness of the whole saying is subtly damaged.

TNIV's change is all the less justified because this verse is a kind of mini-parable. In Greek "no one" and "slave" are both masculine in gender. There is no reason why one should not think of a male slave as an example of a principle. When, in the third sentence, one leaves the realm of the parable and goes to the application to "you," the "you" is obviously inclusive of both men and women. There is no need to tamper with it.

Luke 9:26.
NIV: If *anyone* is ashamed of me and my words, the Son of Man will be ashamed of *him* when he comes in his glory ....
TNIV: If any *of you are* ashamed of me and my words, the Son of Man will be ashamed of *you* when he comes in his glory ....

TNIV's change from "anyone" to "any of you" runs the danger of restricting the range of "anyone." Now it is no longer "anyone at all, throughout all ages," but "anyone of you present to hear." Perhaps one can still infer a broader application, but the broad sweep is not as unambiguous nor as directly and emphatically stated. (Mark 8:38 is similar.)

Matthew 16:26.
NIV: What good will it be for *a man* if he gains the whole world, yet forfeits *his* soul? Or what can *a man* give in exchange for *his* soul?
TNIV: What good will it be for *you* to gain the whole world, yet forfeit *your* soul? Or what can *you* give in exchange for *your* soul?

Mark 8:36 and Luke 9:25 are similar. (It would be allowable to use "a person" here instead of "a man" [Greek *anthropos*].[11] The problematic change lies in the shift to second person ["you"].)

1 John 2:15.
NIV: ... If *anyone* loves the world, the love of the Father is not in *him*.
TNIV: ... If *you* love the world, love for the Father is not in *you*.

1 John 3:17.
NIV: If *anyone* has material possessions and sees *his* brother in need but has no pity on him, how can the love of God be in *him*?
TNIV: If any one *of you* has material possessions and sees *a* brother or sister in need but has no pity on them, how can the love of God be in *you*?

1 John 5:16.
NIV: If *anyone* sees *his* brother commit a sin that does not lead to death, *he* should pray and God will give him life....

---

[11] P. 466n1.

TNIV: If *you* see *any* brother or sister commit a sin that does not lead to death, *you* should pray and God will give them life....

1 John 5:16b.
NIV: I am not saying that *he* should pray about that.
TNIV: I am not saying that *you* should pray about that.

In all the cases from 1 John "you" can refer to the immediate recipients of John's letter. It is not as clear as before that the principle holds in general, not just for the recipients.

C. Change from third person ("he") to first person ("we")

1 John 4:20.
NIV: If anyone says, "I love God," yet hates *his* brother, *he* is a liar. For *anyone* who does not love *his* brother, whom *he* has seen, cannot love God, whom *he* has not seen.
TNIV: If *we* say we love God yet hate *a fellow believer*, *we* are *liars*. For if *we* do not love *a brother or sister* whom *we* have seen, *we* cannot love God, whom *we* have not seen.

The third person, "anyone," leaves open the possibility that, in the historical context of the letter, John is thinking mostly of people who belonged to a dissident group and had already separated themselves from the church (1 John 2:19). Changing to "we" in the TNIV suggests instead that the issue at hand is primarily one of hypocrisy among those whom John is directly addressing. There is a difference of meaning here, affecting how we see the situation that John is addressing.

D. Dropping generic "he"

In some passages TNIV tries simply to drop generic "he." But this too can produce changes in meaning.

1 Corinthians 14:28.
NIV: If there is no interpreter, the speaker should keep quiet in the church and speak *to himself* and to God.
TNIV: If there is no interpreter, the speaker should keep quiet in the church and speak to God *when alone*.

The NIV is correct in translating it "to himself." The phrase is parallel in structure to the phrase translated "to God."[12] TNIV's expression "when alone" not only leaves out completely the idea of speaking to himself, but adds the idea of being alone, which is not there explicitly in the Greek. And it is not clearly implied either, since the person in question could speak in

---

[12] Mark Strauss ("Response to Vern Poythress," *Christianity Today* [Oct. 7, 2002], 45) claims that "the Greek dative *eauto* in 1 Corinthians 14:28 probably means 'by himself' (= 'when alone') rather than *to himself*." But this view must be rejected for several reasons: (1) the dative *eauto* ("to himself") is obviously parallel to the dative *to theo*, "to God," and the parallelism is

tongues quietly, mumbling under his breath while still in the church setting. Or he could speak in tongues out loud in a context of a small number of other Christians who were each praying out loud to God, and with none disturbing another. (I understand that in some cultures, more given to expressing all prayers out loud, the practice of simultaneous vocal prayer by many is common, even outside the context of tongues.) The operative concern for Paul seems to be in not disrupting the church gathering by trying to address it in tongues, not in a literal restriction to being off by oneself.[13]

> 1 John 3:15.
> NIV: Anyone who hates *his* brother is a murderer, ...
> TNIV: Anyone who hates *a* fellow believer is a murderer, ...

E. "They" with singular antecedent

Finally, TNIV uses "they" with a singular antecedent in order to avoid generic "he." Let us consider an example, John 14:23:

> NIV: ... If anyone loves me, *he* will obey my teaching. My Father will love *him*, and we will come to *him* and make our home with *him*.
> TNIV: ... Anyone who loves me will obey my teaching. My Father will love *them*, and we will come to *them* and make our home with *them*.

In the second sentence, TNIV substitutes "them" for "him" three times.[14] To whom does "them" refer? The context is set by the preceding sentence, which uses "anyone." "Anyone" is grammatically singular. It invites us to start with a particular case (one person), but that case is an example of a general principle applying to a whole group, namely all human beings, and

---

reinforced by the word *kai* ("and") linking them together. Thus both datives indicate the addressee, and are properly translated with the English word "to." (2) The clause as a whole (verse 28b) does not fit together well under Strauss's interpretation. One would have to translate, "by himself let him speak *and* to God," or "by himself let him speak *also* to God," or "by himself let him speak *even* to God," all of which are awkward. The problem is to make sense of the word *kai* ("and"; sometimes "also" or "even"). In Greek it is clearly functioning to link the two datives ("to himself" and "to God"). But once Strauss reinterprets the first dative to mean "by himself," it is hard to account for its presence. (3) "By himself" in a spatial sense is not a normal function of the dative in relation to a verb like *laleito*, "let him speak," while the dative of addressee is a normal function (for example, "I have spoken *to you*" in John 6:63).

Strauss compounds his error by citing Robertson and Plummer's and Fee's commentaries as if they supported the meaning "by himself." Actually, both commentaries *explicitly* contain the wording "to himself"! They then *infer* from this meaning that the speaker should wait until he is alone. The inference may or may not be correct, but in any case ought not to be pushed back into translation.

[13] From Vern S. Poythress, "Systematic Pattern in TNIV," *Westminster Theological Journal* 64/1 (2002) 187.

[14] TNIV also changes the NIV by changing a conditional sentence, beginning with "if," to a sentence with a restrictive relative clause, "who loves me." The NIV is a more literal representation of the Greek. The change has the effect of eliminating the offending "he" in the second clause, "He will obey my teaching." The meanings are very similar, but not identical. Using "anyone," the NIV starts with a potential pool of examples as wide as humanity. It considers what may be true, if a sample person out of this wide pool is in fact found to love Christ.

then that large group is narrowed down to "anyone who loves me." The group is composed of a plurality of members, and "they" is sometimes used in contemporary English, as it has been for centuries, as the follow-up pronoun in such contexts.[15] We shall call this usage "'they' with singular antecedent."

How do we evaluate this kind of use of "they," which is fairly frequent in TNIV? The question is complex, partly because different people may react differently to the same verse. A portion of the English-speaking public quite regularly uses "they" with singular antecedent, sometimes without realizing it. On the other hand, some people have heard from school grammarians that this usage is "wrong," and consciously try to avoid it. A portion perceives "they" with singular antecedent as improper, perhaps because of the influence of school pronouncements. A portion would see it as out of place in formal written English, but be more tolerant of its appearance in informal conversation.[16]

The potential for misunderstanding rears its head, because some people may look for a plural antecedent to "they." Others may interpret it as a fully plural usage, and conclude that the Father and the Son will make a single corporate home, "our home," with "them," that is, with all who love the Son. In that case the sentence is interpreted in a corporate sense, as having to do with "them" as members of the group to which God comes and which he loves, rather than as individuals.[17]

We can illustrate this possibility by imagining that Jesus had said something like this: "Anyone who loves me will obey my teaching. My Father will love them, and we will come to them and make our home with them, and *they will share a new life together*." In this new statement, the wording "share ... together" indicates unambiguously a corporate experience. A single person cannot "share" by himself. The word "they" must refer to Christians together, more than one at a time. It has plural *reference*, in spite

---

The TNIV starts with the pool already narrowed to consider only the people who do in fact already love Christ. The NIV is slightly more open-ended, in suggesting a look at people who are not yet Christians but might become so. The TNIV focuses more on those who are already committed. This kind of change occurs in a number of other verses as well, and could easily be made into a sixth category along side the five in the main text of this article.

[15] See p. 328.

[16] The convention distinguishing formal writing from informal conversation may not be as arbitrary as it sounds. Face-to-face communication normally decreases the potential for misunderstanding, because much collateral information is supplied from the situation. Written communication cannot rely on the collateral information, and must take greater care to head off misreadings of potentially ambiguous uses. In some contexts, where both a singular and a plural antecedent offer themselves, "they" is potentially ambiguous. The maxim to allow only plural antecedents helps to disambiguate, if both writer and reader abide by it. The use of generic singular "he" also helps head off the potential ambiguities of "corporate" interpretations.

[17] See pp. 229–30 for a further discussion of the problem of a corporate interpretation of plurals in John 14:23. The example on p. 229 is from the NRSV, which begins with "those who ..." rather than "anyone who ..." (TNIV). "Anyone who ..." is considerably more individualizing, but the danger of slipping into a corporate interpretation later on in the verse does not disappear (see the further discussion in this article).

of the earlier word "anyone," which refers to a single sample person within the group. But this means that, even *before* a reader comes to the key extra expression "share ... together," he must allow for the possibility that the word "they" is referring to a plurality of members. And then one must also allow that this plurality of members might function *together*. And so the expression "our home with them" can mean a single "home" with them *together*, a corporate dwelling of the Father and the Son with "them" *together*, a dwelling of God in the church.

The use of "they" with singular antecedent does have one distinct advantage over all the other routes for avoiding generic "he." In the usual case, at least, it makes it possible for a sophisticated reader to reconstruct accurately what the actual meaning is. Substitute generic "he/his/him" for each occurrence of "they/their/them," and you have it! But of course that also raises a question. Why introduce the ambiguity of a corporate interpretation, when you can just use generic "he" and achieve your purpose immediately?! I know, I know, there are all kinds of concerns generated from ideological sources, and for those I must once again refer readers to the book GNBC and the later discussion (chapters 13–17).

Consider one more case, Revelation 3:20:

NIV: If anyone hears my voice and opens the door, I will come in and eat with *him*, and *he* with me.
TNIV: If anyone hears my voice and opens the door, I will come in and eat with *them*, and *they* with me.

In this case, there is a potential plural antecedent, namely "those whom I love" in 3:19. If "they" refers back to this plural antecedent, then Jesus is saying that if anyone—even one person—opens the door, Jesus will come in and eat with "those whom I love," with the whole group of people in the Laodicean church, and by extension with any other church with similar problems. Such, of course, is not the meaning of the original.

One can hope that many people, because they remember this famous verse from *other translations*, will realize right away that this is not its meaning.[18] Others will quickly realize that the most obvious antecedent is the more immediate one, namely "anyone."

But even so, the potential for a corporate meaning does not disappear. Consider the following sentence: "If anyone hears my voice and opens the door, I will come in and eat with them, and they with me, *and they will share a new life together.*" The final occurrence of "they" has an unambiguously plural reference, and the other extra words speak unambiguously about a corporate experience. This result illustrates the fact that even the earlier words, "eat with them and they with me," *allow* a corporate interpretation.

---

[18] It should go without saying that it is unwise for translators to rely on the clarity of *other* translations as a consolation and a protection, covering the lack of disambiguation in the one they are producing.

Under this interpretation, all the people who fit into the class indicated by the preceding occurrence of "anyone" may *together* have the experience of a communal meal with the Lord. And indeed, the Lord's Supper is just such a communal meal. As long as we do not add extra words like "share... together," the meaning is not unambiguously corporate. But neither is it unambiguously individual. Readers are automatically open to the *possibility* of a corporate function for "they," as the expression "they share" illustrates.[19]

Moreover, the thought of communal fellowship is a reasonable theological inference from teachings elsewhere about the Lord's Supper and about Jesus' fellowship with the church. But it is not directly the meaning of this verse, and opening up a corporate interpretation to this verse changes its meaning.

F. Evaluation

This collection of verses confirms what the book GBNC said two years ago. The techniques for avoiding generic "he" are roughly the same as in earlier gender-neutral translations, though with greater frequency for the use of "they" with singular antecedent. With respect to this last use, reactions may vary. For the other uses, changes in meaning nuances are regularly visible, though the translators tried to keep them small.

My judgment remains what it was in GNBC: the translators should have discarded the underlying policy of avoiding generic "he." In translation, generic "he" is needed for maximal accuracy. The firm commitment to avoid it leads to unacceptable degradations of meaning. We lose a valuable resource in the English language, and with it a whole host of nuances in verse after verse.

The defenders of gender-neutral translation have a raft of replies, for which I must refer readers again to GNBC.[20] The appearance of the TNIV has led to a number of new papers, but for the most part they take up themes already discussed in GNBC (see the response below).[21] For now, let me be brief: generic "he" continues to be used in English in the secular press.[22] For Bible translation, we need it. Then let us use it. I continue to believe what I wrote in 2000 in *The Gender-Neutral Bible Controversy*:

> In fact, the "problem" with generic "he" is not with a single occurrence but with the pattern of thought in the Bible, a pattern that more often than not uses male examples as a starting point to express or illustrate

---

[19] D. A. Carson thinks that the earlier word "anyone" guarantees individuality in this verse ("The Limits of Functional Equivalence in Bible Translation—And Other Limits, Too," manuscript distributed by Zondervan to ETS and IBR members, [Sept. 4, 2002], p. 27). But he fails to realize that the later occurrences of "they/them" reintroduce the possibility of a corporately oriented interpretation of the part in which they occur.

[20] See chapters 13–17 and appendix 3. Opposite to our viewpoint, for the most systematic defense of gender-neutral translation (though with some reservations here and there), see Carson, *Debate*, and Strauss, *Distorting*.

[21] See also footnote 12 for a response to Mark Strauss.

[22] P. 315–24.

truths that apply to both men and women. This pattern of thought a translator is not free to change or tone down in translation.[23]

G. Response to Craig Blomberg

As we have seen, the TNIV changes person and number in order to avoid generic "he" (sections 1–3 above). In defense of the TNIV Craig Blomberg cites a number of cases where parallel passages in the Gospels differ in person or number (Matt. 5:3//Luke 6:20; Matt. 9:17//Mark 2:22; John 3:5//3:7), and passages where New Testament authors shift person or number in stating general truths (John 15:15; Rom. 4:7–8; 13:2; etc.).[24] Much could be said about these and other examples. For the sake of brevity I note only the following points:

First, in each of the passages that Blomberg cites, he perceives no meaning difference. But I find the usual subtle meaning differences due to person and number, just as in other passsages (pp. 224–36). The passages therefore prove nothing.

Second, Gospel parallels are not Bible translations. If they *did* give us a model for what is permissible in translation, then a modern translation could freely interchange the wordings and meanings found in *any* of the parallels, producing a "gospel harmony" without differences between the Gospels. Every New Testament scholar would find this completely unacceptable. Blomberg, who is a New Testament scholar himself and is familiar with Gospel parallels, should see the fallacy in using these examples as if they provided a principle for *translation*.

Third, passages for which New Testament writers are the original authors are not translations. An original author is free to vary person and number. With the third person he makes a statement that directly focuses on the general case, while with the second person he makes a statement that directly focuses on the addressee(s). These complementary foci reinforce one another, rather than proving absolute identity of meaning. They therefore offer no principle by which to justify meaning alterations in translation.

Fourth, Blomberg needs not merely a few examples where (he alleges) person and number make no difference, but a general principle that will justify all the places where the TNIV makes changes. Such a general

---

[23] GNBC 232 (see p. 344). In some ways the single most significant datum confirming this conclusion is the oscillating use of generic "she" and generic "he" in some authors (pp. 262, 282, 474). In these contexts, generic "he" is seen by feminists as acceptable, because it is accompanied by an equal weight of generic "she." This oscillating use also confirms the fact that, with both generic "he" and generic "she," readers easily understand that a general principle is being articulated that applies to both male and female.

On the question of whether the Greek and Hebrew generic masculine forms suggest a male example, see the discussion on pp. 254–58, 447–59.

[24] Craig Blomberg, "Today's New International Version: The Untold Story of a Good Translation," manuscript distributed by Zondervan to ETS and IBR members, [Sept. 4, 2002].

principle is clearly contradicted by any of the passages above that show subtle but demonstrable meaning changes.

In sum, Blomberg fallaciously uses Scriptural examples that are not about Bible translation in order to justify flawed translation.

H. A Response to D. A. Carson

Now let us consider D. A. Carson's recent article, "The Limits of Functional Equivalence."[25] Most of the article discusses the general subject of dynamic equivalent translation, and makes points many of which are compatible with pp. 169–93 below. But when Carson comes to discuss gender, he misrepresents our position. We can only touch on the main problems.

First, Carson criticizes us for permitting some changes but not others: "They are making such changes...all the time,.... But when others make similar changes with respect to the pronoun 'he,' Poythress and Grudem condemn them for distorting the Word of God" (p. 22; see also p. 26 and p. 24n54). Carson's word "similar" makes it sound as if we have no standards or are making arbitrary judgments in permitting some changes but not others. But this is not true. We already explain this issue in GNBC, chapter 5, where we talk about "Permissible Changes"; and the Colorado Springs Guidelines mapped out areas of permissible change.[26] Roughly speaking, changes toward generic English are permissible when we are not losing a male meaning component in the original. And changes with respect to generic "he" are permissible when they do not produce significant meaning loss. (For instance, on p. 223 we permit "he who" being replaced by "anyone who" or "whoever," because there is no significant meaning loss from the original.) Carson is of course free to disagree with where we draw the line. But instead he describes us as if we give no reasons.

Carson also paints a harsh picture of us by saying that we "condemn them," that is, condemn the translators.[27] That is not true. We most

---

[25] See note 18.

[26] See chapter 11 below. There is even more support. It is not widely realized that in 1989 the Lutheran Church—Missouri Synod requested one of its commissions to study inclusive language issues. Nine years later the Commission produced the report "Biblical Revelation and Inclusive Language," A Report of the Commission on Theology and Church Relations of The Lutheran Church—Missouri Synod (February 1998). The report is compatible with the Colorado Springs Guidelines in all the areas on which both speak, but it appears to have been produced independently. The report does quote once from an article by Wayne Grudem, from October 27, 1997 (p. 31). But there are no direct signs of interaction with the Colorado Springs Guidelines. In any case, most of the eight or nine years' work by the Commission was presumably done *before* the Guidelines appeared publicly on June 3, 1997. The Commission's report thus represents an *independent* witness to the fact that our principles have logical coherence, and do not arise merely from arbitrary personal whims.

[27] In the quote from p. 22, reproduced above, "them" might possibly refer to "changes," but is most naturally taken as referring to "others," that is, the translators.

pointedly do not do so. GNBC repeatedly makes a distinction between the translators and the resulting translation:

> We are not criticizing the personal motives of the translators. (GNBC 7) We must be careful not to jump to conclusions about individuals. For convenience we have spoken of what translators do, but all we actually have is the product, the resulting translation. We know neither what was going on in translators' minds nor the motives that underlay their thinking....
>
> Thus, it is inappropriate to make this issue an occasion for personal attacks. We must beware of overreacting and firing ourselves with a zeal that "is not based on knowledge" (Rom. 10:2). (GNBC 293; see pp. 119, 405).

Carson overlooks these explicit statements in suggesting that we are attacking the *translators*.

Carson more than once complains about overheated rhetoric coming from people on our side. But this distortion of our position on his part is not only unfair—it is overheated, and may unwittingly encourage those on our side, if they believe Carson, to imitate the harshness that they mistakenly think we advocate, thereby further heating up the situation. Similarly, on p. 26, Carson says, "… their wrath knows few bounds when the TNIV deploys a plural instead of a singular." Colorful, no doubt, but also unfair and dangerous.

Second, Carson has this to say:

> I cannot help remarking, rather wryly, that in the light of the ESV, the argument of Poythress and Grudem sounds a bit like this: "The language is not changing, so we do not need to respond to the demands of inclusive language. But if it is changing, the changes are driven by a feminist agenda, so they are wrong and must be opposed if we are to be faithful to Scripture. Because of the changes, we will make some minor accommodations in our translations, but if others make any other changes, they are compromisers who introduce distortions and inaccuracies, and should be condemned, because changes aren't necessary anyway!" (p. 24n54)

Carson here uses the unfair language "condemned" and "compromisers," again falsely accusing us of attacking the translators personally. In addition the picture that he paints is totally off-base. Carson's depiction repeats the errors of his earlier caricature of us in *Debate*, 183–184, which we pointedly refuted in GNBC 358–360 (see pp. 470–72), and now he produces an even more distorted version, to which he adds our personal names!

Yes, it is intended to be humorous, but in the context of other misrepresentations the humor may manipulate readers. First it lowers the normal demands for fairness and evidence ("a bit like this"). Then by the effects of witty distortion it leaves a colorful, lasting impression that at bottom our position must be hypocritical and ridiculous. One wants to believe the picture because it is witty, not because it is true. And then, if objection is made, will we be told that it is "only a joke"?

Third, Carson says Poythress and Grudem "abuse their own theory by not admitting that basic translations really cannot frequently rise much beyond level 2." But this statement misrepresents us. Far from "not admitting" translation limitations, in the very chapter to which Carson refers, we explicitly discuss at some length the limitations of translations in conveying meaning (pp. 170–93, especially 191–92). The four levels laid out on pp. 194–202 are *not* levels for translations to achieve, as Carson's wording here makes them out to be, but levels of *analysis of meanings*, whether the analysis is directed toward translations or toward other texts. (The whole section is entitled "Excursus: *Analyzing* linguistic complexity," p. 194) Our point is not that translators can achieve perfect representation of meaning, but that they should not be content with "basic meaning" *in cases in which a fine-grained analysis shows that they can achieve more* (see pp. 301–2). All this is clear in GNBC, and Carson abuses our position by making it sound otherwise.

Fourth, Carson misunderstands my statement that Carson and Strauss "could not frankly discuss the ideological connotation of generic 'he'" (Carson, p. 22). In context, I was obviously not saying that they would find it literally impossible to discuss (which would be a rather absurd claim), but that discussing it in any detail, and genuinely weighing the problems (as on pp. 223–344, and especially 275–287), would weaken the case for gender-neutral translation, by removing some people's impression that it is all a question of "neutral" stylistic preferences or of adjusting to "neutral" facts about the current state of English. Interestingly, in his latest response Carson *still* does not discuss the ideological connotation of generic "he"—in particular, the fact that ideology continuously maintains some people's aversion to hearing it. Instead, he repeats generalities from his book about the influence of feminism, the reality of language change, and the lessening use of generic "he," all points to which we have already responded in GNBC 355–366 (see pp. 467–78). He has shifted the issue instead of discussing it frankly as he claims (p. 22). Ironically, his continued avoidance of this one particular topic confirms rather than undermines the point in my review.

Fifth, Carson has missed the point of the quote from p. 314, which says, "The underlying assumption in this objection is that *only what can easily be conveyed into all languages is worth conveying in English*." On the preceding page (p. 313) we introduce an objection that appears to us to have been made in Carson's book and elsewhere: "Gender systems differ among languages. Therefore, you should not insist on mapping a masculine form in Hebrew onto a masculine in English." We then explicitly indicate that we agree that gender systems do differ (313). We also indicate (314) that we are not talking about *all* masculine forms in Hebrew, but "a third-person-singular masculine pronoun used in a generic statement." (But Carson in spite of this statement describes our position as perfectly general: "where we have the masculine pronoun in Hebrew," p. 25.) With respect to this special kind of use, we offer considerable evidence that the *meaning* match between Hebrew, Greek, and English is generally very good (pp. 447–59). Our argument does *not* rest on the mere assumption that one should always use formal equivalence, as Carson suggests (p. 25; see pp. 173, 197, 198n37, 302–3).

Carson's 1998 discussion of gender in other languages in *Debate*, chapter 4, is relevant and helpful as a general illustration of the form-meaning contrast, which we ourselves recognize (pp. 173, 197, 198n37, 302–3). But in and of itself it cannot settle the questions about how best to translate the *meaning* (not merely form) of masculine singular generics in Hebrew and Greek.

With respect to this narrow question, the discussion of other languages (outside Hebrew, Greek, Aramaic, and English) would have weight only if someone—not necessarily Carson personally—falsely assumed "that only what can easily be conveyed into all languages is worth conveying in English." Without this assumption, the fact that a particular loss of meaning nuance is inevitable in translating into Polish does not lead to the conclusion that a similar loss in English is O.K., *even though it is avoidable in English*. (I do not think that we differ substantively with Carson on this point, only that Carson misunderstands us.)

Of course, with respect to generic "he" Carson might want to claim that there is a trade-off between different kinds of loss, because generic "he" is "offensive" on university campuses (see Carson, p. 21). But this is another topic, to which we respond on pp. 275–87, 292–94.

Sixth, Carson says that he provides many examples pertaining to nonequivalence of gender systems, but "Poythress and Grudem tackle none of them" (p. 25). This is not true. We discuss Numbers 5:6 (from Carson, *Debate* 97) on pp. 453–55, and Carson's discussion on feminine subjects in Hebrew with masculine verbs (*Debate* 96) corresponds to p. 448 (but we mention singular subjects while he mentions plural). In addition, we explicitly indicate our agreement with the main point of Carson's discussion of gender systems in p. 198n37. Carson's word "tackle" suggests that we need to refute his examples. But this completely misses the point. The clear statement in p. 198n37 indicates that our view is completely compatible with his examples.

Carson repeatedly misunderstood and misrepresented us in his book *Debate* (for documented cases, see pp. 189n22, 204n1, 206n3, 219–20, 242n30, etc.). He continues to do so in this latest article. I can only tell readers not to draw conclusions until they read what we say.

CHAPTER 5

Over 100 Christian Leaders Agree ... the TNIV Bible Is Not Sufficiently Trustworthy*

Recently, the International Bible Society (IBS) and Zondervan Publishing announced their joint decision to publish a new translation of the Bible, known as *Today's New International Version* (TNIV). The TNIV makes significant changes in the gender language that is in the NIV. The TNIV raises more concern in this regard than previous Bible versions because, riding on the reputation of the NIV, the TNIV may vie for a place as the church's commonly accepted Bible. We believe that any commonly accepted Bible of the church should be more faithful to the language of the original.

We acknowledge that Bible scholars sometimes disagree about translation methods and about which English words best translate the original languages. We also agree that it is appropriate to use gender-neutral expressions where the original language does not include any male or female meaning. However, we believe the TNIV has gone beyond acceptable translation standards in several important respects:

- **The TNIV translation often changes masculine, third person, singular pronouns (he, his and him) to plural gender-neutral pronouns.** For example, in Revelation 3:20, the words of Jesus have been changed from "I will come in and eat with **him,** and **he** with me" to

---

* This chapter contains the text of a statement that was posted on the CBMW Web site (www.cbmw.org) May 28, 2002, and that subsequently appeared as paid advertisements in *World,* June 15, 2002, pp. 2–3, and July 17/23, 2002, pp. 48–49; *Charisma,* July 2002, pp. 8–9; and in *Christian Retailing.*

"I will come in and eat with **them,** and **they** with me." Jesus could
have used plural pronouns when He spoke these words, but He
chose not to. (The original Greek pronouns are singular.) In
hundreds of such changes, the TNIV obscures any possible significance the inspired singular may have, such as individual responsibility or an individual relationship with Christ.

- **The TNIV translation obscures many biblical references to
  "father," "son," "brother," and "man."** For example, in Hebrews
  12:7, the NIV says "Endure hardship as discipline; God is treating
  you as **sons.** For what **son** is not disciplined by his **father**?" But the
  TNIV translates Hebrews 12:7, "Endure hardship as discipline; God
  is treating you as his **children.** For what **children** are not disciplined
  by their **parents**?" The reference to God as Father is lost. In numerous other verses male-oriented meanings that are present in the
  original language are lost in the TNIV.
- **The TNIV translation inserts English words into the text whose
  meaning does not appear in the original languages.** For example,
  in Luke 17:3, the translators changed "If your **brother** sins, rebuke
  him" to "If any **brother or sister** sins **against you,** rebuke the
  offender." The problem is, the word "sister" is not found in the
  original language, nor is "against you," nor is "offender."

Thus, in hundreds of verses, the TNIV changes language with masculine meaning in the original Greek to something more generic. It does this
in many ways, such as changing
- "father" (singular) to "parents";
- "son" (singular) to "child" or "children";
- "brother" (singular) to "someone" or "brother or sister," and
  "brothers" (plural) to "believers";
- "man" (singular, when referring to the human race) to "mere
  mortals" or "those" or "people";
- "men" (plural, when referring to male persons) to "people" or
  "believers" or "friends" or "humans";
- "he/him/his" to "they/them/their" or "you/your" or
  "we/us/our"; and
- switching hundreds of whole sentences from singular to plural.

We wonder how the TNIV translators can be sure that this masculine
language in God's very words does not carry meaning that God wants us
to see.

Gender problems are not the only serious problems with the TNIV. For
example: How do the TNIV translators know that changing "Jews" to

"Jewish leaders," for example in Acts 13:50 and 21:11, does not make a false claim, and obscure a possible corporate meaning? How do they know that changing "saints" to "those" in Acts 9:13 or to "believers" in Acts 9:32 or to "God's people" in Romans 8:27 does not sacrifice precious connotations of holiness which the Greek word carries? To justify translating "saints" as "believers" because it refers to believers is like justifying translating "sweetheart" as "wife" because that's who it refers to.

Because of these and other misgivings, we cannot endorse the TNIV as sufficiently trustworthy to commend to the church. We do not believe it is a translation suitable for use as a normal preaching and teaching text of the church or for a common memorizing, study, and reading Bible of the Christian community.

Daniel L. Akin, Dean School of Theology, The Southern Baptist Theological Seminary, Louisville, KY

Gregg R. Allison, Professor, Western Seminary, Portland, OR

Kerby Andersen, President, Probe Ministries, Richardson, TX

Neil T. Anderson, Founder and President Emeritus, Freedom in Christ Ministries

Hudson T. Armerding, Past Chairman, National Association of Evangelicals, Quarryville, PA

Edward G. Atsinger, III, President & CEO, Salem Communications Corporation, Camarillo, CA

Ted Baehr, Chairman, Christian Film & Television Commission, Camarillo, CA

Frank M. Barker, Jr., Pastor Emeritus, Briarwood Presbyterian Church, Birmingham, AL

H. F. Bayer, Professor, Covenant Theological Seminary, St. Louis, MO

Tim Bayly, Senior Pastor, Church of the Good Shepherd, Bloomington, IN

Alistair Begg, Senior Pastor, Parkside Church, Chagrin Falls, OH

Joel Belz, Founder and Chairman, *World Magazine,* Asheville, NC

Ron Blue, Ronald Blue & Company

James A. Borland, Professor, Liberty University, Lynchburg, VA

Harald Bredesen, Pastor at Large, St. Paul's Lutheran Church, Westport, CT

Bill Bright, Founder and Chairman, Campus Crusade for Christ, Orlando, FL

Tal Brooke, President and Chairman, SCP, Inc., Berkeley, CA

Harold O. J. Brown, Professor, Reformed Theological Seminary, Charlotte, NC

Larry Burkett, Founder, Crown Financial Ministries, Gainesville, GA

A. B. Caneday, Professor, Northwestern College, Saint Paul, Minnesota

Bryan Chapell, President, Covenant Theological Seminary, St. Louis, MO

E. Ray Clendenen, Executive editor, Bibles and Reference Books, B&H Publishers, Nashville, TN

C. John Collins, Professor, Covenant Theological Seminary, St. Louis, MO

Charles Colson, Founder, Prison Fellowship Ministry, Merrifield, VA

William Cook, Professor, The Southern Baptist Theological Seminary, Louisville, KY

Jack Cottrell, Professor, Cincinnati Bible Seminary, Cincinnati, OH

Darryl DelHousaye, Senior Pastor, Scottsdale Bible Church, Scottsdale, AZ

Nancy Leigh DeMoss, Teacher and Author, Life Action Ministries, Niles, MI

Dennis H. Dirks, Dean, Talbot School of Theology, La Mirada, CA

James Dobson, President, Focus on the Family, Colorado Springs, CO

Daniel Doriani, Dean of Faculty, Covenant Theological Seminary, St. Louis, MO

Ligon Duncan, Senior Minister, First Presbyterian Church, Jackson, MS

Michael J. Easley, Senior Pastor-Teacher, Immanuel Bible Church, Springfield, VA

Tom Elliff, Senior Pastor, First Southern Baptist Church, Del City, OK

Stuart W. Epperson, Chairman, Salem Communications Corp., Winston-Salem, NC

Jerry Falwell, Chancellor, Liberty University; Pastor, Thomas Road Baptist Church, Lynchburg, VA

Steve Farrar, President, Men's Leadership Ministries, Frisco, TX

Ronnie W. Floyd, Senior Pastor, First Baptist Church, Springdale, AR, and The Church at Pinnacle Hills, Rogers, AR

John M. Frame, Professor, Reformed Theological Seminary, Orlando, FL

Jack Graham, Senior Pastor, Prestonwood Baptist Church, Prestonwood, TX

Elisabeth Elliot Gren, Christ Church, Hamilton, MA

Wayne Grudem, Professor, Phoenix Seminary, Scottsdale, AZ

Joshua Harris, Executive Pastor, Covenant Life Church, Gaithersburg, MD

Jack Hayford, Founding Pastor, The Church on the Way, Van Nuys, CA; Chancellor, The King's College and Seminary

Howard G. Hendricks, Professor, Dallas Theological Seminary, Dallas, TX

Ken Hemphill, President, Southwestern Baptist Theological Seminary, Fort Worth, TX

C. E. Hill, Professor, Reformed Theological Seminary, Orlando, FL

Roland S. Hinz, President, Hi-Favor Broadcasting (Spanish Language), Los Angeles, CA

H. Wayne House, Professor, Faith Seminary, Tacoma, WA

R. Kent Hughes, Senior Pastor, College Church, Wheaton, IL

Susan Hunt, Author, Atlanta, GA

W. Bingham Hunter, Pastor/Bible Teacher/Author, Chicago, IL

David Jeremiah, Pastor, Shadow Mountain Community Church

Peter Jones, Professor, Westminster Theological Seminary, Escondido, CA

Mary Kassian, Author & Teacher, Alabaster Flask Ministries, Edmonton, Canada

Charles S. Kelley, Jr., President, New Orleans Baptist Theological Seminary, New Orleans, LA

Rhonda H. Kelley, Professor, New Orleans Baptist Theological Seminary, New Orleans, LA

D. James Kennedy, Senior Pastor, Coral Ridge Presbyterian Church, Ft. Lauderdale, FL

Tim Kimmel, Executive Director, Family Matters, Phoenix, AZ

Chuck Klein, National Director, Student Venture, Orlando, FL

George W. Knight, III, Professor, Greenville Presbyterian Theological Seminary, Taylors, SC

Bob Lepine, Director of Broadcasting, FamilyLife, Little Rock, AR

Robert Lewis, Teaching Pastor, Fellowship Bible Church, Little Rock, AR

H. B. London, VP of Ministry Outreach/Pastoral, Focus on the Family, Colorado Springs, CO

Crawford W. Loritts, Jr., Assoc. USA Director, Campus Crusade for Christ, Atlanta, GA

Erwin W. Lutzer, Senior Pastor, Moody Church, Chicago, IL

John MacArthur, Pastor-Teacher, Grace Community Church, Sun Valley, CA

James MacDonald, Pastor, Harvest Bible Chapel, Rolling Meadows, IL

C. J. Mahaney, Senior Pastor, Covenant Life Church, Gaithersburg, MD

Bill McCartney, President, Promise Keepers, Denver, CO

Josh D. McDowell, Josh McDowell Ministry, Dallas, TX

James Merritt, President, Southern Baptist Convention, Snellville, GA

R. Albert Mohler, Jr., President, The Southern Baptist Theological Seminary, Louisville, KY

Joel Nederhood, Pastor, Director of Ministries, Emeritus, The Back to God Hour

Niel Nielson, President Elect, Covenant College, Lookout Mountain, TN

Marvin Olasky, Editor-in-Chief, *World* Magazine, Asheville, NC

Stephen F. Olford, Founder and Chairman, The Stephen Olford Center for Biblical Preaching, Memphis, TN

Raymond C. Ortlund, Jr., Senior Pastor, First Presbyterian Church, Augusta, GA

J. I. Packer, Professor, Regent College, Vancouver, B.C.

Janet Parshall, Nationally Syndicated Talk Show Host, Janet Parshall's America, Arlington, VA

Dorothy Kelley Patterson, Professor, Southeastern Baptist Theological Seminary, Wake Forest, NC

Paige Patterson, President, Southeastern Baptist Theological Seminary, Wake Forest, NC

John Piper, Senior Pastor, Bethlehem Baptist Church, Minneapolis, MN

Randy Pope, Pastor, Perimeter Church, Duluth, GA

Vern Poythress, Professor, Westminster Theological Seminary, Philadelphia, PA

William Pugh, National Director, Athletes in Action, Xenia, OH

Dick Purnell, Director, Single Life Resources, Cary, NC

Dennis Rainey, Exec. Director, FamilyLife, Little Rock, AR

W. Duncan Rankin, Professor, Reformed Theological Seminary, Jackson, MS

Robert E. Reccord, President, North American Mission Board, SBC, Apharetta, GA

Sandy Rios, President, Concerned Women for America, Washington, D.C.

Pat Robertson, Founder and President, Christian Broadcasting Network (CBN)

Adrian Rogers, Pastor, Bellevue Baptist Church, Cordova, TN

Gary Rosberg, President, America's Family Coaches, Des Moines, IA

Barbara Rosberg, Vice President, America's Family Coaches, Des Moines, IA

Phillip Graham Ryken, Senior Minister, Tenth Presbyterian Church, Philadelphia, PA

Thomas Schreiner, Professor, The Southern Baptist Theological Seminary, Louisville, KY

Dal Shealy, President, Fellowship of Christian Athletes, Kansas City, MO

Paul Sheppard, Senior Pastor, Abundant Life Christian Fellowship, Menlo Park, CA

R. C. Sproul, Chairman, Ligonier Ministries, Lake Mary, FL

Randy Stinson, Exec. Director, Council on Biblical Manhood and Womanhood, Louisville, KY

Charles R. Swindoll, Senior Pastor, Stonebriar Community Church, Frisco, TX; Chancellor, Dallas Theological Seminary

Joni Eareckson Tada, Founder & President, Joni & Friends, Agoura, CA

Terry Taylor, President Emeritus, U.S. Navigators

Derek W. H. Thomas, Professor, Reformed Theological Seminary, Jackson, MS

John F. Walvoord, Chancellor Emeritus, Dallas Theological Seminary, Dallas, TX

Bruce Ware, Professor, The Southern Baptist Theological Seminary, Louisville, KY

Stu Weber, Pastor, Good Shepherd Community Church, Gresham, OR

William C. Weinrich, Professor, Concordia Theological Seminary, Fort Wayne, IN

Dean O. Wenthe, President, Concordia Theological Seminary, Fort Wayne, IN

Donald E. Wildmon, President, American Family Association, Tupelo, MS

Bruce Wilkinson, Global Vision Resources, Norcross, GA

P. Bunny Wilson, Fellowship West International Ministries, Pasadena, CA

CHAPTER 6

Bible Scholars Claim "Gender-Neutral" Bible Distorts Scripture*

Press release from CBMW Feb. 1, 2002
(list updated with over 35 names, Feb. 7, 2002)

More than twenty evangelical scholars today issued a joint statement declaring that the recently released *Today's New International Version,* which news reports on Monday identified as "gender-neutral," should not be commended to the church. The scholars expressed concern about "troubling translation inaccuracies . . . that introduce distortions of . . . meanings." Although their primary concern was over gender language and the removal of many instances of such words as "man," "father," "son," "brother," and "he/him/his," other types of inaccuracies were noted as well, particularly in changing singular pronouns to plural, and in changing "the Jews" to "the Jewish leaders" in John's Gospel. The statement was released by the Louisville headquarters of the Council on Biblical Manhood and Womanhood (CBMW).

A list of over one hundred examples of inaccurately translated verses accompanied the statement.

STATEMENT OF CONCERN:
In light of troubling translation inaccuracies—primarily (but not exclusively) in relation to gender language—that introduce distortions of the meanings that were conveyed better by the original NIV, we cannot endorse the TNIV translation as sufficiently accurate to commend to the church.

---

* This chapter contains the text of a statement that was posted on the CBMW Web site (www.cbmw.org) Feb. 1, 2002.

SIGNERS (partial list):
Gregg R. Allison, Ph.D., Western Seminary, Portland, OR
Henry S. Baldwin, Ph.D., Singapore Bible College, Singapore
S. M. Baugh, Ph.D., Westminster Theological Seminary, Escondido, CA
Hans F. Bayer, Ph.D., Covenant Seminary, St. Louis, MO
James Borland, Ph.D., Liberty University, Lynchburg, VA
Harold O. J. Brown, Ph.D., Reformed Theological Seminary, Charlotte, NC
A. B. Caneday, Ph.D., Northwestern College, St. Paul, MN
E. Ray Clendenen, Ph.D., Lifeway Christian Resources, Nashville, TN
Clifford John Collins, Ph.D., Covenant Seminary, St. Louis, MO
William Cook, Ph.D., Southern Seminary, Louisville, KY
Jack Cottrell, Ph.D., Cincinnati Bible College and Seminary, Cincinnatti, OH
Daniel Doriani, Ph.D., Covenant Seminary, St. Louis, MO
J. Ligon Duncan III, Ph.D., First Presbyterian Church, Jackson, MS
John M. Frame, M.Phil., Reformed Theological Seminary, Orlando, FL
Paul D. Gardner, Ph.D., Church of England Evangelical Council, Hartford,
    England
Wayne Grudem, Ph.D., Phoenix Seminary, Scottsdale, AZ
C. E. Hill, Ph.D., Reformed Theological Seminary, Orlando, FL
H. Wayne House, Ph.D., Faith Seminary, Tacoma, WA
W. Bingham Hunter, Ph.D, Harvest Bible Chapel, Rolling Meadows, IL
Peter Jones, Ph.D., Westminster Theological Seminary, Escondido, CA
Reggie M. Kidd, Ph.D., Reformed Theological Seminary, Orlando, FL
George W. Knight, III, Ph.D., Greenville Presbyterian Seminary, Taylors, SC
J. Carl Laney, Th.D., Western Seminary, Portland, OR
Al Mawhinney, Ph.D., Reformed Seminary, Orlando, FL
R. Albert Mohler, Ph.D., Southern Seminary, Louisville, KY
Raymond C. Ortlund, Jr., Ph.D., First Presbyterian Church, Augusta, GA
Paige Patterson, Ph.D., Southeastern Baptist Theological Seminary, Wake
    Forest, NC
John Piper, D. theol., Bethlehem Baptist Church, Minneapolis, MN
Vern S. Poythress, Ph.D., Th.D., Westminster Theological Seminary,
    Philadelphia, PA
Mark R. Saucy, Ph.D., Kyiv Theological Seminary
Thomas R. Schreiner, Ph.D., Southern Seminary, Louisville, KY
R. C. Sproul, DRS, Ph.D., Ligonier Ministries, Lake Mary, FL
Bruce Ware, Ph.D., Southern Seminary, Louisville, KY
William Weinrich, Ph.D., Concordia Seminary, Ft. Wayne, IN
Dean O. Wenthe, Ph.D., Concordia Seminary, Ft. Wayne, IN
Robert Yarbrough, Ph.D., Trinity Evangelical Divinity School, Deerfield, IL

What's Going On
with Bible Translations?

What is the fuss about?

The Bible is God's own Word to us. We depend on it for instructing us about the crucial issue of salvation: "What must I do to be saved?" (Acts 16:30). We depend on it to guide us in the right way to live: "Your word is a lamp to my feet and a light for my path" (Ps. 119:105). We depend on it for revealing Jesus Christ to us: "these things are written that you may believe that Jesus is the Christ, the Son of God, and that by believing you may have life in his name" (John 20:31). So it is surpassingly important that the Bible be translated accurately.

A. A controversy over gender terms

But now evangelicals are arguing about how to translate the Bible. How should we translate gender-related terms in the Bible? Some recent translations have switched to "inclusive language," replacing "father" with "parent" and "he" with "they."

For example, Proverbs 28:7 says, "He who keeps the law is a wise *son*, but a companion of gluttons shames his *father*" (Revised Standard Version [RSV]). The *New Revised Standard Version* (NRSV) altered the wording. It now reads, "Those who keep the law are wise *children*, but companions of gluttons shame their *parents*." "Son" has become "children," and "father" has become "parents." In addition, the whole verse has been converted into plural forms: the words "Those," "children," "companions," "their," and "parents," are plural, and each replaces a singular form in the RSV and in the original language.[1]

---

[1]See Chapter 10 below for a discussion of the distinction between form and meaning.

Or take a second example. John 14:23 says, "If anyone loves me, *he* will obey my teaching. My Father will love *him*, and we will come to *him* and make our home with *him*" (New International Version [NIV]). Some people today find this "generic" use of "he" and "him" unacceptable. So the *New Revised Standard Version* (NRSV) removed it: "*Those* who love me will keep my word, and my Father will love *them*, and we will come to *them* and make our home with *them*." The singular pronouns "anyone, he, him" have turned into plurals, "those, them." The idea of Jesus and God the Father making their home with an individual person is no longer clearly found in the verse.[2]

At points like these, is the NRSV a thoroughly accurate translation, or has it altered meanings in order to avoid male-oriented terms like "father," "son," and "his"?

The NRSV is not the only translation that has moved in this direction. The *New Century Version* (NCV, 1991), *Good News Bible: Today's English Version* second edition (GNB, 1992), *New International Reader's Version New Testament* (1995 edition, NIrV, 1995), *The Contemporary English Version* (CEV, 1995), *God's Word* (GW, 1995), *New International Version Inclusive Language Edition* (NIVI) published in Britain (1996), and *New Living Translation* (NLT, 1996), all make the same kinds of move.[3]

Many of the translators involved in these projects were doubtless well-meaning people. They were seeking to communicate more effectively by avoiding wording that would irritate or offend. But we believe that in the process they subtly changed meanings.[4] The results, we believe, are not the most accurate translations. And they cannot be trusted to indicate at every point how the Bible deals with the sensitive issues of human sexuality.

Consider some other examples.

Colossians 3:18–19 offers key instructions concerning the relation of husband and wife in marriage. Colossians 3:18 tells us, "Wives, *submit*[5] to your husbands, as is fitting in the Lord" (NIV). You would never know it from the CEV, which has the highly weakened expression, "put others first." "A wife must *put her husband first*. This is her duty as a follower of the Lord" (CEV). What does "put . . . first" mean? Precisely what is a wife supposed to do? It is not clear. Readers might guess that a wife is supposed to put her husband's needs before her own, as Philippians 2:4 says, "Each of you should look not only to your own interests, but also to the interests of others" (NIV). But in such a situation, there is really no sense of being

---

[2]See Chapter 13 for a further discussion of this verse.

[3]GW preserves Proverbs 28:7, but analogous problems occur elsewhere in GW.

[4]As we shall see, *some* of the changes have resulted in an increase in accuracy (Chapter 11). We have to sort out the improvements from the slippages.

[5]The Greek word is *hupotassō*, meaning "*subject oneself, be subjected or subordinated, obey*" (Walter Bauer, *A Greek-English Lexicon of the New Testament and Other Early Christian Literature*, 2d ed. [Chicago: University of Chicago Press, 1979], 848).

subject to or obeying someone else who is in authority, but only a general idea of sacrificially caring for him. In the end, a wife does for her husband exactly what the husband does for her: serve sacrificially. What for Paul are different commands for different roles have become in the CEV equivalent commands for identical roles. The CEV has distorted the picture. The CEV's "translation" harmonizes well with what many modern people might wish that the apostle Paul said. But it does not do justice to what he actually said. The same problem occurs also with the parallel passage in Ephesians 5:21–23.

First Timothy 3:1–7 discusses the qualifications for "overseer" or elder. One qualification is that he be "the husband of one wife" (3:2, RSV). The CEV eliminates all signs that Paul expected the elders to be men. The CEV merely says that a "church official" must be "faithful in marriage." All the "he's" become "they's."

Some people today say that Paul was wrong in these teachings. But the Bible is the word of God, having God's own authority, so the Bible could not be wrong on these issues. Or people may say that Paul was right for his own day, but the changing times call for a different practice today.[6] But even in a case like this where people disagree, we need to have the meaning of the Bible preserved in order to see what the Bible said in its time so that we can see the basis for today's disagreement! Especially when an issue engages debate, translators must not hobble the debate by obscuring the meaning of the text.

Now someone may object that the CEV is an extreme example in its translation of Colossians 3:18 and 1 Timothy 3. The other gender-neutral translations do not do as badly. But consider another, similar passage, Acts 20:30, where Paul says to the elders at Ephesus, "Even from your own number *men* will arise and distort the truth. . . ." The word "men" translates the Greek word *anēr*, denoting male human beings.[7] The reference is to *male* elders. The NRSV, NIVI, NIrV(1995), NLT, CNV, and CEV all omit the male component.[8] This is a serious mistake. The verse is a significant one in the modern debate as to whether women may be appointed as elders in the church. Gender-neutral translations have suppressed significant information pertaining to this

---

[6]We ourselves believe Paul set out permanent principles with respect to both leadership in marriage and rule in the church. Leadership in marriage is based on the permanent example of Christ and the church in Ephesians 5:21–33. The specification that elders are male in 1 Timothy 3 is based on the argument of 1 Timothy 2:11–15 appealing to creation. See John Piper and Wayne Grudem, eds., *Recovering Biblical Manhood and Womanhood: A Response to Evangelical Feminism* (Wheaton, IL: Crossway, 1991), especially Douglas Moo, "What Does It Mean Not to Teach or Have Authority Over Men?: 1 Timothy 2:11–15," 179–193; H. S. Baldwin, A. J. Köstenberger, and T. R. Schreiner, eds., *Women in the Church: A Fresh Analysis of 1 Timothy 2:9–15 in Its Literary, Cultural, and Theological Contexts* (Grand Rapids: Baker, 1995).

[7]See Appendix 2 for detailed discussion of the meaning of *anēr*.

[8]But GNB and GW, to their credit, retain "men."

debate. Again, the result is not accurate, but rather skews the verse in the direction of modern ideas about women's roles.

Some people might think that critics of gender-neutral translations are motivated solely by the desire to protect their complementarian views concerning men and women.[9] But these examples as well as our later discussion should make it clear that though the two issues are related, they are also distinct. *The issue on which we are focusing is accuracy in translation, not egalitarian or complementarian views on men and women.*[10] Some complementarians have argued in support of gender-neutral translations.[11] Conversely, some egalitarians have argued *against* gender-neutral translations, on the ground that they are inaccurate.[12]

---

[9]See, for example, Carson, *Debate*, who says of those who signed the Colorado Springs Guidelines, "I cannot help but conclude that what drew many of them to sign this document is their concern to maintain complementarianism, and this out of strong biblical convictions, and their belief that the question of gender-inclusive translations is a necessary component of this conviction" (p. 37; see also p. 188). Mark Strauss says, "I am well aware of the agendas at work in the present debate. There is no doubt that the push for inclusive language is driven on the one hand by feminist concerns, just as the push against it is driven by complementarian concerns" (*Distorting*, 203). (The term "complementarian" within current evangelicalism means someone who holds that men and women are equal in value before God but have different God-given roles in the home and the church, and specifically that there is a unique leadership role that belongs to men in the home and the church. An "egalitarian" would see no God-given differences in roles for men and women in the home and the church.)

[10]To say that opponents of gender-neutral Bibles are *simply* or *primarily* attempting to protect a complementarian view of men and women would be to say that we are dishonest or deceptive when we repeatedly emphasize that our fundamental concern is faithfulness in translation of the Word of God. Moreover, if a rigid desire to maintain male leadership were our primary concern, why would six of the thirteen Colorado Springs Guidelines (see Appendix 1) encourage *more* use of inclusive language in Bible translation, not less? Such a misleading claim also tends to divert attention from the real questions of faithfulness in translation, questions on which we focus in this book.

[11]D. A. Carson and Mark L. Strauss, both complementarians, have written books supporting gender-neutral translations with some qualifications (Carson, *The Inclusive Language Debate: A Plea for Realism* [Grand Rapids: Baker, 1998]; Strauss, *Distorting Scripture? The Challenge of Bible Translation & Gender Accuracy* [Downers Grove, Ill.: InterVarsity Press, 1998]).

[12]See, for example, the discussion in Chapter 7 of the REB's statement that some kinds of change would be "compromising scholarly integrity" (REB, Preface, ix). The REB was not an evangelical project and a number of the REB translators would not be complementarians.

Note also the comments of Robert Jewett, professor of New Testament at Garrett-Northwestern Theological Seminary. Though Jewett does not hold the same view of the authority of Scripture as conservative evangelicals would hold, he does see an issue of scholarly integrity at stake in the debate over gender-neutral Bibles. He says that gender-neutral language "obscures the genuine revolution that is there in Scripture." He said, with regard to gender-neutral language in the NRSV,

> We're facing, with the NRSV, liberal dishonesty in spades. . . . All the way through the NRSV, implying that Paul has all these liberated concepts and so forth like the current politically correct person in an Ivy League school: I mean that's just ridiculous. Here you have the imposition of liberal prejudice on the biblical text with the ridiculous assumption that our modern liberal views were Paul's. (Reported in *World* 13/6 [Feb. 14, 1998], 20.)

Everyone should want to have in translation the fullest possible representation of what the Bible actually says, as opposed to what we might expect it to say, in order better to weigh the modern arguments about gender.

And so we need to explore these issues with care. We need to investigate the ins and outs of what these translations do, and evaluate the results on the basis of biblical standards.

B. What are these new versions?

Now what shall we call these new versions? They are not all the same. There are a few radical-feminist versions that even undertake to call God the Father "Father and Mother" or to eliminate "Father" language altogether.[13] But these versions clearly reject the authority of the Bible and its claim to be the Word of God, and *they are not the focus of our attention in this book.* We are thankful that most modern versions—including all the versions we examine in this book—have attempted to preserve the language about God, including masculine pronouns referring to God. But even when language about God is preserved, we are concerned that several modern versions, produced for the most part by evangelical translators, have removed important aspects of meaning when they refer to human beings.

The versions that concern us in this book generally eliminate generic "he," avoid using the word "man" as a name for the human race, and systematically exclude many instances of male-oriented words such as "father," "son," "brother," and "man" in cases where (we will argue) a male component of meaning is present in the original text, and where all earlier translations included these words.

Such versions have been called by several names. Some people favoring such translations have called them "gender accurate." But, as we have already seen, they contain some pointed inaccuracies, so the phrase "gender accurate" is misleading. And this phrase takes a position beforehand on the very issue that needs to be debated—are these versions in fact "accurate" in their translation of Scripture?

Others have chosen the phrase "gender inclusive." *The New International Version: Inclusive Language Edition* even contains the word "inclusive" in its title. The idea here is that the new versions have language indicating that women are included in the message of salvation. But earlier versions also made this fact clear. Consider John 14:23 as an example: "If anyone loves me, he will obey my teaching. My Father will love him, and we will come to him and make our home with him" (NIV). When John 14:23 uses the word "anyone" at the beginning, it shows clearly that both men and women are included. The subsequent uses of "he" and "him" in the verse

---

[13]For a detailed analysis of these radical "feminist" versions, see Strauss, *Distorting Scripture*, pp. 60–73. Strauss lists three "feminist versions": (1) *An Inclusive Language Lectionary* (Atlanta: John Knox; New York: Pilgrim Press; Philadelphia: Westminster Press, 1983); (2) *The New Testament and Psalms: An Inclusive Version* (New York: Oxford University Press, 1995); (3) *The Inclusive New Testament* (n.l.: Priests for Equality, 1994). We do not give consideration to these "feminist versions" in this book, but interested readers will find Strauss's analysis very helpful.

refer back to "anyone." So they apply to both men and women. In reality the NIV at this point is just as "inclusive" as the versions that insist on eliminating generic "he," because the sentence as a whole shows that both men and women are included in the meaning. Therefore, the label "gender inclusive" creates a problem. It suggests that any other kind of translation is *not* inclusive. And such is not the case. Hence this label is not really satisfactory either.[14] (We realize, of course, that, if a translation uses "he" and "him," some people may feel that women are not being sufficiently recognized or affirmed. But this is a different problem, which we must take up later [Chapter 15].)

We will therefore mostly use the label "gender neutral." This label comes closer to describing the actual difference between the translations that eliminate generic "he" and those that do not. When used in a generic way, as in John 14:23, "he" includes women as well as men (see above).[15] But it does so using a *masculine* form—the gender of the word "he" is masculine. Gender-neutral translations, one and all, tend to eliminate masculine forms and male connotations in verses that express general truths. In this sense, they strive to be "gender neutral."

But it must be remembered that the translations that we are considering in this book do *not* remove masculine pronouns referring to God and the Persons of the Trinity. In most cases they preserve male markings in historical references. Thus, not everything has been made "neutral," but some specific kinds of statements have been made "gender neutral," as we explain in the rest of this book. We realize of course that no brief label can say everything. In fact, people who use the term "gender inclusive" or "inclusive language" do not imply that everything has been made uniformly "inclusive." Any label we use can only serve as shorthand. In the rest of the book, we look at the versions in detail in order to see just what has been changed, in order to assess these changes fairly.

C. Controversy

We need to examine these gender-neutral translations and the thinking that lies behind them. But the issue is controversial, and when controversy arises, potential for misunderstanding increases. We may misunderstand opponents. Opponents may misunderstand us. Even someone trying to be neutral may misunderstand. Right at the beginning, to guard against misunderstanding, it seems wise to explain our goal.

---

[14]In the course of this book, however, we ourselves from time to time may use the term "inclusive language Bible" to refer to gender-neutral Bible translations, partly because the phrase has become a code-word or technical term to refer to these translations, and partly because its use in the title of the NIVI has made this usage somewhat common in this debate.

[15]See also the extensive discussion of generic "he" in chapters 13–17.

In this book we criticize some decisions that have been made in gender-neutral translations. When we criticize the translation of a particular verse, we do not mean that *every other* verse is badly translated. In fact, in some verses gender-neutral translations, through revision in wording, have increased accuracy (see Chapter 5). Nor do we mean that all gender-neutral translations did the same thing with the same verse.

Second, we are not criticizing the personal motives of the translators. Only God can judge people's hearts. We do not know our own motives perfectly, let alone the motives of others. Moreover, as we shall see (Chapter 4), translation as a whole is complex business, in the midst of which many good and bad motives may operate in subtle ways. And translators may sometimes make mistakes through mere oversight.[16]

Third, in matters of usage in modern English, we see nothing necessarily wrong with a whole spectrum of typical modern uses. Some people may continue to use generic "he," while others may avoid it, and instead use "he or she" or "you" or "they."[17] Some people may use "man" to designate the human race, others may not (see Chapter 12). When we criticize a particular translation, it is not because it is bad English, but because it is not the most accurate translation. A writer today has authority over what he or she writes. A Bible translator does *not* have this authority, because the meaning belongs not to him but to God.

Fourth, in cases where a translation is not the most accurate, it may still capture *some* of the meaning, usually the most central and obvious meaning. Moreover, almost always the translation results in a statement that is theologically true. For example, in 1 Timothy 3:17, even though the NRSV and CEV omit the key information about overseers being men, they include many statements that are indeed true of overseers! Obviously, we are not criticizing translations for saying things that are theologically true, but rather for *omitting* one aspect that they should *also* have included.

Fifth, we commend the many worthy attempts in our society to honor and encourage women. But it is not really honoring to women in the long run if people settle for less than the most accurate Bible translation, just because they *think* it is more honoring to women. In fact, it is dishonoring, because they dedicate to women's honor an exhibit that shows less than fullest respect for the Bible's meanings.

---

[16]For convenience, we will sometimes speak of what translators thought and did. But in reality we have direct access only to the product, the actual translation. It is the translation product about which we are concerned.

[17]We use generic "he" liberally in writing this book, not because there are not legitimate alternative ways of writing, but because we thereby illustrate further the point we will make in Chapters 16 and 17, that generic "he" is understandable and usable *in principle.*

Moreover, in a book like this one, where we must so often discuss general principles, it is helpful to be able to express a principle using a singular example when we need to. See the discussion in Chapter 13.

Finally, we authors (Vern Poythress and Wayne Grudem) are fallible. We continue to learn—in fact, as we look back at what we said and wrote on this subject beginning in 1996, we recognize, in retrospect, that in several cases we would now say things more precisely or guard against misunderstanding more carefully. In this book, therefore, we give our best judgments, but we are open to being corrected by further knowledge.

Examining gender-neutral translations includes several steps. We begin by looking briefly at the history of gender-neutral translations, and the controversy that they stirred up.

CHAPTER 8

The Rise of Gender-Neutral Bible Translations

What is the history behind gender-neutral translations?

A. Earlier gender-neutral Bible translations

1. An unnoticed gender-neutral translation: the ICB/NCV

The earliest complete translations of the Bible to adopt a gender-neutral translation policy were apparently the *New Century Version* (NCV) and the *International Children's Bible* (ICB), both published by Word Publishing Company. The ICB, a simplified edition of the NCV, appeared first, in 1986. The NCV has a copyright date in the following year (1987). (The latest edition, which we cite, has a copyright in 1991.)

The simplified ICB says nothing in its preface about its gender-neutral translation policy. But the NCV gives some explanation. The goal of the NCV was to make a Bible that was clear and easily understood, and the translators based their vocabulary choice on a list of words used by the editors of *The World Book Encyclopedia* to determine appropriate vocabulary ("Preface," xiii). Based on the concern for clarity and simplicity of expression, the NCV translates with considerable recourse to paraphrase.

With regard to gender language, the NCV is strongly gender-neutral, as the preface explains:

Gender language has also been translated with a concern for clarity. To avoid the misconception that "man" and "mankind" and "he" are exclusively masculine when they are being used in a generic sense, this translation has chosen to use less ambiguous language, such as "people" and "humans" and "human beings" and has prayerfully attempted throughout to choose gender language that would accurately convey the intent of the original writers (p. xiv).

This statement indicates what our following analysis will show in some detail, namely, that the NCV does not use "man" as a name for the human race, and does not use "he" in a generic sense.[1]

However, because the NCV and ICB had such a small share of the market for English Bibles, and because they engaged in paraphrase, the gender-neutral translation policies of these Bibles created little stir. In any case, the NCV aimed at a very popular reading level, and such a translation was unlikely to be used or even much noticed by scholars, pastors who engaged in detailed expository preaching, or lay people who engaged in serious, detailed Bible study.[2]

2. The first major gender-neutral translation: the NRSV (1990)

Much more significant was the publication of the *New Revised Standard Version* (NRSV) on September 30, 1990.[3] The NRSV was a revision of one of the most widely used and influential Bibles in the history of the English-speaking world, namely, *The Revised Standard Version*, which was first published in 1946 (New Testament) and 1952 (the whole Bible), and revised in 1971 (New Testament only).

---

[1]We have found a few exceptions, such as occurrences of generic "he" in Luke 14:26 and 17:3–4 NCV.

[2]Mark Strauss, in his book, *Distorting Scripture?* (Downers Grove, Ill.: InterVarsity Press, 1998), pages 7, 47–52, claims that three other versions produced before 1990 were also "gender-inclusive," his term for what we have called gender-neutral Bibles. Strauss mentions the Roman Catholic *New Jerusalem Bible* (1985), another Roman Catholic version, *The New American Bible* (with a revised New Testament in 1988, and revised Psalms in 1991), and *The Revised English Bible* (1989) which was a major revision of the 1961 *New English Bible*. However, it is not at all clear that the REB should be put in this "gender-neutral" category, because it still retains the generic use of "he" (Strauss, 51). The two Roman Catholic versions (NJB and NAB) are only partially gender-neutral in their policies, and of course they were not much noticed among evangelical Protestants.

On pp. 209–213 Strauss gives an extensive chart of different versions, indicating the way they have translated one hundred different verses. It is misleading and not as helpful as it might be in determining the policy of various translations, because in his totals at the bottom of the columns he lumps together problematic and unproblematic translation decisions. More specifically, his totala make no distinction between verses that contain a Hebrew or Greek word with a clear male component of meaning (such as *'îsh* or *anēr*) and verses that contain words that do not always carry such a component (for example, some verses containing *'ādām* and *anthrōpos*, both of which have commonly been translated as "person" or "people" in many contexts long before the rise of any concern for gender language in Scripture). The relevant question is not whether a Bible translation uses an inclusive term like "someone" or "one" or "person" where there is no male meaning component in the original text. The important question, and one that we will return to again and again in this book, is whether the translation uses these inclusive terms in cases where there is a clear male component of meaning in the original text. (Readers could calculate such separate totals from this detailed chart if they wished, but Strauss's own totals do not make such a distinction.)

[3]The copyright for the NRSV is 1989, but the publication was not actually issued until 1990.

The NRSV was of particular interest to both of the authors of this book, since we had both used the RSV as our own personal Bible for over twenty years by the time the NRSV was published. Both of us had looked forward to the publication of the NRSV, because the RSV that we used, though it was an excellent translation, still labored under the difficulty of using "thee" and "thou" to address God (as in the Psalms and all the prayers recorded in Scripture), and these words occurred over 3,000 times.

When the NRSV appeared, however, it was apparent that a thorough-going revision of the gender language in the Bible had occurred. The preface explains the policies that were followed by the translation committee:

> As for the style of English adopted for the present revision, among the mandates given to the Committee in 1980 by the Division of Education and Ministry of the National Council Churches of Christ (which now holds the copyright of the RSV Bible) was the directive to continue in the tradition of the King James Bible, but to introduce such changes as are warranted on the basis of accuracy, clarity, euphony, and current English usage. Within the constraints set by the original texts and by the mandate of the Division, the Committee has followed the maxim, "As literal as possible, as free as necessary." As a consequence, the New Revised Standard Version (NRSV) remains essentially a literal translation. Paraphrastic renderings have been adopted only sparingly, and then chiefly to compensate for a deficiency in the English language—the lack of a common gender third person singular pronoun.

> During the almost half a century since the publication of the RSV, many in the churches have become sensitive to the danger of linguistic sexism arising from the inherent bias of the English language towards the masculine gender, a bias that in the case of the Bible has often restricted or obscured the meaning of the original text. The mandates from the Division specified that, in references to men and women, masculine-oriented language should be eliminated as far as this can be done without altering passages that reflect the historical situation of ancient patriarchal culture. As can be appreciated, more than once the Committee found that the several mandates stood in tension and even in conflict. The various concerns had to be balanced case by case in order to provide a faithful and acceptable reading without using contrived English. Only very occasionally has the pronoun "he" or "him" been retained in passages where the reference may have been to a woman as well as to a man. . . . In such instances . . . the options of either putting the passage in the plural or of introducing additional nouns to avoid masculine pronouns in English seemed to the Committee to obscure the historical structure and literary character of the original. In the vast majority of cases, however, inclusiveness has been attained by simple rephrasing or by introducing plural forms when this does not

distort the meaning of the passage. Of course, in narrative and in parable, no attempt was made to generalize the sex of individual persons. (From "To the Reader" in NRSV, n.p.).

The policy on inclusive language was discussed further by Walter Harrelson in an essay in *The Making of the New Revised Standard Version of the Bible* (Grand Rapids: Eerdmans, 1991). Harrelson says,

> The policy that was developed over the last decade of the Committee's life finally came to have the assent of all members. That policy was quite simple: the Committee should remove all masculine language referring to human beings apart from texts that clearly referred to men. To achieve this, the Committee adopted a number of agreed conventions (chief among them the use of the plural instead of the singular). . . . It was agreed that we would not use "persons" or "people," unless no alternative could be found. We would use "one" or "someone" as necessary, but sparingly. When a Psalmist was referring to an enemy, we sometimes would retain the "he" or "his" in order not to lose the vivid, personal force of the psalm (p. 76).

We will discuss the NRSV more fully in the following chapters. Its concern to combine a gender-neutral translation policy with an "essentially literal" approach to translation means that in many verses we can see exactly what changes have to be made to make a translation gender-neutral. Since it is a revision of an earlier translation, we also have a basis for comparison to determine how many changes need to be made in order to make a Bible gender-neutral in the sense explained above.

3. The Contemporary English Version (CEV) (1995)

The American Bible Society published the *Contemporary English Version* (CEV) in 1995. Once again this was a translation with a high emphasis on readability even for new Bible readers:

> A contemporary translation must be a text that an inexperienced reader can *read aloud* without stumbling, that someone unfamiliar with traditional biblical terminology *can hear without misunderstanding*, and that everyone can *listen to with enjoyment* because the style is lucid and lyrical ("Preface," viii).

With respect to gender language, the translators explained their policy as follows:

> In everyday speech, "gender generic" or "inclusive" language is used because it sounds most natural to people today. This means that where the biblical languages require masculine nouns or pronouns when both men and women are intended, this intention must be reflected in translation, though the English *form* may be very different from that of the original. The Greek text of Matthew 16:24 is literally, "If anyone wants

to follow me, *he* must deny *himself* and take up *his* cross and follow me." The *Contemporary English Version* shifts to a form that is still accurate, and at the same time, more effective in English: "If any of *you* want to be my followers, *you* must forget about *yourself*. *You* must take up *your* cross and follow me" ("Preface," x).

Once again, the inclusive nature of the gender language in this translation was not widely noticed, in part because this, too, was a translation that people would tend to use as a supplement rather than as their main study Bible. In fact, the preface to the CEV explains that in its attention to the way the English Bible would sound when read aloud, the CEV fulfills a special role:

> Each English translation is, in its own right, the word of God, yet each translation serves to meet the needs of a different audience. In this regard, the *Contemporary English Version* should be considered a *companion*—the *mission* arm—of traditional translations, because it takes seriously the words of the apostle Paul that "faith comes by *hearing*" ("Preface").

B. The NIVI controversy

If some earlier gender-neutral translations went virtually unnoticed, and if even the NRSV received only slight criticism for its inclusive language policy, such was certainly not to be the case with the NIV. Among evangelicals in the United States, the NIV is clearly the most widely used Bible translation. Sales figures will of course include all Bible sales in the United States, including sales to Roman Catholics and liberal Protestants as well as evangelicals. Among evangelicals the percentage of use is no doubt higher than total U.S. sales figures would indicate.

I. Prominence of the NIV

For the last half of 1996 (just before this controversy broke), sales of the Bible in the U.S. were as listed in the following table. For comparison, sales for the first half of 1999, the most recent period for which we have information, are also listed.

Bible sales in the U.S.

	July-Dec 1996	Jan-June 1999
New International Version (NIV)	32.1%	30.1%
King James Version (KJV)	23.5%	23.5%
New King James Version (NKJV)	9.4%	9.7%
New American Bible (NAB—Roman Catholic)	6.3%	6.7%
Living Bible (LB)	3.7%	0.6%
Spanish language Bibles	3.1%	3.4%
New Century Version (NCV)	2.6%	1.1%
The Message (MS)	2.6%	2.7%
Bibles on CD (various)	2.5%	1.4%
New Revised Standard Version (NRSV)[4]	2.5%	1.9%
New American Standard Bible (NASB)	2.5%	2.5%
New Living Translation (NLT)[5]	2.4%	7.9%
Amplified Bible (Amp)	1.5%	1.7%
Today's English Version (TEV)	1.1%	1.0%
New International Reader's Version (NIrV)	0.7%	0.9%
Contemporary English Version (CEV)	0.5%	0.6%
God's Word (GW)	0.3%	0.2%
New Jerusalem Bible (NJB—Roman Catholic)	0.3%	0.4%
Other	2.5%	3.2%
(including interlinear, multiple version texts, non-Spanish foreign language Bibles, and other English versions)		
Total	100%	100%

2. Revising the NIV

The NIV was first published in 1973 (New Testament) and 1978 (Old Testament), and a revised version was published in 1984. After the publication of the 1984 edition, the 15-member Committee on Bible Translation (CBT), which had oversight of the actual text of the NIV, began to work on another revision, in its attempt to improve the NIV where advances in scholarship might show a different rendering to be preferable, and also in order to keep it up-to-date in its use of the English language.

Regarding gender language in the NIV, there had been personal conversations and some information about the modifications forthcoming in the NIV, but the extent of these was not known until the *New International Version: Inclusive Language Edition* (NIVI) was first published in Great

---

[4]The NRSV total also includes some sales of the RSV (Revised Standard Version). The amount, though small, is not specified in the data available to us.

[5]The NLT was first published in 1996, and there were no sales in the first part of the year.

Britain in 1995 (New Testament) and 1996 (entire Bible). Even then the NIVI Bible was not available in the United States. As a result, the inclusive language used in the NIVI did not receive much notice among American evangelicals.

Almost simultaneously, a simplified version of the NIV was published under the title *New International Reader's Version* (NIrV(1995)). It adopted gender-neutral language similar to the NIVI, but once again this went largely unnoticed (it was written for children who were just beginning to read, but not many of them were checking the English translation against the Hebrew and Greek originals).

In the spring of 1997, controversy over the NIVI exploded in the evangelical world. The following timeline lists many of the events in this controversy.

3. Timeline of events in the controversy over the inclusive-language NIV

1992

NIV's Committee on Bible Translation decided to begin working to produce an inclusive-language edition of the NIV.[6]

1995

NIV-Inclusive Language Edition (New Testament and Psalms) was published in Great Britain.

1996

NIV-Inclusive Language Edition (NIVI) (whole Bible) was published in Great Britain.

June, 1996

CBMW News, the journal of the Council on Biblical Manhood and Womanhood, published a brief article, "What's Wrong with 'Gender Neutral' Bible Translations? A Review of the *New Revised Standard Version*," by Wayne Grudem (pp. 3–5). The NIV was not mentioned.

Fall, 1996

Priscilla Papers, the journal of Christians for Biblical Equality (CBE), which is an egalitarian advocacy group, published a lead article by David Scholer calling for Zondervan and the IBS to release an inclusive-language NIV in the U.S., as they had done in Great Britain.

---

[6]As reported in *World*, April 19, 1997, 5. D. A. Carson, whose book shows evidence of extensive conversations with members of the CBT, says, "In 1992 they decided to provide an inclusive-language edition" (*The Inclusive-Language Debate: A Plea for Realism* [Grand Rapids: Baker, and Leicester: IVP, 1998], 26).

The New Living Translation was published by Tyndale House Publishers in Wheaton, Illinois. Though it was largely gender-neutral in its translation policies, it was a new translation that was not as widely used as the NIV, and it did not generate much controversy upon its initial publication.

Nov. 21, 1996

Wayne Grudem read a paper, "What's Wrong with 'Gender-Neutral' Bible Translations? A Critique of the *New Revised Standard Version*" at the annual meeting of the Evangelical Theological Society in Jackson, Mississippi. Interest in the paper was surprisingly strong, and during the question and answer session, questions were raised about the inclusive NIV published in England. (Ken Barker, secretary of the Committee on Bible Translation for the NIV, earlier that month had accepted from Grudem 20 copies of the paper that he distributed to all the members of the CBT.)

1997

Mar. 29, 1997

World magazine published a cover story, "THE STEALTH BIBLE: The Popular *New International Version* is Quietly Going 'Gender-Neutral.'" In the article Susan Olasky wrote that the NIV "is quietly going 'gender-neutral'" (p. 12). She noted that Christians might be able to buy only an inclusive-language NIV in the future, or that the "publisher Zondervan may still choose to put out two separate versions." But she also quoted Larry Walker, a member of the NIV's Committee on Bible Translation (CBT) as saying that the "consensus" on the CBT is to have the inclusive NIV "take the place of the other." The article also quoted CBT secretary Ken Barker as saying that "it will be the publisher's decision: 'If our committee had its way there would be no separate inclusive-language edition.' But he says, 'I've heard—I can't say this is actual fact—that Zondervan will keep making the two editions,' at least for a while if the traditional version finds a market niche" (p. 15).

The article immediately met with a huge reaction. Shortly after the article appeared, thousands of copies were reprinted in a special edition of *World* that included only this article and an accompanying article, "Comparing the Two NIV's" by Wayne Grudem, which was scheduled to appear in the next issue of *World*. (Jerry Falwell ordered 50,000 copies of this special reprint to send to people on his mailing list, and it was widely distributed elsewhere as well.)

Apr. 2

Zondervan sent a letter to Ron Wilson, executive director of the Evangelical Press Association, registering a formal complaint against *World* because of the article.

Apr. 3

Zondervan released a "Dear Friend" letter that was widely distributed to bookstores and other outlets. In it, Zondervan Vice President Tom Mockabee said that the *World* story was a "disturbing article of misinformation." He also said, "We see this article as having a predetermined bias without regard to the facts," and that "The Evangelical Press association is reviewing the matter as to a violation of its Code of Ethics."

About this time Zondervan also posted on its Web site a "Frequently Asked Questions" page about the NIV controversy, a letter to *World* magazine, a letter to NIV readers, and a page from the International Bible Society with their "Frequently Asked Questions" and the IBS responses.

The first question on the Zondervan "FAQ" page asked, "Is the *World* magazine article true?" The answer: "No. Zondervan was never questioned by *World* prior to the publishing of this article, which attempts to convey a conspiracy of evangelical Bible translation with radical social feminism. . . . Nothing could be further from the truth . . ."

Apr. 19

World published several articles on the controversy:
(1) "The Battle for the Bible" by Susan Olasky (pp. 14–18, top), including a quote from J. I. Packer, "Adjustments made by what I call the feminist edition are not made in the interests of legitimate translation procedure. These changes have been made to pander to a cultural prejudice that I hope will be short-lived" (p. 16).

(2) "The Ultimate Journalistic Sin: We stand by our story and we didn't make up any quotes," an editorial by Joel Belz. In the editorial Belz says they have rechecked their facts and there was nothing untruthful in their earlier article and they stand by it. He also says, "The really serious journalistic sin has always been to misquote a source. This story about the NIV revision is about people who, for supposedly good reasons, are willing to misquote God" (p. 5).

(3) "Comparing the two NIV's" by Wayne Grudem (pp. 14–18, bottom). This article compared 15 sample passages in the NIV and the NIVI.

Apr.

Donald Wildmon's widely circulated newsletter from the American Family Association, *Christians and Society Today*, featured a cover story, "NIV Bible Going Gender Neutral" (April, 1997), 1.

Apr. sometime

Zondervan replaced its earlier Web pages on the controversy with a less accusatory, more circumspect response.

April–May

> News reports in Christian journals took various sides on the issue. Paige Patterson, President of Southeastern Seminary in Wake Forest and a prominent Southern Baptist leader, and Al Mohler, President of Southern Seminary in Louisville, issued strong statements against inclusive language Bibles. Jerry Falwell's newspaper, *National Liberty Journal* (May 1997), featured a cover story by Paige Patterson opposing "A 'Gender-Neutral' NIV."

May 3

> *World* published its May 3/10 issue, including a guest editorial by James Dobson, "Spooked by the Zeitgeist: Don't Give in to Feminist Pressure to Rewrite the Scriptures" (p. 30). Dobson wrote, "If we would not change a comma in the Gettysburg Address, why in the name of heaven would we tamper with the Word of God?"

> *World*'s May 3/10 issue also included an article, "The Smoking Gun" (p. 7). In it they quoted a letter from Lars Dunberg, President of International Bible Society, sent to *Priscilla Papers*, published by the egalitarian organization Christians for Biblical Equality. The letter was dated Jan. 9, 1997, but just published in *Priscilla Papers* (in mid-April, 1997). In light of Zondervan's repeated claims that the "Stealth Bible" article in *World* was not "true," and was "misinformation," the letter gave surprisingly clear confirmation to *World*'s claim (on Mar. 29) that Zondervan, the IBS, and the CBT were indeed quietly preparing to publish an inclusive NIV in the U.S.

The text of the letter was as follows:

> Dear Dr. David Scholer,

> I read with great interest your article on the *NIV Inclusive Language Edition*, "An Important But Mysterious Event" (*Priscilla Papers*, fall 1996). As the International President of International Bible Society, I'm happy to break the "silence" and solve this mystery for you.

> The inclusive edition of the *NIV* was completed last year. As it was ready to be published, it was decided that because International Bible Society/Zondervan was going to release a *New International Reader's Version*, the *NIV* at the 3.5 grade reading level, during the summer of 1996, the *NIRV* should be released first. This edition is inclusive in its nature.

> As that version was not ready to be launched in Britain until next year, it was decided to go ahead and let Hodder publish the inclusive version this last fall.

> Zondervan and IBS will publish an inclusive version of the *NIV* in the American market. It is not clear yet if that will be done before the major revision that the IBS has been working on with the Committee on Bible

Translation, which has been going on for the last five-six years. It may be that the next edition will include all those changes, and in that case will not be released until the year 2000. These things are still being debated, that's why we have not been public with it.

I trust that this information will be helpful to you.

Lars B. Dunberg

[The letter appeared in *Priscilla Papers* 11:1 (Winter 1997), 33.]

May 5

Joel Belz, publisher of *World*, traveled to Zondervan headquarters in Grand Rapids, Michigan, and met with Bruce Ryskamp, president of Zondervan, to attempt to resolve their differences.

May 13

Moody Radio's national program *Open Line* included a dialogue between Ken Barker, Secretary of the NIV's Committee on Bible Translation, and Wayne Grudem, President of the Council on Biblical Manhood and Womanhood.

May 14

Zondervan and the IBS issued a press release through a professional public relations firm, A. Larry Ross & Associates of Dallas, stating that they would continue to publish the 1984 NIV and at the same time they would "continue to move forward with plans for the possible publication of an updated edition of the present NIV" after the year 2001.

May 14

The Grand Rapids Press, the newspaper in Zondervan's hometown, carried a front-page headline, "Baptists irate over Zondervan plan for new Bible." They reported that Southern Baptists would probably pass a resolution opposing gender-neutral Bibles at their convention next month.

May 19

Representatives from Zondervan and the IBS met in Nashville with leaders of the Baptist Sunday School Board (Southern Baptist Convention) (*World*, June 14, 1997, 13). Baptist leaders indicated their intention to stop using the NIV in their Sunday School curricula and selling the NIV in their Baptist Book Stores if Zondervan and the IBS pursued their plans for an inclusive NIV in the U.S. The meeting reportedly ended abruptly when Zondervan officials indicated their intention to proceed with plans to publish an inclusive-language NIV.

Throughout April and May, Zondervan and the IBS continued to receive protests from individual people and even some denominational groups over plans for an inclusive NIV in the U.S. Some churches sent their current pew Bibles (NIV) back to Zondervan or the IBS.

May 23

The IBS board convened a special meeting by conference call and decided to issue a press release the following Tuesday, May 27 (Monday, May 26, was Memorial Day, a national holiday).

May 27

7:00 a.m. The International Bible Society issued a press release saying it "has abandoned all plans for gender-related changes in future editions of the New International Version (NIV)." It also stated that "The present (1984) NIV text will continue to be published. There are no plans for a further revised edition."[7]

9:00 a.m. Dr. James Dobson convened a group of twelve evangelical leaders who had been invited to his headquarters in Colorado Springs to attempt to bring resolution to the NIV controversy. The meeting included four representatives of the NIV: Bruce Ryskamp, President of Zondervan; Lars Dunberg, President of the International Bible Society; and, at the request of Ryskamp and Dunberg, Ken Barker and Ron Youngblood, two of the principal translators of the NIV (and members of the Committee on Bible Translation).

Others came to the meeting to express concerns about the NIV: Timothy Bayly, Executive Director, Council on Biblical Manhood and Womanhood, and pastor, Church of the Good Shepherd, Bloomington, Indiana; Joel Belz, Publisher, *World* magazine; James Dobson, President, Focus on the Family; Wayne Grudem, President, Council on Biblical Manhood and Womanhood, and Professor of Biblical and Systematic Theology, Trinity Evangelical Divinity School; Charles Jarvis, Executive Vice President, Focus on the Family; John Piper, Senior Pastor, Bethlehem Baptist Church, Minneapolis, Minnesota; Vern S. Poythress, Professor of New Testament Interpretation, Westminster Theological Seminary; R. C. Sproul, Chairman, Ligonier Ministries.

The meeting resulted in a "Statement by Participants" and in a list of "Guidelines for Translation of Gender-Related Language in Scripture." (See Appendix 1 for the full text of the Guidelines [later known as the Colorado Springs Guidelines or CSG] in their final form.)[8]

---

[7]This response was more conservative than anything the critics of gender-neutral translation would have requested. For example, the Colorado Springs Guidelines for translation, which were drafted at a meeting later that same day (see following paragraphs), allowed for and gave explicit approval to several kinds of changes in translation of gender-related terms in Scripture, changes where the original Hebrew or Greek text was itself "gender-neutral" and did not imply any male components of meaning.

[8]Appendix 1 also indicates how refinements of the Guidelines were introduced (and agreed on by all the participants in the original meeting) before they were issued in published form in October 1997.

A subsequent account of the meeting, written by Wayne Grudem and then read and modified on the basis of corrections and comments submitted by most of the other participants before publication, can be found in Appendix 1. The article was approved for publication not only by those who came with concerns about the NIVI, but also by Bruce Ryskamp, president of Zondervan, and Ken Barker, secretary of the CBT.[9]

May 28–29

National newspapers carried stories reporting that plans for a gender-neutral NIV had been cancelled: *USA Today* (May 28, 1997, 3A); *New York Times* (May 29, 1997, A9), and the Associated Press (May 28, 1997, dispatch, subsequently carried by many papers).

May 30

Wayne Grudem, president of CBMW, and James Dobson, president of Focus on the Family, both sent letters to Dr. Gray Allison, president of Mid-America Baptist Theological Seminary in Memphis, urging him not to dismiss tenured faculty member Larry Walker, an Old Testament professor and a long-time member of the NIV's Committee on Bible Translation. Grudem's letter indicated that Larry Walker had read the guidelines produced in the May 27 meeting and was in agreement with them. (Walker was subsequently dismissed from Mid-America Seminary, after refusing a request from the seminary board and administration that he resign from the NIV's Committee on Bible Translation, on which he had served for 30 years, according to a report in *Christianity Today*, July 14, 1997, 62.)

May 28–May 31

Several refinements and modifications were made to the "Guidelines for Translation" that had been drafted at the May 27 meeting. Changes were worked out by phone and fax communications among the twelve participants, and by the afternoon of May 31 a final draft was produced to which all participants could give agreement. Participants then signed a copy of the guidelines and faxed their signatures to Focus on the Family headquarters, where a press release was being prepared.

June 3

A press release from Focus on the Family made public the statement and guidelines from the May 27 meeting.

June 11

The General Assembly of the Presbyterian Church in America passed a resolution: "The PCA concurs with the decision by the (NIV) Committee

---

[9]Due to travel constraints, Ron Youngblood had to leave the meeting late in the morning. Lars Dunberg had a conflicting commitment and had to leave in the early afternoon. Ryskamp and Barker, who read and approved the article for accuracy, stayed for the entire meeting.

on Bible Translation, International Bible Society, and Zondervan Publishing not to pursue their plans to publish a 'gender-inclusive' version of the NIV in the United States, believing that such a version is inconsistent with the Biblical doctrine of divine inspiration" (*Presbyterian and Reformed News*, Summer, 1997, 7). (The actual motion is found in "Minutes of the Twenty-fifth General Assembly," Part Two: Journal, 25–45, 193.)

June 14

The June 14/21 issue of *World* featured the cover headline: "Bailing Out: Plans for 'gender-accurate' NIV are abandoned: Everyone looks for a safe place to land." The story by Susan Olasky, "Bailing out of the Stealth Bible" (pp. 12–17) reported details of the May 27 IBS press release and the May 27 meeting in Colorado Springs.

June 16

Christianity Today published a brief news article, "Hands Off My NIV! Bible Society Cancels Plans for 'Gender-Accurate' Bible after Public Outcry" (pp. 52–53).

June 17

The Southern Baptist Convention passed a resolution opposing "the use of so-called gender-inclusive language" in Bible translation (*SBC Bulletin*, 74 [June 17–19, 1997]: 5).

June 25 (approximate date)

CBMW News published a detailed account of the May 27 meeting, "NIV Controversy: Participants Sign Landmark Agreement," by Wayne Grudem (pp. 1, 3–6; see Appendix 1 for text of the article). The article was read for accuracy, corrected, and approved prior to publication by all the participants who stayed for the entire meeting.[10] This issue of *CBMW News* also included the complete text of the "Guidelines for Translation of Gender-Related Language in Scripture" (p. 6) and the longer "Statement by Participants in the Conference on Gender-Related Language in Scripture" (p. 7).

July 1

The ethics committee appointed by the Evangelical Press Association sent a report to the EPA Board of Directors. The report was generally critical of *World*'s coverage of the controversy with respect to "accuracy" (in presenting a one-sided picture, and in linking Zondervan to "feminist seduction") as well as "distortion" and "sensationalism" (in use of "inflammatory language" and "insinuation"). However, the

---

[10]One participant did not approve of publishing the article in general, but did not note any inaccuracies in it.

report did not say that anything *World* published was false, and in fact said that *"World* published nothing which they knew to be false in advance, and have not demonstrated reckless regard [as to whether a statement is false or not]."

The three members of the ethics committee, Mark Fackler (of Wheaton College), Wesley Pippert, and Beth Spring (of *Christianity Today*) issued the report, but Pippert added a personal addendum that was also critical of public statements made by Zondervan.

By the next day, the report had been made public before the EPA Board had a chance to consider it. The report was later disavowed by the EPA board (see July 27, below).

July 7

Joel Belz sent a letter to EPA executive director Ron Wilson protesting that the ethics committee had been appointed in violation of the EPA bylaws: (1) The executive director appointed the three members of the panel, but the bylaws specify that the president and/or the board of directors are to do this. (2) The three people chosen were not impartial, but all had "strong Wheaton and/or CT ties." Belz said, "Can anyone read these people's backgrounds and not call it a stacked deck? Basic jury selection procedures were ignored." (3) The report was immediately disseminated to the media before the EPA board had a chance to evaluate it. (4) The report "never seriously interacts with our detailed claims of truthfulness, but features instead a preoccupation with issues of tone and balance." Belz requested an immediate phone conference meeting of the EPA board. (Belz had been president of the EPA the previous year.)

July 8

Joel Belz wrote a letter to the EPA board asking that they focus first of all on the fundamental issue of truth. Zondervan, says Belz, has spent "thousands of dollars" to "deny the truthfulness of WORLD's reporting," and adds that "the charge of falsehood not only remained in place, but continued to be repeated and even amplified by ZPH/IBS personnel as weeks went by." Belz says, "If ZPH/IBS are right in their repeated and widely disseminated claims that we have lied, they must be compelled to prove it. If they can't prove it, then they should be asked to be quiet."

July 14

John Kohlenberger III, a frequent Zondervan author, presented a paper, "Understanding the Current Controversy over Bible Translations," at the Christian Booksellers Association (CBA) International Convention in Atlanta, Georgia. He came "at the request of CBA," according to the introduction by Mark Kuyper. The paper defended inclusive-language translations as the most effective and accurate way to translate gender language in Scripture today.[11]

July 14

Christianity Today published a major news article, "Bible Translators Deny Gender Agenda" (pp. 62–64), and an editorial by Mickey Maudlin, "Accusing the Brothers (and Sisters)" (p. 4). Both the article and the editorial were strongly critical of those who opposed the NIVI at the May 27 Colorado Springs meeting, and critical of the translation guidelines written at that meeting.

Not one of the people who had criticized the NIVI at the Colorado Springs meeting was interviewed for the article, and we were uniformly dismayed at the standard of accuracy it exhibited. Seven of the participants in the May 27 meeting sent the following letter of protest to *Christianity Today*. (The letter was published Oct. 6 in CT, 14, with some deletions.)

Dear Editor:

We were identified as "inclusive language opponents" in your July 14 coverage of the May 27 meeting on gender language in translation. The article and editorial left much to be desired in terms of fairness and accuracy. The article mentioned none of the over 4000 Bible verses whose translation is changed to something less accurate in inclusive-language Bibles. You cited ten people or groups who disapproved of our position and only one who approved. The evaluative statements in the article and editorial were imbalanced 37 to 1 against our position. The editorial criticized several extreme positions supposedly held by those who oppose inclusive-language translations, yet none of us holds these extreme positions. Of the thirteen translation guidelines adopted at our meeting, you cited only four, and three of those were cited incorrectly. You cited none of our six guidelines that approved certain kinds of inclusive language that retain accuracy in translation. You called inclusive language by the biased term "accurate language," thus excluding by definition our fundamental claim that it is inaccurate language. Perhaps most disappointing was the failure to mention the grace of God at work to bring a peaceful resolution and a unanimous statement from a meeting of twelve people at the heart of the recent conflict over a planned (and now canceled) inclusive-language NIV. CT has covered

---

[11]It is interesting that Kohlenberger has now become a member of the governing board of Christians for Biblical Equality, an egalitarian advocacy organization that has strongly promoted the gender-neutral NIVI (as reported in the CBE publication *Mutuality* [Spring 2000], 5).

other controversial issues fairly in the past; we hope for better coverage
of this issue in the future.

Sincerely yours,
Tim Bayly
Joel Belz
James Dobson
Wayne Grudem
Charles Jarvis
Vern Poythress
R. C. Sproul

July 22

The EPA Board of Directors met in special session.

July 28

The EPA Board of Directors released a statement saying that "the EPA
has realized that it has made two major errors in handling this process.
First, we violated our own bylaws in appointing the ad hoc ethics committee. Our bylaws require that functioning committees be composed of
members of the EPA. . . . Since the three ad hoc committee members are
not currently members of the EPA, the committee lacked the mandated
qualifications to legitimately perform its task.

"Our second major error was the release of the ad hoc committee's
report before the Board of Directors had an opportunity to formally
review the report. . . . We deeply regret that our improper handling of
this situation has complicated the dispute . . ."

Aug. 6

The faculty of Westminster Theological Seminary in California passed a
resolution stating their opposition to gender-neutral Bible translations:

> We approve the thrust of the guidelines for translation for gender
> related language in Scripture, although we would desire opportunity
> of refinement of the details. We would also wish for a more general
> statement of the underlying principles of translation, including the
> importance of maintaining the inclusive use of the male gender in
> English as in Hebrew and Greek, and the recognition of the Biblical
> patriarchal structure.

Oct. 18

The EPA Board of Directors issued a two-page statement indicating that
they had concluded their involvement in the *World*-Zondervan dispute
"without rendering judgment," noting that "our efforts at mediation
failed." The statement said, with respect to Zondervan's filing of an
ethics complaint against *World*, that "a judgment of right or wrong by
EPA will accomplish no good thing" (reported in Baptist Press dispatch
Oct. 28, 1997).

Oct. 21–22

James Dobson's radio program, *Focus on the Family*, included a discussion of concerns about gender-neutral Bibles, with Wayne Grudem as a guest on the program.

Oct. 27

Christianity Today issue appeared with the article, "Do Inclusive Language Bibles Distort Scripture? Yes (by Wayne Grudem); No (by Grant Osborne)" (pp. 26–39). The editorial by David Neff, "The Great Translation Debate" (pp. 16–17) invited readers to "express your own convictions on this issue by responding to a CT survey on the World Wide Web." (In the Dec. 8 issue, David Neff reported that of the 904 respondents, 27% supported inclusive-language Bibles, 68% opposed, and 5% had no opinion [p. 6].)

This same issue of *CT* included a two-page ad, "Can I Still Trust My Bible?" The ad published for the first time (except for the June issue of *CBMW News*)[12] the full text of the Colorado Springs translation guidelines, and also contained the names of 50 additional endorsers of the guidelines. The ad was placed by the Council on Biblical Manhood and Womanhood, and also appeared at about the same time in *Moody*, *Charisma*, and *World*.

1998

February

The Commission on Theology and Church Relations of The Lutheran Church—Missouri Synod released a study, *Biblical Revelation and Inclusive Language*, a 40-page report which opposed inclusive-language Bible translation (with particular references to the NRSV and the NIVI, but also to other publications which refer to God as "she" and to Christ as the "Child of God" rather than "Son of God"). The commission that produced the report had started its work in 1989 (p. 5). The principles in the report were fully consistent with the Colorado Springs Guidelines (see the "Summary" on pp. 39–40), but did not mention the CSG by name, and seemed to have been produced independently of them.

Sometime during 1998:

Two books on the controversy were published, both claiming to be balanced and fair treatments of the issue, but both in fact arguing strongly in favor of gender-neutral Bible translations, and both strongly critical of the Colorado Springs Guidelines:

> D. A. Carson, *The Inclusive Language Debate: A Plea for Realism* (Grand Rapids: Baker, and Leicester, England, InterVarsity Press, 1998), and

---

[12]Note that further refinements to the guidelines were made between June and the publication on October 27. See Appendix 1 for the full text of this ad.

> Mark L. Strauss, *Distorting Scripture? The Challenge of Bible Translation and Gender Accuracy* (Downers Grove, Ill.: InterVarsity Press, 1998).

Vern Poythress's article criticizing gender-neutral translation practices appeared in *Westminster Theological Journal* (fall 1998).[13]

Vern Poythress critically reviewed D. A. Carson and Mark Strauss's books on the gender-neutral controversy in *World* (Nov. 21).[14]

As a result of the agreement reached at the Colorado Springs meeting, the *New International Reader's Version* (NIrV, 1995) was extensively revised to conform to the Colorado Springs Guidelines, and released in 1998. The preface said, "This edition of the *New International Reader's Version* has been revised so that the gender language more closely matches that of the *New International Version*. When we prepared this new edition, we had help from people who were not part of the first team. We want to thank them for their help. They are Ben Aker from the Assemblies of God Theological Seminary, Paul House from the Southern Baptist Seminary, and Scott Munger from International Bible Society" (NIrV, [1998], x).

1999

May 14

> An International Bible Society press release announced that it was encouraging the NIV's Committee on Bible Translation to continue with its work. Even though the 1984 NIV would continue to be available with no changes, the press release said, "IBS encourages the CBT to continue translating the biblical text with clarity, accuracy, and faithfulness so that this work can be reviewed by the IBS Board for possible publication" of a new English translation.

The IBS Web site included further information in a "Frequently Asked Questions about the NIV" section. It indicated that the new translation will not be called the NIV, but no name had yet been chosen. Regarding a completion date, it said, " The CBT may—or may not—be ready to submit a complete text to IBS for consideration by the end of the summer of 2003. We'll have to wait and see how well their work progresses."

June 5

> *World* published a cover story, "There They Go Again . . ." (pp. 14–16). According to the article, the IBS will not publish a new "edition" of the NIV but will publish a new "rendition" of the Bible. The article also quoted a letter by the IBS Vice-President for Translations, Eugene

---

[13]Vern S. Poythress, "Gender in Bible Translation: Exploring a Connection with Male Representatives," *Westminster Theological Journal* 60/2 (1998): 225–253.

[14]Vern S. Poythress, "Searching Instead for an Agenda-Neutral Bible," *World* 13/45 (November 21, 1998): 24–25.

Rubingh, dated March 19, 1999, in which he said, "I, the CBT and practically everyone involved, thoroughly support gender-accurate language [the IBS expression for regendering]. The matter is one of timing, of finding the appropriate hour to move ahead" (p. 16).[15]

June 24

An online news service, Religion Today, published a feature story, "'Gender-accurate' Bible due to be published," in which it reported an interview with Steve Johnson, communications director for the IBS, who said that a "gender-accurate" translation of the Bible is due to be published in 2003 or 2004. The article reported, "The new translation will not be called the NIV, but will be similar to it, Johnson said. 'The style and character will remain the same.' Wording of the new translation is being researched by scholars who make up the Committee on Bible Translation, the group that originally translated the NIV."

The article continued, "Changes in gender language will be included in the new translation, which has not yet been named. For example, where the NIV says in 1 Corinthians 11:28, 'A man ought to examine himself before he eats of the bread and drinks of the cup,' a possible new translation is, 'A believer ought to examine him or herself,' IBS said. Also, verses about Jews plotting to kill Jesus will refer back to the Pharisees, not the entire Jewish population."

However, the article noted that others were troubled by the plans of the IBS and CBT: "Some critics now say IBS's decision to proceed with the new translation circumvents the 1997 agreement. R. Albert Mohler, president of Southern Baptist Theological Seminary, told Religion News Service that he felt 'a sense of betrayal' because the agreement seems to have 'no effect.'"

C. Personal observations on the events in this timeline

In the following section, one of the authors of this book, Wayne Grudem, gives some personal observations and evaluations of the events, made from a distance of just over two years (I am writing in August 1999).

1. Public reaction

The strong negative reaction of the Christian public to the possibility of an inclusive-language NIV was not, in my judgment, due to misinformation, and was not due to the alleged use of sensational language by *World* magazine but rather was due to one central fact: the people who controlled the NIV were making plans to change it to a gender-neutral translation. Based

---

[15]However, in private conversation with Wayne Grudem, Mr. Rubingh later indicated that he did not intend the expression "gender-accurate" to imply a gender-neutral translation.

on extensive conversations with many Christians in many different churches, I think that the strong reaction of the Christian public was due to a fairly accurate understanding of the central issues involved. Literally thousands of evangelical Christians perceived that there was a tampering with the Word of God that came, however indirectly, as a result of feminist pressures in the general culture. I do not think that Christians generally thought people involved with the NIV were themselves feminists or egalitarians, but they did think that the changes made to produce a "gender-neutral" Bible were (in actual fact, even if not from sinister motives) the result of an unnecessary capitulation to feminist pressures in the culture as a whole. I believe that is still the assessment of the great majority of the Christian public, and it is still my assessment as well.

2. Why did the issue become so heated?

a. The Christian public

On the part of Christian laypersons, the issue provoked an extremely strong reaction. I personally saw this happen several times when I would simply put a comparison list of verses up on an overhead projector transparency in talking to church groups about this issue. When people saw the actual changes in verses, they weren't just puzzled or curious, or even saddened—they were genuinely angry! I think this is because the Bible is in a very fundamental way precious to God's people. They treasure it more than any other book because it is genuinely the words of God, and it is their source of spiritual life and their source for hearing God's voice speak to them through the words of Scripture. Whenever Christians have a sense that the Bible they trust is going to be changed so that it will no longer be trustworthy, they are rightfully upset about it! If they weren't upset about such perceived changes, I would think that they did not care deeply about the Word of God.

I do not agree, however, that the Christian public in general, or inclusive-language opponents in particular, were guilty of "Bible rage," as D. A. Carson puts it. Carson mentions one incident by one anonymous person (someone who drilled holes in a copy of the NIV and sent it back to the IBS). From the actions of this one unknown person, he implies an unwarranted conclusion about NIVI opponents in general, namely that they were guilty of "Bible rage" in this controversy. He compares it to "road rage" where an angry motorist reacts to another motorist who has cut him off in traffic and, as Carson puts it, "Road rage triumphs, and out comes a crowbar or a shotgun, and mayhem is the result."[16] Such a comparison is hardly fair to the

---

[16]D. A. Carson, *Debate*, 15. I do not deny that the event happened, for I saw the mutilated Bible myself when Lars Dunberg of IBS brought it to the May 27 meeting in Colorado Springs.

vast majority of Christians who deeply love God's Word and use the NIV as their own personal Bible and who were honestly troubled over what they perceived as a substantial threat to its trustworthiness in English translation.

b. Christian leaders opposed to the NIVI

People like James Dobson, Paige Patterson, Jerry Falwell, J. I. Packer, Al Mohler, R. C. Sproul, John Piper, and others who spoke out on this issue felt very strongly about it for the same reasons: they perceived a threat to the preservation of an accurate Word of God in the English language. This is a major issue, and, if they were right in their perception, they should have felt strongly and spoken strongly about it.

c. Zondervan Publishing House

On the other side of the controversy, emotions also ran strong and deep. Zondervan Publishing House is a long-established Christian ministry that does an immense amount of good for the kingdom of God through its publications year after year. Yet sales of the NIV (I have been told) accounted for roughly half of Zondervan's annual revenue, and when the controversy posed a threat to that revenue, everyone connected with Zondervan was understandably troubled by it. I am personally acquainted with many people who work for Zondervan. I realize that they all count it as a ministry for the Lord, and they are rightly dismayed if anything threatens seriously to hinder or destroy that ministry. If they weren't upset about such events that posed a major threat to the whole of their ministry, I would think that they

---

(Carson mentions seven copies; I only saw one. I do not know whether the seven copies all came from the same person or from a group.)

But Carson's discussion of "rage" frames the whole issue in a biased and emotionally charged way. In the opening four paragraphs of his book he compares opponents of gender-neutral Bibles to the people who commit murder on the highway, the people who strangled and burned William Tyndale in 1536, the person who destroyed an RSV with a blowtorch in 1952, and the person who drilled holes in an NIV Bible (pp. 15–16). He returns to the "Bible rage" theme on page 35, and then again at the end of the book on page 194 (blaming *World* magazine for an article that "managed to . . . incite enough hate that destroyed Bibles were mailed to IBS headquarters.") Carson does not mention the tears of grief in John Piper's eyes as he sat next to Lars Dunberg and saw the mutilated copy of God's precious Word, or the dismay the rest of us felt. It is always possible to paint one's opponents in an unfavorable light by pointing to some irrational, even criminal act carried out by a loner on the fringe, and then to let readers conclude that people on the other side of a question are filled with "rage" and "hate." But such a portrayal hardly gives one's readers an accurate picture of the responsible advocates of the other position.

Carson at one point does qualify his portrayal: "while on all sides of this debate there are some passionate people—some of them enraged—there are also some people who are extraordinarily self-disciplined and gracious, and many who are between the extremes" (*Debate*, 37). Carson calls for moderation on all sides. Nevertheless, the intense picture of murder and mayhem with which he begins will do little to promote understanding on either side.

did not care deeply about the wonderful, kingdom-advancing ministry that God has entrusted to them.

d. The Committee on Bible Translation

Similarly, the members of the Committee on Bible Translation have, over the last three decades, produced one of the most remarkable accomplishments in the twentieth century—they have provided the entire English-speaking world with a widely used translation that is understandable and that has helped the spiritual life of now more than 150 million people around the world. To be entrusted with the care of this NIV translation is a wonderful stewardship, and they were understandably deeply troubled at a controversy that seriously threatened the ministry of the NIV Bible.

(The fourteen members of the CBT in 1997 were Kenneth Barker, Gordon Fee, Scott Hafemann,[17] R. Laird Harris, Karen Jobes, Walter Liefeld, Donald Madvig, Douglas Moo, Martin Selman, John Stek, Larry Walker, Bruce Waltke, Herbert Wolf, and Ronald Youngblood.)

Reaction to the Colorado Springs meeting: With regard to the May 27 meeting at Focus on the Family Headquarters in Colorado Springs, several members of the Committee on Bible Translation were particularly troubled, partly because a revision of the NIV that they had worked on for several years was apparently canceled in a single day, in a meeting at which only two of them were present (Ken Barker and Ron Youngblood). Moreover, for over 30 years some CBT members had understood that they were the sole custodians of the text of the NIV, and here suddenly they found that Dr. James Dobson, who is not a technically trained Bible scholar, had convened a meeting that had the result of telling them how they could and could not translate the NIV. Moreover, the results of this meeting were endorsed by the president of Zondervan (the company that has exclusive rights to distribute the NIV), and the president of the IBS (the organization that owns the copyright to the NIV). It is understandable that many members of the CBT did not think this was a fair process or one that respected their role as sole custodians of the text of the NIV.

In hindsight, people can always wonder whether the meeting could have been arranged in some better way or whether some other way forward could have been found. I myself think the arrangements were proper and fair and included representatives from all the major groups involved, and I am still (after more than two years) thankful for the good results of the meeting. Moreover, from my perspective as one of the opponents of gender-neutrality that met in Colorado Springs, it seems to me that the IBS

---

[17]Scott Hafemann has since left the CBT and, according to the IBS, has been replaced by R. T. France.

and Zondervan, in canceling plans for the inclusive NIV, made the only decision they could make if they were to preserve the continuing widespread use of the NIV by the Christian public. The simple fact was that the CBT had decided to go forward with an inclusive-language NIV, and the Christian public was deeply opposed to it, much more strongly than any of us had imagined. To go forward with plans for an inclusive-language NIV at that point would have exacerbated the controversy and possibly destroyed the NIV itself.

e. The International Bible Society

In a similar way the International Bible Society has a remarkable worldwide ministry, and sales of the NIV provide much of the income that enables this ministry to continue. It is also understandable that people connected with the IBS were deeply troubled by the controversy, for it seemed to threaten much of the ongoing ministry of the IBS and its translation of the Bible into many languages.

3. What was the fundamental problem?

In my own judgment, refined now by the distance of two years, the fundamental problem was not caused by any *journal articles* (such as the "Stealth Bible" article in *World*). Nor was the problem caused by anything in the *process* (the style of writing in *World* magazine, who was or was not invited to Dr. Dobson's meeting, or which persons talked to which other persons at what time and in what sequence, and so forth).[18] Rather, the entire problem was caused by the fundamental *fact* underneath it all: the people who controlled the NIV were making changes in it that significantly distorted the meaning of the Word of God. Once the Christian public found out about this, they simply were not going to accept it, and the other events in the controversy unfolded as a natural result of that fundamental fact.

4. What decided the issue?

When the IBS and Zondervan saw that the controversy was beginning to threaten not simply a proposed future NIV but the present NIV itself, they gave in to pressure from the Christian public in general, who simply would not allow such changes to be made in their Bibles. It was significant that the criticisms of the inclusive NIV came not only from *World* magazine but also from many other Christian leaders, in particular James Dobson, Jerry Falwell, J. I. Packer, Paige Patterson, Al Mohler, Don Wildmon, and others. These leaders were not persuaded that the *World* articles were false; in fact, they realized that the articles were all too true.

---

[18]People may, of course, debate whether *World* or *Christianity Today* or Zondervan or CBMW or other participants and factors in the subsequent process exacerbated the problem.

Yet it seems to me that the three most significant influences were *World* magazine (with its surprisingly widespread and influential readership), the opposition of James Dobson (with the potential for arousing the opposition of the millions of listeners to his radio program), and the opposition of the Southern Baptist Convention, particularly the Baptist Sunday School Board (now LifeWay Christian Resources) at the May 19 meeting in Nashville.

Some people have criticized this decision as just "giving in to market pressures," and so forth. For my own part, I do not think the decision has to be viewed in such a negative light. Zondervan came to the realization that large segments of the Christian public disapproved of a Bible that they were considering producing and selling. It seems to me that through this process the viewpoints of the general Christian public came to play a significant role in the direction of Bible translation and in the direction of the NIV specifically. This is not a process that we should find objectionable, at least in principle (though I realize that people will differ over the details of this specific instance).[19]

5. Clarity versus unclarity in the issues

As I reread the materials put out in defense of inclusive-language translations during 1997, it seemed to me that the defenders of gender-neutral Bibles left much to be desired in terms of their clarity in presenting the actual substance of the matters in dispute. The July 14 issue of *Christianity Today* provided no way for readers to gain an accurate understanding of what the May 27 Colorado Springs Guidelines actually said, or even the general character of the guidelines, or that all participants had signed them, or that there were serious issues of translation accuracy at stake. This is not fair or accurate reporting. If the editors of *CT* had wished to differ with the guidelines, they surely could have done that. But to give readers no understanding of the content or character of the guidelines that they criticized was just to resort to caricature.

The same lack of clarity in explaining the real issues characterized John Kohlenberger's paper at the Christian Booksellers Association meeting on July 14. His paper focused much attention not on points we objected to in the NIVI, but on areas where what he called "inclusive" language had been used for centuries in Bibles (such as translating Hebrew *banîm* as "children," for example, which is recognized in all the lexicons)—yet these were matters no one disagreed about, and they diverted attention from the central concerns.

The concerns that were at the heart of the issue (the loss of generic "he," the loss of male meaning components, and the systematic change of singulars to plurals, for example) had been clearly evident in *World* magazine

---

[19]See our later remarks in the excursus at the end of Chapter 10.

and in a number of other materials put out in opposition to gender-neutral Bibles, but these genuine concerns were not the focus of attention in many of the responses.

6. The claims of truth and falsehood

It seems to me that subsequent events demonstrated that *World* was correct in the following three fundamental claims of its original "Stealth Bible" article: (1) that an inclusive language NIV was being prepared by the Committee on Bible Translation for publication in the United States, (2) that it had been in process for over four years, and (3) that Zondervan and the IBS were aware of it.

In light of this, it saddened me that Zondervan flooded the evangelical world with charges that the *World* article was not true, all the while failing to answer the central question: *Was the CBT preparing an inclusive-language NIV?* This was the issue that concerned the Christian public, yet Zondervan's Web site opened the NIV discussion by saying, "Is the *World* magazine article true? No. Zondervan was never questioned by *World* prior to the publishing of this article, which attempts to convey a conspiracy of evangelical Bible translation with radical social feminism. . . . Nothing could be further from the truth."

This answer subtly shifts attention from the real question that concerned the Christian public to a question about a "conspiracy" between Bible translators and "radical social feminism." On the real question, whether the CBT was preparing an inclusive-language NIV for publication in the United States with Zondervan's knowledge and approval, Zondervan gave no answer and countered with ethics charges and pages of material that did not address the real question.

There were, I agree, some parts of the *World* article about which Christians might legitimately differ, such as whether there was a connection (it never claimed a conspiracy) between feminism and gender-neutral Bibles, or whether it was appropriate to use some of the language that Zondervan claimed was sensationalistic (such as the phrase "unisex-language Bibles"), or whether it was appropriate to put on the cover a picture of a stealth bomber superimposed on an NIV Bible. I can understand how Zondervan executives differed strongly with these things, and I am not objectiing to their protests against them. But these were matters of atmosphere, style, and analytical judgments, not the central claim, and they were not the matters that deeply concerned readers of *World*. Rather, people were concerned about the central fact claimed in the article: *Was the CBT preparing an inclusive-language NIV for distribution in the U.S.?* It was, and the principal groups responsible for the NIV knew about it.

It would have been understandable if Zondervan had objected to the article in terms of tone and balance (matters on which there can certainly be legitimate differences of opinion), or in terms of analysis of the influence of feminism on trends in the evangelical world. But the outright claim that *World* had published an article that was not true saddened me, for it seriously damaged the reputation of *World* in the eyes of the evangelical public.

D. Developments since the NIV controversy: other translations

After the NIVI controversy died down, several other translations appeared or were announced in 1998 or 1999, and they mostly followed the translation guidelines issuing from the May 1997 Colorado Springs meeting.

1. The *NET Bible, New English Translation* (Biblical Studies Press, 1996, 1997, 1998) is for the most part gender-specific (not gender-neutral) in its translation.

2. The *International Standard Version* (New Testament) (Davidson Press, 1998) quotes many of the Colorado Springs Guidelines in the preface and conforms to them.

3. A new translation sponsored by the Southern Baptist Convention, the *Holman Christian Standard Bible*, will be gender specific when it is published (a Gospel of John was distributed in June 1999).

4. The *English Standard Version* (ESV), an evangelical revision of the 1971 *Revised Standard Version*, announced in February 1999 by Crossway Books, will also be gender specific in its translation policy.[20]

5. Finally, as noted above, the NIrV was reissued in 1998 in a form that conformed to the Colorado Springs Guidelines.

It remains to be seen what may happen with a revision of the NIV. The May 14, 1999, press release from the IBS (see above) mentions an upcoming new Bible version, probably to be released in 2003 or 2004, based on the continuing work of the CBT in revising the NIV text. The new translation will not be called the NIV, but will have some other name yet to be determined. What will this new translation do with gender issues? Will it be gender-neutral, like the NIVI published in Great Britain (and still available in the summer of 2000 in British bookstores)? Or will it only incorporate changes along the lines of the Colorado Springs guidelines? (It also will contain other changes, not related to gender, that have been in the works since the publication of the 1984 NIV.)

On the one hand, it is possible that it will be gender-neutral, like the NIVI. Since most of the translators are the same, and the basic translation philosophy is essentially the same, and the text which is being modified is the previous NIV text (for the CBT is not producing a new translation from scratch), the new version may be similar in gender language to the

---

[20]In the interests of fair disclosure, it should be noted here that both of the authors of this book, Vern Poythress and Wayne Grudem, are members of the Translation Oversight Committee for the *English Standard Version*.

inclusive-language NIV that the CBT was planning before the 1997 controversy. (Perhaps it might just eliminate gender-neutral language from a handful of the verses that received the most criticism.) In that case, even though it would not be named the NIV, in substance it would undo the IBS's cancellation of a gender-neutral NIV in its press release of May 27, 1997.

On the other hand, the new version may follow the Colorado Springs Guidelines. There are several encouraging factors. The CBT and the IBS are understandably anxious to avoid another public controversy like the one that threatened the future of the NIV itself in 1997, and we are aware of a number of helpful private conversations between members of these groups and people who oppose gender-neutral Bibles. Moreover, members of both the CBT and the IBS are aware that significant portions of their target audience would reject any new Bible that is "gender-neutral"[21] and perhaps some would even protest against it. And, since trust in a Bible translation is related to trust in the committee that produced it, the CBT and the IBS wisely realize that any new translation that they issue will also influence to some degree people's confidence in the current NIV. In addition, it is also possible that some CBT members have modified their viewpoints on this matter since 1997 as a result of several books and articles that have been written, as well as many private discussions. So it is too soon to tell what will happen with this new "rendition" of the NIV when it appears in 2003 or 2004. We will have to wait and see.

---

[21]See the report of the readers' poll by *Christianity Today* under October 27, 1997, in the chronology above: 68% of respondents opposed gender-neutral Bibles. In addition, presumably most or all of the evangelical leaders who opposed the NIVI (see the list at Appendix 1, p. 301ff, for example) would also oppose any similar gender-neutral translation if it were to be produced by the CBT.

CHAPTER 9

The Bible: The Word of God

Before discussing Bible translation in detail, it is important to understand what kind of book the Bible is. Most Christians would agree that the Bible is "the Word of God," but exactly what does that mean? And what does the Bible really claim about itself?

We need to begin by examining just what kind of book the Bible claims to be, and then asking how we come to believe its claims. After that, we can ask what those findings mean for how we treat the Bible today.[1]

A. All the words in Scripture are God's words

I. The Bible claims to be God's words

There are frequent claims in the Bible that all the words of Scripture are God's words (as well as words that were written down by the human authors). In the Old Testament, the claim to be God's word is often seen in the introductory phrase, "Thus says the LORD," which appears hundreds of times. In the world of the Old Testament, this phrase would have been recognized as identical in form to the phrase, "Thus says king . . ." which was used to preface the edict of a king to his subjects, an edict which could not be challenged or questioned, but which simply had to be obeyed.[2] Thus, when the prophets say, "Thus says the LORD," they are claiming to be messengers from the sovereign King of Israel, namely, God himself, and they are claiming that their words are the absolutely authoritative words of God.

---

[1]Sections A to E of this chapter are adapted from Wayne Grudem, *Bible Doctrine: Essential Teachings of the Christian Faith* (Grand Rapids: Zondervan, and Leicester: InterVarsity, 1999), 33–48, and are used by permission of Zondervan Publishing House. For further study of the nature of the Bible as the Word of God, see Wayne Grudem, *Systematic Theology* (Leicester: InterVarsity, and Grand Rapids: Zondervan, 1994), 47–138.

[2]See Wayne Grudem, "Scripture's Self-Attestation," in *Scripture and Truth*, ed. by D. A. Carson and John Woodbridge (Grand Rapids: Zondervan, 1983), 21–22.

When a prophet spoke in God's name in this way, every word he spoke had to come from God, or he would be a false prophet. So, for example, when God tells Moses that he will send the people another prophet like Moses, he says, "I will put my words in his mouth, and he will tell them everything I command him. If anyone does not listen to my words that the prophet speaks in my name, I myself will call him to account" (Deut. 18:18–19; see also Num. 22:38; Jer. 1:9; 14:14; 23:16–22; 29:31–32; Ezek. 2:7; 13:1–16).

Furthermore, God is often said to speak "through" the prophet (1 Kgs. 14:18; 16:12, 34; 2 Kgs. 9:36; 14:25; Jer. 37:2; Zech. 7:7, 12). Thus, what the prophet says in God's name, God says (1 Kgs. 13:26 with v. 21; 1 Kgs. 21:19 with 2 Kgs. 9:25–26; Hag. 1:12; cf. 1 Sam. 15:3, 18). In these and other instances in the Old Testament, words that the prophets spoke can also be referred to as words that God himself spoke. Thus, to disbelieve or disobey anything a prophet says is to disbelieve or disobey God himself (Deut. 18:19; 1 Sam. 10:8; 13:13–14; 15:3, 19, 23; 1 Kgs. 20:35, 36).

These verses by themselves do not claim that *all* the words in the Old Testament are God's words, for these verses themselves are referring only to specific sections of spoken or written words in the Old Testament. But the cumulative force of these passages, including the hundreds of passages which begin "Thus says the LORD," is to demonstrate that within the Old Testament we have written records of words that are said to be God's own words. These words constitute large sections of the Old Testament. For example, when Moses read the words that God had given the people up to that point, it was called the Book of the Covenant: "Then he took the Book of the Covenant and read it to the people. They responded, 'We will do everything the LORD has said; we will obey'" (Exod. 24:7). When we realize that all of the words that were part of the "law of God" or the "Book of the Covenant" were considered God's words, we see that as sections were added to the Old Testament, it all claimed that kind of authority. For example, when Joshua added what God commanded him to add, we read, "And Joshua recorded these things in the Book of the Law of God. Then he took a large stone and set it up there under the oak near the holy place of the LORD" (Josh. 24:26; see Deut. 29:21; 31:24–26; 1 Sam. 10:25; 2 Kgs. 23:2–3).

In the New Testament, a number of passages indicate that all of the Old Testament writings are God's words. Second Timothy 3:16 says, "All Scripture is God-breathed and is useful for teaching, rebuking, correcting and training in righteousness" (NIV). Here "Scripture" (*graphē*) must refer to the Old Testament written Scripture, for that is what the word *graphē* refers to in every one of its 51 occurrences in the New Testament.[3] Furthermore, the "sacred writings" of the Old Testament are what Paul has just referred to in verse 15.

---

[3]But see the discussion below, for two instances where the word *graphē* includes New Testament supplements to the Old Testament.

Paul here affirms that all of the Old Testament writings are *theopneustos*, "breathed out by God." Since it is *writings* that are said to be "breathed out," this breathing must be understood as a metaphor for speaking the words of Scripture. This verse thus states in brief form what was evident in many passages in the Old Testament: the Old Testament writings are God's Word in written form. For every word of the Old Testament, God is the one who spoke (and still speaks) it, although God used human agents to write these words down.[4]

A similar indication of the character of all Old Testament writings as God's words is found in 2 Peter 1:21. Speaking of the prophecies of Scripture (v. 20), which means at least the Old Testament Scriptures to which Peter encourages his readers to give careful attention (v. 19), Peter says that none of these prophecies ever came "by the impulse of man," but that "men moved by the Holy Spirit spoke from God" (RSV). Peter does not deny the role of human volition or personality in the writing of Scripture (he says that the men "spoke"), but he says that the ultimate source of every prophecy was never a man's decision about what he wanted to write, but rather the Holy Spirit's action in the prophet's life, carried out in ways unspecified here (or, in fact, elsewhere in Scripture). This indicates a belief that *all* of the Old Testament "prophecies" (and, in light of vv. 19–20, Peter seems to include in this category all of the written Scripture of the Old Testament) are spoken "from God": that is, they are God's own words.

Many other passages could be cited (see Matt. 19:5; Luke 1:70; 24:25; John 5:45–47; Acts 3:18, 21; 4:25; 13:47; 28:25; Rom. 1:2; 3:2; 9:17; 1 Cor. 9:8–10; Heb. 1:1–2, 6–7), but the pattern of attributing to God the words of Old Testament Scripture should be very clear. Moreover, in several places it is *all* of the words of the prophets or the words of the Old Testament Scriptures that are said to compel belief or to be from God (see Luke 24:25, 27, 44; Acts 3:18; 24:14; Rom. 15:5).

But if Paul meant only the Old Testament writings when he spoke of all "scripture" as God-breathed in 2 Timothy 3:16, how can this verse apply to the New Testament writings as well? Does it say anything about the character of the New Testament writings? To answer that question, we must realize that the Greek word *graphē* ("scripture") was a technical term for the New Testament writers and had a very specialized meaning. Even though it is used 51 times in the New Testament, in every one of those instances it refers to words belonging to the books of the Bible, not to any other words or writings outside the canon of Scripture. Thus, everything that belonged

---

[4]Sometimes Christians have used the words "inspired" and "inspiration" to speak of the fact that the words of Scripture are spoken by God. We have preferred the NIV rendering of 2 Tim. 3:16, "God-breathed," and have used other expressions to say that the words of Scripture are God's very words. This is because the word "inspired" has a weakened sense in ordinary usage today (e.g., the poet was "inspired" to write, or the basketball player gave an "inspired" performance).

in the category "scripture" had the character of being "God-breathed": its words were God's very words.

But at two places in the New Testament we see New Testament writings also being called "scripture" along with the Old Testament writings. In 2 Peter 3:15–16, Peter says,

> And count the forbearance of our Lord as salvation. So also our beloved brother Paul wrote to you according to the wisdom given him, speaking of this as he does in all his letters. There are some things in them hard to understand, which the ignorant and unstable twist to their own destruction, as they do the other scriptures (RSV).

Here Peter shows not only an awareness of the existence of written epistles from Paul, but also a clear willingness to classify "all of his [Paul's] letters" with "the other scriptures." This is an indication that very early in the history of the church all of Paul's epistles were considered to be God's written words in the same sense as the Old Testament texts were.

Similarly, in 1 Timothy 5:18, Paul writes,

> for the scripture says, "You shall not muzzle an ox when it is treading out the grain," and, "The laborer deserves his wages." (RSV)

The first quotation is from Deuteronomy 25:4, but the second occurs nowhere in the Old Testament. It is rather a quotation from Luke 10:7. Paul here quotes Jesus' words as found in Luke's Gospel and calls them "scripture."

These two passages taken together indicate that during the time of the writing of the New Testament documents there was an awareness that *additions* were being made to this special category of writings called "scripture," writings that had the character of being God's very words. Thus, once we establish that a New Testament writing belongs to the special category "scripture," we are correct in applying 2 Timothy 3:16 to that writing as well. Hence, the New Testament as well has the characteristic that Paul attributes to "all scripture": it is "God-breathed," and all its words are the very words of God.

Is there further evidence that the New Testament writers thought of their own writings (not just the Old Testament) as the words of God? In some cases, there is. In 1 Corinthians 14:37, Paul says, "If any one thinks that he is a prophet, or spiritual, he should acknowledge that *what I am writing to you is a command of the Lord*" (RSV). Paul has here instituted a number of rules for church worship at Corinth and has claimed for them the status of "commands of the Lord."

One might think that Paul felt his own commands were inferior to those of Jesus and therefore did not need to be obeyed as carefully. For example, in 1 Corinthians 7:12 he distinguishes his own words from those of Jesus: "To the rest I say, not the Lord . . ." (RSV). However, this simply means that he had possession of *no earthly word that Jesus had spoken on this subject*. We can see that this is the case because in verses 10–11 he simply repeated Jesus' earthly teaching "that the wife should not separate from her husband" and "that the husband should not divorce his wife" (RSV). In verses 12–15, however, he gives his own instructions on a subject that Jesus apparently did not address. What gave him the right to do this? Paul says that he spoke as one "who by the Lord's mercy is trustworthy" (1 Cor. 7:25). He seems to imply here that his own judgments were to be considered as authoritative as the commands of Jesus!

Indications of a similar view of the New Testament writings are found in John 14:26 and 16:13, where Jesus promised that the Holy Spirit would bring all that he had said to the disciples' remembrance, and would guide them into all the truth. This points to the Holy Spirit's work of enabling the disciples to remember and record without error all that Jesus had said. Similar indications are also found in 2 Peter 3:2; 1 Corinthians 2:13; 1 Thessalonians 4:15; and Revelation 22:18–19.

2. We are convinced of the Bible's claims to be God's words as we read the Bible

It is one thing to affirm that the Bible *claims* to be the words of God. It is another thing to be convinced that those claims are true. Our ultimate conviction that the words of the Bible are God's words comes only when the Holy Spirit speaks *in* and *through* the words of the Bible to our hearts and gives us an inner assurance that these are the words of our Creator speaking to us. Apart from the work of the Spirit of God, a person will not receive or accept the truth that the words of Scripture are in fact the words of God.

But those in whom God's Spirit is working recognize that the words of the Bible are the words of God. This process is similar to that by which people who believed in Jesus knew that his words were true. He said, "My sheep hear my voice, and I know them, and they follow me" (John 10:27). Those who are Christ's sheep hear the words of their great Shepherd as they read the words of Scripture, and they are convinced that these words are in fact the words of their Lord.

It is important to remember that this conviction that the words of Scripture are the words of God does *not* come *apart from* the words of Scripture or *in addition to* the words of Scripture. It is not as if the Holy Spirit one day whispers in our ear, "Do you see that Bible sitting on your desk? I want you to know that the words of that Bible are God's words." It is rather as people read Scripture that they hear their Creator's voice speaking to them in the words of Scripture and realize that the book they are reading is unlike any other book, that it is indeed a book of God's own words speaking to their hearts.

3. Other evidence is useful but not an ultimate foundation

To say this is not to deny that other kinds of arguments support the claim that the Bible is God's words. It is helpful for us to learn that the Bible is historically accurate, that it is internally consistent, that it contains prophecies which have been fulfilled hundreds of years later, that it has influenced the course of human history more than any other book, that it has continued changing the lives of millions of individuals throughout its history, that through it people come to find salvation, that it has a majestic beauty and a profound depth of teaching which are unmatched by any other book, and that it claims hundreds of times over to be God's very words. All of these arguments are useful to us and remove obstacles that might otherwise come in the way of our believing Scripture. But all of these arguments taken individually or together cannot finally be convincing. As the Westminster Confession of Faith said in 1643–46,

> We may be moved and induced by the testimony of the Church to an high and reverent esteem of the Holy Scripture. And the heavenliness of the matter, the efficacy of the doctrine, the majesty of the style, the consent of all the parts, the scope of the whole (which is, to give all glory to God), the full discovery it makes of the only way of man's salvation, the many other incomparable excellencies, and the entire perfection thereof, are arguments whereby it doth abundantly evidence itself to be the Word of God: yet notwithstanding, our full persuasion and assurance of the infallible truth and divine authority thereof, is from the inward work of the Holy Spirit bearing witness by and with the Word in our hearts (ch. 1, para. 5).

4. Scripture is self-attesting

Thus, Scripture is "self-attesting." It cannot be "proved" to be God's words by appeal to any higher authority. For if we make our ultimate appeal, for example, to human logic or to scientific truth or to historical investigations to prove that the Bible is God's Word, then these things take on an authority that is even higher than that of the Bible. Therefore, the *ultimate* authority by which Scripture is shown to be God's words must be Scripture itself.

5. Objection: This is a circular argument

Someone may object that to say Scripture proves itself to be God's words is to use a circular argument: we believe that Scripture is God's Word because it claims to be that. And we believe its claims because Scripture is God's Word. And we believe that it is God's Word because it claims to be that, and so forth.

It should be admitted that this is a kind of circular argument. However, that does not make its use invalid, for all arguments for an absolute authority must ultimately appeal to that authority for proof: otherwise the authority would not be an absolute or highest authority. This problem is not unique to the Christian who is arguing for the authority of the Bible. Everyone either implicitly or explicitly uses some kind of circular argument when defending his or her ultimate authority for belief. A few simple examples will illustrate the types of circular arguments that people use to support their beliefs:

"My reason is my ultimate authority because it seems reasonable to me to make it so."

"Logical consistency is my ultimate authority because it is logical to make it so."

"The findings of human sensory experiences are the ultimate authority for discovering what is real and what is not, because our human senses have never discovered anything else: thus, human sense experience tells me that my principle is true."

Each of these arguments utilizes circular reasoning to establish its ultimate standard for truth.

How then does a Christian, or anyone else, choose among the various claims for absolute authorities? Ultimately the Bible will convince us of its truthfulness as we see it to be fully consistent with all that we know about the world around us, about ourselves, and about God. In the actual experience of life, other religious books (such as the *Book of Mormon* or the *Qur'an*) or other intellectual constructions of the human mind (such as logic, human reason, sense experience, scientific methodology, etc.) are seen to be inconsistent or to have shortcomings that deny them authoritative status. In this way we see that a candidate for ultimate authority can be *disqualified* by other factors such as internal contradictions, historical errors, or inability to account for large parts of life. But passing these tests does not by itself *qualify* something to be an absolute authority, or convince us that something should be our absolute authority. We can only be convinced of that by the authority itself.

Because of the excellence of the Bible, we would expect that it would commend itself convincingly to all people as God's Word. However, people do not always recognize Scripture for what it really is, because sin distorts our perception of life and causes us to think incorrectly about God and about creation. Therefore it requires the work of the Holy Spirit, overcoming the effects of sin, to enable us to be persuaded that the Bible is indeed the Word of God and that the claims which it makes for itself are true.

In another sense, then, the argument for the Bible as God's Word and our ultimate authority is *not* a typical circular argument. The process of persuasion is perhaps more like a spiral: as we gain a better understanding of Scripture and what it teaches about God, and as we gain a better understanding of the world around us, these will tend to complement each other, with each one confirming the accuracy of the other. This is not to say that our knowledge of the world around us serves as a higher authority than Scripture, but rather that such knowledge, if it is correct knowledge, continues to give greater and greater assurance and deeper conviction that the Bible is the only truly ultimate authority and that other competing claims for ultimate authority are false.

6. This does not imply dictation from God as the sole means of communication

At this point a word of caution is necessary. The fact that all the words of Scripture are God's words should not lead us to think that God dictated every word of Scripture to the human authors.

When we say that all the words of the Bible are God's words, we are talking about the *result* of the process of bringing Scripture into existence. The question of dictation addresses the *process* that led to that result, or the manner by which God acted in order to ensure the result that he intended. It must be emphasized that the Bible does not speak of only one type of process or one manner by which God communicated to the biblical authors what he wanted to be said. In fact, there is indication of *a wide variety of processes* that God used to bring about the desired result.

On the one hand, there are a few scattered instances of dictation explicitly mentioned in Scripture. When the apostle John saw the risen Lord in a vision on the island of Patmos, Jesus spoke to him as follows: "To the angel of the church in Ephesus *write* . . ." (Rev. 2:1); "And to the angel of the church in Smyrna *write* . . ." (Rev. 2:8); "And to the angel of the church in Pergamum *write* . . ." (Rev. 2:12). These are examples of dictation pure and simple. The risen Lord tells John what to write, and John writes the words that he hears from Jesus.

But in many other sections of Scripture such direct dictation from God is certainly not the manner God used to cause the words of Scripture to come into being. The author of Hebrews says that God spoke to our fathers by the prophets "in many and various ways" (Heb. 1:1). On the other end of the spectrum from dictation we have, for instance, Luke's ordinary historical research for writing his Gospel. He says:

> Inasmuch as many have undertaken to compile a narrative of the things which have been accomplished among us, just as they were delivered to us by those who from the beginning were eyewitnesses and ministers of the word, it seemed good to me also, having followed all things closely for some time past, to write an orderly account for you, most excellent Theophilus . . ." (Luke 1:1–3 RSV).

This is clearly not a process of dictation. Luke used ordinary processes of speaking to eyewitnesses and gathering historical data in order that he might write an accurate account of the life and teachings of Jesus. He did his historical research thoroughly, listening to the reports of many eyewitnesses, and evaluating his evidence carefully. The Gospel that he wrote emphasizes what he thought important and reflects his own characteristic style of writing.

In between these two extremes of dictation on the one hand, and ordinary historical research on the other hand, we have many indications of various ways by which God communicated with the human authors of Scripture. In some cases Scripture speaks of dreams, visions, or of hearing the Lord's voice. In other cases it speaks of men who were with Jesus and observed his life and listened to his teaching, and the Holy Spirit made their memory of these words and deeds completely accurate (John 14:26). Apparently many different methods were used, but it is not important that we discover precisely what these were in each case.

In cases where the human personality and writing style of the author were prominently involved, as seems the case with the major part of Scripture, all that we are able to say is that God's providential oversight and direction of the life of each author was such that their personalities and skills were just what God wanted them to be for the task of writing Scripture. Their backgrounds and training (such as Paul's rabbinic training, or Moses' training in Pharaoh's household, or David's work as a shepherd), their abilities to evaluate events in the world around them, their access to historical data, their judgment with regard to the accuracy of information, and their individual circumstances when they wrote, were all exactly what God wanted them to be, so that when they actually came to the point of putting pen to paper, the words were fully their own words but also fully the words that God wanted them to write, words which God would also claim as his own.

B. Because all the words of Scripture are God's words, to disbelieve or disobey any part of Scripture is to disbelieve or disobey God

The preceding section has argued that all the words in Scripture are God's words. Consequently, to disbelieve or disobey any part of Scripture is to disbelieve or disobey God himself. Thus, Jesus can rebuke his disciples for not believing the Old Testament Scriptures (Luke 24:25: "And he said to them, 'O foolish men, and slow of heart to believe all that the prophets have spoken!'" [RSV]. Believers are to keep or obey the disciples' teaching (John 15:20: "if they kept my word, they will keep yours also" [RSV]). Christians are encouraged to remember "the commandment of the Lord and Savior through your apostles" (2 Pet. 3:2, RSV). To disobey Paul's writings was to make oneself liable to church discipline, such as excommunication (2 Thess. 3:14) and spiritual punishment (2 Cor. 13:2–3), including punishment from God (this is the apparent sense of the passive verb "he is not recognized" in

1 Cor. 14:38). By contrast, God delights in everyone who "trembles" at his word (Isa. 66:2).

C. The truthfulness of Scripture

1. God cannot lie or speak falsely

The essence of the authority of Scripture is its ability to require us to believe and to obey it and to make such belief and obedience equivalent to believing and obeying God himself. This leads us to consider the truthfulness of Scripture, because if we do not think some parts of Scripture are true, we of course will not be able to believe them.

Since the biblical writers repeatedly affirm that the words of the Bible, though human, are God's own words, it is appropriate to look at biblical texts which talk about *the character of God's words* and to apply these to the character of the words of Scripture. Specifically, there are a number of biblical passages that talk about the truthfulness of God's speech. Titus 1:2 speaks of "God, who never lies," or (more literally translated), "the unlying God." Because God is a God who cannot speak a "lie," his statements can always be trusted. Since all of Scripture is spoken by God, all of Scripture must be "unlying," just as God himself is: there can be no untruthfulness in Scripture.

Hebrews 6:18 mentions two unchangeable things (God's oath and his promise) "in which *it is impossible for God to lie.*" Here the author says not merely that God does not lie, but that it is not possible for him to lie. Although the immediate reference is only to oaths and promises, if it is impossible for God to lie in these utterances, then certainly it is impossible for him ever to lie.

2. Therefore all the teachings in Scripture are completely true and without error in any part

Since the words of the Bible are God's words, and since God cannot lie or speak falsely, there is no untruthfulness or error in any part of Scripture. We find this affirmed several places in the Bible.

> The words of the LORD are pure words,
> Like silver tried in a furnace of earth,
> Purified seven times (Ps. 12:6, NKJV).

Here the psalmist uses vivid imagery to speak of the undiluted purity of God's words: there is no imperfection in them. Also in Proverbs 30:5, we read, *"Every word of God proves true*; he is a shield to those who take refuge in him" (RSV, author's italics). It is not just some of the parts of Scripture that are true, but every part. In fact, God's Word is fixed in heaven for all eternity: "For ever, O LORD, *your word is firmly fixed in the heavens"*

(Ps. 119:89, RSV, author's italics).[5] Jesus can speak of the eternal nature of his own words: "Heaven and earth will pass away, but my words will not pass away" (Matt. 24:35, RSV). These verses affirm explicitly what was implicit in the requirement that we believe all of the statements of Scripture, namely, that there is no untruthfulness or falsehood affirmed in any of the statements of the Bible.

3. God's words are the ultimate standard of truth

In John 17, Jesus prays to the Father, "Sanctify them in the truth; *your word is truth*" (John 17:17). This verse is interesting because Jesus does not use the adjectives *alēthinos* or *alēthēs* ("true"), which we might have expected, to say "your word is true." Rather, he uses a noun, *alētheia* ("truth"), to say that God's Word is not simply "true," but it is truth itself.

The difference is significant, for this statement encourages us to think of the Bible not simply as being "true" in the sense that it conforms to some higher standard of truth, but rather to think of the Bible as itself the final standard of truth. The Bible is God's Word, and God's Word is the ultimate definition of what is true and what is not true: God's Word is itself *truth*. Thus we are to think of the Bible as the ultimate standard of truth, the reference point by which every other claim to truthfulness is to be measured. Those assertions that conform with Scripture are "true" while those that do not conform with Scripture are not true.

What then is truth? Truth is what God says, and we have what God says (accurately but not exhaustively) in the Bible.

4. Might some new fact ever contradict the Bible?

Will any new scientific or historical fact ever be discovered that will contradict the Bible? Here we can say with confidence that this will never happen — it is in fact impossible. If any supposed "fact" is ever discovered that is said to contradict Scripture, then (if we have understood Scripture rightly) that "fact" must be false, because God, the author of Scripture, knows all true facts (past, present, and future). No fact will ever turn up that God did not know about ages ago and take into account when he caused Scripture to be written. Every true fact is something that God has known already from all eternity and is something that therefore cannot contradict God's speech in Scripture.

Nevertheless it must be remembered that scientific or historical study (as well as other kinds of study of creation) can cause us to re-examine Scripture to see if it really teaches what we thought it taught. For example, the Bible does not teach that the sun goes around the earth, for it only uses descriptions of phenomena as we see them from our vantage point and

---

[5]Hereafter, the authors will show emphasis by inserting italics in Bible passages.

does not purport to be describing the workings of the universe from some arbitrary "fixed" point somewhere out in space. Yet until the study of astronomy advanced enough to demonstrate the rotation of the earth on its axis, people *assumed* that the Bible taught that the sun goes around the earth. Then the study of scientific data prompted a re-examination of the appropriate biblical texts. Thus, whenever confronted with some "fact" that is said to contradict Scripture, we must not only examine the data cited to demonstrate the fact in question; we must also re-examine the appropriate biblical texts to see if the Bible really teaches what we thought it to teach. We can do so with confidence, for no true fact will ever contradict the words of the God who knows all facts, and who never lies.

D. The inerrancy of Scripture

The previous section addressed the topic of the truthfulness of Scripture. A key component of this topic is the issue of Scripture's inerrancy. This issue is of great concern in the evangelical world today, because on many fronts the truthfulness of Scripture has been brought into question or even abandoned.

With the evidence given above concerning the truthfulness of Scripture, we are now in a position to define biblical inerrancy:

> *The inerrancy of Scripture means that Scripture in the original manuscripts does not affirm anything that is contrary to fact.*

This definition focuses on the question of truthfulness and falsehood in the language of Scripture. The definition in simple terms just means that *the Bible always tells the truth*, and that it always tells the truth *concerning everything it talks about*. This definition does not mean that the Bible tells us every fact there is to know about any one subject, but it affirms that what it does say about any subject is *true*.

It is important to realize at the outset of this discussion that the focus of the controversy over inerrancy is on the question of truthfulness in speech. It must be recognized that absolute truthfulness in speech is consistent with some other types of statements, such as the following:

1. The Bible can be inerrant and still speak in the ordinary language of everyday speech

This is especially true in "scientific" or "historical" descriptions of facts or events. The Bible can speak of the sun rising and the rain falling because from the perspective of the speaker this is exactly what happens. From the standpoint of the speaker, the sun *does* rise and the rain *does* fall, and these are perfectly true descriptions of the natural phenomena which the speaker observes.

A similar consideration applies to numbers when used in counting or in measuring. A reporter can say that 8,000 men were killed in a certain battle without thereby implying that he has counted everyone and that there are not 7,999 or 8,001 dead soldiers. This is also true for measurements. Whether I say, "I don't live far from my office," or "I live a little over a mile from my office," or "I live 1¼ miles from my office," or "I live 1.287 miles from my office," all four statements are still approximations to some degree of accuracy. In both of these examples, and in many others that could be drawn from daily life, the limits of truthfulness would depend on the degree of precision implied by the speaker and expected by his original hearers. It should not trouble us, then, to affirm both that the Bible is absolutely truthful in everything it says and that it uses ordinary language to describe natural phenomena or to give approximations or round numbers when those are appropriate in the context.

2. The Bible can be inerrant and still include loose or free quotations

The method by which one person quotes the words of another person is a procedure that in large part varies from culture to culture. While in contemporary American and British culture, we are used to quoting a person's exact words when we enclose the statement in quotation marks, written Greek at the time of the New Testament had no quotation marks or equivalent kinds of punctuation, and an accurate citation of another person needed to include only a correct representation of the *content* of what the person said (rather like our use of indirect quotations): it was not expected to cite each word exactly. Thus, inerrancy is consistent with loose or free quotations of the Old Testament or of the words of Jesus, for example, so long as the *content* is not false to what was originally stated. The original writer did not ordinarily imply that he was using the exact words of the speaker and only those, nor did the original hearers expect verbatim quotation in such reporting.

3. It is consistent with inerrancy to have unusual or uncommon grammatical constructions in the Bible

Some of the language of Scripture is elegant and stylistically excellent. Other scriptural writings contain the rough-hewn language of ordinary people. At times this includes a failure to follow the commonly accepted "rules" of grammatical expression (such as the use of a plural verb where grammatical rules would require a singular verb). These stylistically incorrect grammatical statements (several of which are found in the Book of Revelation) should not trouble us, for they do not affect the truthfulness of the statements under consideration: a statement can be ungrammatical but still entirely true. For example, an uneducated backwoodsman in some rural area may be the most trusted man in the county, even though his grammar is poor, because he has earned a reputation for never telling a lie.

Similarly, there are some statements in Scripture (in the original languages) that are ungrammatical (according to current standards of proper grammar at that time) but still inerrant because they are completely true. God used ordinary people who used their own ordinary language. The issue is not elegance in style but *truthfulness* in speech.

4. It is consistent with inerrancy to have mistakes in later copies of the Bible

Sometimes people object to inerrancy by saying that mistakes have been introduced into copies of the Bible as they have been passed down through the centuries. They say that such mistakes are found not only in modern language copies, such as English, but also in ancient Hebrew and Greek manuscripts. Why should we argue for an inerrant Bible when there are probably some mistakes in all our copies?

When we stop to think about it, it would require a monumental miracle of vast proportions if God were to keep from mistakes every single person in the world who ever wrote down or printed a portion of the Bible, or even a single verse. There are hundreds of millions of Bibles in the world. Even in manuscripts from the ancient world, we have over 5,000 copies of the whole or parts of the Greek New Testament, made by thousands of different people over the course of several centuries, and no doubt thousands more were made that did not survive. Do we really think that God would so intervene at every moment of history when someone wanted to copy a chapter or a book by hand, or even a verse, that the person's hand would be guided (by an angel perhaps?) to make no mistakes in copying, even in spelling? Surely this is a bizarre idea.

Instead, what we find is that ancient Hebrew and Greek manuscripts were for the most part copied very carefully, and with remarkable accuracy, but there are still small variations in spelling or wording here and there (these are called "textual variants," and they are not kept secret from English readers, but are noted in modern English translations by footnotes that say something like, "other ancient manuscripts read . . ."). God did not miraculously prevent mistakes from occurring in the copies.

Is there anything inerrant then? Yes, the original manuscripts were "inerrant," much like the original Ten Commandments that God himself carved in the two tablets of stone. And what we have today are copies that are very, very close to the originals. This is an important difference. If there were errors even in the original manuscript that Moses wrote, for example, or Paul, then there would be nothing that we could trust completely. But if the mistakes have come into the copies, then we can trust the whole text *except* where there are significant differences in the remaining manuscripts, which is very few places.[6]

Another way to say this is that God claims the original manuscripts, the "Scriptures," as his words. Any mistakes in the originals would be God's mistakes! But any mistakes in the subsequent copies are man's mistakes in copying, not God's mistakes in what he originally said to his people.

An analogy from American history is helpful here. The original copy of the Constitution of the United States is housed in a building called the National Archives in Washington, D. C. If through some terrible event that building were destroyed and the original copy of the Constitution lost, could we ever find out what the Constitution said? Of course: we would compare hundreds of copies, and where they all agreed, we would have reason for confidence that we had the exact words of the original document.

A similar process has occurred in determining the original words of the Bible. For over 99 percent of the words of the Bible, the surviving copies agree, and we can say that we *know* what the original manuscript said. Even for many of the verses where there are textual variants, the correct decision is often quite clear (there may be an obvious copying error, for example), and there are really very few places where the textual variant is both difficult to evaluate and significant in determining the meaning. In the small percentage of cases where there is significant uncertainty about what the original text said, the general sense of the sentence is usually quite clear from the context.

This is not to say that the study of textual variants is unimportant, but it is to say that the study of textual variants has not left us in confusion about what the original manuscripts said.[7] It has rather brought us extremely close to the content of those original manuscripts. For most practical purposes, then, the *current published scholarly texts* of the Hebrew Old Testament and Greek New Testament *are the same as the original manuscripts*. Therefore, the doctrine of inerrancy affects how we think not only about the original manuscripts but also about our present manuscripts, and our present Bible translations, as well.

E.   Written Scripture is our final authority

It is important to realize that the final form in which Scripture is authoritative is its *written* form. It was the words of God *written* on the tablets of stone that Moses deposited in the ark of the covenant. Later, God commanded Moses and subsequent prophets to *write* their words in a book.

---

[6]Note Deuteronomy 31:26–29, which makes a distinction between the original that God caused Moses to write and to store beside the ark, and what the people later will do in straying from these words. This passage is not, of course, a technical exposition of text criticism, or even a description of corruption of copies of the words of God, but it is suggestive in the way that it indicates the importance of returning to the original (verse 26) in contrast with the possibility of human sin and corruption that deviates from what God originally said (verse 29).

[7]An excellent survey of the work of studying textual variants in the extant manuscripts of the New Testament is Bruce M. Metzger, *The Text of the New Testament: Its Transmission, Corruption, and Restoration*, 2nd ed. (Oxford: Clarendon Press, 1968).

And it was *written* Scripture (*graphē*) which Paul said was "God-breathed" (2 Tim. 3:16). This is important because people sometimes (intentionally or unintentionally) attempt to substitute some other final standard than the written words of Scripture. For example, people will sometimes refer to "what Jesus really said" and claim that when we translate the Greek words of the Gospels back into the Aramaic language that Jesus originally spoke, we can gain a better understanding of Jesus' words than was given by the writers of the Gospels. In other cases, people have claimed to know "what Paul really thought" even when that is different from the meaning of the words he wrote. Or they have spoken of "what Paul would have said if he had been consistent with the rest of his theology." Similarly, others have spoken of "the church situation to which Matthew was writing" and have attempted to give normative force either to that situation or to the solution they think Matthew was attempting to bring about in that situation.

In all of these instances we must admit that asking about the words or situations that lie "behind" the text of Scripture may at times be helpful to us in understanding what the text means. Nevertheless, *our hypothetical reconstructions of these words or situations* can never replace or compete with *Scripture itself* as the final authority, nor should we ever allow them to contradict or call into question the accuracy of any of the statements of Scripture. We must continually remember that we have in the Bible God's own speech, and we must not try to "improve" on it in some way, for this cannot be done. Rather, we should seek to understand it and then trust it and obey it with our whole heart.

F.   How should we respond to God's Word?

Once we are convinced that the Bible is God's Word, and that every word in the Bible as originally written is a word that God spoke to his people for their benefit, then certain things will follow. Specifically, we should respond to the Bible in a way that is different from the way we respond to every other book in the world.

1.   We should trust every detail of meaning in God's Word

If these are God's very words, we can be confident that every detail of meaning is what God intended. These words are perfect. There is no flaw in them. "And the words of the LORD are *flawless*, like silver refined in a furnace of clay, purified seven times" (Ps. 12:6, NIV). If a refining furnace purges away all impurities in silver, then silver that has been refined not once but seven times is perfectly pure.

It is not as though God is concerned to communicate some main ideas but pays no attention to the details. No, everything that God speaks is perfect: "*Every word* of God is flawless; he is a shield to those who take refuge in him" (Prov. 30:5, NIV).

Jesus also refers to "every word" of Scripture, and has such confidence in it that he says we are to "live" by it: "It is written, 'Man shall not live by bread alone, but by *every word* that proceeds from the mouth of God'" (Matt. 4:4). Though Deuteronomy had been written over 1,400 years earlier, in Jesus' view every word of this Scripture was still the word of God by which people are to live.

In fact, Jesus places confidence in the individual letters of the words of Old Testament Scripture. He mentions the smallest letter of the alphabet and then a small part of one letter when he declares, "For truly, I say to you, till heaven and earth pass away, *not an iota, not a dot*, will pass from the law until all is accomplished" (Matt. 5:18). Every letter was what God had spoken!

In arguing with his opponents, Jesus sometimes based an argument on one letter of one word of the Old Testament, as in Matthew 22:41–46:

> While the Pharisees were gathered together, Jesus asked them, "What do you think about the Christ? Whose son is he?" "The son of David," they replied. He said to them, "How is it then that David, speaking by the Spirit, calls him 'Lord'? For he says, 'The Lord said to my Lord: "Sit at my right hand until I put your enemies under your feet."' If then David calls him 'Lord,' how can he be his son?" No one could say a word in reply, and from that day on no one dared to ask him any more questions.

In order for Jesus' argument to work, he needs to make the point that David calls the Messiah "my Lord." Now the word for "my" in the Hebrew text of Psalm 110 is a translation of just one letter added on to the Hebrew word for "Lord." But Jesus is willing to base an argument on it.[8]

Paul likewise depends on a very small detail when he says, "The promises were spoken to Abraham and to his seed. The Scripture does not say 'and to seeds,' meaning many people, but 'and to your seed,' meaning one person, who is Christ" (Gal. 3:16). Paul pays attention to the difference between singular and plural in quoting Genesis 13:15, and emphasizes that the Hebrew "seed" is singular.

It is evident that Paul does not hesitate to depend on any detail in the Old Testament, for he says that *"whatever was written* in former days was written for our instruction, that by steadfastness and by the encouragement of the scriptures we might have hope" (Rom. 15:4, RSV). He emphasizes the usefulness of every part of Scripture when he says that *"All Scripture* is God-breathed and is useful for teaching, rebuking, correcting and training

---

[8]Other cases where New Testament writers based their argument on one single word of Old Testament Scripture are compiled by Roger Nicole, "New Testament Use of the Old Testament," in *Revelation and the Bible*, ed. Carl F. H. Henry (Grand Rapids: Baker, 1958), 139. He lists Matt. 2:15; 4:10; 13:35; 22:44; Mark 12:36; Luke 4:8; 20:42, 43; John 8:17; 10:34; 19:37; Acts 23:5; Rom. 4:3, 9, 23; 15:9–12; 1 Cor. 6:16; Gal. 3:8, 10, 13; Heb. 1:7; 2:12; 3:13; 4:7; 12:26.

in righteousness" (2 Tim. 3:16). Every single thing written in Scripture—"all Scripture"—is breathed out by God, and every bit of it is therefore "useful" for teaching and training us in the ways of God. Nothing in Scripture is unimportant.

2. We should love and treasure every bit of Scripture

There is something wrong with us spiritually if we do not deeply delight in, and even love, the Word of God. "Oh, how I *love* your law!" says the author of Psalm 119. "It is my meditation all the day" (Ps. 119:97, RSV). Whereas others might tend to delight in material riches, the psalmist sets a higher standard for us: "I *love* your commandments above gold, above fine gold" (Ps. 119:127). Not only are God's words more desirable than gold, they are also more pleasant than the sweetest food: "More to be desired are they than gold, even much fine gold; *sweeter also than honey* and drippings of the honeycomb" (Ps. 19:10, RSV). We should treasure God's Word more than any other possession—"The law of your mouth is better to me than thousands of gold and silver pieces" (Ps. 119:72).

3. We should tremble at God's Word

If we were to come into the very presence of God and hear him speak, we would tremble. But in Scripture we *do* hear him speak, and it should cause us to tremble! God says, "This is the one I esteem: he who is humble and contrite in spirit, and *trembles* at my word" (Isa. 66:2, NIV). The psalmist says, "Rulers persecute me without cause, but my heart *trembles* at your word" (119:161, NIV). If we are to tremble at God's Word, surely we should reverence it and treat it with utmost respect.

4. We should recognize that God's Word is powerful, eternal, and worthy of praise

Perhaps from too much casual familiarity Christians today seldom realize the power of God's Word. It has power to change hearts and even to give unbelievers new life, power of a kind possessed by no other words. Peter says, "For *you have been born again,* not of perishable seed, but of imperishable, *through the living and enduring word of God*" (1 Pet. 1:23, NIV). The Word of God is so powerful it is "like fire" and "like a hammer that breaks a rock in pieces" (Jer. 23:29, NIV). It is like rain that God sends so that it "will accomplish what I desire and achieve the purpose for which I sent it" (Isa. 55:11, NIV). The Word of God is "sharper than any two-edged sword, piercing to the division of soul and spirit, of joints and marrow, and discerning the thoughts and intentions of the heart" (Heb. 4:12, RSV). Yet in all its power it also nourishes us daily: "Man shall not live by bread alone, but by every word that proceeds from the mouth of God" (Matt. 4:4, RSV).

The words of Scripture, like the words that Jesus spoke in his earthly ministry, are "spirit and life" (John 6:63).

In fact, so wonderful is God's Word that we are also to praise it: "In God, *whose word I praise*, in the LORD, whose *word I praise*—in God I trust; I will not be afraid" (Ps. 56:10–11, NIV). Now praise like this is due to God alone, so the psalmist in praising God's Word must understand that he is also praising God himself.

5. We should fill our thoughts and lives with God's Word

We are not to read the Bible once or twice and forget it. We are to meditate on it continually. "But his delight is in the law of the LORD, and on his law he *meditates* day and night" (Ps. 1:2, NIV). Meditation is appropriate to Scripture, because every detail, every word, every nuance of meaning comes to us from God himself, and nothing is to be missed. Of course, included among these details are nuances and aspects of meaning related to gender—the special concern of this book. These details of meaning also belong to Scripture, and along with all other details contribute to making it "profitable" for us (2 Tim. 3:16). They are put there by God for our benefit. Repeated inspection and study will only reveal to us more and more of the rich truths God has put in his Word. This is why Scripture memorization is so valuable: it solidifies in our minds every detail of the words of God. We are to memorize Scripture so that it will be with us always: "I have *hidden your word in my heart* that I might not sin against you" (Ps. 119:11, NIV).

What an amazing gift God gave us when he gave his Word! It is astounding that the infinite, eternal, omnipotent Creator has spoken to us in words we can actually understand, ponder, rely on, and obey. They are words for our benefit and blessing, not for our harm. They are words that bring us into an intimate relationship with God himself. Such a great treasure from God will never pass away: "The grass withers, and the flower falls, but the word of the Lord abides for ever" (1 Pet. 1:24–25, RSV).

G. Faithfulness to God's Word

God warns against confusing his Word with human words, saying to the prophets, "'Let the prophet who has a dream tell his dream, but let the one who has my word speak it faithfully. For what has straw to do with grain?' declares the LORD" (Jer. 23:28). Jesus condemned the Pharisees and teachers of the law who put their own teachings ahead of God's words: "And why do you break the command of God for the sake of your tradition?" (Matt. 15:3).

By contrast, God commends those who so reverence his words that they "tremble at his word" (Isa. 66:2, 5). He prohibits adding to or subtracting from his words in the most severe terms (Deut. 4:2; 12:32; Prov. 30:6).

These commandments apply to our whole life. But they also have implications for the task of translating the Bible. We are to remain faithful to every word, and thus to every part of the meaning of Scripture, as far as we are able, as we deal with translating the very words of God. Faithfulness in translation is one aspect of faithfulness to God himself.[9]

Translators from the past have recognized this obligation. Hear what Martin Luther says:

> I have been very careful to see that where everything turns on a single passage, I have kept to the original quite literally and have not lightly departed from it. . . . I preferred to do violence to the German language rather than to depart from the word.[10]

---

[9]Are we wrong to say that this whole issue is ultimately one of faithfulness to God in the work of translation? We are aware that Carson warns against escalating rhetoric. For example, regarding the change made by the NIVI in Psalm 1:1 from singular ("Blessed is the man . . .") to plural ("Blessed are those . . ."), Carson writes, "But if one side insists that the other, by its translation judgment in this instance, is twisting the very words of God or the like, it should be obvious by now that it is betraying ignorance of translation problems and the nature of gender and number systems in different languages. That side is merely blessing its own translation preferences with divine sanction" (*The Inclusive-Language Debate,* 108). Later Carson says that both sides should "try to avoid manipulative language" and adds that "arguments that tie your opinion to Christian orthodoxy . . . have the effect of marginalizing and manipulating people who, in your best moments, you would happily acknowledge to be orthodox" (196).

We must take Carson's concern seriously. We ourselves have struggled to present a fair and balanced view. On the one hand, we are convinced that some of the changes have unnecessarily sacrificed accuracy. On the other hand, we know that esteemed brothers in Christ disagree with us. Scripture counsels, "If it is possible, as far as it depends on you, live at peace with everyone" (Rom. 12:18, NIV). But if faithfulness to God's Word is indeed at stake, peace may not always be possible.

If we agreed with Carson's premise that if it was just a matter of "translation preferences," we would not make these statements about faithfulness to God's Word. If Carson understood these changes as we understand them, that is, as changes that (1) are not required by the current state of the English language, (2) are not justified by the meaning of the words in the original text, and (3) result in the systematic loss of a certain kind of meaning in English translations (for example, the loss of male-oriented meanings and nuances), then perhaps he too would see this as a matter of faithfulness to God and his Word.

The appropriate answer to make to us, if someone objects to these claims, is not a command or a plea, "Stop making such claims about faithfulness to God and his Word," for that would just be a plea asking us to stop saying what our understanding of the issue makes us think is true.

The appropriate kind of answer rather should be an argument attempting to show us that gender-neutral translations do *not* systematically exclude a certain kind of male-oriented meaning, or an argument showing that certain Hebrew or Greek words do *not* have the male-oriented nuances that we claim, or an argument showing that the problem is not that people dislike gender-specific language but rather that they actually misunderstand the male-specific language in the Bible. (We recognize that Carson and Strauss have attempted to make such arguments elsewhere in their books, and we appreciate the opportunity to interact with them over those arguments.)

[10]Martin Luther, "On Translating: An Open Letter," in *Selected Writings of Martin Luther,* ed. T. G. Tappert, trans. by C. M. Jacobs, rev. by E. T. Bachman, vol. 4 (Philadelphia: Fortress, 1967), 186.

CHAPTER 10

How to Translate

To evaluate the issues properly we need to have a sense for what a translation does. But how can we decide what a "good" Bible translation is? We begin with what the Bible itself says. In fact, the Bible itself provides us with some crucial guidance—not with specific instructions about how to translate, but with the foundation, explaining why Bible translation is part of God's plan for the church.

A. Translation based on the Bible's command

In the Great Commission Jesus instructs the disciples to "make disciples of *all nations, . . . teaching them* to obey everything I have commanded you" (Matt. 28:19–20, NIV). This implies that Jesus' teaching will spread among the nations and will be understood and obeyed. But that means that his teaching has to become available to these nations—and they speak thousands of different languages. Therefore, when Jesus gave the Great Commission it implied that his followers eventually would have to translate his teaching into many different languages. Translation of Jesus' teaching (and, by implication, the message of the whole Bible) plays a part in the total process of fulfilling the Great Commission.

Acts 2 points to the same conclusion. On the Day of Pentecost the Holy Spirit gave the gift of tongues to the disciples, enabling them miraculously to speak the message in other languages. On that day, the day when the gospel began to go to all nations, an amazing miracle from God hinted that translation into other languages (but not necessarily miraculous translation!) would be a part of spreading the gospel message.

But "making disciples" does not mean merely translating the Bible and then throwing the completed version at some prospective disciple. We need to include evangelism and a process of growth that involves much teaching

(Eph. 4:11; 1 Cor. 12:28). A translation of the Bible lies at the base of this process, but afterwards the teaching is built upon the translation.

The Bible defines our goal. But what difficulties confront translators in practice?

B. Difficulties in translating

To appreciate some of the difficulties, we need to take a look at the actual process of translation and at the human languages with which a translator works. God gave us language as one of his greatest gifts. But it is not only a great gift—it is an exceedingly rich and complex gift. That very richness makes translation a challenging operation.

1. Words take different meanings

A single word like "dog" or "trunk" in English reveals vast complexity. One dictionary lists no less than four distinct words "dog." It has only one entry for "trunk," but six distinct senses listed under it.[1] How do we decide among these senses?

Native speakers of English usually decide instantly and without effort which sense of a word is right. They use hints deriving from (1) the grammar (is the word a noun, a verb, a direct object, etc.? And what grammatical construction does it fit into?), (2) the relationship to the larger context — that is, the other words, sentences, paragraphs, and the whole communication ("discourse") and (3) the situation (about what circumstances is the speaker talking, and what does he expect us to do in response?). These three factors can be called the grammatical context, the discourse context, and the situational context. They reveal which of several senses of a word the speaker is using.

But occasionally there are ambiguities. At times it is a challenge to know which sense of a word a speaker is using. In fact, when breakdowns in communication occur, it is often because two people are using the same word in different ways.

When we try to translate between two languages, the challenges become even greater. Suppose that we are translating the Old Testament from Hebrew to English. We must deal with the dictionary definitions for both Hebrew and English words. Though two words from the two languages may roughly correspond in meaning (Hebrew *ben* and English "son," for example), they seldom match *exactly*.

In many cases, because a word has several different possible meanings, no one word in English may match all the uses in another language. For example, consider the word *ruach* in Hebrew. A beginner may be told that

---

[1] *Webster's Ninth New Collegiate Dictionary* (Springfield, MA: Merriam-Webster, 1987).

ruach means "breath, wind, spirit."[2] He might naively assume that this means that the word *ruach* means an amalgamation of "breath, wind, spirit" all at the same time. But no—in any one occurrence, only *one* of these meanings occurs. For example, Genesis 6:17 says, "I will bring a flood of waters upon the earth, to destroy all flesh in which is the *breath* [*ruach*] of life from under heaven; everything that is on the earth shall die" (RSV). The Hebrew word *ruach* is correctly translated "breath" in the KJV, NASB, NKJV, RSV, and NIV. Next, 1 Kings 18:45 says, "And in a little while the heavens grew black with clouds and *wind* [*ruach*], and there was a great rain" (RSV). The same Hebrew word *ruach* occurs, and KJV, NASB, NKJV, RSV, and NIV all correctly translate with "wind." Job 4:15 says, "A *spirit* [*ruach*] glided past my face; the hair of my flesh stood up" (RSV). KJV, NASB, NKJV, RSV, and NIV all have "spirit," in the sense of a ghostly apparition.

In each case the context clearly indicates which of the three main meanings is appropriate. In general, we seek to find the appropriate English expression that matches *the meaning of Hebrew in a particular context.*

2. Sentence formation differs from language to language

In translation we also must deal with the meaning of whole phrases, sentences, and paragraphs, not simply isolated words. Each word in a sentence contributes to the meaning. But we want to translate the message, the meaning of the whole, not simply words in isolation. Translators must take into account the many ways in which word meanings interact when they occur in discourse.

We find, for example, that languages differ in the way they put words and sentences together. Greek may use long sentences: Ephesians 1:3–14 is one sentence in Greek. Current English style prefers shorter sentences. Hebrew sentences tend to be shorter still.

The normal order of words in a sentence may differ between languages. For example, if we translate Ephesians 1:15–16 woodenly, word by word, it comes out like this:

> On-account-of this also I, having-heard the in you faith in the Lord Jesus and the love the to all the saints, not I stop thanking about you mention making at the prayers my.

That is not how we would say it in English! Many factors contribute to the difference. In English, we distinguish subject, predicate, and object mostly by word order. "Man bites dog" differs from "Dog bites man." In Greek, the difference between subject and object is not usually shown by word order, but by the endings that attach to nouns (called case endings). This device leaves the Greek speaker free to rearrange the word order while keeping the same subject and object.

---

[2]BDB gives precisely these three terms at the beginning of its entry for *ruach* (924).

We find also that grammatical features in one language do not match those in another language in a one-to-one fashion. The beginner learns that the Greek aorist tense means "simple past action." For example, Matthew 4:21 says, "Jesus *called* them" (NIV). The simple past tense "called" in English corresponds to the Greek aorist tense. But in other cases the Greek aorist tense has nothing to do with past time. In Matthew 5:16 the commandment "*Let* your light so *shine*" (RSV) uses the aorist tense, referring to what the disciples should do *in the future*. The more advanced student has to learn that such a thing regularly happens with the Greek aorist imperative, which is used to issue commands.

Or again, the beginner learns that the Greek conjunction *hina* means "in order that," and is used to show purpose. For example, Romans 4:13 says, "I have planned many times to come to you ... *in order that* [*hina*] I might have a harvest among you" (NIV). But in other cases the same meaning can be translated with "so that," or "so," or an infinitive in English:

I long to see you, *so that* [*hina*] I may impart to you some spiritual gift . . . (Rom. 1:11, NIV).

Send the crowds away, *so* [*hina*] they can go to the villages and buy themselves some food (Matt. 14:15, NIV).

All this took place *to* [*hina*] fulfill what the Lord had said through the prophet (Matt. 1:22, NIV)

In other cases, the Greek word *hina* does not carry the sense of purpose, and may need a different handling in translation:

"Lord, I do not deserve to [*hina*] have you come under my roof" (Matt. 8:8, NIV).

"If you are the Son of God, tell [*hina* is added here] these stones to become bread" (Matt. 4:3, NIV).

. . . do to others what you would have [*hina* is added here] them do to you (Matt. 7:12, NIV).

In Matthew 4:3 and 7:12, no distinct English word translates the Greek word *hina*. Instead, the sentence as a whole in English enables us to connect two parts together[3] in a manner corresponding correctly to the meaning in Greek.

We could go on and on discussing such differences. Anyone studying a foreign language begins to notice such differences. But he learns the differences only after he passes an initially naïve stage in which he learns over-simple formulas like "The Greek word *hina* means 'in order that.'"

---

[3]Roughly speaking, "tell" and "these stones to become bread" are connected in English in a way corresponding to the function of *hina* in Greek; likewise, "what you would have" and "them do to you" are so connected. But the meaning derives from the whole construction, and cannot be neatly assigned to just one word in it.

3. Form and meaning

The naïve person may think, "Just translate by putting in equivalent words, one by one." But as we have seen, such a procedure often does not adequately capture the meaning of the original. In fact, translators want to express the same *meaning* in English as was expressed in the original. To achieve this goal, they find that many times they must not simply translate mechanically, word for word. That is, they do not preserve *form*. A single word in Hebrew (like *ruach*, "breath, wind, spirit") is not always translated the same way in English. A single grammatical tense (like the Greek aorist) is not always translated the same way. A single construction (like the Greek conjunction *hina*) is not always translated the same way. The translator alters these *forms* in English, precisely in order to express the fullest possible meaning most accurately in English.

This kind of flexibility in translation is not always easy for beginners to achieve. Hence, teachers of translation summarize it in a simple way: "translate *meaning*, not *form*."

Naïve Bible students can easily make a mistake here. They believe, rightly, that every detail in the message of original manuscripts, including every individual word, was breathed out by God (2 Tim. 3:16). But then they may wrongly infer that a *translation* must proceed on a strict, mechanical, word-for-word basis. Such reasoning does not recognize that in the original languages, God himself combined the words into sentences in order to convey a message. We do not do justice to God's speech unless we recognize that he spoke the words *in sentences and paragraphs*, not in isolation. Faithfully rendering his speech in another language means attending all aspects of God's speech, not just the words in isolation. When we read a letter to a friend, we read the message using the words. Just so when we read God's Word, the Bible.[4]

4. The theory of dynamic equivalent translation

Linguists and teachers of translators developed the theory of "dynamic equivalent" translation to spell out in detail the differences between form and meaning, the differences between different languages, and the kind of practices that lead to sound translation.[5] Central to the theory was the principle of translating meaning in preference to form. Thus, "dynamic

---

[4]The New Testament writers frequently quote from the Septuagint, thereby illustrating that a translation that is not always word-for-word is serviceable. The King James Version, in the places that deviate from pure formal equivalence, also recognizes that translation must convey the meaning of the whole, not merely the words in isolation.

[5]See especially Eugene Nida, *Toward a Science of Translating; With Special Reference to Principles and Procedures Involved in Bible Translating* (Leiden: Brill, 1964); Eugene Nida and Charles R. Taber, *The Theory and Practice of Translation* (Leiden: Brill, 1969); both of which were early landmarks in the field. A more recent representative is Jan de Waard and Eugene A.

equivalence" means choosing an expression that yields equivalent *meaning* in the target language. "Formal equivalence," by contrast, means choosing an expression that has one-to-one matching *forms* in the target language, regardless of whether the meaning is the same. The standard theory of dynamic equivalence thus advocates *translating meaning rather than form.*

Such a summary is clearly on the right track. It encourages translators to concentrate on what is important, and to restructure the form when it is necessary to convey the meaning. Such an emphasis is especially helpful in a situation where communication is difficult, because it is better to transmit at least a minimal core content than to produce a formal equivalent that does not work at all.

In addition to this basic principle, early "dynamic equivalence" theory spelled out the implications for various kinds of special cases. For example, it said that you may make explicit in the target language information that is linguistically implicit in the original. For instance, suppose that there is no noun for "love" in the target language, but only a verb. When you have a noun for "love" in Greek (*agapē*), you may have to translate in a way that includes an explicit subject and object in the target, "God loves you" or "you love God."

Consider another, more complex case. Compare two translations of Ephesians 1:18:

... that you may know what is the hope of His calling (NASB)
... that you may know what is the hope to which he has called you (RSV)

The underlying Greek, word for word, runs like this: "the hope of-the calling his." Strictly speaking, neither the NASB nor the RSV (nor the KJV nor any other major English translation) is purely "formally equivalent." A pure word-for-word matching results in ungrammatical English. The NASB has done a minimal rearrangement of the words, in order to achieve grammatical English.

But now there is still a difficulty. "Of" in English is not a perfect match for the underlying Greek construction, which uses the genitive case rather than a separate word like "of." "Of" is not an exact equivalent. And in fact,

---

Nida, *From One Language to Another: Functional Equivalence in Bible Translating* (Nashville, TN: Nelson, 1986).

Carson says that since 1986 advocates of dynamic equivalence have preferred the term "functional equivalence" (Carson, *The Inclusive-Language Debate* [Grand Rapids: Baker, 1998], 71). However, Osborne uses both phrases interchangeably in his argument for inclusive-language translations (Grant Osborne, "Do Inclusive-Language Bibles Distort Scripture? No," *Christianity Today* 41:12 [Oct. 27, 1997], 33–39). Mark Strauss also uses both the phrase "dynamic equivalence" and "functional equivalence" for this theory of translation (Strauss, *Distorting Scripture? The Challenge of Bible Translation & Gender Accuracy* [Downers Grove, IL: InterVarsity, 1998], 82–83). We will use the term "dynamic equivalence theory" to describe the early developments. Later in this chapter we describe later developments, which are probably best described by other labels.

in this case at least, it introduces the possibility of misunderstanding. English readers may easily understand the NASB as meaning "the hope that he will call you." But that is not what Paul means. In Greek the actual meaning is closer to "hope arising from his calling" or "hope pertaining to his calling." The RSV, NIV, and GNB all have "the hope to which he has called you," which heads off the possible misunderstanding, and is one useful solution. They have restructured the form, and thereby clarified the meaning. In the process, they have also put in the extra word "you." That word is not there in Greek. So is it illegitimate in English? No. It is linguistically *implicit* in Greek. If the Greek explicitly speaks of "his calling," that is, God's calling, it *implies* that God is calling *someone*. Who is "the someone?" By implication, it is "you."

The theory of dynamic equivalence allows even more. At times, because of cultural differences, target readers within a particular language and culture are almost *bound* to misunderstand, not so much the words as the cultural significance of the act. In one target culture, meeting someone with palm branches signifies scorn. So what does one do with Jesus' Palm Sunday entry in John 12:13, where the crowds "took branches of palm trees and went out to meet him" (NIV)? In a case like this, the theory allows the translator to put in the necessary cultural information that was not linguistically there in the original. Instead of saying "they . . . went out to *meet* him," one says, "They took branches of palm trees and went out to *welcome* him." The translator compromises on linguistic meaning here (the Greek text does not specify that people were welcoming Jesus), but the theory says it is right to add "to welcome" in order that the total act of communication may be successful.

Dynamic equivalence theory was a useful tool to encourage translators to reckon again and again with *meaning*, not simply *form*. It is particularly important when one is training people who start out with a naïve understanding of language. Their impulse is often to translate mechanically, word for word, *especially* when they have a very imperfect grasp of one of the two languages with which they are working. They have, perhaps, learned a simple beginner's rule, such as "Hebrew *ben* means *son*." The temptation is just mechanically to replace the word *ben* with "son" everywhere, *ignoring context and ignoring the nuances of meaning to which the context points.*

C. Use of early dynamic equivalence theory

We must understand the context in which the theory of dynamic equivalence developed. In the twentieth century an academic field called "structural linguistics" developed theoretical reflections on the issues of translation. At nearly the same time Wycliffe Bible Translators and other translation agencies began the task of translating the Bible into thousands of languages where people were still unreached with the gospel. The theoretical work of the academics and the practical work of the actual translators grew together as people wrestled with the problems of translation.

1. Developing the theory of dynamic equivalent translation

The people doing actual Bible translation into thousands of languages found out that translation into tribal languages involves extra challenges. Many of these languages have grammatical systems very different from Indo-European languages. In addition, the recipients, the people in the "target" group, typically have little or no previous knowledge of Christianity. The target language may not have religious vocabulary directly matching some key ideas in the Bible.[6]

2. Emphasis on clarity

Because translation into tribal languages struggles with such a mass of difficulty, in its early development the theory put a great emphasis on clarity: "Make sure that what you say is clear. Make it understandable, and set it forth in smooth grammatical form."

That is good advice for missionaries when they first enter a culture. But in the long run this great stress on clarity can tempt people to forget that the Bible in the original languages is not always interested merely in simple clarity and immediate understanding. The Bible makes people think. It develops complex theological reasoning. It presents rich poetic expressions. Peter confesses that some things in Paul's writings are "hard to understand" (2 Pet. 3:16), and Daniel 9:27 is about as cryptic in Hebrew as it is in the KJV.[7] We do not mean to say that such passages are *impossible* to understand, but they certainly require study.

Second, because of the unique demands of unreached people, the early theory urged us to make everything explicit. In doing this, it can easily tempt people to believe that there is no difference in meaning *at all* between explicit and implicit information. But in fact, there are subtle differences, as we shall see.

---

[6]The problem can be illustrated from the Septuagint, the ancient Greek translation of the Old Testament. The Greek word for "God," *theos*, in the pagan, polytheistic Greek context, meant one of the "gods" of the Greek pantheon. No word in Greek perfectly meshed with the Old Testament teaching about the one true God. When the Old Testament was originally translated from Hebrew to Greek, the translators had to decide what was the best rendering *within the constraints of Greek vocabulary*.

The Greek word *harmartia*, with the meaning "failure, fault," can mean "guilt" within a philosophical context. But it does not perfectly mesh with Old Testament teaching about sin before a holy, infinite God.

[7]In the KJV, Daniel 9:27 says, "And he shall confirm the covenant with many for one week: and in the midst of the week he shall cause the sacrifice and the oblation to cease, and for the overspreading of abominations he shall make *it* desolate, even until the consummation, and that determined shall be poured upon the desolate."

Finally, though the creators of dynamic equivalence theory recognized in principle that many dimensions contribute to meaning, when it came to putting it into practice, the emphasis on clarity led naturally to a concentration on what is most basic or obvious. As a result, some translators tended to put in the background the other dimensions of meaning.

Much depends on how a translator understands in practice the implications of the theory. The theory can be used very effectively as a guide to all the vexing complexities of real languages. But, if it is oversimplified, it can become an excuse for simply translating a most basic meaning, or most obvious meaning, and ignoring any nuances that go beyond the basics.

Early dynamic equivalence theory worked as well as it did because it was initially applied to translation into tribal languages, translations made for speakers with little or no knowledge of Christianity. In these situations, it was natural to put a high value on simplicity, clarity, and explicit explanation of difficulties.[8]

Subsequently, however, the theory began to be applied to translation into English and European languages. At first, focus tended to be on people with low reading skills: children, people with English as a second language, and people with poor literacy or reading disabilities. But then its use expanded to include the general reading public. The translators may still have had in mind only beginning readers. But marketers would be tempted to spread the completed translation as widely as possible, and to advertise it as if it were ideal for everyone.[9] As this shift occurred, the translation procedures became less appropriate. The marketers were acting almost as if the whole world were able to understand only if everything was carefully digested and simply explained in the actual translation of the Bible.[10]

3. Refinements in recognizing meaning nuances

Fortunately, the actual thinking of translators and translation theorists has continued to develop and to refine the initial emphases. The United Bible Societies speaks of "functional equivalent" translation and the

---

[8]But note Anthony Nichols's criticism of tendencies toward ethnocentrism in actual translation practice: ". . . the emphasis on explicitness in UBS and Summer Institute of Linguistics manuals in practice guarantees that indigenous receptors approach Scripture through a Western grid and denies them direct access to the biblical universe of discourse. . . . In fact, the renderings of the more traditional, "formal correspondence" Indonesian versions were regularly more culturally appropriate. (Anthony H. Nichols, "Translating the Bible," *Tyndale Bulletin* 50/1 [1999]: 160; see also Anthony H. Nichols, "Translating the Bible: A Critical Analysis of E. A. Nida's Theory of Dynamic Equavalency and Its Impact upon Recent Bible Translations," unpublished Ph.D. thesis, University of Sheffield, 1997).

[9]See the discussion of marketing under "niche translations" in Chapter 16.

[10]Note, for example, Stephen Prickett's concern that an emphasis on clarity and simplicity may result in flattening out the depth and complexity of the original text (Stephen Prickett, *Words and the Word: Language, Poetics and Biblical Interpretation* [Cambridge: Cambridge University Press, 1986], 4–35).

Summer Institute of Linguistics of "meaning-based" translation. The Summer Institute of Linguistics, the academic side of Wycliffe Bible Translators, has developed semantic structural analysis and discourse analysis to enable translators to deal more consciously and focally with the structure of whole paragraphs and larger units.[11]

Translation theorists have now seen that there were some limitations in the earlier phases of the theory. Ernst-August Gutt, in working with Wycliffe Bible Translators, saw principial problems with earlier dynamic equivalence theory when it was misconstrued as a complete answer. In practice, it tended to neglect some of the subtler aspects of meaning. After extensive theoretical reflection, he comments, "Translators should have a firm grasp of hitherto neglected aspects of meaning. In particular, they should understand that there are important differences between expressing and implicating information, between strong and weak communication."[12]

Gutt's advice to translators is to look carefully before you leap. He realizes, as all good translators do, that compromises are inevitable. But he also points out that in many situations the translation by itself cannot and ought not to be expected to carry the entire load of communication. People who read and study the Bible can also be helped by footnotes, Bible helps, beginning commentaries, preachers' explanations, and so forth. This is so even in translation into tribal languages—and how much more in English!

To appreciate fully what Gutt says, many biblical scholars may have to expand their point of view. Biblical scholars spend most of their time thinking and writing about the *theological value* and *interpretive implications* of the passages that they study. They write commentaries whose main business is to make *explicit* the many implications of the text. Therefore, if two wordings leave the *theological* implications the same, they might be seen as equivalent from the scholar's point of view. The two seem to be "identical in meaning" from the point of view of theological content. But literary stylists and linguists studying discourse can alert us to broaden our focus on other aspects of the text. They note, for example, that subtle differences exist between explicit and implicated information, direct and indirect address, active and passive constructions, second-person and third-person discourse, and so forth. These produce subtle nuances in the total complex

---

[11]For the beginnings of these developments, see John Beekman and John Callow, *Translating the Word of God* (Grand Rapids: Zondervan, 1974), and Kathleen Callow, *Discourse Considerations in Translating the Word of God* (Grand Rapids: Zondervan, 1974).

[12]Ernst-August Gutt, *Relevance Theory: A Guide to Successful Communication in Translation* (Dallas: Summer Institute of Linguistics, 1992), 72. See also Ernst-August Gutt, *Translation and Relevance: Cognition and Context* (Oxford/Cambridge, MA: Blackwell, 1991).

Mark Strauss says, "The technical writings and research emerging from major international translation organizations like Wycliffe Bible Translators and the United Bible Society view it as a given that dynamic or functional equivalence is the only legitimate method of true translation" (*Distorting*, 83). This statement does not yet acknowledge the complexities with which Gutt wrestles.

of meaning produced in the total act of communication. Thus, at this level of greater refinement, two radically different wordings are typically *not completely identical in meaning*.

D. Types of complexity

Many types of subtlety and nuance thus remain to be considered when we try to refine our understanding of meaning. What are they?

1. Limits in dictionary summaries

We have seen that many words can have more than one sense, depending on context. But even a summary of these various senses is not the whole story. Even within a single main sense we may discover that slightly different connotations or nuances are evoked in different contexts. Dictionary writers undertake to describe the main possibilities for different senses of a word, and they may to some extent note distinct contexts in which different senses occur. But even large-scale descriptions in dictionaries involve summaries and approximations.[13]

2. One word may combine several meanings

In addition, in special situations a word can resonate with more than one of its dictionary meanings. For example, the Bible sometimes uses a play on words or uses two different meanings of a word. In Genesis 1–5, a single word *'ādām* in Hebrew is used as the designation of the human race (Gen. 1:26, 27), as a descriptive term for the first man (Gen. 2:7, 7, 8), and as a proper name for Adam (Gen. 5:1, 3, 4, 5). In Ezekiel 37 the same Hebrew word *ruach* is used for breath (37:5), wind (37:9), and Spirit (37:14)—all within the scope of one passage. In the famous verse about being "born again" (John 3:7), the key Greek word *anōthen* is probably being used with a double sense: both "again" and "from above." It is impossible to reproduce these features perfectly in one word in English or in most other languages, because no one word in our language can function in all these ways.

Now what do translators do with such situations? They have to admit that in a translation they cannot always achieve everything, and they try to do the best they can with the resources of the language into which they are translating.

---

[13]For example, the standard Hebrew-English lexicon (BDB) tells us that the Hebrew word *rimmon* means "pomegranate." It naturally does not include a rather minute detail, namely that in Hebrew the word may possibly have connotative associations with love that are not present in English, but that may be evoked *in some contexts* in Hebrew. When the Song of Solomon says, "Your cheeks are like halves of a pomegranate" (RSV), G. Lloyd Carr's commentary adds, "Pomegranate wine had a reputation in Egypt as an aphrodisiac, where, as in Mesopotamia, pomegranates were used in love potions" (Carr, *The Song of Solomon* [Downers Grove, IL: InterVarsity, 1984], 116–117).

3. Factors that contribute to total meaning

Many additional factors contribute to the overall meaning and impact of a piece of language, often in subtle ways. We may list a few of them.

First, genre matters. That is, it matters whether the communication is prose or poetry, sermon or prayer, letter or historical narrative, reasoned discourse or passionate rhetoric. The genre or type of discourse colors the whole.

Second, metaphors matter. Metaphors do not have quite the same meaning as a literal rendering. They set hearers' minds in motion to work out what analogy exists (say) between sinners and sheep, or between growing plants and the kingdom of God, or between the church and a human body. When feasible, a good translation should preserve metaphors, not flatten them.[14]

Third, the difference between direct assertion and implication matters. Asserting something directly is not the same as implying it, because in the latter case the reader must exert himself to work out the implication. The author, by implying but not asserting, may be conveying to the reader not only a particular truth, but also his confidence that the reader can see the implication without being hit over the head with it. What is directly said also enjoys a kind of centrality in relation to what is implied. A good translation should try to preserve the difference between direct assertion and implication.

As an example, consider Jesus' parables. A story form like a parable can conceal its meaning from some as well as revealing its meaning to others (Mark 4:10–12). There is a key distinction between direct statements about seeds, how some grow and others do not, and indirect claims about people's hearts. This distinction between the two is what makes the Parable of the Sower function as a way of sorting out those who know the secrets of the kingdom of God from those who do not.

Fourth, register matters. The "register" denotes the variety of language appropriate to a particular social occasion: language may be exalted, stiff, technical, formal, intimate, informal, vulgar, or base. The total meaning of a passage depends on where it falls on a spectrum from "formal" to "informal," from technical to colloquial.

Fifth, style matters. Does a writer use high literary style or low, complex or simple vocabulary, complex or simple sentences and paragraphs, elegant or simple structures? All of these choices influence the total impression on readers.

---

[14]As always, there are complexities. In some cases, a metaphor or simile easily intelligible in one cultural and linguistic setting may pose difficulty when minimally translated for people with no knowledge of the original setting. Isaiah 1:18 says that ". . . your sins . . . shall be as white as snow" (NIV). What if we are translating into a tropical culture that has never seen snow?

Sixth, order of presentation matters. The total experience of reading depends on what a reader already knows, and what he knows depends on what has been introduced at earlier points in a discourse.

Seventh, rate of presentation matters. Do we confront a dense, compact theological argument, or rambling, leisurely discussion of the same subject?

Eighth, the relation between author and reader matters. Is the author sympathetic with his readers, or is he castigating them? Is the relation between author and reader affectionate, friendly, tense, or hostile? A tone of joy or sorrow, excitement or boredom, urgency or leisure may come with a particular discourse.

Ninth, focus and emphasis matter. "It's the dog that bit the man" is subtly different from "It's the man that the dog bit," or "The dog—he's the one that bit the man," or "It's indeed the dog that bit the man," or "It's the dog that did indeed bite the man." What is the author emphasizing in each case, what is he focusing on, and with what purpose does he draw our attention in various directions?

Tenth, allusions and connections with other sentences and discourses matter. Genesis 5:3 says, "When Adam had lived 130 years, he had a son in his own likeness, in his own image, and he named him Seth" (RSV). It enriches us to notice that this verse alludes to Genesis 5:1–2 and 1:26–27, where God created man "in his own image." Of course, Adam is not doing the same thing that God did, but he is doing an analogous thing. And then we are still further enriched by noting that the language of re-creation in Colossians 3:10 builds on the language of Genesis: ". . . put on the new self, which is being renewed in knowledge in the image of its Creator" (NIV).

The situation is particularly complex because the allusions and connections among passages may be of different kinds and intensities. We find not only direct quotes, but also reuse of similar language without quotation (as in Col. 3:10). We find not only references to the exodus as a literal event in the past, but also as a model for helping us understand Christian redemption (1 Cor. 10:1–11).

Eleventh, repetition of key words matters. The repetition draws the different places in the text more closely together.

Twelfth, paragraph structure matters. The organization and sequence in an argument, not merely the individual pieces, contribute to the total message.

4. Bible translators should try to capture the richness of the Bible

A good translator, then, should try to capture as much of this richness as possible in translation. He should try to avoid recasting the teaching into a totally different shape, which might convey something close to a basic meaning but lose many of the other factors that convey meaning as mentioned above.[15]

Nor should a translator assume that he can safely ignore some factors that influence meaning, since these are not "the main point" and therefore (he may think) "unimportant." After all, a translator is a finite human being. As human beings, we cannot possibly anticipate all the ways in which God may use his Word in another language, to speak to a variety of people with their varied personalities, ages, circumstances, needs, sins, and failures. Because we cannot second-guess God, we need to strive to represent all the textures of meaning in the Bible, all the ins and outs of its language, as exactly as we can in a second language.

E.   Translation as maximal equivalence

But as we have seen, because the task is so complex, no translation can attain the ideal and communicate into the second language absolutely *everything* that is meant in any speech or writing in the first.

So what do translators do in practice? They try to do the best they can. They make hard choices and settle for compromises. Consider Ezekiel 37. The same word *ruach* occurs several times, with the senses "breath," "wind," and "Spirit" (verses 5, 9, 14). One can represent these different senses in English using the three English words "breath," "wind," and "Spirit." But then one does not adequately show the connection between the three uses, nor the subtlety involved in playing on three different meanings of the same word. English readers may vaguely sense that the three English words "breath," "wind," and "Spirit" are related by analogy, but the impression is not as strong as in Hebrew.

So the translator puts in a footnote, indicating that the same Hebrew word underlies the different English words. This is probably the best solution in English, but it still is not quite the same as the original. Having something in a footnote is not the same as having it in the text. Some readers ignore it, while others interrupt the flow of their reading, which would not be necessary in Hebrew. Moreover, explaining word play *explicitly* creates a different, more pedantic atmosphere than simply letting readers see for themselves.

The other solutions are not nearly as good. For example, one could use the word "breath" in all occurrences. But now this one English word with its English meaning does not seem to fit well in some of its occurrences. The meaning of verses 9 and 14 is no longer as clear in English—in verse 14 the Lord now says, "I will put my *breath* in you and you will live." But compare

---

[15]In addition, another kind of problem arises if the translator tries to make everything *explicit* in translation. Instead of a translation he ends up with a commentary that spells out many implications of the original. The change from implicit to explicit communication is, in itself, a subtle change in meaning.

this verse with Ezekiel 36:26, "A new heart I will give you, and a new spirit [*ruach*] I will put within you" (RSV). The thought of renewing the human spirit is definitely present. This promise finds fulfillment in the pouring out of the Holy Spirit, who in turn renews our human spirit (Acts 2; Rom. 8). If we translate Ezekiel 37:14 using "breath," we miss this implicit reference to the Holy Spirit.

There are still other difficulties. In some verses we are not sure which of two meanings the writer intends. In some of these cases, the writer may intend primarily one, but still evokes some connotation of the other. For example, Job 32:8 says, "But it is the spirit [*ruach* margin has "Spirit"] in a man, the breath [Hebrew *nshāmā*] of the Almighty, that gives him under-standing" (NIV). The Hebrew word *ruach*, meaning either "breath" or "spirit," occurs in the first half of the verse. Which of the two meanings is correct? "Spirit" fits the context, which says that this "spirit" or "Spirit" gives man understanding. The NIV's translation with "spirit" is basically correct. But the parallel line, "the breath of the Almighty," uses a different word for "breath," implying that the connotation of "breath" cannot be elim-inated from the earlier use of *ruach*. The parallel lines play on this second meaning of *ruach* in a way that cannot be perfectly reproduced in English.

When translators confront these hard choices, how do they decide which way to go? They have a sense of priorities. Some things are more important to convey than others. They begin with something like the basic meaning or obvious meaning of a passage, and that must be conveyed, but they should not stop there. They should move out to encompass as many subordinate aspects as they can. In other words, within the limits of proper use of the receptor language, translators should aim at "maximal equivalence."[16]

F.   But a trustworthy translation is still possible

But a word of caution is in order here. A translator might be tempted to focus only on all the tiny details that are "lost," and that simply "can't be translated." In fact, D. A. Carson's recent book on gender language in trans-lation uses the motto that "translation is treason."[17] (Perhaps Carson meant

---

[16]Mark Strauss, *Distorting*, 77, 84, and Carson, *Debate*, 70, both indicate approval of the principle that translators should try to bring over into the receptor language as much of the meaning of the original as they can.

[17]Variations on "all translation is treason" occur at several points (Carson, *Debate*, 47; sim-ilarly, 68, 117, 130, and 187). See especially his Chapter 3, "Translation and Treason: An Inevitable and Impossible Task," and Chapter 4, "Gender and Sex around the World: A Translator's Nightmare."

Though Carson's emphasis is on the difficulty of translation work, he does state at one point that "any element in any text can be translated, except for some forms" (p. 68), and he quotes with approval the statement of Eugene A. Nida and Charles R. Taber, "Anything that can be said in one language can be said in another, unless the form is an essential part of the message" (p. 203, n. 18, quoting Nida and Taber's book *The Theory and Practice of Translation*, Helps for Translators 8 [Leiden: Brill, 1974], 4).

the motto as a humorous exaggeration; but his book is so serious in tone in other respects that we fear that some readers will not realize that it is humorous.) By concentrating on all the difficulties, the book may at times convey to some readers a highly negative impression about the possibility of translating Scripture accurately at all.

But we must not lose perspective here, for several reasons:

(1) "Translation is treason" comes from an Italian proverb, not from the Bible. No such thing can be found in the Bible, for the Bible does not convey anything like this attitude. "Treason" involves aiding one's enemies through a profound betrayal of one's own country or society. Surely translating the Bible is not such an activity! Translation is a wonderful ability that God has given human beings as part of his gift of language. It functions amazingly well in conveying the meaning of the Hebrew, Aramaic, and Greek portions of the Bible into other languages, so that we can read it, understand it, trust it, and obey it.

(2) God is sovereign over the affairs of the world, including the languages spoken by different people, and his Word commands us to make disciples and teach "all nations" (Matt. 28:19–20). He knew and planned that Christians would be involved in the task of translation, and we may rightly expect that he has put in the various language systems of the world the ability to convey the meaning of the Bible accurately. A standard book on translation theory says bluntly, "Anything which can be said in one language can be said in another."[18]

(3) The components that do not carry over easily in a translation generally are not the fundamental or core meanings of passages, but finer details such as additional nuances, overtones, and connections with other words.[19]

(4) At the time of the New Testament, many of the people who became Christians had no ability to read the Hebrew Old Testament. They were able to read a Greek translation, however, called the Septuagint. The New Testament authors have no hesitation in using the Septuagint (even though it had many deficiencies), quoting from it as Scripture, and expecting people to believe

---

[18]Mildred L. Larson, *Meaning-Based Translation: A Guide to Cross-Language Equivalence* (Lanham, MD: University Press of America, 1984), 11. However, the basic truth does need qualification. As Larson explains, sometimes it takes many words or even a longer explanation to signify in one language what is signified by just one word in another language. And some details of nuance, dependent on form, are very difficult to convey fully in another language.

[19]These are the kinds of things that Carson mentions, for example, in *Debate*, 48–65.

and obey it. They did not consider the translation of the Word of God from Hebrew and Aramaic into Greek as "treason"; they considered it a precious gift from God whereby people could read and understand God's words in their own language.

1. The richness and depth of the Bible

We need to bear in mind two complementary aspects of the Bible, its simplicity and its profundity. On the one hand, the Bible's basic message is simple. God designed the Bible so that it can instruct simple-minded people as well as the learned (Prov. 1:4; Ps. 19:7; 1 Cor. 1:18–31). The Bible sets forth the message of salvation in so many ways and so many places that no one has an excuse for missing it. As a result, even a flawed, muddled translation of the Bible can lead people to salvation. We can rejoice in the ways in which God uses even very imperfect translations to convey spiritual food to his people.

On the other hand, the Bible is also an incredibly profound book. The wisdom of God in the Bible is unsearchably rich and deep (Rom. 11:33–36; Isa. 40:28; Eph. 3:18–21). While a simple summary of the Bible may indeed express the meaning of salvation, the summary cannot capture everything. God invites us to go on, to hear more, to learn more, to sit at Jesus' feet (Luke 10:39), to digest the vast richness of biblical wisdom. God calls on us to grow in wisdom by meditating on and absorbing his Word (Prov. 1:2–7; Ps. 1; 119:11,15, etc.).

A translator needs to respect this rich wisdom. Of course a translator needs to present the basic message, but in dealing with the Bible in all its richness and wisdom, no translator should be content with a minimum. Translators of the Bible should represent *as much as possible* of the full richness of meanings, instructions, exhortations, and examples found in the Bible in the original languages.

How much of what the Bible says in the original languages is important, then? All of it is important, for it has all been given to us by God! Paul tells us, *"All Scripture* is God-breathed and is *useful* for teaching, rebuking, correcting and training in righteousness" (2 Tim. 3:16).

God's people have known this instinctively for centuries. They have studied, meditated on, pondered, prayed over, and memorized the Bible as the very Word of God. The more detailed attention they have given to it, the more of its richness they have discovered. In this way, it is vastly superior to every other book in the world. There is more richness of meaning in it than we can ever discover.

How can this be? The main reason is that behind the Bible lies the infinite wisdom of God. In human history great minds have produced great books. But God's mind is infinitely greater than any human mind, and what the Bible says is nothing less than his communication to us.

2. The richness of human language

But a second reason for the richness and complexity of the Bible is that God has created human language in such a way that it is able to convey a vast amount of meaning. The more we look at the Bible, written as it is in ordinary human languages, the more we can see that many dimensions contribute to the total meaning and texture of its message. Of course, there is something like "basic meaning," what a sentence says most obviously. But stylists, students of literature, discourse analysts, and other specialists can see more. By conscious reflection they confirm what Bible students have instinctively known for centuries: the Bible is a highly complex book. At every point multidimensional textures interlock with what is obvious. If we begin to analyze any particular Bible passage, many things contribute to its full meaning.

G. The tension between preserving form and explaining meaning

Once we recognize the richness of the Bible, and once we set it as our goal to bring into English as much of the meaning of the original text as possible, how much should we preserve the form and structure of the original Hebrew and Aramaic and Greek text in our translation? And how much of the form should we restructure in order to convey the meaning more effectively in English?

The obvious answer is, "The translator should do as much restructuring as he needs in order to represent the meaning fully in English."

But in doing a translation there are limits to how much restructuring is appropriate. To take it to the other extreme from a purely word-for-word translation, a systematic theology attempts to represent "the meaning" of the Bible in English by setting out its main teachings in systematic form. It is a radical restructuring and rearranging (and explaining) of the Bible. But that of course is not what a translation should do. The translation should be the base on which English readers build as they formulate their theology, but the translation should not turn into a writing of a doctrinal summary of the Bible.

1. The problem of idioms

So the translator might adopt a more modest goal. He might say, "I will do the minimum of rearrangement necessary to make grammatical English sentences." But some problems still arise. For example, what about idioms? Idioms are groups of words in one language that take on a specialized meaning distinct from the meanings of the individual words considered separately. To "hit the sack" in American English means to go to bed. But if it were translated literally into another language, it would be understood (literally) to mean, "to strike a cloth bag with one's hand." So it is with the

Bible—expressions that were clear in the original languages may not be clear in translation when they are carried over in this minimal way.

2. Other problems

Problems arise not only with idioms but with other kinds of expressions. Remember the example from Ephesians 1:18. A word-for-word translation from Greek produces "the hope of-the calling his." A minimal rearrangement results in "the hope of his calling." But English readers might understand this as meaning "the hope that he will call you," rather than what Paul intended. So the RSV, NIV, and GNB have "the hope to which he has called you."

Restructuring of this kind offers the possibility of improving clarity and understanding. Well and good. But it also introduces the possibility of subtle unanticipated problems. The RSV, NIV, and GNB introduced the word "you." That word is not completely wrong. But it does not correspond to any word in Greek, and in English it results in a meaning slightly more definite than the Greek. "His calling" in Greek has to do with God's calling people. As a word picture, it opens the horizon to anyone whom God calls. "You" is more specific, more concrete, more focused on the Ephesians. In addition, the RSV/NIV/GNB wording suggests that the whole point of God's calling is to have hope. The Greek leaves one more open to the broader possibility, namely that God's call to be a Christian includes many aspects, only one of which is the hope for fulfillment of his plan. This latter view is the one that in fact occurs elsewhere in Paul (Eph. 4:1; 1 Cor. 1:9; etc.).

The differences here are subtle, so it is easy to overlook them. Certainly, we want first of all to make sure that we capture in translation something like the "main meaning," that is, the meaning that is big and obvious. It does no good to go after subtleties if readers are going to miss the main point. "Hope to which he has called you" probably expresses the main point better than "hope of his calling," because it heads off the "big" misunderstanding that many might fall into, namely, misunderstanding it as "hope that he will call you." But the restructuring ("hope to which he has called you") also has potential liabilities, and we need to be aware of that.

3. What about paraphrases?

Approaches that engage in paraphrasing restructure the material more thoroughly and in the process become even more venturesome. For Ephesians 1:18, GW has the expression "the confidence that he calls you to have," and NLT has "the wonderful future he has promised to those he called." In these cases the alterations in meaning are quite noticeable. In GW "confidence" has lost the future-pointing connotation of "hope." Moreover, "confidence" is purely subjective, whereas "hope" in Paul's writings evokes something more, something objective, namely, the future new heavens and new earth, and our life in it. Unlike GW, the NLT's expression "the wonderful future he has promised to those he called" has the future element, all right, but lacks the subjective side of "hope" and introduces from nowhere the idea of "promise." Whereas "the hope to which he has called you" restructured a bit, these paraphrases restructure a lot and use words that convey a smaller part of the original meaning.[20]

Still another problem with the paraphrases is that they undermine the connections between Ephesians 1:18 and other passages where Paul talks about hope. The idea of "hope" is a noteworthy one in Paul, and it hinders deeper understanding of the Bible when English readers are not able to appreciate the connections between passages where Paul uses the same word in approximately the same way.[21]

The problem with changing the word "hope" to something else, and thereby loosening the connections with the idea of "hope" in other Pauline passages, recurs in paraphrases with a huge number of other passages as well. Part of the meaning of a passage comes from the connections that one text enjoys with many others. These connections take the form not merely of direct quotations from earlier parts of the Bible but common wording and subtle allusions. When paraphrases restructure the text, use simpler words that capture a smaller part of the original meaning, and add explanatory phrases, the complex and multiple connections with other texts simply cannot be captured.

There is a lesson here. When people start paraphrasing in the manner of GW and the NLT, changes in meaning result. No doubt the paraphrasers try hard. But some nuances drop out, while other nuances appear out of nowhere. Moreover, greater liberty in paraphrase means greater risks. If a translator abandons the form of the original, any misunderstanding in his interpretation may have drastic effects on the translation. By contrast, if the translator preserves the form of the original when it conveys meaning in a satisfactory way, he may not always have to decide between different

---

[20]These paraphrases do convey genuinely biblical teachings, such as the idea that God gives us promises, and the idea that God wants us to have confidence or trust in him. But these teachings are to be found explicitly in other passages. In translation, we need to convey the meaning of *this passage* (Eph. 1:18), not meanings of other passages elsewhere in the Bible.

[21]On the other hand, one must beware of equating or lumping together all the meanings in all the occurrences of a particular word. For example, the Hebrew word *ruach*, in any one verse, usually takes one of its three main meanings, not all three lumped together. James Barr rightly castigates "illegitimate totality transfer" (*The Semantics of Biblical Language* [London: Oxford University Press, 1961], especially 218–22).

In the situation in Paul's letters, the occurrence of the same word "hope" in several different places, or the occurrence of the same word in Greek for first-century readers, is a subtle extra clue encouraging students to notice the common threads of thought in the different passages and to synthesize the teachings in all the passages into a larger whole. The teaching still arises from the sentences and passages as a whole and is not merely embedded in the word "hope" itself. This sort of concordant reinforcement of teachings is fully compatible with the knowledge that the word "hope" by itself has only a limited dictionary-type meaning.

possible interpretations of the original, because the different possibilities that were there in the original (and that the original readers had to work at understanding) will be carried over into the translation as well.

4. Preserve the form or change the form?

No one simple recipe will always work. "Preserve the form" will not always work because it sometimes obscures the meaning. "Preserve the meaning while ignoring the form" will not work either, because form and meaning are not neatly separable, and the form often affects the meaning.[22]

---

[22]We have never argued for, nor did the Colorado Springs Guidelines advocate, a general principle that "formal equivalents" are always a more accurate method of translating, though supporters of inclusive-language Bibles have sometimes represented us as claiming that. Sometimes there are direct, "formal" equivalents that translate meaning well, but the fact that we argue for some of these does not mean we claim that formal equivalents will always translate meaning well.

Carson sometimes represents our position as a misguided attempt merely to preserve the "form" of expression in Hebrew or Greek: "Dr. Grudem's argument is simply an appeal for formal equivalence" (Carson, *Debate*, 98). He portrays our position as "the argument that attaches a particular equivalent in gender assignment to faithfulness to the Word of God" and says this is "profoundly mistaken in principle" and it "understands neither translation nor gender systems" (ibid.). But our earlier writings repeatedly emphasized loss of *meaning*, not mere loss of similarity in *form*, and we regret that our position has been often misrepresented as merely an ill-informed attempt to preserve forms.

To take one example, here is the rest of Wayne Grudem's section on "representative generics" that Dr. Carson quotes and dismisses as "simply an appeal for formal equivalence" (*Debate*, 98). Readers may judge for themselves whether Grudem's main concern was mere "form" (as Carson claimed) or loss of nuance and therefore loss of some of the details of meaning that were in the original. (Italics have been added wherever the emphasis was on translating meaning.)

> The point is this: the Bible has many "pure generics," and it has many "representative generics." In order to bring over into English the full *sense* of these expressions as nearly as possible, English translations should translate the pure generics in Hebrew and Greek as pure generics in English, and the representative generics in Hebrew and Greek as representative generics in English. That would preserve their distinctive *nuances*.

> However, these more recent gender-neutral Bibles translate the pure generics as pure generics, and they also translate the representative generics as pure generics. "Blessed is the man . . ." becomes "blessed are those. . . ." "I will come in to him" becomes "I will come in to them." Someone may object that these really *"mean* the same thing," but the feminists who protested against representative generics twenty or thirty years ago certainly did not see them as equivalent in *meaning*. They objected to representative generics precisely because they singled out a male human being as representative of a group, and thus they had male-oriented *overtones*. It is precisely these *overtones* that are filtered out in modern gender-neutral translations.

> In these new translations, the *nuances* of the representative generics are lost. Of course, what is lost is precisely what the early feminists objected to—the masculine *overtones* of these representative generics, for they nearly always have a male ("he," "man," "brother") standing for the whole group. Therefore the masculine *overtones* have been systematically filtered out.

> Is this really bringing over *"meaning for meaning"* or "thought for thought" into English? It is not even bringing over *"thought for thought"* as accurately as it could be

Speech and writing operate in too many dimensions for a rough paraphrase to get everything right.[23]

What has been done in actual practice? Translations fall along a spectrum. Some try harder to preserve form; others freely paraphrase. How shall we describe this spectrum?

One common way is to call one end of the spectrum "formal equivalence" and the other end "dynamic equivalence." But now we have a potential problem with terminology. The label "dynamic equivalence" can mean different things to different people. As used by some people, it can mean a highly paraphrastic approach to translation, an approach that in fact does not pay attention to nuances of meaning. Or it can mean all that was best in the early theory of dynamic equivalence. Or it can mean all that is best in the ongoing developments, including refinements that may still come in the future. "Meaning-based translation," the term used at SIL, is probably better as a description of ideal translation. To avoid confusing these many meanings, we will label the one end "preservation of form" and the other "change in form."

The KJV, NASB, and NKJV try harder to preserve the form. They are therefore sometimes called translations that use the principle of formal equivalence. But even these translations from time to time engage in more than minimal grammatical adjustments. They all pay attention to meaning as well as form. Hence, "formal equivalence" is not the best term for them. They do try harder to preserve form, and hence are closer to the end labeled "preservation of form."

The NLT, GW, and CEV freely restructure the form, often paraphrasing, so they belong on the end that changes form. GNB and NCV are usually less paraphrastic, less likely to engage in more venturesome transformations, but are usually considered to be examples that illustrate change in

---

done, for the *thought* is changed: the male *overtones* are filtered out. The male *overtones* are what much of our culture objects to today, and they are the part of the *meaning* that is lost in gender-neutral translations. This does not really increase accuracy or even increase understanding of the representative generic *idea* that is in the original. Rather, it obliterates this *idea*. Accuracy in translation is lost, and the *meaning* is distorted. (Wayne Grudem, "What's Wrong with Gender-Neutral Bible Translations?" [Libertyville, Ill.: CBMW, 1997], 15–16).

Such a concern for preserving meaning can be found over and over again in our previous writings. To claim (as Carson and Strauss do in their books) that we merely seek to transfer the equivalent form from Hebrew or Greek into English is simply to misrepresent our position.

[23]Mark Strauss is technically correct when he says, "The primary goal of a good translation must always be meaning rather than form" (*Distorting*, 83). We ourselves have said the same thing earlier in this chapter. But the interrelationships between meaning and form are complex, so that changes in form frequently entail subtle changes in meaning. Strauss tends to gloss over these subtle changes, and so (though he may not have intended it) he gives people an excuse for settling for a minimum such as may be found in a paraphrase.

form. Other translations are in between, with the RSV closer to the side of preserving form and the NIV in the middle.[24]

We can put these versions on a spectrum to give a visual representation of the range of translation policies. We place translations with more preservation of form nearer to one end and translations with more change in form nearer to the other end. Because there are trade-offs, some of the translations employ policies that place them nearer to the middle.[25]

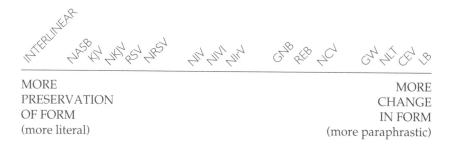

MORE
PRESERVATION
OF FORM
(more literal)

MORE
CHANGE
IN FORM
(more paraphrastic)

In fact, we would expect that in all these cases many of the translators were intuitively sensitive to language. They intuitively knew the basic truths that dynamic equivalence theory has articulated in explicit theoretical form. That is, they knew that their basic task was to translate "meaning," not "form." All of them changed the form of the original when they had to, in order to convey an intelligible meaning. But many of them also knew intuitively that there are trade-offs when one starts radically paraphrasing. So different translations with different purposes, sometimes targeting different audiences, may have ended up at different points along the spectrum, in the degree to which they felt free to restructure or paraphrase. The more radically paraphrastic versions may have had in mind non-Christians and beginning readers, as a result of which they put a very high premium on simplicity and clarity.

We are sympathetic with the struggles that translators have at any point on this spectrum. But we must face a central fact: at a fine-grained level translators cannot avoid trade-offs. The end of the spectrum toward preservation comes closer to a one-to-one match and often retains meaning

---

[24]Kenneth N. Taylor's *The Living Bible—Paraphrased* and Eugene H. Peterson's *The Message* are in still another category. They try to imagine what the Bible's message would look like if set partially in a modern environment, so they could be called very free paraphrases with much explanatory and illustrative material added.

[25]This chart is an approximate summary of complex sets of translation policies. People may differ with the exact placement of one or another translation with respect to the one to the right or left of it, but in general they are at the appropriate place on the spectrum.

nuances that are lost in restructuring. But it loses a little in readability. It tends to produce sentences that have to be thought out rather than have their meaning all "on the surface." And it risks producing some sentences that are in fact misunderstood or produce real struggles for understanding, especially for beginning Bible readers.

Beginning students of Hebrew and Greek are often impressed with preservation of form because it seems to create an "exact match" with the original. But the exactness of the match is sometimes illusory. The match in form may not actually match well in meaning in some specific cases. Hence, translation theory rightly pushes these students to recognize the limitations of preserving form.

At the other end of the spectrum, with paraphrastic translations, the translation has great readability and accessibility even to non-Christians and beginning readers. The text "springs alive," because the idiom is so thoroughly natural and contemporary. It is a pleasure to read—and often an exciting, spiritually enlivening experience.[26] But by putting such a premium on smooth readability, the translation trades off meaning nuances, so that what the reader receives differs subtly from the original.

Naïve readers may easily be overimpressed with these versions and not realize what they are missing. A paraphrastic version seems so effortless. It also seems to be saying the same thing as any other version does unless one makes detailed, verse-by-verse comparisons between two translations. And even if one does, how can one know, without comparison with the original languages, how big the problems are? On the other hand, when a naïve reader takes in hand a translation that preserves form, he intuitively senses some of the strain and difficulty as he makes his way through the more difficult English. To a certain extent, he can judge for himself whether he can deal with it. Thus, preservation-of-form translations make some of their limitations quickly evident. But the other end does not. We need to be aware that, in fact, problems arise at *both* ends.

We think that there is room for a spectrum of approaches here, *provided that readers understand the limitations as well as the advantages of the different approaches.* As a start, one might give to a non-Christian friend a Bible portion, like the Gospel of Mark, from one of the more paraphrastic versions, so that he quickly hears the Bible's main message. But if a person becomes a Christian, one wants him to move beyond this stage. The more mature Bible student will want to have a translation with more preservation of form, like the NASB, NKJV, or RSV. The NIV is a good "middle-of-the-road" compromise that can simultaneously serve many needs—though it is not quite as good for detailed study as translations that preserve form, nor

---

[26]The Holy Spirit uses the text to bring spiritual life, just as he may use a sermon. But the good use of a flawed medium does not constitute an endorsement of the flaws.

quite as easy for a beginning reader to read as the translations that change form.

5. But aren't different translations just different kinds of interpretation?

In the light of the difficulties that attach to translating the Bible, translators may console themselves by saying that "all translation is interpretation." There is some truth in this, in that all translation requires that the translator first *do* interpretation. The most accurate translation can only be accomplished when a translator first interprets thoroughly and understands the meaning of the original, including all its nuances in all their dimensions. Only then is he ready to produce a translation that conveys not only the main meaning but all the nuances of the original. In that sense, every translation represents the translator's best understanding or "interpretation" of the original.

But the motto, "all translation is interpretation," is turned into another meaning if people then use it as a blanket justification for rewriting the text in the way that an interpretive commentary would do. An interpretive commentary *expounds* the implications of a text and *makes explicit* what the original text leaves implicit. This has not generally been the job of mainstream translation, nor do we think it is what a general-purpose Bible translation should do.

However, we must recognize that much of the American religious public has become lazy about the Bible and busy with other affairs. Many ordinary Christians do not read commentaries, and many Christian bookstores (at least the ones that we have visited around the U.S.) do not even stock more serious commentaries. So translators may be tempted to try to "help" the readers of the Bible by including extra information in the text explicitly, in order to make it easy for them. They may put in paraphrases. They may explain metaphors in ordinary prose. They may expand tightly packed theological exposition. By doing so, they attempt to help readers to understand some parts of the Bible's message more easily and quickly. There are benefits here, especially for beginners. But if they label the paraphrases "The Bible" and call them a "translation," they have blurred the line between translation and commentary. Christians need to be aware of the limitations, not only the benefits, of such versions, and to move beyond them as they mature in their own study.

To return to our original claim, we must be clear that the meaning of any Bible passage includes not only its "basic content" but also the nuances arising from style, focus, emphasis, allusion, metaphorical color, and many other dimensions. All translations should endeavor to include as much as they can. But differences of priorities among the different translation strategies will sometimes lead to different solutions in detail.

H. Excursus: Analyzing linguistic complexity

[Note to readers: The following section is more technical, and some readers may wish to skip this section and go immediately to the next chapter.]

In this chapter we have only attempted to summarize some main features among the numerous issues in Bible translation. Our summary is just
that—a summary. It is the tip of the iceberg. Translation specialists have
written whole books on translation theory.[27] These books also invoke a
much larger body of linguistic theory found in linguistic textbooks. But the
books themselves, complex as they may be, only supply a "warm-up" for
the real job, the actual practice of translation. Theoretical generalizations
can never anticipate all the details in complexity that we may encounter in
translating a specific verse into a specific target language. To these specifics
we must turn our attention in subsequent chapters.

I. The naïve approach: word-for-word

But we should first observe that there are several levels of depth at
which people approach translation. First, there is level 1, the naïve
approach. Many people with no experience with a second language naively
imagine that translation is easy. Just find the corresponding word and plug
it in. People just beginning to learn a second language often operate at this
level. They learn quick, oversimplified correspondences. "Hebrew *ben*
means *son*." "Greek aorist tense means simple past action." Such simplifications are natural at the beginning. But of course they are only a beginning. At the next level, level 2, they have to "unlearn" these simple
summaries, as they find out that the simple correspondences were in fact
over-simple. Unfortunately, some students apparently never "unlearn"
them—such is the difficulty of progressing to the stage of theoretical
sophistication in understanding (level 2).

2. The theoretically informed approach: using a linguistic system

Next is level 2, the theoretically informed approach. Aided by teachers
and textbooks, people learn that the naïve approach is oversimple. They
learn standard theoretically informed distinctions between form and
meaning, sense and reference, dynamic-equivalent and formal-equivalent
translation. They learn how to use these theoretical tools to avoid fallacies
in interpretation and in translation. Our discussions above about idioms,
about multiple senses of a single word, about different translations of

---

[27]The books already cited may serve as a sample: Nida, *Science*; Nida and Taber, *Theory*;
de Waard and Nida, *From One Language*; Larson, *Meaning-Based Translation*; Gutt, *Relevance
Theory*; Gutt, *Translation and Relevance*; Beekman and Callow, *Translating the Word of God*;
Callow, *Discourse*.

Greek *hina*, all illustrate this level. The first few sections of this chapter operate almost entirely on this level.[28]

Most textbooks in translation, in linguistics, and in biblical hermeneutics operate at this level, for very good reason.[29] Seminary professors and teachers of would-be translators constantly work at this level in the classroom. They have to work with each new entering class of naïve students in order to make them theoretically informed. Typical texts in translation theory operate at this level, to train naïve students to be theoretically informed about the reasons for restructuring form. James Barr's book *The Semantics of Biblical Language* and D. A. Carson's book *Exegetical Fallacies* are excellent texts operating on this level.[30] Their examples taken from scholarly writings show that not only complete novices but established biblical scholars can commit linguistic "bloopers" when they are not theoretically informed by linguistics.

3. The discerning approach: using native speakers' intuitive sense of subtleties

Then there is level 3, the discerning approach. At this level people recognize, often intuitively, that the theoretical apparatus belonging to the second level is only a summary. The phenomena of language and human communication vastly surpass it in complexity. Theoretical distinctions still have their use in guarding against fallacies. But they cannot substitute for the complex process of weighing the intertwining effects of multidimensional associations and textures in language. We have dipped a little into this level with our list of subtle influences on meaning, such as genre, metaphors, implication, emphasis, and so on. Of course, any particular item on the list can itself be subjected to some theoretical scheme. But the scheme never exhausts the reality. And of course the list is only a summary, and could never be exhaustive. The interlocking of these dimensions, as well as the distinct effect of any one dimension, creates additional richness. Interpretation and translation at this level are arts, not sciences. Translation does not take place by mechanical application of a theoretical formula, but by discernment.

---

[28]Reflective discussions (level 4) of complexities normally intuitively discerned (level 3) begin approximately with the section entitled, "Types of complexity." In fact, this separation into "levels" is itself an idealization; the real situation, as usual, is more complex.

[29]In the field of theoretical linguistics and translation theory, there is another good reason for staying at this level most of the time. Language and translation are in fact *so* complicated that vast simplifications and restrictions of focus were virtually *necessary* to make a fundamental advance in the early days. In addition, in the United States the transformational-generative school as well as earlier behaviorist-leaning approaches prized a more mechanical, formal approach that tended to neglect nuance.

[30]James Barr, *The Semantics of Biblical Language* (London: Oxford University Press, 1961); D. A. Carson, *Exegetical Fallacies* (Grand Rapids: Baker, 1984).

Our examples of subtleties in meaning also operate at this level. The difference between putting in or leaving out "you" in Ephesians 1:18 belongs to this level. The example from Ezekiel 37, where the text plays on three different meanings of *ruach* ("breath, wind, spirit"), also belongs to this level.

4. The reflective approach: explicitly analyzing subtleties

Then there is level 4, the reflective approach. At this level people endeavor theoretically to analyze and make explicit the complexities sensed intuitively at level 3 (the discerning approach), but earlier put to one side at level 2 (the theoretically informed approach).[31] Ernst-August Gutt's refinement to earlier dynamic equivalence theory belongs to this level. Understandably, not as much has been done at this level, and in the existing state of linguistic scholarship, we may not be ready for its execution on a broad scale.[32]

We may sketchily illustrate how the levels (which are themselves idealizations) crop up in the discussion of form and meaning. The naïve approach (level 1) virtually equates form and meaning or confuses them. The naïve approach expects to translate a single word in the same way every time. It thinks that the *form* of the Hebrew word *ruach* matches *meaning* in a one-to-one fashion, so that *ruach* always means "breath, wind, spirit" rolled together in a confused mass.

Or a naïve person introduces an argument based on form. He may say, "The Hebrew word *banîm*, plural of the word *ben* "son," is *masculine* plural. Since it is *masculine*, it should be translated 'sons,' not 'children.'" But in fact this confuses *masculine* gender, a grammatical feature, a *form*, with the *meaning* component "male." In fact, in many contexts *banîm* (masculine form!) means "children" (both male and female included in meaning). This fact is recognized, for example, in the KJV translation "children [*ben* in masculine plural construct state] of Israel."

Or someone says, "The Greek pronoun *auton* in the accusative means *him.*" In fact, the two are related, but the bald generalization is far too simple. Or "we must always translate Greek masculine with English masculine."

---

[31]Teachers operating at a theoretically informed level (level 2) may be aware of the complexities of discerning intuitive subtleties (level 3) and reflective analysis (level 4). But for pedagogical reasons they simplify and avoid these complexities in classroom and textbook discussion. They have their hands full teaching people who still operate naively, at level 1!

In fact, bringing in discerning complexities (level 3) too early simply confuses students. Because the discerning approach threatens to undermine the purity of the theoretically informed distinctions (level 2), any focus on these complexities could be counterproductive, unintentionally encouraging some students to regress to level-1 naiveté.

[32]Some of Kenneth L. Pike's works, such as *Language in Relation to a Unified Theory of the Structure of Human Behavior*, 2d ed. (The Hague/Paris: Mouton, 1967), and *Linguistic Concepts: An Introduction to Tagmemics* (Lincoln: University of Nebraska Press, 1982), suggest a way forward. But Pike, like everyone else, was constrained by the demands of teaching naïve students!

It seems possible also to postulate a fifth level, where we reflect on the theological underpinnings of language found in the Second Person of the Trinity, who is the divine Word.

In fact, translation involves *meaning* transfer, whereas this rule results in preserving masculine *form* at all costs.

The theoretically informed approach (level 2) carefully distinguishes form and meaning, based on the theoretical distinction between "signifier" and "signified" going back to Ferdinand de Saussure (1906).[33]

At this level we observe that in its various occurrences the Hebrew word *ruach* has the same *form* but different *meanings*. We translate the *meaning* in each context (for example, "wind" in 1 Kings 18:45), not the *form*. We note also that there can be idiomatic constructions. For example, the Hebrew phrase *ben hayil*, literally "son of might," is not literally talking about the biological descendent of "might." It is one of a fair number of expressions with *ben* ("son")[34] that is better translated by taking the expression as a whole: thus NIV translates "brave man" (1 Sam. 14:52), and the RSV and NASB translate "valiant man." We preserve the meaning but alter the form.

At this level we likewise observe that the Hebrew word *banîm*, in the plural, often refers inclusively to males and females. The *form* is masculine, whereas the *meaning* is to denote a mixed group.[35] Likewise, one observes that the Greek word *auton* ("him") is used to refer back to *any* masculine antecedent.[36] The masculine in the Greek language does not function in a manner parallel to masculine in English, since gender agreement in Greek affects virtually every noun and adjective. Gender belongs to impersonal as well as personal expressions. "Truth" (*alētheia*) is feminine; "word" (*logos*) is masculine; "fig" (*sukon*) is neuter; "summer fig" (*olunthos*) is masculine. Thus, the masculine gender must be carefully distinguished from the semantic meaning component, "male." We see at this level that the requirement of always translating masculine to masculine confuses form (masculine) with meaning (male).[37]

The discerning approach (level 3) realizes intuitively that form and meaning are not neatly separable. The perfect distinction of form and meaning is an idealization. The distinction is a theoretical construct—useful but dependent on ideally purified conceptions of "form" and "meaning." In

---

[33]One standard English translation is Ferdinand de Saussure, *Course in General Linguistics*, ed. Charles Bally and Albert Sechehaye (New York: McGraw-Hill Book Co, 1966).

[34]See *BDB*, 121, meaning 8.

[35]There is a feminine form *banôt* ("daughters") used when referring exclusively to females. But it and the masculine *banîm* are the only two choices in the plural. So what does one do when referring to mixed groups including males and females? One regularly uses *banîm* in the masculine. The masculine form is the "default" form, used whenever one is not referring to an exclusively female group. In terms of meaning, the masculine plural form *banîm* contains no implication that it is "sons" only and not also "daughters."

[36]As usual, there are exceptions.

[37]Carson, *Debate*, and Strauss, *Distorting*, also operate at the theoretically informed level (level 2) most of the time (though Carson, *Debate*, 47–76, in his chapter on the difficulties of translation, includes quite a few examples of subtle losses in translation, thus illustrating higher levels). With reasonable uniformity they expound theoretically informed principles to

real everyday use, forms may carry subtle meaning associations. For example, consider the following two sentences translating Proverbs 17:11:[38]

> RSV: An evil *man* seeks only rebellion, and a cruel messenger will be sent against *him*.

> NRSV: Evil *people* seek only rebellion, but a cruel messenger will be sent against *them*.

This proverb states a general principle that is applicable to any evil person. The two translations express the truth using different *forms* in two places. But they express approximately the same truth, that is, the same *meaning*. In terms of *form* "man" is grammatically singular and masculine. "People" is grammatically plural and not marked for gender. But in both cases the truth thereby expressed holds for a plurality of people of both sexes. The *forms* differ, but the *meaning* is "the same"—that is, when we ignore subtle nuances and concentrate on "basic" meaning.

But subtle differences crop up when we look more closely. The most obvious difference occurs with the word "man." "Man" in this context can mean either a human being or a male human being. If it means "male human being," the male human being is being used as an example that can be generalized to include females. But the starting point is still a male example. What occurs in the Hebrew original of Proverbs 17:11? The Hebrew here does not use a separate word for "man." It does not convey in a pronounced way, "only male." So the RSV translation may convey to some people a nuance not there in Hebrew. It would be better to translate, "An evil *person* seeks only rebellion, and a cruel messenger will be sent against him."

Another problem arises because of the use of the plural "people" in the NRSV. This change in *form* still conveys the same meaning—approximately. But there are also some differences. The starting picture in the RSV is a singular individual, used to illustrate the general principle. The starting picture in the NRSV is a plurality of people. As a result, the NRSV leaves us with an ambiguity as to how the statement applies to any one individual. Are the "evil people" acting separately, with a cruel messenger beging sent

---

teach naïve readers. Carson's exposition of differences in gender systems is a particularly elaborate case (*Debate*, 77–98). Just such elaborate data sets from many languages form the inductive basis for the theoretically informed general distinction between form and meaning, and the dynamic equivalence theory's principle of preserving meaning, not form. The particularities of any one gender system are "form," while a translation into a particular language using its gender system represents "meaning." Extended exposure to linguistic data like Carson's is very useful in training naïve people to rise to an understanding of what linguistic theory has in mind with the form-meaning distinction.

Carson's exposition of gender is also useful for the purposes of this present book because it also illustrates the fact that theoretically informed principles deliberately leave to one side the complexities and nuances of level 3.

[38]See Chapter 13 for fuller discussion.

to each one? Or are they acting together, with a cruel messenger being sent to them *as a group*? The mention of a single "cruel messenger" suggests that we are to think of a single messenger coming against all of them *together*. The change in form from singular to plural turns out to have subtle meaning implications that the NRSV may not have anticipated. The underlying Hebrew uses singular forms and conveys the idea of an individual as the starting example. In this case using singulars in English is better.[39]

The reflective approach (level 4) brings the intuitions of level 3 to conscious attention and proceeds to analyze their workings. At this level we explore by explicit, disciplined analysis how form and meaning are intimately intertwined.[40] For example, we may explicitly analyze how Ezekiel 37 can achieve its affects by playing on more than one sense of the same word *ruach* ("breath, wind, spirit"). Or we analyze how it is that in general proverbial statements, the distinction in *form* between singular and plural can have meaning implications (see Chapter 13).

Why bother with all these levels? All of us must still come back to weighing the translations of particular verses. But the awareness of vast complexity may help us to remember the two sides: the simplicity and accessibility of the Bible's message on the one hand, and the depth of its wisdom on the other.

It is possible for scholars and professional translators to underestimate this depth. Scholars so commonly deal with naïve students that the challenges we must later pose at levels 3 and 4 may be misheard as simple naïveté at level 1.

Many of the defenders of gender-neutral policy have accused the critics of naively equating form and meaning (level 1). And of course on occasion they may be right, because, as Barr's and Carson's books remind us, even seasoned scholars can commit linguistic bloopers.[41] But at heart, the critics of gender-neutral translations are concerned with discerning subtleties (level 3). In response to the criticisms, the defenders of gender-neutral

---

[39]Note, however, that we do not thereby undermine the valid theoretically informed observation that in *some cases* a singular form in one language may be translated by a plural form in another, in order to convey maximal meaning.

Carson's exposition of gender includes an illustration from discerning approach (level 3) at one point, when it touches on the intricate *details* of finding the right word for "God" in the Pévé language (Carson, *Debate*, 93–95; based on Rodney Venberg, "The Problem of a Female Deity in Translation," *Bible Translator* 22/2 [1971]: 68–70). The translator, Rodney Venberg, guided by theoretically informed analysis, suggested to the Pévé tribe more than one translation option that the native speakers *intuitively* rejected (*Debate*, 94). The complexities exist, but the theoretically informed distinction between form and meaning must pass over them.

[40]Kenneth Pike's conception of the form-meaning composite surpasses in penetration the Saussurian ideal separation of form and meaning. It does so in an explicit, theoretically disciplined discussion, thus illustrating a reflective approach at level 4 (Pike, *Language*, especially 62–63 and 516–17; but the larger context of *Language* must be understood to grasp the full import of his conception).

[41]Barr, *Semantics*; Carson, *Fallacies*.

translations appeal to standard[42] linguistic theory and translation theory (level 2, the theoretically informed approach) to defeat the critics and vindicate gender neutrality. But in doing so they have not touched the real issue, which involves level 3, the subtle interplay of form and meaning in textual detail.

We can now understand sympathetically the reaction of some advocates of gender-neutrality. For example, when the controversy about the NIVI broke out,[43] scholars may have perceived the controversy as a reaction from a naïve Christian public (level 1). This public, being naïve, did not understand the scholarly decisions based on theoretically informed translation theory (level 2). The rolling back of decisions made by the NIV's Committee on Bible Translation might have seemed therefore to be a regression towards incompetence: the CBT, with a base in linguistic theory, felt it was being drowned out by the volume of uninformed, naïve protest from level 1. This result was maddening.

Unfortunately, it may not have dawned on scholars that native speakers of English have very deep sensitivities and intuitions about their native tongue. That is, as native speakers they have an intuitive sense of subtleties (level 3), even when they are totally untrained in linguistics and translation theory (naïve at level 1). These intuitive instincts detected some subtle factors not consciously within the focus of standard theoretical frameworks at level 2.[44]

The situation became more difficult because the scholarly critics of gender-neutral translations as well as the defenders of gender neutrality wanted to address the general Christian public, not just fellow scholars. The scholarly critics therefore simplified their language in order to make plain what the issue was. But since the issue usually involved differences in nuances, the nuances had to be given disproportionate emphasis in order to make them clearly visible to the naïve (that is, those operating at level 1). And the critics often simplified their statements for the sake of communication. These critics' simplifications could easily *appear* to be a result of naïveté on the part of the critics, not just naïveté in the audience. Hence, the scholarly defenders had all the more temptation to regard the scholarly critics themselves as naïve.[45]

---

[42]Of course there is no universally accepted "standard" linguistic theory but rather a variety of competing schools and research programs. But within any one school there is still a core body of established theory that students are expected to learn. This core body, including theoretical framework, theoretical tools, and theoretical generalizations, is what we have in view.

[43]For the history of the controversy, see Chapter 8.

[44]We return to this issue in Chapter 21.

[45]The same observations could apply to various sections of this book. As indicated in the Preface, we are writing to a broad audience. Hence we must simplify. But such simplification should not be misread as level-1 naivete.

As another example we may take Carson's book, *The Inclusive Language Debate*. The book repeatedly gives the impression that opponents[46] lack sufficient competence even to discuss the issue: "The argument . . . is profoundly mistaken in principle. It understands neither translation nor gender systems" (p. 98); "it should be obvious by now that [one side in this conflict] is betraying ignorance of translation problems and the nature of gender and number systems in different languages" (p. 108); "the CSG are open to far more and far more serious linguistic objections than the CBT principles" (p. 111); "where the critics are right, they have not been so on the ground of a linguistically informed critique of gender-inclusive translations" (p. 144); "it betrays a serious ignorance of language structures, including gender systems, and of the nature of translation, when a shift in the system of a receptor language is tagged with evil epithets, or the resulting translations are judged mistranslations" (p. 187); "The undergirding understanding of language and translation (and occasionally even exegesis) is sufficiently flawed that the attack will not long prove successful or widely convincing" (p. 163); "But these principles are profoundly flawed, even when they are saying some important things" (p. 194).

It is unfortunate that in several crucial areas Carson has simply not understood our position or the position of the Colorado Springs Guidelines accurately (we explain this in more detail later in this book). Perhaps some of the fault was ours for failing to represent our position with sufficient clarity. Yet we have never advocated ideas such as "the English language is not changing" (p. 112), or "it is always inappropriate to render a singular by a plural" (p. 105), or that Hebrew and English "have the same gender systems" (p. 97). When Carson's allegations of scholarly incompetence (cited above) are combined with the attribution to us of simplistic and erroneous positions that we do not hold, and when the beginning and the end of the book paint a picture of irrational, violent "Bible rage" that bursts forth from gender-neutral translation opponents (pp. 15–16, 35, 194), the effect on readers (whose only knowledge of our position may be through Carson's book) may be to think of us as incompetent, simplistic, and filled with rage.[47]

---

[46]Several of the people who wrote the Colorado Springs Guidelines had extensive training in Greek and Hebrew and had taught at the graduate level for many years, so Carson's claims may seem implausible. But, as we noted already, it is possible even for experienced scholars to commit blunders. The issue here is not really any amount of expertise in the specialized theories in various fields at level 2, or the ability in practice to stay clear of blunders violating the principles articulated at level 2, but discernment (level 3).

In the end, in the special context of discerning complexities, the "standard" theories (level 2) are irrelevant, because their high generality, their idealization, and their goal of simplifying in order to teach students prevents them from addressing the crucial questions of nuance. Ironically, in this special context, appealing to the standard theoretically informed principles demonstrates ignorance—a failure in understanding the problem.

[47]We would appeal at this point to Carson's statements about taking care how we characterize the other side in this debate: "Slogans and demonizing those who disagree with us will

It is legitimate for Carson to try to address those readers who may have very naïve ideas and simplistically equate form and meaning (level 1). It is legitimate for him to make the point that translation is far more complex than that by offering theoretically informed instruction (level 2). But we confess we are profoundly disappointed with his misrepresentations of our position.

In fact the central issues arise primarily from what is uncovered in a discerning approach (level 3). They involve subtleties. The advice to treat the dispute as level-1 naïveté only blocks rather than encourages discernment. It therefore results in a situation that requires even more effort to overcome (as in the reflective approach). It is primarily the differences in meaning that come to light from the discerning approach (level 3 intuition) and the reflective approach (level 4 analysis) that we consider in the remainder of this book.

---

not help. . . . In large part this little book is nothing more than an attempt to lower the temperature, slow the pace of debate" (p. 37); "Each side needs to try harder to avoid demonizing the other side" (p. 195).

CHAPTER 11

Permissible Changes in Translating Gender-Related Terms

It is now time to consider what different translations do in practice. What actually happens, verse by verse, sentence by sentence? Because of the focus of this book, we will examine gender-related issues, not translation as a whole.

Thousands of verses are potentially affected by gender-neutral translation policies. We would wear ourselves out if we tried to look at each verse, so we begin by looking at a sampling of verses that illustrate the kinds of things that gender-neutral translations undertake to change. For the benefit of English readers, we express the changes mostly in terms of English expressions, with brief references to the underlying Hebrew and Greek texts.

The changes are of two main kinds: (1) Some changes either improve the accuracy of translation or leave it about the same. These we have categorized as "permissible" changes for a translator to make. (2) Other changes alter nuances of meaning in ways that are so significant they seem to us to be unacceptable. These changes we categorize as "impermissible" for a translator for reasons that we will explain in subsequent chapters. Then between changes that are permissible and those that are impermissible are a number of cases that are less clear-cut. These we will examine near the end of our tour (in Chapter 18).

In this chapter we consider permissible changes. A few of the changes made in gender-neutral translations make almost no difference in meaning, and some increase accuracy.

A. Replacing "man" and "men" when the original includes women

A translation can replace "men" with words like "people" when the reference includes women, that is, when "men" denotes "human beings." Here are some examples.

1. Replacing "all men" with "all" or "everyone" when translating Greek *pas*

Romans 3:9

RSV: For I have already charged that *all men*, both Jews and Greeks, are under the power of sin.

NIV: We have already made the charge that Jews and Gentiles alike are *all* under sin.

NRSV: For we have already charged that *all*, both Jews and Greeks, are under the power of sin,

The word "all" indicates that women as well as men are included. The RSV has used the word "men," even though there is no distinct underlying Greek word corresponding to it (the Greek text simply has a form of *pas*, "all"). The NIV and NRSV are at this point more accurate when they dispense with the word "men."

At the time when the RSV appeared (the New Testament in 1946), it could be easily understood because the word "men" was frequently used in a generic sense; that is, women were included. But today in many circles one is expected to use "men" only when referring to male human beings, not when referring to all people. This change—whether one considers it good or bad—has largely come about as a result of the influence of feminism in the larger culture. (At a later point we will have to weigh in greater detail the influence of feminism and consider how to respond, but for the moment we simply observe that feminism has effected a change in English usage.) The net result is that the earlier use of "men" has become potentially confusing. The NRSV in 1989 improved the RSV by eliminating "men"—it headed off this potential confusion without sacrificing anything in the original.

The NIV and even the KJV in 1611 also eliminated the word "men," simply on the basis that it is not needed to represent the Greek. The Colorado Springs Guidelines agreed with this:

> When *pas* is used as a substantive it can be translated with terms such as "all people" or "everyone" (A.8).[1]

---

[1]Why does Carson say that "CBMW scholars devote energy to trying to prove that the English language is not changing. . . . that is a bit like Canute trying to hold back the tide" (*The Inclusive Language Debate*, 112)? The claim is obviously untrue. The accompanying statement

2. Replacing "men" with "people" when there is no masculine term in the original text

Matthew 5:15

RSV: Nor do *men* light a lamp and put it under a bushel, but on a stand, and it gives light to all in the house.

NIV: Neither do *people* light a lamp and put it under a bowl. Instead they put it on its stand, and it gives light to everyone in the house.

There is no Greek term specifying "men" in this verse but only a plural verb *kaiousin* "they light or set on fire." However, there is a difference between the structure of Greek and English here because Greek can say "they light" without using any pronoun at all to specify the subject. To make up for this difference in languages, translators have to supply some plural subject in English. Older versions used "men," but "people" is surely better, since "men" is often today understood to refer only to male human beings, which is not what Jesus intended.

3. Replacing "men" with "people" for Greek *anthrōpos* (plural)

Romans 2:16

RSV: On that day when, according to my gospel, God judges the secrets of *men* by Christ Jesus.

NRSV: On the day when, according to my gospel, God, through Jesus Christ, will judge the secret thoughts of *all*.

NIVI: This will take place on the day when God will judge *everyone*'s secrets through Jesus Christ, as my gospel declares.

The NRSV and NIVI have "all" and "everyone" where earlier KJV, RSV, and NIV had "men." The underlying Greek has the word *anthrōpos* in the plural, which can include women as well as men, and the context in Romans 2 shows that Paul is talking about all human beings. The substitution of "all" (NRSV) and "everyone" (NIVI) avoids the potential confusion and so is an advantage.

On the other hand, NRSV and NIVI also lose something. The Greek word *anthrōpos* denotes a human being, and is thus more specific in meaning than "all" or "everyone." Outside of the context of Romans 2, "all" might include angels and even animals. Of course, the context of Romans 2 narrows things down and shows us that Paul is talking about human

---

that we published with the Colorado Springs Guidelines and that was signed by all participants said, "We all agree *that modern language is fluid and undergoes changes in nuance* that
require periodic updates and revisions" (*CBMW NEWS* 2:3 [June 1997], 7, italics added). In
addition, the Colorado Springs Guidelines themselves contain Guidelines that approve some
changes. (See further discussion in Appendix 6.)

beings and their guilt before God. But NRSV and NIVI rely on the implicit force of the context, whereas the Greek makes explicit the reference to human beings. In addition, the NRSV and NIVI make explicit the universality using the words "all" and "everyone," while the Greek leaves the universality more implicit with the word *anthrōpos* ("people") and does not have any word which specifies "all" or "everyone." Probably an even better result could have been achieved with the phrase "people's secrets," which avoids both of the problems of "all" or "everyone."

The kind of translation of *anthrōpos* mentioned here was never in dispute, and no one is objecting to it. One standard translation of *anthrōpos* was "human being"[2] long before this dispute over inclusive language. Moreover, the Colorado Springs Guidelines specify that "in many cases, *anthrōpoi* refers to people in general, and can be translated "people" rather than 'men'" (A.5).[3]

Unfortunately, Mark Strauss's book, *Distorting Scripture? The Challenge of Bible Translation and Gender Accuracy*,[4] uses loose terminology at this point. It says that such a translation of *anthrōpos* uses "inclusive language" (p. 37). It thereby uses the label broadly, to speak about usages that are not in dispute. But the same label, "inclusive language," has a narrow use to designate usages that *are* in dispute. The entire debate was sparked by the *NIV: Inclusive Language Edition*, and Strauss's own category for gender-neutral Bibles is "Gender-Inclusive Versions."[5]

By using the label "inclusive language" in a broad way as well as the narrower way, Strauss bundles the uncontroversial usages into the same collection with the controversial ones—it is all "inclusive language." One thereby gets the false impression that since the old (undisputed) practices of the KJV and the NIV were all right, so are the new disputed usages.

---

[2]BAGD, 68.

[3]In spite of this explicit statement in the CSG, D. A. Carson claims that the signers of the CSG want to call a mixed group of males and females "men." He says, "Most of the men who signed this document are known to me personally . . ." and then in a footnote attached to the word "men" in that statement he adds, "In deference to their convictions, I use this term in its generic sense; there are three women in this list of names: Vonette Bright, Mary Kassian, and Dorothy Patterson" (Carson, *Debate*, 37 and 201, n. 21.). It may give readers a chuckle to think that we are so ignorant of modern English that we want to call Vonette Bright, Mary Kassian, and Dorothy Patterson "men," but in fact Carson's remark attributes to us a view opposite to the one stated in the CSG, where it says that "people in general" can be called "people" rather than "men" in translating *anthrōpos*. Carson himself seems to be aware of our actual preference in the next chapter, for in a footnote to Chapter 5 (201, n. 5), he quotes Grudem as saying "we surely did not intend" that "women should always be called 'men.'" But no reader of Carson's Chapter 4 would realize this.

[4]Downers Grove, Ill.: InterVarsity, 1998.

[5]Strauss's title for Chapter 2 is "Gender-Inclusive Versions." His list on p. 7 distinguishes "Gender Inclusive" from "traditional" versions such as the NIV, RSV, KJV, and NASB.

Strauss does not define the question clearly. At this point he is talking about things we all agree on. But the label "inclusive" gives the impression that he is establishing a case for "inclusive language" in the actual areas of *disagreement*.[6]

4. Replacing "a man" with "a person" when translating Greek *anthrōpos* (singular) in certain cases

Romans 3:28

RSV: For we hold that *a man* is justified by faith apart from works of law.

NRSV: For we hold that *a person* is justified by faith apart from works prescribed by the law.

The underlying Greek has the word *anthrōpos*, denoting a human being. Translating with "person" is more accurate, now that "a man" can be misunderstood to mean only a male human being.[7]

It is unfortunate that Mark Strauss misrepresents us and other opponents of gender-neutral Bibles at this point. He says,

> To claim that *anthrōpos* must be translated "man" but *tis* may be translated "anyone" or "someone" is a classic confusion of form and meaning. When *anthrōpos* means "anyone," why not translate it that way?[8]

Many people will assume that Strauss is criticizing the Colorado Springs Guidelines, but the CSG never said that *anthrōpos* must always be translated "man." In fact, Guideline A.5 says:

> 5. In many cases, *anthrōpoi* refers to people in general, and can be translated "people" rather than "men." The singular *anthrōpos* should ordinarily be translated "man" when it refers to a male human being.

---

[6]Of course, we allow in principle that one might use the same expression in both a broad and a narrow sense, providing that context shows the difference. But Strauss seldom if ever makes the difference plain. Disputed and undisputed usages are lumped together. As a result, Strauss does not represent clearly what the opponents of gender-neutral Bibles object to.

This failure also mars Strauss's five-page chart in Appendix 2, "Comparing the Gender-Inclusive Versions" (pp. 209-13). The chart is useful for checking individual verses in several translations, but Strauss's total counts of "inclusive verses" are misleading, because they fail to distinguish Greek *anēr*, "man," which is a gender-specific term with a male meaning component, from Greek *anthrōpos*, "human being, man," which sometimes means "person" or "human being" and sometimes means "man, male human being," depending on context. Strauss counts them all together, giving a tally of the times "man" is used to translate them. Such a total is not very relevant to the current debate, because it includes under one total both disputed and undisputed verses. (In the same chart he also lumps together the masculine-specific Hebrew term *'îsh* with the term *'ādām*, which in many contexts just means "person," with the result that the totals for Hebrew are also misleading for any determination of whether the translations engage in neutering gender-specific terms in the original or not.)

[7]The translation of the Greek term *anthrōpos* in various other contexts is a complex question, and we discuss it in Appendix 5.

[8]Mark Strauss, *Distorting*, p. 169.

By specifying that *anthrōpos* should be translated as "man" "when it refers to a male human being," the implication is clear that it does not have to be translated that way when it refers simply to an unspecified person in a general way.

A similar unfortunate misrepresentation of the CSG and the opponents of gender-neutral Bibles is found in the last sentence of the main text of Strauss's book:

> If we ask which translation, ". . . a *man* is justified by faith . . ." (Romans 3:28 NIV) or " . . .a *person* is justified by faith . . ." (NIVI) brings out *better* the inclusive sense so central to this apostolic gospel, the answer appears to me to be obvious" (p. 204).

Strauss is arguing against an artificial position. Nothing in the Colorado Springs Guidelines would object to the translation "a *person* is justified by faith," and so even in the concluding sentence of his book Strauss is arguing against a position that the guidelines do not advocate, and that we do not hold. Unfortunately, Strauss does not say this. He gives no information about whom he is arguing against. In the absence of such information, many an uninformed reader will think that he is dealing with the same controversy and the same critics that he has opposed in the rest of the book. Readers would *think* that we held that unintelligent, uninformed position— and of course would reject such a position, not knowing that it was not one we held. For Strauss to conclude his entire book with such an egregious example of an argument against a "straw man" does not help further clarity or understanding in this important issue.

5. Replacing "a man" with "anyone" when translating Greek *tis*

"A man" can be replaced with "anyone" or "a person" in a general statement that has no male semantic marking in the original.

John 15:6

RSV: If *a man* does not abide in me, he is cast forth as a branch, and withers.

NIV: If *anyone* does not remain in me, he is like a branch that is thrown away and withers.

The Greek text has the word *tis*, "someone, anyone." The translation "anyone" in the NIV is just as accurate as the RSV with "a man." But the phrase "a man," like the word "men," has shifted in meaning over time. Whereas formerly it could be understood as including women, it tends today to be understood as designating male human beings exclusively. Because of the potential misunderstanding, the NIV's "anyone" is now preferable.

The CSG specified this in Guideline A.6:

Indefinite pronouns such as *tis* can be translated "anyone" rather than "any man."[9]

B. Replacing "he who" with "the one who" or "the person who"

In general statements translations may try alternatives to "he who," such as "anyone who," "the one who," "a person who," or "whoever."

Proverbs 14:2

NIV: *He* whose walk is upright fears the LORD.

NIVI: *The person* whose walk is upright fears the LORD.

No words in Hebrew correspond to "he whose" in English, but some English words have to be added because of the difference in the grammatical structure of English. (The Hebrew is a participle of *halak*, "to walk," and means "a walking one," or "one walking.") Thus both versions represent reasonable translations, so long as "he whose" is usually understood in English to represent either a man or a woman. But if "he whose" is perceived as exclusively male, or has a significant potential for being misunderstood in that way in current English, then the NIVI translation is better. Another good alternative would be "the one whose walk is upright."

John 3:18

RSV: *He who* believes in him is not condemned.

NIV: *Whoever* believes in him is not condemned.

---

[9]Once again, Mark Strauss's book is not as clear as it could be. He gives his readers the impression that we would prefer the translation "man" for *tis*, "anyone." Neither the CSG nor any of our writings claimed this. Yet Strauss writes, concerning John 14:23,

Incidentally, it should be noted that in this example the RSV, which Grudem cites as the accurate counterpart to the NRSV, is also wrong according to such a literalist approach, since no word for "man" appears in the Greek. The Greek actually says, "if anyone [*tis*] loves me," using the indefinite relative pronoun *tis*. (*Distorting*, 121)

From this sentence readers might easily think that Grudem supports the reading "man" for *tis*. But this is the opposite of what Grudem actually said in the pamphlet that Strauss frequently quotes. In fact, not just in dealing generally with the pronoun *tis* but when dealing with this very verse (John 14:23), Grudem says, "There would be no problem in beginning the sentence, 'If anyone loves me . . .' because the Greek pronoun *tis* does not specify a man" (Wayne Grudem, *What's Wrong with Gender-Neutral Bible Translations?* [Libertyville, Ill.: Council on Biblical Manhood and Womanhood, 1997], 2). It should be clear to any reader that Grudem's purpose in the pamphlet is not to uphold the RSV at every point (for several times he argues for changes in the gender language of the RSV, as on pp. 1, 2, 4, etc.) but only when it accurately preserves a gender-specific meaning in the original language. Strauss appears to be correcting Grudem for an obviously wrong attempt to preserve more masculine language than the Greek text warrants, but he does so at this point only through misrepresenting Grudem's position.

The underlying Greek phrase *ho pisteuōn eis auton*, translated word for word, would come out "the believing into him," with a meaning close to "the one believing in him." Both "he who" and "whoever" try to make the necessary adjustments to English grammar, and both render the meaning quite accurately in current English. Another good alternative would be "the one who believes in him." The meaning of the Greek is retained in each of these cases.

The CSG stated this principle as follows:

> However, substantial participles such as *ho pisteuōn* can often be rendered in inclusive ways, such as "the one who believes" rather than "he who believes." (A.1, second sentence).

C. Replacing "sons" with "children" when translating Hebrew *banîm*

Exodus 19:6

NASB: "'. . . and you shall be to Me a kingdom of priests and a holy nation.' These are the words that you shall speak to the *sons* of Israel."

RSV: ". . . and you shall be to me a kingdom of priests and a holy nation. These are the words which you shall speak to the *children* of Israel."

KJV: And ye shall be unto me a kingdom of priests, and an holy nation. These are the words which thou shalt speak unto the *children* of Israel.

NIV: " '. . . you will be for me a kingdom of priests and a holy nation.' These are the words you are to speak to the *Israelites*."

NRS: ". . . but you shall be for me a priestly kingdom and a holy nation. These are the words that you shall speak to the *Israelites*."

NLT: " '. . . And you will be to me a kingdom of priests, my holy nation.' Give this message to the *Israelites*."

The Hebrew term here is *banîm*, the plural form of *ben*, "son." It is not a novel idea to translate this common word as "children" rather than "sons" where both males and females are clearly intended, for this was done as long ago as the King James Version in 1611, and was also used in the RSV in 1952. We mention it at this point, however, to indicate another example of a term which need not be translated in a gender-specific way (as is done in the NASB, for example). The NIV, NRSV, and NLT have all translated the expression *benē yisra'el*[10] as "Israelites," which avoids the question of translating the Hebrew plural of *ben* altogether.

---

[10]The word *benē* is another form (the "construct" form) of *banîm*, the plural of *ben*, "son." For a discussion of the translation of singular *ben*, and why it must be treated differently from the plural form, see Chapter 18, below (pp. 347-53).

The CSG stated:

However, Hebrew *banîm* often means "children" (B.2, second sentence).[11]

In sum, a number of types of change either leave meaning the same or result in improvements by adjusting to the fact that for some people, expressions like "a man" and "men" have come to be used only to refer exclusively to male human beings, and "the one who" is more evidently inclusive of all people than "he who," with no significant loss of meaning.[12] Other types of change, however, result in significant alterations of meaning, as we shall see.

---

[11]Carson brings up the translation "children" for Hebrew *banîm* in Hosea 2:4 and says, "It is certainly not the product of a feminist agenda" (pp. 20–21). No opponent of gender-neutral Bibles ever claimed that it was. So what is Carson's point? Perhaps Carson wants naïve readers to see that lack of gender match in English translation may sometimes be OK. Yes, "sometimes." The dispute is over when. Carson has not said anything here that is relevant to this core dispute.

[12]Regarding another type of change that we think acceptable in some contexts and in some translations, the change from "brothers" to "brothers and sisters" to translate the Greek plural *adelphoi*, see the discussion in Chapter 18 below (pp. 360–367).

CHAPTER 12

Unacceptable Changes That Eliminate References to Men

In some verses gender-neutral translations have introduced notable changes that draw them away from the meaning of the original. In this chapter we look first at changes that have eliminated references to men in several biblical texts.[1]

A. Removing references to males in historical passages

Acts 1:21

NIV: Therefore it is necessary to choose one of the *men* who have been with us the whole time the Lord Jesus went in and out among us.

NIVI: Therefore it is necessary to choose one of *those* who have been with us the whole time the Lord Jesus went in and out among us.

NLT: So now we must choose *someone else* to take Judas's place. It must be *someone* who has been with us all the time that we were with the Lord Jesus.

Here the NIVI and NLT introduce an unacceptable change. By replacing "men" with "those" or "someone" they eliminate the male marking that is present in Greek.

If one looks only at the English translations, Acts 1:21 might superficially look like one of the passages like Romans 2:16, where "men" means "people." But the underlying Greek word is different. The Greek has *anēr*, a word that usually designates male human beings, not mixed groups.[2]

---

[1]More examples can be found in Chapter 13 and some in Chapter 12.

[2]The word *anēr* occurs 216 times in the New Testament. It is a strongly male-marked term, in contrast to *anthrōpos*, which can mean either "man" or "person." The BAGD lexicon defines *anēr* as "*man*: 1. In contrast to woman . . . Especially *husband*. 2. *man* in contrast to boy . . . 3. used

Interestingly, in this verse some of the other gender-neutral translations (the NRSV, GNB, and GW) included the word "men," because they recognized that Peter is talking about a male replacement for a male apostle.

The change that deletes "men" is all the more significant because it touches on a theological issue. The Greek text gives evidence that Peter was expecting the apostles all to be male. This expectation in turn suggests that men and women, equally saved and justified in Christ, played complementary rather than identical roles in the early church. The NIVI and NLT, by suppressing this element, skew the verse in another direction.

Acts 20:30

RSV: And from among your own selves will arise *men* speaking perverse things.

NRSV: *Some* even from your own group will come distorting the truth.

Acts 20:30 has in Greek the word *anēr*, with male marking. Paul is addressing the elders of the church at Ephesus, all of whom were men, so he speaks of "men" rather than women who will arise "from among your own selves" and teach perversely. Of course, Paul was aware that women as well as men could hold false teaching, but in this context he is speaking only to elders, and he is speaking about false teachers who will arise from among the elders. Yet the NRSV, NIVI, NIrV(1995), NLT, NCV, and CEV have all omitted the male elements. By doing so, they have obscured the fact that Paul expected elders to be men. This verse is potentially relevant to the theological debate about women holding the office of elder, so it is all the more troubling to see that some gender-neutral translations have omitted significant evidence.

In a number of other verses the same problem occurs. The passage in Greek contains the word *anēr* with its usual sense, yet the male component is omitted in some gender-neutral translations.

1 Timothy 3:2

RSV: Now a bishop must be above reproach, *the husband of one wife*, temperate, sensible, dignified, hospitable, an apt teacher.

---

with a word indicating national or local origin ... 4. Used with adjective to emphasize the dominant characteristic of a man ... 5. *man* with special emphasis on manliness ... 6. Equivalent to *tis*, someone ... 7. *A figure of a man* of heavenly beings who resemble men ... 8. Of Jesus as the judge of the world" (*BAGD*, 66–67).

The verses given from the NT as examples for category 6, "someone," are all texts that refer to men, not people in general (Luke 8:27; 9:38; 10:1; 19:2; John. 1:30; in plural, Luke 5:18 (men carrying a paralytic) and Acts 6:11 (Stephen's Jewish opponents "secretly persuaded some men" to accuse him falsely). The same is true of the LXX examples (Sir. 27:7; 1 Macc. 12:1; 13:34). Therefore this section in *BAGD* is not intended to show that *anēr* loses its male component of meaning but only that the word can be used to mean not just "men" but "some man" or "some men."

For further discussion of *anēr*, including information from the forthcoming new addition of the BAGD lexicon, see Appendix 2, pp. 409–420..

NRSV: Now a bishop must be above reproach, *married only once*, temperate, sensible, respectable, hospitable, an apt teacher.

The fact that the bishop is expected to be male, which is quite clear in the Greek (again using *anēr*, this time to mean "husband"), has dropped out of the NRSV. Later on in the passage the NRSV uses the pronoun "he" to refer back to the bishop. But since this "he" might be generic, the passage in the NRSV still has no clear indication of maleness.

Luke 5:18

NIV: Some *men* came carrying a paralytic on a mat.

NIVI: Some *people* came carrying a paralytic on a mat.

We know that the bearers were men, not women, because the Greek word *anēr* conveys that information. In addition, the situation suggests it. It would have taken men with considerable strength to accomplish the physical task of getting the paralytic on the roof and lowering him down.

Luke 7:20

NIV: When the *men* came to Jesus, they said, "John the Baptist sent us to you to ask, . . ."

NLT: "John's two *disciples* found Jesus and said to him, "John the Baptist has sent us to ask, . . ."

Greek has the word *anēr*, indicating that the two followers of John the Baptist were male.

Luke 22:63

NIV: The *men* who were guarding Jesus began mocking and beating him.

NLT: Now the *guards* in charge of Jesus began mocking and beating him.

Greek has the word *anēr*, indicating that they were male.[3]

Acts 4:4

RSV: But many of those who heard the word believed; and the number of the *men* came to about five thousand.

NRSV: But many of those who heard the word believed; and *they* numbered about five thousand.

Greek has the word *anēr*, indicating that they were male. Note that this passage is similar to Matthew 14:21, Mark 6:44 and Luke 9:14, where Jesus miraculously fed 5,000 *men*. In these verses dealing with the feeding of the 5,000, the gender-neutral translations get it right, and indeed they have no choice, because one of the accounts specifies that the number does not count women and children: "The number of those who ate was about five thousand men, *besides women and children*" (Matt. 14:21). However, as soon

---

[3]In addition, in first century culture, men, not women, performed the function of guarding prisoners.

as such an undeniable parallel is absent, the translations fail to indicate that the numbers apply to the men, not everyone present.

Acts 5:36

NIV: Some time ago Theudas appeared, claiming to be somebody, and about four hundred *men* rallied to him.

NLT: Some time ago there was that fellow Theudas, who pretended to be someone great. About four hundred *others* joined him.

Greek has the word *anēr*, indicating that they were male.

Acts 8:2

NIV: Godly *men* buried Stephen and mourned deeply for him.

NLT: Some godly *people* came and buried Stephen with loud weeping.

Greek has the word *anēr*, indicating that they were male.

Acts 9:7

NIV: The *men* traveling with Saul stood there speechless.

GNB: "*Those* who were travelling with Saul stood there speechless.

Greek has the word *anēr*, indicating that they were male.

Acts 11:20

NIV: Some of them, however, *men* from Cyprus and Cyrene, went to Antioch and began to speak to Greeks also, telling them the good news about the Lord Jesus.

NLT: However, some of the *believers* who went to Antioch from Cyprus and Cyrene began preaching to Gentiles about the Lord Jesus.

Greek has the word *anēr*, indicating that they were male.

Acts 21:38

RSV: Are you not the Egyptian, then, who recently stirred up a revolt and led the four thousand *men* of the Assassins out into the wilderness?

NRSV: Then you are not the Egyptian who recently stirred up a revolt and led the four thousand *assassins* out into the wilderness?

Greek has the word *anēr*, indicating that they were male.

B.   Removing references to males in parables

Some of Jesus' parabolic sayings have been altered to remove the maleness of characters in them.

Matthew 7:24

NIV: Therefore everyone who hears these words of mine and puts them into practice is like a wise *man* who built his house on the rock.

NLT: Anyone who listens to my teaching and obeys me is wise, like a *person* who builds a house on solid rock.

Greek has the word *anēr*, indicating that he was male. (A similar change occurs in Matt. 7:26.)

Luke 14:24

NIV: I tell you, not one of those *men* who were invited will get a taste of my banquet.

NIVI: I tell you, not one of *those* who were invited will get a taste of my banquet.

Greek has the word *anēr*, indicating that they were male.

Luke 11:11

RSV: What *father* among you, if his *son* asks for a fish, will instead of a fish give him a serpent; ...

NRSV: Is there *anyone* among you who, if your *child* asks for a fish, will give a snake instead of a fish?

The original picture of a father and a son has now become a picture of "anyone" and "your child," removing male marking for both the parent and the child. The Greek text has *patēr*, which means "father,"[4] and *huios*, which means "son,"[5] not *teknon*, which means "child."

C. Removing references to males who are examples of principles

Proverbs 5:1

RSV: My *son*, be attentive to my wisdom.

NRSV: My *child*, be attentive to my wisdom.

The Hebrew is *ben*, "son." The father warns his son about an immoral woman in 5:3–23, which confirms that a son rather than a daughter is specifically in view. Other verses in Proverbs contain principles applicable to all, but this fact does not eliminate the male marking intended in Proverbs 5:1.

(Though Mark Strauss claims that Hebrew *ben* (singular) can mean "child,"[6] there is no support for this in the Brown-Driver-Briggs *Hebrew and English Lexicon of the Old Testament*,[7] and Strauss has produced no verses where the established sense "son" could not be used instead of "child."[8])

---

[4]*BAGD*, 635–636.

[5]*BAGD*, 833–835.

[6]Mark Strauss, *Distorting Scripture? The Challenge of Bible Translation and Gender Accuracy* (Downers Grove: InterVarsity, 1998), 157.

[7]The BDB *Lexicon* indicates that Hebrew *ben*, which occurs 4,870 times in the OT, means "son" in singular, though it can mean "children" in plural (BDB, 119–22). If the meaning "child" were possible for the singular form of this word, one would expect to find evidence for it somewhere in thousands of examples. (The 4,870 figure includes both singular and plural forms.)

[8]The evidence Strauss gives is not in any lexicon but is an argument that "child" makes good sense as a translation for *ben* in Isaiah 49:15 and Ezekiel 18:4. While the word "child"

Proverbs 7:1

RSV: My *son*, keep my words.

NRSV: My *child*, keep my words.

Instruction about the immoral woman begins again in verse 5. This shows clearly that a son is in view, but again the NRSV suppresses the male element. The NRSV has "my child" throughout Proverbs 1–9 in the places where Hebrew has *beni* "my son."

Proverbs 3:12

NIV: Because the LORD disciplines those he loves, as a *father* the *son* he delights in.

NIVI: Because the LORD disciplines those he loves, as *parents* the *children* they delight in.

"Father" (Hebrew *'ab*) becomes "parents," and "son" (Hebrew *ben*) becomes "children."[9] The second half of the verse is not a general proverbial saying about parents, but a specific illustration of what the Lord's discipline means. It gains in vividness through its focus on "a father." Even though it is only an illustration, and even though elsewhere the Bible specifically compares God to a *father*, GNB, NIVI, CNV, and CEV could not tolerate the male-oriented meaning of the original.

---

would make sense in these verses, so would the word "son." The context alone is not decisive. Strauss claims that it "probably" means "child," but the translators of the RSV, NASB, KJV, and NKJV did not think the context required that it meant that at all, for they all translated it "son." It is not persuasive for Strauss to attempt to overturn decades of Hebrew scholarship, in which no convincing examples of *ben* in singular have been found to mean "child" rather than "son," simply by appealing to one example of parallelism that has been translated that way in the NIV and asserting that here it "probably" means "child."

This is one of several cases where advocates of gender-neutral Bibles fail to recognize the boundaries of semantic ranges of words, boundaries that have been established through decades and even centuries of lexicographical research. In so doing, gender-neutral Bible advocates fail to follow sound procedures in lexicography when claiming new meanings for Hebrew and Greek words. The general principle of lexicography to be followed here is one stated by the Cambridge Classics scholar John Chadwick, an expert in Greek lexicography, in his book *Lexicographica Graeca: Contributions to the Lexicography of Ancient Greek* (Oxford: Clarendon Press, 1996), 23–24:

> A constant problem to guard against is the proliferation of meanings. . . . It is often tempting to create a new sense to accommodate a difficult example, but we must always ask first, if there is any other way of taking the word which would allow us to assign the example to an already established sense. . . . As I have remarked in several of my notes, there may be no reason why a proposed sense should not exist, but is there any reason why it must exist?

An objector might reply that this is not a "new" meaning, since the meaning "children" is attested for the Hebrew plural form *banîm*. But the general principle is still valid here, because "child" is a postulated new meaning *for the singular form ben*. Innovations of this kind ought always to rely on much more solid evidence than Strauss has produced.

[9]Both words are very common and have unambiguous male markings: Hebrew *'ab*, which occurs 1,191 times in the OT, means "father," not "parent" (see *BDB*, 3), when it occurs in the singular in the context of family relations. Hebrew *ben*, as explained in the previous footnote, means "son" in singular, though it can mean "children" in plural (*BDB*, 119–22).

Proverbs 13:1

NIV: A wise *son* heeds his *father's* instruction.

NIVI: A wise *child* heeds a *parent's* instruction.

A clear male component in the original has been deleted both from "son" and from "father."

Proverbs 28:7

RSV: He who keeps the law is a wise *son*, but a companion of gluttons shames his *father*.

NRSV: Those who keep the law are wise *children*, but companions of gluttons shame their *parents*.

The singular male "son" (Hebrew *ben*) has become the plural and gender-neutral "children," and the singular male "father" (Hebrew *'ab*) has become the plural and gender-neutral "parents."

These changes, and many others like them, are not justified by sound lexicography, but result from a policy that mutes the masculinity (that is, the male components of meaning) of many of God's words.

D. Colorado Springs Guidelines concerning words for "father" and "son"

In order to guard against such changes, the Colorado Springs Guidelines stated the following principles about the translation of words for "father" and "son":

> B. Gender-related renderings which we will generally avoid, though there may be unusual exceptions in certain contexts:
>
> 2. "Son" (*huios, ben*) should not be changed to "child," or "sons" (*huioi*) to "children" or "sons and daughters." (However, Hebrew *banîm* often means "children.")
>
> 3. "Father" (*patēr, 'ab*) should not be changed to "parent," or "fathers" to "parents" or "ancestors."

We recognized that there were unusual instances, so that a guideline like this one should not be made absolute. Therefore these guidelines were classified under the general heading that said we would "generally avoid" them but there may be "unusual exceptions in certain contexts." This still allowed the guideline to warn against a wholesale alteration of dozens or hundreds of examples.

It is disappointing, therefore, to see in D. A. Carson's book a claim that Hebrews 11:23 disproves Guideline B.3. The verse says, "By faith Moses, when he was born, was hid for three months by his parents (plural of Greek *patēr*)." Carson rightly says the word here must be rendered as "parents." The problem is that he claims this verse as an example that proves that "there are some instances when a competent translator ought to do exactly what B.3 forbids."[10] But Carson fails to tell the reader that Guideline B.3 falls under general category B, "Gender-related renderings which we will *generally* avoid, though *there may be unusual exceptions* in certain contexts."[11] The irony of this is that the use of *patēr* in Hebrews 11:23 was explicitly mentioned in discussion as we were writing Guideline B.3 at Dr. Dobson's headquarters in Colorado Springs on May 27. We allowed for cases like Hebrews 11:23 when we included B.3 under heading B. The upshot of it is that a translator does not have to "do exactly what B.3 forbids," as Carson claims, but rather exactly what B.3 allows—"in certain contexts."

E. Why is only the male sex indicator deleted in gender-neutral translations?

Of course, the Bible uses women as well as men as examples. Psalm 113:7 says, "He [the LORD] settles the barren woman in her home as a happy mother of children." Surely the general principle also applies to men who have no children. Should we then translate, "He settles the childless *person* in a home as a happy *parent* of children"? No. We preserve the female orientation of the original example, and let the reader see that it applies broadly by implication but not by explicit statement. We preserve the difference between what is stated explicitly and what is implied.

We should treat other examples of women in the same way, preserving the explicit female indications that are there in the original text. Matthew 25:1–13 introduces "ten virgins" in a parable of Jesus that teaches a lesson about being ready for the coming of God's kingdom. Since the lesson about being ready is a general one, do we conceal the fact that the ten virgins are female?[12] Of course not.

In Luke 15:8–10 Jesus' parable has a woman searching for a lost coin. The woman is an illustration of God searching for the lost. Naturally, the female character of the woman remains in "inclusive language" translations. In Luke 13:20–21 a woman puts yeast into flour. Again, the woman remains in

---

[10]D. A. Carson, *The Inclusive Language Debate: A Plea for Realism* (Grand Rapids: Baker, and Leicester: InterVarsity, 1998), 133.

[11]Carson does not quote the guidelines in full when he criticizes them on pages 111–33. Very few readers of page 133 will take the time to find Guideline B.3 back on page 46 or heading B, which allows for exceptions, back on page 45 in his book. In analyzing the Guidelines, Carson more than once takes a nuanced, guarded statement that allows for unusual exceptions and quotes it in part so that it becomes for his readers an absolute statement. Then he cites an exception in some unusual construction or context and makes the reader think he has shown the guideline to be ignorant of the facts of the Hebrew and Greek Bible. But in fact what Carson has disproven is not the guideline but his own attempt to construe it as an absolute rule with no exceptions.

[12]These "virgins" are definitely women, since the Greek relative pronoun *haitines* ("who") and the participle *labousai* ("having taken, took") in verse 1 are both explicitly feminine, as are other words in subsequent verses. The term "virgin" (*parthenos*) can be used of either men or women (*BAGD*, 627).

translation. But in the parable of the wise and foolish builders in Matthew 7:24 and 7:26, the "man" (Greek *anēr*, indicating a male human being) becomes a "person" in CEV and NLT. All signs of maleness disappear.

Only one out of the two sex indicators gets deleted, the male one. After seeing a number of cases like this, one cannot help raising questions. Why do the gender-neutral translations consistently preserve female examples, but sometimes neutralize the male ones? The only obvious explanations would seem to be prejudice against maleness, or desire to equalize the number of male and female examples, or fear that male examples, unlike female ones, will be irritating to our culture.[13] All of these explanations are, in one way or another, related to one of the fundamental concerns of feminism. As we shall see in Chapter 14, feminism rejects any unequal weight given to the male.

Thus, the changes are of concern, not only because an aspect of meaning drops out, but also because ideology may have entered into translation decisions.

---

[13]The ideas that are unpopular vary from culture to culture, and the pressure to tone down some elements of the Bible's language will always be present in various forms. To put this in perspective, Baylor University English professor David Lyle Jeffrey points to a similar embarrassment with another idea, the idea of Jewishness, in the pre-World War II era in Nazi Germany, and notes how it affected liturgy, hymns, the reading of Scripture in churches, and even Bible translations:

> A notable raluctance to use the words "Jew" and "Israel" had begun to be evident in the German church in the early years of the Nazi era; it expressed itself in the de-judaizing of biblical language in the liturgy and hymns, in changing of worship references from "Jews" to "People of God," and in eschewing of readings which made the Jewish identity of the "chosen" people too transparent to disguise by "re-translation" alone. This felonious and often fraudulent strategy had, predictably enough, voluminous academic defense. . . . What we are now experiencing is essentially the same phenomenon . . . Their claim, after all, was that the changes simply made the text "more inclusive." . . . Why, in our own tremulous time, does the idea of fatherhood, especially of goodly, godly and finally a divinely modeled exemplar of fatherhood, excite such hostility . . . ? ("Death of Father Language: Attacking the Heart of Christian Identity," in *Journal for Biblical Manhood and Womanhood* 4:4 [Spring 2000], 12).

CHAPTER 13

Generic "He"

Now we come to the largest problem, affecting thousands of verses: the problem of generic "he."

A. What is generic "he"?

In English "he" has several functions. It is used to refer to a particular male person identified in the context. It is also used "generically," that is, to make general statements including men and women. Consider Matthew 16:24–26:

> Then Jesus said to his disciples, "If anyone would come after me, *he* must deny *himself* and take up *his* cross and follow me. For whoever wants to save *his* life will lose it, but whoever loses *his* life for me will find it. What good will it be for a man, if *he* gains the whole world and forfeits *his* soul? Or what can a man give in exchange for *his* soul?" (NIV)

The verses contain several occurrences of generic "he," referring back to "anyone." Not only "he" but "his," "him," "himself" can have this function. For convenience, we include he/his/him/himself under the umbrella term "generic 'he.' "

Now we must introduce a distinction. The expression "he who . . ." occurs in general statements, such as "He who guards his mouth preserves his life" (Prov. 13:3, RSV). In such statements "he" is "generic." But there are reasonable translation alternatives to "he who," such as "the one who," "the person who," "anyone who," and "whoever." Such changes are permissible, as we noted earlier. We are here looking at a much more controversial question, whether it is permissible to drop "he" when it refers *backward* to an earlier identifying expression like "anyone."[1] From now on we are talking only about backward-referring generic "he."

---

[1]As we shall see, the issue is controversial mainly because, unlike "he who . . . ," there is often no easy way to eliminate backward-referring "he." Gender-neutral translations have to restructure the whole sentence to get rid of it. In the process they end up altering meanings.

B. Changes in gender-neutral translations[2]

The gender-neutral translations commonly undertake to eliminate this kind of generic "he." The NIVI rewords Matthew 16:24–26 as follows:

> 16:24 *Those* who would come after me must deny *themselves* and take up *their* cross and follow me. 25 For *those* who want to save *their* lives will lose *them,* but *those* who lose *their* lives for me will find *them.* 26 What good will it be for *you* to gain the whole world, yet forfeit *your* soul? Or what can *you* give in exchange for *your* soul? (NIVI).

In verses 24–25 all the singulars, "he/his/himself," are converted to plurals in order to eliminate generic "he." In verse 26 the NIVI adopts a different strategy. It replaces the third person singular "he/his" with the second person "you." The NRSV uses "those/they/them/their/themselves" in all three verses, while the NLT uses "you" in all three verses.

Changes like these are not exceptional. Because generic singular is a convenient and frequent usage in the Bible, gender-neutral translations end up using "they" and "you" in a large number of passages where earlier translations had generic singular "he/his/him." In still other instances the new translations adopt passive rather than active constructions or substitute descriptive nouns for pronouns in order to avoid using "he." The total number of verses affected numbers in the thousands.

Now, let us be clear: The gender-neutral translations still achieve a rough approximation of the meaning of the original when they change the pronouns. But it is an approximation. When we look at finer nuances, shifts from singular to plural and from third person to first or second person result in subtle alterations. "You" begins with the hearer as the starting point in order to make the general statement.[3] "We" speaks to the hearer and includes the speaker, while "anyone/he" pictures a general case "out there," as it were. The relation between a statement and the addressees subtly changes when we shift from third to second person.[4] The relation to the speaker changes if we shift to first person.

---

[2]In this and some other sections, we have reused and revised material from Vern S. Poythress, "Gender in Bible Translation: Exploring a Connection with Male Representatives," *Westminster Theological Journal* 60/2 (1998): 225–53.

[3]The use of "you" and "we" is actually more complex than what we can summarize here. We note some nuances below, but we must stop somewhere in dealing with details. For instance, we do not discuss the difference between second-person singular and plural. The existence in contemporary North American English of only one form, "you," creates a potential ambiguity in English, whereas Greek, Hebrew, and Aramaic have distinct singular and plural forms. Neither do we discuss whether in some kinds of writing "we" may not literally include the reader but includes him only "artificially," from politeness.

[4]Stanley E. Porter analyzes the loss of meaning when the CEV changes to second person "you" in the interests of gender-inclusive language in translating Matthew 16:24, noting that the "sense of wider application" that was evident when "anyone" was used to translate Greek *tis* is now "lost" in the CEV. Porter concludes, "I am not convinced that it is the best interests of making the meaning of the original text clear if the clear meaning that exists is in fact obscured. The attempt to be politically correct may not always be translationally correct"

In addition, "he/his/him" refers to a representative individual person within a group of people, while "they/their/them" refers to the plurality of members of a group. In changing from one to the other the focus shifts from the individual to a plurality.

It is often claimed that no harm is done, since the original meaning of the text is still implied, directly or indirectly, in the translation. A statement about a plurality using "they" still implies truths about each individual ("he") *within* the group. Conversely, a statement about a single sample member using "he" implies truths concerning the plurality of all members of the group. Similarly, readers can infer a general truth from something that starts with "you."

C. Explicit and implicated meaning

But in reality the people who argue this way have already conceded that the meaning has subtly changed in their translation. An *explicit* content in the original has to be *inferred* in the translation, while what was only *inferable* from the meaning in the original becomes *explicit* in the translation. The shift from direct statement to inference is significant. It is a subtle change in meaning. Moreover, a shift from "he" to "you" results in a subtle shift in focus, even though we may express the same general truth through both modes of expression. When we use "he," the pictorial starting point is a sample person who is mentally positioned "out there." When we use "you," the pictorial starting point is "you," the addressee. With "you," the manner of expression invites the addressee to picture himself in the situation. Starting with himself, the addressee then generalizes to others. With "he," the addressee starts with a general instance "out there," and then perhaps applies it to himself. The movement of thought is subtly different.

With this judgment the reference book *A Comprehensive Grammar of the English Language* agrees. After noting that "we" and "they" as well as "you" and "he" have generic uses, it says, "Although used generically, these personal pronouns *we, you,* and *they* retain something of the specific meaning associated with the 1st, 2nd, and 3rd persons respectively. They are therefore not wholly interchangeable."[5] On occasion, even "I" can function generically.[6]

("The Contemporary English Version," in *Translating the Bible: Problems and Prospects*, JSNT Supplement Series 173, edited by Stanley E. Porter and Richard S. Hess [Sheffield: Sheffield Academic Press, 1999], 32–34).

[5]Randolph Quirk, et al., *A Comprehensive Grammar of the English Language* (London/New York: Longman, 1985), 6.21.

[6]One biblical example is 1 Corinthians 13:1: "If *I* speak in the tongues of men and of angels, but have not love, *I* am only a resounding gong or a clanging cymbal." Or someone may say, "A good many readers have childish expectations, because *we* live in a permissive, consumerist society. Advertisements train people to think of themselves as needing to be pleased, entertained, and kept comfortable. Work may still be onerous at times, but when *I* finish work *I* expect to relax."

The ability to use every person, number, and gender in English in a generic way seems to have less to do with peculiar properties of English grammar and more to do with the fact that all over the world speakers find ways to express a general principle using a sample case as their starting point. The starting point can thus be either first, second, or third person, singular or plural.

Does this mean that there are no differences in meaning between generic statements that use first person ("I/we"), second person ("you"), or third person ("he/they")? No, because these different types of generic statements convey somewhat different meanings. The differences due to starting point may be subtle, but they are there—differences in nuance in the total meaning-impact, not merely differences in phrasing with *no* meaning difference.[7] Remember the conclusion of Ernst-August Gutt, "Translators should have a firm grasp of hitherto neglected aspects of meaning. In particular, they should understand that there are important differences between expressing and implicating information, between strong and weak communication."[8]

---

[7]Mark Strauss shows no awareness of such differences in meaning between "he" and "you" used generically (see *Distorting*, 122–24, where Strauss sees generic "you" as one useful substitute for generic "he"). Carson also argues that generic "you" sometimes is a good substitute for generic "he" in gender-neutral versions (*Debate*, 118–20), and, though he concedes that "switching persons is at least potentially misleading" (p. 119), he indicates no aspects of meaning that he thinks might be lost in a switch from "he" to "you" in generic statements. In fact, he says that when Grudem calls attention to subtle differences in meaning introduced by a switch from "he" to "you," Grudem may be guilty of "lexical woodenness" (p. 120), and when Grudem brings up differences in nuance between singular and plural pronouns, this is thinking of language "in the wooden categories of what might be called lexical exegesis" (p. 116).

We reply that careful interpretation requires us to notice nuances and small differences in meaning—to overlook them is to be insensitive to the text; to care about these nuances is to respect the text.

It may aid us to refer again to the differing levels of analyzing linguistic complexity, as noted at the end of Chapter 4. Carson rightly dismisses "lexical woodenness" that belongs to the naïve level 1. This woodenness imagines that "he" or "you" or "they" must always function in exactly the same way with exactly the same nuances and impact. Then at level 2, using the theoretically-informed distinction between form and meaning, Carson might rightly observe that generic "he" and generic "you" are different in form, but that the overall statement has "the same meaning." Hence "lexical woodenness" is refuted.

But one has not yet arrived at level 3, where native speakers are intuitively aware of subtle differences, and where a massively detailed grammar acknowledges them explicitly (*Quick Comprehensive Grammar*, 6.21). It is easy to underestimate the complexity of the discussion.

Carson shows at times that he is aware of difficulties. He says that in John 5:26 translations "'lose' a little something or 'gain' a little something" (*Debate*, p. 115; note similar language on p. 119). But Carson is not interested in elaborating or investigating these details about loss of meaning, so the point is minimized and the casual reader may miss it. In the end, the amount of meaning that is lost is not the focus of his argument, for he retreats to invoking repeatedly the possibility that generic "he" is, or will be, unusable, so that the translators have no choice except to lose some meaning (*Debate*, 106, 117–119, 158; see further discussion in Appendix 6). We will take up these concerns below.

[8]Ernst-August Gutt, *Relevance Theory*, 72.

Stylists trained to be sensitive to nuances recognize that there are differences here. In his book *On Writing Well* William Zinsser discusses generic "he" and its alternatives. Using "they" is not adequate. Zinsser says, "I don't like plurals; they weaken writing because they are less specific than the singular, less easy to visualize."[9] "A style that converts every 'he' into a 'they' will quickly turn to mush."[10]

In the fourth edition (1990) of the book *On Writing Well*, William Zinsser eliminated many of the generic masculines that occurred in earlier editions of his book.[11] But, continuing in the fifth edition (1995), he also says, "Where the male pronoun remains in this edition I felt it was the only clean solution."[12] (See Chapters 15–16, below, for further discussion of whether generic "he" is acceptable and understandable in English today—in fact, dozens of examples from current English-language publications show that it is still useful and still widely understood. The rest of the discussion in this chapter will assume that conclusion, and readers can look ahead to that discussion if they wish.)

D. A failure to recognize the linguistic issue at the heart of this controversy

Carson's and Strauss's discussions regularly fail to discuss the differences between explicit and implied meaning, and the differences in nuance between the starting points for first-person, second-person, and third-person generic statements. For this reason their very definitions of what is meant by "inclusive-language" or "gender-neutral" translation do not really get at the heart of the issue. Carson says:

> By "inclusive-language translations" or "gender-neutral translations" or "gender-inclusive translations" I am referring to English translations of the Bible, or parts of the Bible, that replace male nouns like "man" and "brother" and male pronouns like "he" and "him" with other expressions that clearly include women—hence *inclusive* language. "Man" might become "person," "brother" might become "brother and sister," and so forth.[13]

By this definition, the older translations like the RSV, NASB, and NIV are all gender-neutral translations because they made such replacements compared to the KJV. By this definition, the Colorado Springs Guidelines also endorse exactly what they were written to exclude, because they approve of each of the replacements Carson names (within certain kinds of

---

[9]William Zinsser, *On Writing Well,* 5th ed. (New York: HarperCollins, 1995), 123.
[10]Ibid., 122.
[11]But, consistent with his own principles, he usually did not replace them with plurals.
[12]Ibid., 123.
[13]Carson, *Debate,* 16-17.

expression). In fact, on this definition, every English translation except the KJV is "gender neutral." Since the book begins like this (and under the section "definitions"), one wonders if it can provide an accurate analysis of the real issues in the current discussion.

Strauss similarly fails to define the issue clearly. He says,

> Gender-inclusive versions are those that intentionally use an inclusive term *when this inclusive sense is intended by the author.*[14]

What Strauss does not tell us is whether he means the inclusive sense is *explicitly stated* by the author or that it is *implied* by the author. If he means gender-inclusive versions are those that use inclusive language when an inclusive sense is *explicitly expressed* by the author in the original language, then we would fully advocate such translations, for we want to represent explicitly in English what is explicit in Hebrew or Greek.

But if Strauss means a "gender-neutral" Bible is one that makes explicit in English an inclusive sense that is only *implied* in the original text, then it is hard to know where to stop. What about a passage like Proverbs 13.1, "A wise son heeds his father's instruction" (NIV)? Because the context of Proverbs is full of general principles, we can infer that the writer intended us to see a broad principle here, and therefore to see that a wise daughter heeds both her father's and mother's instruction. That is, the writer intended an implication to be drawn quite broadly. But his formulation nevertheless spoke explicitly of son and father, for concreteness. Must we then eliminate the male meaning components in translation to include explicitly this implication to include women? Why would Exodus 20:17 not change, for it *explicitly says* ". . . you shall not covet your neighbor's wife," but it *implies* that it is also wrong for a wife to covet her neighbor's husband? The upshot of this is that the definition is not precise because it does not recognize what the real issue is.

The real issue is not the *frequency* with which a translation uses masculine terms like "man" and "he" and "father" and "brother," and so on.[15] Nor is the issue whether changes in gender language are made to conform to modern English style.

The issue is whether a Bible translation systematically excludes male components of meaning that are there in the original text. If it does, the translation is "gender neutral," and we argue in this book that such a translation does not properly translate some of the details in the Word of God.

---

[14]Strauss, *Distorting*, 15. Later on the same page he says that the term "gender-inclusive" is "here defined as 'a translation that explicitly seeks to include women when the original author so intended.'" The same kind of statement can be found at the end of his book: "I would suggest that the best policy is to adopt the consistent use of gender-inclusive language whenever the original text clearly intends to include both men and women" (p. 200).

[15]This is why Strauss misses the point in his chart on pages 209–13, where he just counts the total number of masculine-oriented words in various translations.

Generic "he" is also part of the issue because in many cases one cannot eliminate it without altering meanings.

Now, what should we do when translating the Bible? Because the Bible is the very Word of God and because it conveys meaning that is amazingly rich, complex, and multilayered, in the context of doing Bible translation, we ought to convey in the translation *as much of the meaning of the original as we can.* Therefore, with respect to changing generic "he" to some other form of expression, we ought not to tolerate these losses of meaning as long as a way exists of avoiding the losses. And of course a way does exist—namely, continuing to use generic "he."

Translation differs markedly from original writing. Modern writers have authority over their own meanings and can alter them if they choose. They can rephrase or restructure what they are saying in order to eliminate all generic masculines, and they can decide to tolerate the changes in nuance, perspective, and starting point for a generic statement. They can (as Zinsser says) convert their styles to "mush" if they like. But the translator of the Bible does not have the same authority to introduce subtle alterations in the meaning of the biblical text—the meaning of the original does not belong to the translator, and he has no authority to change it.

E. Distortions in meaning

In addition, these changes introduce possibilities for distortion and misunderstanding. For example, consider again Matthew 16:24:

NIV: Then Jesus said to his disciples, "If anyone would come after me, he must deny himself and take up his cross and follow me."

NIVI: Then Jesus said to his disciples, "*Those* who would come after me must deny *themselves* and take up *their* cross and follow me."

In the NIVI, "their cross" in the singular could be construed as a single cross belonging to the whole group of followers jointly. If one reads it this way, the group jointly has responsibility for a single "cross," a group shame. They also have a group life, in which they deny "themselves," their former identity as a group. The focus subtly shifts from individual to group when there is a change from "he" to "they." In a similar way, if nothing but the second-person "you" occurs in a verse, it may become less clear whether the saying applies to all human beings or just to the immediate addressees.

We may further illustrate the difficulties with other passages. Compare two versions of John 14:23:

NIV: If anyone loves me, he will obey my teaching. My Father will love him, and we will come to him and make our home with him.

NRSV: *Those* who love me will keep my word, and my Father will love *them*, and we will come to *them* and make our home with *them*.

The NRSV substitutes plurals for the generic singulars found in Greek and in the NIV. But this step results in an unintended ambiguity in the product. The last clause, "make our home with them," has a plurality of people, "them," combined with a single dwelling place, "our home." Conceivably, it might mean that the Father and the Son make a home with each person. But it might also mean that the Father and the Son make a single home with the plurality of people *together*. That is, they come and dwell with the church corporately. This latter interpretation is closer to the surface or more "obvious" than the first, since it responds to the difference between the singular "home" and the plural "them." Such a thought of corporate dwelling is genuinely biblical (as 1 Cor. 3:10–15 and Eph. 2:22 show), but it is not the thought found in John 14:23. Both the Greek original and the NIV picture the Father and the Son making a dwelling with *each* person, not with the church corporately.

In the illustrations from both Matthew 16:14 and John 14:23, the ambiguity arises because in a generic statement the plural form "they" regularly produces a subtle meaning difference. "They," as we observed, pushes readers to focus on a plurality of people, all the members of some group, as the starting point for the statement of the general truth. At times we can unambiguously infer that the *same* truth holds for each individual member of the group. But at other times the sentence in the plural can affirm a truth about the members taken together in such a way that it is not clear whether an analogous truth holds for one single member rather than for the group as a collective entity.

Now let us return to John 14:23. The clause "my Father will love them" may be understood either corporately or individually. Does the Father love "them" by loving each individual in his individuality? Or does the Father love "them" by loving them as a group, loving the church? Both readings are *theologically* true, as Ephesians 5:25 and Galatians 2:20 indicate. But John 14:23 asserts the former, not the latter.

Love is a multifaceted personal action, with many dimensions and many possible variations in nuance. The connotations change when we shift from loving "him" to loving "them." Consider an example from human experience. We might say, "Mary loves *those* who work for her favorite charity, the Philadelphia Literacy Institute." But the list of workers is long, and Mary does not even know all their names! By contrast, suppose we say, "Mary loves *each person* who works for the Philadelphia Literacy Institute." In fact, she goes to chat with each of them every day. The two modes of expression suggest two loves, subtly different from one another. In the first case, with the word "those," Mary loves the group, while in the second case, with "each person," she loves each individual within the group.

The two modes also tend to suggest two subtly different reasons for the love. In the first case the love is based on attachment to the charitable institute. In the second case the love builds on acquaintance and may have many motives unrelated to the institute. Mary loves John for one reason and Sue for a different reason. Of course we heighten the difference between the two kinds when we add further commentary about Mary not knowing their names (in the first case) or chatting with each one (in the second case). But these details fit the different sentences because they expand on a subtle difference in atmosphere that is already present even without the commentary.[16]

John 14:21

NIV: Whoever has my commands and obeys them, he is the one who loves me. He who loves me will be loved by my Father, and I too will love him and show myself to him.

NIVI: *Those* who have my commands and obey them are *the ones* who love me. *Those* who love me will be loved by my Father, and I too will love *them* and show myself to *them*.

By changing singulars to plurals, the NIVI produces problems similar to what we observed in John 14:23. The nuances of "love" shift depending on whether we are talking about love for a single person or love directed toward a group and its members.

In addition, the focus shifts subtly from an individual to the group of people "who have my commands." We might even imagine that Jesus has in mind two groups, one orthodox and the other heretical.[17] The orthodox group is described as "those who have my commands," whereas heretical groups fail in either of two ways. Either they do not "have my commands," because they replace the apostolic teaching with false substitutes, or they do not "obey them," because they teach that obedience is an optional addition to having the verbal commands. Doubtless all this would be true enough of heretical groups, but it is subtly different from what Jesus is actually saying. His focus is much more directly on individual people. Many such verses that specify a relationship between God and an individual have been obscured in gender-neutral translation.

Interestingly, one gender-neutral translation, *God's Word* (GW), explicitly acknowledges the danger: "However, if a passage focuses upon an individual, *God's Word* does not use plural nouns and pronouns to avoid the gender-specific pronouns *he, him,* and *his.* In these cases the translators considered the text's focus upon an individual more important than an

---

[16]Once again, we are dealing with subtle differences (belonging to the discerning approach, level 3 in the classification at the end of Chapter 10). At level 2, the two expressions are roughly paraphrases of one another, so we could say that they are "the same" in meaning and "different" in form—*at the theoretically informed level* where we are illustrating an idealized kind of form-meaning distinction (a level 2 *approximation*). When we do a fine-grained study, in the discerning approach and the reflective approach (levels 3 and 4), there are fine-grained differences in meaning.

[17]Once again we heighten a subtle difference in order to make it visible and call attention to it.

artificial use of plural pronouns."[18] GW recognizes that the use of the singular may result in "focus upon an individual." A meaning difference is recognized. But then GW goes ahead and transforms to plurals in Matthew 16:24–26, John 14:21, and John 14:23! GW has not consistently followed its own advice.

Consider now the translation of Revelation 3:20:

RSV: Behold, I stand at the door and knock; if *any one* hears my voice and opens the door, I will come in to *him* and eat with *him*, and *he* with me.

NRSV: Listen! I am standing at the door, knocking; if *you* hear my voice and open the door, I will come in to *you* and eat with *you*, and *you* with me.

The NRSV has changed "he/him" to "you." The NRSV again presents us with an ambiguity. The NRSV may mean that Christ will eat with each *individual* "you" who hears his voice. But it may also be a call for the whole church *corporately* to hear his voice and open the door to him. In response Christ then promises to eat with them corporately: "I will . . . eat with *you*." The "you's" in the preceding context of Revelation 3:14–19 all address the angel, and through the angel the church at Laodicea. That is, they address the church *as a whole*. When we come to verse 20, the shift to the individualizing "anyone" is lost in the gender-neutral NRSV.

This removes the ability of this verse to teach us forcefully about the spiritual fellowship that Jesus has with *each individual believer*. This is an important aspect of the Christian life, and it has often been taught from, "I will come in to *him* and eat with *him*, and *he* with me" in Revelation 3:20. But in the NRSV that personal aspect of the Christian life can no longer so easily be derived from Revelation 3:20. One might respond that it can be taught from other passages that speak of the relationship between Christ and the individual believer—but many of those passages also use generic "he" to teach this truth, and they have also been changed in gender-neutral translations.

This loss of the shift to the individual (anyone) in verse 20 may be more significant than we realize from another standpoint. In several of the exhortations to repentance in Revelation 2–3, Christ calls individuals to repentance, even in the face of the possibility that others in the church do not repent (note, for example, Jezebel in Rev. 2:21, and the distinction between the "few" and the many at Sardis, Rev. 3:4; note also "he who overcomes . . ."). The implication of Revelation 3:20 is that *each one* is to hear Christ's voice, even if others in the Laodicean church fail to hear. The NRSV fails to convey this significant dimension of meaning.

John 6:54.

NIV: *Whoever* eats my flesh and drinks my blood has eternal life, and I will raise *him* up at the last day.

---

[18]GW, Preface, xiii.

NIVI: *Those who* eat my flesh and drink my blood have eternal life, and I will raise *them* up at the last day.

The singular "whoever" becomes "those," and the singular "him" becomes "them." The changes were made in order to avoid using "him." But differences in nuance arise from the change. The NIV focuses explicitly on the individual person, while the NIVI uses as its starting point "those," focusing on the plurality of people who "eat my flesh." There are differences between what is explicit and implicit, between direct and inferred aspects of communication. In the NIVI perhaps we can infer an application to individuals, but the NIV has the individual in focus more directly.

Moreover, the NIVI is potentially ambiguous between a group interpretation and an individual interpretation. NIVI is closer to suggesting that eating my flesh and drinking my blood is a communal experience. The Lord's Supper, signifying our union with Christ, is communal in character. So does the NIVI mean that the Christian community has communion with Christ and is communally raised up? Such things may be true, but they do not offer a firm assurance to any individual. A reader may think, "Maybe I could fall away from the community and lose my salvation." The NIV gives a better basis for assurance by focusing the promise on each individual within a larger whole.[19] If anyone eats my flesh, Jesus will raise *that very person*, not simply a group from which some individuals might drop away (see John 6:39).

We have heard people observe, in response to the individual emphasis of these verses, that American Christians are far too individualizing. The danger, they say, is not of missing an individualizing note, but of missing the corporate dimension of New Testament Christianity. So (someone may argue) it might be beneficial to add more emphasis to the corporate nature of the Christian life to some of these texts.

We would probably agree with this assessment of American Christianity as a whole. But we would not agree with the intended conclusion, namely that one can safely reduce the individualizing aspect of *these particular texts*. In the context of doing translation, this sort of argument is an embarrassment, because it indicates that the translator's goal at this particular point is no longer to render faithfully the meaning of the original text but to render a related but different idea that the translator thinks would be *better* for the readers than the idea that is actually in the original text. This is certainly unacceptable: readers' problems with *other* texts and with *other* teachings of the Bible (such as the texts dealing with the corporate nature of the

---

[19]We realize that the doctrine concerning the assurance of eternal salvation is a debated area. But even those who disagree with us will want to know what the text says so that they can reexamine their position if necessary and will not be caught holding their position on the basis of a mistaken impression of what the text says.

Christian life) must not become an excuse for a loose attitude toward translating *these* texts.

Moreover, not all English-speaking readers are the same. The translator does not have the luxury of addressing different groups according to their different problems. No doubt other English speakers who will read a translation need to hear an emphasis on Christ's personal relationship with each individual believer. In addition to tampering with the meaning of the Word of God, it would be paternalistic for a translator to decide what he thinks is "good for current American readers" and then alter nuances of the biblical text accordingly. He would thereby deny them to some extent the freedom to make up their *own* minds about whether New Testament Christianity is really an individual or collective institution and in what ways it is so. Such a translator presumes too much.

Proverbs 17:8

RSV: A bribe is like a magic stone in the eyes of *him* who gives it; wherever *he* turns *he* prospers.

NRSV: A bribe is like a magic stone in the eyes of *those* who give it; wherever *they* turn *they* prosper.

The NRSV has the singular term "a bribe" and singular word "it" combined with the plural "those." The effect is to produce a starting picture with a group of people giving a single bribe. The picture differs from the RSV and Hebrew, where the whole picture is singular.

Proverbs 17:11

RSV: An evil *man* seeks only rebellion, and a cruel messenger will be sent against *him*.

NRSV: Evil *people* seek only rebellion, but a cruel messenger will be sent against *them*.

NRSV has a single messenger coming against a plurality of people, suggesting that the evil people in question are acting together. This alters the meaning present in Hebrew and the RSV.[20]

Proverbs 18:7

RSV: A *fool*'s mouth is *his* ruin, and *his* lips are a snare to *himself*.

NRSV: The mouths of *fools* are *their* ruin, and *their* lips a snare to *themselves*.

The NRSV is vaguer than the RSV. Is each fool a snare to himself, or are a group of fools corporately a snare to themselves when they talk together?

We could multiply examples from Proverbs. Many verses in Proverbs create a difficulty for gender-neutral translation because they express a general principle using a specific example.

---

[20]However, based on Chapter 11, one could improve the RSV by changing "man" to "person."

Note also that the shift to plurals has several times created ambiguity between an individual interpretation and a group interpretation. This phenomenon confirms our earlier observation that, even when there is not such an obvious ambiguity, "they" differs subtly from "he" by inviting the reader to start with the plurality of members rather than an individual sample member.

Proverbs 15:5

RSV: A fool despises *his* father's instruction.

NRSV: A fool despises a parent's instruction.

NRSV eliminates "his." By so doing, it makes it less clear that the proverb pictures a fool despising the instruction of his own father, not the instruction of all the people who happen to be parents.

Old Testament laws also create difficulties because they often use a specific case in order to state a legal principle. Thus:

Exodus 21:14

RSV: But if a *man* willfully attacks another to kill *him* treacherously, you shall take *him* from my altar, that *he* may die.

NRSV: But if *someone* willfully attacks and kills another by treachery, you shall take *the killer* from my altar *for execution*.

By clever rewording the NRSV has succeeded in avoiding generic "he." But in the process, subtle changes enter. The original wording does not quite say that one person actually killed another. It says that one "attacks another *to* kill him." Perhaps attempted murder as well as murder is included. The NRSV excludes this possibility by rewording in order to eliminate the dangerous "him." Moreover, instead of "that he may die," the NRSV has the euphemistic phrase "for execution." By contrast, the Hebrew and the RSV confront readers more pointedly with the consequences of murder.[21]

Exodus 22:5

RSV: When a *man* causes a field or vineyard to be grazed over, or lets *his* beast loose and it feeds in another man's field, *he* shall make restitution from the best in *his* own field and in *his* own vineyard.

NRSV: When *someone* causes a field or vineyard to be grazed over, or lets livestock loose to graze in someone else's field, restitution shall be made from the best in *the owner*'s field or vineyard.

NRSV has converted the second half to passive, "restitution shall be made," instead of the more pointed and vivid "he shall make restitution." Worse, the NRSV has become hard to decipher. Because all "he's" and "his's" have

---

[21]Hebrew does not have a pronoun ("he") at this point but does have the ordinary word for "die." "Execution" is too abstract.

been eliminated, it is no longer so clear who is to make restitution to whom. Who is "the owner" to whom the NRSV refers?

In the RSV (and in Hebrew), the "beast" is specifically labeled with a possessive pronoun to indicate its owner. The "man" who lets the beast loose is also the owner of the beast. The RSV continues with "he" and "his," all referring back to the "man" who is responsible. By contrast, in the NRSV we hear of someone letting loose "livestock," with no explicit specification of the owner. Who is the owner? The livestock might belong to the "someone" who let them loose or to someone else. In fact, the livestock might belong to the same "someone else" who owns the field in which the livestock graze. The only person who has unambiguously been identified as an "owner" is the person who owns the grazed-over field. So is restitution to be made from the injured person's property? Maybe readers can work out a common-sense solution, but the NRSV text does not help them to do it.

The irony here is that, in ancient Hebrew culture, men rather than women would almost always be the ones involved in this kind of legal case. NRSV has needlessly avoided using masculine pronouns.

On and on it goes; verse after verse gets changed, whenever a generic "he" occurs in other versions. Doubtless the translators try hard to preserve what meaning they can, given the fact that they are committed to eliminating generic "he." But over and over again nuances change. One never knows beforehand just what nuances will fade and what new ones appear as the changes are introduced.

And then pity the poor reader who has access only to the resulting English text. When such a reader confronts a general statement in English, it is impossible for him to know more precisely what stood in the original text. "You" and "we" may substitute for a third-person singular in the original, or they may represent a second- or first-person reference in the original. "They" may correspond to either a singular or a plural formulation in the original languages. And how will the reader guess what additional nuances have changed?

F.   Psalm 34:20: Obscuring the New Testament fulfillment

RSV: He keeps all *his* bones; not one of them is broken.

NRSV: He keeps all *their* bones; not one of them will be broken.

NIVI: He protects all *their* bones, not one of them will be broken.

NLT: For the LORD protects them from harm—not one of *their* bones will be broken!

The NRSV, NIVI, and NLT translations replace a singular in Hebrew with the plural "their," in order to avoid generic "he." (NCV and CEV also have "their bones." GW preserves "his bones.")

Psalm 34 is about the Lord's help to the righteous. Some of the verses are formulated in the plural, talking about righteous people (for example, verses 15, 17–18). Verses 19–20 shift to the singular. Some advocates of gender neutrality would like to believe that this shift makes no difference at all, because then they could freely change the singulars to plurals and get rid of the telltale "he."

But, as usual, the singular in Hebrew, as in English, makes the language more vivid, more specific. It offers a picture of a single righteous person, through which one can grasp the generalities. The plural verses also have their strength, in stressing more forcefully that the truths hold with respect to many people. The psalmist writes out of his own experience, but not as if his experience were not replicated in the lives of others. Hence it is wise, unless we have weighty reasons to the contrary, to retain in English the contrast between the singulars and plurals that we see in this psalm.

Now compare Psalm 34:20 with John 19:36, "For these things took place that the scripture might be fulfilled, 'Not a bone of him shall be broken' " (RSV). John is alluding to some "scripture." But scholars debate which one it is. He may be alluding either to Psalm 34:20 or to Exodus 12:46 or to both.[22] (Numbers 9:12, which repeats Exodus 12:46, is also relevant.) Even if he is alluding primarily to one, the other may be more distantly in the background.

Both verses are in fact related to Christ. Christ is "our Passover lamb," according to 1 Corinthians 5:7, and thus fulfills Exodus 12:46. He is also the quintessential righteous man (Rom. 5:19), "the Holy and Righteous One" (Acts 3:14), the perfectly righteous servant who receives God's deliverance from death (Isa. 53:11). Thus he is the fulfillment of Psalm 34. John could easily have been alluding to either Exodus 12:46 or Psalm 34:20, which is why scholars find it difficult to decide between the two. To play it safe, cross-reference Bibles usually mention both verses, and Numbers 9:12 as well.

In fact, it does not matter too much which verse John had in mind. We can see that there is a theological relation between John 19:36 and *both* Old Testament passages. God as the divine author intended us to understand that there is a connection between Christ and the earlier passages about the Passover and about his deliverance of the righteous.

Unfortunately, if Psalm 34:20 is converted to a plural "their bones," the relation is not nearly so obvious. As in other cases, it is not for translators

---

[22]Carson, *Debate*, says he assumes that John 19:36 "is indeed referring to Psalm 34" (p. 210, n. 12). Strauss, *Distorting*, 192, notes plurals in other verses of Psalm 34 and says that this suggests "that the singulars in verses 19–20 are also generic, referring to righteous sufferers in general." But if the psalmist saw fit to switch from plurals to singulars and back to plurals, it represents, as we have observed, a focus at one point on the many instances of application (plural) and at another point the concreteness of an individual case (singular). We should respect these differences in focus and represent them in English translation as well as we can. We should translate the words of *these two verses* for what they are.

to decide prematurely which Old Testament connections are the important ones and which can be obscured by changing the wording out of a desire to avoid elements of meaning that are there in the text.

G. Anything but "he"

God's providential guidance of an individual person's life is quite clear in Proverbs 16:9: "A man's mind plans *his* way, but the Lord directs *his* steps" (RSV). It would not be wrong to translate "A *person's* mind plans his way, but the Lord directs his steps," for the Hebrew word does not designate men alone.[23] The word "his" in English functions like the underlying third-person singular masculine Hebrew pronoun forms to indicate specifically that the person referred to at the beginning of the verse is the one whose "way" and "steps" are in view.

But the offensive word "his" had to go. A comparison of gender-neutral versions shows how translators have tried almost every possible way to avoid literally translating the Hebrew pronoun as "his."

RSV: [literal translation, preserving third-person singular] A man's mind plans *his* way, but the Lord directs *his* steps. (The KJV, NASB, NIV, NKJV, and REB all have "his" as well.)

NCV: [change third-person singular to *third-person plural*] *People* may make plans in *their* minds, but the Lord decides what *they* will do.

NIVI: [change third-person singular to *second-person*] In *your* heart *you* may plan *your* course, but the Lord determines *your* steps.

NLT: [change third-person singular to *first-person plural*] *We* can make *our* plans, but the Lord determines *our* steps. (CEV is similar.)

NRSV: [change third-person singular to *no person*] The human mind plans *the* way, but the Lord directs *the* steps.

Such variation is almost humorous to see. Third-person singular is changed to third-person plural, to second-person, to first-person, to no person—anything is acceptable except a clear, simple, accurate "his."

All of the changes involve *some* change in meaning. The NCV with "they" loses focus on the individual person. Perhaps a group of people are making plans together. The NIVI focuses the sentence on the readers ("you") as the starting point rather than a sample individual "out there." The NLT and CEV focus on the speaker and hearers ("we") as the starting point. In addition, the changes in person undermine the flavor of the proverbs in this section of the Book of Proverbs. The proverbs are characteristically third-person observations about life. A wise person observes the pattern of people's lives out there in the world. In Proverbs 1–9, by contrast,

---

[23]The Hebrew *'adam* has a sense closer to our word "man" without the article, used to designate humanity. "The mind of man [not a man] plans his way, but the Lord directs his steps."

we find many direct second-person exhortations to "my son." One kind of saying may often imply the other, but they are simply not the same in genre or in total meaning effect. Third-person proverbial sayings come to us as general observations about "life." It is not the same if we invent for ourselves proverbial sayings that give the impression of arising directly from our own living ("I" or "we" proverbial sayings) or where the addressee is encouraged first of all to think in terms of checking out in his own life how the saying holds ("you" proverbial sayings).

The NRSV, by leaving out all pronouns, makes the statement less vivid and concrete. The NRSV's phrase "the human mind" reminds us faintly of a philosophical treatise on epistemology that talks in generalities, but never comes to grips with the fact that we are real, living, breathing people. Vividness and specificity are lost.

This passage also illustrates so strikingly the "extra factor" that is driving the translation of these verses. In this kind of verse, we see that gender-neutral translations are not trying to translate all the meaning that is there in the original; rather, they are trying hard *not* to translate a certain component of the meaning (namely, the meaning of the third masculine singular pronoun in Hebrew). Translation is hard enough when we just *try to translate* all the meaning of the original; when also *trying not to translate* a certain type of meaning, the task just becomes worse.

H. Scholarly integrity

Interestingly, an evaluation similar to ours comes from an unusual source: the *Revised English Bible* (REB), a version that pays attention to gender issues.[24] The preface states, "The use of male-oriented language, in passages of traditional versions of the Bible which evidently apply to both genders, has become a sensitive issue in recent years; the revisers have preferred more inclusive gender reference where that has been possible without compromising scholarly integrity or English style."[25]

The REB was published in 1989. As they worked in the years just before 1989, the revisers knew that there was considerable sensitivity over generic "he" and other "male-oriented" terms. They consciously tried to eliminate "male-oriented language" wherever they could. Yet, in every one of the verses that we have considered in this chapter, the REB continues to use

---

[24]The *Revised English Bible* (REB), published in 1989 by the Oxford University Press and Cambridge University Press, is a revision of the *New English Bible* (NEB, 1970). The REB eliminated the uses of "thee" and "thou," adjusted gender language, and tried to make some other improvements to the NEB. Both the NEB and the REB were produced under the oversight of an interdenominational Joint Committee, which included representatives from many of the main denominations of the United Kingdom: the Baptist Union, the Church of England, the Church of Scotland, the Congregational Church of England and Wales, the Methodist Church of Great Britain, the Presbyterian Church of England, and others. The British and Foreign Bible Society and the National Bible Society of Scotland were also represented (REB Preface, viii).
[25]REB, "Preface," ix.

generic "he." We must infer, then, that they thought that eliminating generic "he" would have compromised "scholarly integrity or English style."

Which of these two—integrity or style—is at stake with generic "he"? In many of the verses, style does not appear to be the issue. It is just barely possible that the REB was thinking of the fact that using plurals all the time can turn a style "to mush," as Zinsser says.[26] But the REB freely uses plurals in many places where the original has them. So using "they" is not a big stylistic issue. More probably, REB is thinking of attempts to avoid generic "he" by using "they" to refer back to a singular "anyone," or repeatedly using noun phrases like "the person," "that person," "that one" to avoid using "he." Such changes would produce awkward style.

But now, using "you" is just as acceptable as "he," from a *stylistic* point of view, and changing the whole sentence to plurals ("they") in a number of cases does not produce objectionable style. So the real issue is not style but scholarly integrity. REB implies that the changes made by gender-neutral versions violate scholarly integrity! That is, a scholar who really knows what the original says could not put in plurals or "you" without abandoning his integrity. Integrity demands that he translate the meaning of the original.

I.   How many verses are affected?

How many changes must be made to an English translation in order to avoid generic "he"? An exact count is impossible to obtain without comparing every verse of the Bible, but we can get some idea of the magnitude of the change from a computer count of the words in the RSV and its gender-neutral update, the NRSV. A search using *Bible Works* indicates that the words "he, him, his" occur 4,200 fewer times in the NRSV than the RSV. However, some of these preserve the singular sense of the verse by using the word "one" (this occurs 495 more times) and "someone, anyone, everyone" (264 more times). If we deduct for these, there are still 3,441 times where "he, him, his" are removed. From the sample verses we have examined, time and again generic "he" is eliminated by changing singulars to plurals, changing third-person pronouns to second or first person, changing active verbs to passive and deleting the subject, or changing personal statements to impersonal.[27] Eliminating generic "he" is not a matter of a minor

---

[26]Zinsser, *On Writing Well*, 122.

[27]In a few cases—but they are comparatively few—one can eliminate generic "he" without such wholesale change. For example, in John 6:51, where NIV has "if anyone eats of this bread, *he* will live forever," NIVI has "whoever eats of this bread will live for ever." Generic "he" disappears through cleverly restructuring the relation of the two clauses. There is an "if-then" sentence structure in Greek, so that the NIV is closer to a formal equivalent. Moreover, the NIV captures more nuances of meaning with an "if," since it more directly hints (in a context that includes this theme, and where the Greek construction with *ean* ["if"] hints it) that there is a real possibility of unbelief. Yet the NIVI does pretty well. It captures the main point

difference in a small number of verses. This is a substantial change of nuance, perspective, and other details in thousands of passages of Scripture.

J. The Colorado Springs Guidelines on generic "he"

In order to protect the meaning signified by third-person generic statements in the Hebrew and Greek texts of Scripture, the first two Colorado Springs Guidelines read as follows:

A. Gender-related renderings of Biblical language which we affirm:

1. The generic use of "he, him, his, himself" should be employed to translate generic 3rd person masculine singular pronouns in Hebrew, Aramaic and Greek. However, substantival participles such as *ho pisteuōn* can often be rendered in inclusive ways, such as "the one who believes" rather than "he who believes."

2. Person and number should be retained in translation so that singulars are not changed to plurals and third person statements are not changed to second or first person statements, with only rare exceptions required in unusual cases.

These guidelines are specifically aimed at the question of translating personal nouns and pronouns—they talk about "generic 3rd person masculine singular *pronouns*" and "*third person* statements" compared to "*second or first person* statements." Moreover, they are not talking about every use of the pronoun, for they allow for "rare exceptions in unusual cases."[28] The heading "Gender-related renderings," and the concern of Guidelines A.1 for generic "he," qualified the statement A.2, which otherwise might have been construed as impossibly general. When published, the Colorado Springs Guidelines were accompanied with sample verses and discussion that focused on personal nouns and especially pronouns.

The statements never purported to apply to the translation of *all* Hebrew and Greek singulars and plurals in Scripture (for which there is variation between Hebrew, Greek, and English, as between all languages). They made no claims about the translation of *all* Hebrew and Greek masculine and feminine nouns and adjectives in Scripture (for which there is similar variation between languages).

1. Misrepresentations of the Colorado Springs Guidelines

But critics of the CSG repeatedly misinterpreted them and claimed that they involved sweeping translation demands that were both foolish and

---

and does not run the danger of shifting to a group focus by using plurals. More radical dynamic-equivalent translations have sometimes done such restructuring in contexts unrelated to gender, and so we are not focusing on these few cases in this book.

[28]In the oral discussion during the formulation of the guidelines in Colorado Springs, the puzzling alternation of gender and number in some Old Testament poetic and prophetic literature was specifically mentioned, and we wanted the guideline to allow for flexibility in order to produce a translation in coherent English.

impossible to carry out. Carson says, "The critics seem to assume that it is always inappropriate to render a singular by a plural."[29] More frequently, Carson says of the CSG: "What this assumes is that English generic use of such pronouns exactly mirrors the generic use of the pronouns in the donor languages."[30] But it hardly does that. It only implies that such a choice in English is better than alternatives, not that it is an "exact mirror." (And of course it allows "rare exceptions.")[31]

Similarly, Strauss quotes part of Guideline A.2 and then goes off on a discussion about Hebrew plural nouns:

> The guidelines . . . demonstrate this same confusion of form and meaning. Guideline A.2 mandates that "person and number should be retained in translation." Yet in many cases this is impossible. . . . *'Elohîm*, the Hebrew word for "God," is actually plural in form.[32]

But Strauss does not here complete the quotation of Guideline A.2 so that readers can see that there are exceptions in "unusual cases" (such as some Hebrew plural forms that have a singular sense).[33] Nor does he seem to recognize that the entire statement has to do with "gender-related language in Scripture" (so the title and also headings A and B), not with all language and all singulars and plurals.

What these two guidelines do claim is *not* that Hebrew, Greek, and English are "exactly" the same in pronoun use but that in the generic constructions mentioned they are *substantially* the same—so much so that (with few exceptions) generic third-person singular masculine pronouns in Hebrew and Greek are best translated by generic third-person singular masculine pronouns in English.

---

[29]Carson, *Debate*, 105.

[30]Carson, *Debate*, 111. See also page 98 (criticizing Grudem): "One cannot responsibly translate all Greek-specified genders into English as corresponding English genders, because the gender systems of the two languages are different." Again on p. 117, "Our gender system . . . does not mesh exactly with the gender and number systems of Hebrew, Aramaic, and Greek." And on p. 156, "But the deeper problem with Dr. Grudem's analysis is that it assumes that the gender and number relationships internal to contemporary English are exactly the same as in Greek."

In each of these cases Carson has started from a specific instance (in the last case, for example, Grudem's claim that Greek *autos* should be translated by "him" not "them" in Luke 17:3, "If your brother sins, rebuke *him*"), and then he has turned our claim for *equivalent meaning in that kind of construction* into a sweeping claim for *equivalent form in gender and number in the whole of both languages*. It is easy then for him to refute the latter claim, but in each case it is a claim he wrongly attributes to us, not a claim that we ourselves have made. The discouraging part is that such unjustified generalizing of our statements occurs so often in the book, and forms so much of his argument in the book, that one begins to worry that readers will actually start to believe that we argue for these foolish positions that he attributes to us.

[31]See further discussion in Appendix 3.

[32]Strauss, *Distorting*, 85–86.

[33]Note that *'Elohîm* regularly takes a singular verb and is construed as singular in meaning in the Hebrew Bible.

Carson spends over twenty pages explaining how grammatical gender systems differ among languages of the world.[34] He shows that in many of them Hebrew and Greek grammatical gender cannot be made to match the gender of the receptor language in a translation, so adjustments have to be made. He says, "My point here is that to use in the receptor language a pronoun different in gender from what is used in the donor language is not intrinsically wrong."[35] It is unclear whom he is arguing against up to this point in this long chapter—Colorado Springs Guideline A.1 already affirmed the same point in translating a masculine participle with a gender-neutral expression in English.[36]

On the other hand, to assert that Hebrew, Greek, and English do not match "exactly" in their use of personal pronouns does not disprove their substantial overlap and substantial similarities of use. What we have claimed is that a translation of a personal pronoun that uses the same gender and number often conveys the maximal amount of meaning. And this is nothing new—it has been followed for all English translations until the advent of gender-neutral Bibles beginning in 1986.

Another claim of critics of the CSG is that we confuse grammatical gender with meaning, and we wrongly assume that the grammatical gender of Hebrew and Greek must be preserved in English. Carson writes:

> There are countless passages of similar gender complexity in the Hebrew Old Testament, which cannot be faithfully rendered into English by formal equivalents. So when we are told, in a careful selection of instances, that we must have the masculine pronoun where the Hebrew has the masculine pronoun, or else we are sacrificing or twisting the Word of God, the kindest thing that can be said is that honest concern for the integrity of the Word of God has blinded the critic to two facts: (1) the original words of God were (in these cases) in Hebrew, not English; and (2) Hebrew and English do not have the same gender systems. Formal equivalents are often impossible. . . . everything depends on understanding the meaning in the original and attempting one's best to convey that meaning in the receptor language.[37]

---

[34]Carson, *Debate*, 77–98.

[35]Carson, *Debate*, 96.

[36]When Carson comes to analyze the sentence about *ho pisteuōn* being translated by "the one who believes" in Guideline A.1, he does not modify his incorrect insistence that we require the preservation of grammatical gender across languages but rather says we are inconsistent with our principle in this case! "But strictly speaking, *ho* is the *masculine* article, and the participle, as determined by the article, is masculine as well. . . . Why the double standard, except for the influence of the English gloss? The donor languages do not encourage a distinction in translation approaches based on the gender of these parts of speech" (*Debate*, 112). But it is not a "double standard" at all—it is rather a consistent attempt to preserve meaning in translation as much as it can be done in contemporary English. It is a "double standard" only when measured against a standard of "always preserve formal grammatical gender" that Carson has imposed on us.

[37]Carson, *Debate*, 97.

But such a statement fails to inform the reader that the CSG did not insist on "formal equivalents" but on preserving meaning. It is surprising that Dr. Carson can write this when the CSG themselves affirm at least six examples of translation that do not preserve formal equivalents:

Guideline	Heb. or Greek word or phrase	Grammatical gender in Heb. or Greek	Approved English translation	Sex indicated by English translation
A.1	*ho pisteuōn*	Masculine	the one who believes	unspecified
A.5	*anthrōpoi*	Masculine	people	unspecified
A.7	*oudeis*	Masculine	no one	unspecified
A.8	*pas*	Masculine	all people, everyone	unspecified
B.1	*adelphoi*	Masculine	brothers and sisters	male and female

Carson has simply attributed to the Guidelines a position that exists only in his own mind and one that is explicitly contradicted by the Guidelines. He has, moreover, compounded the error by insinuating that the participants were "blinded" to the fact that "the original words of God were (in these cases) in Hebrew, not English."[38]

K. Making our decision

Given the data that we have seen to this point, we can easily make a decision about generic "he." We need it for Bible translation. Thousands of times we need to use generic "he" in English in order most accurately to express the meaning of the original. Translators ought to use it any time that they need it in order to convey in English the full meaning of the original. They ought not to settle for substitutes or rewording that sounds vaguely the same and conveys a meaning that is more or less similar. Translators should go for the best that we can get in English. The issue here is simply whether we want greatest accuracy in translation. Because of the

---

[38]Among the original signers of the CSG, three had earned doctorates in New Testament (Grudem, Piper, Poythress), two had earned doctorates in Old Testament (Barker, Youngblood), and each of these five had been working with the original Hebrew and Greek texts of the Bible for twenty-five years or more. Others had substantial training in both Hebrew and Greek at the M.Div. level. There must be some more appropriate way to criticize the CSG and those of us who oppose gender-neutral Bibles than to insinuate that we are unaware that the Old Testament is written in Hebrew or that Hebrew and English do not have the same gender systems! In the same sentence Carson tells his readers that he thinks this is "the kindest thing that can be said" about us (p. 97).

number of verses involved, the use of generic "he" is the most decisive issue for gender-neutral translations.

To Bible translators today, we would say, if you refuse to use generic "he" at all, you affect thousands of verses. If you use it even once, you admit that it is serviceable, and then you should use it every place that you need it.[39]

But one and all, the gender-neutral translations (NRSV, NCV, GNB, CEV, GW, NIrV(1995), and NLT) have decided to eliminate generic "he" across the whole Bible, though some have exempted a handful of verses.[40] By eliminating generic "he," they have in practice diminished accuracy in representing meaning. It seems to us that the inescapable conclusion is that these translations have so compromised accuracy in translation that they are not worthy of our trust.

L.   The deeper issue: feminism

Sad to say, not everyone agrees. When confronted with arguments of this kind, a good many people have been worried about the fact that generic "he" is perceived as "insensitive to women" or that feminists have pronounced generic "he" to be "sexist." The alleged problems with generic "he" now need our attention.

(Chapters 14, 15, 16, and 17 will analyze the question of generic "he" in more detail and interact with arguments against its use. Readers who have seen enough and just want to see the wrap-up of our discussion can look at the conclusion of Chapter 17, then go to Chapter 18 for other important issues in translating gender language, and to Chapters 20 and 21 for the conclusion of the whole book.)

---

[39]We shall have to discuss later the issue of "sensitivity," which might lead to minimizing generic "he" without completely abandoning it. See Chapter 15.

[40]GW includes more remaining cases with generic "he" than the others—many more than a handful. REB, as we observed, tries to maintain what they say is "scholarly integrity" in this area, and so we have not classified it as gender neutral.

CHAPTER 14

Feminist Opposition
to Generic "He"

English-speaking people have not always found generic "he" objectionable, but many people object to it today. Why? What is the origin of the objection, and what are the reasons behind it?

Although there have been occasional voices protesting generic "he" for centuries,[1] no widespread opposition to it came to general public attention until influential feminist voices began to mount a vigorous campaign against it in the 1970s.[2] But what is so bad about generic "he"?

First, a caution. We will talk broadly about "feminism," but it is not all the same. Early feminism contained some very legitimate concerns, but also some wrongheaded ideas. But God can bring good results even out of wrong human intentions (Gen. 50:20). And some good results *have* come. Not only society as a whole but also Christians in particular have received a wake-up call to pay more attention to the needs and concerns of women and to value women as highly as they value men. As a result, we hope, Christians have become more alert to the dangers of male domineering and pride and have gone to the Scriptures to learn and obey more thoroughly God's standards for male-female relations.

Moreover, feminism is not a monolithic movement. In the early days some of the most objectionable ideas belonged to people with the loudest mouths, the hottest zeal, and the deepest commitment—and such people

---

[1]Dennis Baron notes that "more than eighty bisexual pronouns—little words such as *ne, ter, thon, heer, et,* and *ip*—have been proposed since the eighteenth century, and because many word coiners worked in isolation and received little publicity, some of the same forms were invented more than once, most notably versions of the blends *hesh, himer,* and *hiser"* (*Grammar and Gender* [New Haven and London: Yale University Press, 1986], 190).

[2]Casey Miller and Kate Swift, in the first edition of their landmark book, *The Handbook of Nonsexist Writing* (New York: Lippincott & Crowell, 1980), 125, listed numerous academic studies in the period from 1971 to 1980 that argued that generic "he" indicated bias against women.

often received disproportionately large press coverage. They exerted influence out of proportion to their numbers. But many others, both men and women, would have sympathized with this or that element, without endorsing the extreme views of a few.

In addition, we must beware of explaining complex historical changes on the basis of single causes. We do not claim that changes in language were produced wholly by a single cause, only that the influences that we look at are *some* of the causes.[3]

It would be fascinating to conduct a full-orbed study of all the variations and nuances within the very complex movement labeled "feminism." But we cannot do it here. We must simplify. We concentrate on some of the main ideas and express them in starkest form. This is still useful, because the core ideas continue to have influence. But in practice we must remember that there is much variation in the degree and subtlety of influence.

So now let us look at some core ideas, particularly as they come to bear on the question of generic "he."

A. The development of the conflict

Transport yourself back to 1965. Most people calmly accept generic "he" without even noticing it. It is a convention of the English language. But then a number of feminists begin to claim that it is "oppressive," "sexist," and "insensitive to women." The claim at that time is hardly persuasive on the face of it, for both men and women have used generic "he" all their lives without intending to oppress women or be insensitive. The average person instinctively senses that the feminist claim is not valid. Nevertheless, feminists achieve some political momentum from their claim. They draw attention to language as an image of thought. To change the language, they hope, is to change the thinking of a whole culture. Language change is a way of changing social and political structures in society.[4] Moreover, by changing language we can free ourselves from the past.[5]

---

[3]D. A. Carson warns against "monocausational analyses" (*The Inclusive-Language Debate* [Grand Rapids: Baker, 1998], 186–187), but also says,

> Second, we cannot deny, I think, that some of the pressure for change [in the English language] springs from a profound abandonment of the Bible's worldview, the Bible's culture, the Bible's story line, as that has been mediated to us by various English Bibles. I mourn the loss. (ibid., 189)

[4]Some feminist writers are explicit in stating their goal of engineering a change in the English language in order to bring about desired changes in society: Ann Pauwels advocates feminist language reform (LR) and language planning (LP) through pressure on governmental agencies, educators, publishers of educational materials, journalists, editors, legislative bodies, labor unions, and professional societies, and tells us that much of this kind of pressure has already succeeded. (Ann Pauwels, *Women Changing Language* [London and New York: Longman, 1988], 7–14, as cited by E. Ray Clendenen, "Inclusive Language in Bible Translation: A Reply to Mark Strauss," a paper read at the 50th annual meeting of the Evangelical Theological Society, Nov. 19–21, 1998, Orlando, Florida.)

[5]For example, Miller and Swift say,

At the same time, feminists also cast aspersions on the past. Granted, generic "he" exists in our language as a heritage from the past, but they argue that the past is suspect because the past oppressed women. Now we live in the present and now we must free ourselves from everything patriarchal. If we declare generic "he" to be "sexist," we also help to prejudice everyone against the English writings of the past, all of which use generic "he." In this way, we help to free ourselves from the authority of the past (including, incidentally, the authority of the Bible).

From a feminist perspective, there is another benefit to opposing generic "he" and other aspects of English that are thought to be "sexist." In doing this, feminists can create a kind of banner for themselves, a mark of allegiance. Feminists themselves, and those who sympathize with them, can express their sympathy by the way they talk. The change in language can thus perform a symbolic function, to indicate allegiance to feminism. And feminists can better identify those who are still ideologically backward, by the fact that they still use generic "he." Those who resist the movement reveal themselves by their speech; and then they can be singled out, in order to be gently persuaded or pestered—or whatever the case may call for.

There is yet another attractive feature of such a language change: It is, for some, a subtle form of self-denial, a new kind of asceticism. One promises to police one's speech to remove generic "he." The bolder person will substitute conspicuous alternatives like "she or he" or "s/he." The shy will shift to the plural "they." Both people, by such linguistic asceticism, show that they are serious about "avoiding sexism" and "being sensitive to women."

The possible ascetic aspects of this practice may have deeper significance than we at first recognize. All over the world people know, deep in their hearts, that all is not well with the world. In fact, the Bible tells us that people know that they are sinners before a holy God (Rom. 1:18–32). But the knowledge is so painful that people suppress it. Nevertheless, they still feel the need for a remedy. The true remedy, we know, is found in Christ and his sacrifice, but if people do not acknowledge that Christ bears our pun-

---

The reason the practice of assigning masculine gender to neutral terms is so enshrined in English is that every language reflects the prejudices of the society in which it evolved, and English evolved through most of its history in a male-centered, patriarchal society. We shouldn't be surprised, therefore, that its vocabulary and grammar reflect attitudes that exclude or demean women. But we are surprised, for until recently few people thought much about what English—or any other language for that matter— was saying on a subliminal level. . . . Many people would like to do something about these inherited linguistic biases, but getting rid of them involves more than exposing them and suggesting alternatives. It requires change, . . .

At a deep level, changes in a language are threatening because they signal widespread changes in social mores. (Casey Miller and Kate Swift, *The Handbook of Nonsexist Writing*, 2d ed. [New York: Harper & Row, 1988], 4.)

See also Dale Spender, *Man Made Language* (London: Routledge & Kegan Paul, 1980).

ishment, they look for another kind of atonement. Fairly often, people imagine that one possible atonement is to punish themselves. A person denies himself certain foods or comforts in hopes that it will help him to cleanse himself morally. He is severe on his body, imagining that the body, rather than his own heart, is the source of sin. However, the apostle Paul observes that these practices do not represent God's way of salvation, but a man-made way:

> Since you died with Christ to the basic principles of this world, why, as though you still belonged to it, do you submit to its rules: "Do not handle! Do not taste! Do not touch!"? These are all destined to perish with use, because they are based on human commands and teachings. Such regulations indeed have an appearance of wisdom, with their self-imposed worship, their false humility and their harsh treatment of the body, but they lack any value in restraining sensual indulgence (Col. 2:20–23, NIV; see also Col. 2:8).

Human asceticism in general introduces rules forbidding us to handle or taste certain things. The rules are religious and moral prohibitions of human invention. They are attractive. They "have an appearance of wisdom." The people who follow them think that they are accomplishing moral progress. The "harsh treatment of the body" eases the feeling of guilt. But it is all of no value, because it is not rooted in Christ's atoning death and resurrection. Paul says about them, "They lack any value in restraining sensual indulgence" (Col. 2:23). People may feel self-righteous because they are keeping the man-made rules. But their hearts are still as corrupt as before.

In the realm of language, the prohibition against generic "he" may sometimes function as just such a man-made ascetic rule. For many people, at least at first, avoiding generic "he" requires concentration and mental work. This extra work shows that people are "serious" about the struggles women face. It is a work that demonstrates their commitment. Moreover, this "work" is appealing because people know that they have sins in the area of sexual desires, and the work may even seem to promise moral cleansing. But in actual fact, keeping the prohibition does not have any value in dealing with sexual indulgence, and it does not do what only Christ can do, namely, root out the corruptions of the heart.

Of course, now that the prohibition on generic "he" has become established and widespread in modern societies, many other people may adopt it just to "fit in" or "to show politeness," and the ascetic factor may be minimized. There may be a variety of motives, some of them commendable.

And—lest readers misunderstand—we *do* commend the good motives. We agree that in our modern speech it is all right in principle to use "you" and "they" as substitutes, or to use "he or she." In many contexts, when these things are done in order simply to affirm the dignity of women, and to encourage them, they are useful variations on the use of generic "he."

Thus, the issue is not whether we can use these variations, but whether we can *also* use generic "he" when we need it. Are we free to use all the options, or does a prohibition, a ban, remove the freedom to use one of them? Especially, can we use generic "he" in Bible translation? As speakers, we have authority over what we say. We can rephrase it if we want, thereby saying something subtly different. But we do not have authority over what the Bible says. We cannot introduce alterations there in the same way that we might alter nuances in our own speech. So the issue of using generic "he" comes to prominence exactly here. In this context, the *prohibition* of generic "he," *not* the use of other alternatives, is what concerns us.

Are feminists right to introduce this prohibition? Christians surely need to respect all human beings, men and women, old and young alike. We are all made in the image of God. In emphasizing this, feminists have touched on one side of a truth, a side that had been neglected. But they have also distorted the truth by erecting man-made rules instead of going to God to receive a transformed heart and guidance for daily life. So a secular version of "sensitivity" will never be the same as the Bible-directed love and compassion that we show on the basis of Christ's salvation, guided by his Word. Behind secular feminism we believe there often lies a desire for a kind of moral reformation, and ultimately we can call it the desire for another way of salvation—another way, less humiliating than the cross, to deliver us from our sinful sexual desires and actions.

B. Egalitarianism in the culture

It is undeniable that in the last three decades feminists have exerted enormous influence on our culture, especially on cultural leaders. Their thinking is attractive partly because it grows out of an even more widespread ideology: egalitarianism. Radical egalitarianism says that all human beings are equal, and therefore they ought to be made to be exactly the same in a whole host of spheres. According to radical egalitarianism, it is "unfair" for anyone to have authority over another, or to have more power or money or influence. If we may exaggerate by putting radical egalitarianism in its most stark form, such a view would hold that those who stand out and excel should somehow be pulled down and made to fit in with the crowd, lest someone feel inferior.

Egalitarianism is seductive because it builds on something close to biblical truth, but then also distorts it. According to the Bible all people are made in the image of God, all are sinners before God, and all can enjoy equal access to God through Christ. There is a kind of equality before God. Egalitarianism appeals to this truth, but it does not acknowledge the complementary truth about human differences.

The Bible also affirms that God ordains the *differences* among people. The members in the body of Christ are different from one another (note the metaphor of one body with many parts in 1 Cor. 12). Some are more prominent than others, though all are necessary. God sets some, not all, in positions of governing authority (Rom. 13). Men and women are created differently, not identically (Gen. 2). In the actual world we live in, God distributes gifts and abilities unequally: "Who gave man his mouth? Who makes him deaf or mute? Who gives him sight or makes him blind? Is it not I, the LORD?" (Exod. 4:11, NIV). With respect to human government and human authority, "it is God who executes judgment, putting down one and lifting up another" (Ps. 75:7, RSV), and "there is no authority except from God, and those that exist have been instituted by God" (Rom. 13:1, RSV).

In a sinful world, the rich, the strong, and the powerful may use their advantages to trample on the weak. Governmental authorities may exploit those under them, and men may selfishly exploit their wives. This exploitation rouses both the anger of God and the indignation of human observers. We have an obligation before God to work to rectify such exploitation. We should work for change both in individuals and in society.

Once again, egalitarianism uses half the truth. It rightly protests exploitation and tries to rectify it, but it goes too far when it proposes to level all distinctions. The true solution must follow God's way, to follow the wise and detailed instructions about daily living that are found in the Bible. Strong and weak alike must submit to Christ's Lordship. Thorough submission to God will remove sin and exploitation, but not level all distinctions.

Many egalitarians of course do not believe in God, so they are not looking for salvation in the traditional sense. But they see the hurts and struggles of life, and feel their effects keenly. Egalitarians want a solution. Even if they ignore God, the solution that they propose is, in a broad sense, a false way of salvation. Egalitarianism offers to solve our problems not by submission to Christ but by human engineering that forcibly reshuffles everyone's lot. Egalitarianism historically originated from non-Biblical sources, especially the French Revolution. The French Revolution enthroned Reason as a goddess. But when people do not acknowledge God but only Reason, the differences that God ordains among people seem not to be "rational." Hence, they must be denied or abolished. Since human sexual differences today do not seem to many people to be "rational," they too must be overcome.

In people's sinfulness they look at differences and distinctions among people and there is a strong temptation to say, "It's unfair!" There is a temptation within us to want to be god. We want to call the shots. And because we will not bow before the depths of the infinity of God's mind, we sometimes cannot accept that one person can see and another is blind (Exod. 4:11), that one is rich and another poor, that one is in authority and another is not. "It's unfair!" we say. Yet Scripture tells us, "Rich and poor have this in common: The LORD is the Maker of them all" (Prov. 22:2, NIV), and, "He changes times and seasons; he removes kings and sets up kings; he gives wisdom to the wise and knowledge to those who have understanding" (Dan 2:21, RSV; cf. 4:25, 37).

Of course, the Bible also indicates that having a wise king is better than having a foolish king (Deut. 17:16–20). And helping your neighbor to climb out of poverty is better than heartlessly ignoring his or her plight (James 2:15–16; 1 John 3:17–18)! The Bible urges us actively to serve our neighbor, not just passively to accept a painful circumstance when we can help to alleviate it. But the command to serve comes within a context that acknowledges God's plan, and recognizes that not all distinctions are "unfair."

In fact, from the Bible's perspective what's "fair" is that we all experience eternal condemnation from God, and enjoy none of his good gifts. "All have sinned and fall short of the glory of God" (Rom. 3:23, RSV), and "the wages of sin is death" (Rom. 6:23, RSV).

We are sinners. We do not deserve even the least of God's gifts. None of us on earth deserves any of the status, authority, ability, or knowledge that he has.

But if we lose sight of God in his majesty, and if we do not learn about life from God's Word, we will arrogantly make our own judgments about what is "right" and "fair." Among people who do not consciously submit to God's sovereign authority, these judgments about what is "fair" will vary from time to time and from culture to culture. Sometimes "fairness" is distorted into the corrupt principle that says, "I want 'fairness' for me, or for my people, but not for those outsiders, because they are inferior." But in our current culture, still under the strong influence of egalitarian thinking that began with the rationalism and egalitarianism that surrounded the French Revolution, people will often decide that it is "fair" for everyone to be exactly the same.

With respect to feminism, this egalitarian tendency quickly leads to the dogma that *men and women must be the same*, not complementary in their differences. Men and women must participate with identical prominence, in identical numbers, and in identical ways in university athletic programs, in high school SAT scores, in doing mathematical research at the university level, in every type of occupation and career in the business world, in serving in combat in the military, in sharing equally in caring for children within a marriage, and so forth. Of course, identical numbers and equal prominence may be natural and appropriate in some areas—but in others they are artificial. But strict egalitarian thinking does not know where to stop, because it is driven by an abstract, rationalistic principle of abolishing differences. In particular, differences based on gender cannot be tolerated.

In sum, there are profound spiritual issues involved here—and ultimately, two very different ways of looking at the world. On one side stands feminism and egalitarianism, promoting its own way of salvation and distorting the truth, insisting that there should be no gender-based differences between status, prominence, or authority of one person and another. On the other side stands the teaching of the Bible that God affirms both the honor of all human beings and the God-ordained differences among them, including differences in men's and women's roles in marriage (Eph. 5:22–33; Col. 3:18–19; 1 Pet. 3:1–7) and in the church (1 Tim. 2:8–15; 3:2; Matt. 10:2–3).

Of course, many other ideologies and religions oppose the Bible in other ways, by serving false gods, or by endorsing human oppression. We focus on feminism here, not because it is worse than other false ways, but because it has generated the particular controversy in language that we are discussing.

C. Generic "he" seen as giving prominence to the male

Now, why do feminists care about generic "he"? "He" is sometimes used *generically*, that is, to speak of *a sample individual to whom a general principle applies*. The general principle typically applies to both men and women. In this sense, "he" encompasses both men and women; it is inclusive. But is it truly "gender neutral"? That is, does there remain no connotation of "male" deriving from the masculine gender of the word "he"? *The American Heritage Dictionary* perceptively comments:

> If *he* were truly a gender-neutral form, we would expect that it could be used to refer to the members of any group containing both men and women. But in fact the English masculine form is an odd choice when it refers to a female member of such a group. There is something plainly disconcerting about sentences such as *Each of the stars of* It Happened One Night [i.e., Clark Gable and Claudette Colbert] *won an Academy Award for his performance*. In this case, the use of *his* forces the reader to envision a single male who stands as the representative member of the group, a picture that is at odds with the image that comes to mind when we picture the stars of *It Happened One Night*. Thus *he* is not really a gender-neutral pronoun, rather, it refers to a male who is to be taken as the representative member of the group referred to by its antecedent. The traditional usage, then, is not simply a grammatical convention; it also suggests a particular pattern of thought.[6]

---

[6]*The American Heritage Dictionary of the English Language* (3rd ed.; Boston/New York: Houghton Mifflin, 1996), 831. But it is easy to exaggerate the supposed oddity. Consider the following: "If a Christian man or woman has widows in the family, he must support them himself" (1 Tim. 5:16, NEB). "He" and "himself" refer to either man or woman. The NEB was written by people sensitive to stylistic issues, yet they did not flag this sentence as stylistically inappropriate.

We also recognize that generic "he" is more difficult to process, and strikes people as more awkward, when the group represented includes only two people and when the two people are specific individuals known to us (as in the Academy Award example above). Generic "he" is much more commonly used to apply to a large or even limitless group of both men and

The idea of "a male who is to be taken as the representative member of the group" becomes evident in other types of sentences as well. Consider the difficulty of the following sentence: "As a typical commuter drives to his workplace, he may find himself caught in traffic. He passes his time by listening to the radio, putting on his lipstick, or thinking through the tasks ahead of him at work." A specifically male detail such as "adjusting his tie" would be less jarring than the specifically female detail "putting on his lipstick." Or again: "At the end of the day, a person wants TV to entertain him, not make him think. He won't be checking out the ideas in an encyclopedia, but will be sitting back with a drink or putting up his hair for the night." In a sentence with generic "he," readers are more prepared to encounter a detail that is specifically male, as opposed to one that is specifically female.

"He" includes both men and women, but does so using a male example as a pictorial starting point. In a subtle way, this use brings along with it an unequal prominence to men and women. Thus feminism attacks it as "unfair." But in doing so, feminism relies on an egalitarian standard antagonistic to the Bible, for the Bible maintains some gender-based differences between men and women, and, in particular, it uses many male examples and male sample cases to express general truths. Of course, it also uses female examples, though not with the same frequency. And we must emphasize again that the Bible does teach the dignity of all human beings. Men and women *alike* are created in the image of God, and all have fallen into sin. But the Bible also indicates that there are *differences* in the gifts that God gives them and the roles that he assigns to them in this life. Feminism and egalitarianism fight against those differences.

Egalitarianism thus rejects the dominance of generic masculines in English. But what about Hebrew, Aramaic, and Greek? Hebrew, Aramaic, and Greek have gender systems of their own. The three languages differ from one another as well as from English. But in all three languages, when singular personal pronouns[7] refer to human beings, the gender usually lines up with sex. The listener's instincts are to try tentatively to identify the sex of human referents by the gender marking of personal pronouns. Of course special contexts may override this tendency. But the tendency is there in listeners because it is one prominent function of pronouns when they refer to human beings.

Hence, in a typical context referring to human beings, the listener to some extent "pictures" a male figure on the basis of a masculine singular

---

women, few or none of whom are individuals that we specifically picture in our minds (and this broader generic sense is the way it is used in the Bible).

[7]We include pronominal affixes in Hebrew and Aramaic.

[8]Plural masculine pronouns in Hebrew, Greek, and Aramaic may refer to all male groups, but they may also sometimes refer to mixed groups, composed of both men and women. (It is

personal pronoun.[8] The context decides whether the reference is literally to a particular male human being, to a male fictional character, or to a male as an illustration or sample from a group. Thus, in Hebrew and in Greek as well as in English, the usage "suggests a particular pattern of thought," namely a picture using a male representative.[9]

We may illustrate with Leviticus 14. Leviticus 14:2 introduces the situation, "This shall be the law of the leper in the day of *his* cleansing. Now *he* shall be brought to the priest" (NASB). Both men and women could contract the infectious skin disease that is termed "leprosy." (The Bible mentions women explicitly in the discussion of leprosy in the previous chapter, in Leviticus 13:29, 38.) The reader easily infers that the instructions in Leviticus 14 are intended to *apply* to both men and women. But the instruction commences using *masculine singular forms.*

The reader *pictures a single sample human being* who will, from then on, represent the procedure to be followed in any number of future cases. But does the reader picture a male, or a female, or both equally? The reader con-

---

a little like the older use of the English word "men.") The possibility of reference to a mixed group makes them differ at this point from the details of the singular pronouns.

[9]Mark Strauss appears not yet to have understood how there can be a male representative or sample case as the starting point for a general principle. He writes:

> There also appears to me to be an internal contradiction in Dr. Grudem's presentation. Throughout his writings he claims, on the one hand, that masculine terms like "man" and "he" are perfectly acceptable generic terms. . . . He then turns around and says these terms must be retained because they are *intended* to be exclusive—that is, referring to a single male representative. They are intentionally male-coded, and this male coding is essential to the meaning. But you can't have it both ways. Either the referent is male or the referent is unspecified. Either the context is generic, or it is one of a male representative (Strauss, "Inclusive Language in Bible Translation," paper presented at the Portland, Oregon, regional ETS meeting, April 10, 1999], p. 13).

But yes, you can have it both ways, because the genius of a sample case is that, precisely in its particularity, it can express a general truth. Would Strauss agree that the importunate widow in Luke 18:1–8 can be female sample case, and at the same time be an example of a general principle about men and women persevering in prayer? Can Proverbs 28:7 make a statement about a father and son from which one can infer a general principle that includes mothers and daughters ("He who keeps the law is a discerning *son,* but a companion of gluttons disgraces his *father,*" NIV)? These, of course, are only analogies to the situation with generic "he," but they are useful analogies. Note again the language from the *American Heritage Dictionary,* "Thus *he* is not really a gender-neutral pronoun, rather, it refers to a *male* who is to be taken as *the representative member* of the group referred to by its antecedent" (p. 831, emphasis ours). We are claiming that an analogous tendency also exists in Hebrew, Greek, and Aramaic.

Strauss's failure to understand what we are saying, or even to grasp the possibility of a both-and combination, seriously undermines his ability to enter into profitable dialogue with our position. In fact, Strauss's either-or dichotomy, when understood rigidly, leads directly to an endorsement of almost everything that gender-neutral translations do. According to this dichotomy, we can have either a general principle or sexual marking, but not both. Thus, general principles must always receive *colorlessly* general expression, with no sexual element occurring in the representative case. Hence, no male-oriented meaning components can be retained in English in any situation where a general principle is exemplified. This may come close to capturing the general pattern of translation exemplified in some of the gender-neutral translations.

tinues meeting masculine forms referring to the leper in verses 7–8. In verse 9 he then reads, ". . . he shall shave his head and his beard and his eyebrows." (NASB). The mention of "beard" confirms that the representative case is a male human being.[10] Now, is the reader surprised at this inclusion? Does he say, "Why are you talking now specifically about a man, when I thought earlier that you were including both men and women?" We think not.

But would he be surprised if the text, after all these masculine forms, were to introduce without warning a reference to some item of women's apparel, such as the "perfume boxes" of Isaiah 3:20? Would the text continue with masculine pronouns if it were to describe some special ceremony involving a woman opening her perfume box?[11]

We realize of course that Hebrew, Aramaic, and Greek do not directly match English. So without being native speakers, no one can say with absolute certainty what the exact effects would be in those languages. But in typical contexts, *singular masculine gender pronouns encourage a starting picture of a male*, not just a totally faceless entity. They ease the reader into a smooth transition to a particular detail like a beard, which we associate with men and not women. (See Appendix 3 for further discussion and illustrations.)

The larger cultural context of the Bible reinforces these tendencies. Within patriarchal cultures people are comfortable with the idea of taking a male person as a sample, as representative of anyone within a larger group. Illustrations abound, many of which do not depend on the pronominal system. David represents the whole Israelite army when he fights Goliath (1 Sam. 17:9). The male leaders are representatives of their tribes (Num. 7:12–84; 17:2). The male priests are representatives of Israel before God.

Most significantly, Adam and Christ are representatives for two cosmic groups. Adam represents all his descendants, and Christ represents all who belong to him: "For as in Adam all die, so also in Christ shall all be made alive" (1 Cor. 15:22, RSV; cf. Rom. 5:12–21; 1 Cor. 15:20–22, 45–49). Husbands are imitators of Christ, and wives of the church which is subject to Christ (Eph. 5:22–33). Yes, the Bible gives honor to all members of the body of Christ (note the importance given to all members of the body in 1 Cor. 12), but it also refutes the erroneous aspects of feminism. Feminism replaces biblical honor with a misguided attempt to wipe out the differences in people with respect to prominence, order, leadership, and representation.

---

[10]Of course, due to hormonal changes, disease, or bodily irregularities, in unusual cases a woman may have hair growth on the face, or a man may lack it. We are not, however, looking at exceptional cases but asking what an Israelite reader would understand concerning the *typical* case.

[11]As we will see in Appendix 3, a masculine verb can be followed by a feminine subject. But the feminine subject, when it refers to a person, uses a feminine form to refer to a female person. The most direct reference to the person still matches the sex of the person.

Generic "he" is thus seen to be simply one aspect of the larger spiritual conflict. Feminists want to abolish generic "he" partly because, by its lack of gender symmetry, it symbolizes a difference between men and women. But the Bible paints a different picture, a picture in which God has ordained men, not women, to serve in certain positions of leadership, first in Adam as representative of the human race, then in Christ, and now in the family and the church. It so happens that generic "he" in English subtly resonates with this truth by suggesting a male case as the starting illustration for a general truth. Most of the time, before the rise of feminism, people paid no conscious attention to it. But it was there. And it is still there, which is one reason feminists are troubled by it. Generic "he" in English accomplishes this symbolization in a manner analogous to what happens in Hebrew and Greek in the Bible. From the standpoint of the most radical feminists, the Hebrew and Greek would also be regarded as offensive and "sexist" where they use a generic masculine singular pronoun. Radical feminism not only denounces a practice in English; by implication it also denounces the same practice in the Word of God in the original languages. And in denouncing the Word of God, it thereby denounces God who caused the words to be written.

Of course, in eliminating generic "he," gender-neutral translations endeavor to retain the general principle expressed in a verse. But they lose part of the meaning by not expressing the fact that the original typically uses a male sample, a male representative who embodies or illustrates the principle in operation. In addition, as we saw in the preceding chapter (Chapter 13), because there is no effective substitute for generic "he," they lose other significant aspects of meaning by changing singulars to plurals, third person to second or first person, active verbs to passive, and so forth. In fact, the losses through such rephrasing are generally far more noticeable and far more damaging to meaning than the losses that concern a male starting point.[12] In fact, much of what we have written in this book concentrates on the more important issue, the losses through such rephrasing. But the fact that feminism focuses on the issue of a male example causes us to focus some attention on this fact too.

The pattern with respect to generic "he" matches what we have seen in other kinds of cases where gender-neutral translations have made impermissible changes, such as deleting "men" (referring to males) or "father" or "son." All the verses of this kind involve a male human being, or else a masculine term with an associated male semantic component. In each case the semantic maleness occurs in a context where the verse as a whole expresses, or at least implies indirectly, some general truth that applies to both men and women.

---

[12]As usual, we should preserve in translation all the nuances we can. But we must also have a sense of degrees of loss, so that when we come to hard cases where there seems to be no good way to express every nuance in translation, we make the wisest choice.

Such is clearly the case with proverbial statements and with Jesus' parables. It is also so even in historical passages like Acts 1:21, at least in terms of secondary implications. In Acts 1:21 Peter looks for a replacement for Judas as an apostle. Now, the apostles were all men. But others besides the apostles followed Jesus and were witnesses to his teaching and his suffering. Some of these witnesses were women (Luke 8:2–3; 23:49, 55). The apostles, even though unique in some respects, are in other respects examples of what all believers ought to be like. Unfortunately for modern cultural prejudices, when the apostles are examples, they are still all *male* examples, and such is not easy for feminists to accept. Similarly, the men who buried Stephen (Acts 8:2) are examples of what every believer should do in honoring Christians who die for the faith—but these examples were all males.

In all these cases the gender-neutral translator—let us call him Jerry—eliminates the fact that the representative instance is male, while trying to retain the general principle.[13] Why should he even attempt to do such a thing? Why not do what translators have always tried to do, namely represent in English a maximum amount of meaning from the original?

The obvious answer is, some people would not like it. To begin, radical feminists would not like it. In addition, feminists have deeply influenced many other people who would not consider themselves radical feminists or perhaps even feminists at all. The influence begins with cultural leaders and filters down through educational institutions and media to many others. Now Jerry, as a translator of the Bible, does not want his Bible translation needlessly to irritate all these people. So he makes a gender-neutral translation. In so doing, is he compromising the meaning of the Bible for the sake of peace with modern culture?

Jerry would probably deny it. He would claim, perhaps, only to be "following good grammar." But *grammatical experts* in English have stated that the problem is not grammar but ideology. *The American Heritage Dictionary* (1996) states:

> In contrast to these innovations [using "she," "s/he," "hiser," etc.], many writers use the masculine pronoun as generic in all cases. For the same series of sample sentences, the average percentage of Usage Panel members [writing experts] who consistently completed the sentences with *his* was 37. This course is grammatically unexceptional, but the writer who follows it must be prepared to incur the displeasure of readers who regard this pattern as a mark of insensitivity or gender discrimination.[14]

---

[13]It would deflect from our main argument to observe that, even though there is a common pattern, the different cases are far from being on the same level. In some cases, as in Acts 1:21 and 20:30, the texts are directly addressing a specific historical situation, and the broader general principles lie far in the background. In other cases, such as Matthew 7:24, 26, the individual male figure is introduced only for directing people's attention to a principle.

[14]*American Heritage Dictionary*, 831.

Generic "he" is "grammatically unexceptionable." That is, you cannot argue on *grammatical grounds* that it needs to be eliminated. The *American Heritage Dictionary* (1996) polled the 173 members of its Usage Panel of experts in the English language on how to complete a series of sentences such as, "A patient who doesn't accurately report ____ sexual history to the doctor runs the risk of misdiagnosis" or, "A child who develops this sort of rash on ____ hands should probably be kept at home for a number of days." In their responses, an average of 46 percent of panel members used combination forms such as "his or her" or "her/his" (this 46 percent thus combines several different replies), 37 percent used "his," 3 percent used "their," 2 percent used "her," 2 percent used "a" or "the," and 7 percent gave no response or felt no pronoun was needed, and a few gave other responses.[15] But if 37 percent of these experts (the largest for any one specific response, since the 46 percent was a combined total) continued to use "his" as their most preferred word in these sentences (and many more would have said it is acceptable but not preferred), then no one can rightly claim that generic "he, him, his" is improper English today. In spite of several decades of discussion, no substitutes have gained general acceptance.

But the *American Heritage Dictionary* says generic "he" creates "displeasure" because some consider its use to be "gender discrimination." Here the label "gender discrimination" indicates the influence of feminist ideology. Only by assuming the truth of feminism can anyone move from the mere fact that "he" is masculine to the conclusion that using a male as an example is morally wrong, that it is "gender discrimination" in an age when such discrimination is deplored. In effect, the *Dictionary* hints that the motive for avoiding generic "he" is not to offend those who have (perhaps unknowingly) swallowed a piece of feminist ideology.

At an earlier point the *Dictionary* says that generic "he" "is not simply a grammatical convention; it also suggests a particular pattern of thought." Once again it distinguishes between "grammatical convention" and "a particular pattern of thought," that is, the male orientation. Later it adds that the writer who goes on using generic "he" "may invite the inference that there is some pointed reason for referring to the representative instance as male."[16] The ideological rejection of male orientation, not the grammar, makes it unacceptable.

D. Generic "she"

In telling the story we have still oversimplified. We must still consider generic "she."

At present, many people have settled into a pattern of avoiding generic "he," for a variety of reasons. But generic "he" still occurs in major secular

---

[15]Ibid.
[16]Ibid.

news media, as we shall confirm below (see Chapter 16). In addition, some modern writing uses generic "she." That is, "she" is used to refer to a sample person in making a general statement. "If anyone wants to read a good book, she should go to the library and pick out something she is interested in." "She" refers back to "anyone" or "everyone" or "whoever" or some other generalizing antecedent. In this use, generic "she" has the same basic functions as generic "he." We also find some writers who *oscillate* between generic "he" and generic "she," perhaps using "he" for one or two paragraphs, then "she" in the next two pages, then back to "he."[17]

We have talked loosely about a "prohibition" on generic "he." But strictly speaking, generic "he" is not prohibited, so long as generic "she" is used just as much. At an earlier point in time, it may have looked as if feminists wanted simply to prohibit generic "he" completely. In 1988 Miller and Swift's *Handbook of Nonsexist Writing* rejected generic "he" and devoted a whole chapter to discussing alternatives to generic "he."[18] The book went through the usual list: writers should substitute "they" with singular antecedent, or "he or she," or try pluralizing ("they" plural), or use "you." Using "she" or oscillating between "he" and "she" did not come up for discussion.[19]

But now generic "she" is apparently occurring more frequently. D. A. Carson reports his own observations to this effect.[20] As we mentioned before, the *American Heritage Dictionary* (3d ed., 1994)[21] polled its Usage Panel with a series of sample generic sentences. Two percent of the Panel chose the feminine pronoun ("she/her/hers/herself"). Two percent is not a large percentage, but it still represents a very significant amount within the totality of English language usage.

What are the implications? The increasing occurrence of generic "she" shifts the ground under us, because it opens the possibility of oscillating between "he" and "she." Feminist ideology does not prohibit this oscillation. Generic "he" may occur freely, provided that generic "she" appears elsewhere to balance it. Thus, generic "he" *as such* is no longer an ideological problem. It is not insensitive, or offensive, or objectionable, *provided* "she" occurs elsewhere or there are other clear assurances of ideological sensitivity.

---

[17]Carson says, ". . . some use 'he' generically and then a few pages on use 'she' generically" (*Debate*, 189). Carson further elaborates on p. 190, citing as an example Cornelius Plantinga, Jr.'s recent book *Not the Way It's Supposed to Be: A Breviary of Sin* (Grand Rapids: Eerdmans, 1995).

[18]Miller and Swift, *Handbook*, 43–58.

[19]The *Handbook* does observe briefly that "she" and "her" have been used in generalizations about secretaries and nurses, but it does not approve of this practice, which is obviously still "sexist" from its point of view (p. 46).

[20]Carson, *Debate*, 189–90.

[21]*American Heritage Dictionary*, 831.

As another kind of illustration we may take Zinsser's book *On Writing Well*.[22] Beginning with the fourth edition, Zinsser eliminated many of the generic "he's" that occurred in previous editions. But he decided against using generic "she" or oscillating between "he" and "she."[23] He used other alternatives such as "you." But he also retained generic "he" in a few places.[24] Though some egalitarians might quarrel with Zinsser's stylistic advice to others, few would object strenuously to his own personal stylistic decision to retain a few generic "he's." Zinsser has obviously shown his sensitivity to ideological issues by making many changes and by discussing the whole subject openly. He thus reassures the wondering reader that no insensitivity or ideological chauvinism is intended with the remaining "he's."

Of course there may be a few egalitarians who object even to what Zinsser has done. But most egalitarians are reasonable. They want reassurances, and Zinsser gives such reassurance. For other writers, the use of generic "she" alongside generic "he" also provides just such a reassurance. It shows that a writer is politically aware, and may hint also that the writer is sympathetic with egalitarianism.[25]

What is the point of this for our discussion? (1) It shows that generic "she" is understandable to people today as a pronoun that causes a reader to think of a female person as a starting point for a general statement that applies to males and females alike. (2) If the innovative generic "she" is understandable today and people recognize that it is used to state a generally applicable truth, then surely generic "he," which has a long history of use in English, is also understandable. (3) If no one objects to generic "he" when used in equal proportions with generic "she," this indicates that the real objection is not that readers will *misunderstand* generic "he," but that they think it is *unfair* or *discourteous* to give disproportionate prominence to male examples. Thus, the real objection is directly related to egalitarian thought and, more specifically, to feminist ideology.

E.   The "mandate" of the National Council of Churches of Christ

The explanations that gender-neutral translations give in their prefaces show some telltale signs that translators were not completely unaware of

---

[22]William Zinsser, *On Writing Well*, 5th ed. (New York: HarperCollins, 1994).

[23]Ibid., 123–24.

[24]"Where the male pronoun remains in this edition I felt it was the only clean solution" (ibid., 123).

[25]Note what we said earlier about certain language usages having a symbolic function. Exclusive use of generic "she" or oscillation between "he" and "she" both tend symbolically to connote sympathy with feminism. They are thus even more reassuring to language police than using "you" or "they." "You" and "they" are used by traditionalists as well as feminists, so they do not by themselves have any symbolic overtones. On the other hand, occurrence of

these issues. Let us begin with the earliest prominent gender-neutral translation, the NRSV. The preface explains:

> During the almost half a century since the publication of the RSV, many in the churches have become sensitive to the danger of linguistic sexism arising from the inherent bias of the English language towards the masculine gender, a bias that in the case of the Bible has often restricted or obscured the meaning of the original text.[26]

The phrase "the inherent bias of the English language towards the masculine gender" may perhaps include many items, but generic "he" is clearly one of them.[27] The word "bias" already suggests some ideological loading. It is not just a mere asymmetry. It is "bias," a term that implies a negative moral evaluation. Just in case we do not grasp the point, the sentence associates it with "sexism." "Sexism," of course, is a term of moral condemnation. Generic "he" is bad because it is linked to "linguistic sexism." How? Because it gives prominence to the male. The "Preface" is simply following, step-by-step, the assumptions of feminists. Any prominence or asymmetry is "unfair." So it must be eliminated.

Moreover, the NRSV "Preface" quite remarkably claims that this bias "in the case of the Bible has often restricted or obscured the meaning of the original text." But the translators of the NRSV were experts, and they must have known that the Hebrew and Greek of the Bible display the same masculine gender "bias" as English—even more so, in some ways. So it is simply untrue that generic "he" and similar masculine language "restricted or obscured *the meaning of the original text.*" And it would be misleading to suggest that such "bias toward the masculine gender" was a problem for English that did not exist in Hebrew and Greek.

Hebrew and Greek, though different in structure from English, definitely do exhibit an "inherent bias . . . toward the masculine gender."[28] In fact, in some ways the Hebrew and Greek exhibit even more "bias" than English, in ways that cannot even be fully reproduced in English. For example, the Ten Commandments in Exodus 20 in Hebrew use mostly a second-person singular *masculine* prefix form. "You [masculine singular] shall not

---

generic "he" when not balanced by generic "she" gives more prominence to the male and is a sure sign to the language police of ideological backwardness (or disagreement).

[26]NRSV (Cambridge: Cambridge University Press, 1993), "Preface to the New Revised Standard Version," x.

[27]Could it be that the NRSV "Preface" is talking merely about changes in the meaning of "a man" and "men," leading to the permissible changes that we have catalogued in Chapter 5? No. For one thing, such a narrow interpretation leaves us with no explanation for why the NRSV undertook to eliminate generic "he." For another, the NRSV is then killing a gnat with a sledgehammer. Why bring in the highly charged language about "bias," "sexism," and "conflict," when all you have to do is say that you are being more accurate, because the meaning of "a man" and "men" is no longer clearly inclusive?

[28]Another preface, that to the GNB, speaks more directly of "the built-in linguistic biases of the ancient languages and the English language."

kill. You [masculine singular] shall not commit adultery. You [masculine singular] shall not steal." We cannot reproduce the masculine "bias" in English, because English has only one form "you" where Hebrew has four distinct forms (masculine singular, masculine plural, feminine singular, and feminine plural). As we have seen, generic "he" reproduces in English the effects of the Hebrew and Greek use of masculine singular generics. The "bias" of putting a picture of a male example before one's eyes is present in all three languages. That is one reason generic "he" is an excellent resource to use in translation. But the NRSV "Preface" appears to deny this reality, pronouncing that generic "he" "obscured the meaning."

We are left to wonder if the real problem is not obscurity but its opposite, clarity. If translators do not obscure the meaning, they might carry over into English the connotation of a male example which is in the original text thousands of times. But this use of a male example offends some people.

The NRSV "Preface" explains that the translators themselves did not have much choice in this matter, for they were under a mandate from the Division of Education and Ministry of the National Council of Churches of Christ, requiring the elimination of much "masculine-oriented" language from this translation:

> The mandates from the Division specified that, in references to men and women, masculine-oriented language should be eliminated as far as this can be done without altering passages that reflect the historical situation of ancient patriarchal culture. As can be appreciated, more than once the Committee [the committee of translators, who actually had to wrestle with the text of Scripture] found that the several mandates stood in tension and even in conflict.[29]

Among other things, the mandate required the elimination of generic "he" as one element of "masculine-oriented language." But the elimination of generic "he" was to be done "without altering passages." As we have seen, in many verses this is impossible.[30] The translating Committee found that there was "conflict." The Committee, we presume, tried to make the best of a bad situation.

F. The explanatory statement of the NIVI

Next, consider the *New International Version: Inclusive Language Edition* (NIVI). The Committee on Bible Translation included an explanation of their thinking in the preface to the NIVI. For the sake of giving an adequate context, we quote an extended passage:

---

[29]NRSV, "Preface," x.

[30]Again, there are exceptions, when translators have a passage to which they can make tiny changes without restructuring it. But in most cases, they find themselves resorting to "you," "they," passives, and other problematic rephrasings.

The first principle [on gender] was to retain the gender used in the original languages when referring to God, angels and demons. At the same time, it was recognized that it was often appropriate to mute the patriarchalism of the culture of the biblical writers through gender-inclusive language when this could be done without compromising the message of the Spirit. This involved distinguishing between those passages in which an activity was normally carried out by either males or females, and other cases where the gender of the people concerned was less precisely identified. While in cases of the former the text could be left unaltered, in cases of the latter words like "workmen" could be changed to "worker" or "craftsman" to "skilled worker."

A further problem presented itself in handling pronouns. In order to avoid gender-specific language in statements of a general kind, it was agreed that the plural might be substituted for the singular and the second person for the third person.[31]

The key expression is found in the second sentence: "It was often appropriate to mute the patriarchalism of the culture of the biblical writers." This statement is vague, and the vagueness opens the door to massive changes that would virtually rewrite the English Bible. All the translators have to do is preserve "the message of the Spirit," which might be understood to include whatever minimal core of meaning the translators decide on.

Of course, the translation committee did not mean to open the door this wide. What did they mean? It is impossible to say. Maybe different members of the committee meant different things. Rather than trying to guess, it is more useful for us to understand how such an explanation will serve to encourage people who defend gender-neutral translations.

Once again, consider our hypothetical translator, whom we have called Jerry. Jerry takes comfort from this explanation. He says, "Possibly, the meaning is revealed in the next two sentences. The next two sentences say that when the Bible describes an activity by men, we can say that it is men. With women, we can say that it is women. When it might be a mixed group, we use a gender-neutral term like 'worker.'"

This practice is reasonable. But it has nothing to do with "patriarchalism." A translator describing mixed groups is not "muting" or downplaying the "patriarchalism" of the culture. He is just reporting which groups in the culture contained men and which contained women. The same practice might be used in reporting about any culture whatsoever, without "muting" anything about the character of that culture. The second sentence simply does not connect with the third and fourth sentences.

But then Jerry suggests, "I am thinking of the fact that many Hebrew and Greek words used to describe mixed groups are marked as masculine

---

[31]"Preface to Inclusive Language NIV," NIVI, vii.

in gender. Masculine is used when the gender of the group is unknown or mixed." These usages may indeed be one part of what the NIVI has in view. In fact, the NIVI may be talking about the sorts of permissible change that we discussed in Chapter 11. About these there is no dispute, and if the NIVI had made only those sorts of changes, we would have no objections.

But in fact, the NIVI made hundreds of other changes, changes which we seriously dispute. Many of these involve singular masculine terms, in verses that appear to take a male representative as a starting point for enunciating a general principle.

Now the question arises, as it does with generic "he," whether the use of the masculine gender in such verses represents not merely a grammatical convention but "a particular pattern of thought." The pattern of thought would be what we have already seen, the use of a male example as the representative when talking about a broader principle. For example, a verse from Proverbs may speak of a "father" and a "son" in order to express a principle that would apply to a mother or a daughter as well.

In this case, a defender of gender-neutral translations like Jerry is in a dilemma. If there is *no* pattern of thought, but merely a grammatical convention with no meaning at all, then nothing is being "muted" in English. If, on the other hand, there is a pattern of thought, what is "muted" is not merely something out there in the *culture*, but in the thought, in the *language*. It is not merely in the language in general, but in the particular sentence that one is struggling to translate. What is "muted" is not patriarchalism in the culture, but an aspect of *meaning* in the sentence in question.

So Jerry tries again, "Perhaps, then, 'muting the patriarchalism' refers to the next paragraph, which discusses generic 'he.' "

Does removing generic "he" "mute the patriarchalism"? How so? Consider, for example, John 14:23:

> NIV: If anyone loves me, he will obey my teaching. My Father will love him, and we will come to him and make our home with him.

> NIVI: *Those* who love me will obey my teaching. My Father will love *them*, and we will come to *them* and make our home with *them*.

As we saw earlier, John 14:23 in the NIV and in the original Greek has singular generic pronouns. In the NIVI, these are converted to plural forms, "those," "them."

Here is the dilemma: Either the NIVI's rewording changes the meaning of the earlier NIV, or it does not.

If it does not change the meaning, then the result does not alter readers' perceptions of the "patriarchalism of the culture of biblical writers." Nothing has been gained. Why change the wording?

But if the NIVI does change the meaning, then Jerry cannot continue to use the argument that there is no change in meaning.

Jerry might respond, "Well, there are slight changes of meaning in *English*. But the NIV and the NIVI convey equally well the meaning of the Greek."

But a dilemma still remains. If both do equally well in conveying the meaning of the Greek, then neither is "muting" anything in ancient culture. Then why make the change?

In fact, Jerry knows that there are masculine generics in John 14:23 in Greek. Either the masculine marking conveys a sense of a male representative example, or it does not. If it does not, then the supposed "patriarchalism" is not in the original text, and there is nothing to "mute." In this case, the NIVI explanation does not apply. But if the "patriarchalism" *is* in the original text, then it should be translated. Why does Jerry resist translating part of the meaning?

Language, thought, and culture, though distinguishable, are interlocked in countless ways. A simple recipe to translate meaning while cutting out cultural influences is unworkable. Accurately translated meaning inevitably *includes* subtle clues giving readers insights into the surrounding culture.

We need to distinguish a minimum of three different possibilities. First, patriarchal practices in the culture may show no effects on a particular text. Second, a text may *mention* patriarchal practices, without necessarily approving them. Third, the text may set forth *thought patterns* influenced by patriarchy.

In the first instance, patriarchy has no direct effect on the text, so the translator has no problem. He "mutes" nothing.

In the second instance, the text *mentions* a patriarchal practice. Then the translator should translate it. For example, in 1 Samuel 2 Eli's sons take advantage of their privileged position in order to exploit the people. The Bible condemns this exploitation, but does not refrain from describing it. In like manner, it can describe various aspects of a patriarchal culture without approving of things that are bad about this culture. Translators should not "mute" any of this. If the Bible says something in the original, say it in translation as well.

But what about the third situation, where the text's own thought patterns show "patriarchal" influence? In what ways might such influence exert itself? The text might concentrate on the history of male characters. It might use predominantly male examples. It might use masculine forms to designate groups of mixed sex. It might use male-oriented terms as a depiction of a representative case in expressing a general truth. Strictly speaking, such usages are not directly "patriarchal." In theory, they might occur in texts written in many different cultural settings. We do not know how far such usages are directly reinforced by patriarchy, and how far they are independent of a culture. Hence, the textual patterns in question should be labeled "male-oriented textual meanings."[32] Thereby we distinguish the issue of the orientation of a *text* from the social organization of a *culture*.

Our third category, then, consists in texts that shows male-oriented meanings. Then, when feasible, we must translate those meanings *in order to remain faithful in representing every aspect of the original meaning.*

At this point in the discussion, suppose that Jerry (our hypothetical advocate of gender-neutral translations) now brings into our discussion the guideline that the Committee on Bible Translation for the NIVI formulated for its own internal use:

> The patriarchalism (like other social patterns) of the ancient cultures in which the Biblical books were composed is pervasively reflected in forms of expression that appear, in the modern context, to deny the common human dignity of all hearers and readers. For these forms, alternative modes of expression can and may be used, though care must be taken not to distort the intent of the original text.[33]

What do we make of this? Patriarchalism is "pervasively reflected in *forms of expression*." "Forms of expression" have to do with linguistic forms that appear in texts, not merely with the surrounding culture as such. Is this guideline talking about forms in English or in ancient Hebrew and Greek? It must be the ancient languages, since it is these that would "pervasively reflect" "the ancient cultures." The forms of language in the Hebrew and Greek Bible pervasively reflect patriarchalism!

Jerry may nevertheless heave a sigh of relief that these forms are not available to modern people. Most modern people do not read Hebrew and Greek fluently. So, Jerry thinks, modern people are mercifully protected from these forms that would appear "to deny the common dignity of all hearers and readers." So there is no danger.

Then why the fuss? Apparently there still *is* a danger. What is it? There is a danger that these very forms of language would be carried across in translation. If they did, "modern context" would be offended.

Of course, if these "forms of expression" are *mere* forms, without meaning, we can freely alter them in translation.[34] But the NIV's Committee on

---

[32]But there might also be forms like *banîm* ("children") that are masculine in form, but that in a particular context do not carry a male meaning component. They would not carry "male-oriented textual meanings," except possibly in a very reduced sense. In that case, of course, they could be translated in English with a gender-neutral term ("children").

[33]D. A. Carson, *The Inclusive-Language Debate: A Plea for Realism* (Grand Rapids: Baker, 1998), 41, guideline I.D. Carson gives in full the "CBT Policy on Gender-Inclusive Language," quoting from a copy sent to him from the CBT.

[34]Carson thinks that perhaps this CBT principle may refer only to changing *grammatical* gender, not forms that in Hebrew or Greek carried male *meaning* (*Debate*, p. 103). This is doubtful, for why would the CBT decide to say that "patriarchalism (like other social patterns) . . . is reflected in [grammatical gender]"? Moreover, the practice of changing grammatical gender, when appropriate for expressing the meaning, is as old as the KJV, as Carson himself illustrates by mentioning the phrase " 'sons [or children] of Israel' in Hebrew" (p. 103). If this is all that the principle meant, it says nothing new, and does not give any rationale for the new types

Bible Translation, in its guideline, has already told us that these are not mere forms, completely empty of all significance. They have a culturally related overlay of meaning—they "pervasively reflect" patriarchalism, a meaning-rich cultural institution. Meaning is at stake here.

Now in translation, we try to carry over meaning, do we not? So our first attempt would be to try to find analogues in English for these forms, which is what all translations did before 1989 in using generic "he" in English Bibles.

"But," says Jerry, "we cannot. If we try to use generic 'he,' people will be offended. 'He' appears to deny the common human dignity of all hearers and readers."

Just what offends them, Jerry? Just how does "he" "deny the common human dignity of all hearers and readers"? It uses a male starting point as a representative sample for a general statement—and this is "unfair." At this point we are straight back into feminism. Feminism says that using a male starting point is unfair.

We must not spare Jerry from looking more closely at what he himself has said. He started, not with generic "he," but with "forms of expression" in an ancient cultural context, forms of Hebrew and Greek. *These* forms, not merely modern generic "he," "appear, in the modern context, to deny the common human dignity. . . ."

So the objection is not just against English. The objection is against "forms of expression" *in any language* that reflect "patriarchalism" and thereby "deny the common human dignity of all hearers and readers." Of course, feminism is not limited to English-speaking countries. It is an international movement. Feminists work in other languages, not merely in English, to abolish "linguistic sexism," and feminist dogma applies in principle across all languages. The principle runs, "Any preference for the male *in any culture* is objectionable. Any mode of expression that has male-oriented meanings is 'linguistic sexism.'" Our hypothetical gender-neutral translation defender, Jerry, is right to say that in this "modern context" of feminism, the ancient forms of expression in Hebrew and Greek are unacceptable, as unacceptable as their nearest English equivalents.

---

of change that the CBT introduces. The entire statement was approved at the time when the CBT embarked on its project of producing an inclusive-language NIV (1992).

It is interesting to see Dr. Carson stretch again and again to find a sympathetic reading of the CBT's principles, arguing that several of them are not as objectionable as they first appear (see p. 100: "Principle I.C could be understood in a good sense or a bad sense"; p. 103: ". . . principle I.D could be understood in a good sense or a bad sense"; p. 105: "Principle II(6) needs some explanation or clarification."). By contrast, though the book claims to be evenhanded, Carson again and again subjects the Colorado Springs Guidelines to the most unsympathetic reading, failing not only to consider a "good sense" in which they could be read, but even failing to interpret them in a way consistent with the heading under which they occur (see, p. 99, on B.3 regarding "father") or the context of the other guidelines (see, p. 118–21 on *ho pisteuon* and the alleged requirement of retaining grammatical gender).

But now let us apply the feminist principle to a section of the Ten Commandments, the commands in Exodus 20:13–17:

> You shall not murder. You shall not commit adultery. You shall not steal. You shall not give false testimony against your neighbor. You shall not covet your neighbor's house. You shall not covet your neighbor's wife, or his manservant or maidservant, his ox or donkey, or anything that belongs to your neighbor.

When God gave these commandments by speaking from Mt. Sinai, he spoke in Hebrew (for the Hebrew-speaking people of Israel understood him), and he spoke with masculine singular forms. In Hebrew each command "you shall not" includes the equivalent of a masculine singular "you," which is also the form that would normally be used in addressing a single male person. Of course, here and in many other instances, the masculine singular is used in addressing a whole community. Men and women are both included as addressees, by implication from context. But the starting point is masculine singular.

When God wrote these same words on two stone tablets (Exod. 31:18; Deut. 9:10), he wrote in Hebrew, and he wrote with masculine singular forms.[35] The male orientation is very clear in the statement, "You shall not covet your neighbor's *wife. . . .*," for here God used a male starting point (a husband who should not covet) to teach a general truth that applies to both husbands and wives. Now Jerry tells us that these masculine singular forms "appear, in the modern context, to deny the common human dignity of all hearers and readers."

But God used these forms when he spoke from Mount Sinai! We will stand against the whole world, if necessary, to maintain that God is right and that "modern context" is wrong in its moral judgment condemning God's Word. *That* is the issue.

Note also that Jerry's argument slides by the key distinction between patriarchal culture and male-oriented textual meanings. He claims that the "forms of expression," that is, the male-oriented textual meanings, reflect the culture of patriarchy. In fact, culture and language do not map into one another directly, since male-oriented textual meanings can occur in many languages and cultures. But by using the term "patriarchalism," instead of talking about male-oriented meanings, Jerry can deflect attention from textual meaning onto the surrounding culture. Jerry gives the impression that the culture, not the text, is the problem. He obscures the fact that the adjustments he contemplates mute male-oriented textual meanings, not patriarchal culture as such. He wants the culture, not himself, to take the blame for altering meanings.

---

[35]Exodus 20 and Deuteronomy 5 are, of course, a written record of that original speech of God from Mount Sinai.

In sum, Jerry's thinking in defending gender-neutral translations does not make sense. It is muddy at best, and at worst it has just absorbed into itself feminist propaganda. Such is not an adequate basis on which to undertake to change thousands of verses in English to eliminate generic "he."

G. The explanatory statement of the NLT

Another gender-neutral translation, the *New Living Translation*, gives this explanation in its introduction:

> The English language changes constantly. An obvious recent change is in the area of gender-inclusive language. This creates problems for modern translators of the ancient biblical text, which was originally written in a male-oriented culture. The translator must respect the nature of the ancient context while also accounting for the concerns of the modern audience. Often the original language itself allows a rendering that is gender inclusive. For example, the Greek word *anthrōpos*, traditionally rendered "man," really means "human being" or "person." A different Greek word, *anēr*, specifically means a male.[36]

The example that the NLT offers concerning *anthrōpos* and *anēr* agrees with what we have established in Chapters 11 and 12 concerning permissible and impermissible changes. To a casual reader, the NLT appears to be talking only about permissible changes. Thus, the reader is reassured.

Unfortunately, the assurance is illusory. The permissible decision to translate *anthrōpos* with "person" has nothing to do with "male-oriented culture" and "ancient context," but only with a clarification *in English* due to changes in *English* usage. The example (*anthrōpos*) has nothing to do with the three immediately preceding sentences, which one suspects were intended to cover all sorts of *other* decisions, including impermissible changes. In particular, the NLT's words give no hint of the fact that the NLT itself sometimes[37] removes male marking in translating *anēr*, a word that it says "specifically means a male."

So let us look at the actual wording of NLT's general principle in the first four sentences of the above quote. "An obvious recent change is in the area of gender-inclusive language." Does the NLT just have in mind the changes with respect to "every man" and the like, the permissible changes of Chapter 11? But in its practice the NLT does much more.

So what are "the concerns of the modern audience"? The NLT does not say. But the specter of feminist objections to "linguistic sexism" hovers just below the surface. Moreover, one can see again the desire to squeeze out of

---

[36]NLT, "Introduction to the New Living Translation," xliv.
[37]See Matthew 7:24, 26; 12:41; 14:35; Luke 7:20; 14:24; 22:63; Acts 1:21; 5:36; 8:2; 11:20; 20:30; 21:38; 1 Corinthians 13:11; Ephesians 4:13.

the problems by appealing to the distinction between culture and message. The ancient *culture* was "male oriented," and the modern one is not—at least not as much.

But, as before, the attempt to build gender-neutral policies on this observation produces insoluble dilemmas. If the problem is *merely* the culture, then let the Bible describe the culture accurately without approving of its bad aspects. But if the "problem" is the text of the Bible itself, then you had better think again. If the problem in the text is "mere" mode of expression, and not meaning, then it does not create any problem in English, which will simply express the meaning. So what is the problem? Evidently something deeper, *something embedded in the total texture of meaning that the original text generates*. In fact, the "problem" is male textual meanings.

Since the initial publication in 1996, the NLT has been revised, and the material in the "Introduction" altered. In 1999 the revised NLT[38] has deleted the earlier statement and replaced it with the following:

> One challenge we faced was in determining how to translate accurately the ancient biblical text that was originally written in a context where male-oriented terms were used to refer to humanity generally. We needed to respect the nature of the ancient context while also trying to make the translation clear to a modern audience that tends to read male-oriented language as applying only to males. Often the original text, though using masculine nouns and pronouns, clearly intends that the message be applied to both men and women.[39]

The NLT then uses as an example the cases where New Testament letters address believers as *adelphoi* ("brothers"). The NLT translates with "brothers and sisters," which the Colorado Springs Guidelines allow. (And we also would allow it: see Chapter 18 below.)

But the example does not really match the general statement of principle that precedes it. The general statement talks about "male-oriented terms." *Adelphoi* is masculine in gender. The gender, that is, the grammatical *form*, is masculine. But what about the *meaning*? "Male-oriented" suggests a meaning component. But in the context of addressing Christian believers, *adelphoi* is not in fact very "male oriented." It more or less *means* "brothers and sisters,"[40] which is why it is permissible for the NLT to translate it that way. As in the earlier edition, the NLT has taken a permissible example, not really related to its general principle, in order to reassure us

---

[38]The revised NLT still has the same copyright date of 1996, and the copyright page seemed otherwise unchanged, so that it is difficult to tell the two editions apart without detailed comparison. In addition to the changes in the "Introduction," about 165 verses have been revised.

[39]NLT(revised), "Introduction to the New Living Translation," xliv. There are other changes, but we will not enter into them here.

[40]See Chapter 18 for a detailed discussion.

that the general principle is not dangerous. Likewise, when the introduction talks about "a modern audience" tending "to read male-oriented language as applying only to males," what springs first to a casual reader's mind is perhaps the change in English usage with respect to generic use of "a man" "any man," and "every man." Once again, this falls within the category of permissible changes (Chapter 11). And it has nothing to do with "male-oriented terms" in the original but only with a change in English. The NLT does not give us any clear sense of when and where it will feel free to delete male meaning components *in the original text.* It does not address the *disputed* cases head-on.

Thus, the translators by their faltering explanations (or sometimes, lack of explanation) indicate that they are uneasy about what they are doing. At some level, they must intuitively sense that in the disputed cases they are suppressing in English a male meaning component that was present in the original *text* (not merely the surrounding culture). It is not merely a change of form but a subtle change in meaning. They have not succeeded in spelling out for themselves, let alone for their critics, reasons that would give an adequate basis for what they are doing.

H. Objections

Many of the translators and supporters of gender-neutral policy are well-meaning people. Many of them are "complementarians," believing in God-ordained differences in roles for men and women in marriage and in the church, and they object to any analysis that lumps them with feminist doctrine, which they explicitly oppose. But then how do they answer the indications in this chapter, suggesting that in supporting gender-neutral translations they have unwittingly supported part of the agenda of the feminist movement and have compromised accuracy for the sake of fitting in with feminist-influenced cultural preferences? They give several types of reply. We consider these in the next three chapters.

CHAPTER 15

Arguments for Avoiding Generic "He" for the Sake of Acceptability

Our opponents' arguments for eliminating generic "he" in Bible translation fall into three main groups: (1) arguments for making the Bible more acceptable to modern readers, (2) arguments based on analyzing either ancient or modern languages, and (3) an argument for avoiding misunderstanding. We take up these arguments in three successive chapters.

In this chapter we consider the first group, the arguments for making the Bible more acceptable to modern readers.

A. "Bible translations should avoid controversy where possible"

A translator might say, "I avoid the loaded use of generic 'he' and generic 'she,' as well as 'he or she.' Wherever I can, I use expressions that do not draw attention to themselves."

Response: What the translator might more accurately say is he does not *intend* for the expressions in his new translation to draw attention to themselves. He intends that they be free from the political fray, so that people can hear the Word of God clearly. So he intends.

However, gender language in English is currently in a peculiar condition precisely because people are paying attention to it. They have made it into a cultural theme.[1] Usually we use our native tongue without conscious reflection, but people now *notice* generic "he" and "she" in a way that is untypical of pronouns in general. In addition, the cultural discussion has

---

[1] It is also related to the larger theme of political correctness in language. See Valerie Becker Makkai, "Correctness in Language: Political and Otherwise," 1996 Presidential Address, *The Twenty-Third LACUS Forum 1996*, ed. Alan K. Melby (Chapel Hill, NC: Linguistic Association of Canada and the United States, 1997), 5–25; and "Berger Declines to Salute," *The Religion & Society Report* 5/6 (June 1988): 2–3 (reprinted in *CBMW News* 1/4 [October 1996]: 7–8).

attributed to certain uses a politico-symbolic value. Certain uses symbolize an attitude toward feminism and egalitarianism, and therefore some people think that they can measure ideological progress using linguistic markers. Especially on many university campuses, "language police" attempt to search out and destroy pockets of ideological resistance on this basis.

The political dimension motivates people to look again and again at pronouns, rather than release their attention in other directions. Hence, no matter what you say, you may create waves and political repercussions that you did not intend. Precisely weighed translation nuances can become difficult to achieve in such a situation, because some readers load the translation with unwanted political overtones.

Boston University sociology professor Peter Berger describes the dilemma by comparison with an analogous situation in the Italian language:

> In modern Italian *tu* ["you"] is the intimate form of address, *lei* ["you"] is the formal address. *Lei* happens to be third person plural. I do not know the history of this, but it has been a pattern of modern Italian for, I would imagine, some two hundred years. No one paid any particular attention to this. Even as a child, I knew what one said in Italian. It meant nothing.

> But Mussolini made a speech in which he said that the use of *lei* is a sign of effeminacy, a degenerate way of speaking Italian. Since the purpose of the fascist revolution was to restore Roman virility to the Italian people, the good fascist did not say *lei*; the good fascist said *voi*—from the Latin *vos*, which is the second person plural. From that point on, everyone who used *lei* or *voi* was conscious of being engaged in a political act.

> Now, in terms of the empirical facts of the Italian language, what Mussolini said was nonsense. But the effect of that speech meant an awful lot, and it was intended to mean an awful lot. Because from that moment on, every time you said *lei* in Italy you were making an anti-fascist gesture, consciously or unconsciously—and people made you conscious of it if you were unconscious. And every time you said *voi* you were making the linguistic equivalent of the fascist salute.

> That is what inclusive language means. And that is why it should not be used in the Church.[2]

A similar point is expressed in a gentler way by writer Kristen West McGuire in the *New Oxford Review*:

> As a Protestant seminarian, I used inclusive language regularly because it was expected by my professors. I often found it awkward and imprecise. At the same time, I am no stranger to gender bias. I have been

---

[2]"Berger Declines to Salute," *The Religion & Society Report* 5/6 (June 1988): 3; reprinted in *CBMW News* 1/4 (October 1996): 8. (Peter Berger is a renowned sociologist of religion.)

hurt deeply over the years by disrespect for my intelligence and contributions as a woman. Yet, I question what end is furthered by the use of inclusive language. . . . Inclusive language runs the risk of imposing a particular ideology on the listener. When working in a small blue-collar Protestant church, I found many parishioners very hostile to inclusive language. They saw it as elitist—a statement of my educational "superiority." There was a certain truth in their appraisal. Clearly, inclusive language doesn't necessarily communicate the gospel effectively.[3]

This situation is especially touchy with translations of the Bible, for several reasons. First, many people know at least some Hebrew or Greek. Second, many other people possess earlier translations, and they make comparisons. Any time that someone reads one translation out loud and listeners have another in their hands or in their memory, they can notice differences, and they begin to ask questions. At this point the existing cultural situation inevitably enters. "He" means what it means in contrast to "she" and "you" and so on, but always *within* the context of a politico-symbolic load imposed from the culture. Likewise, a gender-neutral translation means what it means *in the context of contrasts with other translations, and in the context of the politico-symbolic load imposed from the culture.* Cultural forces load "he" with politico-symbolic significance. The same forces immediately load with politico-symbolic significance any translation that that does somersaults to *avoid* generic "he." A gender-neutral Bible may avoid generic "he" because it is politically loaded, but a significant portion of Bible readers will avoid such a translation precisely because it is *just* as politically loaded.[4]

The gender-neutral translator may say, "But I do not intend to be political." But given our cultural atmosphere, any move you make will be interpreted politically. A gender-neutral translation is politically loaded for the same reasons that generic "he" is.

The gender-neutral translator might claim that the political effects are less in one direction than in the other. Generic "he" is immediately visible if it occurs even once. By contrast, the practice of avoiding generic "he" is only indirectly detectable by comparing the patterns of translations over many verses.

But what are the long-range effects? If a translator retains generic "he," even readers who at first dislike it gradually adjust to recognize that no slight to women is intended (because the context shows this again and

---

[3]Kristen West McGuire, "A Case Against 'Inclusive Language," *New Oxford Review* (January–February 1997), 15–16.

[4]This reaction need not involve only Christians. Perhaps some non-Christians, on hearing the news of a gender-neutral translation, will rejoice that Christians themselves are finally admitting how outmoded the nonegalitarian thinking of the Bible is. Others, who think ancient source documents should be preserved and respected, will be dismayed to hear of such changes and will not consider a gender-neutral Bible to be a "real" Bible.

again). Moreover, because the Bible derives from another culture, it contains innumerable signs warning people that it cannot be expected to conform to every modern stylistic preference. On the other hand, if the translator avoids generic "he" throughout, the shocks to more conservative readers, as well as to many serious Bible students, increase as the number of affected verses mounts into the thousands. People may think, *Look how much the translator was willing to sacrifice on the altar of cultural respectability. The price is too high.* The result is long-range loss of trust.

Because of many years of feminist propaganda and the reactions to it, the battle is already taking place on the playing field of language. The translator cannot calmly stand in the middle of the field and expect that by doing so he will avoid all the bullets!

In fact, there is *no* translational solution that will raise us above the political fray. In his hope to avoid politics, the advocate of a gender-neutral translation is unrealistic about what a translator can achieve.

B. "Bible translations need to be sensitive to women"

An advocate of gender-neutral translations might say, "But generic 'he' is perceived as insensitive to women. We want to avoid generating this perception, which is not actually part of the Bible."[5]

Response: First, let us say most emphatically that the concern to honor and encourage women is valid and important—particularly in translating the Bible, which is a book intended for women and men alike.

The Bible contains numerous examples displaying special concern for women: the Old Testament and New Testament instructions about caring for widows, the laws protecting women in cases of rape, Jesus' attention to women disciples, the use of women as examples of faith. As men today, we too must continue to be sensitive to women in this sense. One of the ways that we can do this is to use women as well as men in our own examples and to listen to, respect, and honor women as well as men in our conversations.

But within our politically charged atmosphere, we must be especially careful when it comes to Bible translation. We do not have freedom to alter meanings in the Bible just because, in the short run, it might appear to help a noble cause.

And the problem may not be as great as it initially sounds in this objection, because people readily recognize that the Bible is an ancient

---

[5]Grant Osborne quotes *The American Heritage Book of English Usage*: "It is undeniable that large numbers of men and women are uncomfortable using constructions that have been criticized for being sexist. Since there is little to be gained by offending people in your audience, it makes sense . . . to try to accommodate at least some of these concerns" (Osborne, "Do Inclusive-Language Bibles Distort Scripture? No," *Christianity Today* 41:12 [Oct. 27, 1997], 34). Mark Strauss, *Distorting Scripture? The Challenge of Bible Translation and Gender Accuracy* (Downers Grove: InterVarsity, 1998), says, "If a large percentage of contemporary readers have the impression of being excluded by generic masculine terms, then those terms are inaccurate and should be revised in ways that convey more precisely the author's intention of inclusion."

document, containing innumerable signs of its origin in cultures different from ours (see below). Even rather unsophisticated people see this easily. They can therefore see that they must not willy-nilly impose their modern cultural expectations on an ancient document.

Then what should translators do to be sure they are sensitive to women readers as well as to men? We should do what we can to express more clearly the meaning of the original through the permissible changes mentioned in Chapter 11. "Every man" becomes "everyone," and "no man" becomes "no one," and so forth. Such changes represent improvements, because they more accurately express meaning. But then we come to a massive number of cases that use a male example as the starting point to express a general truth. Not only generic "he" but instances with "father," "son," "man/men" (designating males) form part of this pattern. The pattern is a *thought* pattern of the quantitative dominance of male examples used to express general truths. This thought pattern is really what generates the resistance, because it runs contrary to the modern concern for balanced attention and equal prominence. This thought pattern constitutes the real offense to egalitarians. And behind this pattern in English is a matching thought-and-meaning pattern in the original, which one is not free to change.

So what does a translator do? He must be faithful to the original text at all costs. A translator must not despair just because he cannot instantly produce complete understanding of biblical thought patterns in the mind of every reader. In a sense, the problem is the same as what evangelists and pastors and Christian witnesses have always experienced. Many passages and ideas and thought patterns in the Bible are difficult for people to swallow instantly. To a first-time non-Christian reader, the Old Testament food laws in Leviticus 11 look silly. The account of creation in Genesis 1 looks scientifically out-of-date. The Israelite conquest of Canaan looks immoral. Hell sounds cruel. The atonement seems unjust and crude. The promise of the Second Coming seems fantastic. The resurrection of Christ appears to be a scientific impossibility. The translator ought not to load himself down with the obligation of making all this transparently easy. Translate accurately, and let Christian witnesses and teachers explain these difficult parts to those who cannot accept the thought patterns readily.

At this juncture we should also note certain other warning signs in the wings.

First, the charge of insensitivity has affinities with a larger political agenda. On many university campuses, advocates of "political correctness" appoint themselves as language police, laying down rules for what language to use in order to be "sensitive" to various minority groups. Of course, there is some initial appeal to this procedure, since it does echo a biblical theme, namely that we are to love our neighbor as ourselves. But as usual in a secular culture, biblical ideas are distorted and replaced by politicized counterfeits—in this case, a valid goal of being thoughtful toward others in how we speak has been replaced by a nonbiblical, egalitarian goal of denying all differences and distinctions between groups of people. The whole issue is highly charged with political ideology and needs critical inspection.[6]

Second, we must recognize frankly that in our culture people can use the language of "sensitivity" for manipulation. A woman may say, "As a woman, I feel undervalued and left out by language that is constantly thrusting maleness in front of me. If you were sensitive, you would avoid usage that has these connotations for me." Such expressions of concern ought, of course, to be taken most seriously. We should do what we can to help and reassure such people, out of common courtesy as well as Christian love.

But, in some people who use them, we find a deeper side, whereby the language of "victimization" can be used to achieve political ends. Some groups have learned to push people into action by putting them in a position where refusal to agree with something would allegedly show heartlessness or "insensitivity." This kind of manipulation has become so common that many may use it sincerely, that is, without consciously realizing that they are manipulating through distortion of the actual situation. They have absorbed the distortions unconsciously—they have become convinced they are victims of mistreatment by a whole group (such as men).[7] But letting such people (and there may be very few of them in this particular controversy) continue to play the victim in order to manipulate others shows love neither for the people who are caught nor for the truth that they are evading.

Third, there are in fact a variety of different views and different "sensitivities" on these issues. We must reckon with them all, not just one kind. To some women, the *prohibition* of generic "he" seems insulting. National Public Radio commentator and syndicated columnist Frederica Mathewes-Green, commenting on the 1997 NIVI controversy and the articles in *World* magazine, wrote,

> Speaking as one of the party whose tender feelings are under consideration, I don't *want* the Bible rewritten so it won't offend women. . . . If someone thinks I'm incapable of reading "Blessed is the man" and figuring out it applies to me too, I'm insulted.[8]

---

[6]See Makkai, "Correctness."

[7]Some people, of course, *really are* victims in suffering injustice at the hands of others. But a sense of being victimized by men *in general* or by governmental authorities *in general* is a distortion.

[8]Frederica Mathewes-Green, "Go Ahead, Offend Me," in *First Things* 83 (May, 1998), 12–13.

To people like Mathewes-Green, the prohibition seems obliquely to hint that women are so obtuse they cannot understand generic "he." Or it suggests that women are so fragile they need to have constant stroking, and such "strokes" are to be generated by making sure that female-oriented terms occur with the same frequency or greater frequency than male ones.

In fact, the situation is even worse. In the end, it seems to us insulting to women to imagine that lessening accuracy in Bible translation could be a fitting expression of a desire to honor them or to be "sensitive" to them. Shall we erect as a permanent monument, supposedly "for women's sake," a Bible translation policy that systematically changes nuances of meaning? Such a thing is a monument of dishonor, not honor. If we are sensitive to women, would we not recoil in horror from the prospect of such a travesty of honor?

There is yet a more grievous insensitivity. Changing meanings in the biblical text in order to avoid generic "he" is insensitive to those who love the Bible and expect every possible nuance to be translated. It may even be "insensitive" to God and his demands for faithfulness to his Word. Once again, we come back to a major point—that a translator does not have the freedom to change meanings in the same way as a modern author can change the text that he or she creates.

C. "Bible translations should avoid the negative connotations that attach to certain words"

Another argument says, "Bible translations should avoid the negative connotations that attach to certain words such as the generic use of 'he.'"[9]

In this argument, the supporter of gender-neutral translations may try to salvage something from the previous argument by shifting to a more technical-linguistic viewpoint. He says, "Accurate translation includes connotations as well as denotations. Generic 'he' may *denote* everyone, but it includes the negative *connotations* of sexism. Hence, we reject it according to widely understood translation principles."

Response: There is indeed a valid translation principle that affirms that we should attend to connotations. Connotations, like many other dimensions of communicative texture, belong to the total texture of meaning. Our argument for translating all the aspects of meaning includes translating connotations.

---

[9]D. A. Carson says sometimes translators may be faced with "awkward choice: Preserve the singular form and project bigotry, or go with a plural form and lose the individual reference" (*The Inclusive Language Debate: A Plea for Realism* [Grand Rapids: Baker, and Leicester: InterVarsity, 1998], p. 106; italics added). Mark Strauss says, "However, when a large percentage of the translator's target population gives a particular connotative value to a word, the translator must take notice and adjust the translation accordingly" (*Distorting?* 102).

But what are the "bad connotations" in the case of generic "he"? The bad connotations are the connotations of sexism. Sexism might involve discrimination against women or prejudice against them—both serious moral failures. But in the modern context, "sexism" might also include any acknowledgment of differences between men and women, or any unequal prominence given to male and female meaning components in one's speech. Radical feminists might call someone "sexist" if he or she does not agree with the whole of their doctrine. Just what are we talking about?

In fact, the "bad connotation" of generic "he" is difficult to pin down. Some people have vague feelings of uneasiness about it. What the objection most probably has in view is one of several factors, or a combination of them: (1) generic "he" involves a pattern of thought starting with a male example to express a general truth; and (2) generic "he" may well indicate that the speaker has an unenlightened ideological point of view; and (3) the speaker is not recognizing or affirming women by putting them in equal prominence with male examples.[10]

Factor (1) is about a pattern of thought. The pattern of using a male starting example is there in generic "he," but it is usually also there in the original languages as well. This is not really "bad connotation," in the normal sense of the word "connotation," but a meaning aspect that some readers may not like.

Factor (2) is again about ideology, and about sensitivity, because the person with another ideological point of view is under suspicion of being insensitive to the concerns of women.

Factor (3) is about the pattern of unequal prominence, which we already discussed under sensitivity.

It seems, then, that the "bad connotations" are really the connotations of insensitivity, or else ideology, which we have already discussed. In substance, this argument is only a variation on the two preceding ones. But superficially it appears more sophisticated because it appeals to "translation principles."

But we still need to explore the idea of "connotation" a little more thoroughly.

First, remember that some writers today get around the problem through the oscillating use of generic "he" and generic "she." In the context of this oscillating use, generic "he" has no bad connotations. Hence, the bad "connotations" are not innately bound up with the use of generic "he," but spring from a quantitative pattern of using generic "he" and other male-oriented terms with greater frequency than corresponding female-oriented terms.

---

[10]People may also *feel* as if women are subtly "excluded" in some vague way, even when they know that generic "he" includes women by implication. On the question of whether people actually misunderstand generic "he," see Chapter 17.

Second, for the sake of argument, let us suppose hypothetically that the "bad connotations" are in some way innately bound up with generic "he," so that even one occurrence of "he" provokes the opposition.[11] We still have to recognize that "connotations" are of many kinds. It depends on what we mean by "connotations."

Consider John 19:26:

RSV: Woman, behold your son!

NIV: Dear woman, here is your son.

Jesus is addressing his mother Mary from the cross. To English ears the translation "woman" sounds distant, perhaps disrespectful. The NIV removes this impression by saying "dear woman."

The underlying Greek word is *gunē*, a word meaning "woman" or "wife." This word is clearly not completely identical to the English words "woman" or "wife." Even where it means roughly the same as "woman," its connotations may be different from the connotations of "woman" in English. Several times in the New Testament *gunē* is used in addressing women: Matthew 15:28; Luke 13:12; 22:57; John 2:4; 4:21; 8:10; 19:26; 20:13, 15. In most of these instances the context gives no hint of distance or disrespect, but rather the contrary. The standard Greek lexicon confirms the impression: "*gunai* is by no means a disrespectful form of address."[12]

Yes, the connotations are different. To overcome this difference, the NIV translates "dear woman." We do not object to this kind of change in principle—here it can be seen as a helpful attempt to avoid negative connotations in English that would not be there in Greek.

But now consider another kind of case, the use of "atone" and "atonement" in a Bible translation. Christians rejoice that Christ atoned for our sins and set us free from the guilt and punishment of sin. But not everyone is so pleased. Many non-Christians despise the idea of atonement, especially the idea that Christ was our substitute, taking the penalty of sin on our behalf (1 Pet. 2:24). For these non-Christians, "atonement" has a bad "connotation." They associate it in their minds with distasteful feelings. To some of them it connotes injustice, cruelty, or crudity. For some, it is also an insult to their sense of being basically good people. So should we avoid these connotations by looking for another translation, perhaps "reconciliation"?

---

[11]We recognize that someone may hear one instance of generic "he" from the Bible and take offense, loading the verse with all kinds of bad connotations. But if the translator then rewords the verse to remove the supposed prejudice, and then the person who objected finds out about the change, he may accuse the translator of lacking integrity.

These problems are virtually insuperable. The translator cannot take upon himself the obligation single-handedly to eliminate the long-standing prejudices and anti-Christian antipathy of a whole culture. Again, he must leave space for evangelists and the gentle witness of ordinary Christians.

[12]BAGD, 168.

Of course not. We must preserve the meaning of the original. In this case the problem is not with the word "atonement," but with those who dislike its meaning.

Thus, in one case, with "woman," avoidance of bad "connotations" is legitimate, but in another, "atonement," it is not. What is the difference?

Several test questions show clearly that the negative reactions to generic "he" are not the same as the negative reactions to "woman" used in John 19:26.

1. Some questions to help decide when to seek to avoid a connotation in English

First, *does every native speaker react to the word in the same way?*[13] With the word "woman," yes. With generic "he," no. Many people do not find anything wrong with generic "he," while others do. The divide down the middle of the English-speaking public is an obvious symptom of the fact that we are not dealing with a simple issue of idiomatic English.

Second, *does the connotative reaction change rather than remain stable over decades? And does the reaction change in step with the dominant worldview of the society?* With the word "woman," there appears to be little reason why things would change. On the other hand, generic "he" acquires negative connotations as feminist claims and arguments work more and more widely to persuade people that asymmetrical prominence given to male examples is "unfair."

Third, *can we perceive a possible influence from theological views or tendencies of thought that are contrary to the Bible's standards?* In the case of "woman," it is difficult to see any influence. But in the case of generic "he," as we have seen, people are influenced by feminism and by the larger egalitarian principle that requires equal emphasis for various groups of people.

We can also ask whether some ideological or moral issue controls how people *learn* the connotations. People learn about the connotations of "woman" by seeing that other terms of address are used in English today when speaking on intimate terms. It is not a matter of discussion and debate.

Now, how do people learn the negative connotations of generic "he"? Certainly they will not absorb negative connotations just by not hearing it very often. When we look at how children learn, we observe that they generalize patterns, which leads naturally to understanding generic "he" and "she" (see Chapter 16). When and where are negative connotations laid on top of apparently colorless usage? The negative connotations have to be *taught*—students have to be told explicitly that generic "he" is

---

[13]We are aware of the phenomena of dialects. But the reaction against generic "he" matches ideological rather than regional or ethnic dialect distinctions.

"unacceptable" or "insensitive" or "unfair," even though their intuitions have not so notified them beforehand.

And how will they be taught these things? The student on whom the teacher (or university professor) imposes these standards asks, "Why is it unfair?" The obvious answer is that men and women are equal, and that any practice in language or society that gives asymmetrical attention to the two shows sex discrimination. So might run a typical answer from a high school teacher or a college professor. In short, we are dealing again with an aspect of egalitarian and feminist ideology, pure and simple. The taboo against generic "he" is artificial,[14] and it is maintained only by constant feminist pressure. Children growing up would naturally revert to an innocent understanding of generic "he" unless cultural leaders unwearyingly reinforce the taboo. *The* basic reason why people attach negative "connotations" to generic "he" is that egalitarian ideology says that it is unfair, and that means that the negative connotations are an overflow of ideological influence. The connotations would largely go away if the ideological reinforcement disappeared.[15]

In addition, as we have seen, in actuality no taboo exists against generic "he," provided that it occurs at the same frequency as generic "she." The inhibition concerns not generic "he," but any style that does not give equal prominence to the sexes. The ideological character of this stylistic preference lies right on the surface.

Fourth, *does an explanation concerning different connotations in different languages defuse the problem?* With "woman" in John 19:26, we could explain in a footnote that the equivalent of "woman" as a form of address in Greek is not disrespectful. The average English reader would be satisfied with such

---

[14]*God's Word* (GW) comments in its "Preface":

However, if a passage focuses upon an individual, GOD'S WORD does not use plural nouns and pronouns to avoid the gender-specific pronouns *he, him,* and *his.* In these cases the translators consider the text's focus upon an individual more important than an artificial use of plural pronouns ("Preface," xiii).

Since *God's Word* is a gender-neutral translation in its overall policy, and since it took great care to employ "full-time English editorial reviewers" (p. xi), its use of the word "artificial" here is especially telling.

[15]However, Carson, *Debate*, 186–187, says, ". . . the underlying pressures for change have been there for centuries. We should therefore be exceedingly careful about monocausational analyses of the changes taking place."

While we agree with Carson that some people from time to time have tried various alternatives to generic "he" for centuries (something well documented in any study of gender in English language), these pressures pale in significance compared to the enormous pressures originating with the feminist movement in this century, and the earlier experiments by a few individuals did not have the same ideological underpinnings connected with the same kind of enforcement of a "taboo" against generic "he" that we have seen in this century.

We must also distinguish a *preference* for alternatives from an out-and-out *prohibition* of generic "he." And we must distinguish the bare-bones fact that some avoid using generic "he" from the connotations that are generated when generic "he" is nevertheless used. The connotation, not the fact of avoidance, is what we are focusing on here.

an explanation. Now what about generic "he"? Do we defuse the problem by saying, "Using a male example to express a general truth was not seen as a slight to women in the original context"?

It might give pause to the critic. But the modern oscillating use shows that people already understand this principle when they apply it to an occurrence of generic "he" in the context of generic "she." That is, they already understand that generic "he," with its evocation of a male example, involves no slight to women. It is doubtless reassuring for some people to be reminded of the same principle with respect to ancient culture. Some people would be satisfied.

But others probably would not be.[16] The critic thinks again and asks, "I readily admit that a single case of generic 'he' is OK, if it is not part of a larger pattern. But what about the overall pattern? Is it prejudicial?" When the critic discovers the real truth about the Bible, he may say, "To put males constantly in prominence indicates the failure in moral awareness within the thought pattern of the biblical writers."[17] The modern critic has already decided that the practice of male prominence is in principle to be rejected. It is not *merely* a debate about a nicety of English style. The same conclusion follows from the observations that we have already made, to the effect that the debate over generic "he" is not merely about generic "he," but about many cases in the Bible where male representatives are used.

In sum, an explanation might help some readers greatly, others not so much, others hardly at all. The variations in effect are not really surprising, given what we have already observed about the tasks of evangelists and Christian witnesses. Modern readers confront many thought patterns in the Bible that are not easy for them to accept. Some people accept a simple explanation, and adjust to the thought pattern in the Bible. Others require a more extended explanation. Still others fail to accept even after an extended explanation.

We would now invite readers to use the same test questions with respect to the words "atone" and "atonement." The answers show, as they do in

---

[16]We are not as confident as Carson, who says, "Similarly if a modern woman went back in time to that culture with a profound grasp of the language and literature of that culture, she would be unlikely to take umbrage" (*Debate*, 157–58). It all depends on *which* woman. Many a non-Christian modern woman might completely despise the whole scene and become even more alienated from the Bible than before.

At this point, at least, Carson depicts the problem as basically linguistic, a difference between two language structures that could be overcome in principle by learning the second language. Of course language learning might help in some cases. But the deeper problems lie in cultural assumptions that are correlated with patterns of thought.

[17]Recall the statement about the need to "mute the patriarchalism of the culture of the biblical writers" in the "Preface" to the NIVI, and the statement in NIVI internal guidelines that "the patriarchalism (like other social patterns) of the ancient cultures in which the Biblical books were composed is pervasively reflected in forms of expression that appear, in the modern context, to deny the common human dignity of all hearers and readers" (Carson, *Debate*, 41, guideline I.D. Carson gives in full the "CBT Policy on Gender-Inclusive Language," quoting from a copy sent to him from the CBT).

the case of generic "he," that ideology is at the root of the bad "connotations" that some people would find in those words.

Of course, the rejection of generic "he" and the rejection of "atonement" are far from being on the same level. Atonement is a central doctrine of the Bible. Generic "he" is not.[18] But precisely for this reason, the temptations may be more subtle. Christians easily see the obvious ideological bias against atonement, precisely because it is obvious. But the ideological influence behind attitudes toward generic "he" is not obvious. It is easy for us to be influenced by a subtle atmosphere from the world, even without being aware of it.

In conclusion, we believe that there is plentiful evidence, from several angles, showing that the supposed "negative connotations" are ideologically produced and maintained. If we say these connotations are "just there" in the language used by our culture, and then yield to the cultural pressures not to use certain expressions, we overlook the fundamental egalitarian assumption that is needed to support these connotations. We dare not assume that cultural trends, even trends in patterns of speech, are always morally and spiritually neutral. Sometimes we must recognize that a trend runs counter to the patterns of thought and meaning found in the Bible itself. In this case, for example, we must reject the argument that the claim of "negative connotations" provides adequate grounds for rephrasing every generic "he."

2. Translators should not eliminate the evidence

One final point needs emphasizing. At any point where theological differences are at stake or where heated arguments are being generated over the implications of biblical texts, translators must avoid prematurely deciding the issue. Let readers battle out the issue for themselves on the basis of the fullest information and fullest meaning that the translator can give them. One of the more severe problems with gender-neutral translations is at this very point. The translators overstepped their bounds. They took sides on a very debatable issue, namely whether the use of males as representative or as more prominent has any theological implications from which we can learn. And—what is even more remarkable—they did so in an environment where feminism had already drawn attention to this question and made it into a cultural theme.

D. "Bible translations need to be updated for modern culture"

Another argument says, "Bible translations need to be updated for modern culture."

---

[18]On the other hand, the fact that Adam and Christ are representatives for all those under them is central.

In this argument the proponent of gender-neutral Bible translation appeals to the idea of ideological progress. He might say, "The biblical writers were people of their own time, living in patriarchal culture. They inevitably took on some of the assumptions of their time. They spoke using male representatives because everyone did it. But our times are different—today attention has been drawn to the use of gender language as a moral issue. Given the attention now drawn to gender language, the biblical writers themselves would have spoken differently had they addressed our time. We are simply updating their mode of expression to indicate the way they would have said it had they been here today."[19]

Response: Of course, no one knows what the biblical writers "would have spoken" if they lived now. It is a highly speculative question, impossible to answer with certainty. It is not the kind of speculation on which one can base any sound policy for Bible *translation*.

But there are also other serious difficulties with this proposal. *First, it opens the door to tremendous abuse.* Theological liberals might claim, "Our gospel of human self-improvement is what the biblical writers 'would have spoken' if they were enlightened as we are to appreciate the innate goodness of human beings and their potential to save themselves by using positive thoughts about God."

Second, this proposal simply assumes, without argument, that *we already know what the right moral views are* with respect to the use of male examples in writing. This procedure has a disconcerting similarity to the methodology of theological liberals, who first decide what religion and morality are viable for our times, and then come to the Bible and decide how to update it. But this process destroys biblical authority.

Rather than simply assuming what "must" be morally right with regard to gender language, we first have to hear the Bible for what it is and let it transform our spiritual and moral values. Gender-neutral Bibles are in danger of short-circuiting this process by withholding from modern readers some of the information that they need in order for the Word of God to criticize modern culture.

Third, as even the preface to the NRSV recognizes, *translation ought to be done "without altering passages that reflect the historical situation of ancient patriarchal culture."*[20] Jesus was born in Bethlehem in first-century Palestine, not in twentieth-century Chicago. We must insist on the uniqueness of the Incarnation and of God's work in history once and for all. It is thus theologically important for every Christian to learn about

---

[19]Strauss says, "After translating a passage, a translator should stop and ask, 'Is this how the biblical writer would have said this if he were writing in contemporary English?'" (*Distorting*, 85). Osborne says, "the biblical writers themselves would most likely [use inclusive language] . . . on the principle of becoming 'all things to all people,' since many in our culture could be confused or offended by masculine language" ("Distorting? No," 38).

[20]NRSV, "Preface," x.

other cultures, especially the cultures of the Bible, and not merely to equate them with his or her own.

As a consequence, translators must not try to update ancient cultural institutions, as if these could be replaced with our own. Nor are they to update ancient patriarchy, as if it were identical with our own preferences. If the problem is only that "we would not do it that way," let Bible readers observe that the Bible was written centuries ago in another culture! Even very naive readers can see this fact, because the Bible contains innumerable signs of it.

For example, Paul addresses the "churches in Galatia" (Gal. 1:2), not us directly. Every reader can see that the Letter to the Galatians is relevant to us. But the relevance is best judged only when the modern reader genuinely perceives the differences: the threat in Galatia came from Judaizers advocating circumcision, not from modern forms of legalistic teaching. A translator would only obscure the text by concealing the differences between the Judaizers and modern false teachers, and so forth.

Fourth, *ordinary readers can distinguish between the particularities of history and the general principles that history illustrates.* We all know that David and Goliath were particular people who fought a particular battle. We can nevertheless learn general spiritual and moral lessons from the battle. Likewise, we know that the Judaizers were particular people who troubled first-century Galatian churches. We can learn general lessons from Paul's response to them. We recognize that the biblical writers lived in particular patriarchal societies. We can learn general lessons from how they addressed their societies in the name of God. In none of these cases is it the job of *translators* to obscure the historical particularities. In fact, the opposite is true. Preachers, teachers, and ordinary readers need the translator to preserve the original context so that they may accurately understand it. Then they may more accurately infer the general principles and their application to today's circumstances.

I. An analogy: "updating" the Bible's descriptions of earth?

Consider an example. Psalm 93:1 says, "The world is firmly established; it cannot be moved." Some people have inferred that the Bible teaches that the earth is the center of the solar system and that modern astronomical views are wrong. Others have cited verses like this one in order to claim that the Bible has errors and is outmoded. Is a translator then tempted to alter the meaning? Does a translator undertake to "update" the psalm by speaking of the earth going around the sun? He might argue, "If the psalmist had lived in our day, he would have praised God for the wisdom and power that God displays in the results of modern astronomy." Yes, perhaps he would have. But the expression "would have," as we have seen, is uncontrollably speculative. It is the job of preachers and modern readers to think about implications for today.

Even supposing that the psalmist, by special miraculous revelation, knew all the theories of modern astronomers, he does not speak of them explicitly in the psalm. If he does not speak of them, neither should the translator. As usual, we distinguish what is stated from what may be inferred.

Hence, it is not the job of a translator to save ancient writers from "embarrassment." In fact, the translator who tries to do so will miss part of the actual meaning of the original text. The psalmist in Psalm 93:1 is not speaking of modern astronomy, but neither is he advocating some alternative technical scientific theory. The language is ordinary. It is "phenomenal" language, describing the world as it actually appears to ordinary human observers. As such, it is completely true: the ground underfoot is not constantly shifting around; it is quite firmly in one place, or we would not be able to walk on it! By implication, the psalmist is saying, "You walk around on the ground without thinking about it. You rely on the fact that it will be there, that it will not shake underneath you. Things are this way because that is the way that God specified it to be. You must thank God for all these little stabilities in your life. And these little stabilities point to God who is the greatest 'stability' of all, the one that you can rely on never to be moved away from who he is." The psalmist is saying something true and important, but we might easily miss it if we were embarrassed by the ancient culture in which it is set.

The application to the issue of patriarchy is obvious. If patriarchy is suggested by the language of Scripture, we should translate the language accurately and let the effects of patriarchy be visible in English. We should not be embarrassed by it, or we will miss things that we could otherwise understand more deeply.

In the case of patriarchy, the stakes are higher than they are in the case of modern astronomy, because we cannot be certain beforehand what answers are right. In a case like the astronomical theory of the solar system, we may be reasonably certain that modern science has genuinely uncovered truths about how God governs the world. It has advanced over the knowledge of the ancient world.[21]

But now, have we "advanced" by going from patriarchal society to modern postindustrial society? We have advanced in technology and in sophistication. Have we advanced morally and spiritually? How do we know? If we have swallowed the modern ideology of progress, which says that man is always getting better and better, we just assume that we are superior. But World War I, World War II, the Gulag Archipelago, and the widespread moral rottenness of the late twentieth century and the early twenty-first century should give us pause. It is exceedingly difficult to separate good from bad, especially when we are immersed in the society that

---

[21]Of course, even with all the advances in this field, we may still have lost something in our appreciation of how we depend on God for the firmness of the ground underfoot!

we are trying to criticize, and so share its blind spots. All the more reason why we desperately need the Bible to instruct us (Ps. 119:105!). And of course we then need a Bible in its full integrity, not a Bible subtly tailored to cater to modern prejudices.

In sum, the Bible enables us to discriminate between good and bad in cultures, *both* the good and bad in ancient patriarchal cultures *and* the good and bad in modern cultures. But it can do so most accurately if we see accurately the ancient cultures that it was directly addressing, and hear accurately what it had to say to them. "Updating" undermines this accuracy. In the end it thus undermines rather than advances the very thing that translators hope it will accomplish, namely to help us see the implications for our modern cultures.

E. "The audience today is no longer mainly men"

Another argument runs, "The Bible when written was primarily addressed to men, but today Bible translations should be addressed to men and women alike. Perhaps the Bible uses generic masculines because in its original context the people addressed were mostly men."[22]

Response: First, this objection is really a variation on the idea of "updating." In the process of translation, we ought not to conceal information about the original people to whom the Bible was addressed—if the Bible were mainly addressed to men, then we should translate it accurately in order to indicate this.

Second, there are plenty of obvious counterexamples to this claim. The New Testament letters were intended to be read out loud in the churches (see Col. 4:16; Rev. 1:3), and these churches included both men and women in the assembly. How can anyone say that these letters were addressed "mainly to men"? Paul even speaks directly to certain women, such as Euodia and Syntyche (Phil. 4:2), and several verses in the epistles speak directly to "wives" (Eph. 5:22; Col. 3:18; 1 Pet. 3:1).

Surely we cannot say that the Bible used generic masculines because God intended the Bible to be mainly heard and read by men! From the very beginning of the time when God gave people a written collection of his words (in the Ten Commandments), God spoke to *both* men and women, and yet he spoke from the top of Mount Sinai using masculine second-singular markings in the Hebrew text of these commandments (see Exod. 20:13–17). Jesus similarly used generic masculines even when talking with

---

[22]Osborne writes, "Jesus addresses crowds. In the ancient setting, most of them were males, and the original text uses *he* and *him* throughout (NIV on [Luke] 14:27: 'Anyone who does not carry his cross . . . cannot be my disciple'). But in the modern setting, men and women are assumed to be numbered among those called to be disciples, so we prefer *you* (NLT: 'And you cannot be my disciple if you do not carry your own cross') or *they* (NIVI: 'And those who do not carry their cross . . . cannot be my disciple')" ("Distort? No," 35–36).

the Samaritan woman (John 4:14) and with Martha (John 11:25–26). This argument is simply contrary to fact.

F.   "Gender-neutral Bibles are needed for evangelism"

This argument says, "Gender-neutral Bibles are needed for evangelism on university campuses. If the Bible we use contains generic 'he,' we will lose our audience before the gospel is even heard and considered, because this form of expression is so foreign to university contexts today."[23]

Response: We agree that evangelism is important. By all means, let us write good evangelistic literature and use our creativity to develop ways of reaching out. In addition, many of us have occasions when we want to give a Bible or a Bible portion to a non-Christian. In such situations we want to have available a translation that is easy to read.[24]

But danger arises if we let the demands of evangelism take control of *translation*.[25] In its original setting almost every book of the Bible was addressed first of all to the people of God, not to outsiders. If we translate *primarily* with outsiders in mind, we already run the danger of distorting our perception of the purposes of the Bible.

In addition, this argument hints at a desire to translate the Bible in a way that would smooth over the difficulties for unbelievers. This sort of goal is dangerous because it opens the way to compromise elements of the Bible that are unpalatable to unbelievers.

The problems increase when we ask why university campuses are mentioned rather than prisons or drug recovery centers or shelters for the homeless. There are many needy people in the world, many people who need to hear the gospel. Why does this argument mention only university campuses? On university campuses are those with intellectual gifts, with advanced education, with sophisticated skills for interpretation, and with exposure to literature from other times and cultures. Compared to other

---

[23]Osborne writes, "Gender-specific translations would be counterproductive on secular college campuses" ("Distort? No," 39). Carson writes, "I do not want the old NIV when I am expounding the earlier chapters of, say, Romans in an evangelistic setting in a university. Nothing is gained by it, and too much is lost. I'd much rather use the NIVI" (*Debate*, 191). Actually, Romans is not a very good example to illustrate the real point of debate. Romans in the NIV contains only a few verses with generic "he" and other types of language that belong to the "impermissible" category of Chapters 6–7. On the other hand, it contains quite a few verses that can be improved by making the permissible changes of Chapter 5. Because the NIVI has made improvements in these permissible cases, it may on the average be a better translation of Romans than the NIV, for the purposes that Carson has in mind.

[24]See our earlier discussion in Chapter 4 on the trade-offs between readability and maximal accuracy.

[25]At this point we differ in emphasis with the last paragraph of Osborne's article, in which he writes, "Finally, I want to emphasize the evangelistic purpose of Bible translation. Both the NIV and NLT are trying to get into the Wal-Mart and Barnes and Noble markets. Unbelievers are offended by the generic *he*" ("Distort? No," 39). See also our discussion below of niche translations.

parts of the culture, university students have wide vocabularies and advanced facility in understanding language. They are the ones who should need the least help in reading and understanding documents from an ancient culture. Surely these people will have the least problem interpreting anything difficult or challenging in the Bible.

But no. We are being told that they cannot handle generic "he." They cannot understand that women are included in the verse "If anyone hears my voice and opens the door, I will come in and eat with him, and he with me" (Rev. 3:20)! Do people really intend to claim that university students are so incompetent in interpreting elementary sentences?

And if university students cannot understand generic "he" in an ancient document like the Bible, how then will they understand Thomas Paine, or Abraham Lincoln, or anything written in the history of the world before language police began to dominate our universities in the 1970s? Earlier writings are replete with generic "he" and "man" used to name the human race. How in fact will they understand a current issue of *USA Today*, or *Newsweek*, or a dispatch from the wires of the Associated Press, which may contain generic "he" (see Chapter 16 for examples)?

Why should university campuses, of all places, need a gender-neutral Bible translation? We all know the answer. Most universities today are hotbeds of feminism and egalitarian ideology. It is not the mere use of generic "he" that is suspect; it is the idea of giving male examples more prominence in the text of Scripture. "He" is a symbol of the larger ideological conflict between egalitarianism and the Bible. We cannot really "adapt" the Bible to the university without changing the very content of the Word of God.

Moreover, the argument for change assumes that generic "he" is foreign to universities. Is it? Or does it occur when accompanied by generic "she"? The real problem seems to be, not foreignness in a single utterance, but foreignness of the Bible's thought pattern. Its thought pattern is not hypersensitive to egalitarian ideological red flags. The Bible's pattern of thinking, not the wording of a single verse, generates the problem.

In any case, we really won't get very far in removing the offense of the Bible on university campuses by merely removing generic "he." In the same passage already quoted earlier, columnist Frederica Mathewes-Green continues,

> Besides, updating gender references won't go very far toward a goal of making the Bible palatable. Someone who balks at "a man" is really going to be thrown for a loop when she hits "Take up your cross."[26]

I. The ideological clash

The basic problem therefore is ideological clash. The "negative connotations" and the university campuses about which gender-neutral Bible

---

[26]Frederica Mathewes-Green, "Go Ahead, Offend Me," 12–13.

supporters worry are symptomatic of a deep cultural sickness that has boiled over into elitist standards of linguistic usage. Any culture is sick if it stumbles over a story of a wise man building his house on the rock, or stumbles when in Proverbs the father warns his son about the immoral woman. Such a culture is resistive, as *The American Heritage Dictionary* puts it, to "a particular pattern of thought."[27] It resists using a male representative to express a general truth. Many things, deep things, are needed for its healing. At the center is the gospel of Christ himself. But if there is sickness in the culture, we do not help the sickness by diluting the Bible a little in order that the culture can be more at home with it.

The elite of our culture have grown allergic to saying or hearing anything that might use a male term to express a larger general truth, or using language that invokes the picture of a male figure to stand for a generality—unless it is reassuringly accompanied by a balancing "she" and a female example.[28] "Whoever eats my flesh and drinks my blood has eternal life, and I will raise him up at the last day" (John 6:54, NIV). What could be plainer than "whoever"? But some people are afraid to let the passage stand this way, because "him" is supposedly "sexist."

But the language of the Bible demonstrates again and again the ethical principle that it is all right to use a male figure or a male-marked term as representative of a truth applying to both men and women. In fact, in view of the representative character of Adam as head of the whole human race, of men as heads of their families (Eph. 5:22–33), and of Christ as head of his people, it is singularly appropriate. We need not be embarrassed.

G. "There is a need for niche translations"

At this point the gender-neutral Bible defender could respond by proposing "niche" translations, that is, translations aimed at particular groups or "constituencies." Jerry says, "Let us have one translation for people who want gender-neutral language in their Bible, and another for those who

---

[27]*American Heritage Dictionary*, 831.

[28]Both Carson and Strauss overlook this opposition to biblical *content* that can be found in people's attitudes toward language patterns. They tend to assume that, though ideology may generate trends, the resulting preferences are morally and spiritually neutral (though Carson qualifies slightly in *Debate*, 187–189). Therefore Carson says, in apparent criticism of our position, that "it betrays a serious ignorance of language structures . . . when a shift in the system of a receptor language is tagged with evil epithets" (*Debate*, 187). Strauss insists that the NIVI was not "driven by the agenda of radical feminism" and that "there were no insidious motives behind the translation" (*Distorting*, 29). Carson and Strauss both mention the fact that many or most of the members of the NIV's CBT are complementarians, and they imply that this fact shows there is no feminist agenda.

But they fail to consider the explanation that we offer here, namely, that many people who are complementarian with regard to male-female relationships in the *family* and the *church* might still unconsciously absorb from the surrounding culture a judgment concerning *human language usage* that, on inspection, turns out to be in conflict with the Bible's own use of human language, and turns out to be rooted in feminist assumptions that are not made explicit in the arguments over proper language today.

don't." The idea behind this argument is that we may need different trans-lations to reach different groups of people. Doesn't Paul himself say, "I have become all things to all people so that by all means I might save some" (1 Cor. 9:22)? And if the older, gender-specific translations cause some people to stumble over their use of gender language, shouldn't we remember Paul's statement, "We put no stumbling block in anyone's path, so that our ministry will not be discredited" (2 Cor. 6:3, NIV)?[29]

Response: We agree with the concern not to give unnecessary offense, and we agree (as we noted in Chapter 11) that some gender language can be changed without compromising part of the meaning of Scripture. We are not objecting to those things in this book.

But the gender-neutral translations we criticize in this book change many other things, things such as generic "he" and the use of "father" when the original is talking about a father. Where these "offensive" things accurately express the Bible's meaning, they cannot be evaded. We have no right to change these things.

In addition, a *translator* cannot in every respect imitate Paul's travels through the Greco-Roman world when he became "all things to all people" (1 Cor. 9:22). He cannot adjust his manner of behavior for the benefit of some part of his readership. He cannot say one thing to university students and another to middle-aged suburban Christians and yet another to inner-city elementary schoolchildren. Once he puts out a translation, everyone can pick up the translation and read it. The present state of the English-speaking cultures produces a situation where a translator is inevitably going to offend someone. The translator must not write to please (an impossible task), but write to be faithful.

We do admit that there is room for a translation in very basic English, with very simple vocabulary, to aid young children and second language learners.[30] But beyond this there are significant liabilities to adopting a policy of niche marketing on a large scale.

1. Some problems with niche translations (constituency translations)

First, the production of different translations for different groups tends subtly to break apart the unity of Christian believers. Will Christians have to be separated into different congregations, or even different denominations, on the basis of what Bible is used in the pew? Will we have egalitarian congregations and complementarian congregations?

---

[29]Carson hints at a possible need for niche translations on page 192; Osborne approves of both gender-specific and gender-neutral translations for different purposes (p. 38).

[30]Such a simplified version should, however, be clearly labeled, "The Bible Rendered in Basic English," or "The Bible in Simplified Language," or the like. The Preface should carefully and honestly explain its purposes and limitations, to avoid giving readers a false impression. Note what we say below concerning marketing.

To some extent we have them already, but translations catering to the demands of different groups increase the problem.

Second, this policy makes it increasingly difficult to have one standard Bible to memorize.

Third, we have no easy way of addressing a group that contains people from many viewpoints.

Fourth, translating for the express purpose of targeting people with an ideological viewpoint reinforces people's tendency to regard religion as a consumer commodity. I pick off the supermarket shelf the cereal that I like. I pick off the bookstore shelf the political book whose ideological orientation I like. I pick off the shelf the Bible translation whose ideological orientation I like. The unintended message is, "We have a Bible available that will suit any ideological position." The Bible becomes a wax nose that we may bend to fit to any face.

Fifth, because of the pressure to make money and to maximize one's market, Bible publishers tend to maximize their claims that their Bible version can serve everyone. A Bible consistently using gender-neutral techniques could market itself in two ways:

> This rendering of the Bible is intended for the use of those who are uncomfortable with the use of male-oriented terms to illustrate general truths. It has sacrificed nuances of meaning for the sake of removing these offending bits, so we cannot recommend it for the general reader. But if you have trouble in this area, this book may be for you.[31]

Or, alternatively,

> This Bible is for everyone. It has been translated on the basis of the most informed scholarship, and with careful attention to contemporary English style. It is suitable for private reading, devotional reading, public reading and preaching, and careful study.

Toward which description will marketing pressures push the publishers?

2. Content versus palatability

But let us return to the main issue of adapting to one's audience. The niche marketer points to 1 Corinthians 9:22, "I have become all things to all people so that by all possible means I might save some." We would point to 1 Corinthians 1:18–2:5, where Paul refuses to conform to the expectations of his audience, even refusing to use "eloquence or superior wisdom" which the Corinthians would have esteemed, or the "wise and persuasive words" which would have been popular with such audiences (1 Cor. 2:1, 4, NIV).

---

[31] ☺

While Paul was willing to modify some of his patterns of behavior regarding human customs, he was uncompromising in his refusal to change one bit of the message of Scripture: "We have renounced secret and shameful ways; we do not use deception, nor do we distort the word of God. On the contrary, by setting forth the truth plainly we commend ourselves to every man's conscience in the sight of God" (2 Cor. 4:2, NIV).[32]

What is the difference between these passages that resist cultural conformity and the earlier passages that embrace it? Paul avoids *unnecessary* offense, but he will not shade the *truth* of the gospel or change the *content* of his message. Nor will he cater to pretentious rhetorical standards in order to avoid the gospel's intrinsically offensive elements, its weakness, and its grating against human pride.

Today, as the Bible confronts secular culture, one of its intrinsically offensive elements is the idea that any one man, Jesus Christ in particular, could be set in authority over people and deny them their egalitarian "equality." It is offensive that any message should come claiming authority but refusing to conform to modern secular standards for how people—especially educated, cultured people—should speak and think. It is even offensive that such a message should come out of backward, "patriarchal" cultures.

So we are dealing here with a conflict between modern culture and the Bible. The culture says you may not use predominantly male representatives. The Bible by many examples in its pages shows that you may. Since the Bible's speech is ethically pure, we infer that the culture is wrong. And we should not be surprised that the culture resists biblical claims at this point.

But we may not "mute" the claims of Scripture in order to appease the culture. The difference between us and supporters of gender-neutral translations, even "niche" translations, is that where they see neutral adjustment to current style, we see a subtle (and, yes, often unintentional) capitulation to one aspect of the broad cultural rebellion against the Lord and his Anointed (Ps. 2:2).

Let us be bold. Let us be bold to believe that the Word of God works salvation in the midst of our resistance to it as well as our happy acceptance of it. It works salvation through our resistance by provoking, jostling, undermining, and finally overthrowing resistance. It can do so all the better if we leave in the translations of the Bible plenty of the signs that are there in the original, signs that it is after all ethically legitimate for a male figure to represent or stand for a whole group.

---

[32]As we will show later (Chapter 16), there is a noteworthy difference between Paul's sermons or uses of the Old Testament, on the one hand, and the task of the translator on the other. But general principles about offense are indirectly relevant to all communication.

Why not believe that God will use these differences between the Bible's way of talking and that of our modern cultural elite in order subtly to rebuke and reform us, to give us life and healing and peace? Precisely at these points the Bible can enrich us if we stand firm rather than simply caving in to what the world says is now the new standard for "offense" and "sensitivity."[33]

H. The slippery slope

On the other hand, if we follow the advocates of gender-neutral translations, how far will we go with the principle of conforming to cultural sensitivities for the sake of avoiding offense? Proponents of gender-neutral translations say, "We won't change the basic meaning." But suppose that we can capture some *nuance* of meaning only at the cost of provoking a bad feeling in some modern readers. Then the translator considers dropping the *nuance* for the sake of "greater accuracy," claiming, "Otherwise they may misunderstand—they may incorrectly read in a discriminatory nuance."

But now let us follow this way of reasoning a little further. What about calling God "Father"? The gender-neutral translator says, "Of course we translate using 'Father,' because that is necessary for accuracy."

But then a voice comes disturbingly back:

> Some people will be offended, you know. Some people will misunderstand. In our society, some people have had sinful, oppressive fathers, or no fathers at all. Some people will feel that women are excluded or slighted. Some will feel that you are claiming that God is just a male human being writ large, the ultimate chauvinist. They will think that we are saying that God belongs literally to the male sex. Or even if they do not, the feeling and connotation of it will remain beneath the surface. It is a subtle turn-off. Our culture does not associate with the word "father" the same exact things that ancient culture associated with the words *patēr* and *'ab* in Greek and Hebrew. Language and culture have changed, and we must change too. Admittedly, we lose some nuances. But we gain enormously: we gain clarity and head off all these odious misunderstandings and distortions. We may submit to a tiny loss of nuance for the sake of avoiding the big distortion, the one that will keep people from coming to God or listening to the Bible at all.
>
> Surely the *main point* in the Bible's language about God as Father is that God loves us, protects us, cares for us, gives us wise guidance. Surely we do not want to claim that God is literally of the male sex. Wouldn't we make the point even clearer, and so be more accurate, if

---

[33]See the end of Chapter 17 for a further illustration with a hypothetical niche translation targeted specifically to feminists.

we translated with "parent"? "Our Parent, who is in heaven, let your name be precious. . . ."

Similar reasoning applies to the use of a masculine pronoun to refer to God or to Christ. Granted, Christ is a male human being. But why continually draw attention to his maleness in a culture that finds this fact difficult?

If we allow these concessions, others will enter from the wings, seducing us into an indefinite series of modifications of the Bible for the sake of not "unnecessarily offending" modern readers. We cannot call God a warrior, because our culture sees war as ugly, vicious, uncivilized. We cannot call God king. "King" is male and connotes oppression under arbitrary orders. God cannot be wrathful because it connotes that he has lost control of himself and harbors destructive emotions. God cannot threaten us with hell because that connotes cruelty.

Thus, the gender issue will not be the only place where trends in the culture bring pressure to bear on the language and pressure to bear on Bible translation. In fact, the CEV has already removed another supposed source of modern "offense": it changes "the Jews" to "the people" or "the crowd" in passages where they oppose Jesus, as Matthew 28:15; John 10:19, 31; 18:31; 19:7, 12.[34] And one prominent reviewer of the NRSV complained that the NRSV had not gone far enough, because it "makes not the slightest gesture toward minimizing masculine pronouns for God." He calls this "the single deficiency of the NRSV which is of such magnitude as will render it in its present form unusable for many believers."[35]

Such pressure to change the text of Scripture will be relentless. It will be applied to every Bible translation, and it will not be satisfied merely with the kinds of changes in the NRSV. If evangelical translators and publishers give in to the principle of sacrificing accuracy because certain expressions are thought to be offensive to the dominant culture, this altering of the text of Scripture will never end. *And then readers will never know at any verse whether what they have is the Bible or the translator's own ideas.*

---

[34]Apparently the planned "gender-accurate" translation being prepared now by the NIV's Committee on Bible Translation will also change references to "the Jews" to "the Pharisees," at least according to International Bible Society communications director Steve Johnson in an interview with the online news service *Religion Today* (religiontoday.com article for Thursday, June 24, 1999). The article said, "Verses about Jews plotting to kill Jesus will refer back to the Pharisees, not the entire Jewish population."

For a discussion of the problem, see Terry L. Schram, *The Use of IOUDAIOS in the Fourth Gospel: an Application of Some Linguistic Insights to a New Testament Problem* (Utrecht: Schram, 1973).

[35]Burton H. Throckmorton Jr., "The NRSV and the REB: A New Testament Critique," *Theology Today* 47/3 (1990): 286.

CHAPTER 16

Other Objections against Generic "He"

Several objections have been raised against generic "he" based on ideas about the meaning of the original languages and about the state of English. We pursue these objections one at a time.

A. Objections related to the meaning of the original text

1. "The basic meaning is still preserved"

The first objection says, "The basic meaning is still the same when we rephrase to 'they' or 'you' in order to avoid generic 'he.'"[1]

Response: There is an initial plausibility to this objection. As we have seen from the examples in Chapter 13, translators can find ways to eliminate generic "he" while preserving a good deal of what a passage says. However, subtle changes almost always occur, and in some cases the changes are not so subtle. The word "basic" in this objection already indicates a problem, and demonstrates exactly what we claim, namely, that some aspects of meaning, though perhaps not a minimal "basic" core, do change.

Why then do people advocate this position? One reason may be the realization that translation in general does not succeed in capturing absolutely everything. This general observation then becomes a basis for excusing the

---

[1]This often seems to be the underlying assumption in Strauss, *Distorting Scripture? The Challenge of Bible Translation and Gender Accuracy* (Downers Grove: InterVarsity, 1998), 112–27. (Perhaps Strauss is aware of the changes in nuance, but he does not discuss them.) D. A. Carson, *The Inclusive Language Debate: A Plea for Realism* (Grand Rapids: Baker, and Leicester: InterVarsity, 1998), 107, 117–20, admits that there are problems, but (with some qualifying "if's") thinks that the English language is changing and that we have no choice; we must simply sacrifice the extra meaning. See footnote 37 in Chapter 13. On the qualifying "if's," see Appendix 6.

fact that gender-neutral translations have settled for less accuracy than what they could have had.

Another reason may be a failure to distinguish between a translation and an interpretive commentary or a failure to note that the degree of explicitness or directness is also an aspect of meaning.

In some cases people who make this objection may not be sensitive to nuances, and may even deny that there is any change at all. But in that case, the objector simply shows that he does not have the skills necessary to do a careful evaluation of translations or to appreciate important aspects of the debate.

In each case, however, our response must be: why do you want to translate only the basic meaning when English allows you to translate more of the meaning than that? And why is it only the male-oriented aspects of meaning that you are willing to lose?

2. "Critics are confusing form and meaning"

Another objection says, "You are confusing form and meaning. Gender-neutral translations preserve the meaning of the original, even though they use different forms in English. You are insisting on preserving form, and this is not a good translation principle—in fact, it produces sentences that make no sense in English."[2]

Response: First, the objection simply misrepresents our position. What we have said in the previous chapters, and the examples we have given, show that at every point we are concerned to preserve *meaning* in translation. We have not argued that the *form* of the original always has to be preserved

---

[2]This objection is made frequently by Carson, *Debate* (see, for example, his emphasis on semantic equivalents rather than formal equivalents on pp. 17, 20, 97–98), and by Strauss, *Distorting;* see pp. 29, 82–87, 195. Strauss gives a number of examples where certain Hebrew or Greek nouns with plural form need to be translated by singular nouns in English, or where grammatical gender is not carried over into biological gender in English (pp. 86–87), but such examples were obvious to the drafters of the CSG and are not relevant to the discussion of *singular and plural personal nouns and pronouns* in translation, and specifically the translation of third-person masculine singular pronouns.

Strauss quotes a fragment of Guideline A.2 without context and thus misinterprets it as a foolish and impossible general statement. He says, "Guideline A.2 mandates that 'person and number should be retained in translation.' Yet in many cases this is impossible" (pp. 85–86). What he does not tell the reader is that Guideline A.2 immediately follows Guideline A.1, which is specifically about generic "he," and that it appears under the section heading, "*gender-related renderings* of Biblical language which we affirm." Guideline A.2 in context is not articulating an impossible general rule about person and number but is still focused on generic "he." It criticizes the attempts by gender-neutral translations to avoid generic "he" by substituting "you," "we," and "they."

Strauss also omitted to quote the part of the guideline that makes it clear that gender-neutral shift away from generic "he" is in view: "Person and number should be retained in translation so that *singulars* are not changed to plurals and *third person statements* are not changed to second or first person statements, with only rare exceptions required in unusual cases." The Guideline A.2 specifically singles out "singulars" and "third person," thus zeroing in on generic "he."

(such as Greek or Hebrew word order, for example, or the grammatical gender of Hebrew and Greek words), but we have argued that as much of the *meaning* as possible should be brought over in the translation.

Second, as we indicated in a previous chapter, the objection fails to recognize that form and meaning are often interlocked in a more subtle way than the simple slogan "preserve meaning, ignore form" can indicate.[3] For example, the plural *form* "they" results in more focus on the plurality of members of a group, while the singular *form* "he" results in more focus on the individual member of the group. The difference in focus is a difference in *meaning*. In this case, in changing the form one also changes the meaning. Similarly, in changing from "he" to "you," subtle meaning differences intrude. The objection has ignored these aspects of meaning, just as the expression "basic meaning" ignores the fact that there are other aspects of meaning that contribute to the total textual complex. In other words, while this objection appears to be more sophisticated than the previous one (about preserving "basic meaning"), it is actually only a variation on the same theme.

In addition, as we have seen, generic "he" carries with it some of the connotations of its masculine form. In the sphere of meaning, it suggests the picture of a male example, and that picture is related to the masculine form of "he."

Likewise generic "she" in English conveys some meaning through the feminine form "she": the ordinary use of "she" in English "bleeds over" into the interpretation of generic "she." Generic "she" suggests a female example embodying a general truth. Even apart from the modern ideological overlay that feminism imparts, the forms "he" and "she" both carry meaning with them. Even when used generically, they carry connotations of maleness and femaleness, respectively. In these cases, form is not "mere" form but carries meaning connotations.

3. "We are just ignoring what is not 'intended' in the original language"

Another objection says, "In the original languages the use of pronouns is just a part of grammar. Ancient writers really had no choice. They did not

---

[3]See the discussion of the rich complexity of the Bible, and the interrelationships between form and meaning, in Chapter 10, pp. 168–69 and 174–75.

In terms of the categories developed at the end of Chapter 10, the dispute about meaning involves different levels of refinement. Carson and Strauss, in talking to naïve readers (level 1), can validly make the point that changing a generic statement from singular to plural or from third person ("he") to second person ("you") changes "form" but preserves "meaning." They are talking about the same point that theoretically informed linguistic theory makes about the distinction between form and meaning. But all this discussion focuses only on "basic" meaning, an elementary core, in order to make a pedagogical point. At a later point in learning, when we refine our analysis, we discern the different nuances generated from such changes (level 3), and now at level 4 we explicitly analyze them.

intend to put in a male orientation when they used masculine pronouns. In fact, they did not even perceive a male meaning component in these pronouns. For example, the original 'Introduction to the New Living Translation' says, 'There are other occasions where the original language is male-oriented, but not intentionally so.'[4] These cases we may safely ignore in translation."

Response: Despite the difference in phraseology, this is still another variation on the "basic meaning" objection. The pronouns, we are told, are *"just a part of grammar,"* and the masculine grammatical gender for a pronoun did not convey any idea of a male person to the ancient speakers and hearers.

In this way of stating the objection, the word "just" is minimizing. The pronouns have no male component of meaning, but they are "just" form, "just" grammar.

But we have seen above that these pronouns do carry meaning overtones. It is not "just" an issue of form. Nor are the occurrences of different pronouns in the original languages "just" form, for "he" in English and third-person masculine singular generics in Greek and Hebrew carry an orientation toward thinking in terms of male examples. This orientation constitutes a meaning component, not "just" form. (We discuss this matter at more length in an appendix.)[5]

To say that the ancient writers had no "choice" is also problematic because good writers are often aware of the complexities of meaning that attach to the words they use. For example, in Hebrew the same word *ruach* can have several different senses: "breath," "wind," "spirit." Hypothetically, one could argue that the prophet Ezekiel, as an individual writer, had "no choice" about how the word *ruach* functions in Hebrew—the word was "just there" for him to use. However, Ezekiel uses the existing resources of Hebrew when, in Ezekiel 37, he plays on all three meanings and makes them interact (Ezek. 37:5, 9, 14). He creates meaning using resources of the Hebrew language that he did not "choose"—the language just "was" that way, but *he knew that* and *he used it with an intuitive knowledge of the complexity of meanings* for *ruach*.

Likewise, whenever writers evoke connotations already attached to words or to customs, they use connotations that they did not "choose" to put into the words and customs, but they still do use them. For example, in 1 Corinthians 9:24, Paul uses the example of a race. Paul did not "choose" to set up the Greek practice of having foot races—it was already there in the culture. His reference to the custom is nevertheless meaningful.

In a broader sense these passages are all the more meaningful because of the fact that God in his sovereign control of history *did* choose that just

---

[4]NLT, Preface, xliv. The revised edition of the NLT (see Chapter 14) deletes this statement.
[5]See Appendix 9: "The Relation of Generic 'He' to Third-Person Generic Singulars in Hebrew and Greek," 421–32.

these resources would be available to biblical writers. What is not a "choice"[6] from the standpoint of a human author (because there may be no other options in the language he is using), it is still a choice from the standpoint of the divine author who controls language, culture, and history and uses it as he wills.

The word "intention" is just as slippery as the word "choose." "Intention" can be used in a narrow or a broad way. It could be used in a narrow way to talk only about what an author plans in the most explicit and self-conscious way—that is, the basic or core meaning of a passage. In this narrow sense, "intention" is just another word for the objection that tells us to translate "basic meaning."

However, we can scarcely justify saying that an author only *intended* the basic or core meaning of what he wrote. This is because good authors often incorporate complex and multilayered meanings in a single passage, not just one core idea. Moreover, good authors do many things instinctively, without *consciously* planning them, so talking about how consciously an author "intended" some meaning gets us into inconclusive speculation about an author's state of mind. *How do we know what an author "intended" except by looking at what he actually wrote?* If what he wrote evokes certain connotations and associations, then those things are to be translated along with everything else.

We agree, of course, that biblical writers *explicitly* teach on some subjects and not on others. For example, the Bible does not contain a passage that is explicitly devoted to teaching about the moral standards that apply to using grammatical gender. Neither does it contain a passage that explicitly teaches about how to fill out a modern personal income tax form, or the ethics of abortion, or genetic engineering.

But that does not mean that the Bible says nothing about these topics. Everything that the Bible says, and even the manner in which it says it, involves subtle moral implications, because the Bible is, among other things, a definitive example of morally pure speech. The translator's job is not *merely* to make sure that the most explicit teaching subjects are conveyed in English. His job is to carry over all the nuances that he possibly can. If the nuances are there in the original, they belong in the translation, whether or not they are "intended" in some artificially narrow sense.

4. Differing views of translation

Another objection says, "This is just a dispute over different views of translation" (what in Chapter 10 we called translation with preservation of form or translation with change in form).[7]

---

[6]That is, a choice among alternatives.

[7]"Whether or not to use inclusive language in Bible translation is not a gender issue but a matter of translation theory. . . . The true question is whether formal equivalence or functional

Response: This objection misjudges the real issue.[8] The real issue is whether, within a particular translation policy, the translators preserve as many nuances of meaning as they can. This issue arises *both* with translations that tend to preserve form and with translations that tend to change form, as well as those in between. We may recall the chart from Chapter 10, showing a range of approaches to translation.[9]

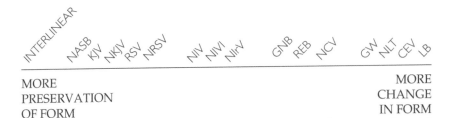

MORE
PRESERVATION
OF FORM
(more literal)

MORE
CHANGE
IN FORM
(more paraphrastic)

Both ends of the spectrum confront the same issues in dealing with gender. What happens in particular cases? The NRSV, the RSV, and the NKJV all tend toward more preservation of form. We criticize the NRSV because it drops male meanings, while we approve the RSV and the NKJV.[10] The REB, the NLT, and the LB all tend toward more change in form. We criticize the NLT because it drops male meanings, while we approve the REB and the LB on this issue.[11] In the middle we find the NIV, the NIVI, and the NIrV. We criticize the NIVI and the NIrV's 1995 edition, while we approve the NIV and the NIrV's 1998 edition. The difference between the two editions of the NIrV (1995 and 1998) shows exactly what the problem is. Using the same general approach, somewhere between the extremes of preservation of form and change in form, the two editions differ *only* in the way that

---

equivalence, as Bible translation theories, produces the best translation for our day. . . . The use of inclusive pronouns in translations falls within the realm of dynamic translation theory" (Grant R. Osborne, "Do Inclusive-Language Bibles Distort Scripture? No," *Christianity Today* 41:12 [Oct. 27, 1997], 33).

[8]It may be just another form of objection 2, which refuses to admit that meaning changes are involved, not just alterations of form.

[9]This chart is an approximate summary of complex sets of translation policies. People may differ with the exact placement of one or another translation with respect to the one to the right or left of it, but in general they are at the appropriate place on the spectrum.

[10]But, as we noted in Chapter 12, the RSV and the NKJV could be improved through changes that would *not* compromise meaning nuances but would reflect more current use of English.

[11]We would still see some problems with the REB and the LB, but both use generic "he" when they need it, and both for the most part preserve male meaning components from the original.

they choose to convey or fail to convey male meaning nuances and to use generic "he." The two editions have exactly the same general translation philosophy but differ on policies concerning gender language.

So the dispute is not a matter of differences in translation theory. To say that this is the issue is to divert attention from the real question, the question of maximal translation of meaning *within the parameters allowed by each kind of translation practice.* We object to preservation-of-form translations that systematically remove male components of meaning, and we object to change-in-form translations that systematically remove male components of meaning. Conversely, we do not object to the translation of gender language in translations that do not have policies that remove such male components of meaning.

B. Objections that minimize the problem

1. "The problem is with isolated mistakes, not with the policy"

Another objection says, "We admit that existing gender-neutral translations have made some mistakes and misjudgments in dealing with individual verses, and we are glad you have found these so we could correct them. But these blemishes do not invalidate the principle that gender-neutral translations are trying to follow. The policy is good, though its implementation is flawed in some cases."[12]

Response: The mistakes and misjudgments are precisely our concern— if there were none of these, we would not be writing this book. But we must also raise questions about the underlying principle or policy, because the policy has brought about the mistakes.

What policy is intended by this objection? If it is only a policy that makes the permissible changes that we mention in Chapter 11, and perhaps a few gray areas that we mention later, then we have no quarrel with it. But much more is involved in all the gender-neutral translations that we criticize in this book. For example, if we look at the policies that the translators express in the prefaces, the prefaces to the NRSV and the NIVI contain problematic formulations.[13] Other prefaces are so vague that they do not

---

[12]This is the approach of Carson when he sees mistakes in the NIVI and simply encourages the translators to be more cautious in applying their principles in the future. He says, "It appears that the critics have scored some points in particular passages . . . , and the CBT should take the most telling of these criticisms seriously and be even more careful in the future than they have been" (p. 162; compare p. 154). Strauss is more explicit: "Critics have tended to find a few examples of poor translation in a particular version and then draw sweeping conclusions about the inaccuracy of inclusive language" (*Distorting*, p. 28). He says, "It is a very common fallacy among those who oppose inclusive language to find a few inaccuracies in one version and then jump to the conclusion that the methodology itself is flawed. This is not valid" (Ibid., 127).

[13]See discussion above, in Chapter 14.

help. Nearly everyone talks about conveying meaning accurately, but the results belie the hope.

Those who favor gender-neutral translations may say, "Translators should conscientiously strive to represent every aspect of meaning,"[14] but the actual practices of gender-neutral translations are *systematically* in tension with this goal.[15]

Because generic "he" is the biggest issue, let us consider what gender-neutral translations attempt to do in this area. They say, in effect, "We will not use generic 'he,' but we will preserve all the meanings in the original." In one sense this policy would be acceptable if it could actually be achieved (for who could object to a translation that preserved "all the meanings of the original"?). But it is completely unrealistic. You cannot achieve political correctness and maximal accuracy at the same time.

There are several reasons. First, the Bible itself, in its explicit teaching, contradicts the egalitarian ideology that drives "political correctness," and we would therefore expect there to be some explicit conflicts (as with the requirement that elders be the "husband of one wife," which was omitted from the NRSV). Second, the Bible generates tension with egalitarianism through subtleties of nuances in its very manner of formulation (as with the

---

[14]We agree with this point when affirmed both by Carson, *Debate*, 68, 70, and by Strauss, who quotes with approval the statement of Herbert M. Wolf, "The goal of a good translation is to provide an accurate, readable rendition of the original that will capture as much of the meaning as possible" (*Distorting*, 77).

[15]We say "systematically" because the underlying theme (in the verses to which we object) is always an attempt to remove from English translations some male-oriented components of meaning that are there in the original text.

Indeed, one paragraph in the CBT's internal guidelines articulates such a tendency:

Where the original cultural context shows a distinctively male activity (bowman, workman, oarsman), characteristic, or relationship, male references may be retained, but if suitable alternatives are available (such as archer, worker, rower), these are usually to be preferred. (Guideline II.5, as reproduced in Carson, *Debate*, 42.)

Unfortunately, the guideline does not specify whether the male component belongs specifically to the Hebrew text (typically in the form of a masculine gender, but sometimes a distinct word, which native speakers would have in these cases understood as reinforcing the fact that these people were male). Or is maleness only inferred from the cultural context without being specified in the text? In the latter case it does not have to be represented *linguistically* in the target language. In the former, it should be so represented, if feasible. (We are translating textual meaning, not general cultural facts.) The lack of distinction between these two situations opens the door to replacing in wholesale fashion "father" (singular) with "parent" or "parents," and "son" with "child," as we have illustrated in Chapter 13. (Is not a father-son "relationship" one of the possible instances of a "male . . . relationship" that the guideline permits to be neutered?)

It is interesting that when D. A. Carson comes to this CBT principle, he says, "The reasoning behind principle II(5) escapes me" (p. 104). It escapes him because he does not consider that the switch to gender-neutral translations is not merely a question of conformity to modern English style; it is an attempt to eliminate as many of the male-oriented components of meaning as possible within the constraints of the kind of translation being produced. Changing "oarsman" to "rower" fits perfectly within that agenda. It should cause no surprise or bewilderment.

male overtones that attach to Hebrew *'adam* as a name for the human race, or with generic "he" that often pictures a male sample case). Third, the taboo against generic "he" restricts our ability to represent in the fullest and most nuanced way the meaning-complex that we want to put into English.

It is sheer delusion to think that you can tie one hand behind your back and still carry on an exhibition in gymnastics with maximal efficacy. Likewise, it is delusive to think that you can follow an artificial taboo against using part of the resources of English and still attain maximal representation of meaning. The prohibition of generic "he" is the equivalent in the field of translation of the command to make bricks without straw (cf. Exod. 5:6–9). We marvel in admiration at the translators' long-suffering toil in trying to make linguistic "bricks" in this way; but we also protest against their enslavement to feminist taskmasters who refuse to let them use some of the resources of the English language.

The preface to the NRSV is more candid than most in admitting that there is a "conflict."[16] One simply cannot achieve the incompatible goals that gender-neutral translations set for themselves, translating maximal meaning and also restricting oneself to gender-neutral language.

2. "But many verses are still OK"

The next objection says, "But you are harping on the worst problems. Look at all the things that these translations got right. For one thing, most of them have preserved the distinction between commands to husbands and those to wives in Ephesians 5:22–33, and the distinctions regarding men and women in the church in 1 Timothy 2:11–15. Moreover, in some of the verses you cite as bad examples from gender-neutral versions, *other* gender-neutral versions have avoided those problems. You are exaggerating the problems."[17]

Response: We are grateful for what the versions got right. We are grateful that the distortions are not even more numerous. And when we examine a bad example, we do not mean that all the gender-neutral translations did just as badly in translating the same verse.

But three issues arouse our concern.

First, the accumulation of so many mistakes—more than three thousand changes need to be made just to eliminate generic "he," to say nothing of other changes—shows that the fundamental policy of gender-neutrality needs to be challenged. The fundamental commitment to eliminating some male components of meaning even when they are there in the original language is a commitment incompatible with trustworthy translation of the Bible.

---

[16]NRSV, x.
[17]See, for example, Strauss, 26, 45.

Second, none of the translations has found a way to escape using generic "he" without damaging meaning. They are trying to make bricks without straw.

Third, the ordinary reader, with no training in Hebrew and Greek, and without the time to compare several English translations line by line, has no way of knowing where the mistakes occur. How can ordinary readers know where they can trust the details and where they can only trust the (apparent) "main point" of a verse? Mistranslation of details undermines trust.

Many gender-neutral translations proclaim that they make the Bible more accessible to ordinary people by making it clear and putting it in up-to-date style. But the version that they offer eliminates aspects of meaning that people need in order to have the most accurate understanding. In the worst case, like NRSV and CEV's elimination of maleness from 1 Timothy 3:2, the "experts" decide for you beforehand what the doctrinal answer is for today, leaving you no opportunity to decide for yourself. The "experts" tell you, not what Paul said, but what they think is good for you to know, so that you will not have to struggle with the knotty issues of theology yourself. This move makes things "easy" for you if you do not want to think. But it leaves you at the mercy of experts, who alone have competence in the original languages. This is a paternalistic tyranny of the experts. Feminism claimed that it would save us from paternalism, but ironically in this respect it has caused it to reappear even more hideously.

An objector may respond, "If people have a problem, let them use another translation." To which we reply, "And how will they decide on a translation if people like you are saying that all the translations are A-OK?" This is precisely why we are writing this book.

C. Objections based on comparisons with other Bible translations and other languages

1. "New Testament writers and authors change person and number when using the Old Testament"

Another objection says, "The New Testament writers and the Septuagint sometimes make shifts of person or number in dealing with the Old Testament. Therefore translators can legitimately change person and number, in order to avoid generic 'he.'"[18]

Response: The Septuagint is the ancient Greek version of the Old Testament, sometimes quoted by the New Testament authors. This objection has in mind cases like 2 Corinthians 6:18, where Paul builds on

---

[18]See Carson, *Debate*, 19–20, 115, 175–81; Strauss, *Distorting*, 125–26, 192; and Osborne, "Distorting? No," 34, 37.

2 Samuel 7:14, and perhaps also on Isaiah 43:6, but uses a plural "sons and daughters" where 2 Samuel 7:14 has "son."

But this objection fails to take into account what the NT writers were doing. In quoting the OT, they are like preachers making an application. They are not translators producing a base translation on which everyone will rely. A preacher is not *claiming* to give the most accurate translation for general purposes but rather an interpretive rendering that brings out some of the implications of the original. The NT offers interpretive renderings rather than a uniform model that endorses a particular brand of translation.

This distinction between a New Testament use and a translation has been recognized for a long time. In the nineteenth century, opponents of biblical inerrancy were using an argument similar to this objection, saying that we do not need to insist on the truthfulness of every word of Scripture, because even the NT authors adapt and quote quite freely when using the OT. But defenders of inerrancy such as A. A. Hodge and B. B. Warfield replied in 1881 as follows:

> Nor is quotation to be confounded with translation. It does not, like it, profess to give as exact a representation of the original, in *all* its aspects and on *every* side, as possible; but only to give a true account of its teaching in *one* of its bearings. There is thus always an element of application in quotation; and it is, therefore, proper in quotation to so alter the form of the original as to bring out clearly its bearing on the one subject in hand, thus throwing the stress on the element in it for which it is cited. This would be improper in a translation. The laws which ought to govern quotation seem, indeed, to have been very inadequately investigated by those who plead the New Testament methods of quotation against inspiration[19] (emphasis in the original).

In fact, 2 Corinthians 6:18 is a good illustration of the kind of thing that the New Testament can do. Paul uses language similar to 2 Samuel 7:14. But 2 Samuel 7:14 in its original context is God's promise to David that he will be a Father to David's son. The immediate fulfillment is in Solomon, and then climactically in Christ the son of David. Through Christ, God becomes Father to us also. Hence, similar language applies to us. Paul therefore applies the language to us and writes not "son" but "sons and daughters."

Paul's purpose is not to give a translation of 2 Samuel 7:14, since the Septuagint already exists. Rather, he is stating a truth for his hearers using language appropriated from 2 Samuel 7:14. But he may not be thinking of 2 Samuel 7:14 alone. He may be combining its ideas with the teaching of Isaiah 43:6, which pictures the restoration from Babylon and final salvation

---

[19]A. A. Hodge and B. B. Warfield, "Inspiration," *The Presbyterian Review* 2/6 (April 1881), 256. (We wish to thank Tim Bayly for calling our attention to this quotation.)

as including an action in which God brings back "my sons . . . and my daughters." Paul is engaging in a complex reflection in which he weaves together Old Testament ideas and their fulfillment in Christ.

If the principle espoused in this objection were followed, it would make translation impossible. Look, for example, at what Paul does in 2 Corinthians 6:16–18. Second Corinthians 6:16 probably quotes from Leviticus 26:12, but combines it with the third-person language in Jeremiah 32:28 and the idea of God's dwelling in Ezekiel 37:27. Second Corinthians 6:17 probably quotes from Isaiah 52:11, but the last part of verse 17 adds a piece from Ezekiel 20:34 or 41. It also adds "says the Lord," which is common in the Old Testament but does not occur in Isaiah 52:11. Now, if the principle stated in this objection were followed, a translator could imitate Paul—a translator could combine several verses from different parts of the Bible into a single whole, and could freely rearrange verses into new combinations, and add whole phrases here and there. This conclusion is absurd, and the starting assumption reduces to absurdity.[20]

What about the Septuagint in its translation of the Hebrew and Aramaic Old Testament? It is not flawless as a translation. At times is it quite accurate, but at other times it was apparently using a different original text from what is available to us today, and at still other times the translators simply misunderstood the Hebrew or Aramaic they were translating. The Septuagint served its purpose reasonably well, as do most English translations with their flaws. But its varying practices should not become the standard for our modern translations.

Though the New Testament use of the Old Testament is not a model for *translation*, it does provide some food for thought when it comes to *evangelism* and preaching. As A. A. Hodge and B. B. Warfield point out, it is legitimate for New Testament writers to "so alter the form of the original as to bring out clearly its bearing on the one subject in hand, thus throwing the stress on the element in it for which it is cited."[21] Likewise, it is legitimate for an evangelist or a Christian who is witnessing to give a less-than-exact quotation in order to throw stress on an element that is pertinent. An evangelist might say, "The Bible says, . . ." after which he might summarize the teaching of the Bible, without quoting any one verse. Or he might say, "It says in Romans that people are justified by faith, not by works." He is not giving an exact quotation. In written material we even have a convention, where we use quotes only in case of a verbatim quotation. A nonverbatim

---

[20]It is disconcerting to see defenders of gender-neutral Bibles use this argument, for it is so evidently incorrect. For a generation New Testament scholars have subjected to intense scrutiny the New Testament uses of the Old Testament. The issues are complex and continue to generate debate. How then can these proponents present an argument that depends on ignoring the many differences between New Testament use and guidelines for an English Bible version?

[21]Hodge and Warfield, "Inspiration," 256.

quotation, without quotes, can express the gist without preserving the wording and without necessarily preserving all the nuances of meaning present in a translation.

These observations also help us in addressing the concerns from Chapter 15 about evangelism. Let us do evangelism. And let us understand that we can re-express the truth of the Bible in a great variety of ways. We may legitimately avoid bringing up gender issues if we want to pursue more major issues. But this is *evangelism*, not *translation*.

2. "Gender systems differ among languages, so no one can make them match perfectly in translation"

Another objection says, "Gender systems differ among languages. Therefore, you should not insist on mapping a masculine form in Hebrew onto a masculine form in English."[22]

Response: We agree that gender systems differ among different languages.[23] We could go on for a long time boring readers by describing detailed ways in which Hebrew and Greek uses of grammatical gender differ from one another as well as from English. But such general observations about differences are not relevant for the point under consideration. We are debating a fairly narrow question, how to deal with translation problems involving generic third-singular masculines. In these cases the nearest *meaning* equivalent in English would often involve generic "he." In Hebrew and Greek, as well as in English, a generic masculine pronoun evokes the picture of a singular male example used to express a general truth.

The underlying thought behind this objection may be something like this: "If we look at the languages of the world, we find many different gender systems. All of them can deal with general statements, but they do so in different ways. Generic statements and general principles may not be marked for gender at all. Or they may even be marked feminine. Since the Bible can be translated into these languages, we can assume that gender markings of generic statements are irrelevant to meaning."

But we must pull the argument relentlessly back to the real issue. We are not debating how best to translate the Bible into Polish or Zande, but into

---

[22]This is a frequent claim of D. A. Carson: See pages 96–98, 114, 117, 156, 158. In criticizing Grudem, he says, "Dr. Grudem's argument is simply an appeal for formal equivalence. . . . One cannot responsibly translate all Greek-specified genders into English as corresponding English genders, because the gender systems of the two languages are different" (p. 98).

[23]Carson discusses extensive differences in gender systems among different languages on pp. 77–99. His survey is interesting, but it entirely misses the point, because we do not claim, nor did the CSG claim, that *grammatical gender* has to be preserved in translation. He has constructed an extensive argument against a position we do not hold.

Strauss also implies that we are seeking to preserve "grammatical gender" or "form," and says, ". . . to mandate a particular form without consideration of the meaning is inherently flawed." He goes on to characterize our position as "the literalist argument of mandating form" (p. 87).

English. Nor are we debating how much of some basic meaning we could translate into Polish.[24] The underlying assumption in this objection is that *only what can easily be conveyed into all languages is worth conveying in English.* When we draw this assumption out into the open, it refutes itself. It is another form of the idea that we can be satisfied with a minimal "basic meaning," rather than seeking to translate all the aspects of meaning that we can.

Of course, we agree that some languages in the world may not have all the capabilities for expression that English does, and in those cases translators will have to do the best they can with those languages. In fact, yet other languages may have more capabilities than English in some types of expression, and then translators can bring over even more aspects of meaning in those expressions than they can in English (some languages still have singular and plural forms of the second person pronoun, for example, where English just has one form, "you"). But all of those considerations are simply changing the subject, which is how to translate the Bible into English today. On that question, we continue to insist that translators are responsible for bringing as much of the meaning as they can *into English*—regardless of whether all of that meaning can be brought into other languages or not.

The objector may then shift the argument to person and number, saying, "You cannot just automatically transfer person and number from Greek to English. For example, Greek has two distinct second-person forms, one for a singular "you" and the other for plural "you" ("you all"). Neither of these forms in Greek functions in exactly the same way as does the English word "you."[25]

Once again, the premise is technically correct (number systems between Greek and English are not identical), but it is not the point we are considering. Even to talk about how "all" third-person statements should be translated is changing the subject. The question at hand is about *a third person-singular masculine pronoun used in a generic statement,* and the point is that the use of a generic third-person masculine singular in Greek or Hebrew evokes the picture of a male "out there" as the starting point for a general statement. So does generic "he" in English. And generic "you," "we," and "they" differ from "he" in their starting point. Generic "he" is then the appropriate meaning equivalent. Most of these objections change the subject in order to escape the specific point under consideration.

---

[24]This is the kind of argument Carson uses when he says, "Dr. Grudem's argument is simply an appeal for formal equivalence. Try applying it to Qafar, where the distances are immediately more obvious" (*Debate*, 98). He also says, with respect to Grudem's analysis of James 5:14–15, "I invite him to apply the same sort of criteria as what he here presupposes when we translate the biblical texts into some of the more alien languages whose gender systems I briefly summarized in chapter 4" (p. 117).

[25]See further discussion in Appendix 3.

D. Objections based on the current state of the English language

I. "People are unfamiliar with generic 'he'"

Another objection says that some people are unfamiliar with generic "he," and therefore some people will misunderstand it.[26]

Response: People still encounter generic "he" in standard secular writings, and they understand it easily. Moreover, people also read books and stories written more than a few years ago, and they encounter generic "he" with no apparent difficulty in understanding.

Consider the following quotations, arranged in chronological order, taken both from standard secular writings and Christian writings. Remember, in reading this list, that critics of generic "he" decided to omit it from the NRSV long before the NRSV was published in 1990, and the NIV's Committee on Bible Translation decided in 1992 to omit it from the NIVI. The NIVI decision was based in part on an expectation that generic "he" would soon disappear from standard English. It hasn't.

These quotations begin before the March 1997 controversy over the plans for publishing a gender-neutral NIV in the United States, and continue for nearly three years after that time (up to the time this manuscript was being prepared for publication). Almost all of these examples were noticed by one of the authors of this book, Wayne Grudem, in the course of ordinary reading, but a few were sent to him by interested friends.

(In the following quotes, italics are ours.)

If a timid person who wants to be more assertive at work takes Prozac without dealing with the issues that make *him* timid, the message becomes the opposite of what we try to do with therapy (*Christianity Today*, Aug. 14, 1995, 36, quoting Wheaton psychologist Karen Maudlin).

During the 22 minutes an average person spends grocery shopping each week, 70 percent of *his* purchasing decisions are made in the store (*Chicago Tribune*, July 29, 1996, sec. 4, p. 1).

---

[26]Carson says, "If for some sections of the reading populace "he" is never or almost never used in a generic sense anymore, then fidelity to the original demands the choice of an expression that is less formally proximate, or we lose some part of what the original text says" (p. 158). Osborne, "Distort Scripture? No," says, ". . . those who have not grown up in the church can misunderstand such male-oriented language" (p. 34). Carson also says, "Regardless of the source of the pressure for linguistic change, the changes (I shall argue) are here. If that is the case, *this is the language that, increasingly, we have to work with*, even if we may not approve all the reasons that have brought these changes about" (*Debate*, 188). But Carson and Osborne do not really specify in any detail just what they think the changes are, in the current state of English. Osborne says people "can misunderstand," but do they? On p. 188 Carson talks about "the changes," at a very general level. But just what changes are in view? Later, on pp. 189–90, Carson does become specific, but the evidence he presents confirms our case. (See also Appendix 6.)

Wages are flat, hours are up, bosses are morons and everyone's stuffed into a cubicle—if *he's* lucky enough to have a job (*Newsweek*, Aug. 12, 1996, p. 3).

A reverse mortgage can allow a senior citizen to remain in familiar surroundings for the rest of *his* life (*Chicago Tribune*, Oct. 31, 1996, sec. 6, p. 3).

. . . every college professor doesn't need to put *his* main energy into expanding the frontiers of knowledge (*U.S. News and World Report*, Dec. 30, 1996, 45–47).

What happens when you tell the average American adult that *he* needs to reduce *his* spending in order to build wealth for the future? *He* may perceive this as a threat to his way of life (Thomas J. Stanley and William D. Danko, *The Millionaire Next Door* [New York: Simon and Schuster, 1996], 30. The cover says this book was "more than one year on the *New York Times* bestseller list").

. . . even if a person has gotten enough sleep, *he* is likely to be irritable or blue if *his* waking hours center on a time when *his* biological clock tells *him he* "should" be asleep. Conversely, even if a person stays awake 36 hours straight, *he* may say *he* feels terrific if you ask *him* about *his* mood at an hour when *his* biological clock tells *him he* is supposed to be awake, findings suggest (Associated Press dispatch downloaded from America Online, Feb 12, 1997. There are twelve uses of generic "he" in those two sentences).

If the person involved thinks the code has been misapplied, or that the code itself is defective, *he* goes to the courts for relief (*Christianity Today*, May 19, 1997, 28, quoting Robert Bork on the American legal system).

. . . to whom much is given, from *him* that much more shall be expected (*U.S. News & World Report*, May 19, 1997, 30, in a column by Arianna Huffington).

When a judge is ready for a jury, *his* Court Security Officer requests the Assembly Room Clerk to use the computer to randomly select the number of jurors *he* needs from those available in the Assembly Room (pamphlet on "Jury Service" distributed July 22, 1997, in the Lake County Courthouse, Waukegan, Illinois [there are female judges in the courthouse]).

A student who pays *his* own way gets the tax credit (*USA Today*, July 30, 1997, p. 3B, discussing the 1997 tax bill and its tax credits for college tuition. This is an interesting quotation—would gender-neutral Bible supporters think that female college students were likely to misunderstand this sentence, thinking that the tax law only applied to male students?).

The Cardmember agrees to use the service only for *his* benefit and for the benefit of members of *his* immediate family ("Your Personal Benefits Guide," a terms of service brochure received from Discover Card Aug. 8, 1997, 14).

. . . technology now enables physicians to watch a patient's condition almost as if they'd shriveled themselves up and traveled inside *his* body (*Chicago Tribune*, Aug. 17, 1997, sec. 5, p. 1).

Or is it when someone with a heavy accent calls up (a news organization), *he* tends to be dismissed more readily than someone who speaks standard English? (*USA Today*, Aug. 21, 1997, 3D, quoting Ted Koppel, who was preparing a *Nightline* broadcast on claims of police brutality in New York City).

Anyone can do any amount of work, provided it isn't the work *he* is supposed to be doing at that moment (*Reader's Digest*, Sept., 1997, 61, quoting Robert Benchley).

If a worker tells the boss *he* needs time off because *he* is "depressed and stressed," then a "reasonable accommodation" should be made (*Reader's Digest*, Sept., 1997, 126, quoting James Brady's summary of government regulations in *Crain's New York Business*).

. . . the first evidence of whether or not a person has a "politically correct" attitude is often *his* use of politically correct or incorrect language . . . there is considerable resistance to [PC language], a good deal of it taking the form of humor or mocking. . . . For example, a high school student calls one of *his* friends who is rather short in stature "vertically challenged" . . . (Valerie Becker Makkai, "Correctness in Language: Political and Otherwise," the 1996 Presidential Address of the Linguistic Association of Canada and the U.S., published in *The Twenty-third LACUS Forum 1996*, ed. Alan K. Melby [Chapel Hill, NC: The Linguistic Association of Canada and the United States, 1997], 5–6).

For example, a patient who has stabilized on an antidepressant can take months to adjust to a new medication, or *he* may fail completely and revert to a suicidal state (*US News and World Report*, Sept. 1, 1997, 73).

The latest PBM strategy is to woo the pharmacist *himself*—a practice that druggists fear could undermine confidence in their profession (*US News and World Report*, Sept. 1, 1997, 71).

A student should also make a habit of coming home, emptying *his* backpack in a certain location and figuring out exactly what schoolwork has to get done that night (*Chicago Tribune*, Sept. 7, 1997, sec. 13, 8).

. . . when you buy a new customer with a check, you've bought a temporary customer who will jump when *he* gets another check from someone else (*Chicago Tribune*, Sept. 9, 1997, sec. 3, 3).

That's because if an employer compensates you with a dollar's worth of health care insurance, that dollar is tax free to you, whereas if *he* pays you a dollar in salary . . . (James K. Glassman, "Treating the Symptoms," *U.S. News & World Report*, Feb. 9, 1998, 54).

If you want someone to laugh at your jokes, tell *him he* has a good sense of humor (*Readers Digest*, March 1998, 144).

When used in this publication, "*he*," "*him*," "*his*," and "*men*" represent both the masculine and feminine genders unless otherwise noted (U. S. Army Chaplain Officer Basic Course: Parish Development 3: Subcourse No. CH 0569, Edition 8 [U.S. Army Chaplain Center and School: Fort Monmouth, New Jersey], March 1998, ii).

The Internet: Why nobody keeps *his* homepage up to date (*Chicago Tribune*, Sunday, April 12, 1998, sec. 5, 5).

After the caller identifies himself, ask *him* to spell both *his* first and last names. Then ask *him* to spell the company name. Then ask where the company is located. Then ask *him* . . . (*Reader's Digest*, May 1998, 60H).

. . . a technology by which the operator performs functions not by typing at the keyboard but by clicks of *his* mouse. . . (p. 2), so the combination offered by the manufacturer must be different from what the purchaser could create from the separate products on *his* own. (p. 17) (United States Court of Appeals for the District of Columbia Circuit, No. 97–5343, April 21, 1998, United States of America, *Appellee vs. Microsoft Corporation*, Appellant Consolidated with 98–5012).

The court defined an "integrated product" as one that "must be different from what the purchaser could create from separate products on *his* own (*Chicago Tribune*, June 28, 1998, sec. 1, 14).

When companies rely heavily on voice mail to do business, Saffo said, it is common for one person to leave a long message detailing *his* thoughts and ideas (*Chicago Tribune*, July 6, 1998, sec. 1, p. 8).

Is your spouse a secret tax cheater? Formerly, the IRS could come after you, if your spouse underreported *his* taxes on your marital return (Jane Bryant Quinn, "New law gets spouse off tax cheater's hook," *Chicago Tribune*, August 2, 1998, sec. 5, 3).

In the House, which would conduct any Congressional investigation and initiate any impeachment process, one member of the Republican majority, Representative David M. McIntosh of Indiana, said: Every member has to be reflecting in *his* own mind, "Is this a question we have to resolve?" (Katharine Q. Seelye, "G.O.P. Hopes Starr Report Won't Be Summer Reading," *New York Times*, August 7, 1998, A14).

The reader who wants to refresh or deepen *his* acquaintance with Western religion and philosophy . . ." (Michael Lind, "Western Civ

Fights Back," a review of a new book by Daniel Boorstin, *The Seekers: The Story of Man's Continuing Quest to Understand His World* [New York: Random House] in *The New York Times Book Review*, September 6, 1998, 10. Boorstin is a former Librarian of Congress and the review notes that he has won the Pulitzer Prize, the National Book Award, the Bancroft Prize, and the Francis Parkman Prize).

Like a patient who finally recognizes *his* condition, the Japanese government today acknowledged that its economy is in deep trouble (CBS World News Roundup, national radio broadcast, heard at 7:03 A.M., October 6, 1998, on WBBM Radio, Chicago).

And the most complex ads are likely to become more common: Advertisers contend that consumers remember pop-up ads about twice as well as typical banner ads on a Web site. "The user feels as though *he's* watching a TV show where the commercials occupy the majority of the time," said Jason Catlett, who runs New Jersey-based JunkBusters Corp., which offers free blocking software (*Minneapolis-St. Paul Star Tribune*, August 27, 1998, D2).

Every student wanting to grow in *his* faith to Christ should be considering one of the colleges described in this helpful resource guide—Billy Graham, evangelist and author (*Peterson's Christian Colleges & Universities 1999*, Princeton, NJ: Peterson's, 1998, back cover).

What can you do if your child's interest in reading begins to wane? . . . Set a good example for your child . . . make sure *he* sees you reading. . . . Let *him* stay up an extra half hour as long as *he's* reading in bed . . . (". . . I'm Pat Carrol for *Parent Magazine*, on the CBS Radio Network," heard on WBBM radio, Chicago, September 6, 1998, 4:21 P.M.).

Given that no rational attorney would risk sacrificing *his* career by knowingly deceiving the court, Mr. Bennett must have been, like the rest of us, "misled" by his client Mr. Clinton (*Wall Street Journal*, Sept. 24, 1998, A18).

"We're going to give free college tuition and fees to any high school student in the top 25% of *his* class if they will commit to teach for four years after they graduate," Massachusetts Gov. Paul Cellucci said (*USA Today*, Nov. 23, 1998, 10A).

It's easy to give a poor person something *he* needs. . . . If the recipient has a relatively tough time doing something, *his* disadvantage can be turned into great gift ideas (*Wall Street Journal*, *An Economist's Christmas*, Dec. 1, 1998, A22).

Presumably, anyone who criticizes how the autoworkers' union built *his* car is "anti-transportation" (Mallard Fillmore cartoon in *Washington Times, National Weekly Edition*, December 7–13, 1998, 43).

To the extent that any lawmaker was thinking about taking it easy on the President for fear of looking partisan or extreme, *he* should take note: *he* will still be denounced by those currently doing the denouncing; *he* will win no laurels for *his* wisdom and sweet reason (*The Washington Times, National Weekly Edition*, Dec. 7–13, 1998, 41).

A child who watches *his* parents fight every day is likely to absorb the lesson that violence is the appropriate solution to problems (*The Washington Times, National Weekly Edition*, Dec. 21–27, 1998, 30).

. . . one child strangled in the netting since the kiddie play sets' introduction in 1976. That's a mortality rate of less than a thousandth of that the average American faces every time *he* gets into an auto (*Wall Street Journal*, Dec. 23, 1998, A14).

But Marvin Kosters of the American Enterprise Institute argues the data are severely misleading. . . . Kosters estimates that in constant dollars, the typical worker has seen *his* wages rise by 15 percent in the past quarter-century (*The American Enterprise*, January/February 1999, 86).

This is the most significant fact at the end of the twentieth century: All the major ideological constructions have failed, tossed on the ash heap of history. For all were based on the same underlying theme: Liberate the individual from the oppression of family, church, and local custom, and *he* would be autonomous and free (Charles Colson and Nancy Pearcey, "The Sky Isn't Falling," *Christianity Today*, Jan. 11, 1999, 104).

Even a moderate phone user should be able to shave 25 percent off *his* monthly bill by shopping around (*Readers Digest*, Feb. 1999, 135).

Moltmann never allows us to relax. . . . The argument often proceeds by way of image and suggestion rather than by way of clarification and analysis. As a result, the reader is liable to go away stimulated, yet less enlightened than *he* thinks (Donald Macleod, "The Christology of Jürgen Moltmann," *Themelios* 24:2 [February 1999], vol. 24:2).

The individual is expected to provide for *himself* through *his* company's scheme and through other investments (Lady Margaret Thatcher, "Resisting the Utopian Impulse," *American Outlook*, Spring 1999, 20).

Anybody in the world can download it off the Internet and install it on *his* computer. . . . A kid could bypass college and launch *his* career in computers by simply learning how to work Linux (*WORLD*, April 3, 1999, 29).

You don't have to answer a school official if *he* questions you; a teacher can't make you do anything that violates your conscience . . . (*Wall Street Journal*, "How the Courts Undermined School Discipline," May 4, 1999).

They might, for example say that because two teen-agers did something heinous with guns in Colorado, everyone everywhere else must drop *his* weapon and put *his* hands up (*The Washington Times, National Weekly Edition*, May 17–23, 1999, 37).

Full-time writing demands a certain amount of entrepreneurship and, like all authors, I worry that every commission will be my last. But a quick straw poll of my writing friends confirmed my feelings. None of them regrets *his* choice (Amanda Foreman, "Take me away from the dreaming spires,"*The Sunday Times* [The London *Times*], May 30, 1999, sec. 5, 4).

"Even with normal memory scores, a person's perception of frequent forgetting and having recalled things better at younger ages correlates with *his* chances of having the APOE-4 gene," says psychiatrist Gary Small of UCLA Medical School ("Alzheimer's clue: Knowing you forget," *USA Today*, July 1, 1999, 1).

Everyone with a computer—and even those without—has had *his* life improved thanks to Mr. Gates (*The Washington Times, National Weekly Edition*, July 5–11, 1999, 33).

Doctors who have exaggerated the severity of a patient's condition to get health plan coverage for *him* (Title of an illustrated statistical pie chart in *USA Today*, August 16, 1999, 1).

Nobody comes off a trans-Atlantic flight looking better than when *he* got on it (*Chicago Tribune*, August 22, 1999, sec. 8, 3).

Little is more incendiary than a member of Congress who feels *he* has been misled—unless it's a law enforcement agency that fans conspiracy theories through incompetence (*USA Today*, Aug. 31, 1999, sec. A, 14).

Because everyone is master of *his* own element . . . we integrate your systems while your company focuses on business (*American Way* (passenger magazine of American Airlines), full page ad for Gedas North America software company, Oct. 1, 1999, 134).

[According to deconstructionism] . . . truth is relative and personal. Each person creates *his* own inner world by acceptance or rejection of endlessly shifting linguistic signs. . . . There is only unlimited opportunity for the reader to invent interpretations and commentaries out of the world *he himself* constructs (Harvard professor Edward O. Wilson in his new book *Consilience: The Unity of Knowledge* [Knopf, 1998], as quoted in *Harvard Magazine* (Harvard's alumni publication), Sept.–Oct., 1999, 99).

[Regarding a Graduated Driver Licensing program advocated by AAA and the Insurance Institute for teenage drivers] To graduate to the second stage, the novice must pass a road test and have no moving violations or at-fault accidents. If *he* does, *he* remains at the first stage while *he* takes a driver-education refresher course (*Reader's Digest*, Dec., 1999, 129).

[On an article about alarmist food scares] Anyone pushing such an agenda knows *he* can win by camping up the media drama. The legal merits of a subsequent lawsuit hardly matter . . . (*The Wall Street Journal*, Feb. 22, 2000, A40).

The Taiwanese voter is a bundle of contradictions: *He* isn't keen on reunification, but doesn't want war just for the sake of a declaration of independence, yet *he* wants to be proud of the island nation, too (*The Wall Street Journal*, Feb. 23, 2000, A22).

If your caller listens carefully, *he* can almost hear the oceandome (ad for WorldCell, showing that the global cell phone can be used in Tokyo, in *American Way* [passenger magazine of American Airlines], Mar. 1, 2000, 105).

"Scots, Croats, Chechens—everybody seems to want a country of *his* own" (Harvard professor Samuel P. Huntington in *Time*, May 22, 2000, 113).

These quotations indicate that the use of generic "he" is still found regularly in all sorts of standard publications today. It is hard to imagine how the reading audience for a modern Bible translation would be significantly different from the reading audience that apparently does not stumble at the use of generic "he" by *USA Today*, *Reader's Digest*, the *New York Times*, the *Times* of London, the *Chicago Tribune*, and the *Wall Street Journal*, or that these readers would have an understanding of English that is different from the passengers on American Airlines, the alumni of Harvard University, or the listeners to CBS radio.

Yet some defenders of gender-neutral Bible are apparently convinced that generic "he" will not be understood by Bible readers today.

In fact, generic "he" is still the standard style used by the Associated Press. *The Associated Press Stylebook and Libel Manual* (1994, and 2000 revision also) directs, "Use the pronoun *his* when an indefinite antecedent may be male or female: *A reporter attempts to protect his sources*. (Not *his or her* sources.)"[27] This book is so widely used that the cover proclaims, "Used by more than 1,000,000 journalists."

Strunk and White's *The Elements of Style*, perhaps the most widely acclaimed and most respected handbook for good writing in the English language, was just reissued in a fourth edition.[28] In it we find the following advice:

Do not use *they* when the antecedent is a distributive expression such as *each, each one, everybody, every one, many a man*. Use the singular pronoun.

---

[27]Norm Goldstein, ed., *The Associated Press Stylebook and Libel Manual* (Reading, Mass.: Addison-Wesley, 1994), 94. The updated edition for 2000 contains the same guideline (Norm Goldstein, ed., *The Associated Press Stylebook and Briefing on Media Law* (Cambridge, Mass.: Perseus, 2000), 114.

[28]William Strunk, Jr., and E. B. White, *The Elements of Style*, Fourth Edition (Boston: Allyn and Bacon, 2000).

Then follow these examples of incorrect and correct usage:

[incorrect] Every one of us knows they are fallible.

[correct] Every one of us knows he is fallible.

[incorrect] Everyone in the community, whether they are a member of the Association or not, is invited to attend.

[correct] Everyone in the community, whether he is a member of the Association or not, is invited to attend.

The book then says, "The use of *he* as a pronoun for nouns embracing both genders is a simple, practical convention rooted in the beginnings of the English language."[29]

After this the book mentions that many writers object to the use of generic "he," and it goes on to allow for the use of "he or she" as an alternative, but says "it often doesn't work, if only because repetition makes it sound boring or silly."[30] Then it mentions the other standard alternatives such as changing the whole sentence to plurals rather than singulars, or eliminating the pronoun altogether, or substituting second person for third person, or trying generic "she."[31] Regarding the option of changing everything to plurals, it says this is acceptable, "although you may find your prose sounding general and diffuse as a result." In the last paragraph of the discussion it returns to generic "he," saying, "No one need fear to use *he* if common sense supports it."[32] Although allowing for the use of alternatives [as we would also do], the clear preference of the entire entry is for generic "he."

It is significant that this new Strunk and White has a copyright date of 2000, as does the new update of *The Associated Press Stylebook*, whereas the decision of the NIV translators to abandon generic "he" in what became the NIVI was made as early as 1992, in the anticipation that generic "he" would soon disappear. But if generic "he" is still entrenched in such standard English handbooks in 2000, its acceptable use will surely continue for at least as long as current Bible translations need be concerned.

Major dictionaries all recognize generic "he," not as archaic but as current English. The definition of "he" as a pronoun that is "used to refer to a

---

[29]Ibid., 60.

[30]Ibid.

[31]What the book actually says about generic "she" is just one conditional sentence with a hint that they know its use can incur the disapproval of other readers: "If you think *she* is a handy substitute for *he*, try it and see what happens" (p. 61).

[32]Ibid. Even stronger is Wilson Follett, *Modern American Usage*, revised by Erik Wensberg (New York: Hill and Wang, 1998), 31-34, who gives seven columns to advocating generic "he" (what he calls "figurative he") and explaining the deficiencies of substitutes such as generic "she" ("distracting"), the use of "his or her" ("annoying"), or changing of active to passive verbs ("wordy and weak"). He admits that using plurals ("they," "their") to refer to a singular antecedent goes on all the time in colloquial speech, then says, "But no esteemed writer of English, early or late, has been cited as using this oddity page after page, in work after work" (31). So generic "he" persists, he says, because "The evidence suggests . . . that many practicing writers choose their pronouns for reasons of economy and sense, not in obedience to prohibitions" (32).

person whose gender is unspecified or unknown" is given in *The American Heritage Dictionary of the English Language* (1992).[33] Similar definitions are found in *Webster's New World Dictionary* (1994), the *Random House Unabridged Dictionary* (1993), *Webster's Third New International Dictionary* (1981), and *Merriam Webster's Collegiate Dictionary* (1995).[34] Sample sentences include, "He who hesitates is lost," "No one seems to take pride in his work anymore," and "One should do the best he can." In the dictionaries there is no dispute over whether such generic usage is understandable in ordinary English today.

When we come to *recommendations* for how people should speak and write today, there is simply no consensus. As we mentioned in a previous chapter, the *American Heritage Dictionary* (1996) polled the 173 members of its Usage Panel of experts in the English language on how to complete a series of sentences such as, "A patient who doesn't accurately report _____ sexual history to the doctor runs the risk of misdiagnosis." In their responses an average of 46 percent of panel members used forms such as "his or her" or "her/his" (this statistic combines several forms), 37 percent used "his," 3 percent used "their," 2 percent used "her," 2 percent used "a" or "the," and 7 percent gave no response or felt no pronoun was needed, and a few gave other responses.[35] But if 37 percent of these experts (the largest for any one specific response) continued to use "his" as their most preferred word in these sentences (and many more would have said it is acceptable but not preferred), then no one can rightly claim that generic "he" is improper English today. In spite of more than thirty years of discussion, no substitutes have gained general acceptance.

2. "Generic 'he' is infrequent"

Another objection says, "Of course we admit that generic 'he' still occurs here and there. But it is not used as frequently as it once was. We need to beware of using uncommon expressions in Bible translation."[36]

Response: There is no reason we have to avoid infrequently used expressions in Bible translation. Some words like "heron," "amethyst," "blasphemy," "elder," and "apostle" may not occur with high frequency in secular writings today, but they are intelligible. Translators can use such words when they need them. The same is true of generic "he" when it is needed to express the meaning accurately.

---

[33]*American Heritage Dictionary*, 831.

[34]*Webster's New World Dictionary*, 3rd college edition (1994), 820; *Random House Unabridged Dictionary*, 2nd ed. Revised (1993), 879; *Webster's Third New International Dictionary*, unabridged edition (1981), 1041; *Merriam Webster's Collegiate Dictionary*, 10th edition (1995), 534.

[35]*American Heritage Dictionary*, 831.

[36]Carson agrees that there are still examples of generic "he" to be found in current English literature today, but says that many examples of gender-neutral language that avoids generic "he" are also easy to find. He concludes that "the changes are farther advanced in the English

And the charge of "infrequency" is a matter of personal judgment. For scholars who read only academic publications that have been sanitized by overly vigilant language police, generic "he" may seem infrequent. But for people who read the ordinary English that is found in newspaper articles written by the "more than 1,000,000 journalists" who follow the Associated Press *Stylebook,* or for writers who follow the guidelines in the Fourth Edition (copyright 2000) of the widely respected Strunk and White's *Elements of Style,* it may not seem nearly as infrequent as some scholars think.[37]

3. "Everybody uses gender-neutral language today"

The next objection says, "But everybody uses gender-neutral language. Sophisticated speakers and writers are steering away from generic 'he.' Are you saying that any time an author rephrases a sentence to move out generic 'he,' the author is a feminist?"

Response: As we observed before, authors and translators have different responsibilities. Authors have power to rephrase their material, even at the cost of losing nuances or (as Zinsser says) turning their style to "mush" if they wish. But translators, especially Bible translators, do not have authority to rewrite the material they are translating—or to advise God on what he should have said or how he should have phrased it.

4. "Generic 'he' will soon disappear"

This objection says, "Since generic 'he' has declined markedly in recent years, it will soon disappear. In Bible translation, we should take account of future trends in the English language, so that our translation will not quickly become out of date."[38]

Response: Several different points respond to this guess about the future.

First, it is a guess. It is unsubstantiated. And predictions of the future have a remarkable way of turning out to be false.

---

language than the critics think, even if not as far advanced as some feminists think" (*Debate,* 190). "But if 'he' in English, complete with gender specification, is used in a generic sense somewhat less frequently than it used to be, and if for some sections of the reading populace 'he' is never or almost never used in a generic sense anymore, then fidelity to the original demands the choice of an expression that is less formally proximate, or we lose some part of what the original text says" (ibid., 158).

The reasoning from infrequency to "demand" is incorrect. Frequency has very little to do with understandability, that is, with actual loss of meaning. People can understand words and complicated sentences that they might very seldom *use* in their own speech. (See further discussion in Appendix 6.)

[37]See footnotes 27 and 28 above with references to the AP *Stylebook* and to Strunk and White, *Elements of Style.*

[38]Grant Osborne says, "Even if the inclusive *he* is retained in some stylebooks, it is impossible to deny that its occurrence is becoming rarer or that ultimately it is on its way out in modern language" ("Distorting? No," p. 34). See also Carson, *Debate,* 117–18.

Second, several factors argue against this prediction. English stylist William Zinsser says, "Let's face it: the English language is stuck with the generic masculine."[39] The current *American Heritage Dictionary* (1996) concludes a long discussion on generic "he" with this prediction: "The entire question is unlikely to be resolved in the near future."[40] And Strunk and White's year 2000 edition of *The Elements of Style* still favors generic "he" over alternatives.[41] Contrary to the unsupported assertions of supporters of gender-neutral Bibles, these standard authorities on the use of English see no clear indications that generic "he" will disappear.

The reason that people who speak and write English resist abolishing generic "he" is that there are times when clear and accurate writing requires the use of a third-person singular pronoun with the person's sex unspecified or unknown. Zinsser says, "A style that converts every 'he' into a 'they' will quickly turn to mush. . . . I don't like plurals; they weaken writing because they are less specific than the singular, less easy to visualize."[42] And Strunk and White warn the reader who changes everything to plurals, "You may find your prose sounding general and diffuse."[43]

Three professional linguists have told us they knew of no major human language that lacked a singular pronoun that was used generically.[44] Therefore, people who predict that English will soon relinquish generic "he," when there is no commonly agreed singular substitute, are predicting that English—perhaps the most versatile language in history—will lose a capability possessed by all major languages in the world. Should we believe such an unlikely prediction? Should we base our Bible translations on it?

Third, at the moment avant-garde circles seem to include not only people who totally avoid generic singulars, but others who use generic "she," or who oscillate between using "he" and "she."[45] This use of "he" keeps it in circulation, and hence means that it is not in fact disappearing. The use of "she" keeps "he" understandable, because the two usages are structurally analogous.

Fourth, generic "he" is not quite like an ordinary noun or verb. An ordinary vocabulary item can fade from the language merely by not being used. Once it becomes unknown, then if someone uses it again, people have no clue to its meaning, and communication fails. But generic "he" is dependent on "he," and its meaning can be inferred from "he" (just as generic "she" is dependent on "she," and its meaning can be inferred from "she").

---

[39]Zinsser, *On Writing Well*, 123.

[40]*American Heritage Dictionary*, 831.

[41]Strunk and White, *Elements*, 60–61 (see longer discussion above).

[42]Zinsser, *On Writing Well*, 123.

[43]Strunk and White, *Elements*, 61.

[44]Even if a few unusual languages in the world lacked a singular pronoun that was used generically, the general principle would still stand.

[45]Carson, *Debate*, 189–90.

Fifth, the pronoun "he" can be used to refer to a male individual in other kinds of examples that are not fully generic but yet give expression to a general principle (see examples at the end of Appendix 4). For example, the good Samaritan, referred to as "he," is an example of what every follower of Christ—male or female—should be like. Understanding of generic "he" flows naturally from the broader principle that in many situations a single case can be used to express a general principle.

Because of all this, it is unlikely that generic "he" will disappear from English until "he" disappears from English—something that may never happen.

Finally, it is unwise to try to jump the gun. People use translations now, not only twenty years from now. If a particular word is serviceable now, translations should use it now. If it disappears in the future, then *in the future* they can revise the English version accordingly.[46]

E. The inevitability of generic "he"

In this last section we do not respond to objections, but rather reflect a bit on how pronouns work. Consider the following utterance, "Sally cannot see the kingdom of God unless she is born again." "She" refers back to "Sally." The speaker who composes the sentence understands this, and so does the hearer who hears. "She" is feminine because it refers backward to "Sally," and Sally is female. Similarly, "Tom cannot see the kingdom of God unless he is born again." These two sentences and many other similar sentences have meaning because of the way in which pronouns like "she" and "he" work.

Now suppose the speaker wants to generalize. "No one can see the kingdom of God unless _____ is born again" (from John 3:3). Because of the large-scale structural correspondences between this sentence and others,

---

[46]Carson agrees that generic "he" has not disappeared from current English when he says, "But let us suppose that English moves on to the place where 'he' refers *exclusively* to the male" (*Debate*, 117–18). He also says, "It is . . . unsurprising that there are still many, many examples around of the unreconstructed generic 'he.' No one is arguing that the change has been universal" (p. 189).

The fact that generic "he" is still used fairly often in current English means that Carson's repeated comparisons to the loss of "thee" and "thou" (and therefore the loss of a distinctly singular second person pronoun) are not particularly relevant (see Carson, *Debate*, 109, 190, 206). Current English has long ago lost "thee" and "thou" and, though most people would know they were an alternative way of saying "you," probably 100% of English speakers today would say they are archaic, and probably less than 1% would understand that they were *singular* pronouns to be distinguished from the *plural* pronoun "you." Therefore "thee" and "thou" have completely lost the ability to convey meaning accurately in English today. But generic "he" is far different, since it is still widely used and widely understood today.

Therefore Carson is incorrect when he says, with reference to Grudem's objection to the switch to plurals in Psalm 1, "That is exactly the argument used to defend the preservation of singular 'thou' a few decades ago" (p. 206). Singular "thou" was gone from current English a few decades ago, so the arguments are not parallel.

and because of the needs in the real world to express general truths, this sentence begs to be able to be completed.

Suppose now, in a hypothetical world, Sue has grown up with English but has never heard generic "he." How will she complete the sentence? She may say, "No one can see the kingdom of God unless *they* are born again." The plural "they" refers back to the singular "no one." Though such a mode of expression may seem awkward, it is not impossible. A similar use has been attested in the English language for centuries. *The Oxford English Dictionary* says under the entry for "they," "2. Often used in reference to a singular noun made universal by *every, any, no,* etc., or applicable to one of either sex (= 'he or she'). . . . He neuer forsaketh any creature vnlesse they before haue forsaken themselues (*sic* from 1535)."[47]

In some ways the logic of the English language is at work to produce such a usage. Any use of a particular pronominal form in English is related to the real-world referent, the "thing in the world" to which the pronoun refers. But in cases like these, the real-world referent is in one sense a potential multitude. "Any creature" focuses on a sample "creature" using a singular grammatical form, but it uses this sample creature in order to make a general statement about a plurality of creatures. The universalized form of the assertion gives it both an aspect of plurality and an aspect of singularity. The same is true with our example above, "No one can see the kingdom of God unless ___ is born again." According to Sue's point of view, she could treat the referent as if it were either single or multiple. By using "they" she chooses to focus on the multiplicity of possible referents, rather than the singularity of the sample case, "no one." In our day quite a bit of spoken English and at least one British publisher have taken over this pattern and used it much more frequently in order to avoid generic "he."[48]

However, there are liabilities to a usage like this one. For one thing, the antecedent may become ambiguous. The NRSV contains a startling example of the problem. "Moreover by them [the ordinances of the LORD] is your servant warned; in keeping them there is great reward. But who can detect *their* errors? Clear me from hidden faults" (Ps. 19:11–12, NRSV; similarly NIVI). Occurrences of "they" and "them" throughout verses 10 and 11 all refer to "the ordinances of the LORD." Verse 12 continues with "their errors," which one would think at first would have the same reference as

---

[47]*The Oxford English Dictionary,* ed. J. A. Simpson and E. S. C. Weiner (2d ed.; Oxford: Clarendon, 1989), 17:928. See Dennis Baron, *Grammar and Gender* (New Haven/London: Yale University Press, 1986), 191–97.

[48]"At least one major British publisher has recently adopted this usage ["they" with singular antecedent] for its learners' dictionaries. . . . But in formal style, this option is perhaps less risky for a publisher of reference books than for an individual writer, who may be misconstrued as being careless or ignorant rather than attuned to the various grammatical and political nuances of the use of the masculine pronoun as generic pronoun" (*American Heritage Dictionary,* 831).

the earlier plurals "they/them." Thus, verse 12 would be saying that the ordinances of the LORD have errors! But the intended reference in the Hebrew text, and in all earlier English translations, is actually to the singular "who": "but who can discern *his* errors?"

The fact that the intended antecedent is singular creates the problem. Consider again, "No one can see the kingdom of God unless _____ is born again." With a slight change, we would obtain, "no one sees the kingdom of God unless _____ is born again." This change forces us to use "sees" as the third *singular* form of the verb "see" (whereas "see" would be used for a plural subject). But that means that we know that the subject "no one" is grammatically singular. In the structure of English there exists a pronounced preference for matching singular pronouns with singular antecedents, for obvious reasons, and "no one" is singular. Thus, commenting on this use of "they," *The American Heritage Dictionary* observes, "What is more, this solution ["they"] ignores a persistent intuition that expressions such as *everyone* and *each student* should in fact be treated as grammatically singular. Writers who are concerned about avoiding both grammatical and social problems are best advised to use coordinate forms such as *his or her*."[49]

This "intuition" is confirmed by linguistic analysis. "Everyone likes ice cream" and "Each student sits at his own desk" both contain third-person singular verbal forms, "likes" and "sits." We are not allowed to replace them with plural verbs in order to produce "Everyone *like* ice cream" and "Each student *sit* at his own desk." "*People* like ice cream" and "*Students* sit at desks" are acceptable, because they contain grammatically plural subjects, "people" and "students." The distinction between singular and plural cuts a large swath through the grammar of the English language, so that it is impossible to excise it. Within this system "no one," "anyone," and "whoever" are grammatically singular. Hence, sentences like, "No one can see the kingdom of God unless *they* are born again" do not simply require us to adjust for a different usage of the word "they," but rather require us to set aside the deeply ingrained sense of concord between singular nouns, verbs, and pronouns, on the one hand, and between plural nouns, verbs, and pronouns, on the other hand, that we read and use hundreds of times every day. People may increasingly use "they" to refer to a singular antecedent, but the grammatical concord fights against it, and therefore we doubt that the majority of careful speakers and writers will ever regularly adopt it. (It is not surprising that only 3 percent of the *American Heritage Dictionary*'s Usage Panel chose a plural pronoun in such sentences, or that this dictionary says that individual writers who adopt it "may be misconstrued as careless or ignorant.")[50]

---

[49]Ibid.
[50]Ibid.

Putting in "they" works even less well in other circumstances. Proverbs 16:26 says, "A worker's appetite works for *him*; *his* hunger urges *him* on" (NASB). Can we change it to "A worker's appetite works for *them*; *their* hunger urges *them* on"? The reader is likely to wonder whether the worker is working for a group of people who have been mentioned in context. "A man who is kind benefits *himself*, but a cruel man hurts *himself*" (Prov. 11:17, RSV). Can we change it to "A person who is kind benefits *themselves*, but a cruel person hurts *themselves*"? This is impossible English.

So Sue abandons her attempt to complete the sentence with "they," and tries again, "No one can see the kingdom of God, unless *he or she* is born again." Sue has now solved the problem of grammatical number. And such a solution may be adequate for some uses and some contexts.[51] But the result is cumbersome, overprecise. Moreover, it undermines vividness, concreteness, and communicative power by flipping the reader's mind back and forth between two alternative pictures rather than sticking with one. The problem becomes worse if we have more than one occurrence. Proverbs 16:26 becomes "A worker's appetite works for him or her; his or her hunger urges him or her on." This monstrosity does not fit into the Book of Proverbs, because it does not have the crispness of a proverb, and is scarcely recognizable as smooth English.

Structurally, the use of "he or she" does not match the ability of other, analogous sentences to use only a single noun or pronoun to do the job. Zinsser says of this solution, "To turn every 'he' into a 'he or she,' and every 'his' into a 'his or her,' would clog the language."[52] One may go through similar analyses of other alternatives that have been tried;[53] there is no obvious solution.

---

[51]But not for Bible translation. "He or she" draws attention to itself, and also suggests that the authors in the ancient context were making a conscious effort to be explicit in including women. Once again, implicated information in the original has become *explicit* information in the translation.

[52]Zinsser, *On Writing Well*, 123. Baron, *Grammar and Gender*, 191, says that language authorities reject "he or she" as "ugly and cumbersome."

[53]Zinsser, *On Writing Well*, 122–25. Regarding the suggestion to alternate between "he" and "she" in successive paragraphs, Zinsser rightly observes, "That struck me as too confusing. My cardinal goal in writing . . . is clarity. Anything that gets in the way of clarity is bad, and a reader suddenly confronted with alternating pronouns would end up constantly wondering, "Who's *she*" and "Where did *he* come from?" The device is also too self-dramatizing; it calls attention to itself as a political statement and pulls the reader's attention away from where it belongs: on the writing" (pp. 123–24).

A similar decision was made in a manual published by the American Academy of Pediatrics. The preface says,

> PLEASE NOTE: The information and advice in this book apply equally to babies of both sexes. It is awkward and confusing to shift constantly from he to she and his to hers. We have chosen to handle this problem by using the masculine form of pronouns exclusively when referring to children and physicians. For example, "*He* gives you *his* love, . . . *he* gets older, *he* will show this love, . . . *His* love is filled with admiration . . . ." (The American Academy of Pediatrics, *Caring for Your Baby and Young Child: Birth to Age 5*, editor-in-chief Steven P. Shelov [New York: Bantam, 1993], xx).

Sue's problem is to find a pronoun, from within the existing English pronominal system, that would refer easily and unambiguously back to "no one." In all innocence, with no knowledge of the previous use of generic "he," she searches. The pronoun must be a third singular personal pronoun to refer to the singular antecedent "no one." Sue has three choices: "he," "she," or "it." "It" will not do, because "no one" refers to human persons, and we do not use "it" to refer to people. So Sue has only "he" and "she." She then quite naturally "reinvents" the usage of "he" as generic singular. Or alternatively she reinvents the use of "she" as generic singular.

Now, in a typical case, a native speaker of English does not do all this reasoning *consciously*. The system works unconsciously. But the system is not a rigid system with no room for innovation, for play, for expanded usage. Thus, granted even the initial hypothesis of total ignorance, the proposed expansion or "reinvention" is reasonable.

The situation is even easier for Sue if she reads a sentence already formulated by someone else. "No one can see the kingdom of God unless he is born again." The sentence goes smoothly until Sue meets "he." Does she then stumble because she has never seen such an odd or unheard-of barbarism? We do not think so. Unconsciously, using the language system that she has already learned, she moves as follows. "He" is a third singular masculine personal pronoun. Look for an antecedent that is third singular. "The kingdom of God" is singular, but it is not a person. It would be referred to by "it." "God" is singular, but the meaning does not fit. "No one" is singular. Is it male? It is a sample including males and females. Does it work as antecedent in terms of meaning? Yes.

Sue may not even notice that she has met with a construction never before seen: generic "he." She may not notice because this use harmonizes so well with what she has already seen innumerable times, namely the backward-referring use of the third-person singular personal pronoun. Generic singular "he" is easy for Sue. She takes it in stride. It is a natural part of the structure of the English language. Without using so much linguistic apparatus, Zinsser observes the same thing: "But let's face it: the English language is stuck with the generic masculine."[54]

Of course, in Sue's world there remains a shortfall in perfect structural symmetry. Sue's extended use of "he" cannot fully resolve the shortfall, even though her extension is based on the inherent logic of the English pronominal system. The shortfall is, of course, the one with which we have wrestled from the beginning. "He" is grammatically masculine, while the referent includes both men and women in the range of the sample. The range for the sample is not exactly proportional to the usual semantic load of the pronoun.

---

[54]Ibid., 123.

But at a microscopic level of analysis, such asymmetries occur scattered throughout language, and language users seldom even stop to notice them. For example, in the quote from Zinsser, he says that the English language "is stuck." The abstract term "the English language" does not exactly match the word "stuck," which we usually expect to find applied either to material objects (a peg stuck in a hole) or people who are baffled. But readers immediately perceive that Zinsser is talking about people being unable to dislodge the language from its structural positioning or "hole." Readers resolve the problem so fast that they do not even notice it. A few sentences earlier we asked whether Sue "stumbles." The context does not match the idea of physically pitching over. Readers automatically perceive that the stumbling is figurative. Elsewhere in this book we have used the phrase, "male meaning component." "Male" modifies animate nouns; it presupposes that the entity it describes is a creature with sex. But the word "component" is an abstract noun, not possessing sexuality. Technically speaking, the two do not match. But readers see that "Male meaning component" means "the meaning component 'male,'" that is, a semantic feature of "maleness" attaching to some word or some part of an utterance.

There is a deep principle at work here. In situations of real-world use of language, interpreters' expectations about meaning drive communicative understanding in a remarkably powerful way. Thus generic "he" creates no structural difficulty.

Let us make the point more vividly. Let us consider a "thought experiment," by envisioning a science fiction scenario. Suppose that, unknown to everyone, an alien superrace invades the earth. The aliens have power to remain invisible, and also possess incredibly developed powers of mind manipulation. Suppose the aliens remain invisible at all times. And suppose they do nothing with their power of mind control except one thing: they wipe out generic "he." They prevent all living speakers of English from ever using an expression with generic "he" or generic "she." They secretly alter all the books and documents from the past to eliminate generic "he." They alter the memories of those who remember the use of generic "he."

Once all the changes are in place, the aliens resolve not to interfere with the newborns. "Aha!" they say, "The newborns now have no chance of learning generic 'he.' Let us see what they will do instead." The aliens resolve to continue their experiment for thirty years, to allow plenty of time for the newborns to grow to a mature use of English. What will happen? Within a few years, the newborns would eventually "reinvent" generic "he" or generic "she" or both, just as Sue did in our example above.

Language learning involves generalizations of patterns. The child grows and learns the systematic difference between singulars and plurals: "dog/dogs," "cat/cats," "boy/boys," "boat/boats," etc. So the child then says "foots" as the plural of "foot." Eventually, this mistake gets straightened out, either through someone correcting the child, or, more often, through more listening to English. The child learns that "feet" is *irregularly* the plural of "foot."

Similarly, in learning a pronominal system the child learns regularities. He learns "I/me/my/mine/myself," "we/us/our/ours/ourselves," "he/him/his/his/himself," etc. The aliens' suppression of generic "he" leaves a gap in the system at the point when the child fills out the sentence, "No one can see the kingdom of God unless _____ is/are born again." The child fills the gap, just as Sue did, by extending a regular pattern. The child sees no problem.

In the case of "foots," a real existing usage, namely "feet," can substitute for "foots." Hence, the child can adjust to the irregularity. But the child can never adjust to the irregularity of not having generic "he" unless there is a suitable substitute for it to fill out the sentence, "No one can see the kingdom of God unless _____ is born again." As modern stylists have observed, and as analysis of the pronominal system confirms, there is no adequate substitute. The child therefore latches onto generic "he" (or "she") as "obvious." He never looks back unless corrected by the punishments and lectures of others. Even if he does not latch onto this innovation himself, he would understand generic "he" the first time that he opened a Bible that the aliens had somehow overlooked and left unaltered.

In sum, native speakers of English have the linguistic ability to understand generic "he." Unless, in some hypothetical world, we see the triumph of a gender-ambiguous term like the proposed third-person singular personal pronoun "thon,"[55] or succeed in tearing up the English language to the point of total destruction or unrecognizable alteration, no one can abolish this ability to understand and use generic "he." This ability is deep. It belongs to human beings who use language.

All this analysis is confirmed by a simple observation. A number of people have told us that they understood generic "she" the very first time that they heard it! They understood not only the basic referential function, but the political connotations as well. If generic "she" can be understood this easily, so can generic "he." Both in fact are immediately intelligible by natural analogy with ordinary, nongeneric uses of "he" and "she."

---

[55]See Zinsser's sarcastic dismissal in ibid., 124–25: "Maybe I don't speak for the average American, but I doubt that thon wants that word in thons language or that thon would use it thonself."

Even if English could be altered so as to possess the extra pronoun "thon," we would guess on the basis of the arguments already given that native speakers would still be able to understand generic "he" and generic "she," though they would see in such a use a focus being given to a male or female sample out of the general case.

CHAPTER 17

Ordinary People Can Understand Generic "He"

In this chapter we take up one final objection, the claim that translations that use generic "he" are likely to be misunderstood by at least some modern readers.

A. Objection: People will misunderstand generic "he"

One objection says, "Generic 'he' is confusing. Some people may misunderstand it and interpret it as exclusively designating males."

Response: This claim of "misunderstanding" is suspect. For one thing, this is not the concern expressed in the books on English style. They warn about "displeasure," but not about misunderstanding.

Second, generic "he" continues to occur in much standard writing in English. Prominent publications (*USA Today, U.S. News, Reader's Digest, The New York Times*, CBS radio broadcasts, and Associated Press dispatches, for example) do not seem to be aware of a danger of misunderstanding.[1]

Third, some people today use generic "she," and a number of people have testified they understood it *the very first time* they encountered it. Ardent feminists themselves use generic "she" knowing that they are including males. By symmetry, generic "he" is also understandable.

In addition, generic "he" and generic "she" both work because their function derives from the broader functions of "he" and "she." Consider again a particular example. "If anyone loves me, he will obey my teaching." Everyone can see that "anyone" is generic, and therefore that the word "he," which refers back to "anyone," includes women. It takes little brainpower to see that this generic "he" is not in danger of being misunderstood.

---

[1]See the examples given in the previous chapter, pp. 215–22.

Understanding of generic "he" is built into the language. People may dislike it, but they will not misunderstand it.

B. Objections based on psychological studies

Another objection says, "Psychological studies show that people do misunderstand generic 'he.'"

This objection comes from Mark Strauss, who in his book about gender-neutral translations cites psychological studies that at first appear to indicate that people do misunderstand generic "he" and "man" used to refer to both men and women.[2]

Response: First, we should be clear about exactly what sort of English usage we have in view. Strauss begins his discussion of experiments not with generic "he" but with the use of "man."[3] We agree with Strauss that usage of "man" and "men" has shifted somewhat. In the last few years expressions like "a man" or "all men" are more often used when only males are in view.[4] These points are not in dispute.[5]

C. Experiments related to "man" for the human race as a whole

But there is more than one kind of usage of the word "man." In addition to the use with "a man" or "the man," to refer to an individual, "man" can be used to refer to the human race: "God created *man* in his own image." It always takes the form "man" *in the singular* ("man" not "men") and *without an article* ("man" not "the man" or "a man"), and thus it can be clearly distinguished from the other uses. Strauss reports the following experiment concerning this usage of "man":

> Joseph Schneider and Sally Hacker (1973) gave college students hypothetical chapter titles for a textbook on sociology and asked them to bring in pictures that could be used in the chapter. Among students who were given titles using generic "man," such as "Industrial Man" and

---

[2]Mark L. Strauss, *Distorting Scripture? The Challenge of Bible Translation & Gender Accuracy* (Downers Grove, IL: InterVarsity, 1998), 140–44.

[3]"'Man' as Male and Female" and "Studies of Generic 'Man'" (ibid., 140–41) are the first two section headings in the larger unit, "Excursus: Contemporary English Usage: Are 'Man' and 'He' Inclusive Today?" See also our later discussion in Chapter 18 of "man" for the human race.

[4]It is difficult to understand why Carson says that "CBMW scholars devote energy to trying to prove that the English language is not changing. . . . That is a bit like Canute trying to hold back the tide" (*The Inclusive-Language Debate*, 112). The accompanying statement published with the Colorado Springs Guidelines and signed by all participants said, "We all agree that modern language is fluid and undergoes changes in nuance that require periodic updates and revisions" (*CBMW News* 2:3 [June 1997], 7). (See Chapter 12, footnote 1, above.)

[5]The Colorado Springs Guidelines accordingly allow Bible translations to use expressions like "anyone who . . ." and "all people" instead of "all men" in cases where such is the meaning of the original.

"Economic Man," 64 percent of the pictures submitted showed only men. When gender-neutral terms like "Industrial Life" and "Economic Life" were used, only half of the pictures contained only male images.[6]

But what exactly does this demonstrate? The experiment in fact showed exactly what we would expect. The word "man," used generically for the human race, conveys simultaneously two aspects of meaning. First, it refers to the race, including both men and women in the scope of the discussion. Second, it does so using a word that evokes connotations of a male representative or male example who stands for the race. When the researchers ask students to bring pictures, they are in effect asking for a pictorial example or illustration matching the title. The closest match can be obtained by picking an example in harmony with the idea of a male representative. Thus it is no surprise that the students bring representative examples where males appear prominently. Similar analysis applies to most of the other experiments involving the word "man." (The one possible exception would be with studies of children, which are not a reliable guide to current English usage. This is because young children are still learning the ins and outs of the English language, and on occasion they make mistakes.)

Strauss concludes, "There seems little doubt from these studies that when 'man' is used as a generic term, it is often misunderstood to refer only to males. At the least, a certain level of confusion and ambiguity often results."[7] But Strauss has missed the real significance of the data. They show not "misunderstanding," "confusion," and "ambiguity," but rather positive evidence for the way that "man" (used for the race) evokes the connotation of a male representative for a whole. Strauss has simply failed to distinguish between this representative connotation of generic "man" and an actual misunderstanding.

D. Experiments related to generic "he"

Next we come to the use of generic "he." Strauss says, "Both women and men reported that they usually pictured men when they read or heard the masculine generic."[8] Note the word "pictured." Generic "he," like generic "man," evokes a male example or male representative to express a general truth. *Of course* people "picture" a man more often than not. At the same time people can still recognize the inclusion of women in the general truth when a term like "anyone" is followed by "he."

---

[6]Strauss, *Distorting*, 141; from J. W. Schneider and S. L. Hacker, "Sex Role Imagery and Use of the Generic 'Man' in Introductory Texts: A Case in the Sociology of Sociology," *American Sociologist* 8 (1973): 12–18.

[7]Strauss, *Distorting*, 142.

[8]Ibid., 143.

Strauss fails to notice that these two things are quite compatible. As in the case of "man" for the human race, he falsely equates the fact that men were "pictured" with the supposition that women are *excluded*.

Consider another experiment. Strauss reports:

> In an experiment conducted by Wendy Martyna, students were asked to judge whether pictures of either a male or a female could apply to sentences containing generic "he," "they" or "he-or-she." For example, a student would be given a sentence like "When someone listens to the record player, he will often sing along." The student would then be shown a picture of either a male or female performing this action and asked whether the picture applied to the sentence. While male pictures were judged unequivocally to be applicable to sentences containing all generic forms, and female pictures to be applicable to sentences containing "they" or "he-or-she," 20 percent of the students reported that female pictures did not apply to sentences containing the generic "he."[9]

But again Strauss has missed the significance of the experiment, and he has misunderstood just what it shows. The use of a picture in the experimental situation introduces an important subtlety. A picture cannot directly express a *general* truth. A picture, by its very nature, is *particular*. It shows an image of a particular person listening to a particular record player. Now the sentence uses generic "he." Generic "he" evokes a particular male example to represent the general truth. How do we represent this feature in a picture? Obviously, by using a male example in the picture. Using a female example in the picture is not quite as appropriate.

Some people may focus on the general nature of the sentence ("When *someone* . . .") and decide a picture of a female is applicable, while others will focus on the single example used to represent the general truth ("*he* will often sing along"), and they will decide that a picture of a female is not appropriate at all. This is because the picture cannot directly represent the general truth expressed with "someone" or "anyone." The best that it can do is to give a particular example. Following the lead of the male-marked generic, the best example to give is male. A picture of a female does not exactly "apply to the sentence," in the sense that it does not match the male representative element present in the sentence.

Thus, what the experiment actually shows is that people are sensitive to the male-marking of generic "he." It does not show that anyone misunderstood anything. The students were not asked whether *by implication* the sentence included females. They were asked whether a picture "applied to the sentence," and "applied to" is a very vague phrase. Some students

---

[9]Ibid., 142–43; from W. Martyna, "Comprehension of the Generic Masculine: Inferring 'She' from 'He,'" paper presented at the American Psychological Association, 85th Annual Convention, San Francisco, August 1977.

understandably would look for a close "match" between the picture and the sentence (including a representative male), and others would not. The experiment shows no more than what we have already observed in our earlier discussion of generic "he" (Chapters 13–14).

E. The limitations of decontextualized experiments

Some general features of experiments of this kind should also produce caution. Psycholinguistic experiments typically take place in carefully isolated and controlled "experimental environments." A student comes into a room with a researcher and is given a sentence to interpret. But the sentence has no context from real-life communication. This lack of ordinary context produces unusual effects. As we say in biblical interpretation, "a text without a context is a pretext." Without the full context of human living, sentences take on ambiguities that they do not possess in real life. Context becomes particularly important in dealing with pronoun reference and indeed all kinds of reference. Reference is reference to something *in the situation, in the context*. Without a context in life, reference is bound to go astray.

For example, take the sentence, "When someone listens to the record player, he will often sing along." The researcher gives a student this sentence as an isolated test sentence, but there is no effective human communicative context. In the absence of a specific context, listeners must invent contexts in their minds, and any number of possibilities present themselves.

One possible context a listener might picture is where Abe, speaking to Barbara, has a definite person in view but does not care to identify that person by name. Abe says, "When someone [a definite person whom I know and am thinking of] listens to the record player, he will often. . . ." In this context, "he" gives away the sex of the person, because "he" is not generic. It refers only to the one person that Abe has in mind. Another context might be one in which Abe has been talking to Barbara about a certain musical society that in fact only has male members. "When someone [in the society] listens . . ." Clearly "someone" has exclusively male range, and so therefore does the word "he." Or we picture a context in which Abe and Barbara are talking about how people in general use record players. Then the context indicates that Abe's "someone" applies broadly, including men and women.

Students being tested cannot focus on just one of these contexts, and so it is no wonder that results appear to show "confusion" or "ambiguity." Any of us could look "confused" if we had to interpret sentences without a context.

What is behind this pattern of experimentation? Many experiments in linguistics and psychology take place in carefully isolated and controlled environments. In imitation of the natural sciences, social scientists may try to fix and control all but one or two "variables" in an experiment. They carefully isolate the experiment from the full flux and multidimensional complexity of human interaction in the world. No doubt certain interesting results accrue from such isolation. We can study with great intensity the patterns produced in a small piece of human behavior.

But when we deal with human communication, there is also a danger. The danger is that we underestimate the importance of contexts—contexts of situation and contexts of the full persons whose personal histories are stored up in them as they participate in a supposedly controlled experimental environment.

Linguists themselves are of two minds here. Some like the advantages and the apparent "rigor" deriving from an experimental environment. Others stress again and again the importance of context as indispensable for human communication.[10] Whatever our preferences for linguistic specialization, we must recognize that, when dealing with issues of pronouns and reference, *decontextualized experiments will regularly produce anomalous results*.

F. The greater importance of data from ordinary usage

We conclude, then, that *data taken from ordinary use are of much greater weight*. Observations about pronominal use in the secular press and secular publications, and about how ordinary people interpret such use, are of much greater weight than any amount of antiseptic experiments with artificially produced sentences.

The full weight of human experience through the centuries confirms this conclusion. Hundreds of languages, through centuries of human communication, have used generic pronouns. The particular structures of pronominal systems and gender systems differ from language to language. But throughout human experience gender-marked generics are intelligible. Given a *real* context of real human communication, the alleged misunderstandings disappear.

---

[10]References to the indispensability of context are legion. To cite a few instances at random: Kenneth L. Pike, *Language in Relation to a Unified Theory of the Structure of Human Behavior*, 2d ed. (The Hague/Paris: Mouton, 1967), 25–27, 33; Kenneth L. Pike, *Linguistic Concepts: An Introduction to Tagmemics* (Lincoln, NB: University of Nebraska, 1982), 107–36; Victor H. Yngve, *From Grammar to Science: New Foundations for General Linguistics* (Amsterdam/Philadelphia: John Benjamins, 1996), 6; Robert E. Longacre, "Discourse Analysis: Its Continuing Relevance and Its Relation to Cognitive Studies," *LACUS Forum XXIV*, ed. Sheila Embleton (Chapel Hill, NC: Linguistic Association of Canada and the United States, 1998), 463–64; Ferenc Havas, "On the 'Logicist' Paradigm in Linguistics and Some of Its Possible Alternatives," *LACUS Forum XXIV*, ed. Sheila Embleton (Chapel Hill, NC: Linguistic Association of Canada and the United States, 1998), 449–50.

Finally, we must remember that our actual focus is Bible translation. How can we test whether people understand a Bible translation? The most relevant "experiment" of all would be to circulate among Christians, who are the primary people who actually read the Bible and pay attention to the Bible's intended *context*. We then open the Bible to a passage that uses generic "he," such as Matthew 16:24,

> Then Jesus said to his disciples, "If anyone would come after me, he must deny himself and take up his cross and follow me."

We ask our fellow Christian first to look at the context of the passage, to read the whole passage, and then to tell us whether Debbie (a particular woman known to the person) is included in the implications of the passage.

Why did Strauss not mention an experiment like this one, which he could easily have performed himself? And what would the results of this experiment be? We hardly need to perform the experiment, because we already know what the results would be—people would immediately agree that Debbie is included in the implications of the passage. The problem, if there is one, is not that some people *misunderstand* the inclusion of women, but rather that some people *dislike* the connotations that they may see in male representation.

G. The deeper issue: ideology

We return, then, to the main point. In modern life, the egalitarian ideology of "fairness" has become so ingrained that it is second nature. Producing predominantly male examples or pictures is politically unacceptable. What more argument do the researchers need?

The issue, as usual, is ideology. Ideology says that unsymmetrical use of male representatives or pictures is wrong. This ideology is the necessary undercurrent that moves people from the actual experimental data to the conclusion that "man" (for the race) and generic "he" must be eliminated. The experimental data do not show "misunderstanding." They only confirm our position.

H. What about a niche translation for feminists?

We have now completed our survey of the responses and objections that arise from people defending gender-neutral translations. It is time to come to a conclusion. But first, now that we have all the arguments in hand, we should take up again the point raised in Chapter 15 about niche translations, that is, translations targeted at specific needs and even specific ideological positions.

In Chapter 15 we indicated that we are opposed to producing a niche translation for particular ideological groups. But to further illustrate the debate, let us suppose that, against all wisdom, we have decided to produce such a niche translation. Perhaps we want especially to address those who perceive generic "he" as "insensitive." No, let us make it hard for ourselves. Let us suppose that we have targeted only a much narrower group, namely hard-core non-Christian feminists and egalitarians. Then what?

How would we determine translation policy? We would do just as we have done in the preceding chapters. We must determine whether generic "he" and various other options are usable or unusable. If they are unusable, we must find usable alternatives, even if we lose some meaning nuances in the process.

Very well. How do we determine usability? Partly, by seeing whether generic "he" is understood, whether it is still in use among the target addressees, whether it is perceived as "insensitive," whether it has bad connotations, and so on.

What is the result? Lo and behold, we find that generic "he" is still understood. Psychological experiments, when properly interpreted, are quite compatible with such understanding (Chapter 17). Feminists still read secular publications like newspapers and magazines (Chapter 16).

We also find that generic "he" is currently used by some feminists, in the form of the oscillating use. In this context, it is not insensitive or offensive (Chapter 15). And if its use were to become less frequent they could infer its meaning from the ordinary use of "he," or by analogy with generic "she" (Chapter 16).

Well and good. So we would decide to go ahead and use it when we needed it to express nuances of meaning faithfully. If we use generic "he" in a Bible verse, the offensive element is not in generic "he," but in the context, that is, the Bible's pattern of thought, which we are not at liberty to change (see Chapter 15). We conclude that to avoid generic "he," even in the case of this hypothetical niche translation, would be unfaithful to the Word of God, because it would unnecessarily forfeit nuances of meaning that we could otherwise convey.

Suppose now that, abandoning our obligation to be faithful to God's Word, we nevertheless go ahead and produce a gender-neutral niche translation that eliminates generic "he." It goes out and circulates among non-Christian feminists. One of their number, Carol, comes upon a copy. She begins to read it. Through the work of the Holy Spirit in her heart, she puts her faith in Christ. She joins a church, grows, and eventually moves on to using a mainstream translation. After some years, she goes to seminary, learns Greek and Hebrew, and becomes a Bible scholar. She evaluates what our translation did. Eventually, she meets us, the ones who produced the niche translation. She says:

> So you are the ones who produced the translation for non-Christian feminists. I appreciate what you were trying to do with it. And God used it in my life. I was so extreme a feminist in those days. Who

knows? If I had picked up a mainstream translation, I might have been so turned off by the generic "he's" that I would have put it down and refused to read further. Instead, I did read further, and eventually I came to faith in Christ.

I praise God for bringing me to faith through your translation, and I praise God that in his providence he brought the translation into my life.

But I have one complaint. In spite of the best of intentions, your translation was not fully faithful to the pattern of thought in God's Word. And you were not fully faithful to me either, because you shaded the truth rather than giving it to me as straight as you could. If, when I was beginning to read your translation, I had found out about what you had done, I probably would have thrown the translation in your face, and told you that I am not impressed with people who claim to follow truth alone and then succumb to pragmatism.

God did use your translation in my life, and it became a great blessing. But he used it in spite of your less-than-perfect faithfulness. He brought good out of a wrong that was done, as he always does. But the fact that he brought a good result does not imply that the means that you used were also good.

Perhaps you thought you were being faithful. In fact, you thought that you were being more faithful by removing the bad connotations. But the "bad connotations" that I would have seen were there in the original too. You didn't recognize it, but you were not making just a neutral adjustment to style, but an adjustment to a modern pattern of thought that does not like male examples. Hence, you were not being fully faithful to God's Word.

And even if we were to look at the question from a pragmatic angle, we cannot second-guess God. We cannot guess all the ways that God may use his Word. In his wisdom he could have used another way to overcome my resistance to the gospel, a way that did not involve this compromise. Why might there not be occasions when radical non-Christian feminists are uninterested in the Bible until we point out that it has nonegalitarian thought patterns, extending down even to the level of its pronouns? And then the feminists may be interested because they are angry enough to engage us in conversation. And then they may hear the real message that otherwise they might not have stayed long enough to hear.

The fact is, if we try to become too smart in adjusting to all the alleged problems that readers will have with the Bible, we end up in spite of our best intentions trying to be wiser than God. But we are not. "The fear of the LORD is the beginning of knowledge" (Prov. 1:7, NIV).

I.   Conclusion

Where have we come? We have seen that we need generic "he" in order to convey meaning with maximal accuracy (Chapter 13). We have seen that resistance to it is ideologically generated (Chapter 14). We have looked at the concerns of those who fear using generic "he" in translation, and have seen that they do not stand up (Chapters 15–17). Generic "he" is still being used (Chapter 16), and many examples can be found in the secular press. Hence, it is usable.

In fact, the "problem" with generic "he" is not with a single occurrence but with the pattern of thought in the Bible, a pattern that more often than not uses male examples as a starting point to express or illustrate truths that apply to both men and women. This pattern of thought a translator is not free to change or tone down in translation.

CHAPTER 18

More Issues in Translating Gender: Man, Son of Man, Fathers, Brother, Son, and the Extent of the Changes

In this chapter we consider other kinds of expressions that gender-neutral translations undertake to change—changes in terms such as "man" (used as a name for the human race), "the man" or "a man" (used to specify a male example), "son of man," "fathers," "son/sons," and "brother/brothers."

A. The use of "man" for the human race

Where other translations have "man" as a designation for the human race, gender-neutral translations look for a replacement. This is evident in two passages in Genesis.

Genesis 1:26–27

RSV: Then God said, "Let us make *man* in our image, after our likeness; and let them have dominion. . . ." So God created *man* in his own image, in the image of God he created him; male and female he created them.

NRSV: Then God said, "Let us make *humankind* in our image, according to our likeness; and let them have dominion . . ." So God created *humankind* in his image, in the image of God he created them; male and female he created them.

NIVI: Then God said, "Let us make *human beings* in our image, in our likeness, and let them rule . . ." So God created *human beings* in his own image, in the image of God he created them; male and female he created them.

NLT: Then God said, "Let us make *people* in our image, to be like ourselves. They will be masters over all life . . ." So God created *people* in his own image; God patterned them after himself; male and female he created them.[1]

Genesis 5:1–2

RSV: When God created *man*, he made him in the likeness of God. Male and female he created them, and he blessed them and named them *Man* when they were created.

NRSV: When God created *humankind*, he made them in the likeness of God. Male and female he created them, and he blessed them and named them *"Humankind"* when they were created.

NIVI: When God created *human beings*, he made them in the likeness of God. He created them male and female and blessed them. And when they were created, he called them *"human beings."*

NLT: When God created *people*, he made them in the likeness of God. He created them male and female, and he blessed them and called them *"human."*[2]

I.   Is the name "man" important for the human race?

Is there any problem with such translations? The problem has to do with the name the Bible gives to the human race. Naming, in the context of the Bible, is not merely a matter of assigning some arbitrary sound to a particular object. According to Exodus 34:5, the "name" of God is a summary of God's character (see also Exod. 3:13–15). Likewise, a name that God assigns to a human being makes a statement about God's designs for that person: note the change of Abram to Abraham (Gen. 17:5), or Sarai to Sarah (Gen. 17:15), or Jacob to Israel (Gen. 32:28).

Therefore the name God gives the human race is significant!

Now in Genesis 1–5 we see a use of words that connects the naming of man, woman, and the race with the headship of Adam. In English there are different words for "Adam" and "the man" but the Hebrew word is the same, *'ādām*. The Hebrew word *'ādām* is both a designation for the first man ("Then the LORD God said, 'It is not good that the *man* should be alone,'" Gen. 2:18), the name of Adam ("When *Adam* had lived a hundred and thirty years . . . ," Gen. 5:3), and the word used for the whole human race ("Then God said, 'Let us make *man* in our image, after our likeness; and let them have dominion . . . ,'" in Gen. 1:26–27).[3] The matter comes into some particular focus in Genesis 5:2, because of the explicit mention of naming. God "named them *Man* [*'ādām*] when they were created" (RSV). If we translate

---

[1]The marginal note attached to "people" in the NLT says, "Hebrew *man*; also in 1:27."
[2]The marginal note attached to "people" and "human" in the NLT says, "Hebrew *man*."
[3]All three senses are found in other occurrences in Gen. 1–5 as well.

'ādām as "man" here, we see some of the connection that is there in Hebrew because the person Adam is called "a man" and the race is called "man."[4]

Of course, the modern objection to such a use of the word "man" as a name for the human race (such as in Gen. 1:26, 27, and 5:2) is the fact that the English word "man" has clear male overtones. Is it then proper to translate 'ādām in Genesis 1:26–27 and 5:2 as "man" and include male overtones in the name of the race, or should we translate with "humanity" or "humankind" or "human beings," words with no male overtones?

The question goes back to the Hebrew word 'ādām. Does the word 'ādām have male overtones? Perhaps not always in the Bible,[5] but certainly in the early chapters of Genesis, where God names the human race. Consider these uses of 'ādām:

Gen. 2:22   and the rib which the LORD God had taken from the *man* he made into a woman and brought her to the *man*.

2:23   Then the *man* said, "This at last is bone of my bones and flesh of my flesh; she shall be called Woman, because she was taken out of Man."

2:25   And the *man* and his wife were both naked, and were not ashamed.

3:8   and the *man* and his wife hid themselves from the presence of the LORD God . . .

3:9   But the LORD God called to the *man*, and said to him, "Where are you?"

3:12   The *man* said, "The woman you put here with me—she gave me some fruit from the tree, and I ate it."

3:20   The *man* called his wife's name Eve . . .

---

[4]D. A. Carson, *The Inclusive Language Debate: A Plea for Realism* (Grand Rapids: Baker, and Leicester: InterVarsity, 1998), says, "Dr. Grudem is partly right: it would be nice to use an English word that would cover both senses, namely, the human race and the male of the human race. But . . . what is really required is not a word that will include only these two senses, but one that will include a third as well, namely, the proper name 'Adam'" (p. 168). We agree that it would be nice if one English word covered all three senses, but of course there is none. Far better, however, to have a word that covers two senses ("man" as a name for the race and as a male human being), and that is clearly connected in the passage to the man Adam, than three different words (such as "humanity," "man," and "Adam") for the three senses, thus showing no connection at all.

[5]Mark Strauss, *Distorting Scripture? The Challenge of Bible Translation and Gender Accuracy* (Downers Grove: InterVarsity, 1998), says, with reference to Wayne Grudem's article in *Christianity Today* (Oct. 27, 1997, p. 28), that "it is sometimes argued that terms like 'ādām and anthrōpos always carry male overtones or connotations." This is another example of taking a specific, narrow statement that we have made and turning it into a sweeping generalization that we did not make (see also p. 130, n. 30, above, and also p. 190, n. 2). What Grudem did claim on the page cited by Strauss was that 'ādām has male overtones *in the opening chapters of Genesis.* The sense it has elsewhere in the Bible is another matter. Grudem similarly did not claim that anthrōpos always carries male overtones, for Colorado Springs Guideline A.5 allows the plural of anthrōpos to be translated as "people," not "men."

When we come, then, to the naming of the human race in Genesis 5:2 (reporting an event before the Fall), it would be evident that God was using a name that had clear male overtones. In the first four chapters the word *'adam* had been used thirteen times in a male-specific way: eight times to mean "man" in distinction from woman, and a further five times (Gen. 3:17, 21; 4:1, 25; 5:1) as a name for Adam in distinction from Eve. (The number is actually greater than this, because in the larger narrative it is clear that references to "the man" prior to the creation of Eve are also referring to a specific male human being: see the twelve additional instances of *'adam* in 2:5, 7 [twice], 8, 15, 16, 18, 19 [twice], 20 [twice], and 21.)

Then after these thirteen (or more) male-specific uses of *'adam*, we read Genesis 5:2:

> Male and female he created them, and he blessed them and named them *Man* (*'adam*) when they were created.

The male overtones attaching to *'adam* in the first four chapters would certainly remain in the readers' mind at this verse.

We are troubled to see that Mark Strauss apparently denies that some of the connotations or overtones attaching to this Hebrew word in this context are part of the meaning of the Bible at this point.[6]

2. Conclusion: "Man" is the most accurate translation for the name of the human race in Genesis 1–5

In any case, in Genesis 1:26–27 and 5:2 the word "man" occurred in all previous English Bibles (that is, all Bibles known to us prior to the inclusive language Bibles in the 1980s). Translators apparently thought that, in translating *'adam* in Genesis 1:26–27 and 5:2, one might best use an English word "man" that is both a name for the human race and that carries male overtones.

Moreover, these Genesis passages in their foundational character create the potential for subtle connotative resonances with the total thinking of Hebrew speakers about sexuality. For example, the fact that Adam has a name that is also the name for the whole race suggests that he is a

---

[6]Mark Strauss at this point objects that there may be "baggage" attaching to the Hebrew word *'ādām* which was not in the words God originally spoke "when he named the human race." Strauss says,

> How do we know what language God and Adam spoke together? The language used by the author of Genesis could well have arisen millennia after the creation of the world, and the Hebrew *'ādām* could itself be a translation (with cultural and societal baggage) of an entirely different term (Strauss, *Distorting*, 138).

Of course we do not know what language God used in speaking to Adam. But with the issue of the name of the human race, the two main passages in view are Genesis 1:26–27 and Genesis 5:2. In Genesis 1:26, God speaks to himself, not to Adam. In Genesis 5:2 it says simply "And when they were created, he called them 'man'" (NIV). It does not say that God announced a specific name *to Adam*. Perhaps it is referring back to Genesis 1:26–27, where God

representative for the race. And of course, later passages, Romans 5:12–21 and 1 Corinthians 15:21–23, directly assert that he is a representative, whose pattern passes to all his descendants. He is also a representative for his wife, as appears in the fact that a commandment addressed to him in Genesis 2:16–17 applies also to his wife in Genesis 3. The complementary relation between Adam and Eve sets a pattern for complementary, rather than interchangeable, egalitarian roles later in Scripture (see Eph. 5:22–33).

Of course, we cannot capture everything in translation, so the word "man" in English, used to designate the human race, is not an absolutely exact equivalent to 'ādām in Genesis 1:26 and 5:2. But we cannot find anything better—"man" in English is the only word that can be used to designate the race and also carry male overtones and associations,[7] which is just what 'ādām does in the Hebrew text of Genesis 1 and 5. Moreover, it is easy to overestimate the alleged problems with using "man" with this meaning. For the most part, it is not that people do not understand such a meaning, but that some people do not like it. Neither would they like what Genesis 1–2 and 5:2 do in the original Hebrew—for more or less the same reasons. In both Hebrew and English a term with male connotations designates the whole human race.

---

speaks to himself. Strauss apparently overlooks this fact when he focuses on God's speaking to Adam.

(Of course God did speak to Adam [as Gen. 1:28–30 and 2:16 show], but Genesis does not say that within one of these speeches he announced to Adam the name of the human race. Strauss is also wrong to state that "Grudem's claim" includes "his assumption that God was necessarily speaking Hebrew when he named the human race" [*Distorting*, 138]. Grudem did not assume this, and it is irrelevant to the issue.)

But the deeper problem is that Strauss's statement deflects us from what God actually says in Genesis to uncontrolled speculations about what God might have meant but did not say in Genesis. As a result, it tempts people to doubt some of the subtle connotations of what God *did* say. For one thing, Strauss's statement appears to suggest that the connotations of 'ādām in Hebrew are "baggage" to be ignored. That is, we can safely cut away those aspects of meaning. But that implies that Genesis 5:2 in Hebrew, which is what God spoke as his own Word to us, does not represent precisely what Strauss thinks we should pay attention to. We hope that Strauss will reconsider this statement, since it implies that the words in the Hebrew text of Genesis are not totally reliable. It implies that the original words of the Bible (the Hebrew text, not an English translation) have a meaning that we cannot trust, a meaning some aspects of which ought to be ignored. This position seems inconsistent with a belief in biblical inerrancy, which we believe Strauss does hold. It is a troubling statement. (Strauss's response to this point [in private correspondence] is to say that two different senses of a lexeme "do not necessarily impose their meaning on each other," as he explained just after the passage we quoted from his page 138. We agree with the principle in general but stand by our argument here that the close contextual relationship between the examples in Genesis 1–5 makes it inevitable that Hebrew readers would see the connections and hear the male overtones, which should not be concealed from an English reader.)

[7]Actually, the related word "mankind" can also designate the race and carry male overtones at the same time. However, the intertextual connections with the same Hebrew word used to mean "man" as a male individual are lost with the translation "mankind," for we cannot say, "the *mankind* and his wife were naked and they were not ashamed" (Gen. 2:25). So it is not clear that anything is gained by the word "mankind."

Gender-neutral translations, while preserving the main point of God's creation of the human race, nevertheless leave out the connotation of a male representative by translating Genesis 1:26–27 and 5:1–2 with "humankind," "human beings," or "people" instead of "man." Commendably, they may include a footnote with some explanation of the connection with Adam.[8] However, footnotes do not solve all the problems, for most readers do not read footnotes, and many who do will not consider the footnote part of the translation, part of the "real Bible." In addition, some electronic versions do not include the footnotes.[9]

Because of concerns like those outlined in the discussion to this point, the Colorado Springs Guidelines affirmed the following:

A.3. "Man" should ordinarily be used to designate the human race, for example in Genesis 1:26–27; 5:2; Ezekiel 29:11; and John 2:25.

Supporters of inclusive-language Bibles at this point fail to explain why they would choose an English translation (such as "humanity") that will bring over into English one significant *part* of the meaning of *'ādām*, while rejecting an English translation ("man") which brings over *more* of the original meaning into English.

And here the question must be faced, why would we seek to have a translation that *conceals* the male overtones of the Hebrew word? Does this preference really indicate a desire for greater accuracy in translation, or do we prefer it because we are somehow embarrassed by the male overtones of the Hebrew word, and we recognize that modern readers will find that part of the meaning to be offensive?

In fact, it is precisely the male overtones of the word "man" which led feminists in the first place to say that such a name for the human race was offensive. It is reasonable to conclude that such feminists would have objected to the procedure of God himself described in Genesis 5:2: "male and female he created them, and he blessed them *and named them 'ādām when they were created.*"

3.   The unity of the human race obscured by plural terms

There is an additional problem with the NIVI's plural term "human beings" and the NLT's plural term "people"—they obscure the unity of the human race that is hinted by the singular term "man." God's statement, "Let us make *man* in our image, after our likeness; and let them have dominion . . ." includes both the singular unity of the race ("man") and the

---

[8]In Genesis 1:26 and 5:2 (but not Genesis 1:27 and 5:1), the NIVI includes a footnote: "Hebrew *'ādām*, traditionally *man*." With all four verses the NRSV includes the footnote, "Heb[rew] *'ādām*." The NLT also includes footnotes, cited above.

[9]For example, *Bible Windows* 4.0 includes the NRSV without footnotes.

plurality ("and let them"), but "Let us make *people* in our image" diminishes the sense of the unity of the race.

4.   The use of "man" for the human race in English today

But is "man" with this meaning still part of English? In fact, we still find the word used in this way in standard secular publications.
(In the following quotations, italics are ours.)

Early *Man's* Journey out of Africa (*U.S. News & World Report*, Nov. 27, 1995, 18, headline).

Somewhere between the law of the wild and the nature of *man* lies . . . *The Edge* (August, 1997, movie preview for the movie *The Edge*, starring Anthony Hopkins as billionaire lost in frozen wilderness).

For *man*, autumn is a time of harvest, of gathering together. For nature, it is a time of sowing, of scattering abroad (*Reader's Digest*, September 1997, 61).

The contest for supremacy between *man* and machine may in fact be the dominant struggle for the Air Force in coming years (*U.S. News and World Report*, Sept. 29, 1997, 24).

After showing how a new navigational system lets a driver avoid a traffic jam caused by turtle migration, the commercial says that "*man* has finally caught up with nature (October 12, 1997, national network television commercial for new car navigation system from Phillips).

"But it's already out of the hands of God, Charlie," she argued. "This is modern technology created by *man*, pushing the envelope . . ." (Nancy Snyderman, ABC television's medical correspondent for *Good Morning America*, in an interview on Oct. 30, 1997, in a comment about the McCaugheys' decision to keep all their babies, as quoted in *World*, November 15, 1997, 21).

Louise Cooper-Lovelace has just completed the 1997 Discovery Channel Eco-Challenge, one of the toughest of a proliferating series of *man*-against-nature sporting events. She and her mates of the Endeavor team have raced nonstop for six days, 18 hours, and 33 minutes . . . (*Hemispheres* [passenger magazine for United Airlines], April, 1998, 73).

[writing about authors Mark Twain, Herman Melville, and William Faulkner] What all of them carry away from the ruins of their religion is a deep uncertainty that *man's* destiny is really in his own hands and a powerful anger that it cannot convincingly be made to seem so (David Lyle Jeffrey, "A Literary God: The novelist as lapsed Calvinist" (a review of Alfred Kazin's book *God and the American Writer*), *Christianity Today* [April 6, 1998], 66).

Man and nature in the hills of Kansas (headline, *Chicago Tribune*, August 2, 1998, sec. 8, 1).

The Seekers: The Story of Man's *Continuing Quest to Understand His World* (title of 1998 book by Daniel Boorstin (New York: Random House) as reported in a review by Michael Lind in *The New York Times Book Review*, September 6, 1998, p. 10). The review notes that Boorstin is a former Librarian of Congress and that he has won the Pulitzer Prize, the National Book Award, the Bancroft Prize and the Francis Parkman Prize, all distinguished literary achievements.

History is not *man's* only teacher and guide (*Arkansas Democrat-Gazette*, Sept. 13, 1998, editorial page retrieved from AOC compilation of today's editorial pages).

Holy Days a time to right yourself with *man*, God [headline] . . . I use the secular New Year to "revisit" my vows to God and my fellow *man*. Happy New Year and Shana Tova (G. Joel Gordon in the *Daily Herald*, [suburban Chicago], Saturday, Sept. 26, 1998, sec. 5, 2).

Man depends primarily on his sense of sight . . . but in water vision is more limited (Shedd Aquarium, Chicago, notice explaining exhibit on "Fish Senses," November 29, 1998).

The neverending battle between *man* and nature has fascinated film-makers for years (Blockbuster in-store video ad for the movie *Twister*, heard in Libertyville, Ill., Blockbuster store, December 15, 1998).

Thus in their darkest economic days, Americans were both invoking *man's* oldest symbols of durable success and praying to the gods for help. . . . *Man's* natural environment comes with diseases and a short life expectancy (MIT economist Lester C. Thurow, *Building Wealth: The New Rules for Individuals, Companies, and Nations in a Knowledge-Based Economy* [New York: Harper Collins, 1999], xi, 181).

Cold, snow good for *man's* soul (by Jeremy Manier and Sue Ellen Christian, *Chicago Tribune*, January 10, 1999, 1).

We hope this means they are retiring the awful word "contagion," suggesting as it did that forces beyond the control of mortal *man* were causing these countries' economic problems (*Wall Street Journal*, May 4, 1999, sec. A, 22)

Approximately how many *man*-made objects are orbiting the earth today? (*USA Today*, May 12, 1999, B.1).

American campuses can foster some of the most craven and anti-intellectual behaviour known to *man* (Amanda Foreman, "Take me away from the dreaming spires," *The Sunday Times* [London *Times*], May 30, 1999, sec. 5, 4).

And they envision a world in which supercomputing power is so pervasive and inexpensive that it literally becomes an integral part of every *man*-made object (*New York Times*, July 16, 1999, 1).

Why *man* was given five senses (caption with a picture of a glass of Guinness beer on a billboard seen on Dan Ryan expressway, Chicago, July 28, 1999).

HOW *MAN* EVOLVED: Amazing new discoveries reveal the secrets of our past (*Time*, front cover, Aug. 23, 1999).

This team brings medical miracles to *man's* best friends: Emergency Vets (*Reader's Digest*, October, 1999, front cover).

The theory of evolution . . . said that differences among species like *man* and apes were the result of different mechanisms of natural selection; *man* and apes, though descended from a common ancestor, the theory holds (*Chicago Tribune*, Oct. 24, 1999, sec. 1, 10).

Whether or not modern *man* acknowledges having some Neanderthal genes . . . (Kathrine E. Bobick, letter to the editor, *Time* magazine, Nov. 1, 1999, 15).

Man and the Economy (headline from editorial in *The Wall Street Journal*, Dec. 28, 1999, A18).

Man and Democracy (headline from editorial in *The Wall Street Journal*, Dec. 29, 1999, A14).

Man and Poverty (headline from editorial in *The Wall Street Journal*, Dec. 30, 1999, p. A12).

Man and Governance (headline from editorial in *The Wall Street Journal*, Dec. 31, 1999, p. A10).

Man has worked hard these many centuries to organize his complex self . . . into a social organization that is at once civil and free (*The Wall Street Journal*, Dec. 31, 1999, A10).

The World Almanac is the most useful reference book known to modern man. (*Los Angeles Times*, as quoted on the back cover of *The World Almanac and Book of Facts 2000* (Mahwah, NJ: Primedia, 1999). The front cover proclaims this book "#1 New York Times Bestseller."

I do not expect that machines will be built which can understand abstract concepts or exercise the other powers that philosophers traditionally attributed to the 'active intellect' in *man*. . . . As a human enterprise, science magnifies *man*. . . . The scientist who succumbs to materialism is conflicted in his view of *man* (University of Delaware theoretical particle physicist Stephen M. Barr, writing in *First Things*, Jan., 2000, 18).

Years ago, *man* thought everything revolved around the earth . . . (cartoon caption in *USA Today*, Jan. 18, 2000, A14).

Does that mean *man* is to blame for the increase [in the earth's temperature]? No, the panel said (*The Washington Times, National Weekly Edition*, Jan. 24–30, 2000, 37).

Man has an instinctive need to find a better place to live. Proof: you moved out of your first place after only nine months (caption on advertisement with photo of ultrasound of unborn child in *The Wall Street Journal*, Feb. 3, 2000, B17).

Man has been obsessed with death as long as obsessions have been around (University of Louisville biology professor Lee Alan Dugatkin, in the *Louisville Courier-Journal*, Feb. 7, 2000, A7)[10]

The Associated Press Stylebook and Libel Manual (1994) says of the terms *"man, mankind"* that "Either may be used when both men and women are involved and no other term is convenient" (p. 120; repeated in updated 2000 edition, p. 153).

"Man" with this meaning (referring to the human race as a whole) always occurs in the singular in English (never "men"). Also, it always occurs without any article or quantifier (not "a man" or "the man"; also not "no man," "any man," or "every man"). It is thus easy to distinguish from uses of the word "man" to designate male human beings exclusively.[11]

B. Eliminating "son of man" in the Old Testament

In the interests of gender sensitivity, the NRSV systematically removed the phrase "son of man" from the Old Testament. It occurs 106 times in the RSV Old Testament, but zero times in the NRSV Old Testament. Especially troubling is Daniel 7:13, "with the clouds of heaven there came one like a son of man" (RSV), which is changed to "one like a human being" (NRSV).

---

[10]The following examples are different from those in the list above, in that they illustrate the use of "men" (not "man") to mean "people in general." We are not arguing that this use is necessary to convey essential meaning in Bible translation today, but we list these recent examples only to show that even this use of the plural word "men" to mean "people, human beings" is not entirely obsolete:

The equality of all *men* before the law is as precious to Americans as any of the animating national traditions elsewhere (*The Wall Street Journal*, October 9, 1998, sec. A, 12).

The critical leap from mice to *men* (headline, *Chicago Tribune*, October 17, 1999, front page).

Responsibility without accountability 'according to law' undermines the core foundation of the Constitution, the principle known as the Rule of Law (as opposed to the rule of *men*), without which our Constitution is no more than a piece of paper . . . (Thomas Moorer, "Making an example of . . . ," *The Washington Times, National Weekly Edition*, December 21–27, 1998, 30).

Indeed, one of the greatest ideas to emerge during the millennium we are leaving is that all *men* are equal in the eyes of the law (*The Wall Street Journal*, Dec. 29, 1999, A14).

[11]Mark Strauss appears to have overlooked this clear distinction between "man" without any article, referring to the human *race*, and "man" with an article or quantifier, referring to individuals. As we have already made clear in Chapter 11, both we and the Colorado Springs

Readers of the NRSV could easily miss the fact that Jesus refers to this passage when he tells the high priest, "Hereafter, you will see the Son of man seated at the right hand of Power, and coming on the clouds of heaven" (Matt. 26:64, RSV). The phrase in Daniel 7:13 is made gender neutral, breaking the force of the linkage with the New Testament.

The NRSV also changes "son of man" in Psalm 8:4. "What is *man* that thou art mindful of him, and the *son of man* that thou dost care for him?" (RSV) becomes, "What are *human beings* that you are mindful of them, *mortals* that you care for them?" (NRSV). The NRSV introduces almost identical changes in Hebrews 2:6, which quotes Psalm 8:4 as follows: "What are *human beings* that you are mindful of them, or *mortals*, that you care for them?" In another passage (Ps. 80:17, NRSV), "son of man" is neutralized to "the one."

The NCV is also consistently gender neutral in these passages. It changes "son of man" to "human being" in Daniel 7:13 and "human beings" in Psalm 8:4, and has God repeatedly calling Ezekiel "human" rather than "son of man." (The NIVI, however, only avoids "man" and "son of man" in Psalm 8:4, not in Psalm 80:17, Daniel, or Ezekiel.)

"Son of man" in the Old Testament presents complex difficulties for translators who want to avoid the male connotations of the phrase. In some

---

Guidelines (A. 5, 6, 7, 8) affirm that in generic statements translators can use words like "anyone," "a person," and so on, instead of the generic use of "a man."

Now Strauss has a whole chapter entitled "Inclusive Language Related to Human Beings: Generic 'Man' and 'He'" (*Distorting*, Chapter 5, 103–39). In one subsection, entitled "Common Techniques for Avoiding the Masculine Generics 'Man' and 'He,'" he clearly deals with cases of the generic use of "a man" being replaced with "someone," "everyone," and so on (117–27), a procedure that is not in dispute.

But then at a later point he refers to uses of "man" for the human race using the same term, "generic 'man'" (p. 141 title of the section). In a single paragraph he lumps together "man, being a mammal, breastfeeds his young" with "a man for all seasons" and "no man is an island" (p. 142). "Man, being a mammal . . ." uses "man" without any article for the human race. (The particular expression startles us, of course, because "man" still contains a meaning aspect suggesting a male representative, and this is not in tune with breastfeeding.) "A man for all seasons" represents a completely different phenomenon, because for some hearers it refers to a particular male human being, Sir Thomas More. In that case, it is not a generic use at all. "No man is an island" may be generic, but might also be a statement to the effect that men need women. Such lumping together does not further the discussion, but only confuses it by failing to distinguish disputed usages from undisputed ones.

Strauss exhibits the same confusion when he discusses our position directly. Referring to a previously published version of much of the list of examples of "man" for the race, he says, "Grudem provides an extensive list of examples of generic 'man' and 'he' from the popular press and contemporary literature" (Strauss, *Distorting*, 144–145). Strauss then says, "Grudem is building a straw man. . . . The question that Grudem should have asked is not *can* 'man' still mean 'human being,' but rather is this the *best* rendering?" (p. 145). Strauss here shifts the discussion from "man" used as a name for the human race to the generic use of "a man." Strauss says, "Someone could argue, of course, that 'Sophia is a man' is a perfectly acceptable sentence, since 'man' here means 'human being' . . . but the sentence still sounds wrong to the reader" (p. 144). Strauss has himself built a "straw man" argument, for he is arguing against a position we do not hold.

instances, as in Daniel 7:13, the phrase definitely has a meaning pointing forward to Christ the Son of Man. In other instances, as in Psalm 8:4, 80:17, and Ezekiel, it is part of a broader, dimmer picture of the idea of representative man.[12] Psalm 8:6 speaks of man's rule over the world, using language reminiscent of Genesis 1:28: "You made him ruler over the works of your hands; you put everything under his feet" (NIV). In particular, God gave dominion to Adam, who represented all human beings. Hebrews 2:6–9 applies the quotation to Christ as the final representative man, the "last Adam" (1 Cor. 15:45), who tasted "death for everyone" (Heb. 2:9).[13] Christ acted as representative, in such a way that the benefits of his work flow to all those who belong to him.

The language in Daniel 7:13 about "one like a son of man" also occurs in a context that suggests the idea of representative man. The "son of man" in Daniel 7:13 receives dominion and is superior to the rule of the kingdoms represented by beasts that preceded him (7:2–8). Adam's rule over the beasts in Genesis is analogous to the dominion of the son of man over bestial kingdoms in Daniel 7.

The idea of representative man appears also to be in the background of Ezekiel. Ezekiel as a prophet is in some respects representative of the remnant of Israel who remain faithful to the Lord. Ezekiel is "son of man." We can add also Psalm 144:3, which uses much of the same language as Psalm 8:4, and Psalm 80:17, which calls the heir to David's throne "the son of man." In Psalm 80:17, the king in David's line is a representative for all the people. Thus the idea of representative man, as well as the phraseology "son of man," connects Psalm 8:4, 80:17, Ezekiel, and Daniel 7:13. By not using "son of man" phraseology in these passages, NRSV obscures the connection of these passages to Christ's self-designation as "Son of man."

We recognize, however, that in other passages "son of man" seems to be a fairly colorless poetic parallel to "man": "God is not a man, that he should lie, nor a *son of man*, that he should change his mind" (Num. 23:19, RSV)." . . . how much less man, who is but a maggot—a *son of man*, who is only a worm!" (Job 25:6, NIV).

In a very loose sense, all the Old Testament passages with "son of man" are connected to the New Testament. When Jesus used the phrase "Son of

---

[12]See, for example, Dan G. McCartney, "*Ecce Homo*: The Coming of the Kingdom as the Restoration of Human Vicegerency," *Westminster Theological Journal* 56/1 (1994): 1–21.

[13]"This [dominion] is predicated not of the individual but of the race, which lost its perfection in Adam and recovers it in Christ" (Joseph A. Alexander, *The Psalms Translated and Explained* [reprint; Grand Rapids: Zondervan, n.d.], 39). "The application to Christ of what this psalm [Ps. 8] says about man is explained by the fact that the incarnate Son was the perfect, indeed the only perfect, man, and that the intention and achievement of his incarnation was precisely to restore to fallen man the dignity and the wholeness of his existence as he reintegrated in himself the grand design of creation. Psalm 8 relates to the whole of mankind, but it finds its true focus pre-eminently in him who is uniquely the Son of man and in whom alone the hurt of mankind is healed" (Philip E. Hughes, *A Commentary on the Epistle to the Hebrews* [Grand Rapids: Eerdmans, 1977], 84).

Man," it is almost certainly built not only on the key passage in Daniel 7:13, but also on the common broader use of "son of man" as a parallel to "man." Christ underlined his identification with humanity using a common Hebrew and Aramaic phrase "son of man." The phrase may have been something of a "mystery title" for some of his hearers, because it was not always transparent that he intended to link it with Daniel 7:13. Only at the end of his earthly life, in a passage like Matthew 26:64, does it become crystal clear even to his enemies that with the title "Son of Man" he was claiming all along to be the fulfillment of Daniel 7:13.

The complexity of the meanings here, as well as the uncertainty about the nature of some of the tantalizing associations, make it impossible for a translator to do everything. For translations that preserve form, the safest option is clearly to preserve "son of man" everywhere. Though it is not idiomatic English, the English reader can analyze it as meaning "someone who is a son of a human being." By implication a person described in this way would himself be human. That is actually not far from the meaning in Hebrew and Aramaic. In addition, many of the occurrences of "son of man" are in poetic contexts. One of the ways in which English poetry distinguishes itself from prose is through phrasing that is strange. Hence the strangeness of "son of man" in English is not in every respect a liability.

Translations that change form will have to find their own way. Because "son of man" does not represent idiomatic English, these translations understandably search for some idiomatic equivalent—but nothing quite does the job. The danger is that in the process they may obscure significant connections with the New Testament title "Son of Man." In the present culture, where the pressure is to *remove* male connotations and male components of meaning, translators should beware of any desire to remove the phrase "son of man" just because the words have male-meaning components that are unpopular in the culture.

Certainly translators should at least preserve "son of man" in those passages where there is a serious possibility of a more direct link to the New Testament: Daniel 7:13; Psalms 8:4; 80:17; and Ezekiel. Psalm 144:3 needs to preserve "son of man" as well, because of its link to Psalm 8:4. Maybe there are other passages with links that we do not see immediately—which is one reason why translations that change form have problems. They never know for sure when they are destroying significant cross-links between verses that use similar phrasing.

The Colorado Springs Guidelines safeguarded against such loss of meaning in Guideline A.9:

> The phrase "son of man" should ordinarily be preserved to retain intra-canonical connections.[14]

---

[14]Carson, *Debate*, has a helpful discussion of the phrase "son of man" (pp. 170–175). He says, "As cumbersome as it is, therefore, on the whole I favor a retention of 'son of man,' at

C. Individual male examples changed to plural groups

When a male figure serves as an example of a general principle, the maleness may disappear in gender-neutral translations.

1.   Old Testament examples with Hebrew *'îsh* ("man") or *geber* ("man")

Psalm 1:1

RSV: Blessed is the *man* who walks not in the counsel of the wicked, nor stands in the way of sinners, nor sits in the seat of scoffers; . . .

NRSV: Happy are *those* who do not follow the advice of the wicked, or take the path that sinners treat, or sit in the seat of scoffers; . . .

NIVI: Blessed are *those* who do not walk in the counsel of the wicked or stand in the way of sinners or sit in the seat of mockers.

NLT: Oh, the joys of *those* who do not follow the advice of the wicked, or stand around with sinners, or join in with scoffers.

The change from singular "man" to plural "those" alters nuances, as we saw in the discussion of generic "he." Moreover, with the singular, the reader tends to picture a single man standing against a multitude of wicked people, sinners, and mockers (the words for evil people here are all plural in Hebrew and in nongender-neutral translations). The contrast between the single man and the plurality of sinners simply drops out when we convert the singulars to plurals.

In addition, Psalm 1:1 starts with the picture of a person who happens to be male. The native speaker of Hebrew reads *ha'îsh*, "the man." The word *'îsh* is frequently used in other places to designate a male human being, as in Genesis 2:24 ("a *man* will leave his father and mother and be united to his wife")—in fact, its most common meaning by far is "man" in the sense of a male human being.[15] Nothing in the immediate context overturns the instinct to assign tentatively the meaning "the man" and to think first of all of a male human being rather than a female.

The native speaker of Hebrew knows, in the back of his mind, that a male-oriented rather than a female-oriented term is likely to be used in a context where the author wants to talk about a sample human being from

---

least in the majority of its Old Testament occurrences, and probably with a brief note to accompany most of them."

[15]See BDB, 35–36. There are special expressions and idioms where the word has other meanings, such as "each" (person), but these do not apply to Psalm 1:1. We do not lack examples to use in determining the meaning, for the word is extremely common, occurring 2,166 times in the OT.

Mark Strauss has a helpful section on the need to retain masculine language in cases "where the principle is general but the illustration envisions a male" (p. 129), but then he fails to apply this sound principle to the case of Psalm 1:1 (pp. 131–132).

within a group composed of both sexes. The sex of the sample person may or may not be germane to the point that the author wishes to make. That is, the reader must determine from the larger context whether the sex of the sample person functions to limit the range of application of the sentence. In some verses it does by virtue of the subject matter. In Exodus 22:16, "A man [Hebrew *'îsh*] seduces a virgin."[16] The context clearly restricts the general principles to males.

But in Psalm 1:1 the context does not restrict the principle. The native speaker therefore holds open the range of application. But meanwhile, partly because of the possibility that the text may actually be specializing to male human beings, the reader pictures a man, a male. This male is then a representative for a truth applying to a larger group. But temporarily the exact composition of the group remains undetermined. (See also the example in Ezekiel 18:5, which begins with a "man" (*'îsh*): "If a man is righteous and does what is lawful and right . . .")

After reading Psalm 1, readers know that the psalm as a whole offers the "man" as a representative, an ideal, to be emulated by readers. He is a model for both men and women. The implicated meaning includes application to many. But the starting point is the picture of one, and that one is male. The maleness is not essential to the *main* point that the psalm makes. But it is there, as a semantic (meaning) component, to the original readers. Gender-neutral translations simply eliminate this meaning component.

In order to prevent such loss of meaning, the CSG stated:

A.4. Hebrew *'îsh* should ordinarily be translated "man" and "men," and Greek *anēr* should almost always be so translated.

A broader summary with regard to *'îsh* may help at this point. We are not saying that "man" or "men" is *always* the appropriate translation of the Hebrew word *'îsh*. The word "ordinarily" in the CSG acknowledges a considerable scope for other kinds of situation. For example, *'îsh* can be used idiomatically with the sense "each one" (as in "each of them [*'îsh*] gave him a piece of money and a ring of gold" (Job 42:11 RSV).[17] *'Îsh* can occur in Hebrew parallelism with other words for human beings, perhaps suggesting that in these contexts the male component of *'îsh* is not prominent (see, for example, Job 32:21; 33:15–17; 34:11; 35:8; 37:7; 38:26). Caution is needed in evaluating these examples, however, since Hebrew parallelism can show contrast or heightened emphasis as well as identity or comparison.[18]

In any case, Psalm 1:1 does not include such parallelism with another term for "man" or human beings. We are trying to be fair to the particular context of Psalm 1:1. As usual, the possible uses of *'îsh* in various contexts,

---

[16]See also Leviticus 15:16; Deuteronomy 22:13; Psalm 80:17; and Proverbs 6:27.
[17]Brown, Driver, and Briggs, *A Hebrew and English Lexicon of the Old Testament* (Oxford: Oxford University Press, 1907), 36.
[18]See the following footnote.

together with the context in any one use, determines the meaning in that use. We are back to the "default" meaning of *'îsh*, "male human being," or "man." If we are to bring over into English as much of the meaning as possible, as accurately as possible, we need to translate Psalm 1:1 "Blessed is the *man* . . ."

Psalm 40:4

NIV: Blessed is the *man* who makes the LORD his trust, . . .

NIVI: Blessed are *those* who make the LORD their trust, . . .

NRSV: Happy are *those* who make the LORD their trust, who do not turn to the proud, to those who go astray after false gods.

NLT: Oh, the joys of *those* who trust the LORD, who have no confidence in the proud, or in those who worship idols.

The underlying Hebrew word is *geber*, a word even more strongly marked than *'îsh* for maleness.[19] Gender-neutral translations try to retain the general principle in the plurals, while deleting the male representative of the principle. This cannot be justified on the basis of sound lexicography

---

[19]"Man as strong, distinguished from women, children, and non-combatants whom he is to defend" (BDB, 150).

Carson cites a number of passages in Job where *geber* occurs in a parallel line with other terms like *'enôsh* ("man, mankind") and *'ādām* ("man, mankind") (Job 4:17; 10:4–5; 14:10; 16:21; 33:17; 34:34; Carson, *Debate*, 122–23). He concludes, "It follows that sharp distinctions in meaning between any two of these terms of the sort that says they cannot occupy the same semantic space, given the right context, is wrong" (p. 124). That is, Carson claims that *geber* has become synonymous with *'ādām* or *'enôsh* in these parallelistic contexts, and has lost its male meaning component. In response, several things need to be said.

First, Hebrew parallelism often uses similar terms, without necessarily collapsing meaning differences between them. James Kugel has effectively argued that parallelistic constructions frequently add extra meaning in the second half, "A, and what's more, B," rather than being purely synonymous restatement, "A and A again" (Kugel, *The Idea of Biblical Poetry: Parallelism and Its History* [New Haven: Yale University Press, 1981]). Carson's very first example, from Job 4:17, says, "Can *'enôsh* ["man"] be more righteous than God? Can *geber* ["man"] be more pure than his Maker?" Does Carson claim that, because of the parallelism, there is no difference in meaning between "righteous" and "pure"? Then how does he know there is no difference between *'enôsh* and *geber*?

Second, Carson here makes a mistake similar to a later one with *huios* and *teknon* (see section F below). He assumes that just because he cannot any longer *see* the difference between two terms within a particular context, there must not any longer *be* any difference. But this is like arguing that there is no difference between "righteous" and "pure," just because Job 4:17 makes the same general theological point about the sinfulness of mankind using either term. Of course, Carson may be right, that the male meaning component of *geber* disappears in contexts like this one. But he may also be wrong. The mere citation of parallelistic occurrences is not decisive one way or the other.

Third, given that BDB, the standard lexicon, indicates there is a male meaning component, the burden of proof is on those who say that it has totally disappeared. Ambiguous cases, such as the cases in Job give us, are not enough.

Fourth, both BDB and Koehler-Bahmgartner (*The Hebrew and Aramaic Lexicon of the Old Testament* [Leiden: Brill, 1994]) acknowledge a usage with the meaning "each" in parallel with *'îsh* in Joel 2:8. But the context is that of war, so one cannot use this passage to prove that *geber*

(the study of the meanings of words). The word *geber* specifically means "man," not "person" or "those who."

Such a procedure is common when gender-neutral translations encounter this type of verse, a verse that uses a specific male example to teach a general truth. (A similar example is Jesus' parable about the wise *man* that built his house on a rock.) The author no doubt expected readers to be able to visualize this specific example and then *apply* it more broadly to people in general, but that broader *application* must be kept distinct from the *example set before readers in* the verse itself.

Micah 2:2

RSV: . . . they oppress a *man* and *his* house, a *man* and *his* inheritance.

NRSV: . . . they oppress *householder* and *house*, *people* and *their* inheritance.

NIVI: They defraud *people* of their homes, they rob *them* of *their* inheritance.

NLT: *No one*'s family or inheritance is safe with you around!

The word underlying the first occurrence of "man" is *geber*, definitely indicating a male human being. In the second occurrence the word is *'îsh*, which also usually designates a male. In the culture of Old Testament times, a man rather than his wife was the owner of the house, and men rather than women passed on the inheritance of their portion in the promised land. Gender-neutral translations just suppress this aspect of meaning. In addition, they convert the second half of the quotation to plurals, in order to avoid the feared word "his." (The NLT opts for a very loose paraphrase.)

Habakkuk 2:5

RSV: . . . the arrogant *man* shall not abide. *His* greed is as wide as Sheol; like death *he* has never enough. *He* gathers for *himself* all nations, and collects as *his* own all peoples.

NRSV: . . . the *arrogant* do not endure. *They* open *their* throats wide as Sheol; like Death *they* never have enough. *They* gather all nations for *themselves*, and collect all peoples as *their* own.

NLT: . . . the *arrogant* are never at rest. *They* range far and wide, with *their* mouths opened as wide as death, but *they* are never satisfied. In *their* greed *they* have gathered up many nations and peoples.

---

has lost its normal male meaning component. Koehler-Bahmgarter also cites passages such as Proverbs 28:21 and the Job passages as having the meaning "person," but these are indeed ambiguous evidence.

Hence, Carson is wrong bluntly to state that the opposite claim "is wrong." As we attempt to show in Appendix 2, lexicographical research is difficult and error prone, especially when the amount of data for use of a term is limited. Carson has underestimated the difficulty of lexicographical analysis, and overestimated the value of the parallelistic evidence that he cites.

Finally, note that, even if Carson is right about neutralization in cases in Job, it still does not affect judgments with respect to cases where *geber* is used outside of parallelistic contexts.

The word *man* (RSV) translates the Hebrew word *geber*, definitely indicating a male human being. The preceding context deals with the Babylonian army coming with its violence and might. To "gather all nations" or "collect all peoples" is the task of an army, and the singular seems to be a generic statement about these soldiers. Within the ancient world, we are clearly dealing with men, not women. But NRSV and NLT cannot bear to say so. To avoid the dreaded generic "he," they convert to plurals, as usual weakening the vividness of the verse.

2.   But don't these passages *apply* to women, too?

Of course, we do not deny that such verses also *apply* to women as well. There are many gender-specific passages in the Bible that apply to the other gender. For example, the parable of the prodigal son (Luke 15:11–32) also *applies* to prodigal daughters. But the parable itself does not speak about a prodigal daughter or a generic prodigal "child"—it speaks about a prodigal *son*. The parable of the good Samaritan (Luke 10:25–37) also *applies* to women, but the specific person in mind is a man who had compassion on the injured traveler. The parable of a woman with the lost coin (Luke 15:8–10) also *applies* to men and even to angels who rejoice over a sinner who repents, but the parable specifically talks about a *woman* who had ten silver coins and lost one and sought it diligently, and "when she has found it, she calls together her friends and neighbors, saying, 'rejoice with me, for I have found the coin which I had lost'" (Luke 15:9). The parable of the five wise and five foolish virgins (Matt. 25:1–13) also *applies* to men and encourages them to be ready for the Lord's return as well as women. But the parable does not specifically speak of ten "servants" or "people" who took their lamps and went to meet the bridegroom, but of ten female "virgins."[20] Accurate translation requires that we keep the gender that is specified in the Greek text in each of these passages and not obliterate it simply because we want to be sure people realize that they apply to men as well, or women as well.

D.   "Mortal" for "man"

The NRSV often substitutes the word "mortal" where the RSV and other versions have the word *man*. For example, when Cornelius fell down and began to worship Peter, Peter lifted him up and said, "Stand up; I too am a man" (Greek *anthrōpos*) (Acts 10:26, RSV). But in the NRSV Peter says, "Stand up; I am only a *mortal*."[21]

---

[20]The subsequent relative pronoun and participle, together with feminine adjectives and definite articles in the subsequent verses, indicate quite clearly that ten women or "virgins" (NIV; "maidens," RSV; Greek *parthenos*) are specified in this parable.

[21]The CEV, NCV, NLT, and NIVI all have "human" here rather than "mortal." NIVI puts it, "I am only human myself." This rendering is much better than "mortal," because it does not

The shift from "man" to "mortal" changes the focus from one's humanity to one's mortality (that is, one's liability to death). The same group, namely the group of human beings, is being described in both cases. But the two descriptions evoke different features and different meanings in order to characterize the group. It is true that dictionaries, under the entry "mortal," give the meaning "a human being."[22] But the word still carries an association with mortality; its connotations are not identical with "human being."

When God speaks to Ezekiel in the NRSV, he no longer says, "*Son of man*, stand upon your feet, and I will speak with you" (Ezek. 2:1, RSV), but now says, "*O mortal*, stand up on your feet, and I will speak with you" (NRSV). The repeated use of "O mortal" in Ezekiel (NRSV) would easily lead an attentive reader to think that the book has some special interest in mortality.

The NCV has God calling Ezekiel by the name "Human": "He said to me, '*Human*, stand up on your feet'" (2:1), and "*Human*, go to the people of Israel and speak my words to them" (3:4). This terminology may be "politically correct" in some university circles, but it is unnatural English. The classic literal translation "son of man" is really not any less natural.

We readers even find ourselves addressed by the designation "mortal": "He has told you, O *mortal*, what is good; and what does the LORD require of you but to do justice, and to love kindness, and to walk humbly with your God?" (Mic. 6:8). And the famous chapter on love now begins, "If I speak in the tongues of *mortals* and of angels, but have not love, I am a noisy gong or a clanging cymbal" (1 Cor. 13:1, NRSV). This is not ordinary English usage today. It is artificially contrived English for the purpose of politically correct speech.

E. Words for ancestors

How should we translate the words for "father" in Greek (*patēr*) and Hebrew ('*āb*)? Many contexts are uncontroversial, for a human father is in view, and "father" is a good equivalent in English, used by virtually all the translations. But some contexts are more difficult. Both the Greek and the Hebrew terms can refer to more distant ancestors as well. But if the same word in singular ('*āb*) means "father" and in plural ('*āboth*) can be used to denote several previous generations, how should we translate the plural? Should we translate it as "fathers" or "forefathers" or "ancestors"? The tendency in gender-neutral translations has been to use "ancestors" rather

---

bring in the connotation of mortality, which is not present in Greek. While the translation of *anthrōpos* is sometimes a complex question (see Appendix 5 for a discussion), in this context there need be no objection to retaining "man" in Peter's statement, for surely Peter was both a human being and male, and both facts are conveyed by the statement, "I too am a man."

[22] See, e.g., *American Heritage Dictionary*, 1176.

than "fathers" in these cases (as usual, eliminating male components of meaning).

Here we have a difficulty. As expected, the standard lexicons, in addition to the meaning "father," offer the meaning "ancestor," in order to indicate that more distant generations are sometimes included.[23] But, on closer inspection, it turns out that instances of this kind usually refer to grandfathers, great-grandfathers, and other *male* ancestors.[24] It appears that the word retains the suggestion of maleness. Thus a translation with the word "forefather" or even "father" (which can be used more broadly in English!)[25] captures this element of meaning, whereas "ancestor" does not.

In a subtle way some focus or greater prominence belongs to male ancestors in this Hebrew usage. This is in fact consistent with an Old Testament pattern by which the tribal and clan structures are traced through the males in each generation. Because of this, the translation "ancestor" obscures the patriarchal character of Old Testament thinking about family lines.

Therefore, the Colorado Springs Guidelines say:

B.3. "Father" (*patēr*, *'āb*) should not be changed to "parent," or "fathers" to "parents" or "ancestors."

Gender-neutral translations have sometimes obscured this male component, as the following examples show:

Genesis 47:3

RSV: "Your servants are shepherds, as our *fathers* were" (Hebrew *'ābot*, plural of *'āb*, "father").

NRSV: "Your servants are shepherds, as our *ancestors* were."

---

[23]BDB, 3, meaning 4. Koehler-Baumgartner, *The Hebrew and Aramaic Lexicon of the Old Testament* (Leiden/New York: Brill, 1994), 1:1, under meaning 1, "father," indicates that more distant ancestors may be so designated.

[24]For example, *'āb* ("father") refers to Abraham (Gen. 17:4; 28:13; 32:10), David (1 Kings 15:3, 11, 24; 2 Kgs. 14:3; 15:38; 16:2; 18:3; 22:2), Shem (Gen. 10:21); Moab (Gen. 19:37); and the patriarchs (Exod. 3:15). Other instances are less obvious. First and Second Kings mention repeatedly that such-and-such a king died and "slept with his *fathers*" or "was buried with his *fathers*" (for example, 1 Kgs. 14:31; 15:24; 22:50[51]). Is the reference to the male ancestors, or to both male and female ancestors? It is impossible to be certain. Surely female ancestors as well as male ancestors had died earlier. But the context of Kings may suggest that the unity of the male kingly line is at issue. Being buried with the earlier kings, not just with ancestors generally, may be significant. Thus, the reference may in fact be exclusively to male ancestors. Or it may intend to highlight the male ancestors while not absolutely excluding the female ones. Even if it were established that *'ābot* ("fathers," plural) is inclusive in some of these uses, it may still evoke the picture of males as representatives for all. In this respect, it may be like the modern use of the English word "man" to refer to the human race as a whole, or the earlier use of "every man" to refer inclusively to women, but with the picture of a male as the typical representative. As a translation, "ancestor" then still suppresses a male connotation in the representative example.

[25]For example, under "father" *The American Heritage Dictionary* offers "a male ancestor" as meaning 3 (3d ed., 664).

NLT: "We are shepherds like our *ancestors*."

In the ancient context the men rather than the women carried on the ancestral line with its occupation. The sons of Israel were shepherds, not because Leah or Rachel or Rebekah were shepherds before they were married, but because Jacob and Isaac had been shepherds. If a translation is going to capture the male component of the meaning of the Hebrew text, it must translate this verse with "fathers" or "forefathers," not "ancestors." Why remove the male meaning that is there in the text?

Numbers 36:4

RSV: . . . and their inheritance will be taken from the inheritance of the tribe of our *fathers* (Hebrew *'ābot*, "fathers").

NIV: . . . and their property will be taken from the tribal inheritance of our *forefathers*.

NRSV: . . . and their inheritance will be taken from the inheritance of our *ancestral* tribe.

NIVI: . . . and their property will be taken from the tribal inheritance of our *ancestors*.

NLT: . . . causing it to be lost forever to our *ancestral* tribe.

Inheritance of land normally passed through the men and their tribal connection. That is exactly why at this point, in the context of Numbers 36, the daughters of Zelophahad asked for an exceptional ruling in their case. In Numbers 36:4 the daughters are describing how things normally took place: "the inheritance of the tribe of our *fathers*." The NRSV, NIVI, and NLT by evasive changes show a tendency to remove maleness. For what reason? The male connotations would have been evident to the original hearers. Why should they be hidden from modern readers?

Acts 7:12

NIV: When Jacob heard that there was grain in Egypt, he sent our *fathers* (Greek *patēres*, plural of *patēr*, "father") on their first visit.

NIVI: When Jacob heard that there was grain in Egypt, he sent our *ancestors* on their first visit.

NRSV: But when Jacob heard that there was grain in Egypt, he sent our *ancestors* there on their first visit.

The text in Genesis does not indicate that any women went on the first visit to Egypt—Jacob sent his "*sons*" to find food (Gen. 42:1). We read, "So ten of Joseph's *brothers* went down to buy grain in Egypt" (Gen. 42:2). In the nature of the case, because of the dangers and hardships of travel, it is unlikely that any women accompanied them. The biblical text talks about Joseph's brothers, who were *men*. The NIVI elsewhere uses "fathers" to designate Abraham, Isaac, and Jacob (Acts 7:32), so it should not be argued that readers are too dull to understand this extended sense of "fathers," encompassing more distant ancestors. If translators are nevertheless worried about "fathers," they could use "forefathers," as the NIV sometimes does. But "ancestors" *misses the male component in the original*—that is the reason "ancestors" was chosen by the gender-neutral translations, and that is exactly the reason why "ancestors" should not be chosen by anyone who wants to represent the full meaning of the original text.

Acts 7:45

RSV: Our *fathers* (Greek *patēres*) in turn brought it in with Joshua when they dispossessed the nations which God thrust out before our fathers.

NRSV: Our *ancestors* in turn brought it in with Joshua when they dispossessed the nations that God drove out before our *ancestors.*

NLT: Years later, when Joshua led the battles against the Gentile nations that God drove out of this land, the Tabernacle *was taken* [verb changed to passive so no subject is expressed] with them into their new territory.

What people brought in the ark of the covenant and the tent of meeting? The Levites and priests did, all of them men. What people engaged in the "dispossession" of the nations? The men were the ones fighting in battle. But these elements of male prominence disappear with the word "ancestors," and with the NLT's complete omission of the subject "fathers." Male components of meaning that are in the original text are singled out for removal again and again.

Hebrews 12:7–10

NIV: 7 Endure hardship as discipline; God is treating you as sons. For what son is not disciplined by his *father* (Greek *patēr*)? 8 If you are not disciplined (and everyone undergoes discipline), then you are illegitimate children and not true sons. 9 Moreover, we have all had human *fathers* (Greek *patēres*)[26] who disciplined us and we respected them for it. How much more should we submit to the Father of our spirits and live! 10 Our fathers (Greek *hoi,* "they") disciplined us for a little while as they thought best; but God disciplines us for our good, that we may share in his holiness.

The NIVI, NRSV, and NLT replace the references to a human father in verse 7 by references to "parents":

NIVI: God is treating you as children. For what children are not disciplined by their *parents?*

NRSV: God is treating you as children; for what child is there whom a *parent* does not discipline?

---

[26]We recognize that the Greek term *patēres* (plural) can occasionally mean "parents" (so Heb. 11:23; BAGD, 635), but that sense is not justified in this context, which is a comparison with our heavenly Father. Note also that the previous verse, verse 7, has used *patēr* ("father") in the *singular,* in the context of a nuclear family. This context clearly sets the meaning of the subsequent references as "fathers," not "fathers and mothers."

NLT: God is treating you as his own children. Whoever heard of a child who was never disciplined?[27]

Of course, this change loosens the comparison with God as heavenly *Father*. The point of the passage is not to teach about parents but to develop an illustration that underlines the meaning of what God does for us. It is a comparison between human fathers and our heavenly Father. Why could the translations not leave the illustration as it is? No, they had to go in and tamper with it, because "father" is too male-oriented for modern taste.

F.   Words for children

How do we translate words for "son," *ben* in Hebrew and *huios* in Greek? The Hebrew plural *banîm* sometimes means "children," including both sexes. But, except in special contexts, the singular *ben* in Hebrew regularly refers to *male* children.[28] Similarly, the singular *huios* in Greek regularly refers to *male* children.

For this reason, Colorado Springs Guideline B.2 said:

B. Gender-related renderings which we will generally avoid, though there may be unusual exceptions in certain contexts:

2. "Son" (*huios*, *ben*) should not be changed to "child," or "sons" (*huioi*) to "children" or "sons and daughters." (However, Hebrew *banîm* often means "children.")[29]

But the gender-neutral translations sometimes ignore the established lexical meanings for these words for "son." For example, "my son" in the early chapters of Proverbs becomes "my child" in the NRSV, even though Proverbs 5–7 includes warnings against the adulterous woman that would be appropriate only when directed to a son, not a daughter.

---

[27]The NLT does revert to "earthly fathers" in verses 9–10.

[28]We are aware of no example where a woman is called a *ben* (singular) in Hebrew, even in special or idiomatic constructions. A woman is called a *bat*, "daughter," not a *ben*. This is significant, especially in light of the abundance of occurrences—*ben* (singular and plural forms) occurs 4,870 times in the OT, and in the singular it always refers to a male human being (except when it is used in uncommon constructions to refer to nonpersonal things such as plants). If it could be used in singular without a male component of meaning, we would expect *some* clear examples to be found. (See Chapter 12, n. 8, above, concerning Strauss's argument for a different sense for *ben* in Isa. 49:15 and Ezek. 18:4.)

[29]Carson, *Debate*, says that Guideline B.2 "does not stand up very well to hard data" (p. 133), but, interestingly, he focuses only on the Greek terms for "son" and "child," and provides no evidence showing that singular Hebrew *ben* could mean "child" rather than "son."

The "hard data" to which Carson refers are passages where *teknon* ("child") refers to a son, plus passages where *teknon* is used in the context of inheritance, plus Romans 8, where both *teknon* ("child") and *huios* ("son") occur (Mark 12:19; Luke 1:7; 15:31; Acts 7:5; Rom. 8:14, 16–17, 19, 21). These data are only indirectly relevant, since we are debating the meaning of *huios* ("son"), not the meaning of *teknon* ("child"). Readers can judge for themselves, from our further discussion of *huios* in this chapter, whether Carson has not misjudged the significance of the hard data to which he appeals. (See especially footnote 34 on the burden of proof.)

Proverbs 5:1–4

NIV: My *son*, pay attention to my wisdom, listen well to my words of insight, that you may maintain discretion and your lips may preserve knowledge. For the lips of an adulteress drip honey, and her speech is smoother than oil; but in the end she is bitter as gall, sharp as a double-edged sword.

NRSV: My *child*, be attentive to my wisdom; incline your ear to my understanding, so that you may hold on to prudence, and your lips may guard knowledge. For the lips of a loose woman drip honey, and her speech is smoother than oil; but in the end she is bitter as wormwood, sharp as a two-edged sword.

What can be the benefit from removing the male designation that is in the Hebrew text, both in the use of the word *ben*, "son," and in the clear sense of the subject matter? Did the translators really think that ancient Hebrew *daughters* were also being warned about sexual relationships with immoral women? The drive to eliminate male meaning components from the text can produce strange results.

Galatians 4:4–7

RSV: But when the time had fully come, God sent forth his Son, born of woman, born under the law, to redeem those who were under the law, so that we might receive adoption as *sons*. And because you are *sons*, God has sent the Spirit of his Son into our hearts, crying, "Abba! Father!" So through God you are no longer a slave but a *son*, and if a *son* then an heir.

NRSV: But when the fullness of time had come, God sent his Son, born of a woman, born under the law, in order to redeem those who were under the law, so that we might receive adoption as *children*. And because you are *children*, God has sent the Spirit of his Son into our hearts, crying, "Abba! Father!" So you are no longer a slave but a *child*, and if a *child* then also an heir, through God.

NLT: But when the right time came, God sent his Son, born of a woman, subject to the law. God sent him to buy freedom for us who were slaves to the law, so that he could adopt us as his very own *children*. And because you Gentiles have become his *children*, God has sent the Spirit of his Son into your hearts, and now you can call God your dear Father. Now you are no longer a slave but God's own *child*. And since you are his *child*, everything he has belongs to you.

The NIVI also uses "child" in Galatians 4:7 where the Greek has the singular *huios* for "son."

The previous context (Gal. 3:26–29) shows that in Christ both men and women can become "sons" of God and "sons" of Abraham ("you are all sons of God through faith in Christ Jesus," Gal. 3:26). When we come then to chapter 4, generations of Bible interpreters have always understood Galatians 4:4–7 as including both men and women within its scope. Galatians 4:4–7 uses "son" in the context of a fresh metaphor. That is, we have here not just a well-worn, stock phrase, but a creative illustration using an analogy between a literal son and a son in a metaphorical sense.

In Galatians 4:1–2 the picture of an heir inheriting an estate becomes the model for understanding that believers inherit God's spiritual blessings (Gal. 4:3–7). Just as a literal biological son has a time of minority (a time when he is not yet of age) and then enters into his inheritance, so also, through Christ the unique Son (Gal. 4:4, 6), we have had a time of minority and then enter into the status of sons, metaphorically speaking. A male marking still belongs to the lexical item "son," in the base meaning on which the metaphor builds. The context shows that the use is metaphorical and that it applies to both men and women.

In a gender-neutral translation, the result is a *similar* meaning, in that now men and women are declared to be *children* of God through Christ the Son. But this similar meaning is not identical to the original. A nuance has been changed. In the original meaning we, men and women alike, were compared with literal sons by means of a metaphorical analogy. In the changed meaning, we are compared with literal children (with no male meaning component in the base meaning). The main theological conclusion to which the metaphor points is the same whether we use "son" or "child." But the basic picture on which the metaphor builds is somewhat different in the two cases, because in the second translation ("child") we have eliminated a meaning component that is present in the original, and the close parallel with Christ the elder "son" is diminished in force.

In the ancient world inheritance characteristically passed through the *male* offspring. Thus, when Paul was talking about inheritance in Galatians 4:1–7, it was natural for him to speak of "sons" (*huios*), and not simply "children" (*teknon*). Of course, there were exceptions to male inheritance, like the daughters of Zelophehad (Num. 36). And the NT can talk about "children" (*teknon*) inheriting, because a subset of the children, namely the sons, customarily did inherit, and on occasion daughters could inherit property. When the NT uses the word for "children," it more forcefully stresses the fact that women as well as men receive the eternal, spiritual inheritance found in Christ. When it uses the word for "sons," it more forcefully stresses the typical ancient pattern for inheritance within this world. Both uses have a function. But their functions are not completely identical.[30] And the word for "son" is not synonymous with the word for "child."

Some people may still say, "But what practical difference does it make?" It makes a difference because we should translate the Word of God in a

---

[30]This is the case even though both Carson (pp. 132–33) and Strauss (pp. 160–61) rightly point out that both *huios* and *teknon* can be used in a context discussing inheritance.

manner that is faithful in every respect, not just in a minimal way. The minimum is not our goal. We ought not to be satisfied with a rough translation, of which we may only say that we think it is close enough for our most immediate practical purposes. We should aim at *maximal* representation of every aspect of meaning —*even when we cannot now say exactly how all the aspects of meaning may be important to some parts of the church some day.* It is God's business to decide what meaning components are important to include in the Bible, not ours!

Let's look at another aspect of this problem. Suppose, for the sake of argument, that it truly "makes no difference" which way we translate, whether "son" or "child." Suppose someone says, "There is no difference in meaning; the meaning is just the same." Then why not translate it using "son"? Ah, there's the rub. Such a translation is now thought to be "offensive" or "insensitive." It might be misunderstood as "excluding" women. But that means that the meanings are not "just the same." No, "son" has a male component of meaning that "child" does not have.

Is it true, however, that "son" is likely to be misunderstood, when it is read after Galatians 3:26–29 where we see that "there is neither . . . male nor female, for you are all one in Christ Jesus"? Can't even a fairly dull person see that we have a metaphor? The difference of meaning is that "son" preserves the male meaning component that is there in the original, and it is that component that gender neutral translations find offensive and seek not to translate into English.

Romans 8 contains another example. The words *teknon* ("child") and *huios* ("son") occur scattered throughout the passage, with no apparent reason why "child" occurs in one place and "son" in another. Surely the main theological points could be made using either word. Both words are used metaphorically, to speak not of a social and legal relation to a human parent, but a Christian's relation to God (note Rom. 8:15: "For you did not receive the spirit of bondage again to fear, but you received the Spirit of adoption by whom we cry out, 'Abba, Father' " [NKJV]).

Since Romans 8 oscillates between *teknon* and *huios*, some people have argued that in this context the two terms are synonymous and should both be translated "children." But this argument is fallacious. The fallacy becomes obvious if we consider that we can do the same thing in English. The NIV, RSV, KJV, NASB, NKJV, GNB(1976), NEB, and REB[31] oscillate in English between "children" and "sons" in exact parallel to the oscillations in Greek. The occurrence of both words in a common context does not destroy the meaning difference between them when the passage is read for English-speaking readers. They still know there is a difference between

---

[31]Once more, the appearance of REB on our side is significant. REB tried to move toward gender-neutral language where it reasonably could. In this case it could not "without compromising scholarly integrity" ("Preface," REB, ix).

"son" and "child" even if the terms are interchanged in a single passage. Likewise, the parallel phenomenon in Greek does not destroy the meaning difference in Greek. If, for the sake of argument, we grant that the context destroys meaning difference, then the context in English also destroys meaning difference.[32] Hence, in Romans 8, "children" and "sons" mean the same thing. So we can leave "sons," and no one should have any problem!

Let us consider a related example. A person can say, "I am a slave of Christ, a servant of Jesus my Lord." The virtual interchangeability of "slave" and "servant" does not imply that they are synonymous, either in English in general or in this sentence in particular. "Slave" in its base meaning indicates a relation more comprehensive and less easy to free oneself from than the word "servant." The differences in meaning remain even in a context where both terms are used in a metaphorical sense. Or again, "My employer acts like a general toward his employees. He orders them about like a ship's captain." "General" and "ship's captain" are not synonymous. The one is a ruler in an army, the other in the navy. Both terms are used in a simile, but the simile does not destroy the difference in meaning in the two comparisons.[33]

From a linguistic point of view, oscillation between two terms proves nothing except that, in a particular context, an author can oscillate. Several

---

[32]As usual, we are not equating Greek and English linguistic systems! Our point is a very narrow one, concerning Romans 8 in particular. Carson and Strauss suggest (though, commendably, they do not assert it as beyond doubt), that there is no difference in meaning between *huios* and *teknon* in Romans 8 (Carson, *Debate*, 132–33; Strauss, *Distorting*, 160–61). But they have not, up to this point, offered any observations *specifically about Romans 8* that would not apply equally well (*mutatis mutandis*) to an English language version of Romans 8.

Suppose, two thousand years from now, a Swahili-speaking philologist examines a copy of Romans in the NIV, looking at it simply as data used to explore the meanings of the English words "sons" and "children." Would he conclude, using similar arguments about oscillation in terminology within a single passage, that "sons" and "children" are identical in meaning in Romans 8? An argument about Romans 8 would "prove too much" by "proving" that there is no difference in meaning in an English (!) version of Romans 8. Hence, there is no real weight to such an argument. (We know that Romans 8 in Greek is different from English, because it is not a translation. But we can readily imagine someone writing something like Romans 8 in English, not based on a previous text in another language. English, like Greek, allows in principle the kind of flexibility we see in oscillating between "sons" and "children.")

[33]In private correspondence D. A. Carson suggested that our examples were not suitable. Instead, he wanted the example of "God is my King" and "God is my Sovereign." Suppose then that these two statements occur at two different points in a paragraph. Is there any difference between them? In both cases we assert the same basic reality, namely God's authority and right to command, and my submissive, obedient relation to him. But in the two metaphors the words "king" and "sovereign" still appear to us to retain something of their original meanings. In particular, "king" retains associations with maleness and long-standing position of honor—that is exactly why some feminist Bible translations have routinely changed "king" to "sovereign." (Queen Elizabeth is a sovereign but she is not a king.) A translator should, if possible, convey the meaning difference between "king" and "sovereign" in translation. In fact, then, Carson's example is not different in principle from ours. We chose examples with a more striking meaning difference, so that people could grasp the point. But Carson's own example still possesses a meaning difference and still confirms our point.

factors may be behind this oscillation. First, in some cases the two terms may indeed be synonymous in nearly every respect. Second, the two terms may be used to make two distinct but related points. Third, the two terms may have differences in lexical meaning but be used in a context where the differences are neutralized. Fourth, the two terms may have differences that are still present in context but that make little difference in the overall thrust of what is being said. The fourth possibility is the one illustrated in the examples above. In such cases, translation ideally preserves the nuances involved in the distinct senses and preserves distinct metaphors and similes arising from the meaning differences.[34]

In Romans 8, *huios* continues to possess the semantic component "male" in the base meaning on which the metaphor builds. So there is good reason to translate using "son" and to preserve in English the shifts between "son" and "child" that mirror what we find in Greek. Moreover, there is a further bonus to preserving the word "son." The model of Christ the Son, visible in Romans 8:29, as well as verses 3 and 32, resonates with the occurrence of *huios* ("son") elsewhere in Romans 8. Retaining the translation "son" as the English rendering of *huios* enables us to retain the connection between Christ's Sonship and our *sonship*. The connection recedes if we consistently translate using "children."

In sum, in Galatians 4:4–7 and in Romans 8 a term with male marking is used to represent a group including both men and women. The usages in Romans 8 and Galatians 3:26–4:7 appear to rest partly on the fact that a single male, namely Christ himself, has represented us and achieved deliverance for us. Gender-neutral translations preserve the main point but delete

---

[34]Remember that *huios* means "son," not "child," when used in the context of family relations. The burden of proof is on those who would deviate from the natural lexical meaning in a context that evokes an analogy with the literal family status of "son" (note the reference to God as "Father" in Rom. 8:15).

Carson seemed to have missed the significance of burden of proof in this matter. He rightly observes that it is possible *in principle* for a word to have one meaning component neutralized:

> Just because some passages in the New Testament *can* distinguish between *huios* and *teknon* does not necessarily mean that the two words cannot share identical semantic ranges in pragmatic circumstances (*Debate*, 132).

But then what evidence does he present that the meaning component has in fact been neutralized in the case of *huios* in Romans 8? He cites passages where the word *teknon* ("child") is used to refer to a son, some of them in the context where inheritance is in view. This is interesting; but it is not really surprising. In English today we can obviously use the word "child" to refer to a son, because a son is in fact also a child. Evidence like this does indeed show that *teknon* or another word meaning "child" could *in principle* be used in a context like Romans 8 or Galatians 4:1–7 that talks about inheritance.

But we are not dealing with a merely hypothetical question of what is possible with a previously unknown word. We already know the meaning of *huios* from the evidence in the standard Greek lexicons. The burden of proof is on Carson or any other opponent to show that *huios* has lost the male meaning component that the lexicons say it normally has when used in family contexts.

the male marking, so there is some loss of meaning. "Son" for *huios* would be a better translation, and should be preserved.

Hebrews 12:5–8

NIV: And you have forgotten that word of encouragement that addresses you as *sons*: "My *son*, do not make light of the Lord's discipline, and do not lose heart when he rebukes you, because the Lord disciplines those he loves, and he punishes everyone he accepts as a *son*." Endure hardship as discipline; God is treating you as *sons*. For what *son* is not disciplined by his father? If you are not disciplined (and everyone undergoes discipline), then you are illegitimate children and not true *sons*.

The word *huios* occurs six times in the verses, three times in the singular. The gender-neutral translations NRSV, NIVI, NIrV(1995), NCV, GW, CEV, and NLT consistently use "child" and "children," not "son." But the meaning of *huios* (singular) is "son." When the word occurs in the singular in a family context like this one, it always has this meaning. The meaning is only confirmed by the quotation from Proverbs 3:11–12, which occurs in the context of a father giving advice to his son. Wisdom, pictured as feminine, is the son's proper consort (Prov. 3:13–18; 8:1–9:18), rather than an immoral woman (Prov. 5:1–20).

Once again, it is interesting that the REB (1989) consistently has "son" translating the Greek word *huios* in Hebrews 12:5–8, as well as Galatians 4:4–7. Remember that the REB strove for gender-neutral expressions "without compromising scholarly integrity or English style."[35] Since there is no stylistic reason for preferring "son," the reason must be that they thought using "child" would be "compromising scholarly integrity."

I.   More difficult cases with "son"

Not all translation cases are clear-cut. We mentioned earlier (Chapter 11) that the plural word *banîm* ("sons") in Hebrew can be used to describe mixed groups. In these contexts it is not really equivalent to "sons," but closer to our word "children." Indeed, the KJV regularly translates it "children" in the expression "children of Israel."

A quick overview of Greek and Hebrew vocabulary suggests why there is a fundamental difference between Greek and Hebrew in this regard. Greek has a three-way contrast between "son" (*huios*), "daughter" (*thugater*), and "child" (*teknon*). Hebrew has a two-way contrast between "son" (*ben*) and "daughter" (*bat*). Hebrew does have a word for "child," *yeled*, but it usually applies to youngsters only, not to grown-up sons and daughters.[36] In Hebrew, without a wide-ranging word for "children,"

---

[35]REB, "Preface," ix.

[36]Isaiah 29:23 looks like an exception. But here *yeled* appears in a poetic context; it may represent a metaphorically expanded use, beyond the norm for *yeled*. In addition, *yeled* has

banîm (the plural "sons") must cover mixed groups of males and females that include adults, because there is no convenient third term. In Greek, the term *tekna* (plural of *teknon*, "child") does the job, so there is no pressure to make the plural *huioi* ("son") serve this purpose and produce contexts where the male semantic component is neutralized.

In the Old Testament this situation leads to difficult cases, where translators must decide whether the text is talking only about males or about mixed groups. Some cases may not be clear, and we must simply do our best.

More difficulties arise because in the New Testament some of the uses of *huios* may be influenced by Hebrew.[37] For example, Matthew 5:9 and 5:45 speak of "sons of God," "sons of your Father," using *huios* in the plural. Does this use of "sons" imitate the Old Testament use of *banîm* for children? Possibly. It is a debatable issue, and scholars may disagree over the exact nuances.

But we believe that certain factors still tip the balance toward translating with "sons." It is still valid to distinguish between Hebrew on the one hand and Greek "influenced" by Hebrew on the other. The influence, not only from the Septuagint (the Greek translation of the Old Testament), but also from bilingual speakers, makes it possible to use *huios* in an extended, expanded, or semi-metaphorical sense matching the Hebrew. When someone does that, he is quickly understood by others familiar with the Hebraic influence. But such an extended use does not cancel out what the native speaker knows, namely that *huios* when used less innovatively means "son," not "child." Even in the instances of extended use there is a background in which the native speaker knows that male marking is part of the base meaning.

We preserve this complex interplay between a base meaning and an extended sense when we regularly use "son" as the English translation of *huios*.[38] In the cases where the English New Testament has an extended

---

both masculine and feminine forms, thus duplicating the limitations of *ben* and *bat*. By contrast, the Greek word *teknon* ("child") is neuter, giving no indication whether the child is male or female.

[37]For example, the expression "sons [*huioi*] of Israel" (Rom. 9:27) in the New Testament clearly builds on the Old Testament expression "children [*benē*] of Israel." The expression "sons [*huioi*] of the living God" in Romans 9:26 derives from Hosea 10:1 (in Hebrew, Hos. 2:1), "sons (or children) [*benē*] of the living God." In the treatment of the Greek word *huios* ("son") the Colorado Springs Guidelines allow "unusual exceptions in certain contexts." Contexts influenced by Old Testament manners of expression must clearly be considered carefully, and the Guidelines did not intend to settle the questions prematurely.

[38]In both Hebrew and Greek there also are specialized uses, like "sons of the bridegroom" (Matt. 9:15), describing followers. We may legitimately consider the possibility of idiomatic translations like "guests of the bridegroom" (NIV). But this use is distinguishable from the uses about which we are talking. The language "sons of God" appears to build more directly on the family analogy, not on the idea that we are in some loose sense followers of God (note Rom. 8:15; Gal. 4:1–7).

usage, everyone knows that it is an extended usage, and easily adapts, all the while knowing that the base meaning of "son" continues. The relation between extended use and base meaning in English mirrors the analogous relation in Greek. All this worked easily in English until feminists began to object to male prominence anywhere in any literature.

We get a similar phenomenon in pre-1960 English, where "brother" was used metaphorically for Christians. Christian congregations would be addressed as "brethren," as they are still addressed as "beloved" or "loved ones." Among some Christians, this usage was so well established that most of the time no one thought about it. But if asked, everyone would have told you that, of course, this was a special use, a metaphorical use, and that on a literal level "brother" basically meant "male sibling." The extended use, in direct imitation of English translations, which in turn imitated the Greek New Testament, did not result in any broadening of the base meaning to eliminate its male component.

G. Brothers

Translating the Greek word for "brother" (*adelphos*) presents special challenges, especially in the plural forms. Subtle differences exist between the Greek word and the corresponding English word "brother."

Although in many cases the plural word *adelphoi* means "brothers," and refers only to males, there are other cases where *adelphoi* is used to refer to a brother and a sister or to brothers and sisters. Consider the following quotations from Greek literature outside the New Testament:

> That man is a cousin of mine: his mother and my father were *adelphoi* (Andocides, *On the Mysteries* 47 [approximately 400 B.C.]).

> My father died leaving me and my *adelphoi* Diodorus and Theis as his heirs, and his property devolved upon us (*Oxyrhynchus Papyri* 713, 20–23 [A.D. 97; Diodorus is a man's name and Theis is a woman's name]).

> The footprints of *adelphoi* should never match (of a man and of a woman): the man's is greater (Euripides, *Electra* 536 [5th cent. B.C.]).

> . . . you [an impatient and critical man] find fault even with your own parents and children and *adelphoi* and neighbors (Epictetus, *Discourses* 1.12.20 [approximately A.D. 130.]).

In standard English, we just don't say, "My *brothers* Dave and Sue." So the Greek plural *adelphoi* sometimes has a different sense from English "brothers." In fact, the major Greek lexicons for over 100 years have said that the plural *adelphoi* sometimes means "brothers and sisters."[39]

---

[39]So Bauer, *Greek-English Lexicon* (1957 and 1979); Liddell-Scott-Jones, *Greek-English Lexicon* (1940 and as early as the 1869 edition).

We find a similar use in the New Testament. The word *adelphoi* is used by itself when both men and women are addressed: "Therefore, I urge you, brothers (*adelphoi*), in view of God's mercy . . ." (Rom. 12:1). Surely Paul intends to include both male and female hearers in this one word *adelphoi*, and surely his readers would all have understood that fact.

This kind of use is natural to Greek, because the masculine form *adelphos* ("brother") and the feminine form *adelphē* ("sister") are just different forms (masculine and feminine) of the same word, with the root *adelph-*.[40] The plural form of this word would be *adelphoi* when talking about a group of all men, and it would also be the same form (*adelphoi*) when talking about a group of both men and women. Only the context could tell us whether it meant "brothers" or "brothers and sisters." This makes Greek different from English, where "brother" and "sister" are completely different words. We would not call a mixed group of men and women siblings "brothers."

To be exact, the masculine plural form *adelphoi* does not literally mean "brothers and sisters," but something like "brothers, and maybe sisters as well (look at context to see)." Depending on context, it may or may not refer to a mixed group. Thus, if need arises, a Greek writer can also use *both* the masculine *and* the feminine forms, side-by-side, to make explicit the inclusion of women. For example, Matt. 19:29 says, "And everyone who has left houses or *brothers or sisters* [feminine, *adelphas*] or father or mother or children or fields for my sake will receive a hundred times as much and will inherit eternal life.")?[41]

In sum, the meanings of the plural word *adelphoi* in Greek and the word "brothers" in English do not exactly match.[42] Neither does the meaning of plural *adelphoi* exactly match "brothers and sisters." "Brothers and sisters" in English makes the inclusion of "sisters" explicit, whereas the Greek word leaves it to context to decide. Given the lack of exact match, *any* translation is going to be less than ideal. Translators have a hard decision to make. Several options should be examined, each with its own advantages and disadvantages.

In a number of passages *adelphoi* is used to designate literal brothers. Matthew 1:2 speaks of Judah's "brothers," and Matthew 4:18 speaks of two "brothers," Peter and Andrew. In these cases the translation "brothers" presents no problem, for only male siblings are in view.

The problem arises when the word is used as a designation for Christians. Christians are "brothers" (*adelphoi*) to one another. "Brothers" is a frequent designation, built on the fact that God is our Father and that Christ is our elder brother (Rom. 8:29; 8:15–17).

---

[40]The root *adelph-* is from *a-*, which means "from," and *delphus*, "womb" (ibid., 20) and probably at an earlier point had the sense of "from the same womb."

[41]See also Mark 10:30.

[42]There are other subtle differences as well, which one can see by carefully comparing Greek and English dictionaries. But we avoid these technicalities.

Of course, this use is a metaphorical use. Christians are not literally all children of the same human father and mother. Rather, they are members of the family of God. Their status is analogous to the relations within a human family. Their relation to God is analogous to the relation of children to a human father. Without hesitation the average Christian reader immediately grasps the metaphorical character of this expression.

The distinct character of this usage, applying to God's family rather than a human family, gives scope for some flexibility. For example, Christians can be called "sons" of God, by analogy with Christ's Sonship, and have a masculine word "son" applied to all of them (Gal. 4:4–7). Collectively, they are the "bride" of Christ, with a feminine word "bride" applied to them (Rev. 19:7). Christians for generations have read English translations with the word "brothers," used in this metaphorical sense.[43] They have seen, as they have seen with the word "son," that both men and women are included.

But the analogy here between a human family and a divine family extends to include the sexuality of the persons involved. For example, Paul instructs Timothy to "treat the younger men as brothers, older women as mothers, and younger women as sisters" (1 Tim. 5:1–2). He is to do so because the church is "God's household" (1 Tim. 3:15).[44] Thus, in at least some places in the Bible, the analogy includes the analogy between a human family with brothers and sisters and God's family with "brothers" and "sisters." In the analogy, the people in the group are not compared simply to human brothers, but to sisters as well. The translation with "brothers and sisters" in places like Romans 12:1 helps to capture this aspect of the analogy.

Thus, the translation "brothers and sisters" has some definite advantages.

(1) It conveys explicitly in English the fact that *adelphoi* in Greek can include sisters.

(2) It underlines in English the fact that both men and women were being addressed in a particular verse.

(3) It expresses in English the full analogy between a human family with brothers and sisters and the family of God, which includes "brothers" and "sisters" in the metaphorical sense.

However, there are also advantages in keeping the single term "brothers" to translate the Greek term *adelphoi*.

(1) Because earlier English Bible translations used "brother" in this way, it has become an established meaning of the word. *The American Heritage*

---

[43]Actually, the word with this meaning has often taken the form "brethren."
[44]See Vern S. Poythress, "The Church as Family: Why Male Leadership in the Family Requires Male Leadership in the Church," in John Piper and Wayne Grudem, eds., *Recovering Biblical Manhood and Womanhood: A Response to Evangelical Feminism* (Wheaton: Crossway, 1991), 233–47.

Dictionary (1992) reports under meaning 4c, ". . . A fellow member of the Christian church."[45] This meaning is in fact *inclusive*.

(2) In a considerable number of places it is not clear whether a specific passage intends to include women among the addressees. If we consistently translate "brothers," we create for ourselves no special difficulties when we come to such places. But if we translate "brothers and sisters," we have to make an explicit decision, every time, as to whether the passage intended to address the "sisters" as well. Sometimes the evidence is just not there.

James 3:1: "Let not many of you become teachers, my brethren, for you know that we who teach shall be judged with greater strictness" (RSV).

If the translation has "my brothers and sisters," as the NRSV and NIVI do, the text seems to suggest that women are allowed to be teachers in the church, contrary to 1 Timothy 2:11–15. Actually, however, the text in Greek offers no such support, because Greek readers would not automatically assume that the term *adelphoi* included women unless the context somehow led them to think that. Of course, James 1:1–2 starts by addressing all Christians as "my brothers." But by the time we come to James 3:1, James may be focusing on men as the ones who (in the first-century church) would be expected to become the teachers. "Brothers" is flexible, in that it can include or exclude women according to context. "Brothers and sisters" is not flexible but forces an interpretation in which the "sisters" are included, even where that was not the intention of the original author.

Acts 9:30: "When the *brothers* learned of this, they took him down to Caesarea, and sent him off to Tarsus" (NIV).

It is impossible to say whether the group that accompanied Paul to Caesarea included women. The NRSV, NIVI, and NLT skirt the issue by using "believers." But they thereby lose the distinctly family flavor of "brothers." They also fail to indicate the regularity with which this designation is used to denote Christians. GW has "the disciples." NCV and CEV have "the followers."

Acts 10:23: ". . . The next day Peter started out with them, and some of the *brothers* from Joppa went along" (NIV).

For a journey like this one, it seems historically likely that all the travelers were men. But we do not know for certain.

Acts 17:6: ". . .they dragged Jason and some other *brothers* before the city officials . . . " (NIV).

We do not know whether the group included women.

Acts 17:10: ". . . the *brothers* sent Paul and Silas away to Berea. . . ." (NIV).

Were "the brothers" all the Christians, or leading men who represented the whole body? It is impossible to know. Similar problems occur with still other verses in Acts.

---

[45]*American Heritage Dictionary*, 243.

If the rest of the New Testament regularly uses "brothers," in the established sense of "fellow member of the Christian church," it creates no special difficulties for these passages. It even sets up an expectation that "brothers" may or may not include women. If, however, we use "brothers and sisters" in passages like Romans 12:1, we push people toward understanding "brothers" only as a designation for *male* believers. Then we have to solve the problems in Acts in some other way. The best solution, though not a pretty one, is probably to translate using "brothers," whenever we cannot be sure that women were included, and add a footnote with each of these occurrences, which would read, "Greek *adelphoi* may include women. The context must decide."

Thus, we have two main solutions: the consistent use of "brothers" or the use of "brothers and sisters" wherever the context clearly indicates the inclusion of women. Both of these translation procedures are reasonable. Neither is ideal in all respects. We expect that different translations will choose different directions, depending on the nature of the translation and its relation to previous translations in English.

There are still potential problems with connotations. To people familiar with the previous history of using "brothers/brethren" in the Bible, a new usage like "brothers and sisters" stands out. It is conspicuous because people remember what earlier versions said. It thus conveys to some readers a pro-feminist overtone. On the other hand, given the feminist-generated antipathy to male-oriented terms, "brothers" undoubtedly has an unnecessarily restrictive male overtone in some people's ears.

What should a translator do in such a case? In our judgment, these two factors nearly cancel each other out. We should, of course, be concerned not to cause needless offense. But we should be far more concerned to translate the Bible with faithfulness to meaning. Hence, both of the two translations are in principle acceptable.

The CSG put the principle this way:

B. Gender-related renderings which we will generally avoid, though there may be unusual exceptions in certain contexts:

1. "Brother" (*adelphos*) should not be changed to "brother or sister"; however, the plural *adelphoi* can be translated "brothers and sisters" where the context makes clear that the author is referring to both men and women

It is more questionable, however, whether a translator may avoid the difficulties by resorting to other terms besides "brother" and "sister." In the passages in Acts involving "brothers" (*adelphoi*), the gender-neutral translations use other terms: "believers," "disciples," "followers," and sometimes still other expressions. All these expressions, like "brothers," designate a group of fellow Christians. The *referent* (the group being referred to) is the same, no matter which expression we use. But the *meaning* (the total idea conveyed to the reader by the word) is not the same. "Believing" and "following" and "being a disciple" are descriptions with meanings distinguishable from one another. And all three are distinguishable from the meaning of "brothers." The gender-neutral translations are simply ignoring the specific meanings and translating according to reference alone (using another term for the thing referred to). But modern semantic theory, the theory of meaning, rightly asserts the distinction between reference and meaning. And sound translation theory requires that we translate meaning, not merely reference.

The objection may come that the point of these passages is merely to identify the participants, not to make a statement about their character. But this objection repeats the earlier excuse about "basic meaning." As long as we get the main point, according to this view, we can ignore the nuances carried by the specific descriptive terms that a verse uses. But this view does not provide us with an adequate philosophy of translation. As we explained above,[46] translators must endeavor to represent every aspect of meaning.

In addition, when translations vary their terminology in English, they conceal the fact that the first-century Christians had a common, distinctive term for themselves: "brothers." The sense of intimacy, of community, of belonging to one spiritual family under God the Father, was strong. But we conceal it in English if we start shifting the terms around.

H. Brother (singular)

We must also consider what to do with the singular forms of *adelphos*. Consider some examples.

Matthew 5:22

RSV: But I say to you that *every one* who is angry with *his brother* shall be liable to judgment; *whoever* insults *his brother* shall be liable to the council.

NRSV: But I say to you that if *you* are angry with *a brother or sister*, *you* will be liable to judgment; and if *you* insult *a brother or sister*, *you* will be liable to the council.

NRSV has made several changes. The one that we want to concentrate on at the moment is the change from "brother" to "brother or sister." Is this change a problem?

We have observed that sometimes the plural *adelphoi* can include both brothers and sisters, so that its meaning is similar to "brothers and sisters." By logical parity, would not the singular *adelphos* mean "brother or sister"? It may seem logical, but language does not always operate by pure abstract

---

[46]See Chapter 10, pages 165–95.

logic. In fact, the plural is used to cover mixed groups, but the singular always covers only one person. That one can be either male or female. If the one is male, *adelphos* is the appropriate term. If the one is female, *adelphē*, with a feminine ending, is the appropriate term. Thus, the singular and the plural do not behave in the same way, because only in the case of the plural do we have to deal with mixed groups. Hence, in ordinary cases the masculine *adelphos* in the singular unambiguously means, "brother," not "sister." So it is with Andrew, the brother of Peter (Matt. 4:18) and John the brother of James (Matt. 4:21), while Mary the sister of Martha (Luke 10:39) is described using the feminine form *adelphē* ("sister").

But what happens when one uses *adelphos* in an example like Matthew 5:22, which is intended to express a general truth? The effect is somewhat like what we have seen with generic "he." The masculine form of *adelphos* leads the listener to picture in his mind a male example. But the male example illustrates a general truth. The context shows that the truth applies to both men and women.

Perhaps, because the feminine form *adelphē* is only another form of the same root *adelph-*, the effect of the masculine is less pronounced. But we must still remember that in all such cases the context, rather than the grammatical form of the sentence, tells us how far the generality extends. Only from context would a reader know whether the general principle holds for brothers alone or for both brothers and sisters. Thus, some tendency to think in terms of a male example remains. Hence, "brother" is a good translation in English.[47]

But does not "brother or sister" say the same thing? It expresses the same general principle. But it does so in a way that makes explicit different aspects. What was implicit in the original has become explicit in the translation. Moreover, the rhetorical effect is slightly different. Putting in an explicit "or" causes listeners to create in their minds two pictures rather than one to illustrate the general truth. No doubt Scripture itself in the original lan-

---

[47]Carson objects to the CSG's insistence that singular *adelphos* should not be changed to "brother or sister" while plural *adelphoi* can be translated "brothers and sisters." He says, "Why it insists on excluding inclusive language for the singular form quite escapes me. . . . Why concede the point for the plural and deny it for the singular?" (p. 131).

Carson apparently does not consider that such a distinction has been maintained in the standard lexicons for over a hundred years (see n. 37, above). The lexicons have recognized the inclusive sense of the plural form because that sense was attested by ancient usage. The reason for the difference should not be hard to understand: the masculine plural (*adelphoi*) in Greek was used for mixed groups of men and women but the singular masculine form (*adelphos*) would be used for a male sibling, the singular feminine form (*adelphe*) would be used for a female sibling. When people spoke about family relations, the sex of the person in question would almost always be known. In the few cases where it was not, some alternative wording such as *teknon* ("child") might be used. Or one could resort to "brother or sister," or conceivably one could use the masculine form as a default (we do not know any case of a literal use of this kind, but it is theoretically conceivable). But this last case, because it was infrequent, would, we suspect, still carry over the picture of a male example for an unknown case.

guages can produce two pictures if it wants, as in James 2:25, where "brother or sister" is explicitly in the Greek. But the rhetorical effect is different than what we produce by using a single example to illustrate a generality. The strength of the single example is in its greater concreteness, vividness, and crispness. The strength of the dual example is in making explicit that the author wants us to think of various types of cases, to all of which the principle would apply.

Still more subtle effects arise from the fact that an author tacitly knows what a reader experiences. He knows that "brother or sister" generates a double picture in the reader's mind. So he avoids it unless that is what he wants. The reader in turn tacitly knows that authors do such things. Therefore, when the reader sees "brother or sister," he senses that there is some special reason for including the "sister" explicitly.

These effects undoubtedly occur in the original languages as well as in English. So, apart from unusual cases, it would seem wisest to maintain the distinction in our translation. In other words, we translate "brother" (*adelphos*) in the original with "brother"; and we translate "brother or sister" (*adelphos ē adelphē*, with "sister" mentioned explicitly) with "brother or sister."

The NRSV has also introduced some other changes. The word "his" in "his brother" has twice dropped out:

> RSV: But I say to you that every one who is angry with *his* brother shall be liable to judgment; whoever insults *his* brother shall be liable to the council.

> NRSV: But I say to you that if you are angry with *a* brother or sister, you will be liable to judgment; and if you insult *a* brother or sister, you will be liable to the council.

Why? The NRSV must not allow a male marking in a pronoun referring back to "everyone" or "whoever." In the process, however, it has slightly distorted the meaning. "His brother" indicates clearly that the text is contemplating anger between two people both of whom are part of the same "brotherhood" or religious community. Omit the "his," and the text might be about an unbeliever who is angry with a Christian ("if you are angry with a brother or sister," where the "you" need not be limited to Christians). The NRSV may have tried to minimize this possibility by changing from "anyone" to "you," but the third person "every one" and "whoever," corresponded accurately to the Greek. As usual, this change has shifted the starting point of the illustration from a person "out there" to the addressee, "you."

Matthew 18:15–17

> RSV: If your *brother* sins against you, go and tell *him his* fault, between you and *him* alone. If *he* listens to you, you have gained your *brother*. But if *he* does not listen, take one or two others along with you, that every word may be confirmed by the evidence of two or three witnesses. If *he*

refuses to listen to them, tell it to the church; and if *he* refuses to listen even to the church, let *him* be to you as a Gentile and a tax collector.

The RSV follows fairly closely the structure of the Greek, and in doing so makes good sense. But the passage creates severe difficulties for gender-neutral translations. The opening word "brother" is only the beginning. We must also deal with the later references to the brother using masculine pronouns. If a translator replaces "brother" with "brother or sister," the difficulties only increase, because then it becomes more awkward to refer back to the offender with a masculine "he." The option of converting to a second person "you" is not really open, because "you" already occurs in the passage to refer to the person sinned against. The option of converting to plurals is not good, because the meaning of the passage depends strongly on the picture of a single individual person who has offended. The NCV, GNB, and GW wisely give up and sprinkle the passage liberally with generic "he." But for other versions, the prohibition against generic "he" takes priority even when the difficulties are severe.

> NRSV: If *another member of the church* sins against you, go and point out the fault when the two of you are alone. If *the member* listens to you, you have regained *that one*. But if you *are not listened to*, take one or two others along with you, so that every word may be confirmed by the evidence of two or three witnesses. If *the member* refuses to listen to them, tell it to the church; and if *the offender* refuses to listen even to the church, let *such a one* be to you as a Gentile and a tax collector.

"Another member of the church" replaces "your brother." "Your brother" is far more intimate, and offers far more motivation for caring about the brother enough to go to him. NRSV has endeavored to specify the reference (a fellow Christian), but has not succeeded in capturing the meaning as distinct from the reference. Moreover, even the reference is not perfect. "Another member of the church," in a modern context, might easily be interpreted as meaning only "another member of the local church of which I am a member." With this interpretation, it would leave out Christians who are members of other churches and also people who claim to be Christians but are not formally members of any church. "Brother" focuses on the spiritual bond with fellow participants in the spiritual family of God. "Member of the church" focuses on the technical question of who has gone through a formal process leading to being recorded on the roll.

Moreover, "member of the church" introduces the idea of church membership into the first century, even into Jesus' teaching. While there may be very good theological and practical reasons for the practice of church membership today, it is historically inaccurate to indicate that Jesus mentioned the idea in such an explicit way. In fact, no explicit mention of the idea of church "membership" ever existed in the New Testament—until the NRSV added it to this verse!

In the second sentence, NRSV has "the member" instead of the natural "he." The result is not smooth English. Here as elsewhere the NRSV injects noun phrases in order to avoid the normal English tendency to use a backward referring pronoun "he/him." As these noun phrases multiply, the passage as a whole takes on a more technical, formal, legal cast.

NRSV's "point out the fault" replaces "tell him his fault." "To him" is doubtless *implicit* in the NRSV. But it is not explicit. Making it explicit, as the RSV and the Greek do, makes the matter more concrete.

NRSV's "that one" replaces "your brother." Again, "your brother" is much more intimate and gives much more motivation. "That one" is awkward English to avoid "your brother" and "him."

NRSV replaces "if he does not listen" in verse 16 with a passive, "if you are not listened to," in order to avoid "he." The passive is rhetorically weak and makes less explicit the personal character of the refusal. It is not simply that, in some vague way, communication has failed. Rather, "*he*," the person, has not listened. Responsibility by an individual human being is more evident in the original wording than in the NRSV.

In verse 17 NRSV again chooses a noun phrase, "the member," in order to avoid "he." Then it must produce still another noun phrase, "the offender," to avoid a second "he." The result is not normal fluid English style but more formal. "Such a one" also fails as a translation. Both the RSV and the Greek remain concrete. It is "him," the very one that we have been talking about, that is now like a Gentile. NRSV seems only to say that someone *of that kind* must be like a Gentile. The NRSV has prematurely made a transition that moves us out of the concrete story and into a general statement about the lesson that we must learn from the story. The decision does not show respect for the text. It only shows desperation to find some other way to avoid "him."

> NIVI: If your *brother or sister* sins against you, go and show *them their* fault, just between the two of you. If *they* listen to you, you have won *them* over. But if *they* will not listen, take one or two others along, so that 'every matter may be established by the testimony of two or three witnesses.' If *they* refuse to listen to them, tell it to the church; and if *they* refuse to listen even to the church, treat *them* as you would a pagan or a tax collector.

After the introductory "brother or sister," the NIVI has converted everything to plurals.[48] The difficulty is that by the time one gets to the end of

---

[48]In fairness to the NIVI, note that the NIVI was produced specifically for a *British* readership. We have been told that the use of "they" with a singular antecedent is more common in Britain than in American English (we have not been able either to verify or to falsify this claim). If this is so, the NIVI may sound odder in these constructions to Americans than to its intended readers. In any case, American English versions have not widely imitated the NIVI's technique (though it does occur, for example, in Psalm 19:12 NRSV, in Matthew 18:15–17 NIrV [1995], and in Luke 17:3–4 NIrV[1995]).

verse 17, one has well nigh forgotten that we are really talking about *one* person. The plural "they" blurs out the picture. As Zinsser says, "I don't like plurals; they weaken writing because they are less specific than the singular, less easy to visualize."[49] There is also an oddity in verse 15, in the expression, "show them their fault, just between the two of you." The "two of you" are, of course "you" and "them." Has someone miscounted?! In addition, "gained your brother" in verse 15 has become the colorless "won them over."

> NLT: If *another believer* sins against you, go privately and point out the fault. If the *other person* listens and confesses it, you have won *that person* back. But if you are *unsuccessful*, take one or two others with you and go back again, so that everything you say may be confirmed by two or three witnesses. If *that person* still refuses to listen, take your case to the church. If the church decides you are right, but the *other person* won't accept it, treat *that person* as a pagan or a corrupt tax collector.

The NLT engages in more paraphrase, so that nuances appear and disappear for various reasons unrelated to gender issues. But through paraphrase the NLT can also produce sentence structure that makes less conspicuous the absence of generic "he." The NLT is nevertheless attempting translation with one hand tied behind its back. Would more accurate paraphrase have appeared if the NLT had allowed itself to use generic "he"? Because so many factors go into paraphrasing, it is hard to prove it one way or the other.

We will note only a few obvious problems with the NLT rendering. "Another believer" more or less succeeds in referring to the same sample individual as does "your brother." But the meaning (as distinct from the reference) is different. "Brother" carries family connotations and therefore a stronger motive for reconciliation. (To its credit, NLT revised edition has a marginal note "Greek *your brother*.")

"Go privately" is less specific and less concrete than "between you and him alone." It leaves open the door for someone to interpret it as meaning, "as long as I don't put it in the newspapers, it does not matter whether I take a few friends along to support me." Fortunately, the next verse makes it reasonably clear that "privately" means "with no one else beyond you and him." But of course, one has shifted what is explicit and what must be inferred.

"Point out the fault" is less specific, vivid, and personal than "tell *him his* fault."

"Other person" and "that person" throughout the passage are attempts to avoid "he." The first such is the worst, because it replaces the much more intimate expression, "your brother."

---

[49]William Zinsser, *On Writing Well*, 123.

"Unsuccessful" replaces the much more concrete, "if he does not listen."

In verse 17 the NLT inserts the explanatory phrase, "If the church decides you are right." That is making explicit what is implicit in the original. One suspects the reason. It is not that the reader could not understand the passage without this addition, but that introducing another clause makes less awkward the following phrase, "the other person."

Luke 17:3–4

RSV: Take heed to yourselves; if your *brother* sins, rebuke *him*, and if *he* repents, forgive *him*; and if *he* sins against you seven times in the day, and turns to you seven times, and says, "I repent," you must forgive *him*.

Translating this short passage presents similar problems to the preceding one. But in some ways it is even worse, because the picture of a brother sinning seven times in the day is very concrete. It operates almost like a parable to illustrate a principle of larger scope. The passage gains considerable force by focusing concretely on a singular example, not merely on a vague, plural generality about forgiving "people." We lose this focus if we convert to third person plurals.

NCV, GNB, GW, and NLT wisely retain generic "he's." But by so doing, they are witnesses in our favor. They admit that in spite of their desire to avoid generic "he," they need it here in order to express meaning most exactly. Moreover, they admit by their practice that generic "he" is still understandable and usable in contemporary English![50]

---

[50]The admission is all the more telling because these four specific translations, in their overall policy directions, set a high premium on achieving very smooth, idiomatic, readable English.

We revert to the point made in Chapter 16, that refusing generic "he" is like doing a gymnastic routine with one hand tied behind one's back. It is as if, when the difficulty of the performance becomes too severe, the gymnast suddenly whips out his hand from behind his back in order to surmount the difficulty. Having safely propelled himself through the crisis, he immediately restores the hand to its confined position, and goes through the rest of the routine, hoping that no one will notice the momentary breaking of the "rules."

But then why confine the hand the rest of time? To us as part of the audience, the one telltale moment imparts a faintly ludicrous air to every other part of the performance.

We admire the diligence and dedication of all gymnasts, including gender-neutral gymnasts, and we would by no means want to suggest a mocking or flippant reaction. Their performance is truly remarkable. But we cannot rid ourselves of the conviction that they made at least one poor strategic decision, the decision to confine the one hand. And it does not help their case when we see a feminist performer enter and use each of the two hands half the time, to the delight of the feminist spectators.

By rebinding his hand, the gymnast shows that he has learned nothing from the fact that for one moment he enjoyed liberty. He displayed both to himself and to the whole audience what one can achieve with both hands. The hand is not in fact crippled or bound irrevocably. The limitation is not natural, but represents an artificially imposed "rule," for the sake of "sensitivity." Whether this behavior is really sensitive we already discussed in Chapter 15. We think that it detracts from the very real concerns of women to link them with this artificial— and ultimately ludicrous—constraint.

NRSV: . . . If *another disciple* sins, you must rebuke *the offender*, and if there is repentance, you must forgive. And if *the same person* sins against you seven times a day, and turns back to you seven times and says, "I repent," you must forgive.

The NRSV does a remarkable job within its straitjacket policy of avoiding male overtones. But it cannot avoid all the problems. As we have seen, "another disciple" has the same reference but not the same meaning as "your brother."[51] "Your brother" retains the family connotations and is far more intimate. It gives better motivation to rebuke your brother.

"The offender" is a heavy, stylistically awkward substitute for "him." Moreover, the word "offender" makes explicit in English what is not expressed explicitly within the corresponding clause in Greek.

"You must forgive" omits to tell us whom we must forgive. We can infer it, but the expression is less vivid.

"The same person" is ambiguous. It might mean the same person referred to in the preceding verse, namely "another disciple." Or it might mean that now we are talking about a general case where someone (otherwise unspecified) sins seven times in a day. That is, the word "same" is not referring backward to the preceding verse, but indicates that you are dealing not with seven different people sinning, but with the *same* person sinning all seven times. This person is then perfectly general, *not just* another disciple. We may suppose that a theological principle with this generality is valid, but it is not what the passage says in Greek. The passage is referring to "your brother" all the way through. NRSV has failed to represent accurately what the passage actually means, and has substituted its own more general principle.

NIVI: . . . Rebuke *a brother or sister* who sins, and if *they* repent, forgive *them*. If *anyone* sins against you seven times in a day, and seven times comes back to you and says, "I repent," you must forgive *them*.

The NIVI tries its usual device of plural "they" with singular antecedent. But note that it has fallen into the same error as the NRSV: by placing "anyone" at the beginning of verse 4, it misrepresents the degree of generality in the principle in verse 4.

CEV: 3 Correct any followers of mine who sin, and forgive the ones who say they are sorry. 4 Even if one of them mistreats you seven times in one day and says, "I am sorry," you should still forgive that person.

In the CEV, verse 3 loses force by being put entirely in plurals. Verse 4, fortunately, reverts to singular, but then must finish with the stylistically awkward "that person" where "him" would be cleaner and more appropriate.

---

[51]But, in fact, *adelphos* ("brother") in a context like this one is slightly vaguer than "another disciple." It may designate more broadly a person with whom one is on more intimate terms. Some speeches in Acts use it in addressing fellow Jews (Acts 2:29; 7:2; see Rom. 9:3).

Luke 6:41–42

RSV: Why do you see the speck that is in your *brother's* eye, but do not notice the log that is in your own eye? Or how can you say to your *brother*, "Brother, let me take out the speck that is in your eye," when you yourself do not see the log that is in your own eye? You hypocrite, first take the log out of your own eye, and then you will see clearly to take out the speck that is in your *brother's* eye.

NRSV: Why do you see the speck in your *neighbor's* eye, but do not notice the log in your own eye? Or how can you say to your *neighbor*, "Friend, let me take out the speck in your eye," when you yourself do not see the log in your own eye? You hypocrite, first take the log out of your own eye, and then you will see clearly to take the speck out of your *neighbor's* eye.

The RSV (and NIV) translates four occurrences of the Greek word *adelphos* with "brother." The NRSV translates three times with "neighbor," once with "Friend." "Neighbor" and "friend" are more distant than "brother," and neither carries the family connotations.[52] Of course, "brother" in undoubtedly being used here in a metaphorical sense. But the metaphor belongs as much to the entire saying as it does to one word. The saying invites us to picture even what we might do with someone who was a literal (male) brother, as an illustration of the broader principle of what we should do to one who is a "brother" in the religious sense. When we take into account the context of Jesus' teaching, the word "brother" also hints at an application focused specifically on the Christian "brotherhood." This specific focus is lost with the word "neighbor."

To translate *adelphos* ("brother"), the NIVI uses "someone else," then nothing, then "friend," then "the other person." This is colorless and weak, worse than the NRSV's "neighbor." NCV has "friend" four times. GNB has "brother" four times! What is the matter with "brother," that the NRSV, NIVI, NCV, NLT, and CEV had to avoid this obvious equivalent? (The problems are similar in the parallel passage, Matt. 7:3–5.)

All in all, the translators have tried their hardest to do a good job with a bad set of tools. One may admire how well they have done under such limitations, and still protest, as we do, the slavery to the unnatural prohibition under which they labor and which makes it impossible for them to do better.

---

[52]BAGD gives *neighbor* as a gloss for *adelphos* under meaning #4, citing Luke 6:41–42 and a few passages like it. The gloss *neighbor* was almost certainly not intended to say that the word *adelphos* here loses its family connotations, but only that it is being used to refer to an associate, not a literal sibling. All the passages from early Christian literature probably have either the sense of religious "brotherhood" or use the literal "brother" as an example to state a general principle.

I. The extent of the changes

We have looked at dozens of specific examples of changes in gender-neutral Bibles. But is it possible to quantify the total number of changes? A precise count would be impossible without comparing every verse in each gender-neutral version, line by line. But an approximate sense of the number of changes can come from a comparison of the number of times certain words are used in the RSV and NRSV.[53]

1. The changes from singular to plural

A computerized word count shows that the words "he, him, his" occur 4,200 fewer times in the NRSV than in the RSV. However, in some cases the singular sense was preserved in an acceptable way using the words "one, someone, anyone, everyone, whoever" (plus their possessive forms). These words occur 900 more times in the NRSV.[54] Now there may be an occasional verse where changes have been made for reasons other than gender language concerns, but the vast majority were changed because of the desire to eliminate the "masculine" words "he, him, his." These figures suggest, then, that the offending words "he, him, his" were either eliminated or changed to plurals, to second person, or to first person, about 3,300 times in the NRSV.[55] The change to the plurals "they, them, their, those" probably accounts for over half of these instances, since those words occur 1,732 more times in the NRSV. In many other cases, the pronouns have just been dropped and the sentence recast in different ways. As we have seen in many examples above, such changes frequently introduce losses of meaning.

2. Changes in other words

A computer analysis can also show us the extent of other word changes, at least for the NRSV. The word "father" (including plural and possessive forms) occurs 601 fewer times in the NRSV than in the RSV. The word "son" occurs 181 fewer times (including the loss of "son of man" 106 times in the

---

[53]The statistics in the following two paragraphs were compiled using *BibleWorks* (Hermeneutika Bible Research Software). Statistics are given for the RSV and NRSV because the one is a revision of the other, and because both are available on this same Bible search program. The NIV is also on this program, but not the NIVI, so a similar statistical analysis is not possible. The NLT is available on *BibleWorks 4*, but since it is not exactly a revision of an earlier version comparative statistics cannot be compiled. (*The New Living Translation* is a new translation following change-in-form translation philosophy similar to *The Living Bible*. Perhaps, because it was done under the sponsorship of Tyndale House Publishers, the publisher of *The Living Bible*, it may have used wording from the *Living Bible* here and there, but in many places the wording shows no relation to *The Living Bible*.)

[54]These numbers are not rounded off, but the statistics happened to result in even hundreds (1546 + 953 + 1701 = 4200, and 495 + 25 + 105 + 45 + 114 + 8 + 108 = 900).

[55]This number differs from the count of 3,408 given by Wayne Grudem in an earlier writing because the earlier figure did not take into account the word "whoever," which occurs 108 more times in the NRSV.

Old Testament). The terms "brother" and "brethren" (including plural and possessive forms) occur 266 fewer times, and "man/men" is apparently changed to "mortal, mortals" 205 times.[56]

We are not saying, of course, that every last one of these changes is unjustified, for one would need to examine each verse individually to make such a claim. But we are saying that in the dozens of examples that we have examined in detail, there are unacceptable changes that involve loss of nuance, change of perspective, loss of individual emphasis, and a frequent failure to translate male components of meaning that are in the original text. And these examples, in conjunction with the word counts listed here, lead us to think that the *total number of unacceptable changes in meaning* in this one gender-neutral translation alone would be *somewhere in excess of 4,600.*

Probably this estimate is somewhat high, because sometimes acceptable renderings may have been found using other ways of restatement. But if even *half* of the changes result in significant loss of meaning (and we think the total is much higher than that), then we are still left with a Bible in which over 2,300 places the translation is untrustworthy.

3. Why make these changes?

Why make these changes? There have been no new archaeological discoveries, no changes in our knowledge of Greek and Hebrew, no ancient texts discovered that would suggest that we put plural pronouns instead of singular in these places, or first or second person in place of third person. There have been no linguistic discoveries showing that the words previously translated "father," "son," and "brother" (singular) have lost their distinctive male meanings. No, the changes have been made in the NRSV because the NRSV translators were required by a division of the National Council of Churches of Christ to remove "masculine oriented language" from the Bible. And similar changes were also made in the NIVI, CEV, NCV, and NLT because of policy decisions to eliminate much male-oriented language in the Bible.

This is not a small difference in a few verses. The systematic change from singulars to plurals alters the flavor and tone of the Bible, with a significant loss in the Bible's emphasis on God relating directly to a specific, individual person. The loss of these other masculine words significantly diminishes the degree to which male examples and male imagery in the Bible are accurately translated into English. And in thousands of cases the translations lose accuracy in other ways, because of the way translators

---

[56]The word "mortal," which is generally introduced as a substitute for "man" in the verses we have examined, occurs 117 more times and "mortals" 88 more times in the NRSV than in the RSV, making a total of 205 additional times. (The words "man" and "men" occur a total of 2,462 fewer times, but as explained above, many of these are cases we would not dispute because no male component of meaning is found in the original Hebrew or Greek text.)

must rephrase, reword, and recast sentences, simply to avoid using the offending masculine words. The result is indeed a more "gender-neutral" Bible, for male components of meaning are eliminated from thousands of verses. But it is not a more accurate Bible, or a more trustworthy one.

4. After all these changes, how many pronouns can you actually trust?

There is one other consideration. Such changes in gender-neutral translations will undermine readers' trust in *many other pronouns in the Bible.* Think about it for a moment: imagine that you have a translation such as the *New Living Translation* that tells you in its Preface that "in many instances *we have used plural pronouns (they, them) in place of the gender-specific singular (he, him)*" (p. xlv, NLT).[57] Or imagine that you have the NIVI that tells you, "In order to avoid gender-specific language in statements of a general kind, it was agreed that *the plural might be substituted for the singular and the second person for the third person*" (p. vii, NIVI).

Now when you are reading this Bible, imagine that you want to make a point in a sermon (or contribute something in a Bible study) based on one of those plural pronouns. How do you know you can depend on it? Maybe it is accurate, but then again maybe it is one of those "substitutes" that replaced "patriarchal" language, and maybe the original Hebrew or Greek text really has a third person singular, not a plural as your translation would indicate. Then how do you know that the "they" or "we" or "you" corresponds most exactly to what God's Word said? How can you base any trust in it at all? Unless you can check the Greek or Hebrew text yourself, you simply will not be able to trust any of those pronouns anywhere in that gender-neutral Bible.

How much difference does that make? For the NLT,[58] the possible substitute pronouns that sometimes were used to avoid generic "he" occur as follows: we (2,350), us (1,589), our (1,317), ours (23), ourselves (42), you (14,811), your (6,299), yours (84), yourself (178), yourselves (175), they (7,435), them (5,033), their (4,133), theirs (15), themselves (257). That is a total of 43,741 words in the Bible. Now even if half of these occur in historical narratives or other contexts where no changes would be made because "you" refers to the individual being spoken to and "they" refers to an identifiable group of people, that still leaves over 20,000 cases where you can have no confidence that the pronoun faithfully represents the meaning of the Hebrew or Greek text. Such erosion of trust in our English Bibles is a high price to pay for gender-neutral translations.

---

[57]The NLT revised edition says, "In many instances we have used plural pronouns (they, them) in place of the masculine singular (he, him)" (p. xliv).

[58]The count might be slightly different for the NLT revised edition.

CHAPTER 19

More Examples
Concerning Man, Father, Son

In this chapter we look at more examples of changes in gender-neutral translations. The words we consider here are "man," "men," "father," "son," "fatherless," and some instances of male human beings used as examples for general cases or general truths. Still more examples can be found in Appendix 4.

(Readers who think they have seen enough examples may simply skip to the next chapter.)

A. Deleting "man" and "men" for a male human being: more examples[1]

In Greek the word *anēr* almost always has the sense "husband" or "man" (male human being),[2] while there is another word (*anthrōpos*) that can mean "man" or "person," depending on context. Until recently, English translations included the male semantic component of *anēr* in translation. But gender-neutral translations show some changes that obliterate the male meaning that attaches to this term. (For further discussion of the meaning of *anēr*, see Appendix 2.) The following examples illustrate such loss of meaning.

Acts 4:4

NIV: But many who heard the message believed, and the number of *men* (Greek *anēr*, plural) grew to about five thousand.

---

[1]This first section continues the discussion of references to men that was begun in Chapter 12, above.

[2]Colorado Springs Guideline A.4 says, "Hebrew *'îsh* should ordinarily be translated 'man' and 'men,' and Greek *anēr* should almost always be so translated."

NRS: But many of those who heard the word believed; and *they* numbered about five thousand.

CEV: But a lot of people who had heard the message believed it. So by now there were about five thousand *followers* of the Lord.

NCV: But many of those who had heard Peter and John preach believed the things they said. There were now about five thousand in the group of *believers*.

The different numbers are significant in understanding the history of the remarkable early growth of the church. Were there five thousand *men*, which indicates a very large congregation when women and children are also taken into account? This would make a congregation of at least 10,000 assuming an equal number of women, and more with children. Or were there just five thousand *believers* in total?

The word *anēr* indicates there were five thousand "men."[3] It is not foreign to New Testament writers to give such a count (note Matt. 14:21, where Matthew specifies that he is excluding women and children from the total: "The number of those who ate was about five thousand men, besides women and children"; similarly, 15:38). Gender-neutral translations reduce the size of the church at this point by more than half.

Acts 9:38

RSV: . . . the disciples, hearing that Peter was there, sent two *men (anēr,* plural) to him.

NCV: . . . the followers in Joppa heard that Peter was in Lydda, they sent two *messengers* to Peter.

Here the NCV omits that the "messengers" were male. For what purpose?

Acts 11:3

RSV: Why did you go to uncircumcised *men* and eat with them?

NCV: You went into the homes of *people* who are not circumcised and ate with them!

Since only men could be circumcised, the "people" referred to were all men. The Greek text has the word *anēr*, specifically indicating *men*.

Matthew 12:41

RSV: The *men* (Greek *anēr*, plural) of Nineveh will arise at the judgment with this generation and condemn it.

---

[3]F. F. Bruce says, "The number of the men alone now totaled some five thousand," and his footnote explains, "'of the men' as distinct from women and children" (*The Book of the Acts*, NIC [Grand Rapids: Eerdmans, 1954], 96). Craig Keener says that the population of Jerusalem at that time was between 25,000 and 85,000, and that Josephus gives the total number of Pharisees in Palestine as 6,000. He then adds, "A total of 5,000 Christian Jewish Christian 'men' in Jerusalem, not including women and children (so the Greek here) is thus quite substantial" (*The IVP Bible Background Commentary: New Testament* [Downers Grove, Ill.: IVP, 1993], 333).

NRSV: The *people* of Nineveh will rise up at the judgment with this generation and condemn it.

The NIVI, NIrV(1995), NCV, and NLT also have "people."[4]

The word *anēr* occurs here. Mark Strauss writes, "Since females were certainly among those converted at Nineveh, the sense here appears to be 'people.'"[5] But the fact that females were converted at Nineveh does not imply that Matthew mentions them. The pressure is on to think that he does mention them, because that is how we moderns would think. But the ancient world was not so caught up in the pressures from egalitarianism. Perhaps Matthew singled out the men because within the ancient world men would more typically be the ones to appear in court. Or perhaps he mentioned the men as representative of all. Because Strauss fails to recognize the established lexical boundaries for *anēr*, he is forced to guess from the context again and again whether "men" is intended—and in dozens upon dozens of contexts there is not enough contextual information to decide.

However, prior to the modern push to eliminate male meanings from the Bible, the overwhelming evidence for a male sense to *anēr* would have made this an easy decision. But today, while the word *anēr* with its male component pushes strongly toward one conclusion, translators who neglect this are left to modern guesses as to what Matthew might most reasonably say, and these guesses push in the other direction. In all cases like this, the gender-neutral translations can be expected to lean toward eliminating maleness.

Matthew 14:35

RSV: And when the *men* (Greek *anēr*, plural) of that place recognized him, they sent round to all that region and brought to him all that were sick.

NRSV: After the *people* of that place recognized him, they sent word throughout the region and brought all who were sick to him.

Nothing from the context indicates decisively whether men and women were both involved, whether men only were involved, or whether Matthew wishes to single out the men as the primary ones responsible for the activities. The word *anēr*, however, normally designates men. Thus, the meaning evidence from the text says "men." But our modern guesses about what might generally happen in such a scene lead people to suggest that women might have been involved. This situation is precisely the kind of case where

---

[4]GW and REB have "men." The contrast between GW and other gender-neutral translations is revealing. Despite having in its preface a statement leaning toward gender neutrality (p. xiii), GW has refused to alter historical passages that have *anēr*.

[5]Mark L. Strauss, "Linguistic and Hermeneutical Fallacies in the Guidelines Established at the 'Conference on Gender-Related Language in Scripture,'" *Journal of the Evangelical Theological Society* 41/2 (1998): 244.

the pressures for neutrality weigh heaviest. It is not surprising then that the NRSV, NIVI, NIrV(1995), NLT, NCV, and CEV all have "people" and fail to translate the male meaning component in *anēr*.[6]

There is a similar example of eliminating male meaning in an Old Testament passage quoted in Matthew:

Zechariah 13:7

NIV: Awake, O sword, against my shepherd, against the *man* who is close to me! . . . Strike the shepherd, and the sheep will be scattered.

CEV: My sword, wake up! Attack my shepherd and *friend*.

CEV has eliminated the male marking of the word for "man" (*geber*). In the New Testament Jesus quotes this verse as fulfilled in him (Matt. 26:31). The "man" in question is Jesus. So why did CEV obscure the maleness here?

In Chapter 13 we already mentioned similar examples in the Gospels and Acts where the male-specific term *anēr* is translated without male meaning in English: Matthew 7:24 (the wise *man* who built his house on a rock becomes a wise "person" in the NLT and CEV); Luke 5:18 (the *men* who came carrying a paralytic and who dug a hole in the roof of the house become "some people" in the NIVI and CEV); 14:24 (the *men* who refused the banquet invitation are called "those who were invited" or "the guests I first invited" in the NRSV, NIVI, NLT, CEV, and NCV); Acts 1:21("one of the *men*" from whom a new apostle would be chosen to replace Judas is now "one of those who have been with us" in the NIVI); 5:36 (the four hundred *men* who followed the revolutionary Theudas have become four hundred "others" in the NLT); 8:2 (CEV, NCV: the godly *men* who buried Stephen are called "faithful followers of the Lord" in the CEV and "religious people" in the NCV); 9:7 (the *men* traveling with Saul on the road to Damascus are called "those" in the NIVI and "people" in the NCV); 11:20 (the *men* from Cyprus and Cyrene who went to Antioch to preach are "believers" in the NLT, "followers" in the CEV, and "people" in the NCV).

1 Corinthians 13:11

NIV: When I became a *man*, I put childish ways behind me.

NIVI: When I became an *adult*, I put childish ways behind me.

Since the apostle Paul is speaking in the first person, "I," with himself as the principal illustration, the normal male component in *anēr* is undoubtedly still present. "Man" is more accurate than "adult."[7]

Ephesians 4:13.

RSV: Until we all attain to the unity of the faith and of the knowledge of the Son of God, to mature *manhood*, to the measure of the stature of the fulness of Christ.

---

[6]GW, to its credit, retains "men."

[7]We agree with Carson on this verse: "This change is silly. Paul grew up to be a man, a male human being" (p. 159).

NRSV: Until all of us come to the unity of the faith and of the knowledge of the Son of God, to *maturity*, to the measure of the full stature of Christ.

NIVI: Until we all reach unity in the faith and in the knowledge of the Son of God and become *mature*, attaining to the whole measure of the fulness of Christ.

NLT: Until we come to such unity in our faith and knowledge of God's Son that we will be *mature* and full grown in the Lord, measuring up to the full stature of Christ.

The picture is not of each individual Christian separately coming to maturity, but of all together, as a body, becoming mature, with the goal of attaining "the full stature of Christ." "Manhood" is thus used metaphorically for the whole church. The Greek text (*eis andra teleion*) could more literally be translated, "until we arrive at a mature man," and the word *anēr*, used in this verse, has connotations not only of maleness but of maturity. But since the goal is being like Christ, who is male, the male connotations do not completely disappear from the word in this passage. The whole church is viewed here metaphorically as male, after the pattern of Christ, just as she (!) is viewed as metaphorically female in Ephesians 5:22–33.

But of course egalitarians are uncomfortable with such sexually loaded metaphors, because they are a reminder that human sexual complementarity includes differences, differences that make a difference.

B.   Changing "father" to "parent"[8]

Psalm 103:13

NIV: As a *father* has compassion on *his* children, so the LORD has compassion on those who fear him.

CEV: Just as *parents* are kind to *their* children, the LORD is kind to all who worship him.

CEV changes "father" to "parents," suppressing the fact that the comparison of the Lord to a father is a regular feature in the Old Testament. By turning the singulars into plurals, CEV has also made the first part less vivid, and weakened the effectiveness of the comparison to the Lord, who is after all like a single father, not a plurality of parents. All this to avoid mentioning a male person.

Proverbs 15:5

RSV: A fool despises his *father's* instruction, but he who heeds admonition is prudent.

NRSV: A fool despises a *parent's* instruction, but the one who heeds admonition is prudent.

---

[8]This section continues the discussion of words for "father" (Hebrew *'ab* and Greek *patēr*) that was begun in Chapter 12.

"Father" has been changed to "parent."

Proverbs 17:21

RSV: . . . the *father* of a fool has no joy.

NRSV: . . . the *parent* of a fool has no joy.

The Hebrew word '*ab* (singular) indicates a male parent. Why not translate that meaning?

Proverbs 27:10

NIV: Do not forsake your friend and the friend of your *father*.

NIVI: Do not forsake your friend and the friend of your *parent*.

Proverbs 28:7

NIV: He who keeps the law is a discerning *son*,
but a companion of gluttons disgraces his *father*.

NIVI: Those who keep the law are discerning *children*,
but companions of gluttons disgrace their *parents*.

Proverbs 29:3

NIV: A man who loves wisdom brings joy to his *father*,
but a companion of prostitutes squanders his wealth.

NIVI: Those who love wisdom bring joy to their *parents*,
but companions of prostitutes squander their wealth.

Not only has the NIVI replaced "father" with "parents," but turned everything into plurals in order to avoid the masculine terms "man" and "his." That is foolish, because the phrase "companion of prostitutes" obviously has in view a son and not a daughter. NIVI alters the meaning by throwing away the male markings, presumably in order to suggest that the verse has in mind daughters who may become "companions of prostitutes" in another sense, that is, by *becoming* prostitutes. But that meaning still does not work well, because it is hard to see how daughters who become prostitutes thereby "squander their [parents'] wealth." The daughters are earning money, not squandering it. No, the passage is about a man. So why does the NIVI try to avoid expressing that fact?

Isaiah 38:19

NIV: . . . *fathers* tell their children about your faithfulness.

NIVI: . . . *parents* tell their children about your faithfulness.

The underlying Hebrew has '*ab* ("father") in the singular.

Acts 7:20.

NIV: For three months he was cared for in his *father's* house.

NIVI: For three months he was cared for in his *parents'* home.

CEV: For three months his parents took care of him in *their* home.

NLT: His *parents* cared for him at home for three months.

Acts 7:20 is clearly referring to Amram, the father of Moses (the Greek text specifies "the house of his father," with "father," *patēr*, in singular). NIVI removes the specific reference to the male parent and replaces it with both parents.

CEV and NLT specify that Moses' parents cared for him, though the Greek does not say that either parent did this. It says only that he "was cared for." What is explicit in the translation is only implicit in the original. In fact, it is not even implicit. The text gives no hint as to whether Miriam the sister of Moses cared for him, or a friend or relative, or the mother alone while the father was out of the house working elsewhere. CEV and NLT have just imported into the text their own unfounded guesses.

Isaiah 39:6

NIV: . . . and all that your *fathers* have stored up until this day, will be carried off to Babylon.

NIVI: . . . and all that your *predecessors* have stored up until this day, will be carried off to Babylon.

The reference is to Hezekiah's male ancestors in the kingly line, his "fathers." The underlying Hebrew word is *'ab* ("father") in the plural. It does not mean merely "predecessors," but "fathers," or "forefathers" (including grandfathers and previous generations). The word "predecessors" is much too vague, because it simply means people who came before him, whether or not they were related to him.

Nehemiah 1:6

NIV: I confess the sins we Israelites, including myself and my *father's* house, have committed against you.

NIVI: I confess the sins we Israelites, including myself and my *family*, have committed against you.

Hebrew has the word *'ab* ("father") in the singular. The NIVI has changed the meaning. Whereas the NIV and the original Hebrew refer to Nehemiah's *father's* house and descendants, the NIVI is most naturally understood as referring to *Nehemiah's immediate* family, that is, his wife and children, thereby excluding his father, mother, brothers, sisters, and other close relatives.[9] Of course, these relatives are still included in the larger group of "we Israelites." But the NIVI has changed what Nehemiah actually said.

---

[9]BDB writes "=family" to indicate one of the meanings of "father's house" (p. 3). But it means extended family, descendants of one's father or grandfather or great-grandfather, as one can easily see from the verses that BDB cites (Gen. 24:40; 41:51; 46:31; Num. 18:1; and others). NIVI has either not realized this fact, or has not realized that for a typical modern reader of English, "my family" will include only the nuclear family.

C. Changing "son" to "child"[10]

Proverbs 10:5

RSV: A *son* who gathers in summer is prudent, but a *son* who sleeps in harvest brings shame.

NRSV: A *child* who gathers in summer is prudent, but a *child* who sleeps in harvest brings shame.

NLT: A wise *youth* works hard all summer; a *youth* who sleeps away the hour of opportunity brings shame.

The word for "son" is the masculine word *ben*, in the singular. The picture is of a single individual. The reader pictures a male child, though the example is clearly generalizable. In addition, in the ancient Israelite context, sons rather than daughters would be the ones expected to be engaged in the hard manual labor of harvesting.[11] The NRSV and NLT fail to translate the male component of the Hebrew word *ben*, "son." In addition, by using "youth" the NLT has removed any hint that the proverb is thinking of the son's responsibility to his father as the background for his toil in the field. The hint at responsibility to parents is gone.

Proverbs 10:1

NIV: A wise *son* brings joy to his father,
But a foolish *son* grief to his mother.

NIVI: Wise *children* bring joy to their fathers,
But the *foolish* bring grief to their mothers.

The word for "son" is the masculine singular word *ben*. The reader pictures a male child. The NIVI deletes the male component, and pluralizes to avoid two occurrences of "his." Similar treatment occurs in Proverbs 15:20.

Proverbs 13:24

NIV: He who spares the rod hates his *son*,
but he who loves *him* is careful to discipline *him*.

NIVI: Those who spare the rod hate their *children*,
but those who love *them* are careful to discipline *them*.

Proverbs 17:25

NIV: A foolish *son* brings grief to his father
and bitterness to the one who bore him.

---

[10]This section continues the discussion of words for "son" in Chapter 11, pp. 200–201.

[11]Ruth 2:8 indicates that women were sometimes out in the fields for harvest. But that does not destroy our point, to the effect that it is natural for Israelites, when picturing a landowner whose fields are ready for harvest, to think in the first instance of the responsibility of the owner's son. The son should be out there even without being told. The daughter has responsibilities in the house. It would not follow as a matter of course that she would go out to the field.

NIVI: Foolish *children* bring grief to their fathers
and bitterness to those who bore them.

Proverbs 19:13

NIV: A foolish *son* is his father's ruin, . . .

NIVI: A foolish *child* is a father's ruin, . . .

Proverbs 19:18

NIV: Discipline your *son*, . . .

NIVI: Discipline your *children*, . . .

Proverbs 19:26

NIV: He who robs his father and drives out his mother
is a *son* who brings shame and disgrace.

NIVI: Those who rob their father and drive out their mother
are *children* who bring shame and disgrace.

Proverbs 29:17

NIV: Discipline your *son*, and *he* will give you peace; . . .

NIVI: Discipline your *children*, and *they* will give you peace; . . .

D. How can an "orphan" have a living mother?

Job 24:9

RSV: There are those who snatch the *fatherless* child from the breast.

NRSV: There are those who snatch the *orphan* child from the breast.

The picture is of a child nursing at the breast, hinting that the mother is still alive and feeding the child, though the father is dead.[12] NRSV's "orphan" deletes the male component of "fatherless," resulting in a statement that bewilders the reader: if the child is an orphan, it has no father or mother—so how could it be nursing at it's mother's breast?

E. More examples

We could go on. So as not to weary readers, we have transferred to Appendix 4 some other examples.

---

[12]The Hebrew word *yatom* means "fatherless," and the BDB lexicon says, "in no case clear that both parents are dead" (p. 450).

CHAPTER **20**

Practical Application Questions

In wrapping up our discussion, we turn now to some common questions.

A. Tests for gender-neutral policy

"How can I tell whether a translation is gender-neutral?"

The *New Revised Standard Version* (NRSV), *New International Version Inclusive Language Edition* (NIVI), *New Century Version* (NCV), *Contemporary English Version* (CEV), *Good News Bible* (GNB), *New Living Translation* (NLT), and *God's Word* (GW) are gender-neutral.[1] We base the judgment primarily on their decision systematically to avoid generic "he." That one choice is the most decisive, because it affects thousands of verses. But all these versions also drop male-oriented markings in other passages. You can test a version for yourself by looking up any of the passages that we have discussed, and comparing the test version with a reliable translation like the *New American Standard Bible* (NASB) or *New International Version* (NIV).

The best quick test is to look at John 14:21 and 14:23. You can also check Matthew 16:24–26. The particular meanings expressed in these verses in Greek require a translation that uses generic "he." If a particular version uses generic "he" in these verses, it will probably use "he" elsewhere in order accurately to represent the full meaning. If, on the other hand, generic "he" does not appear, you know that the translation has restructured the verses, altering nuances of meaning in the process. If it restructures these

---

[1]The *New International Reader's Version* (NIrV[1995]) was gender-neutral when first published in 1995 and 1996, but it has now been revised to bring it into conformity with sounder principles. In the 1998 edition, the preface says, "This edition of the New International Reader's Version has been revised so that the gender language more closely matches that of the New International Version" (NIrV[1998], x).

verses, it probably does the same throughout the whole Bible in order to avoid male-oriented meanings.

Regarding the word "man" (another telltale sign), a quick test would be to see if it uses the word "man" as a name for the human race in Genesis 1:26 and 5:2, or if it uses the word "man" in Psalm 1:1, "Blessed is the man . . ."

B. Isn't this controversy for experts only?

Some readers might think, "Shouldn't I just leave questions of Bible translation to the experts?"

Many detailed issues in translation require knowledge of the original languages. But in the case of eliminating generic "he," you can see for yourself the changes that gender-neutral translations introduce. In these verses, no change has occurred in scholars' understanding of the meaning in the original. The changes result from alleged changes in the English language. If you are a native speaker of English, you have as much right as any biblical scholar to decide whether such changes are wise.[2]

In this kind of verse, as well as in many others, any competent speaker of English can ask the appropriate questions. Which English expressions best translate the meaning that is there in the original? Is generic "he" understandable and proper English today? Is the word "man" without the article an understandable and proper name for the human race? Does a change from "he" to "you" or "we" or "they" distort the meaning or not?

Everyone who speaks and writes English can contribute legitimately to that discussion and can come to an informed decision on it. That is why the decisions of whole churches and whole denominations are significant in this matter: these are people who speak and write English, and many of them understand very well what the issues are and consider this an important issue for preserving accurate translations of the Word of God. You as an individual Christian, along with individual churches and denominations, will ultimately decide this issue, because you will decide which Bible translations you will buy and use. Scholars of course should have a role in the discussion, but it is also possible for scholars to become too isolated in the academic world and lose sight of the "large picture," even on the state of the English language itself.[3]

---

[2]There are a few technical dimensions to the question, because we must consider whether the original has any male overtones parallel to those of generic "he" and whether the third-person wording in the original carries a force analogous to the third person in English (see Appendix 3). But the technical details are very minor in comparison with the overarching question, "Should we allow all this restructuring and changing of nuances?"

[3]Note our earlier remarks in the excursus at the end of Chapter 10. Even people with no special training in linguistics or a second language (the naïve level 1 approach) have profound skill in using and understanding their native tongue. They exhibit intuitive discernment (level

C. What about the translators of gender-neutral versions?

"How could this happen? Doesn't it show that a lot of translators have given in to feminist claims, and that they do not respect Scripture?"

We must be careful not to jump to conclusions about individuals. For convenience we have spoken of what translators do, but all we actually have is the product, the resulting translation. We know neither what was going on in translators' minds nor the motives that underlay their thinking.

In addition, the translators were not a uniform group. Many of the translators involved in gender-neutral translations were in fact complementarian in their own views about women. Others, however, favored egalitarian or feminist positions. In each Bible translation, teams of people worked together to produce the translation. In fact, we know from private conversations that some of the scholars connected with some gender-neutral translations produced early drafts that did not contain the problems that we see in the final version. They must not be held responsible for changes that were introduced at a later point without their consent.

Others may have been outvoted in key decisions. Others may have looked over part of a version but not the verses that exhibit the problems. Others may have worked under a "mandate" like what the National Council of Churches of Christ gave for the NRSV, requiring certain directions to be taken in producing the translation. While disagreeing with the mandate, they may have continued to work on the project in order to ensure that the resulting translation was as good as it could be given the constraints under which it was produced. Others may have agreed with gender-neutral changes because they were told by some experts in English style that these changes were necessary due to the state of the English language, and that using generic "he" and using "man" to refer to the human race were no longer acceptable in English today. If translators begin to believe such statements about English, we must recognize that they have few options left. They may have thought, reluctantly, that they were just agreeing with "modern English style."

Thus, it is inappropriate to make this issue an occasion for personal attacks. We must beware of overreacting and firing ourselves with a zeal that "is not based on knowledge" (Rom. 10:2). "For man's anger does not bring about the righteous life that God desires" (James 1:20). The law of

---

3) when it comes to the nuances of their own language. Therefore, experts (with the theoretically informed apparatus of level 2) must pay attention to their instincts on these matters. They must beware of brushing aside this level-3 discernment merely on the ground that it does not mesh well with their level-2 theories.

Carson rightly cautions us about hasty generalities. "Arguments about what 'sounds' right turn out to be remarkably subjective" (*The Inclusive-Language Debate* [Grand Rapids: Baker, 1998], 192). There are variations in English, so that any one person's judgment may not always represent the whole spectrum of variations. But neither can one hastily dismiss widespread reactions from many people.

love requires us to hope for the best concerning other people's motives (1 Cor. 13:7), while we are scrupulously critical of our own.

However, precisely because we know something of our own sinful tendencies, and because we share with Christians a common life in the body of Christ (1 Cor. 12) and a common zeal for the glory of Christ, it is not amiss to warn others about temptations that we see impinging. We would be unwise if we minimized the significance of the misjudgments in gender-neutral translations and did not speak of the spiritual dangers.

We are also disturbed that some evangelical defenders of gender-neutral translations have not been forthright about the problems. Let Jerry, our hypothetical advocate of gender-neutral Bibles, serve as our example once more. Jerry in his explanations gives the impression that there are very few changes in meaning and that in gender-neutral translations all is well, apart perhaps from a few accidental oversights. Contrast his approach with the candor that we see from two more liberal sources, the National Council of Churches responsible for the NRSV and the consortium of British churches responsible for the REB. From the Preface to the NRSV comes the admission that the goals of gender neutrality and preserving "passages that reflect the historical situation of ancient patriarchal culture" stand "in tension and even in conflict."[4] From the Preface to the REB comes the observation that avoiding generic "he" can mean "compromising scholarly integrity."[5] Why does Jerry try to assure us, while the NRSV and the REB do not? Does Jerry really understand the issues? Are there reasons why he is minimizing the difficulties, the genuine changes in meaning?

In the end we have to let Jerry judge his own motives. But we still have the duty to evaluate the products, the actual versions produced. We are justified in criticizing gender-neutral versions themselves. They have instituted a systematic policy that has resulted in compromising faithfulness to the meaning of the original.

D. Helping out

"What can I do to help?"

First, pursue godliness and purity in your own life in your response to issues of human sexuality. Feminism, though it is wrongheaded in many ways, is partly reacting against human sin. We hinder the cause of truth if we do not display godliness in responding. In particular, we need to follow the Bible as it calls us to respect and honor women as well as men. We should look for biblical ways in which we may honor and encourage women. In our own daily speech and writing, we should look for ways to be sensitive to the interests and concerns of women as well as men, and this

---

[4]NRSV, Preface, x.
[5]REB, Preface, ix.

may involve some changes in habitual patterns of speech that actually are insensitive to women or that appear to fail to include them (though such appearance was not our intention). Remember also that several times in this book we have said that alternative forms of expression (such as using "he or she," or changing a sentence to plurals) are often very appropriate in our own speech and writing today, since an author has freedom with his or her own composition in a way that a translator of another person's writing does not.

We should also encourage Bible translations to make legitimate, acceptable changes in translation where meaning is not sacrificed and where the inclusion of women could be made more explicit than it has been in the past. In addition, we should look for ways in which we may encourage men to be men who imitate Christ and not the patterns of this world (Rom. 12:1–2). We should display graciousness and patience in dealing with those influenced by the negative, unbiblical aspects of feminism, both men and women (1 Tim. 2:23–26; Col. 2:12–15).

Second, use a reliable translation in your own study and Bible reading. We can recommend the NKJV, NASB, the RSV,[6] and the NIV. (The KJV was reliable in its time and is still used by people who are accustomed to it, but now it has become difficult for people to understand if they themselves have not grown up using it.) Other reliable translations may appear in the future.[7] We may hope that one or more of the presently available versions may undertake a small revision to include permissible changes indicated in Chapter 11, in order that it may become still better. But we must pray that they will not undertake the impermissible changes discussed in Chapters 13–19.[8]

Third, alert your pastor to the issues, and urge him to be aware of them when the church decides to purchase a new set of pew Bibles. As occasion arises, alert other people to the problems that exist in a translation that they may be using.

---

[6]We are aware, as many are, that the RSV shows doctrinal problems in a handful of verses (the most famous being Isaiah 7:14). But these are not gender related. No translation is flawlessly perfect. Conversely, no translation in common use is so bad that people cannot hear from it the message of salvation and be saved. As usual, we are here addressing most focally the problems introduced by gender-neutral translation principles.

[7]As we mentioned in Chapter 8 (p. 147), several new Bible translations have been announced recently, all of which give indication of conforming to the principles upheld in this book and expressed in the Colorado Springs Guidelines. These translations include the NET Bible, New English Translation (NET), The International Standard Bible (ISB), the Holman Christian Standard Bible (HCSB), and the English Standard Version (ESV). The first two of these have already released entire New Testaments, and we look forward to the release of the entire Bible in these new versions in the next few years.

[8]But note that in a few of the sections at the end of Chapter 18, we indicate that in our judgment the decisions are not as clear-cut, for example with respect to the translation of *anthrōpos* ("man, person") or the translation of plural *adelphoi* ("brothers, brothers and sisters").

Finally, pray for the work of translation and for the church, that the church as a whole may have discernment in its use of the translations on the market.[9]

---

[9]As further developments take place, you may receive up-to-date information from the Council on Biblical Manhood and Womanhood, P.O. Box 7337, Libertyville, IL 60048, which takes a continuing interest in the issue of gender-neutral translation as well as the broader issues concerning men and women. Their Web site is at www.cbmw.org.

CHAPTER 21

Conclusion

Our friend Jerry, our hypothetical advocate of gender-neutral translations, can sound so reasonable. He says,

> Gender-neutral translations are just adjusting to changes in English usage and using sophisticated translation theory. You wouldn't want me to continue using the word "gay" for "joyful" now that it has taken on another meaning. So it is with the other changes—the language has changed, and we must adapt accordingly. There is no need for concern. Trust me.

Then we look at Proverbs 3:12.

NIV: Because the LORD disciplines those he loves, as a *father* the son he delights in.

NIVI: Because the LORD disciplines those he loves, as *parents* the children they delight in.

The NIVI has changed "father" to "parents."[1] The underlying Hebrew word *'ab* means "father." The meaning is clear in Hebrew. So why change the English? Has the English language changed, so that "father" no longer means "father"? No, "father" means what it did thirty years ago or three hundred years ago. Or have we discovered new information about the Hebrew of Proverbs in the last thirty years? No, the Hebrew words mean the same things we previously thought they did. There is no excuse for the

---

[1]Similarly, GNB, NCV, and CEV have "parents." On the other hand, KJV, RSV, NASB, NKJV, The New Berkeley Version (1969), GNB(1976), NRSV, GW, and NLT have "father." NEB has the translation, "for those whom he loves the LORD reproves, and he punishes a favourite son." The REB has a similar wording, and so does the quotation of Proverbs 3:12 in Hebrews 12:6. (See our discussion in Chapter 10 on the difference between quotation and translation.) NEB is based on the Septuagint, the ancient Greek translation, which may represent a different underlying Hebrew text. Except for NEB and REB, modern translations have followed the Hebrew in the Masoretic text. The variation in the Septuagint has nothing to do with gender issues, so we need not discuss it further here.

change, other than willfully avoiding maleness. Despite Jerry's assurances, this change is not the product of advanced scholarship.

This sort of evasion in Bible translation can only make one shake one's head. How could they do it? This verse is not a proverb about parenting in general. Rather, *it expresses what God is like*. The relation of a father to a son illustrates the character of God. God is elsewhere described as Father. So the illustration is even more pointed if it uses a human father as the example.

The NIVI was not fighting for some worthy theological principle here. Quite the contrary—the sheer pettiness of this change makes one marvel. What possible motive could a translator have to evade the meaning "father"? Nothing is achieved here except conformity to a general modern cultural antipathy to maleness. For this flimsy purpose the translation tampers with the meaning and weakens the tie between God and human father. Will we betray translation responsibility and faithfulness to every word that comes from the mouth of God for the sake of a passing cultural fad?

When we see this kind of alteration of Proverbs 3:12, and in hundreds upon hundreds of other verses, we wonder what has happened to the reverence for every word of Scripture that was so common in the church in previous generations. The words of Scripture are not ours to tamper with as we please.

Some people might say that we are being "petty" by focusing on minor matters. No, it is gender-neutral translations that show pettiness by distorting Proverbs 3:12 and hundreds upon hundreds of other passages. Our respect for the Word of God should extend to minor matters as well as major ones. Otherwise, we are not fully faithful.

Make no mistake. We are grateful for the degree to which the majesty and truthfulness of God's Word sounds out even through flawed and biased translations. In addition, we recognize that even the best translators may on occasion make mistakes. No one should feel less respect for translators if someone uncovers a few minor lapses in accuracy, due to general human frailty and not systematic policy. Translations are not flawless, and often a translator may find no way to convey in English every bit of nuance in the original. We are deeply sympathetic for the difficulties that translators face and grateful for their labors.

But the grip of feminist dogma on the modern psyche confronts us with a particular danger. Feminism attempts systematically to ban from the language patterns of thought that would be contrary to its program. The omissions and alterations in gender-neutral versions are systematic in character and line up with this program. The integrity of the meaning of the Word of God has been compromised in the process.

The issue is therefore tied in with the doctrine of Scripture and its authority. Do we follow the Bible alone, submitting to all its teachings and all its nuances? Or do we trim it in order to fit in more comfortably with modern thought patterns?

Colorado Springs Guidelines

In this appendix we reproduce in full the Colorado Springs Guidelines, and assess their significance. The Colorado Springs Guidelines were originally drawn up at a meeting convened by Dr. James Dobson in Colorado Springs, on May 27, 1997.[1] After some further refinement, they were published in the final version, to which we refer throughout this book.

A. The Guidelines, with the accompanying comments

The Colorado Springs Guidelines were first officially published in Christian magazines. They appeared in the context of an advertisement, of which the Guidelines form the central portion. Below is the text of a paid advertisement that appeared in *Christianity Today* October 27, 1997 (pp. 14–15), and also in *Charisma*, *Moody*, and *World* at about the same time.

Can I Still Trust My Bible?

In recent controversies over gender-neutral translations, Christians have begun to wonder which Bibles they can trust to translate gender-related language accurately.

Here are some guidelines endorsed by Christian leaders who agreed that "it is inappropriate to use gender-neutral language when it diminishes accuracy in the translation of the Bible." These guidelines were written at a meeting convened by Dr. James Dobson in Colorado Springs on May 27, 1997.

If you want to know what Bible translations you can trust, one place to start is to ask your Christian book dealer or your pastor if your translation meets these

---

[1]For the historical time line of events into which they fit, see Chapter 8.

guidelines. Several widely-used translations already meet these guidelines, including the NIV, NASB, RSV, KJV, and NKJV.

COLORADO SPRINGS GUIDELINES FOR TRANSLATION OF GENDER-RELATED LANGUAGE IN SCRIPTURE[2]

A. Gender-related renderings of Biblical language which we affirm:

1. The generic use of "he, him, his, himself" should be employed to translate generic 3rd person masculine singular pronouns in Hebrew, Aramaic and Greek. However, substantival participles such as *ho pisteuōn* can often be rendered in inclusive ways, such as "the one who believes" rather than "he who believes."

2. Person and number should be retained in translation so that singulars are not changed to plurals and third person statements are not changed to second or first person statements, with only rare exceptions required in unusual cases.

3. "Man" should ordinarily be used to designate the human race, for example in Genesis 1:26-27; 5:2; Ezekiel 29:11; and John 2:25.

4. Hebrew *'ish* should ordinarily be translated "man" and "men," and Greek *anēr* should almost always be so translated.

5. In many cases, *anthrōpoi* refers to people in general, and can be translated "people" rather than "men." The singular *anthrōpos* should ordinarily be translated "man" when it refers to a male human being.

6. Indefinite pronouns such as *tis* can be translated "anyone" rather than "any man."

7. In many cases, pronouns such as *oudeis* can be translated "no one" rather than "no man."

8. When *pas* is used as a substantive it can be translated with terms such as "all people" or "everyone."

9. The phrase "son of man" should ordinarily be preserved to retain intracanonical connections.

10. Masculine references to God should be retained.

B. Gender-related renderings which we will generally avoid, though there may be unusual exceptions in certain contexts:

1. "Brother" (*adelphos*) should not be changed to "brother or sister"; however, the plural *adelphoi* can be translated "brothers and sisters" where the context makes clear that the author is referring to both men and women.

---

[2]The Colorado Springs Guidelines were first published in ads: "Can I Still Trust My Bible?" *World* 12/23 (Oct. 25, 1997): 2–3; "Can I Still Trust My Bible?" *Christianity Today* 41/12 (October 27, 1997): 14–15.

2. "Son" (*huios, ben*) should not be changed to "child," or "sons" (*huioi*) to "children" or "sons and daughters." (However, Hebrew *banîm* often means "children.")

3. "Father" (*patēr, 'āb*) should not be changed to "parent," or "fathers" to "parents" or "ancestors."

C. We understand these guidelines to be representative and not exhaustive, and that some details may need further refinement.

Some examples you can check for yourself

The following verses illustrate the guidelines for translation of gender-related language in Scripture. For Guideline A1 (first sentence): John 14:23; Rev. 3:20; (second sentence): John 3:18. A2: Psalm 1:2; 34:20; Gal. 6:7; James 5:14-15. A3: See guidelines for examples; also Psalm 90:3. A4: Hebrew: Psalm 1:1; Greek: Acts 20:30; 1 Cor. 13:11. A5 (first sentence): Matt. 12:36; (second sentence): 1 Cor. 15:21; 1 Tim. 2:5. A6: Matt. 16:24. A7: Gal. 3:11. A8: John 12:32. A9: Psalm 8:4; Dan. 7:13. A10: Matt. 6:9; John 3:16. B1: Matt. 18:15; Rom. 12:1. B2 (first sentence): Gal. 4:7; (second sentence): Exod. 19:6. B3: Gen. 48:21. (This list of verses was not part of the original signed statement.)

Affirmed at a meeting at Focus on the Family headquarters, May 27, 1997 (and revised Sept. 9, 1997), by:

Ken Barker, Secretary, Committee on Bible Translation; Member, Executive Committee of Committee on Bible Translation

Timothy Bayly, Executive Director, Council on Biblical Manhood and Womanhood; Pastor, Church of the Good Shepherd, Bloomington, Indiana

Joel Belz, Publisher, God's World Publications

James Dobson, President, Focus on the Family

Wayne Grudem, President, Council on Biblical Manhood and Womanhood; Professor of Biblical and Systematic Theology, Trinity Evangelical Divinity School

Charles Jarvis, Executive Vice President, Focus on the Family

John Piper, Member, Council on Biblical Manhood and Womanhood; Senior Pastor, Bethlehem Baptist Church, Minneapolis, Minnesota

Vern S. Poythress, Professor of New Testament Interpretation, Westminster Theological Seminary

R. C. Sproul, Chairman, Ligonier Ministries

Ron Youngblood, Member, Committee on Bible Translation; Professor of Old Testament, Bethel Theological Seminary West

These guidelines have also been endorsed by Gleason Archer, Hudson Armerding, Clinton E. Arnold, S. M. Baugh, Alistair Begg, James Montgomery Boice, James Borland, Bill Bright, Vonette Bright, Harold O. J. Brown, Bryan Chapell, Edmund Clowney, Robert Coleman, Charles Colson, Jack Cottrell, Jerry

Falwell, John Frame, W. Robert Godfrey, Jack Hayford, H. Wayne House, Elliott Johnson, Peter Jones, Mary Kassian, D. James Kennedy, George W. Knight III, Andreas Köstenberger, Beverly LaHaye, Tim LaHaye, Gordon R. Lewis, Robert Lewis, Erwin Lutzer, Richard L. Mayhue, R. Albert Mohler, Jr., J. P. Moreland, Joel Nederhood, J. Stanley Oakes, Stephen Olford, J. I. Packer, Dorothy Patterson, Paige Patterson, Dennis Rainey, Pat Robertson, Adrian Rogers, Paul Sailhamer, Robert Saucy, Jerry Vines, John Walvoord, Bruce Ware, Stu Weber, William Weinrich, David Wells, John Wimber.

Resolutions opposing gender-neutral Bible translations were also passed in the summer of 1997 by the Southern Baptist Convention, the Presbyterian Church in America, and the Conservative Congregational Christian Conference.

When these guidelines were published in *CBMW NEWS* [now *Journal for Biblical Manhood and Womanhood*], and when they were released in the June 3, 1997, press release from Focus on the Family, the guidelines were accompanied by the following statement, signed by all twelve participants at the meeting:

Statement by Participants in the Conference on Gender-Related Language in Scripture

Focus on the Family's Headquarters; Colorado Springs, Colorado
May 27, 1997

Over the past two months evangelical leaders have engaged in a serious debate concerning the use of gender-inclusive language in English Bible translation. Dr. James Dobson called a meeting of concerned individuals to discuss together and seek the leading of the Holy Spirit in these matters. Those who participated in this meeting give glory to God for His grace evident among us as we worked together this day, and with hope we offer the following statement with the prayer that it will be of use to the Church for the glory of God.

All participants agree that our overarching concern in Bible translating is to preserve the sanctity of the truth of sacred Scripture by rendering the most accurate translation possible. In the interests of such accuracy, we all agree that modern language is fluid and undergoes changes in nuance that require periodic updates and revisions. We agree that Bible translations should not be influenced by illegitimate intrusions of secular culture or by political or ideological agendas. Specifically, we agree that it is inappropriate to use gender-neutral language when it diminishes accuracy in the translation of the Bible, and we therefore agree to the attached guidelines for translation of gender-related language in Scripture.

We agree there are limited times when the use of gender-neutral language enhances the accuracy of translations, but that the trend in usage of gender-inclusive language can easily become—and because of overuse, in too many cases, already has become—an instrument of distortion of the Biblical text.

We agree that many of the translation decisions made by those who produced Hodder and Stoughton's *New International Version Inclusive Language Edition* in the

United Kingdom were not the wisest choices. Further, the statement in the Preface saying "it is often appropriate to mute the patriarchalism of the culture of the biblical writers through gender-inclusive language" (*Preface to the NIVI*, vii) was regrettable and sadly misleading.

We agree that it was also regrettable that the *New International Reader's Version* (*NIrV*), released also as *The Kid's Devotional Bible*, was released with a Preface which did not explicitly notify parents that gender-related changes were made in this version. We commend Zondervan for offering to refund the purchase price of any *NIrV's* to anyone who makes a request. We agree that families that wish to be reimbursed for the cost of *The Kid's Devotional Bible* (*NIrV*) should also be granted a refund.

Focus on the Family was distressed to learn that its own *Adventures in Odyssey Bible*, the International Children's Bible of Word Publishing, is also a gender-neutral translation (in the Old Testament). Focus on the Family is working with Word, Inc. and has withdrawn that edition from its distribution channels. Focus plans to reimburse parents who request a refund (see attached Focus on the Family press release). We commend Focus on the Family for its decisive and straightforward actions.

It is ironic in light of the present controversy that Zondervan's sales of inclusive language Bibles (*NIrV* and *New Revised Standard Version*) are only five percent of all their Bible sales, and in fact most inclusive Bibles are sold by other publishers: Thomas Nelson/Word (*New Century Bible, International Children's Bible, Contemporary English Version*, and *NRSV*), Tyndale House Publishers (*New Living Translation*), World Bible Publishers (*God's Word* and *NRSV*), and Baker Book House (*NRSV*). We commend the openness with which Zondervan approached this meeting, and we are encouraged by the willingness of the International Bible Society to revise the *New International Reader's Version* so that the revision (which will be completed later this summer) will eliminate the gender-related changes that had been made, bringing it into line with the current NIV.

This throws into stark relief our wider concern with the translation of God's Word among evangelical publishers at large and the necessity within Bible publishing for greater accountability to the Church concerning the matters here raised. The willingness of the IBS to re-examine the language of the *NIrV* and to move away from changes made to its text is greatly encouraging to us, and we call on the other publishers and copyright holders to issue similar public statements demonstrating similar reappraisals of their translation principles (see attached International Bible Society press release of May 27, 1997).

We agree that the discussions were transacted in a spirit of mutual trust and charity. Further, the policy statement issued by the IBS and the press release from Focus on the Family evoked profound gratitude and thanksgiving by all present.

With glory to God, and thanksgiving;

  Ken Barker, Secretary, Committee on Bible Translation; Member, Executive Committee of Committee on Bible Translation

Timothy Bayly, Executive Director, Council on Biblical Manhood and Womanhood; Pastor, Church of the Good Shepherd, Bloomington, IN

Joel Belz, Publisher, God's World Publications

James Dobson, President, Focus on the Family

Lars Dunberg, President, International Bible Society

Wayne Grudem, President, Council on Biblical Manhood and Womanhood; Professor of Biblical and Systematic Theology, Trinity Evangelical Divinity School

Charles Jarvis, Executive Vice President, Focus on the Family

John Piper, Member, Council on Biblical Manhood and Womanhood; Senior Pastor, Bethlehem Baptist Church, Minneapolis, MN

Vern S. Poythress, Professor of New Testament Interpretation, Westminster Theological Seminary

Bruce E. Ryskamp, President and CEO, Zondervan Publishing House

R. C. Sproul, Chairman, Ligonier Ministries

Ron Youngblood, Member, Committee on Bible Translation; Professor of Old Testament, Bethel Theological Seminary West

B.   A description of the meeting

Shortly after the conclusion of the meeting in Colorado Springs (May 27, 1997), Wayne Grudem wrote an account of the meeting. This account was sent to all participants, to check it for factual accuracy. It has been approved as accurate both by those of us who came to the meeting with concerns about the inclusive NIV, and also by Bruce Ryskamp, President of Zondervan, and Ken Barker, Secretary of the NIV's Committee on Bible Translation. Both Mr. Ryskamp and Dr. Barker were present for the entire May 27 meeting, and they along with other participants suggested changes that have been incorporated into the account as it now stands. We believe it is an accurate record of what happened. It was published, in the form that appears below, in *CBMW News*.[3]

NIV SUPPORTERS AND CRITICS AGREE ON HOW TO TRANSLATE GENDER-RELATED LANGUAGE IN SCRIPTURE

Wayne Grudem
President, CBMW

If you put twelve men with strongly differing viewpoints on a controversial issue in one room, what do you get? If they are Christian men who are willing to pray together, and who share a desire that the Bible be translated accurately, then you just might get a surprising agreement.

---

[3]Wayne A. Grudem, "NIV Controversy: Participants Sign Landmark Agreement," *CBMW News* 2/3 (June 1997): 1, 3–6.

That was exactly what happened May 27 at the Focus on the Family head-quarters in Colorado Springs. James Dobson had asked that the main defenders of the New International Version meet with a group concerned about its "inclusive language" editions in England (NIVI) and the United States (the NIrV).

The participants: The meeting included four representatives of the NIV: Bruce Ryskamp, President of Zondervan; Lars Dunberg, President of the International Bible Society; and, at the request of Ryskamp and Dunberg, Ken Barker and Ron Youngblood, two of the principal translators of the NIV.

Others came to the meeting to express concerns about the NIV: I was there as President of CBMW, along with our executive director, Tim Bayly, and John Piper, pastor of Bethlehem Baptist Church, Minneapolis (and a CBMW Council member). Also at the meeting were Vern Poythress, professor of New Testament, Westminster Theological Seminary (and a contributor to CBMW's book, *Recovering Biblical Manhood and Womanhood*), R. C. Sproul, Chairman, Ligonier Ministries (and a member of CBMW's Board of Reference), Joel Belz, Publisher of *World* magazine; Charlie Jarvis, Executive Vice President of Focus on the Family; and James Dobson, President of Focus on the Family, who had convened the meeting.

What happened at the meeting? The meeting began at 9:00 A.M. with an extended time of prayer around the table. We sought God's help for what was becoming a major controversy in the evangelical world. We soon saw those prayers answered, as open, frank discussion led to expressions of sincere desire, on the part of all participants, to translate God's Word accurately. The NIV representatives were dismayed that criticism of a proposed inclusive-language NIV for the U.S. had spilled over into widespread distrust of the current NIV. They were also troubled that they had been linked with secular feminism in the minds of many people, even though the majority of NIV translators were complementarian, not egalitarian, in their personal convictions.

Our "NIV concerns group" then presented a statement we had prepared the previous day. R. C. Sproul opened with an expression of the importance of accu-racy in translation, the realization that language does change over time, and the caution that Bible translators must be very careful not to be influenced by wrong-ful intrusions of secular culture. Then John Piper presented a ten-page list of spe-cific translations in the NIVI and the NIrV which we thought to be inaccurate. Third, Vern Poythress, who had previously studied Bible translation and taught classes in linguistics at Wycliffe Bible Translators' Summer Institute of Linguistics in Norman, Oklahoma, gave his perspective on the difficulties Bible translators face. Dr. Poythress said that, while he appreciated the desire of the NIV translators to communicate effectively in contemporary English, these concerns have to be weighed against some important losses in the accuracy and content of what was actually communicated by the revisions. Fourth, I presented a list of suggestions for guidelines involving the translation of gender-related language in Scripture. Finally, Tim Bayly presented some actions that we were asking the NIV represen-tatives to consider in light of our concerns.

The surprise press release, and some common ground: However, *two hours before* our meeting had started, the International Bible Society had issued a press release that contained many of the very points we were prepared to request from them! The surprise press release announced: (1) that the IBS was abandoning all plans for gender-related changes in the NIV, (2) that the present NIV would continue to be published unchanged, (3) that the NIrV would be immediately revised to bring its treatment of gender into line with the current NIV, and (4) that the IBS would immediately negotiate with the British publisher (Hodder & Stoughton) to cease publication of the inclusive language NIV in the United Kingdom. We were both amazed and delighted at these actions. But one aspect still troubled us: the press release said the reason for the decisions was the strong desire of the Christian public for an unchanged NIV, and it said that many scholars still thought the inclusive versions rendered the original texts "more precisely" into current English.

As our discussions continued through the morning, however, we found that we shared even more common ground. The NIV representatives agreed with the concerns about accuracy and cultural pressures that R. C. Sproul had expressed, and also shared concerns over many of the specific translation items that John Piper had raised. In addition, we found that Ken Barker had a list of translation guidelines that he had prepared in recent thinking about these issues, and his list was similar to the list that our group had presented. Several of us saw this as evidence that God had prepared the way for us to reach agreement on a wide number of these issues. From that point on in the meeting, we began to work on a joint statement that could be issued as a press release from Focus on the Family.

What were some specific problems with the inclusive language translations? First, the loss of generic "he, him, his": We had expressed concern that the rejection of generic "he, him, his" had obscured the personal application of Scripture to the individual in cases like, "I will come in and eat with *him*" (Rev. 3:20, where the Greek pronoun is masculine singular). The NIVI had changed this to "I will come in and eat with *them*," which represents Jesus eating with a whole church, not just an individual. Similarly, John 14:23 had been changed from "If anyone loves me, *he* will obey my teaching. My Father will love *him*, and we will come to *him* and make our home with *him*" in the current NIV, to the NIVI rendering, "*Those* who love me will obey my teaching. My Father will love *them*, and we will come to *them* and make our home with *them*." Such a loss of teaching about personal fellowship between God and an individual Christian affected numerous verses. (We pointed out similar changes that had been made in many but not all of the cases in two children's versions, the NIrV and, in the Old Testament, the *Adventures in Odyssey Bible*, but I will focus on the NIVI in this report.) Because of these concerns, we agreed on guideline A.1., *The generic use of "he, him, his, himself" should be employed to translate generic 3rd person masculine singular pronouns in Hebrew, Aramaic and Greek.*

We were aware that the rejection of generic "he, him, his" had led to the changing of person and number in thousands of cases in yet another translation, the *New Revised Standard Version* (NRSV), and we suspected that at least several hundred verses had been changed in the NIVI (though no computer count was yet available).

To prevent such changes in person and number in translation, we agreed on guideline A.2., *Person and number should be retained in translation so that singulars are not changed to plurals and third person statements are not changed to second or first person statements, with only rare exceptions required in unusual cases.* This meant that Greek and Hebrew terms for "he" would not be changed to "they" or "you" or "we," in an attempt to make the translation "gender-neutral."

But is generic "he, him, his" acceptable in English today? We all agreed that this usage is less common today, but the question remains, is it still correct, and understandable, even to say things like, "No one seems to take pride in *his* work anymore," and "One should do the best *he* can," and "*He* who hesitates is lost," and "He keeps all *his* bones; not one of them is broken" (Ps. 34:20), and "*He* who believes in me will live, even though he dies" (John 11:25)? To answer this question, our group also presented evidence from contemporary dictionaries, style books, and articles in secular journals showing contemporary uses of "he, him, his" in a generic way, and indicating expert testimony that the English language was unlikely to resolve differing preferences about the generic use of "he, him, his" in the near future. We also cited at least one linguist who knew of no human language that lacked a singular pronoun that was used generically (in some languages it is a masculine singular pronoun; in others, a neuter singular pronoun). Therefore, people who predict that English will soon relinquish generic "he, him, his," when there is no commonly agreed singular substitute, are predicting that English—perhaps the most versatile language in history—will lose a capability possessed by all major languages in the world. To say the least, this is unlikely to happen.

What if women feel excluded? During the morning one important difficulty was raised: Some women Bible readers do not feel included by such generic uses of "he, him, his." In response to this, Vern Poythress commented on how easily people learn hundreds of variations in different dialects, even dialects of English when they move from one part of the country to another. Our response to women who say they do not feel included by such language should be to teach[4] them that such usage does *not* in fact "exclude women"—the original author did not intend such an exclusive meaning, the translators did not intend such a meaning, and that is not the meaning the words have when interpreted rightly in their contexts. People who aren't aware of an inclusive, generic meaning for "he, him, his" can learn it in a moment. But we also must say that we have all been *told a lie*—for it is a lie that such usage is "exclusive." We have been told this not by Bible translators but ultimately by secular feminism, which is trying to make these patterns of

---

[4]Strauss criticized this statement as being "extraordinarily condescending" (*Distorting Scripture? The Challenge of Bible Translation & Gender Accuracy* [Downers Grove, IL: InterVarsity, 1998], 145). But in his citation Strauss omitted the explanation of what Grudem meant by "teach," namely, to point out that "the original author did not intend such an exclusive meaning, the translators did not intend such a meaning, and that is not the meaning the words have when interpreted rightly in their contexts." Grudem's intent was not condescending (though we can see how the word "teach" could be misunderstood in that way), but was only to point out commonly accepted standards for determining meaning of a text—consider the intention of the author (and translator in this case), and consider the context.

speech illegitimate. Joel Belz said, and Poythress agreed, that we have all been affected by such feminism, whether we are aware of it or not. It becomes a problem when it tells us that we cannot use certain forms of English expression which are needed for precise Bible translation. We need to be aware of such pressure in our culture, and not give in to it but teach otherwise.

The name "man" for the human race: We were concerned at verses which had rejected the word "man" as a name for the human race, so that these inclusive versions said, "Let us make human beings in our image" rather than "Let us make man in our image" (Genesis 1:26; the Hebrew word is singular collective noun 'ādām, the same word used as the name of Adam, and the same word used of man in distinction from woman in Gen. 2:22, 25). We agreed therefore on guideline A.3., *"Man" should ordinarily be used to designate the human race or human beings in general, for example in Genesis 1:26–27; 5:2; Ezekiel 29:11; and John 2:25.*

Should men be called men? In many cases we were concerned that the words "man" and "men" were omitted from the NIVI and the NIrV for no apparent reason, especially when male human beings were referred to in the text. For example, in referring to warriors in Judges 18:7, the NIV spoke of "five *men*," but the NIVI changed it to "five *of them*." Nicodemus in John 3:1 was changed from "a *man* of the Pharisees" to "a *Pharisee*" (thus obliterating the connection with the previous verse, which said that "Jesus knew all *men*." The apostle who was needed to replace Judas was chosen from "one of the *men* who have been with us" in the NIV (Acts 1:21, precisely representing the Greek word *anēr*, which designates a man in distinction from a woman), but it was changed in the NIVI to "one of *those* who have been with us." The men in the boat with Jesus during the storm at sea were changed from "*men*" to "*disciples*" in the NIVI (Matt. 8:27; the word *anthrōpoi* means "men" here). In a similar way, the NIV had rightly said that the Old Testament high priest was selected "from among *men*" (Heb. 5:1) but the NIVI changed it to "from among *human beings*." (Are we to think that a woman could have been a priest in the Old Testament—to say nothing of high priest?) Similarly, the writing prophets of the Old Testament included no women, but still these writing prophets were changed from "*men*" to "*human*" in 2 Peter 1:21. We could see no reason for such changes except a general antipathy toward the word "men."

Although we had not found the following additional verses by the time of the May 27th meeting, we subsequently have found that similar changes were made in other passages where the Greek word *anēr* (or its plural *andres*), which nearly always means a man in distinction from a woman, was "neutered" in the NIVI. Therefore, Jesus' disciples were changed from "*men* of Galilee" to "*you* Galileans" in Acts 1:11. The representatives Judas and Silas who were sent from the Jerusalem council were changed from "two *men* who were leaders" to simply "who were leaders" in Acts 15:22. The false teachers who would arise from the midst of the Ephesian elders were changed from "*men*" to "*some*" in Acts 20:30. The Jewish men who were summoned to help drag Paul out of the temple area (where no women were allowed) were changed from "*men* of Israel" to "*people* of Israel" in Acts 21:28. And Paul himself, instead of saying "when I became a *man*," in the NIVI says "when

I became an *adult*" (1 Corinthians 13:11). With regard to the Old Testament, we were concerned that the Hebrew word *'ish*, which ordinarily means "man" in distinction from woman, had also been "neutered" in a number of cases. Once again, such "neutering" of language about people who were evidently male human beings, and who were described with such a distinctively male Greek term, simply diminished accuracy in translation.

Should Jesus be called a man? In a similar way, the masculinity of Jesus was downplayed in six verses that we found in the NIVI: the words of Caiaphas were changed from "it is better for you that one *man* die for the people" to "it is better for you that one *person* die for the people" (John 11:50, and similarly in John 18:14; see also John 10:33). Paul's statement that "the resurrection of the dead comes also through a *man*" was changed to "through a *human being*" in 1 Corinthians 15:21. In a similar way, Philippians 2:8 was changed from "being found in appearance as a *man*" to "being found in appearance as a *human being*." Finally, 1 Timothy 2:5 was changed from "the *man*, Christ Jesus" to "Christ Jesus, *himself human*." Such translations obscure the theological truth that it was Christ as a man, in parallel to the man Adam before him, who was the representative head of his people.

Because of these concerns, we agreed on guideline A.4., *Hebrew 'ish should ordinarily be translated "man" and "men," and Greek* anēr *should almost always be so translated.* We also agreed on the second part of guideline A.5., *The singular* anthrōpos *should ordinarily be translated "man" when it refers to a male human being.*

Legitimate uses of inclusive language: On the other hand, we recognized that there were times when some forms of "inclusive language" were appropriate in translation when the original Hebrew or Greek text was not specifically male in its meaning and when the other kinds of inaccuracies prevented by the other guidelines were not introduced. Therefore we agreed with the first part of guideline A.5., *In many cases,* anthrōpoi *refers to people in general, and can be translated "people" rather than "men."* For example, it is perfectly acceptable to translate Matthew 12:36, "On the day of judgment, *people* will have to give an account for every careless word they speak." We also agreed on guideline A.6., *Indefinite pronouns such as* tis *can be translated "anyone" rather than "any man."* For example, Matthew 16:24 should be translated, "if *anyone* would come after me . . ." Similarly, guideline A.7 affirms, *In many cases, pronouns such as* oudeis *can be translated "no one" rather than "no man,"* as in Galatians 3:11, "*no one* is justified before God by the law." Guideline A.8. affirms, *When* pas *is used as a substantive it can be translated with terms such as "all people" or "everyone."* This is seen in verses such as John 12:32, "I will draw *all people* to myself." None of us objected to any of these kinds of "inclusive language," and in fact these principles had been largely followed several years ago in the current NIV.

The phrase "son of man": We were also concerned that in some cases the phrase "son of man" had been omitted, as in Psalm 8:4, "What is man, that you are mindful of him, *the son of man*, that you care for him?" which in the NIVI was changed to, "what are mere mortals that you are mindful of them, *human beings* that you care for them?" This obscured the connection to Hebrews 2:6, where the verse is quoted. We agreed therefore on guideline A.9, *The phrase "son of man" should ordinarily be preserved to retain intracanonical connections.* And of course all participants wanted to clearly affirm guideline A.10, *Masculine references to God should be retained.*

Brothers, sons, and fathers: We recognized that the biblical authors were perfectly capable of saying "brothers and sisters" when they wanted to (as in Josh. 2:13; Mark 10:30), and we were concerned that the NIVI had added the phrase "and sisters" in many cases where the original text had not done so, as in Romans 8:29, "in order that he might be the firstborn among many *brothers and sisters*" (the Greek text has only *adelphoi*, brothers, referring to all Christians—it was not our concern to decide how we today might speak of a group of Christians, but to represent faithfully in translation how Paul spoke of a group of Christians). We agreed on guideline B.1., *"Brother"* (adelphos) *and "brothers"* (adelphoi) *should not be changed to "brother(s) and sister(s)."*

In the same way, guideline B.2. affirmed, *"Son"* (huios, ben) *should not be changed to "child," or "sons"* (huioi) *to "children" or "sons and daughters."* (However, Hebrew banîm *often means "children."*) This was because the New Testament authors were able to speak of "children" (*tekna*) when they wanted to do so (as in John 1:12, "He gave power to become *children* of God," and Romans 8:16–17, "bearing witness with our spirit that we are *children* of God.") But in other verses the Bible spoke of us as "sons," and faithful translations should not change this to "sons and daughters" or "children" as the NIVI did in Galatians 4:7, "Since you are no longer slaves, but God's *children,* and since you are his *children,* he has made you also heirs." The problem with this translation is the Greek text specifies "sons" (*huioi*), not "children" (*tekna*), and to translate it "children" obscures the connection with Christ *as son* in that very context, and also obscures the fact that we all (men and women) gain standing as "sons" and therefore the inheritance rights that belong to sons in the Biblical world. (Similarly, it should also be noted that we all—men and women—have a sort of female identity as the bride of Christ in 2 Cor. 11:2; Eph. 5:25–33; and Rev. 19:7, and we should not "neuter" these references to make us the "spouse" of Christ.)

Finally, we recognized that the words "father" and "fathers" faithfully represent the male leadership present in Biblical families, and we agreed in guideline B.3., *"Father"* (patēr, 'āb) *should not be changed to "parent," or "fathers" to "parents" or "ancestors."*

However, we recognized that in unusual cases exceptions to these statements about brothers, sons, and fathers might have to be made to produce legitimate English, so we spoke in heading B of *Gender-related renderings which we will generally avoid, though there may be unusual exceptions in certain contexts.*

Finally, we realized that these guidelines probably did not cover every case, so we added guideline C., *We understand these guidelines to be representative and not exhaustive.* We thought that if translators were willing to follow these guidelines, the principle of precision in rendering the gender orientation of the original Hebrew and Greek texts would be established, even though we may not have spoken about every possible type of translation problem.

Summary statement: We left the meeting with a strong sense of thanksgiving to God for the broad agreement he had enabled us to reach. We rejoiced that at least our two groups, seemingly so far apart before the meeting, had been willing to say in a public statement, "*We agree that it is inappropriate to use gender-neutral language when it diminishes accuracy in the translation of the Bible, and we therefore agree to the attached guidelines for translation of gender-related language in Scripture.*" In affirming this statement, we put ourselves on record as saying that translations that violated these guidelines did in fact "diminish accuracy in the translation of the Bible." We also affirmed that there are some kinds of "inclusive language" that are valid, because we affirmed, "*We agree that there are limited times when the use of gender-neutral language enhances the accuracy of translations,*" and we specified several such valid uses. As a result of the discussion, and after much reflection in the past several weeks, the NIV translators and publishers joined us in agreeing that "*many of the translation decisions*" in the NIVI "*were not the wisest choices.*" Finally, we expressed hope that other translators and publishers would decide to follow the guidelines we agreed on as well.

Publishers' commitments: We also rejoiced that Zondervan's president Bruce Ryskamp expressed willingness to give refunds to customers who ask for them for their current NIrV Bibles. In addition, James Dobson clearly wanted to state that Focus on the Family had ceased distributing their *Adventures in Odyssey Bible*, which was a children's Bible based on the *New Century Version*. Focus on the Family said it would give refunds for this Bible to anyone who asked for them. (We were also happy to hear a few days later that Thomas Nelson/Word Publishers had agreed to remove the gender-neutral language from this Bible.) We called on other publishers of gender-neutral Bibles to issue similar public statements showing similar reappraisals of their translation principles.

One issue remained unresolved. Zondervan Publishing House continued to state publicly that *World* magazine was unethical and untruthful in its coverage of this issue. Although *World's* publisher Joel Belz, Zondervan's president Bruce Ryskamp, and the president of IBS, Lars Dunberg, were present at our meeting, they graciously decided not to make these differences a major agenda item of our meeting, since they felt (and we agreed) that the far more important issue was reaching agreement on issues of accuracy in translation of the Word of God into English. These differences between Zondervan and *World* are yet to be resolved as I write this article, and we need to pray for God's grace especially for these three men, that their differences will be resolved in a way that is pleasing to the Lord. (Readers who wish to see the charges that Zondervan has filed with the Evangelical Press Association, and responses from *World*, can find the entire text of them at: www.worldmag.com.)

We reached substantial agreement on all of these points before the meeting broke up about 2:30 in the afternoon on May 27, but the document had to be circulated by fax and phone three times throughout the subsequent five days, before total agreement was reached on the final wording of all of the guidelines. Then on Saturday night, May 31, complete agreement on the wording of the guidelines was finally reached by phone. By Monday morning, June 2, all twelve participants had signed the final document and faxed their signatures to the Focus on the Family headquarters. The press release was then issued on June 3.

The influence of many others: This meeting had been preceded by several weeks of public and private discussions among many Christians. Those of us who came to the meeting with concerns about the NIV were thankful for the prominent Christian leaders who had spoken out against inclusive language translations, or whose publications had voiced serious concerns. These leaders included not only James Dobson, who had convened the meeting, but also J. I. Packer, Jerry Falwell, and R. C. Sproul (all of whom are on our CBMW Board of Reference). In addition, we knew of other leaders who were concerned and would also have spoken out if necessary. We thought that the influence of the Southern Baptist Convention, as voiced through Paige Patterson, President of Southeastern Seminary, and Al Mohler, President of Southern Seminary, had been especially significant. In addition, Southeastern Seminary professor Andreas Köstenberger (editor of *CBMW News*) had provided extensive research for us on over 700 uses of Greek words for "man" in the NIV and the NIVI in preparation for our meeting. And we all knew of many people who were praying regularly for the meeting.

Our overall assessment of this meeting (and I think I speak for all twelve participants) is one of thankfulness to God that we were able to reach such a broad and significant agreement in such a short time. We are all hopeful that the Lord will use this as a positive influence on Bible translation into English for many years to come.

C. Refinement of the Guidelines

As indicated above, refinements of the Guidelines took place through faxes during the days following the meeting on May 27. Final agreement on the refinements was reached on June 2, 1997, and a press release issued the Guidelines on June 3, 1997. But subsequent interaction with many scholars resulted in three further refinements. These refinements were again submitted to all the participants for approval, and approved on September 9, 1997. The official published Guidelines given at the beginning of this appendix include these refinements.

The refinements included the following three changes:

Guideline A.3 originally read,

"Man" should ordinarily be used to designate the human race or human beings in general, for example in Genesis 1:26–27; 5:2; Ezekiel 29:11; and John 2:25.

The expression "or human beings in general" turned out to be unclear and led to a misunderstanding the guideline. Some people thought that it was talking about the generic use of "any man" or "every man" (as in Guidelines A.5-A.8), rather than the use of "man" in a general statement about human nature (as in the verse cited with the guideline, John 2:25: "because he knew all men and needed no one to bear witness of *man*; for he himself knew what was in *man*").

We deleted the extra words ("or human beings in general") to clarify the guideline.

Guideline B.1 originally read:

> "Brother" (*adelphos*) and "brothers" (*adelphoi*) should not be changed to "brother(s) and sister(s)."

Examination of further lexicographical data (as indicated in Chapter 12) showed that this guideline was too narrow. Data from outside the New Testament indicated that the plural *adelphoi* could refer to a literal brother and sister. Of course we already knew that the New Testament used *adelphoi* in a metaphorical sense to refer to Christians, including men and women. But if this usage were merely a metaphor, it might still be based on a ground-level male meaning component in the normal use of *adelphoi*. The additional data dispelled this doubt, opening the way to the following refined Guideline B.1:

> "Brother" (*adelphos*) should not be changed to "brother or sister"; however, the plural *adelphoi* can be translated "brothers and sisters" where the context makes clear that the author is referring to both men and women.

Guideline C originally read:

> We understand these guidelines to be representative and not exhaustive.

But we recognized that further study and reflection might possibly result in more precision and more refinement at a later time. Therefore we added another clause to Guideline C, so it now reads:

> We understand these guidelines to be representative and not exhaustive, and that some details may need further refinement.

Notice of the refinement of the Guidelines appeared in *CBMW NEWS* 2:4 (Sept., 1997), p. 9, in the following brief article (reprinted here in full):

Three small changes to translation guidelines

After considering comments from many people, the signers of the May 27 translation guidelines have agreed to the following changes:

CHANGE #1: A.3. "Man" should ordinarily be used to designate the human race [DELETE: or human beings in general], for example in Genesis 1:26–27; 5:2; Ezekiel 29:11; and John 2:25.

> This is because the phrase was confusing and widely misunderstood. Many people thought we meant that women should always be called "men," which we surely did not intend!

CHANGE #2: B.1. "Brother" (*adelphos*) should not be changed to "brother or sister"; [ADD: however, the plural *adelphoi* can be translated "brothers and sisters" where the context makes clear that the author is referring to both men and women.]

> This does not say it *has* to be translated that way, but that it can be. (Translators still might want to keep "brothers" for the sake of continuity in Bible translations, for example.) This change is a result of much evidence from Greek lexicons and Greek literature that we were unaware of earlier (see further information below).

CHANGE #3: C. We understand these guidelines to be representative and not exhaustive, [ADD: **and that some details may need further refinement.**]

The endorsers of the statement recognize that there may yet be new information or more precise ways of formulating certain things, but they would only be refinements, not fundamental changes.

Evidence regarding *adelphoi* as "brothers and sisters"

Many times the plural word *adelphoi* means "brothers," and refers only to males. But in Greek, the masculine plural form of a word is also used when referring to a mixed group of men and women. In the following actual sentences from Greek literature, the sense "brother and sister" or "brothers and sisters" seems to be required:

1. That man is a cousin of mine: his mother and my father were *adelphoi*.

2. My father died leaving me and my *adelphoi* Ted and Thelma as his heirs, and his property devolved upon us.

3. The footprints of *adelphoi* should never match (of a man and of a woman): the man's is greater.

4. An impatient and critical man finds fault even with his own parents and children and *adelphoi* and neighbors.[5]

In standard English, we just don't say, "My *brothers* Ted and Thelma." So the Greek plural *adelphoi* sometimes has a different sense from English "brothers." In fact, the major Greek lexicons for over 100 years have said that *adelphoi*, which is the plural of the word *adelphos*, "brother," sometimes means "brothers and sisters" (see BAGD, 1957 and 1979; Liddell-Scott-Jones, 1940 and even 1869).

This material was new evidence for those of us who wrote the May 27 guidelines—we weren't previously aware of this pattern of Greek usage outside the Bible. Once we saw these examples and others like them, we felt we had to make some change in the guidelines.

One other factor influencing our decision was that the masculine *adelphos* and the feminine *adelphē* are just different forms (masculine and feminine) of the same word *adelph-*, which is again different from English where bro- and sis- are completely different roots. (The root *adelph-* is from *a-*, which means "from," and *delphus*, "womb" [LSJ, p. 20] and probably had an early sense of "from the same womb.")

Therefore in the New Testament, when Paul wrote,

Therefore, I urge you, brothers (*adelphoi*), in view of God's mercy . . . (Rom. 12:1),

it seems that the original hearers would have understood him to mean something very much like "brothers and sisters" in English today. (Or technically "siblings,"

---

[5]The quotations are found in the following sources: (1) Andocides, *On the Mysteries* 47 [approx. 400 B.C.]; (2) *Oxyrhynchus Papyri* 713, 20–23 [A.D. 97; with Greek names Diodorus and Theis, not Ted and Thelma]; (3) Euripides, *Electra* 536 [5th cent. B.C.]; (4) Epictetus, *Discourses* 1.12.20–21 [approx. A.D. 130].

but that is not the way anyone speaks to anyone else today: would we say, "Therefore, I urge you, siblings . . ."?)

Why then does the New Testament sometimes specify "brothers and sisters," putting both masculine (*adelphoi*) and feminine (*adelphai*) forms (as in Matt. 19:29 or Mark 10:30)? Sometimes the authors may have specifically included feminine forms in order to prevent any possible misunderstanding, to make it very clear that women as well as men were included in a certain statement.

These changes will now be included in all future printings of the guidelines. I think they make the guidelines stronger, more accurate, and more likely to gain general acceptance from the broader Christian world.

Wayne Grudem
President, CBMW

D. Explanation[6]

We would now like briefly to explain the Colorado Springs Guidelines, paying special attention to guidelines that some people have misunderstood or challenged. We (authors Wayne Grudem and Vern Poythress) were participants in the meeting at Colorado Springs and signers of the Guidelines. But readers should understand that the following explanations are ours, not necessarily those of all the signers.

To begin with, the Colorado Springs Guidelines are just that—guidelines. They show a *general direction* for sound translation of gender-related language. They are not the final word, nor are they intended to cover all the details. Guideline C says it explicitly: "C. We understand these guidelines to be representative and not exhaustive, and that some details may need further refinement."

The guidelines do not deny that complexities exist. What they desire to insist on is that translators remain within the bounds of sound lexical research and faithful translation of meaning. Such insistence has become necessary because the gender-neutral translations that have appeared in print fail in certain key areas: (1) they fail to translate a male semantic marking in quite a few instances in which it is there in the original; and (2) they regularly lose nuances and full accuracy in meaning by restructuring sentences in order to avoid using generic "he."

The guidelines did not suddenly create "out of thin air" new restrictions on the translation of gender-related language. Rather, they reflected the consensus of generations of biblical scholarship regarding the appropriate range of meanings that could attach to various Hebrew and Greek expressions. Considering the state of the English language in 1997, we were proposing English renderings that fell *within* the known range of meanings

---

[6]Some of this material has been taken from Vern S. Poythress, "Explanation of the Colorado Springs Guidelines," at the Web site of the Council on Biblical Manhood and Womanhood, www.cbmw.org.

and rejecting other English expressions that fell *outside* the known range of meanings for each kind of expression in the original language.

Let us begin with Guidelines A.1 and A.2, which go together.

1. The generic use of "he, him, his, himself" should be employed to translate generic third-person masculine singular pronouns in Hebrew, Aramaic, and Greek. However, substantival participles such as *ho pisteuōn* can often be rendered in inclusive ways, such as "the one who believes" rather than "he who believes."

2. Person and number should be retained in translation so that singulars are not changed to plurals and third-person statements are not changed to second- or first-person statements, with only rare exceptions required in unusual cases.

These two guidelines focus on the problems that arise when translators try systematically to avoid using generic "he" in English. As we have seen in Chapter 7, gender-neutral translations convert "he" to "they," "you," or "we" in order to avoid using a male-oriented term. In the process, they regularly alter nuances of meaning.

The guidelines do *not* mean that every grammatical singular in the Hebrew or Greek language in every context must be forced to correspond to a grammatical singular in English. If sentence 2 is read in its entirety, it is evident that the guideline is talking about "singulars" and "third-person statements" that should not be changed to "plurals" and "second- or first-person statements," and all of this is in the context of "gender-related renderings of biblical language." Therefore, if this statement is read in its immediate context, it should be evident that the subject matter is still the use of "he, him, his, himself," and that this statement is the complement to statement 1. Guideline 1 affirms generic "he," and Guideline 2 denies that it should be changed to "they" or "you" or "we."

These guidelines are not of course insisting that we preserve grammatical form in every case and pay no attention to meaning (see Appendix 3). Rather, they are mainly saying that in the particular instances related to generic "he," changing to plurals and changes of person involve subtle meaning changes, and therefore should be avoided. It was therefore surprising, and in fact disappointing, to see some critics of these guidelines pay no attention to the context or even the whole of the sentence in Guideline 2 but criticize a fragment of Guideline 2 lifted out of the context in which it occurred.

Guideline A.3 says,

"Man" should ordinarily be used to designate the human race, for example in Genesis 1:26–27; 5:2; Ezekiel 29:11; and John 2:25.

Note that this guideline says nothing directly about Hebrew and Greek terms, but only about English usage. In fact, it talks about using English "man" when the *meaning* of the original involves "the human race." Thus, it invites attention to the context of the original. It is not a sweeping state-ment about *'ādām* ("man, mankind, human being, Adam") in Hebrew or *anthrōpos* ("man, human being") in Greek.

This guideline is tied to the conviction that "man" in the singular, with-out any article, is used for the human race in ordinary English up to today. In addition, "man" with this meaning has connotations of a male represen-tative, like the ties of the Hebrew in Genesis 1:26, 27; 5:2 to the person of Adam. See the further discussion in Chapter 18.

Next, consider Guideline A.4:

Hebrew *'îsh* should ordinarily be translated "man" and "men," and Greek *anēr* should almost always be so translated.

We and some of the other participants were well aware of the use of *'îsh* in idiomatic constructions with the sense "each one." That (among other reasons) is why we introduced the word "ordinarily" in the guidelines. The problem is that gender-neutral translations on the market eliminate male marking in other passages where they have no lexicographical warrant.

Anēr ordinarily has the meaning "man" in distinction from "woman." (It can also have the meaning "husband.") Gender-neutral translations took liberties with some of the verses using this word. See Appendix 2 and the examples in Chapters 13 and 19.

Guideline B.1:

"Brother" (*adelphos*) should not be changed to "brother or sister"; how-ever, the plural *adelphoi* can be translated "brothers and sisters" where the context makes clear that the author is referring to both men and women.

This guideline attempts to follow the lexicographical evidence. As we indicate in Chapter 18, the plural *adelphoi* can designate a mixed group con-sisting of literal brothers and sisters, according to evidence from outside the New Testament. The singular *adelphos* normally means "brother," because in the typical case a particular individual is in view: Andrew, the brother of Peter (Matt. 4:18), or John the brother of James (Matt. 4:21), or Philip the brother of Herod (Matt. 14:3). When the singular *adelphos* is used in a *generic* statement, the statement implies that the principle holds for both men and women. However, the picture still starts with a male example. See Chapter 18.

Guideline B.2:

"Son" (*huios, ben*) should not be changed to "child," or "sons" (*huioi*) to "children" or "sons and daughters." (However, Hebrew *banîm* often means "children.")

Again, we may debate about exceptions. But gender-neutral translations have wiped out gender markings in quite a number of cases where the sin-gular word for "son" occurs. This procedure is not justifiable on the basis of standard lexicography. See our discussion in Chapter 18.

Guideline B.3 says:

"Father" (*patēr*, *'āb*) should not be changed to "parent," or "fathers" to "parents" or "ancestors."

The tendency in existing gender-neutral translations has been to obscure the patriarchal character of Old Testament thinking about family lines. In many of the salient usages, *'ab* is not simply "ancestor," but something more like "forefather." Translations have also replaced "father" in the singular with "parent(s)," without any lexicographical warrant. See Chapters 13, 18, and 20.

Hebrews 11:23 is a clear exception ("By faith Moses' parents [Greek *patēr*, plural] hid him for three months after he was born, because they saw he was no ordinary child, and they were not afraid of the king's edict"), and in fact we explicitly mentioned this verse in oral discussion when drafting the guideline, but we felt that such unusual exceptions would be adequately covered in the qualifying phrase, "though there may be unusual exceptions in certain contexts." Maybe the guidelines should have gone into more detail about the character of the exceptions. But beyond a certain point, going into detail would have deflected from the main points, and would have gone beyond what we intended to do with the guidelines.

E. Assessment

We continue to believe that, when understood as indicated, the Guidelines offer a very helpful starting point for Bible translation. Looking back after two years and hundreds of hours of discussion and research, we still see no need to change any of them in any significant way, and we think that they summarize clearly and briefly the appropriate boundaries for accurate translation of gender language in the Bible into current English.

As we have explained in many places throughout this book, however, the Guidelines are not what several opponents have made them out to be—in fact, in a number of cases we could not recognize these guidelines from the way they were reported by critics.

The Guidelines acknowledge exceptions and the need for further work on details (Guideline C; introduction to Guidelines B; expressions like "often," "ordinarily," "almost always"). They offer in effect a quick sketch of the sort of problems that we discuss at much greater length in this book, problems that any analyst can see for himself as he examines gender-neutral translations.

Of course, one can look back from the space of two years and ask whether issuing these guidelines was a helpful step. We realize that they provoked some intense reaction, and in expressing that reaction, advocates of gender-neutral translations succeeded to some degree in deflecting attention from the failures of gender-neutral translations and focusing attention instead on other issues: complexities in translation theory, alleged failures in the Guidelines, the way in which the Colorado Springs meeting came about, who was represented there and who was not represented, and so forth.

Yet if we had given no such guidelines, we suspect that the confusion and controversy would have been much worse. Stating one position clearly and succinctly is a great benefit in bringing understanding and ultimate resolution to a controversy. If we had issued no such guidelines, or had only said something very brief (such as: retain generic "he" and "man" [designating the race] where needed, and retain male meaning components in translation), other problems might have ensued. Some of the advocates of gender-neutral translations might have claimed that it was all a false panic, because gender-neutral translations were already trustworthy!

Some of these advocates still claim that we do not need generic "he" or "man" for the race; and some would say that, apart perhaps from a few minor accidents, gender-neutral translations have successfully represented meaning. Both claims are false; but they are being made nevertheless. The Colorado Springs Guidelines chose to begin to specify in detail where the problems were, in order to show that the problems were real and had specific solutions. The rest is history.

Analyzing the Meanings of Words: "Man" for *Anēr*

A thorough analysis of meaning involves great complexities. In learning a language, we infer the meaning of particular words from the context of their occurrences in sentences, conversation, and social settings. But not every idea generated from the context as a whole is actually a part of the meaning of a new word that we are trying to learn.

For example, I may say, "When I was in Ohio, I saw a sow nursing her young." People learning English, who do not yet know the meaning of the word "sow," may infer that a "sow" is some kind of animal that nurses its young. From the context, they know that the particular animal in question was in Ohio and was a female. But without further information, they would not know whether the word "sow" designates *only* females or whether it includes males as well. That is, "sow" might be a synonym for "pig," or it might designate only *female* pigs. Nor would they know whether the word was even more specialized, designating only those animals that were currently nursing mothers.

The question here is, how much information from the context also belongs to the meaning of the word "sow," and how much is extraneous to the word "sow." How do we separate the contribution of the context from the contribution of the word? It is not easy. In fact, ultimately an absolute and strict separation is impossible.

A. The Greek word *anēr*

The problem is easily illustrated by the occurrences of *anēr* ("man") in the New Testament. In some contexts *anēr* means "husband." Some other occurrences clearly have the meaning "male human being."[1] But many

---

[1]For example, Matthew 14:21 says, "The number of those who ate was about five thousand *men*, besides women and children." The sentence cannot mean, "about five thousand *per-*

other contexts do not, by themselves, conclusively show that *anēr* has a semantic component of "male"; neither do they show that the word lacks the semantic component of "male." Many uses where *anēr* refers to a male human being will not serve as conclusive evidence, because a word meaning "person" could also be used in such contexts. The maleness of the person in question would then be inferred from the information in the context but would not necessarily be contained in the word itself. Equally, the examples that some people cite in the other direction are not conclusive, because there are other possible readings of the situation.

For example, Matthew 14:35 depicts a situation "when the men (*anēr*) of that place recognized Jesus." Some have claimed that both men and women were involved.[2] But how do they know it? Perhaps the men as opposed to women were exclusively or more prominently involved in the process, so that Matthew decided to focus on them.

Another example is Ephesians 4:13, which uses *anēr* in a strikingly creative (and metaphoric) way:

> Until we all attain to the unity of the faith and of the knowledge of the Son of God, to mature *manhood*, to the measure of the stature of the fulness of Christ (RSV).

Here Paul is probably connecting the church to the thought that Christ is the perfect man. So it is not at all clear that the male marking has disappeared from the base meaning on which the metaphor builds.

The fact that there are many inconclusive cases with regard to *anēr*, as there are in many other cases of lexicographical analysis, means that there is considerable scope for reading evidence in more than one way. Now, this situation would not be so bad were it not for the fact that people on all sides of the modern cultural controversies have a heavy emotional stake in issues of sexuality. It is therefore painfully easy for people to read in their own biases.

---

sons (or "human beings"), besides women and children." Therefore, the word *anēr* in this case is seen to mean "man in distinction from women and children." Similarly, Acts 8:3 says that Saul was going from house to house, and "he dragged off *men* and women and put them in prison."

[2] Johannes P. Louw and Eugene A. Nida, *Greek-English Lexicon of the New Testament*, 9.1, claim that *anēr* has the meaning "person, human being, individual" in Matthew 14:35 and Romans 4:8 (they cite only these two, but of course it is possible that they may have in mind a number of other cases). Yet it is not at all clear that Louw and Nida's evidence proves their claim—surely Matthew 14:35 does not provide sufficient evidence, nor does the only other verse they cite in support, Romans 4:8, for that is a quotation from Psalm 32:2, a psalm in which David is speaking in the first instance about himself. That a man can be a representative of a general truth appears from Psalm 1 and Psalm 32:2. But, as we have seen in discussing *'îsh* and *geber* ("man"), this observation does not eliminate the existence of a male semantic component in the representative, the single person who embodies the general truth.

In a similar manner, the information on *anēr* presented in Horst Balz and Gerhard Schneider, eds., *Exegetical Dictionary of the New Testament* (Grand Rapids: Eerdmans, 1990), 1:99, needs critical sifting.

The burden of proof is nevertheless on those who claim that in a particular context *anēr* has lost all of its male semantic component. Why? Because this semantic component is definitely there in some of the occurrences,[3] and the existence of *anthrōpos* ("human being, person") as a more neutral designation fills the need to talk about mixed groups, individuals whose sex is unknown, and so on. It is linguistically improbable that we would find *anēr* moving toward near synonymy with *anthrōpos* ("human being, man, person") in many contexts, leaving Greek with no obvious, convenient term to use when one wants to specify that one is talking about male human beings.

B. Interpreting Bauer's *Lexicon*

Another reason for claiming that *anēr* retains its male semantic component is that this is how standard lexicons have understood the word for generations. When we argue that *anēr* usually and perhaps always in the New Testament means "man" (in distinction from woman) or "husband," we are simply reflecting the definitions given in the Bauer-Arndt-Gingrich-Danker *Greek-English Lexicon of the New Testament and Other Early Christian Literature* (Chicago: University of Chicago Press, 1979). As we noted in Chapter 13, the BAGD lexicon defines *anēr* as:

> "*man*: 1. In contrast to woman . . . Especially *husband*. 2. *man* in contrast to boy . . . 3. used with a word indicating national or local origin . . . 4. Used with adjective to emphasize the dominant characteristic of a man . . . 5. *man* with special emphasis on manliness . . . 6. Equivalent to *tis*, someone . . . 7. *A figure of a man* of heavenly beings who resemble men . . . 8. Of Jesus as the judge of the world" (BAGD, pp. 66–67).

The verses given from the New Testament as examples for category 6, "someone," are all texts that refer to men, not people in general (see discussion below).[4] Therefore this section in BAGD is not intended to show that *anēr* loses its male component of meaning but only that the word can be used to mean not just "men" but "some man" or "some men." After that BAGD provides some examples of an idiom *anēr tis*, which BAGD defines as *a man*. The entry then lists an idiomatic use, *kat' andra*, which means "man for man" or "individually," and which can be applied to people generally, but no New Testament occurrences are listed.

The second English edition of this lexicon (1979, a translation of Walter Bauer's fifth edition of 1958) inserted another sentence at the end of meaning 1: "But cf. Ac 17:34, where ἀνήρ = ἄνθρωπος" (p. 66). The claim is that in

---

[3]See footnote 1, above, as well as all the instances where *anēr* means "husband," as well as other instances cited in BAGD, meaning 1 (p. 66).

[4]The texts are Luke 8:27; 9:38; 10:1; 19:2; John 1:30; in plural, Luke 5:18 (men carrying a paralytic) and Acts 6:11 (Stephen's Jewish opponents "secretly persuaded some men" to accuse him falsely). The same is true of the LXX examples (Sir. 27:7; 1 Macc. 12:1; 13:34).

this one instance, Acts 17:34, *anēr* has the meaning "people" (not specifically males, "men"). This sentence, interestingly, was not in the fifth German edition of Bauer's lexicon, from which this English edition was translated;[5] nor does it appear in the sixth German edition of Bauer's lexicon which appeared in 1988.[6] It is a peculiarity of the English translation to add this sentence.

But does Acts 17:34 demonstrate that *anēr* could equal *anthrōpos* in meaning and therefore could have little or no male marking at times and be translated "person" rather than "man"? The verse says, "But some *men* [*andres,* plural of *anēr*] joined him and believed, among whom also were Dionysius the Areopagite and a woman named Damaris and others with them" (NASB).

Is the "woman named Damaris" included among the "some men" in the first part of the verse? Probably not. F. F. Bruce's commentary on the Greek text says, "'Including in particular Dionysius the Areopagite; and (in addition to the men) a woman named Damaris', etc. There is no need to suppose that *kai gunē* [and a woman] is included in the *tines andres . . . en hois* [some men . . . among whom]."[7] The Greek text of the verse is: τινὲς δὲ ἄνδρες κολλυνθέντες αὐτῷ ἐπίστευσαν, ἐν οἷς καὶ Διονύσιος ὁ Ἀρεοπαγίτης καὶ γυνὴ ὀνόματι Δάμαρις καὶ ἕτεροι σὺν αὐτοῖς.

In fact, the forthcoming new edition of the BAGD *Lexicon*, scheduled for release in September 2000, from the University of Chicago Press, seems to correct the earlier edition which had claimed that *anēr* = *anthrōpos* in Acts 17:34. We had an opportunity to see the entry for *anēr* in the proofs that were displayed at the University of Chicago Press booth at the Society of Biblical Literature convention in Boston November 20–23, 1999. The new entry defines *anēr* as "an adult human male, *man, husband.*" It also says, "In Ac 17:34 ἀνήρ appears to = ἄνθρωπος but the term was probably chosen in anticipation of the contrasting γυνή (is Damaris the wife of one of the men?)."

The expression is in fact not too hard to understand in this context. Paul had just given an address at the Areopagus, apparently before the official court that presided at that spot. The court officers were almost certainly all men. Others, of course, may have gathered to hear the proceedings. Given the context, Luke focuses first on the "men" who believed, from among the men who formed the official Areopagus court. Then he mentions "also" another person who believed, Dionysius "the Areopagite." Then, realizing that there was also a woman who believed, he adds her name but thinks it necessary to specify that she is a woman: "and a woman named Damaris."

[5]Walter Bauer, *Griechisch-Deutsches Wörterbuch zu den Schriften des Neuen Testaments und der ürchristlichen Literatur* (Berlin: A. Töpelmann, 1958), 132.

[6]Walter Bauer, *Griechisch-deutsches Wörterbuch . . .* (Berlin: de Gruyter, 1988), 132.

[7]F. F. Bruce, *The Acts of the Apostles: The Greek Text with Introduction and Commentary* (Grand Rapids: Eerdmans, 1951), 341.

The sentence makes sense and need not be understood to include Damaris among the "men" (*andres*).

The principle that would keep us from adopting the additional sense "person" for *anēr* is that if a well-established meaning makes sense in the context, then we should not adopt a previously unattested meaning in its place. Such a general principle of lexicography is well stated by Cambridge lexicographer John Chadwick, whose book *Lexicographica Graeca: Contributions to the Lexicography of Ancient Greek* is a collection of specialized studies that reflect his years of experience on the team overseeing a supplement to the Liddell-Scott *Lexicon*:

> A constant problem to guard against is the proliferation of meanings. . . . It is often tempting to create a new sense to accommodate a difficult example, but we must always ask first, if there is any other way of taking the word which would allow us to assign the example to an already established sense. . . . As I have remarked in several of my notes, there may be no reason why a proposed sense should not exist, but is there any reason why it must exist?[8]

In other words, the burden of proof is on the person who postulates a new sense. If an already established sense can account for a particular use, one must not postulate a new sense.

In the case of *anēr*, out of 216 occurrences in the NT, a great majority of them clearly refer to a man or men, not to "persons" generally, and the sense "man" fits well even in Acts 17:34, where the context does not absolutely require that sense. This and perhaps a few other ambiguous cases are just that—ambiguous—and therefore they do not constitute a persuasive argument that *anēr* at times loses its distinctively male sense.

The Liddell-Scott *Greek-English Lexicon*, Ninth Edition with Supplement (Oxford: Clarendon Press, 1968), gives the following meanings for *anēr*:

> I. *man*, opposed to *woman* (*anthropoi* being *man* as opposed to *beast*). II. *man*, opposed to *god*. III. *man*, opposed to *youth*, unless the context determines the meaning . . . but *anēr* alone always means *a man in the prime of life*, esp. *warrior*. IV. *man* emphatically, *man indeed*. V. *husband*. VI. Special usages [several idioms are given] (p. 138).

It is significant that neither of these two standard lexicons indicates that the word loses its male marking in any of its usages. In the present controversy we should be suspicious of any attempts to overthrow such well-established boundaries to the range of meanings of a word, especially in a time when major forces in the culture are pressing us to eliminate male-oriented language (and therefore male markings on words!), and especially if these attempts are accompanied by no new data but only appeal to the

---

[8]John Chadwick, *Lexicographica Graeca: Contributions to the Lexicography of Ancient Greek* (Oxford: Clarendon Press, 1996), 23–24.

same old data that scholars have seen for centuries. Once again Chadwick's warning is pertinent: "We must always ask first, if there is any other way of taking the word which would allow us to assign the example to an already established sense . . . there may be no reason why a proposed sense should not exist, but is there any reason why it must exist?"[9]

C. Dealing with possible multiple senses

One other principle of semantics needs consideration: where a word takes different senses, we should be able to specify contextual markers that indicate which sense a word is taking. This is the case for many words that have more than one sense. Even for those words where one sense in dominant, there may be special idiomatic constructions that bear an altered or extended sense. And there may be contexts where some normal semantic component of the sense is neutralized. For example, though the Hebrew *ben* in the singular usually bears the sense "son," it can be used in the plural to designate a group of children of both sexes, and it can be used in idiomatic constructions like *ben hayil*, "son of might, mighty man."[10] But we expect that nearly always contextual clues will supply indications as to which sense or which idiom is being used at a particular spot. (Thus, the plural form of *ben* is a contextual factor indicating the possibility of absence of a male semantic component.) Differences in sense are thus *controlled* by context. Ambiguities in meaning are usually resolvable through context, though any language supplies occasional cases where a speaker wittingly or unwittingly leaves an ambiguity that cannot be resolved from context and fails to make himself clear.

Now, what happens when we apply these insights to *anēr*? Some people would claim that *anēr* at times means "person" or "people" *without a male semantic component*. But these people still have to admit that *elsewhere* (and not just where it means "husband") *anēr* sometimes carries a male semantic component.[11] That is, according to these people, sometimes *anēr* means (roughly) "person," and sometimes "male person, man."

But then we must ask, *can we specify contextual clues that determine which of these two senses occurs in any one particular place?* If not, we are making the very implausible claim that the two different senses occur in free variation—and we can never tell which is which. In such a hypothetical case, consider what would be going on in the ancient world with native speakers of Greek. Suppose that one generation of speakers uses the two senses of *anēr* in such a way that no contextual clues indicate which sense is being used. The next generation of native speakers, growing up and listening to

---

[9]Ibid.

[10]Brown, Driver, and Briggs, *Hebrew and English Lexicon*, 121b, meaning #8.

[11]The existence of the male semantic component is recognized in the standard lexicons, as noted above. See, for example, Matthew 14:21 and Acts 8:3, and footnote 1, above.

this usage, cannot distinguish the two senses, and so in their own minds they collapse the two into one sense. The next generation would, perhaps, see *anēr* as just meaning "man," because the contexts never distinguish this sense "man" from the hypothetical sense "person." In fact, then, in any real situation of continued use of human language, a usage involving two distinct senses must include contextual factors that distinguish the senses.

So, someone who claims that *anēr* sometimes means "person" must admit that there have to be some contextual markers that tell us when a male semantic component is present. But what are those contextual markers? Suppose we were to say that the only contextual clue to a male semantic component is a context that shows that in fact male human beings are being referred to. But it is then the context, either textual or situational, that contains the information about maleness. Again, how would language learners be able to distinguish this situation from one in which *anēr* simply meant "person" and the context indicated maleness? Therefore, we can exclude the possibility that the sense "male human being" occurs *only* where the context provides information that only men are in view. It is far more likely that the "default" sense for *anēr* includes maleness. Maleness is included in the meaning in typical, ordinary contexts.

If it turns out that some occurrences of *anēr* do not include this semantic component, it is some special factor (such as the presence of a specialized idiom) in the context that neutralizes it. The lexicographer then tries to describe just what contexts lead to neutralization. Such contexts, if they exist, will be specialized contexts.

D. Possible origins of mistakes

How did the gender-neutral translations get skewed? It could have happened in several ways.

(1) The more recent lexicon by Louw-Nida gives three entries for *anēr*, one with the meaning "husband," one with the meaning "man" ("an adult male person of marriageable age"), and one with the meaning "human being."[12] Translators may have looked at this last entry and simply followed it. They used "person" or "human being," thus eliminating the male semantic component in *anēr* from dozens of passages. However, this procedure was not justified in light of the actual entry in Louw-Nida, because (a) they give no information as to what contexts the supposed gender-neutral meaning is found; (b) they also acknowledge that *anēr* can mean "man, male human being"; (c) they give no new information that would lead us to over-

---

[12]Johannes P. Louw and Eugene A. Nida, editors, *Greek-English Lexicon of the New Testament Based on Semantic Domains*, 2 vols. (New York: United Bible Societies, 1988), 104. The entry under "human being" says more specifically, "a human being (normally an adult)—(in the singular) 'person, human being, individual,' (in the plural) 'people, persons, mankind'" (section 9.1).

throw established meanings for *anēr*, and (d) more significantly, *they make no distinction at all between the meanings of* anēr *and* anthrōpos, *but treat both words under the same two entries* (9.1 for "human beings" and 9.24 for "males").[13] With no new lexical evidence given to support this entry, and with the entire history of Greek lexicography clearly recognizing that *anēr* and *anthrōpos* are not exact synonyms, but that *anēr* is the male marked term, we may conclude that the Louw-Nida lexicon at this point is insufficiently careful, and that following Louw-Nida in this case is simply a mistake.

(2) Translators may have followed the new sentence in BAGD, mentioned above, where the editors of the English edition added a sentence not in the German original: "But cf. Ac 17:34, where *anēr = anthrōpos*" (p. 66). But, as we noted above, Acts 17:34 is insufficient reason for introducing a new meaning for *anēr*—and certainly insufficient reason for introducing wholesale changes in the translation of dozens of other examples.

(3) Translators may have looked at meaning 6 in BAGD, which gives as one of the meanings of *anēr* "someone," and in the plural "*some* people" (p. 67). This datum could then be viewed as justification for translating with "someone" or "people" almost everywhere, or at least wherever the context does not *clearly* indicate that men only are in view. In fact, such a procedure reverses the burden of proof. Rather than seeing "someone" as a specialized usage, it becomes the general usage imposed on passages where it does not belong.

E. Analyzing particular cases

But before making such a major change in the translation of a common New Testament word, it would be appropriate to look carefully at when and where the sense "someone" can be expected, and what the BAGD entry meant by this meaning. When we look in Bauer's lexicon under the sense "*someone*," a most interesting fact comes to light. The passages that are cited involve *men*. As we mentioned above, this suggests that this specific entry in BAGD is not intended to show that *anēr* loses its male component of meaning but only that the word can be used to mean not just "a man" or "men" but "some man" or "some men" (often, one who had not been previously mentioned or had not yet been introduced in the narrative). Let us consider the ones that come from the Bible.

Luke 9:38 uses *anēr* "man" to describe the man who brought his demonized son to Jesus. Luke 9:42 describes the man as the boy's "father" (Greek *patēr*), indicating that he was indeed male.

Luke 19:2 uses *anēr* to describe Zacchaeus, a man.

---

[13]Louw and Nida also give a third meaning, "husband," for *anēr*; and in the case of both *anēr* and *anthrōpos*, they have special entries for some idioms.

John 1:30 uses *anēr* in John the Baptist's prediction, referring to the coming of *Jesus*.

Luke 5:18 uses *anēr* to describe the men who carried the paralytic. Nothing in the context suggests that they were not men, and indeed, in the ancient world, the activity of lifting him up to the roof and digging a hole in it would almost certainly have been done by men.

Acts 6:11 uses *anēr* to describe the people who brought false accusations against Stephen. Again, nothing suggests that these were not all men—and the bearing of testimony in ancient Jewish society would have most likely been done by men. The gender-neutral translations NRSV, NIVI, NCV, NIrV(1995), NLT, CEV, and GW all say "men"!

Acts 8:27 uses *anēr* to describe the Gerasene demoniac. In the subsequent narrative he is described using masculine participles, indicating that he was in fact male.

Acts 10:1 uses *anēr* to describe Cornelius the centurion, a man.

Romans 4:8 uses *anēr* to describe the person whose sins are forgiven. Paul quotes from Psalm 32:2 (which is renumbered as Psalm 31:2 in the Septuagint version). The Septuagint has *anēr*. The underlying Hebrew has *'ādām*. The people who translated the Septuagint would have seen *'ādām* in Hebrew. *'Adām* has some male associations in Hebrew because of its connection with Adam. Moreover, Psalm 32 has the superscript, "Of David. A maskil." Bearing in mind that the psalm speaks of David's personal experience of forgiveness, the Septuagint seizes on the male associations, and translates using *anēr*. Paul simply takes over the Septuagint without change, probably seeing no difficulty in the use of *anēr* with its male marking here because it is a psalm written by David out of his own experience.

James 1:12 says, "Blessed is the *man* (*anēr*) who perseveres under trial, . . ." Clearly James is making a statement of general applicability. It *applies* to both men and women. An analyst with a modern mentality is tempted to conclude immediately that every element of male semantic component is gone. But *anēr* can still mean that James is starting with a male example illustrating the general truth, just as blessing statements in the Old Testament may begin with the example of an individual man:

> Blessed is the *man* who does not walk in the counsel of the wicked or stand in the way of sinners or sit in the seat of mockers (Psalm 1:1).
>
> Blessed is the *man* whose sin the LORD does not count against him (Psalm 32:2).
>
> Blessed is the *man* who takes refuge in him (Psalm 34:8).
>
> Blessed is the *man* who makes the LORD his trust (Psalm 40:4).
>
> Blessed is the *man* who trusts in you (Psalm 84:12.)
>
> Blessed is the *man* you discipline, O LORD, the man you teach from your law (Psalm 94:12).

Blessed is the *man* who fears the L ORD, who finds great delight in his commands (Psalm 112:1).

Blessed is the *man* whose quiver is full of them (Psalm 127:5).

Thus is the *man* blessed who fears the L ORD (Psalm 128:4).

Blessed is the *man* who finds wisdom, the man who gains understanding (Proverbs 3:13).

Blessed is the *man* who listens to me, watching daily at my doors (Proverbs 8:34).

Blessed is the *man* who always fears the L ORD (Proverbs 28:14).

The Greek version (Septuagint) corresponding to Psalms 1:1; 32:2; 34:8; 40:4; 112:1; Proverbs 8:34; and 28:14 has *anēr*. Other passages have *anthrōpos*. But the context usually shows that there is some focus on a male example. In Psalm 128, verse 3 mentions the man's wife, showing that the "man" is male. Job 5:17 makes a general statement, but in the context of exhorting Job. Psalms 32, 34, and 40 are psalms of David. Even the psalms that are not ascribed to David are more loosely connected to the figure of the king as the chief representative of the people.

Psalm 84:12 has a more general context, but then the preceding verses talk about the blessedness of dwelling "in your [God's] house," which in the fullest sense was open only to priests. And the Old Testament priests were all male.

Psalm 94:12 talks about being taught "from your law," an opportunity more often open to men than to women. The underlying Hebrew word is *geber*, which explicitly denotes a male. In Psalm 127:5 the metaphor of a quiver evokes the context of fighting and war, in which almost exclusively males engaged. The underlying Hebrew word is once again *geber*. In Proverbs 3:13–18 wisdom is pictured as feminine. The man who finds her is like one who finds a good wife (Prov. 31). The context is instruction to a son.

Now such an Old Testament theme dealing with the "righteous man" is appropriate to James. In fact, James has many thematic similarities to Old Testament wisdom literature. The expression in James 1:12, "Blessed is the *man* (*anēr*) who perseveres under trial," though not a direct Old Testament quotation, picks up on the similar language in the Old Testament. The use of *anēr* is probably imitative of the translation style of the Septuagint. It does not therefore establish that James knows about another, gender-neutral sense of *anēr*, or that he intends *anēr* to be understood in a completely gender-neutral sense here. Rather, a man is used to represent a truth applying to men and women and children as well.

Thus it seems likely that the word *anēr* retains the connotations of maleness even in these contexts. The general principle *applies* to men and women, but the specific statements make the principle vivid by expressing it using an individual male as the embodiment and starting point. The situation is somewhat analogous to Psalm 113:9, where the Lord "settles the barren woman in her home as a happy mother of children." The Lord shows kindness to childless men as well as childless women. The general principle applies to both. But the specific expression uses a woman as the specific object of the Lord's kindness.

Another possible example where it might be claimed that *anēr* means "person" not "man" is found in James 1:20:

RSV: . . . for the anger of *man* does not work the righteousness of God.

NRSV: . . . for *your* anger does not produce God's righteousness.

The underlying Greek word is *anēr*. The NRSV, by changing to "your," makes the addressees the starting point for generalization, whereas the Greek and the RSV present us with the generalization directly. In addition to this change, the NRSV makes less forceful the contrast between God and man.

Modern thinking would guess that James must be thinking simply of *human* anger generically, not only because of the contrast with God's action, but also because the preceding verse contains the generic term *anthrōpos*, used inclusively of all human beings. But in James's context, men were more likely than women to show anger in obvious and violent ways, leading to murder and mayhem. James may want to use this vivid picture of *men*'s anger in order to make a point that is valid for all. In addition, James may still have the Old Testament pattern of the "righteous man" in the background of his teaching (see 1:12; 3:2, and the discussion above), and this statement of the anger of man would provide a clear contrast to the pattern of the righteous man.

All in all, the evidence for another sense of *anēr* is quite weak and must be used with great caution. In fact, it seems likely that *anēr* has stronger and more exclusive associations with maleness than does the English word "man." Even up to the present, because the changes have not registered in all subgroups of the English-speaking world, and because we retain knowledge of previous generations of use, people know that the English word "man" can sometimes denote a person of either sex, whereas *anēr* appears to denote a male even in cases where the male is an example or illustration of a general principle.

In spite of these facts, gender-neutral translations have gone ahead and introduced a meaning "people" in quite a few cases. The pressure is on from the culture not to put in a male marking unless the context absolutely requires it, even if this means acting contrary to centuries of Greek lexicography.[14] This pressure from the general cultural climate has reversed the

---

[14]Mark Strauss follows this procedure, assuming that *anēr* can mean "man" or "person" depending on the context, and then reasoning at length from context in order to try to decide whether *anēr* should be translated "man/ men" or "person/ people" in specific verses. He says, "in other cases, a decision on whether males or males and females are intended is very

burden of proof in some people's eyes and led to a skewed reading of the lexicographical evidence.

F. *Anēr* in words of address

There is one other specialized use of *anēr* that deserves comment. In a particular idiom used when addressing an audience, *anēr* can occur in the plural along with another noun referring to the hearers (such as, literally, "men, brothers," or "men, Galileans"). Again, it is probable that *anēr* retains male overtones. Even if some of the time the speaker is addressing mixed groups, the men may be singled out, viewed as more prominent, or as representative of all. In a large number of cases, there is no decisive information as to whether the groups contained women or not.

Acts 1:11

NIV: *"Men* of Galilee," they said, "why do you stand here looking into the sky?"

NIVI: *"You* Galileans," they said, "why do you stand here looking into the sky?"

The backward reference is apparently to the apostles (1:2), all of whom were men. In addition, the word *anēr* occurs. But the NIVI removes the male marking.

Acts 1:16

NIV: "Brothers, the Scripture had to be fulfilled . . ."

NRSV: "Friends, the scripture had to be fulfilled . . . "

NIVI: "Brothers and sisters, the Scripture had to be fulfilled . . ."

The Greek has *andres adelphoi,* literally "men, brothers." We do not have an exactly equivalent phraseology in English. We can translate idiomatically simply with "brothers" (NASB, RSV "brethren"). The Greek has a male component that is very difficult to account for if Peter were making a deliberate attempt to include the "sisters," as the NIVI represents him as doing. In the parallel verses in Acts 15:7 and 13, where the context may make it a little clearer that men were in view, NIVI has only "brothers."

Acts 1:14–15 makes it look as though Peter is addressing a group composed of both men and women. So it is tempting to assume that *andres* "men" has no meaning. But Peter is probably looking forward in his mind to the specific issue of choosing a replacement for Judas (Acts 1:21–26). In such a weighty decision the men would, in first-century Jewish culture,

---

difficult" (p. 109). The decision would not be difficult at all if he would pay attention to the established lexical meaning of *anēr* as "man." But by relying on slim evidence that *anēr* might mean "person" in very rare cases, and then using that doubtful evidence as a wedge to open the door so that all instances of *anēr* are called into question, he has introduced a vagueness into the translation process that is simply not justified by the lexical evidence.

play a leading role. In view of this purpose, Peter may already introduce in 1:16 some indication that he is addressing them especially and distinctively.

Acts 2:22

NIV: "Men of Israel, listen to this: . . ."

NIVI: "People of Israel, listen to this: . . ."

No one knows whether Peter's address took place in the "Court of Women," where women could enter, or in one of the inner temple spaces where only men could enter. The translation "men of Israel" is not obviously incorrect, nor is there clear reason to think that "people of Israel" is required by the context here.

These examples show some of the difficulty of estimating from context where a male semantic component occurs and with how strong a force it occurs. In some special constructions and contexts, there may be disagreement. But because of modern biases, the tendency is not to see a reason for male marking, even when it is there, and as a result to wipe it out in translation.

G. Conclusions

We could go on with further examples from the New Testament, but the analysis would be similar. There are many cases in which the context by itself would not *require* the meaning "man." But in all of these cases the meaning "man" makes sense and is not foreign to the context. Our approach here is just the same that Greek lexicographers regularly use in studying the meanings of the word. We are not arguing that *anēr* could never lose its male semantic component in specialized idioms, but only that the argument that it loses its male marking in any New Testament examples is based on very doubtful evidence and is not sound lexicography.

We can underline what we hope should be obvious. In cases of disputes about word meaning throughout this book, we as well as those with whom we disagree are fallible. It is always possible that scholars will make advances in fine-tuning lexical descriptions. In fact, the ability to conduct exhaustive computer searches through the body of Greek literature in the *Thesaurus Linguae Graecae* opens exciting possibilities in this area. On this basis scholars may on occasion find good grounds for adding detail to lexicons and changing the interpretation of some individual verses. But, except in the case of very rare words or other special cases, sound interpretation remains within the bounds laid out by specific lexical evidence. If, instead, scholars postulate meanings merely on the ground that they fit the immediate context and could theoretically be established by evidence not yet uncovered, they rightly evoke the complaint that they appear to be driven by subjective preferences or ideologies rather than hard evidence.

The Relation of Generic "He" to Third-Person Generic Singulars in Hebrew and Greek

D oes generic "he" represent a good match with the functions of third-person singular generics in Hebrew and Greek?

A. Differences among gender systems

The gender system of each language has its own character, distinct in detail from the systems of other languages. Thus, there is no perfect matching. But pronouns serve similar communicative functions in many languages, because they are used to refer to items that have already been identified or will shortly be identified by other means. Thus, Hebrew, Aramaic, and Greek, as well as English, have resources for using pronouns to refer to people in the ways that John 14:23 does it: "If anyone loves *me*, *he* will obey *my* teaching. *My* Father will love *him*, and *we* will come to *him* and make *our* home with *him*."

In Hebrew, Aramaic, and Greek, the forms indicating person and number often occur as affixes attached to nouns or verbs, but this difference is a technicality. The functions are still similar. Since there is much similarity in meaning and communicative function in the use of pronouns, translation chooses in the great majority of instances to preserve person and number in translation of pronouns. There are nevertheless fascinating differences in some areas. For example, Greek has three genders, masculine, neuter, and feminine, while Hebrew and Aramaic have only two. In Greek a neuter pronoun can refer to a person or group of people, when its antecedent is neuter (as with the word *teknon*, "child"). In Greek a neuter plural subject can be followed by a singular verb. In Hebrew, a masculine singular verb can be followed by a feminine singular subject.[1]

In addition, in Hebrew, Aramaic, and Greek gender markings attach not merely to words referring to human beings, but to almost all nouns and adjectives. Gender applies even to words designating inanimate objects. For example, "sea" (*thalassa*) in Greek is feminine. The corresponding Hebrew word *yam* ("sea") is masculine. One word for "speech, word" is masculine in Hebrew (*dābār*), while another, nearly synonymous word is feminine (*'imrah*). Hence grammatical gender cannot simply be equated with sexual differentiation. In Hebrew and Aramaic, gender markings attach also to the verbs in second-person forms and in the third-person singular and some third-person plural forms.

B.   Third-person singular statements about human beings and ordinary speaker expectations

We are not directly concerned with all these areas but specifically with third-person statements *about human beings*. When gender-marked nouns, adjectives, participles, and pronoun forms are *used to refer to human beings, the gender usually lines up with the sex.*[2] This is natural, because it is one of the main useful functions of having gender marking when referring to human beings. With plural pronouns, masculine is used in referring to mixed groups as well. But with most sentences using singular forms, the listener tends tentatively to identify the sex of the person on the basis of gender marking.

Of course, we must also leave to one side the use of singular *collective* terms. Hebrew, Aramaic, and Greek, like English, have collective terms like "crowd," "group," and "church" for designating groups as a whole. We are not concerned with these cases, but with pronouns that refer to members of a group, whether a single member (with singular pronoun) or several members together, with a plural pronoun. In particular, what happens with third person pronouns?

In Chapter 14, we offered an example from Leviticus 14. Here, in a case covering both men and women lepers, the repeated use of a masculine singular pronoun sets up a male as the principal example of the general

---

[1]Gesenius, *Gesenius' Hebrew Grammar*, 2nd ed. (Oxford: Oxford University Press, 1910), section 145.

[2]Al Wolters states that, as far as he knows, in all Semitic languages, grammatical gender designations for persons always correspond to the personal gender of the person being referred to—not only for human beings, but also for pagan deities, demons, etc. (Information taken from tape of "The Gender of the Holy Spirit," a paper presented at the 1998 ETS annual meeting, November 19–21, 1998, in Orlando, Florida. Wolters's statement occurred during question-and-answer session after the paper itself. Copies of the tape are available from ACTS, Inc., 14153 Clayton Rd., Town & Country, MO 63017.) This claim, though it might have to be qualified if unusual exceptions were found, reinforces the point that we are making.

principle, so that when a reader comes to Leviticus 14:9, he is not surprised to hear the mention of the leper's "beard."[3]

Other cases in the Bible confirm that masculine singular pronouns, nouns, adjectives, and participles produce similar expectations.

Consider Ezekiel 18:5–9. Ezekiel 18:5 begins with the expression, "Suppose there is a righteous man ['*îsh*] . . ." (NIV). Even without further context, we can probably guess that the principle here will be universal, applying to both men and women. But then in verse 6 we meet the expression, "He does not defile his neighbor's wife or lie with a woman during her period" (NIV). Clearly a male example is being used to illustrate the general truth.

But what if, after introducing the example of a righteous man in verse 5, verse 6 had read instead, "She does not commit adultery with her neighbor's husband"? Or what if it had said, "He does not commit adultery with her neighbor's husband"? There would be a jarring effect. Suddenly the beginning picture has changed, and we are picturing a female example, though we are still looking at the same general principle.

As long as we are looking at the same general principle, why do the pronouns matter? They matter precisely because they focus in on an example, a representative case. And when we come to particular details in which the sex of the representative comes into play more directly, we clearly are expecting the sex to match the sex that was hinted at in the earlier pronouns.

Now as a reader reads a passage for the first time, he does not at first know when and in what way the sex of a representative will be relevant in an illustration. When he reads the first part of Leviticus 14, he does not know that verse 9 will mention the leper's beard. More generally, he does not know whether something mentioned later on in the text will apply literally only to a male example. Hence, he must keep somewhere in the back of his mind the fact that the representative sample is male, in order to be prepared for a possible detail that further exemplifies this maleness. In other words, the maleness of the representative is there, subtly in the back of the reader's mind, *before* he encounters something like Leviticus 14:9 or Ezekiel 18:6 that makes the maleness more undeniably central to the character of the example.

As another example, consider Deuteronomy 15:12–17. Deuteronomy 15:12 begins with language that explicitly mentions both sexes:

If your kinsman, a Hebrew man or woman, is sold to you, then he [masculine singular attached to the verb] shall serve you . . . (NASB).

The passage then continues with masculine singular forms and some forms not marked for gender until 15:17. Then 15:17 completes the instructions by saying,

---

[3]See Chapter 14, pp. 256–57.

then you shall take an awl and pierce it through his [masculine singular] ear into the door, and he [masculine singular attached to the verb] shall be your servant [masculine singular] forever (NASB).

But the verse concludes, "And also you shall do likewise to your maid servant" (NASB). This final addition of the "maid servant" indicates clearly enough that, in the course of using so many masculine singular forms throughout the paragraph, the writer and the reader alike have slipped into a pattern of thinking of a male servant as the focal illustration of the principle. The addition of a specific application to a "maid servant" shows that there was a need to signal to the reader that the focal illustration was changing to a female.

The Septuagint, the ancient Greek translation of the Old Testament, shows analogous phenomena in Leviticus 14, Ezekiel 18:5–6, and Deuteronomy 15:12–17, and so do the Aramaic versions.[4] Thus, there is reason to believe that in Greek and Aramaic as well as Hebrew a masculine singular personal pronoun encourages readers to picture a male representative in expressing a general principle.

From the New Testament we may add an example from Luke 18:23–35, the parable of the unmerciful servant. In verse 24 the servant appears, described as "one debtor, " with masculine gender. Verse 25 continues with two masculine singular pronouns, then mentions "his wife." As with the Old Testament examples, when a masculine singular form is used in this way, the reader must be prepared for the possibility that later information will give a detail that makes the sex of the sample person more central to the narrative. In the back of his mind the reader already knows that the story is considering a male example, *before* he hears about the wife in verse 25.

Or consider Luke 14:16–24, the parable of the banquet. In verse 18 "the first" invited person, masculine gender, responds. In verse 19 "another," masculine gender, responds. In verse 20 still "another," with masculine gender, says, "I have married a wife." At the end of the narrative it speaks of the "men" (*anēr* in the plural, for male human beings, not *anthrōpos*) who were invited (Luke 14:24). The transition from generic third masculine singular pronouns to specific male details is seamless and natural and causes no difficulty for the reader. But a transition to a specifically female example (if the guest in v. 20 had said, "I have married a husband," for example) would have been jarring to the reader's expectations.

Sometimes a passage may use the very same masculine forms to make a general statement that applies only to men. Titus 2:2 exhorts the "older men," using masculine plural forms. The masculine plural could presumably be

---

[4]We have checked Targum Onkelos in Leviticus and Deuteronomy, and Targum Jonathan in Ezekiel. Of course, translations may choose to follow the original literally, even when it results in awkward phrasing in the target language. One must therefore exercise caution in evaluating linguistic evidence arising from a translation.

used to designate a mixed group. But when we come to the next verse, Paul exhorts the "older women," showing that the earlier verse refers to men in distinction from women. In 2:2 the reader must hold in mind the male-oriented meaning element of the masculine gender until he arrives at verse 3, in order to determine the scope of the group addressed. Thus the masculine gender has not lost all of its potential meaning contribution in this case. Thus, in many situations dealing with human beings, masculine forms tend not merely to be grammatically masculine, but to suggest the picture of a male as the example.

In conclusion, when we have a story or a series of statements referring to a single human being, using a series of masculine pronouns, the gender of the pronoun indicates the sex of the person. If the context makes a general (generic) statement, as in the third-person generic singular use, the sex is the sex of the sample person, who is an example of the general principle. This situation is similar to the situation in English with generic "he" (Chapter 14).

We recognize that there may be additional subtle differences from English. On the one hand, in the original, the net effect of the masculine marking may be subtly weaker than in English, because grammatical gender occurs in other uses besides the cases that identify the sex of the referent.

But on the other hand, in generic statements, masculine forms tend to occur more frequently in Hebrew and Greek than in English (because most nouns, adjectives, and participles are gender-marked in Greek and Hebrew, and verbs are also gender-marked in Hebrew). This greater frequency of gender-marked words referring to persons may push listeners in the opposite direction, toward reinforcing the impression of a predominance of male orientation in generic statements. These two effects are both extremely subtle. Because they work in opposite directions, the net effect is probably still similar to the use of generic "he" in English.

C. What does the study of linguistics imply?

People who have studied linguistics may still have questions about the analysis above.[5]

1. Gender systems as form

One question is, "Do the differences between gender systems in different languages mean that gender in generic statements is mere convention, mere form with no meaning?"

---

[5]The difficulty arises because, as the excursus in Chapter 10 indicated, introductory linguistic theory distinguishes form and meaning, but does not touch on the subtleties involved in the possible meaning influence of a masculine gender within the context of a generic statement. The theoretically informed approach (level 2) lays aside subtleties that typically operate intuitively with native speakers (level 3).

Gender systems differ from language to language. Indeed, a catalog of different languages shows striking variations. Some have no gender. Some have two genders, but the line between the two may vary. One language may distinguish between male and nonmale (which includes inanimate), another between female and nonfemale. Other languages may have three or four or more grammatical genders (the extra genders being used to some extent in classifying nonhuman entities).[6]

People translating from one language to another make silly mistakes if they try to force grammatical genders to match. Instead, they need to respect the particular rules of each language. A simple guideline would say, "Translate meaning, while letting the grammatical genders, as forms, follow the normal grammatical contours of each language."

But the simple guideline, rightly understood, leaves open the question of whether *nuances in meaning* attach to a masculine form like generic "he." We must look at each language to see. This more detailed study is precisely what we have done above. In cases where two languages have substantial similarities in their generic statements, we should not hesitate to strive for the best match in meaning that we can achieve.

2. Perception in English

Another question: "Does generic 'he' really retain any connotation of a male example or starting point? Some native English speakers see it as purely neutral."

Generic "he" may, to some people, "feel" purely neutral. They may say, "I do not think of a male example, but simply of the general truth." Before the rise of feminism, most people did not consciously focus on generic "he," but took it for granted. They naturally focused on the main point, the general truth, not on tiny details in its manner of expression. But even though conscious attention naturally focuses elsewhere, generic "he" still sets up a kind of slant or preference toward a male example, as we saw from examples in Chapter 14.[7] A specifically female detail is disruptive:

> The average American needs the small routines of getting ready for work. As he shaves or blow-dries his hair or pulls on his panty hose, he is easing himself by small stages into the demands of the day.[8]

The native speaker is usually focusing conscious attention in other directions, until the phrase "his panty hose" forces him to attend consciously to the fact that he has been assuming a male example in the process of digesting the

---

[6]See, e.g., D. A. Carson, *The Inclusive Language Debate: A Plea for Realism* (Grand Rapids: Baker, 1998), 78–89.

[7]See Chapter 8, 142–48.

[8]Miller and Swift, *Handbook*, 46, quoted from C. Badendyck in the *New York Times Magazine*.

general statement. As we have seen, the effect in Hebrew and Greek seems to be similar.

3. Meaning arising from choice

Another question may arise: "Do not linguists say that meaning arises from *choices* within the possibilities of a language? But with generic statements in English, Hebrew, and Greek, a masculine is used automatically. The speaker does not consciously choose it. So how can male meaning attach to it?"

It is true that in generic singular statements about human beings in English, Hebrew, and Greek, the masculine pronoun is the normal one. It is called the "default" form or "unmarked" form because one uses it if there is no special need to use another form. By contrast, a feminine form is "marked." One would not choose it automatically. So it indicates prominently that a female example is in view. Typically, it would be used to formulate a truth holding only for women, or especially for women (as in Ps. 113:9, "He settles the barren woman in her home as a happy mother of children"). On the other hand, using "he" in a general statement does *not* indicate that we are dealing with a truth holding only for men. It indicates mainly that we are not dealing with women only. We may be speaking about men only, or about both men and women. Thus, a default masculine singular is not completely "neutral."

Moreover, the example of English use of generic "he" shows that the idea of a male example can attach to an unmarked form. It is simply much more subtle than the effect of the feminine form. The general truth expressed with generic "he" holds for both men and women, but the specific manner of formulation still suggests the starting picture of a male example.

D. Shifts in number

Some fine-grained differences between languages now need our attention. In Hebrew, we find on occasion shifts from singular to plural in generic statements, as in Numbers 5:6–7. An illustrative translation would go as follows:

A man or a woman, when they [masculine plural] commit [a sin] from among all the sins of mankind ['ādām, masculine singular collective], to break faith with the LORD, and that soul [feminine singular][9] is guilty [feminine singular], they [masculine plural] shall confess their [masculine plural] sin that they [masculine plural] committed, and he [masculine singular] shall pay back his [masculine singular] guilt in full, adding [masculine singular] a fifth

---

[9]The Hebrew word *nepesh*, meaning "soul, life, self," has the feminine gender.

to it, and he [masculine singular] shall give to the one against whom [masculine singular] he [masculine singular] was guilty.

The shift from plural to singular is disconcerting in English. But it is not illogical in Hebrew. As we observed earlier, even in English, "they" can sometimes be used to refer back to a generic singular (though this usage has its own problems and is widely rejected in written English). Generic singular statements have an aspect of singularity, in focusing on a particular sample case, and an aspect of plurality, since they apply to a plurality of persons. In a case like this one, however, English idiom prefers consistency in number more than Hebrew does. The most attractive solution in English is to use all singulars, as do the RSV and the NIV. But it is at least arguable that one could use all plurals in a case like this. Translation cannot capture absolutely everything.

However, advocates of gender-neutral translation are tempted to leap from this difficult example to a general permission to use plurals indiscriminately. Certainly it would be convenient for them if they could always use "they" and avoid the taboo generic "he." But we must not leap to a conclusion just because it is convenient. In fact, a number of factors counsel caution.

First, the use of both singular and plural forms in the context of a tightly woven generic statement seems *not* regularly to characterize Greek[10] but only Hebrew (and perhaps Aramaic as a language akin to Hebrew). Hence, this example does not address the problems of New Testament translation.

Second, the use of both singular and plural forms makes sense in view of the character of generic statements. Such statements often include both a sample case and a general area to which the sample case applies. The intersection of these two aspects creates the opportunity for using both singular and plural. Likewise, when we use a collective term like "committee" or "humanity," the sense involves both the singular nature of the group as a whole and the plurality of members of the group. Hence, the mixing of singular and plural forms may in some languages and in some contexts make sense. But we do not thereby destroy the difference in meaning between one and many. The use of a singular pronoun undoubtedly still focuses on the singularity of a sample or the unity of a collective, while the use of a plural pronoun still focuses on the plurality of members of the whole. Thus, meaning differences remain. When feasible, these meaning differences still need representation in translation.

Third, though Hebrew and English differ, the differences must not be exaggerated. American English can shift from singular to plural, though usually not within the bounds of a single sentence. In this book we occasionally shift within a short space from talking about a sample translator in

---

[10]The Septuagint, the Greek translation of Numbers 5:6–7, uses all singulars.

the singular to talking about translators in the plural. A casual observer might therefore suppose that the two modes of expression are completely identical in meaning. But in fact they have the usual differences in nuance.

Fourth, the phenomena in Numbers 5:6–7 actually move in the opposite direction from what gender-neutral policy demands. Gender-neutral policy wants to use plural forms *in English* as if these were freely interchangeable with singular forms *in English*. What the Hebrew demonstrates is only that in certain paragraphs in Hebrew, singular and plural forms *in Hebrew* perform closely interlocking functions. In reality, such might easily become an argument for paying special respect to those cases in Hebrew where the singular *alone* is used throughout a passage, with no oscillation into the plural. Since the Hebrew has its plural forms available more readily than English, the consistent use of the singular is then all the more significant. So, it might be argued, when Hebrew consistently uses singular, we have *even more* reason in English to use the singular.

Such a case occurs, for example, in Leviticus 14:1–33. In the entire passage every pronoun or substantive that refers to the leper is masculine singular. But the NLT shifts from plurals to singulars and back: plurals occur in the NLT in 14:1–3a, 8–9, 32; singulars in 14:3b–7, 10–31. Even where singulars occur, the NLT is careful not to introduce generic "he." The whole effort is slightly ridiculous, because in verse 9 the leper shaves off his beard, indicating that a male example is in view.

E.   Shifts in person

Consider another difference, this time in the use of second and third person. Hebrew can move rapidly from second person to third person forms in generic statements. For example, Leviticus 1:2–3 runs,

> Speak to the people [masculine plural] of Israel, and say to *them* [masculine plural], When *any man* [*'ādām* masculine singular] of *you* [masculine plural] brings an offering to the LORD, *you* [masculine plural] shall bring *your* [masculine plural] offering of cattle from the herd or from the flock. If *his* offering is a burnt offering from the herd, *he* shall offer (RSV).

But even here, the shifts do not seem to be arbitrary. The third person singular (equivalent to "he") continues from verse 3 to the end of Leviticus 1. The beginning of verse 3 is a paragraph break. It introduces the first of three sections dealing with different kinds of offering, from the "herd" (cattle, verses 3–9), from the "flock" (sheep and goats, verses 10–13), and from birds (verses 14–17). Hence, the change to third person in verse 3 actually helps to mark a major break between the general command in verse 2 and the special instructions for particular offerings in the rest of the chapter. Leviticus 2 specifies the grain offering using an opposite pattern. The general instructions in 2:1–3 come in the third person, perhaps continuing the third person from Leviticus 1. The details for various special types of grain offering are then described in the second person in 2:4–17.

Our observations concerning these phenomena are similar to those concerning singular and plural in Hebrew.

First, the quick transition may occur more readily in Hebrew than in Greek.[11] But in this case it is a useful transition in English as well, because of the way in which it helps to set apart one section of discourse from another.

Second, the use of both second person and third person makes sense in generic statements, since the sample person that is the starting point for a general statement can often be chosen either to be the addressee or a person "out there." As we have observed, the use of both second person and third person in general statements does not collapse the differences between the two, with respect to whom one uses for the sample person.

Third, though Hebrew and English differ marginally, English also can use second as well as third person in general statements.

Fourth, if indeed Hebrew shifts more readily, then it is easy to argue that there is all the more reason to retain person markings in those passages that consistently use one form rather than another. But of course gender-neutral translations do not do that. Leviticus 27:2b–33 uses third person masculine singular and second person in a consistent way. But most gender-neutral translations turn the passage around in various ways in order to avoid generic "he."

Certainly we need to exercise appropriate caution in translation. Languages do not exactly match in their use of singular and plural pronouns, nor in their use of second and third person. But what sort of caution is appropriate? In the absence of complete understanding of phenomena like those in Numbers 5:6–7 and Leviticus 1:2–3, caution counsels *us not to move further away than necessary from the most obvious equivalents.* And caution must lean on what understanding we do have, not on a desperate desire to avoid generic "he." Above all, exceptional cases must not become a sweeping license to change person and number wherever we want.[12]

Finally, English differs from Hebrew, Aramaic, and Greek in the precise places where pronouns normally would occur. English generally requires that verbs have an explicit subject, while Hebrew, Aramaic, and Greek can use the verb together with an affix to indicate the subject. The result is that in translation English will sometimes have an explicit pronoun where Hebrew, Aramaic, or Greek does not.

---

[11]John 15:5–7 and some other passages shift the person. But a literal reproduction of the shift in English does not result in English that is perceptibly awkward.

[12]This is precisely the point of Colorado Springs Guideline A.2. At the time of the Colorado Springs meeting, some of us at the meeting explicitly discussed the sort of switches found in Numbers 5:6–7 and Leviticus 1:2–3. That is the reason for the qualifying phrase, "with only rare exceptions required in unusual cases."

Let us take John 14:23 as our example. In English it runs, "If anyone loves me, *he* will obey my teaching. My Father will love him, and we will come to him and make our home with him." Greek has pronouns corresponding to each English pronoun except "he." The verb for "obey" in Greek has a third-person singular ending, so that by itself it means "he will obey," even without an added pronoun.

Now this verb in Greek has no gender marking. It can be used equally for "he will obey" or "she will obey." In that respect it does not perfectly match the translation "he will obey." We insert "he" in translation because it is customary in English, not because we can exactly match the gender in Greek. But the pronouns in Greek corresponding to the occurrences of "him" are all masculine in gender.

In many other cases, explicit gender-marking occur in Hebrew, Aramaic, and Greek that cannot necessarily be easily represented in English. We have already mentioned that the commandments in Exodus 20:13–17 have masculine singular verbs: "You [masculine singular] shall not murder." In generic statements Greek substantive participles are typically masculine in gender: "Whoever [masculine singular article plus masculine singular participle in Greek] has my commands and [masculine singular] obeys them, he [masculine singular] is the one who [masculine singular article plus masculine singular participle] loves me" (John 14:21). The use of masculine singular in cases like this one is grammatically conventional. But, as in English, it also "suggests a particular pattern of thought."[13] It suggests a male example and so has a contribution to meaning. It is not mere empty form.

This sort of fine detail cannot be carried over directly into English. A translation does what it can in English. But it is another matter when a translation fails to do as well as it can by deliberately avoiding generic "he."[14]

Despite some smoke-screen-like rhetoric, the driving force for gender-neutral policy is *not* trying to do justice to fine-grained differences between Hebrew and Greek and English. The real issue is only English. Even casual observers can see that the taboo against generic "he"—not peculiarities in the number, person, and gender systems of Hebrew or Greek—drives many of the changes in gender-neutral translation. For those who still doubt it, we can easily present confirming evidence.

Consider the NIVI of Leviticus 20.

Verses 1, 27: No generic "he" is in the NIV, so no change is needed.

Verses 2–6, 9: Singulars are converted to plurals to avoid generic "he."

---

[13]*American Heritage Dictionary*, 831.
[14]Concerning the translation "the one who" rather than "he who" for a definite article plus a participle, see footnote 16 below.

Verses 7–8, 19, 22–26: "You" occurs, so no change needed.

Verses 10–18, 20–21: Third singulars all remain third singular. Why? Because the laws concern forbidden sexual relations. The general principle applies only to one sex. Hence, a "he" or a "she" can be permitted.

The NIVI's pronouns match the NIV and the Hebrew in number and in person whenever they can do so, *except* where it would lead to generic "he" in a principle that includes women. The need to avoid generic "he," not the meaning of person or number in Hebrew, determines the changes.

In Ezekiel 18, the person, number, and gender markings are carefully orchestrated in Hebrew. The Lord directly addresses the people in the second person plural in verses 2–3, 19, 25, and 29–32 (with a few interspersed third singulars to express what happens in an individual case, and a third plural for "the house of Israel"). Outside of these verses of direct address, and the summary statements in verses 4 and 20a, the designations of a sample righteous or wicked person use the third masculine singular (verses 5–19, 20b–24, 26–28). So what might you expect in English? The RSV follows the pattern of the Hebrew point by point. But the NRSV changes it, using singulars in verses 5–20, then plurals in 21–24, 26–28. Why? In verses 5–19 we meet three times the expression "defile(s) his neighbor's wife" (6, 11, 15), indicating clearly that the sample cases in verses 5–19 are male. Accordingly, NRSV is not afraid to use "he." But there are no such indicators beyond verse 19. NRSV therefore feels that it cannot use generic "he." The loss of that option forces everything into plural.

Leviticus 27 consistently uses the third person to describe the person who vows an item. It uses the second person exclusively for the community as a whole and the priest who represents them in determining the valuation of the vowed item. GNB exactly reverses this practice, regularly using the second person for the person who vows, and the third person for the priest and his actions. Why? It can thereby avoid generic "he."

In all these cases, and many more, constraints with respect to generic "he" result in otherwise unaccountable changes in person or number.

Remember also that some of the committees responsible for translation already had policies in place from the beginning. From the beginning NRSV had a "mandate" to eliminate generic "he." NIVI had an internal policy agreement (as of August 1992):

> To avoid gender-specific language in general statements, a third-person sentence may be changed to second person where this adequately conveys the meaning, and a singular sentence may be recast in a plural form provided this does not obscure a significant individual reference.[15]

---

[15]"CBT Policy on Gender-Inclusive Language," quoted in Carson, *Inclusive Language Debate*, 43, guideline II 8.

Changes were based on a general principle that generic "he" would be eliminated wherever possible. It remained for the Committee on Bible Translation (CBT) to decide what kind of accuracy was "adequate" (not necessarily best). And they decided what counted as "significant individual reference," as opposed to a more subtle individualizing nuance. They had to cut off or ignore meaning nuances, but they tried to minimize the effects. We are glad that they tried to minimize the damage, but we regret that they consented to the damage in the first place.

In responding to gender-neutral policies, we have three principles. First, translators need to do grammatically appropriate things in English. They need not try *artificially* to make gender or number markings appear or disappear in English in exact correspondence with gender and number in the original.

Second, it is grammatically appropriate in English to use generic "he" in translating third-person singular generic statements. We should not avoid a good equivalent when we have one.

Third, in a large number of cases, the original also evokes a picture of a male example of a general truth, so that in fact even on a fairly minute level generic "he" results in excellent meaning representation in English, closely corresponding with the meaning of the original. Hence, we have all the more reason not to be intimidated out of using generic "he."[16]

---

[16]Some people may wonder about our attitude toward the construction "he who . . ." "He who" in English translation often corresponds to a *masculine* participle in Hebrew or Greek. If the masculine is there in the original, with male connotations, should not it always be translated as "he who"? But translation must bear in mind many aspects of meaning, not merely the male connotations of one item. Thus, even prior to the gender-neutral controversy, some translations have chosen to use expressions like "the one who," "whoever," and other alternatives (as in the NIV of John 14:21). Moreover, when a sentence opens with "he who," there is no preceding referent in the passage to which "he" refers. In the absence of an earlier referent, indicating that "he" is in fact inclusive, the problem of potential misreading does rear its head.

But this potential for misreading can easily be overestimated. "He who . . ." is a regular construction in English introducing generic statements. But "he who . . ." is probably fading in frequency of use, so it is difficult to say what will happen with it in the future.

The Colorado Springs Guidelines explicitly allow translations other than "he who": "However, substantival participles such as *ho pisteuōn* can often be rendered in inclusive ways, such as "the one who believes" rather than "he who believes" (Guideline A.1).

The Spectrum from "He" in a Story to "He" in a General Statement

There is a spectrum of uses of the pronoun "he." We can lay out a transition in small steps, starting with a typical parable and ending with a typical general statement using generic "he."

We begin with Luke 10:30–35, the parable of the good Samaritan. The parable illustrates what all of us Christians should do,[1] using a specific story. The story involves "a man" who was attacked by robbers, as well as "a Samaritan." NRSV, NIVI, NIrV(1995), NCV, GNB, GW, NLT, and CEV all use masculine singular "he/him" to refer to both characters. A male character, the Samaritan, can clearly represent what all of us are to do. Similarly, in the parable of the unmerciful servant in Matthew 18:23–34, a male servant represents anyone who is unmerciful. NRSV, NIVI, NIrV(1995), NCV, GNB, GW, NLT, and CEV all use "he."

The parable of the lost sheep in Matthew 18:12–14 is likewise a detailed parable, and NRSV, NIVI, NIrV(1995), NCV, GNB, GW, and NLT all retain "he" to refer to the shepherd. But the introductory remark, "What do you think?" (18:12, NIV) involves the listener more closely, inviting application. The CEV turns the whole story into the second person "you."

Next, in Matthew 24:48–51 a servant represents in a particular story form what is true for many. CEV avoids using "he," but NRSV, NIVI, NIrV(1995), NCV, GNB, GW, and NLT use "he/him." This story is shorter

---

[1]In fact the story has other dimensions, including the shock to Jews of having a Samaritan as the "hero." But we need not enter into these.

than the parable of the good Samaritan, and so has fewer details. More of the elements that are left are immediately transferable into a general lesson.

Matthew 24:46–47, the story of the responsible servant, is even shorter. And it is preceded by a generalizing rhetorical question in verse 45, "Who then is the faithful and wise servant?" (RSV). It stills uses a particular servant as an example, but the generality to which the example points is closer to the surface. NCV, NLT, and CEV eliminate all masculine indicators,[2] but NRSV, NIVI, NIrV(1995), GNB, and GW do not.

Matthew 24:43–44 has a compressed story followed immediately by the application to "you":

> But understand this: If the owner of the house had known at what time of night the thief was coming, *he* would have kept watch and would not have let *his* house be broken into. So you also must be ready, because the Son of Man will come at an hour when you do not expect him (NIV).

NCV, NLT, and CEV eliminate "he." The NRSV, NIVI, NIrV(1995), GNB, GW retain "he."

Now consider Luke 15:4–6, the parable of the lost sheep in Luke. This story is longer and has quite a bit of detail, so it is in some ways more "particular"; the general lesson is more in the background. But it begins with "one of you" (15:4, NIV), more directly inviting the audience to generalize. It then continues in the third person ("he"). GNB, NLT, and CEV use "you" all the way through, converting the whole of a particular story into a more directly general saying. NRSV, NIVI, NIrV(1995), NCV, and GW retain "he."

Luke 17:7–9 is a similar passage beginning with "one of you" (NIV), then continuing with third person ("he"). But it continues with rhetorical questions, never producing a single-stranded story line. Thus, the general principle is closer to the surface. NRSV, NCV, NIrV(1995), GNB, and CEV use "you" throughout, even though this greatly weakens the transition to the application in verse 10, where for the first time the Greek (and RSV and NIV) returns to second person ("you"). NIVI, GW, and NLT retain "he."

The general principle is even closer to the surface in Luke 12:58:

> As you go with your accuser before the magistrate, make an effort to settle with *him* on the way, lest *he* drag you to the judge, and the judge hand you over to the officer, and the officer put you in prison (RSV).

---

[2]In this and some other instances below, the disappearance may, however, be a product of paraphrasing rather than deliberate avoidance. With a shorter piece, it is hard to say for sure. The substitute "that servant" in Matthew 24:47 sounds clunky and overemphatic as a translation of a simple *auton* ("him") in Greek. But one cannot be absolutely sure that it was introduced to avoid "him." The main point is not whether a more paraphrastic version actually uses "he" in every single instance, but whether it is *willing* to do it in order to express meaning most accurately.

The application to "you" is right at the surface. At the same time, the verse retains some of the qualities of a story, and is clearly a particular example illustrating how one is to be reconciled to any neighbor or to God. NRSV, NIVI, NIrV(1995), NCV, GNB, NLT, and CEV eliminate all masculines. GW retains "he/him."

We take another step toward the prominence of the general principle in third-person general statements. For example, Luke 6:40 says, "A student is not above *his* teacher, but everyone who is fully trained will be like *his* teacher" (NIV). In the context of first-century Jewish culture, male teachers taught male students. But the general principle expressed in the saying would apply to men and women disciples of Jesus. The NIVI and GW are willing to preserve "his" in English, corresponding to a Greek masculine pronoun.[3] NRSV, NIrV(1995), NCV, GNB, NLT, and CEV lack all masculine pronouns.

We also find third-person general statements that retain some of the illustrative punch characterizing parables, as in Luke 17:3–4:

RSV: If your *brother* sins, rebuke *him*, and if *he* repents, forgive *him*; and if *he* sins against you seven times in the day, and turns to you seven times, and says, "I repent," you must forgive *him*.

The mention of sinning seven times in one day has illustrative punch. The NRSV, NIVI, NIrV(1995), and CEV eliminate all masculines. The NCV, GNB, GW, and NLT do not.[4]

Again, consider Luke 14:26–27:

RSV: If any one comes to me and does not hate *his* own father and mother and wife and children and brothers and sisters, yes, and even *his* own life, *he* cannot be my *disciple. Whoever* does not bear *his* own cross and come after me, cannot be my *disciple.*

The hyperbolic use of "hate," the illustrative multiplication of kinds of relatives, and the picture of bearing one's cross, all have literary sparkle, giving the saying some of the illustrative power of Jesus' parables. But now the opening words, "if anyone," are even more pointedly generalizing than was the expression "if your brother" in Luke 17:3–4. By this point, the generalized principle is so much at the front that almost all the gender-neutral translations—NRSV, NIVI, NIrV(1995), GNB, GW, NLT, and

---

[3]In Greek the pronoun attaches only to the last occurrence of "teacher." The first has the definite article, which can function in Greek as a weakened substitute for the possessive.

[4]We suspect, but of course cannot prove, that more of the gender-neutral translations would have eliminated masculines in a generic statement like this one, if they could have found a reasonable way to do so without seriously damaging the force of the saying. Luke 17:3–4 is impossible to express cleanly and accurately if you do not allow yourself to use a third-person singular generic pronoun—illustrating once again that language as a whole cannot easily dispense with the third-person singular generic. See also the discussion of this passage in Chapter 18.

CEV—eliminate the masculine singular "he/his." In this case the NCV, interestingly, does not.

Finally, in more purely general statements, like John 6:56, 14:21, and 14:23, the generic "he" disappears in all gender-neutral translations: NRSV, NIVI, NIrV(1995), NCV, GNB, GW, NLT, and CEV.

Our purpose here is not to go into the specific details of individual translations of these verses,[5] but to make a point about using "he." Actual usage of the third person singular, within Scripture itself, shows a whole spectrum of cases involving *both* a more individualizing concrete case *and* a more general truth expressed through this case. At one end of the spectrum, in detailed parables, the concrete case is in the forefront. At the other end, in general statements with "anyone" and "whoever," the general principle is in the forefront.

Ordinary English readers can understand an ordinary "he" at one end of the spectrum. Therefore they can understand it at the other end. There is really no sharp break in principle. Communication rests on the natural ability of speakers to see general implications through a particular expression. This task is common to every point of the spectrum. The labors of gender-neutral translations to evade "he" are quite unnecessary.

Defenders of gender-neutral practices might like to think that the fully generic use of "he" in John 6:56, at one end of the spectrum, is a very special, very isolated, and very peculiar use. But in fact it is an integral part of the English language. Language hangs together at this point, so that an artificial ban cannot succeed in abolishing linguistic reality.[6]

In short, gender-neutral practices concern a whole spectrum, a spectrum that travels from generic "he" all the way over into the ordinary use of "he" and male examples in story telling. The evasion concerns not one isolated usage, but the canceling out of male representatives wherever it seems feasible. The issue, then, is not whether a certain very specific usage is becoming "infrequent," nor whether readers can "understand," but whether translators can risk offending readers by retaining the male-orientation overtones in the original text.

---

[5]In *some* cases, especially in the context of more paraphrastic translation policies, the substitutes have at least found reasonable paraphrastic ways of eliminating masculines.

[6]See also the discussion in Chapter 16 of the inevitability of generic "he."

Translation of *Anthrōpos*

Challenges arise in translating the Greek word *anthrōpos* that are not quite parallel to most of the other cases that we have seen. *Anthrōpos* can mean "man," but it can also mean "human being" (including women). It depends on the context. Whereas the Greek *anēr* ("man") is strongly marked as male (see Appendix 2), *anthrōpos* is used generically in a considerable number of cases. For example, 1 Timothy 4:10 speaks generally of God's salvation to all:

NIV: . . . the living God, who is the Savior of all *men* [*anthrōpos*, plural], and especially of those who believe.

NIVI: . . . the living God, who is the Saviour of all *people*, and especially of those who believe.

NIVI's word "people" is accurate. In fact, it is an improvement on the NIV "men," now that "men" has come to be used in some circles exclusively of male human beings.

The Colorado Springs Guidelines recognize this situation in Guideline A.5:

In many cases, *anthrōpoi* refers to people in general, and can be translated "people" rather than "men."

The same is true of the singular form *anthrōpos*, used to refer to people in general, as we see in Romans 3:28:

NIV: For we maintain that a *man* [*anthrōpos*, singular] is justified by faith apart from observing the law.

NIVI: For we maintain that a *person* is justified by faith apart from observing the law.

Once again, the NIVI is accurate and improves the NIV.

In other instances, *anthrōpos* in the singular refers to a particular historical individual. In cases like these, Greek speakers would ordinarily use *gunē,* "woman," if the individual in question were female. Hence, *anthrōpos* in such a context does not just mean "human being," with no hint of gender, but "a man," even though the word in itself is not *strongly* marked as male in the way *anēr* ("man") is. Fortunately, gender-neutral translations have usually preserved the male aspect in translating cases of this kind.

The Colorado Springs Guidelines again recognize the situation in the last half of Guideline A.5:

> The singular *anthrōpos* should ordinarily be translated "man" when it refers to a male human being.[1]

---

[1]The Colorado Springs Guidelines do not say explicitly what happens in other cases (such as the case when *anthrōpos* in the singular refers to a sample case, illustrating a general principle). Why? The explanation is simple enough: the Guidelines do not attempt to cover every instance, but focus on those that may be more controversial. In addition, they attempt to provide enough examples of permissible changes to show that we are not forbidding change where there is no accompanying loss of meaning. But they do not produce explicit rules to cover every case.

Likewise, in this book we do not devote extensive attention to *anthrōpos,* because, from the sample cases that we have checked, it appears that its treatment by gender-neutral translations is in most cases not as serious a problem as are other areas.

Strauss unnecessarily suggests sinister possibilities when he says, "There seems to be a marked reticence by the authors of the guidelines to affirm positively that *anthrōpos* and *'ādām* are accurately and precisely translated as 'person' or 'human being' in many contexts" (*Distorting Scripture? The Challenge of Bible Translation & Gender Accuracy* [Downers Grove, IL: InterVarsity, 1998], 106). For the record, we freely (not "reticently") agree with Strauss's positive affirmation about *anthrōpos* and *'ādām.* We reject the term "reticence" as a misconstrual of the actual reasons for omission.

The Evaporation of an Argument: D. A. Carson's Lack of Evidence for the Unusability of Generic "He" in English

Carson's book *The Inclusive-Language Debate*[1] is articulate and winsomely written. In the key debate about generic "he," it is easy to overlook the number of times that the book conducts arguments based on unestablished suppositions. These suppositions sometimes take the form of "if" statements or "suppose" statements that help to carry the argument forward. (The underlining in the following statements is ours.)

1. If the only corresponding individual expression in English [generic "he"] is one which is gender-specific and will be read in those parts of the English-speaking world where such gender specificity carries overtones of bigotry *not carried by the donor text*, then the responsible translator is faced with an awkward choice: Preserve the singular form and project bigotry, or go with a plural form and lose the individual reference (p. 106).

2. But let us suppose that English moves on to the place where "he" refers *exclusively* to the male (pp. 117–18).

3. But some of us are convinced that the language is changing [with respect to "he"] (p. 118).

4. If the English language is changing in the way the translators of the NRSV and NIVI believe it is, they cannot responsibly leave all those

---

[1] D. A. Carson, *The Inclusive-Language Debate: A Plea for Realism* (Grand Rapids: Baker, 1998).

gender-specific words in the English text precisely because to do so would be bad translations (p. 119).

5. Regardless of the source of the pressure for linguistic change, the changes (I shall argue) are here. If that is the case, *this is the language that, increasingly, we have to work with* (p. 188).

6. But if "he" in English, complete with gender specification, is used in a generic sense somewhat less frequently that it used to be, and if for some sections of the reading populace "he" is never or almost never used in a generic sense anymore, then fidelity to the original demands the choice of an expression that is less formally proximate, or we lose some part of what the original text says (p. 158).

A. Answering the suppositions

We have responded to each of these suppositions in the body of this book.

The first supposition, from page 106, says, "If [generic "he"] . . . carries overtones of bigotry not carried by the donor text . . ." The term "bigotry" is a strong term and ratchets up the emotive content of the discussion another notch. The heart of the supposition, however, is the claim that generic "he" carries negative connotations, a matter that we discussed in Chapter 15 under the objection "Bible translations should avoid the negative connotations that attach to certain words."[2] We will not repeat that discussion here, but only say that the matter needs argument, not a mere "if . . ." statement, if it is to supply a persuasive reason for readers to agree with Carson.

The second supposition ("But let us suppose that English moves on to the place where 'he' refers *exclusively* to the male," pp. 117–18) requires the actual disappearance of generic "he" from modern English. We have addressed this matter in Chapter 16: Generic "he" has not disappeared from contemporary English.[3] Carson himself admits that it has not disappeared, for he says, "It is therefore unsurprising that there are still many, many examples around of the unreconstructed generic "he." No one is arguing that the change has been universal."[4]

The third, fourth, and fifth suppositions talk in general terms about language "change": " some of us are convinced that the language is changing" (p. 118); "If the English language is changing in the way the translators of the NRSV and NIVI believe it is" (p. 119); "Regardless of the source of the pressure for linguistic change, the changes (I shall argue) are here" (p. 188). But these vague statements say nothing about whether generic "he" is

---

[2]See Chapter 15, sec. C, 281–87.
[3]See extensive list of examples, and further discussion, in Chapter 16, 315–25.
[4]*Debate*, 189.

unusable today. We agree that language is always changing, and we agree that there have been changes with respect to gender language. Several of the Colorado Springs Guidelines were specifically formulated to take account of such changes. What we are waiting to hear in Carson's book is an argument showing that generic "he" can no longer be used effectively.

The sixth and final supposition involves the *infrequency* of generic "he": "But if 'he' in English, complete with gender specification, is used in a generic sense somewhat less frequently that it used to be, <u>and if</u> for some sections of the reading populace 'he' is never or almost never used in a generic sense anymore . . ." (p. 158). We have responded to that objection in Chapter 16, under the objection, "Generic 'he' is infrequent." It is enough to repeat here that (1) we agree that it is less frequent than, say, twenty years ago; (2) its infrequency is exaggerated; (3) it is still usable and still used in a wide variety of publications; (4) we know of no section of the population that does not understand generic "he" (and generic "she"!) today; (5) good Bible translation will often require us to use less common but understandable words and expressions in order to translate accurately.

But now we notice a common pattern. All of these suppositions involve the possibility *that generic "he" is, or will be, unusable, so that the translators have no choice* except to lose meaning.

The "if" clauses, together with the conclusions drawn from them, are a decisive point in the debate. *If* generic "he" were absolutely unusable, then the alternatives would be all that we have available. In many cases gender-neutral translations would be the best we could expect. *If* the crucial assumption held, there would be no real alternative. It all depends on the "if." Carson's repetition of "if's" shows that he himself understands this point.

So the attentive reader waits for Carson to settle these "if" questions. In fact, Carson heightens the sense of expectation, for after setting out supposition 6, Carson says explicitly, "I shall come to that question in chapter 9" (*Debate*, 158). After raising the question about using "man" for the human race, Carson says, "Once again, I must postpone discussion until chapter 9" (*Debate*, 169).

B. Chapter 9: But where is the argument?

Finally, the reader comes to Chapter 9, entitled "But Is the English Language Changing?" (pp. 183–92). The title "But Is the English Language Changing?" poses the question only in a very vague way. We might respond, "Of course the English language is changing. We do not need to talk about that well-known fact, but quite narrowly about the question of whether the changes are of such a kind as to make generic 'he' unusable." But perhaps this general title will introduce the evidence and arguments we have been waiting for, the evidence on which so much earlier has been made to rest.

The book now has ten pages in which to address the crucial question: is generic "he" usable or not? The chapter begins auspiciously: "The question that is the title of this chapter raises *the issue* that lies behind so much of the rest of the debate" (p. 83, italics ours). This sentence suggests that this issue may be in one way *the* issue, "the issue that lies behind so much of the rest of the debate."

So what does this chapter do? It is a strange disappointment. The first section of the chapter, entitled "The Debate," occupies pages 183–85. Rather than zeroing in on whether generic "he" is usable, Carson continues to follow the vague theme of the chapter title, by speaking of change only in general terms:

> If spoken and written English have not changed, or have changed very little, then why this push to change translations. . . . On the other hand, if the language is changing, then two options are possible. We may update our translations to accommodate the changes so that our Bibles will not be linguistically out of date. Alternatively, we may ascribe whatever gender changes that are developing in the language to feminist influence and then heartily oppose them.
>
> The latter course is being pursued by the critics of gender-inclusive translations. At the risk of caricature (in which on this issue I really do not wish to indulge), their argument runs something like this: (1) The English language is not changing, or not changing much. (2) If it is changing, we should oppose the changes because the feminists are behind the changes (pp. 183–184).

But general questions about quantity of change or an alleged strategy of opposing changes are irrelevant. The issue, we repeat, is whether, *given the existing changes*, and *given the existing state of the English language*, generic "he" is still usable. At this point Carson's discussion confuses rather than focuses the issue. Unfortunately, the confused focus on *quantity* of change continues to influence the discussion in later sections.

C. A caricature of "the critics"

Now consider in more detail Carson's summary of "the critics of gender-inclusive language." These critics, he says, "ascribe whatever gender changes that are developing in the language to feminist influence and then heartily oppose them" (p. 183). And they think that the English language is "not changing much" (p. 184).

Carson says that in his description he runs "the risk of caricature." He realizes that it is a simplification.

First, let us assure readers that Carson's description is indeed a caricature. The accompanying statement that we published with the Colorado Springs Guidelines and that was signed by all participants said, "We all agree *that modern language is fluid and undergoes changes in nuance that* require periodic updates and revisions" (*CBMW News* 2:3 [June 1997]: 7, emphasis added). In addition, the Colorado Springs Guidelines themselves contain guidelines that approve some changes. The following all approve changes in translations due (at least in part) to changes in English: Guidelines A.1 (approving "the one who . . ." rather than "he who"), A.5 (approving "people" rather than "men" for plural Greek *anthrōpoi*), A.6 (approving "anyone" rather than "any man" for Greek *tis*), A.7 (approving "no one" rather than "no man" for Greek *oudeis*), and A.8 (approving "all people" rather than "all men" for Greek *pas*).[5]

More accurately stated, our position would be: (1) Many changes in the use of gender language in current English should be reflected in modern translations, and these changes can be made with no significant loss of meaning (see Chapter 11). (2) In other kinds of words and expressions, changes in Bible translation have been proposed that result in significant loss of components of meaning that are there in the original text (see Chapters 12–13, 18–19). (3) This second group contains many cases where losses could have been avoided if the translations had been willing to use English words and expressions (generic "he" and "man" as a name for the human race, for example) that are used less frequently but still quite widely today, and they are still fully understandable. Where necessary to preserve significant components of meaning in translation, they should be retained.

We discussed the question of feminist influence on changes in English in Chapter 14, but it should be noted here that the CSG give approval to several changes in translation that reflect changes in English due at least in part to feminist influence. To say that we "ascribe whatever gender changes that are developing in the language to feminist influence and then heartily oppose them" (p. 183) is simply untrue. But Carson says in the very next sentence, "The latter course is being pursued by the critics of gender-inclusive translations" (p. 183). Furthermore, to say we hold that "If [the English language] is changing, we should oppose the changes because the feminists are behind the changes" (p. 184) is also simply untrue, in light of our explicit endorsement of many changes in translation due to these very changes in English.

Of course, Carson has already put in a disclaimer with his expression "at the risk of caricature." Someone might think, "So what if the description is a caricature? That is OK, because Carson does not claim it is anything more." But if the caricature is so off-base, what is the point of bringing it up at all? Unfortunately, rather than directing us to the central issue, the usability of generic "he," Carson has directed us away from it into the broad question of language change, and toward the irrelevant issue of whether some people are reacting out of linguistic conservatism.

---

[5]See Appendix 1 for the complete text of the Guidelines.

The book has set up a "straw man": it sets up a weak opponent, easy to knock down, leading onlookers to think he is opposing the actual position of "the critics of gender-inclusive translations" (p. 183), whereas in actual fact he is opposing a mirage, a position not held by us. After this weak opponent is knocked down, it appears to Carson's readers that only the gender-neutral position remains, and it then appears to be the only reasonable option.

In the next paragraph the book then claims to look at an illustration of this linguistic conservatism: "Several essays and short articles have been put forward along these lines [i.e., the lines that Carson summarized in his two-point caricature]" (p. 184). The example that immediately follows is Grudem's "two and a half pages of examples of generic 'he' and related pronouns, all drawn from recent newspapers" (p. 184). The fact that Grudem cites recent newspapers clearly indicates that Grudem is not "opposing changes," as Carson claims, but *recognizing the existing state of the language* after changes have already taken place. Moreover, Carson gratuitously hypothesizes, on the basis of Grudem's list (a mere *list!*), the implication that Grudem thinks language "is not changing, or not changing much." Grudem makes no such claim! The claim is only that generic "he" remains in use, and that "man" as a name for the human race remains in use, not that *other expressions* have not become more common alongside of these. Carson has misconstrued Grudem's point, and therefore does not represent Grudem accurately.

Carson's book then gives a long quote from a letter to the editor from Professor D. F. Wright (pp. 184–85). Wright laments that the Colorado Springs meeting "evinced so little sensitivity to the cultural and social changes that have brought about significant linguistic shifts in common English" (p. 184). Wright is also speaking in vague generalities. As we just demonstrated, the participants at Colorado Springs specifically acknowledged "linguistic shifts." Wright compounds the problem by giving, as his lone example, the problems in using " 'man' and 'men' in contexts where male(s) are not indicated" (p. 185). Wright seems to be talking about permissible changes (Chapter 11), such as the Colorado Springs Guidelines explicitly allowed, for we too encouraged other terms than "man" and "men" to be used in contexts where (to use Wright's wording) "male(s) are not indicated." Wright has either misunderstood the Guidelines, or chooses to set up a straw man in order to make it easy to knock down.

So far in Chapter 9, there is no real argument. Carson is in dialogue with an artificial opponent.

The next section, entitled "Some Reflections," is the final section in the chapter (pp. 185–92). It has several subsections, which we take up one at a time.

The first subsection, entitled "History of the Issue" (pp. 185–87), reviews the history of alternatives to generic "he" over three centuries, including primarily "they" with a singular antecedent, but also other alternatives. This does not address the central issue, because we are not concerned to argue that no alternatives have been used, but only to argue that generic "he" is still usable *as well as* alternatives.[6]

The next subsection, entitled "Causes of Language Change" (pp. 187–89),[7] is also irrelevant to the issue. The issue is not what has caused change, but whether generic "he" is still usable in English.

D. The long-awaited discussion of generic "he"

Next comes a subsection entitled, "Generic 'He.'" Carson observes that there are "still many, many examples around of the unreconstructed generic 'he.' No one is arguing that the change has been universal" (p. 189). Yet in this sentence he speaks of "the change." "Change to what?" we would ask. Since in this context he sees the remaining examples of generic "he" as indicating that "the change" has not been "universal," he must mean *the change from using generic "he" to using alternatives to generic "he," such as "he or she," or "they," and so forth*. This change has happened, but it has not been "universal."

So here is the heart of Carson's evidence for the unusability of generic "he," the premise on which so much of the book depends: *He says that many people have stopped using generic "he" and use alternatives.*

We agree that many people have stopped using generic "he" and use alternatives. There is no argument on this point. But that does not establish what Carson needs to establish, namely, that generic "he" is unusable, or that people will not understand it, or that we cannot use it in Bible translation. Similarly, many people today have stopped using "man" as a name for the human race. But that does not prove that "man" as a name for the race is unusable, or that people will not understand it, or that we cannot use it in Bible translation. We have treated this question at length in Chapter 16, under the objection, "Generic 'he' is infrequent."[8] To put the matter briefly,

---

[6]Within this section Carson also rejects "monocausational" explanations for generic "he" (p. 187), and so do we (see Chapter 14, footnote 1). This section is helpful for information, but does not touch the main issue.

[7]Carson admits that feminism has been instrumental in "changes in the area of grammatical gender" (p. 187). In addition, Carson has three points. (a) The system resulting from change is not "evil" (p. 187). (b) ". . . the changes (I shall argue) are here" (p. 188). (c) We should beware of overreacting (pp. 188–89).

The first point, point (a), we have already had to qualify (see Chapter 15, footnote 28). First, though a system for grammatical gender is not "evil" in itself, people's *attitudes* toward certain usages may contain many moral and spiritual influences, good and bad. Second, the continued use and ability to understand generic "he" shows that it too is part of "the system." The debate is over the state of the system, and Carson's point (a) bypasses this main issue.

Points (b) and (c), rightly understood, are both valid, but they also are irrelevant. The question, as before, is just *what* changes we are talking about. Carson is vague.

[8]See Chapter 16, p. 325.

Bible translations regularly use words and expressions that are somewhat less frequent but that ordinary English speakers understand.[9]

The rest of the subsection includes observations that generic "she" is often used alongside generic "he," and observations from Carson's own reading, mentioning the lesser use of generic "he," and the use of generic "she." He says no more than what we could confirm from our own observation.

In fact, his observations confirm the usability of generic "he." Every case in current literature in which generic "he" occurs alongside generic "she" reinforces readers' ability to understand generic "he" in future instances. Every occurrence of generic "she," by itself rather than alongside generic "he," also reinforces readers' ability to understand generic "he," because generic "he" can be understood by analogy with generic "she." Just as listeners have found that they understood generic "she" the *first time* they heard it, so they can (by analogy) understand generic "he" if they have been raised on a steady diet of generic "she."[10]

In sum, Carson's observations in this key section do not disprove our position, and some observations support our position. Up to this point we have looked in vain for an argument showing that generic "he" is unusable in Bible translation today. Where is the argument?

E. An argument from frequency of use

Carson is also occupied with the question of *frequency of use* of generic "he" and alternatives. Within a single paragraph (p. 189) he has the following expressions:

---

[9]Or does Carson intend more? He speaks elsewhere in a very general manner of "change," without specifying exactly what precise changes he has in mind, and says at other times that "the language is changing" (supposition 3, p. 118), that is, continuing to change, and that "the changes are farther advanced" (p. 190), and so on. He also draws an analogy with the discussions fifty years ago over "thee" and "thou" (p. 190). He may thus convey to readers the impression that there is a monolithic direction of change, leading clearly and inexorably toward the total disappearance of generic "he" in the future. If this is his intent, it is a form of the argument for disappearance, which we already considered in Chapter 10. But Carson does not pursue this supposition. It is impossible to say what he thinks an argument for disappearance would look like, nor is it clear whether he thinks it has any weight.

Because some readers are likely to think that the book is hinting at such an argument, the effect on them can in some ways be just as great as if the book actually spelled out an argument. It is as if the book appealed to a reader's good sense for the direction where things are "obviously" headed, and asked, "Do I really need to belabor the obvious?" At the same time, the book avoids the implausibilities, the ungrounded speculation, and the statements vulnerable to attack into which it would have to enter if it actually tried to produce an argument (see our Chapter 16).

Maybe Carson intended none of this. He does not spell anything out. We are not criticizing Carson's intentions, but alerting readers not to be swayed by a phantom argument, an argument that Carson's book does not give, and that Carson himself nowhere endorses (except, of course, when it comes in the form of an unestablished supposition like supposition 2).

[10]See also our arguments in Chapter 16, pp. 326–34.

. . . to quote examples . . . , all on one side, does not fairly assess *how far* the changes have gone.

. . . *how many* of these same sources[11] alternate between gender-neutral language and more traditional language?

Above all [!], what is the *balance* of gender-neutral usage in current English as compared with, say, thirty years ago? I know of no study that has tried to probe this carefully, but I would be surprised if such a study did not reveal a *very substantial shift* indeed (p. 189; italics ours).

In addition, supposition 6 above (from p. 158) focuses almost entirely on the question of frequency.

But this still does not address the essential point, nor does it establish the essential "if" statements on which so much of the previous chapters depended. Frequency of use for a word or expression has very little to do with understandability or usability. People can *understand* words and complicated sentences that they *use infrequently* in their own speech, or that they hear infrequently in the speech of others. The word "albatross" occurs infrequently in the books we read, but we understand it when we read it. Moreover, as we observed in Chapter 16, even if generic "he" were to occur *very* infrequently (which we doubt will happen), it would be understandable as a natural extension of the ordinary use of "he."

A preoccupation with frequency also fails to distinguish between performance and competence. Roughly speaking, performance means actual usage. Competence means what I am *able* to do and understand, even though I am not actively *using* all my abilities frequently. For example, on the level of competence, people can understand vocabulary that very seldom appears in performance. "Albatross," "sapphire," "municipality," and "pneumonia" are not words that I encounter frequently in reading, nor do I use them often in my speech, but I understand them if I do encounter them. Another example is the use of "whom" as the objective case of "who." The word "whom" is undoubtedly less frequent today than it was forty or fifty years ago, when people were better trained in traditional English grammar and took care to use "whom" as the direct or indirect object in a sentence, or as the object of a preposition. People today are less aware of this distinction and many never use "whom." But they understand it readily.

---

[11]The "sources" to whom Carson alludes are the kind that Grudem has cited as examples of using generic "he." Many of these sources are newspapers and major magazines. They may be following the recommendation of *The Associated Press Stylebook and Libel Manual* (1994), 94, which directs, "Use the pronoun *his* when an indefinite antecedent may be male or female: *A reporter attempts to protect his sources*" (Not *his or her* sources). The press stylebook actually excludes two typical alternatives, the use of "his or her" and (by implication) the use of "her" by itself (generic "she"). But, as usual, the point is *not* frequency of alternatives.

In like manner people can understand grammatical constructions or complex sentences that they do not actively *use* themselves, and that they encounter only *infrequently*. Infrequency is no barrier to understanding, unless the infrequency diminishes virtually to a zero point.[12] The same holds for generic "he." Even those who do not use it understand it.

Remember also the point that we have already made in Chapter 10. Generic "he," unlike an ordinary noun or verb, has a meaning derivable from "he" even when it has *never* been heard before, just as generic "she" has a meaning derivable the first time that it is heard.

In short, even if generic "he" is infrequent, there is no loss of meaning, just as there is no loss with other infrequent uses.

The issue, as we have endlessly repeated, is not whether we can use other alternatives, nor whether we use them with high frequency, but whether we can *also* use generic "he" when we need it. And if not, why not? Carson's entire discussion effectively bypasses the question. It also ignores the key difference between obsolescence in language and ideological prohibition. For language police to *prohibit* generic "he" (except when accompanied by "she") and for many people then deliberately to *avoid* using it, even though they understand it when others use it, is very different from a situation where it has effectively disappeared (as with "thee" and "thou").

F.   Constituencies

Carson's key chapter has one more subsection, on "Varieties of English." It does not constitute an argument, but contains very general observations to the effect that there are variations in English, even internationally. With this we agree. It is irrelevant to the main issue.

In this subsection Carson also contemplates the possibility of niche translations, designed for different audiences. Since some of the audiences may be large, rather than minor "niches," Carson uses the term "constituency." Superficially, it might appear from pages 191–92 that Carson favors this option. ". . . with the extraordinary variations now operative in worldwide English, perhaps constituency Bibles, even if inevitable, are in part a good thing" (p. 192). But the tone is resigned: "I wish Bibles did not have constituencies; I wish there were one English Bible used everywhere. But that day is past. The fact is that this wishful thinking cannot be imposed" (p. 192). Carson clearly senses some of the same problems that we have indicated in discussing constituency translations (see Chapter 9)—though neither he nor we may be able to alter a less-than-ideal situation.

---

[12]The possibility of decrease to the zero point returns us to the argument from disappearance (see Chapter 16).

Carson is correct that such divisions into constituencies are probably going to happen no matter what we do. But the question remains: is it wise to produce a gender-neutral translation with this purpose in mind? And is it *right*? (Not: will it happen anyway?) Is a gender-neutral policy faithful to original meaning, and faithful to God, given that the translation is designed to address such-and-such a group of potential readers? Carson does not discuss the *rightness* of it. There is no argument or evaluation.

But let us consider ourselves whether it is right. As we indicated in Chapter 15, there are serious problems with constituency translations, and we are not in favor of one in this case. Even if we attempt to produce a constituency translation, faithfulness to God's Word requires that we do not tone down the pattern of thought in the Bible (see the end of Chapter 17).

G. The great omission

In the end Carson has not given us any substantive argument why generic "he" is unusable. He tells the readers at several points that he will deal with the question in Chapter 9, and when we read Chapter 9, the next-to-last chapter of the book, we find that he has simply omitted the topic. As a result, the entire debate is left unfinished. It is as if readers have followed the flow of thought through the whole book up to this point, only to find that the stream, instead of running to the sea, simply loses volume until it evaporates into the hot air of the desert.

Where is the burden of proof on whether generic "he" is usable? Its use by the secular press and the oscillating use by feminists give simple evidence. (Carson himself presents this evidence on pp. 184, 189–90 and see our extensive list of examples in Chapter 16, pp. 315–22 above.) It is usable because they use it. Then the burden of proof is on those who claim that it is not usable. Carson's book provides no argument, and therefore leaves the other side victorious in the debate, *even if* the other side chooses not to mount a single positive argument.[13] But in this case we have presented in this book much positive argument and evidence for the continuing usability of generic "he."

---

[13]One may make similar observations about another, very distinct issue, namely, the use of "man" for the human race. In the course of his book, Carson provides no substantive examination of whether "man" for the race is still usable. On page 169 he says, "I must postpone the discussion until chapter 9" (*Debate*, 169). Then, when we come to his Chapter 9, he never discusses specific data about "man" in that use. The discussion is once again unfinished.

Now, as our Chapter 18 shows (see many examples above, pp. 351–54) "man" is currently used in this way (and Carson agrees, *Debate*, 184). Hence, it is usable. The burden of proof is on those who claim otherwise. Carson gives no argument and so gives the victory to the other side.

H. Conclusion

Is generic "he" usable?[14] It is. In this book we have endeavored to give supporting evidence and arguments (Chapters 15–17). Carson's book, as we have seen, omits answering the question, but unwittingly supports our position with his recognition that there are "many, many examples around of the unreconstructed generic 'he'" (p. 189), and with his data on the continued occurrence of generic "he" and "she" (pp. 189–90). Since generic "he" is usable, the key decision by translators of gender-neutral versions to eliminate generic "he" has *unnecessarily* resulted in meaning losses. The result goes astray from maximal fidelity to the Word of God.

---

[14]That is, *in addition to* alternatives. We are not closing down alternatives but pointing out that this one is still open too, in spite of strident voices trying to pronounce a prohibition. We are advocating freedom on this issue—freedom for translators to use whatever expression most fully conveys the meaning of the original text—rather than any restriction or prohibition that says that generic "he" cannot be used.

Scripture Index

Index of Persons

Index of Subjects